OBLIGATIONS *ERGA OMNES* AND INTERNATIONAL CRIMES

Obligations *Erga Omnes* and International Crimes

A Theoretical Inquiry into the Implementation and Enforcement of the International Responsibility of States

by

André de Hoogh
Lecturer in International Law,
University of Utrecht

KLUWER LAW INTERNATIONAL
THE HAGUE / LONDON / BOSTON

A C.I.P. Catalogue record for this book is available from the Library of Congress

ISBN 90-411-0232-9

Published by Kluwer Law International,
P.O. Box 85889, 2508 CN The Hague, The Netherlands.

Sold and distributed in the U.S.A. and Canada
by Kluwer Law International,
675 Massachusetts Avenue, Cambridge, MA 02139, U.S.A.

In all other countries, sold and distributed
by Kluwer Law International,
P.O. Box 85889, 2508 CN The Hague, The Netherlands.

Printed on acid-free paper

Printed in the Netherlands

DEDICATION

To my parents Thom M. de Hoogh and Wil J.F.M. de Hoogh-Leijten

TABLE OF CONTENTS

PREFACE

The very first beginning of the work on this book began when my supervisor to be, professor Karel Wellens, of the University of Nijmegen, proposed that I would select a subject for a Ph.D. research project. At the same time he provided guidelines in that the subject selected should not be too well known so as to ensure at least some degree of originality, and that there should certainly be a certain minimum of literature on the subject so as not to be at a loss for starters. Having done some surveying I came up with the subject of obligations *erga omnes*. To some extent this was the logical follow-up to my graduation thesis, which concerned the subjects of *jus cogens* in a humanitarian context, chemical warfare and reprisals.

After a year or so it seemed to me that the topic of obligations *erga omnes* could not form the basis of the entire thesis except in relation to the subject of international crimes of State. So my research shifted substantially towards the works of the International Law Commission on State responsibility. The reports of the special rapporteur for the topic, professor and judge Arangio-Ruiz, allowed in depth investigations into the theoretical underpinnings of the responsibility of States.

This thesis then started off by examining the legal interests of States and the United Nations in relation to obligations *erga omnes* and international crimes. It continued to discuss the issues of reparation, countermeasures, and the use of armed force, as well as the restrictions thereto, with special reference to the (possible or potential) consequences of a régime applicable to international crimes. The final chapter investigated certain problems the Court might encounter in settling a dispute or giving advice regarding international crimes.

Within the time span of the six years that it took to complete this thesis interest in the topics discussed soared. This has been due, at least partly, to the coming into power of Gorbachov, the resultant end of the Cold War, and the consequent capability of the Security Council to act where it could not act before. By now it cannot be said that there is only a minimum of literature on the subjects investigated. This book now lying before you, which is based, with only minor alterations, on my Ph.D. thesis defended at the University of Nijmegen in January 1996, will probably not be the last on these subjects. Indeed, in the light of the approaching completion by the Commission of its efforts to elaborate draft articles on the international responsibility of States, these central, controversial and captivating subjects will undoubtedly draw much future attention from international legal scholars.

André de Hoogh
Nijmegen, 1996

ACKNOWLEDGEMENTS

As is the case with so many books, this book could not have been written without the support and assistance of many people.

I would like to express my appreciation to the staffs of the various law libraries I visited during my research period, namely those of the University of Nijmegen, the Peace Palace and the T.M.C. Asser Institute in the Hague, the Max Planck Institute for Public and International Law in Heidelberg, the Palais des Nations in Geneva, and the Office of Legal Affairs and Columbia University in New York. As a follow-up I would like especially to thank professor Frowein of the Max Planck Institute and professor Gellhorn of Columbia University for arranging my stays there and for providing access to their respective libraries.

My gratitude goes to the T.M.C. Asser Institute for hosting my stay in the Hague during the Second Phase Researchers' Course in 1990, and for providing financial support for my stays at the Palais des Nations in Geneva and the Max Planck Institute in Heidelberg.

Similarly I would like to express my appreciation to the Law Faculty of the University of Nijmegen, and all those previously or presently employed within it, for making my time spent there so memorable. Special mention may be made of Anita van Loon, our former secretary, who, as with so many others, took the time to listen to all my plans, troubles and goings on.

Naturally I would like to thank all those, whether family, friends or colleagues, that listened willingly, patiently or not noticeably reluctant, to my comments on all kinds of international developments. As so many fall within this category, I will refrain from naming any specifically, thus averting any risk of oversight.

My brother Thom de Hoogh has played a crucial role regarding the preparation of this book. Were it not for him I doubt I would have finished in time. Notwithstanding my lack of pace, and my urge to constantly keep on changing the text and adding improvements, he remained patient and insistent. All the work on the layout of the text has been his affair, and I would like to express my deep appreciation for all the effort, skill and experience he has put into the preparation of the camera-ready manuscript.

My gratitude goes in no small measure to professor and judge Arangio-Ruiz, who in 1990 provided me with a recommendation for participation in the International Law Seminar held in the context of the annual meetings of the International Law Commission. Furthermore, ever since judge Arangio-Ruiz has sent me his reports on State responsibility which formed the invaluable bases of discussion for this thesis.

Penultimately I would praise professor Ben Vermeulen and doctor Colin Warbrick for their no small efforts to read and provide valuable criticism within such a minimal period of time as five weeks.

Finally my gratitude goes to my supervisor in this Ph.D. enterprise, professor Karel Wellens. It is he who some seven years ago put his faith in me, when he asked me to prepare a proposal for a Ph.D. research project. In the end the outcome of all my research has been as much his effort as it has been mine.

Of course none of the mistakes or errors that may be found to exist in the text of this book can be attributed to any of the persons that contributed to its inception.

LIST OF ABBREVIATIONS

ACSIL	Annals of the Chinese Society of International Law
ADV	Archiv des Völkerrechts
AFDI	Annuaire Français de Droit International
AJIL	The American Journal of International Law
AJPIL	Austrian Journal of Public and International Law
AMBB	Adviescommissie Mensenrechten en Buitenlands Beleid
Assembly	General Assembly, United Nations
ASZIW	Aussenwirtschaft, Schweitzerische Zeitschrift für internationale Wirtschaftsbeziehungen
BJIL	Brooklyn Journal of International Law
BYBIL	British Year Book of International Law
CAVV	Commissie van Advies voor Volkenrechtelijke Vraagstukken
CDE	Cahiers de droit européen
CJIL	Cornell Journal of International Law
CMLR	Common Market Law Review
Commission	International Law Commission, United Nations
ConnJIL	Connecticut Journal of International Law
Council	Security Council, United Nations
Court	International Court of Justice, United Nations
CWILJ	California Western International Law Journal
CYIL	Canadian Yearbook of International Law
DA	Deutsche Außenpolitik
DJILP	Denver Journal of International Law and Policy
Ed.	Editor
Eds.	Editors
EEC	European Economic Community
EI	Études Internationales
EJIL	European Journal of International Law
EPIL	Encyclopedia of Public International Law
FA	Foreign Affairs

GA	General Assembly, United Nations
GATT	General Agreement on Tarifs and Trade
GIELR	The Georgetown International Environmental Law Review
GJICL	Georgia Journal of International and Comparative Law
GYIL	German Yearbook of International Law
HILJ	Harvard International Law Journal
HJLP	Hitotsubashi Journal of Law & Politics
HRLJ	Human Rights Law Journal
HRQ	Human Rights Quarterly
HYIL	Hague Yearbook of International Law
IA (Moscow)	International Affairs (Moscow)
ICJ	International Court of Justice, United Nations
ICLQ	The International and Comparative Law Quarterly
IJIL	Indian Journal of International Law
ILC	International Law Commission, United Nations
ILC-draft	ILC draft articles on the international responsibility of States
ILM	International Legal Materials
ILR	International Law Reports
IO	International Organization
IowaLR	Iowa Law Review
IR	International Relations
IS	International Spectator
IYHR	Israel Yearbook on Human Rights
IYIL	The Italian Yearbook of International Law
JDI	Journal du Droit International
LJIL	Leiden Journal of International Law
MJIL	Michigan Journal of International Law
MLR	The Modern Law Review
NILR	Netherlands International Law Review
NJ	Neue Justiz
NJB	Nederlands Juristenblad
NTIR	Nederlands Tijdschrift voor Internationaal Recht
NTRR	Nederlands Tijdschrift voor Rechtsfilosofie & Rechtstheorie
NVIR	Nederlandse Vereniging voor Internationaal Recht
NYIL	Netherlands Yearbook of International Law
NZIR	Niemeyers Zeitschrift für Internationales Recht
Organization	United Nations Organization
OZOR	Österreichisches Zeitschrift für öffentliches Recht

PCIJ	Permanent Court of International Justice
Permanent Court	Permanent Court of International Justice
PLO	Palestine Liberation Organization
PUSL YIL	Pace University School of Law, Yearbook of International Law
PYIL	Polish Yearbook of International Law
RBDI	Revue Belge de Droit International
RCDIP	Revue critique de droit international privé
RDC ADI	Recueil des Cours, Académie de Droit International
RDILC	Revue de droit international et de législation comparée
RDISDP	Revue de Droit International, de Sciences Diplomatiques et Politiques
RGDIP	Revue Générale de Droit International Public
RIAA	Reports of International Arbitration Awards
RICJ	The Review, International Commission of Jurists
RIW	Recht der Internationalen Wirtschaft
RPF	Rwandese Patriotic Front
SAYIL	South African Yearbook of International Law
SFDI	Société Française pour le Droit International
SJILC	Syracuse Journal of International Law & Commerce
SJIR	Schweizerisches Jahrbuch für internationales Recht
SLR	Shudo Law Review
SR	Staat und Recht
UN	United Nations
UNTS	United Nations Treaties Series
Vienna Convention	The 1969 Vienna Convention on the Law of Treaties
VJIL	Virginia Journal of International Law
WTO	World Trade Organization
YAAA	Yearbook of the Association of Attenders and Alumni of the Hague Academy of International Law
YBILC	Year Book of the International Law Commission
ZAORV	Zeitschrift für Ausländisches öffentliches Recht und Völkerrecht
ZOV	Zeitschrift für öffentliches Recht
ZVR	Zeitschrift für Vergleichende Rechtswissenschaft

INTRODUCTION

This is a world of contradictions, but it may well turn out to be one of paradoxes. In this world States have traditionally created international law, whether expressly by means of the conclusion of treaties, or tacitly by means of contributing to a general practice accepted as law; after having created international law States have violated it; and in response other States have performed as law enforcers. In doing all these things States have not acted, predominantly, according to legal principles, but rather according to political expediency and the needs perceived to exist either within their national communities or within the international community. Insofar as relations within the international community are concerned, they have tended to guard their sovereignty by opposing centralization, whether that would relate to law-making or to law enforcement.

With regard to both the former and the latter this has manifested itself in the requirement of consent. Thus States claim to be bound by international law only to the extent that they have expressed their consent to treaties, generally by way of ratification, or to customary international law, by way of contributing to a practice accepted as law or otherwise persistently objecting the formation or existence of a rule. In a similar vein they have tended to enforce international law only if that suited their own self-interest, which in their perception lay with *ad hoc* alliances. It should come as no surprise then that States have neither proved consistent or reliable in their action, in their choice of allies, or in the choice of causes worthy of their attention.

A break in these traditional patterns occurred due to World War I, which caused devastation on such a scale that, in order to prevent the repetition of such events, article 11 of the Covenant of the League of Nations declared war or the threat of war, whether immediately affecting members of the League or not, a matter of concern to the whole League.[1] The members undertook, in articles 13 and 15, not to go to war against any Member which complied with the arbitral award or the recommendations contained in a unanimous Council of the League of Nations report. If a member breached its covenants not to resort to war under articles 12, 13 and 15, article 16 provided that this would *ipso facto* constitute an act of war against the other members, which undertook immediately to subject the law-breaking State to the severance of trade, financial and certain other relations. Significantly the Covenant only stipulated that the Council of the League of Nations would "recommend" what effective military forces the members would severally contribute to the armed forces to be used to protect the covenants of the League.

Yet the efforts of the League to maintain international peace and security proved ineffective, and after World War II another attempt was made to construe an effective collective security system. In contrast with the League system, article 2, paragraph 4, of the Charter of the United Nations [hereinafter "Charter"] did not only prohibit recourse to war, but the threat or use of force by members against States generally (with qualifications).[2] That prohibition has been complemented by the obligation, expressed in article 2, paragraph 3, that members shall settle their disputes in such a manner that international peace and security, and justice, are not endangered. Furthermore, under Chapters VII and VIII of the Charter the Security Council is endowed with the power to determine, in an exclusive manner, the existence of a threat to the peace, a breach of the peace, or an act of aggression, and to decide on the measures or action to be taken to maintain or restore international peace and security. The only exception to that monopoly is constituted by article 51 on the right of individual or collective self-defence against armed attacks. Yet even that right is limited by the phrase "until the Security Council has taken measures necessary to maintain international peace and security".

Due to the existence of the Cold War, and the consequent frequent exercise of the veto power by the permanent members, the Security Council has not been able to function as it had been envisaged. One of the reactions to the Security Council's near impossibility to act has been the adoption of General Assembly resolution 377 (V), in which the Assembly claimed, in situations of threats to the peace, breaches of the peace and acts of aggression, the competence to recommend measures, including the use of armed force, in case of breaches of the peace and acts of aggression, if the Security Council's inaction resulted from the lack of unanimity of the permanent members. Another reaction by governments, but also by legal scholars, has been an attempt to reinterpret the basic Charter prohibitions on the use of force, and the circumstances under which a justifiable use of force in self-defence could take place.

On the legal level a number of interrelated developments has occurred, linked in one way or another to the existence of an international community.

The 1969 Vienna Convention on the Law of Treaties contains some provisions on *jus cogens*.[3] Its basic article 53 stipulates that any treaty in conflict with a peremptory norm of general international law is void. And a peremptory norm exists if a norm is accepted and recognized by the international community of States as a whole as a norm from which no derogation is permitted. In its commentary the International Law Commission [hereinafter "Commission"] had indicated that the law of the Charter concerning the prohibition of the use of force constituted a conspicuous example of a peremptory norm.[4]

One year later the International Court of Justice [hereinafter "Court"] proclaimed, in the Barcelona Traction Case, the distinction between obligations vis-à-vis States in the field of diplomatic protection and obligations towards the international community as a whole (or obligations *erga omnes*).[5] As examples of obligations in the latter category it named the prohibitions of aggression and genocide, and the principles and rules concerning the basic rights of the human person, including protection from slavery and racial discrimination.

And finally the Commission adopted in 1976, as part of its effort to elaborate a draft on the international responsibility of States, article 19, Part One, on the distinction between international delicts and international crimes.[6] Article 19, paragraph 2, provides that: "An internationally wrongful act which results from the breach by a State of an obligation so essential for the protection of fundamental interests of the international community that its breach is recognized as a crime by that community as a whole constitutes an international crime." In paragraph 3, subs (a) to (d), the Commission went on to list a number of spheres of obligations of essential importance to the community, and specific examples of international crimes within such spheres. The spheres mentioned by the Commission related to the maintenance of international peace and security, the right of self-determination, the protection of the human being, and the protection of the human environment. As specific examples the Commission named aggression; colonial domination; slavery, genocide, and *apartheid*; and massive pollution of the atmosphere or the seas.

A little bit over three months after the actual work on this thesis began, Iraq invaded Kuwait, occupied it, and eventually annexed it. Fortunately the Cold War had not only ended after the coming into power of Gorbachov, it even led to veritable co-operation between the superpowers. Nowhere was this shown as clearly as with the Iraq-Kuwait crisis, regarding which the Security Council adopted resolution after resolution. At a point in time that already five of those had been adopted (including a comprehensive trade embargo and a call for maritime enforcement of that embargo), then president Bush of the United States, addressing a joint session of Congress, observed:[7]

> "Out of these troubled times a new world order can emerge, a new era, freer from the threat of terror, stronger in the pursuit of justice, and more secure in the quest for peace. An era in which the nations of the world, east and west, north and south, can prosper and live in harmony."

This apparent promise of a "New World Order" also gained attention from international legal scholars. The question in the mind of the present writer has been whether such a New World Order would and could be grafted upon the old legal structures, or whether it required the modification of those old structures, going as far, possibly, of amendments to the Charter or the Statute of the Court [hereinafter "Statute"].[8] From that perspective the subject of this thesis, dealing in a broad sense with issues of community enforcement, has offered ample opportunities for reflection.

The starting-point of this thesis lay with the (obiter) dictum of the Court in the Barcelona Traction Case on obligations towards the international community. Regarding those the Court claimed that they are the concern of all States, and that in view of the importance of the rights involved all States can be held to have a legal interest in their protection: they are obligations *erga omnes*.[9] On the basis of those pronouncements claims have been made that all States possess a legal interest regarding violations of the prohibitions of aggression and genocide, and regarding violations of the basic rights of the human person (slavery and racial discrimination).

Questions of legal interest are generally considered to relate to the right of a State to invoke the responsibility of a State engaged on the basis of its commission of an internationally wrongful act. The State committing an internationally wrongful act is nowadays generally referred to as "author State". The State entitled to invoke the author State's responsibility has been termed "injured State" by the Commission. On that it has adopted, in 1985, article 5, Part Two, which provides both a definition and certain preconceived categories of injured States.[10] Paragraph 3 of the said article states that, in addition, all States are injured States if an internationally wrongful act constitutes an international crime. In view of the text of article 5, Part Two, as well as

the reports of special rapporteurs and the discussion within the Commission, the research on this thesis shifted, in the course of time, from obligations *erga omnes* towards international crimes. Over and above issues of legal interest on the part of States, the question arose whether the existence of obligations towards the international community (obligations *erga omnes*) should not also lead to a right of a personified international community, that is, the United Nations, to invoke the responsibility of the author State of an international crime (see chapter two).
From questions of legal interest this thesis developed in the direction of the question what States or the United Nations could do on the basis of their right to invoke the responsibility of the author State of an international crime. Which forms of reparation could be demanded? Could they resort to economic and other measures to pressure a State into acceding to their demands? Could they resort to the use of armed force and implement the author State's responsibility themselves? And finally, to what extent would it be possible to invoke an author State's responsibility for an international crime before the Court.

The point of departure for the specific chapters in this thesis has been the Commission's definition of the phrase "international responsibility" in the commentary to article 1, Part One, which would cover:[11]

> "(...) every kind of new relations which may arise, in international law, from the internationally wrongful act of a State, whether such relations are limited to the offending State and the directly injured State or extend also to other subjects of international law, and whether they are centred on the duty of the guilty State to restore the injured State in its rights and repair the damage caused, or whether they also give the injured State itself or other subjects of international law the right to impose on the offending State a sanction admitted by international law."

In view of this very broad definition few restrictions to the present thesis could be imposed. However, some limits result from the title of this thesis: "Obligations *Erga Omnes* and International Crimes: A Theoretical Inquiry into the Implementation and Enforcement of the International Responsibility of States".
First of all this thesis is devoted to questions related to the responsibility of "States". Generally therefore it will not discuss the responsibility of any other actor or subject of international law. Consequently the responsibility under international law of individuals, corporations, non-State entities or international organizations, inclusive the United Nations, is excluded from the scope of this thesis.
Secondly, only the "international" responsibility of States will be discussed. Issues regarding any kind of responsibility which a State might incur due to the operation of rules within its own domestic legal system are excluded from the scope of this thesis.
Thirdly, this thesis will not deal in any way with another topic under consideration by the Commission, namely "Liability for Injurious Consequences Arising out of Acts not Prohibited by International Law".[12] Only responsibility incurred on the basis of an internationally "wrongful" act will be considered in this thesis.
A fourth restriction is based on the theoretical nature of the research. In the light of the broad scope of the issues involved, the present writer deemed it both impractical and inadvisable to engage in an in depth research of the State practice of the differing

fields. Going into all the State practice related to the responsibility of States generally, and reparation and reprisals in particular, the law on human rights, self-determination of peoples, and the use of armed force, did not present itself as the most appropriate way to approach the underlying and common questions which are central to this study.

Regarding the choice of sources it may be said that the reports of the special rapporteurs on the topic of State responsibility, the discussion on that topic within the Commission, the texts of draft articles and their commentaries adopted by the Commission, have formed the basis of discussion for a large number of the issues argued on in this thesis. Though these texts and documents do not present a formal source of law in the sense of article 38 of the Statute, their influence on judicial decisions and teachings of the mostly highly qualified publicists of the various nations can already be verified. More importantly they influence both the practice of States and their juridical opinions on the rules of State responsibility. The latter takes place especially through the reports of the Commission to the General Assembly, as discussed by the Sixth Committee.

As to the formal sources of law the present thesis has taken into account a number of treaties, mostly multilateral ones, in the field of international peace and security and human rights. With regard to rules of customary international law it may be said that at times instances of State practice have been referred to, though such reference should be considered to be of illustrative character in relation to the particular legal argument made in the text. Certain general principles of law, such as *ex injuria jus non oritur*, have been quoted in particular contexts. The bulk of the judicial decisions reviewed as to their relevance to the topics has been the jurisprudence of the Permanent Court of International Justice [hereinafter "Permanent Court"] and the Court. Certain pertinent arbitral and claims commission awards have been taken into account though. As to the publicists, that is literature and doctrine, preference and precedence has been given to those authors commenting upon the topics of obligations *erga omnes* and international crimes.

With the particular topics in mind, and especially the consequences which the commission of an international crime might entail for the maintenance of international peace and security, the practice of the Security Council, as laid down in its resolutions, has been reviewed as to its relevance. The choice for restricting the review to Security Council resolutions, to the exclusion of General Assembly resolutions, has been made taking into account the fact that the members of the United Nations have conferred on the Security Council, under article 24, the primary responsibility for the maintenance of international peace and security; and the fact that under article 25 members have agreed to accept and carry out decisions of the Security Council taken in accordance with the Charter. The absence, generally, of any power to make decisions binding on members of the United Nations was another reason for the exclusion of Assembly resolutions.

From a temporal point of view research has been limited, generally, to the twentieth century. However, although the jurisprudence of the Permanent Court has been taken fully into account, the practice related to the League of Nations has been disregarded. In contrast to the continuity as regards the Statutes of the Permanent Court and the present Court, as expressed also in article 92 of the Charter, the Charter of the United

Nations has not been based upon the Covenant of the League of Nations. Nor can the United Nations be considered, generally, a successor in law to the League of Nations. Considering the divergent and innovative features of the Charter, no useful purpose would have been served by examining also the practice related to the League.

The end date of the research has been set at 30 June 1995. This has given the present writer the chance to take into account the latest report of special rapporteur Arangio-Ruiz,[13] the first devoted exclusively to international crimes, as well as the judgment of the Court on the East Timor Case.[14] Account has been taken also of the 1001 resolutions adopted by the Security Council by that date.

Although the thesis is focused on the topics obligations *erga omnes* and international crimes, the theoretical nature of the research, as well as the relative novelty of the topics, has dictated a broad range of attention being devoted to matters not directly related to those topics. Thus the theory of State responsibility generally, that is, regarding international delicts, is discussed within the specific sections or subsections before attention is turned towards either obligations *erga omnes* or international crimes. The main reason for this is that up to a relatively short time ago the rules on State responsibility had been considered to be of unitary character, that is to say that there existed only one régime of responsibility for all internationally wrongful acts.[15] Special rapporteur Arangio-Ruiz proposed, and acted upon that proposal, to first elaborate the régime of responsibility applicable to international delicts, and afterwards attempt to elaborate the régime applicable to international crimes.[16]

The Commission has claimed, in 1976, that more severe consequences would attach to crimes than are applicable to delicts, but it indicated that it did not need to address those questions at that stage of drafting.[17] However, an important final, but preliminary, question must be addressed, namely whether there are two régimes of State responsibility, one for international delicts and one for international crimes, or whether there are more. That question has been triggered by some observations of the Commission in the commentary to article 19 to the effect that:[18]

> "(...) it would be wrong to believe that there is a single basic régime of international responsibility which is applicable to all internationally wrongful acts without distinction, and that all that is required is to add extra consequences to it for wrongful acts constituting international crimes. That may be true for some particular crimes, but there is no gainsaying the possible existence of others with respect to which the applicability of certain specific forms of responsibility would exclude the applicability of the consequences prescribed for other wrongs. The idea that there is some kind of least common denominator in the régime of international responsibility must be discarded."

These remarks were made mostly in order to rebut a stance implying that the Commission should restrict itself to stating a general régime of State responsibility, and that it would leave it to customary or conventional law to lay down the régime applicable to international crimes.[19] Yet it cannot but be noted that it had stated earlier on in the commentary when positing the more severe consequences in case of international crimes:[20]

> "This does not, of course, mean that all these crimes are equal – in other words, that they attain the same degree of seriousness and necessarily entail all the

more severe consequences incurred, for example, by the supreme international crime, namely, a war of aggression."

There can be no doubt that the international crime of aggression takes a prominent position in international law. While most international crimes have been regulated, to differing degrees, in conventional instruments, the only conduct regarding which collective enforcement has been envisaged concerns also the crime of aggression. It cannot be doubted that the crime of aggression is the supreme crime in international law, though that position is due more to the fact that its commission disturbs the relations between States in the most serious way. It cannot be said, at least not *a priori*, that the commission of other international crimes causes less damage, or that their commission would be any less abhorrent than the crime of aggression.

Now while there are certainly grounds to single out the Charter of the United Nations for differential treatment,[21] that is not the same as saying that the régime applicable to cases of aggression should be different from the régime applicable to the other international crimes. Furthermore, one would wonder whether it would be feasible for the Commission to embark on the codification or progressive development in regard to crimes in total disregard of the régime of State responsibility developed over the years. The Commission posited its distinction between delicts and crimes on the view that it existed *de lege lata*. Yet it would seem that one of the difficulties encountered during the elaboration of the régime of crimes has been the lack of any clear idea as to which aggravated consequences could be envisaged in case of crimes. In that light one would expect any régime applicable to crimes to be grafted upon the general régime of State responsibility applicable to delicts. The elaboration of a régime on crimes should therefore proceed on the assumptions that all those consequences which attach to the commission of an international delict also attach to the commission of a crime,[22] that there are only two régimes of responsibility, and that those régimes are substantially uniform in character.

The purpose of the research has been to investigate, from a legal perspective, whether it is possible to fruitfully elaborate a régime of responsibility applicable in case of crimes, that is, a substantially aggravated régime. To that end it has been attempted to identify features of the régime of responsibility applicable to international delicts which could or should be modified in order to impose more severe consequences on the author State of an international crime. In the same vein the assumptions that there are only two régimes of responsibility, and that those are uniform in character, will have been put to the test, and they will be reverted to at the end. Furthermore, it will be, and has been, assumed that the underlying purpose for imposing more severe consequences on the author State of an international crime lies with the perceived need, lacking in regard to delicts, to provide for the more effective suppression of conduct constituting crimes.

On the basis of the foregoing observations this thesis will be subdivided into the following chapters. Chapter one will investigate the structures related to interests, rules, obligations and rights in international law and the legal interests of States. Chapter two will deal with obligations *erga omnes*, international crimes, and the legal interests of the international community and the United Nations. Chapter three will concern the obligation of an author State to provide reparation, and the corresponding right of (an) injured State(s) and the United Nations to demand such reparation, in case of international crimes. Chapter four will examine the right of (an) injured State(s) and the United Nations to resort to non-military countermeasures in response to international crimes. Chapter five will look into the right of (an) injured State(s) and the United Nations to resort to armed force in response to international crimes. Finally chapter six will discuss the right of (an) injured State(s) and the United Nations to have recourse to the International Court of Justice in relation to international crimes.

NOTES

[1] The 1919 Covenant of the League of Nations, 13 AJIL 1919, Supplement, pp. 128-140.
[2] The 1945 Charter of the United Nations, 39 AJIL 1945, Supplement, pp. 190-215.
[3] The 1969 Vienna Convention on the Law of Treaties, 63 AJIL 1969, pp. 875-903.
[4] Text and Commentary Article 50, Law of Treaties, YBILC 1966, Volume II, pp. 247-249, 247.
[5] Barcelona Traction, Light and Power Company, Limited, Judgment, ICJ Reports 1970, p. 3, 32.
[6] Text and Commentary Article 19, Part One, YBILC 1976, Volume II, Part Two, pp. 95-122.
[7] Transcripts of President's Address to Joint Session of Congress, N.Y. Times, 12 September 1990, A20.
[8] The 1945 Statute of the International Court of Justice, 39 AJIL 1945, Supplement, pp. 215-229.
[9] Barcelona Traction Case, 32.
[10] Text and Commentary Article 5, Part Two, YBILC 1985, Volume II, Part Two, pp. 25-27.
[11] Text and Commentary Article 1, Part One, YBILC 1973, Volume II, pp. 173-176, 175.
[12] On the Commission's project on "Liability for Injurious Consequences Arising out of Acts not Prohibited by International Law", see Report of the International Law Commission on the work of its forty-sixth session, 2 May – 22 July 1994, General Assembly, Official Records, Forty-ninth Session, Supplement No. 10 (A/49/10), pp. 367-437.
[13] Arangio-Ruiz, G., Seventh Report on State Responsibility, 9 May 1995, A/CN.4/469, 49 pp.; 24 May 1995, A/CN.4/469/Add.1, 4 pp.; and 29 May 1995, A/CN.4/469/Add.2, 3 pp.
[14] Case concerning East Timor (Portugal *v.* Australia), Judgment, 30 June 1995.
[15] Commentary Article 19, Part One, 97.
[16] Arangio-Ruiz, G., Preliminary Report on State Responsibility, 18 May 1988, A/CN.4/416, 34 pp., 4-6.
[17] Commentary Article 19, Part One, 117.
[18] Commentary Article 19, Part One, 117.
[19] Commentary Article 19, Part One, 117-118.
[20] Commentary Article 19, Part One, 109.
[21] Commentary Article 19, Part One, 118.
[22] C.f. Riphagen's proposed article 14, paragraph 1, Part Two. Riphagen, W., Fifth report on the content, forms and degrees of international responsibility (part 2 of the draft articles), YBILC 1984, Volume II, Part One, pp. 1-4, 4; and Arangio-Ruiz' proposed article 15, Part Two. Arangio-Ruiz, Seventh Report, Addendum 1, 2.

CHAPTER 1

STRUCTURES RELATED TO INTERESTS, RULES, OBLIGATIONS AND RIGHTS IN INTERNATIONAL LAW AND THE LEGAL INTERESTS OF STATES

1.1. Introduction

The present chapter deals with questions of legal interest generally, and culminates in an examination of issues related to *jus cogens*, obligations *erga omnes* and international crimes. The starting-point was constituted by the observation of the Commission that the relations resulting from the commission of an internationally wrongful act might be established between:[1] "(...) the offending State and the directly injured State or extend also to other subjects of international law, (...)." The term "directly injured State" will be taken to mean a State against which an internationally wrongful act is directed, or a State which is in one way or another affected, in an exclusive manner, by the wrongful act of the author State.

It seems appropriate to start the present chapter by investigating the notion of interest, notwithstanding that that notion does not appear to have any specific legal connotation. The notion of interest, when addressed by jurists, is usually supplemented by adjectives, such as in "legal interest", "interest of a legal nature", and "political interest". The latter two phrases are not relevant for the examination in this chapter, which concerns primarily the issue of legal interest. After having explored, generally, the notion of interest, the distinction between interests *pur sang* and interests protected by international law will be reflected upon. A further topic of discussion will be the way in which interests come to be protected by international law, that is, through the elaboration of primary rules of international law.[2]

Primary rules of international law can be said to lay down obligations or rights for those bound by the rule concerned. In regard to obligations and rights alike the question may be raised whether there do not exist obligations correlative to rights and/or rights correlative to obligations. This latter correlation, rights correlative to obligations, leads to observations regarding the possession of a correlative right as a prerequisite to demand the performance of obligations by other States. Another point of discussion concerns the sources laying down the rules that provide for the correlative rights to demand the performance of obligations by other States. Finally the exercise of such correlative rights will be linked up to the notion of legal interest.

At this point the criteria to determine whether a State can be held to possess a legal interest in the performance of obligations by other States must be examined. Consecutively will be discussed the criteria of the general interest in the performance of obligations, the common interest in the performance of obligations, and the performance of obligations towards specific States. Finally attention will be devoted to the notions of damage (material, moral and legal) and the effects resulting from an internationally wrongful act. The examination of criteria provides the basis for establishing an *a priori* categorization of legal interests regarding the performance of obligations by States. Apart from certain non-problematical categories the following will be discussed: legal interests, prejudice and the individual interest of States; legal interests, prejudice and the collective interest of States; and legal interests and the posited collective interest.

From these attention is turned towards a final category of legal interests, to be determined by reference to the content, or subject-matter, of certain rules and their recognized importance for the international community. In positive law the recognized importance of certain rules constituted the basis for the introduction of the concept of *jus cogens* in the Vienna Convention on the Law of Treaties.[3] Subsequently, so it seems, the Court picked up on this development and proclaimed, in the Barcelona Traction Case, the existence of obligations *erga omnes*.[4] The Commission in turn took note of these and certain other developments, and adopted, in article 19, Part One, of its draft on State responsibility, the distinction between international delicts and international crimes.[5]

It is proposed to examine, in section 1.2, interests and their expression in international law. Section 1.3 will discuss obligations, rights and their correlation in international law. This is followed, in section 1.4, by certain observations on the necessity of correlative rights, their sources, their exercise and the requirement of a legal interest. Section 1.5 then examines the criteria to determine the existence of a legal interest in the performance of obligations. Section 1.6 goes on to postulate certain categories of legal interests of States. The concept of *jus cogens* will constitute the subject of section 1.7. In section 1.8 then the Court's dictum on obligations *erga omnes* will be discussed. Finally section 1.9 will examine the theory of international crimes.

1.2. Interests and their legal expression in international law

1.2.1. A DEFINITION OF INTERESTS?

The question has to be raised what the real meaning is of the notion of "interest". It is clear that, grammatically speaking, it is mostly used in context with "have an interest in something". But of course this begs the question, because "interest" is supplemented by the adjective "in". Gervais nevertheless offers a definition of what an interest should be considered to be:[6]

> "La notion d'«intérêt» se développe sur un plan pratique, celui de «l'existence» ou plus concrètement de l'utilité. Un «intérêt» peut se définir comme une utilité, qui peut être matérielle ou morale, actuelle ou future, qui est en général égoïste mais peut aussi être altruiste. Cette «utilité», caractéristique de l'intérêt, consiste à avoir la *possibilité matérielle* soit de satisfaire ses besoins, soit d'obtenir des avantages, soit d'éviter des inconvénients. Cette notion abstraite de l'«intérêt» en général a un contenu indéfini, en tant qu'elle recouvre toutes les utilités imaginables, «les divers intérêts concrets» correspondant chacun à une utilité particulière ayant un contenu determiné identifiable par sa spécificité et

qui, de ce fait, pourraient être appelés intérêts «nommés»."

It may be granted to Gervais that interests will normally be directed towards the fulfilment of needs, obtaining advantages, or avoiding disadvantageous effects. But States have many interests, and it may happen that a State will choose for the prevailing of the one that is more favourable to another State than to its own. Thus the altruistic (social or humanitarian) interest, which Gervais mentions, but fails to relate to his definition of "utilité", may have as strong an impetus as interests of an egocentric nature. Furthermore, Gervais construes "utilité" as the material possibility of achieving a certain goal. However, an interest does not of necessity relate to the possession of the means necessary for achieving that goal, but to the realization of what an interest stands for, whatever the means.

Though it is clearly possible to mention the existence of an interest, still the expression "have an interest in something" seems to be inadequate, because, although it states the object "something", it fails to make clear what the objective is with regard to that object. Thus the owner of the interest has, with regard to that "something", a certain objective in mind in the sense that a certain course of conduct is contemplated to the exclusion of others. This objective in regard to such course of conduct relates either to maintaining a certain status quo, or to changing it. In this respect Arató observes:[7]

> "Die Rechtssubjekte begleiten den Verlauf der Dinge mit Werturteilen und qualifizieren den Eintritt oder Nichteintritt gewisser Umstände, die Fortdauer oder Veränderung der Zustände als erwünscht. Der Wert, den der Eintritt oder Nichteintritt einer bestimmten Veränderung für den Betreffenden hat, ist das Interesse."

This objective will inevitably have to be implemented by means of certain acts or omissions on the part of States,[8] and this whether or not the status quo is to be maintained or changed. The Dictionnaire published by the Union Académique Internationale refers to an interest ("intérêt") as follows:[9]

> "Terme désignant ce qui affecte matériellement ou moralement une personne physique ou juridique, l'avantage matériel ou moral que présente pour elle une action ou abstention, le maintien ou le changement d'une situation."

It seems, however, that "interests" do not have an autonomous existence of their own. From these observations it will be clear that an interest cannot be divorced from the actual circumstances in which it exists. Normally if an interest is advanced regarding a certain subject-matter,[10] without specifying the objective to be pursued therewith, it will retain its inherently abstract character. This situation does not change, not even when it relates to a certain concrete situation, for so long as it is not indicated to what extent such an interest is to result in the maintenance of, or change in, the status quo. Nevertheless it is possible to hold, in the abstract, that an interest always manifests itself in relation to a certain desired course of conduct, the realization of which is sought to be achieved by States or other subjects of international law. Brunnée for instance states:[11]

> "At the same time, however, the level of 'coinciding interests' provides the foundation for the 'common interests' concept's significance on the legal level. This flows from the fact that the existence of (coinciding) interests generally inspires efforts to see them realized. (...) Such realization is, in its scope and

effectiveness, dependent on the degree of agreement between the parties concerned. This agreement, in turn, is most stable and of greatest continuity if it can crystallize into a rule of international law. (...) Accordingly, international law in general is a result of the 'common interest' of the states in dependable relations guided by certain basic principles."

Most of the time an interest, a desired course of conduct, will be advanced by States or other subjects of international law, and allocation will thus be instantly made.[12] However, it may happen that a State claims that an interest advanced by another State, in the sense of a desired course of conduct, is not in the interest of the State advancing it, or that its very existence is being denied. Indeed, for the most part a claimed interest will be considered, by the State advancing it, also to be in its interest. To put it differently: that the realization of a certain course of conduct is, subjectively speaking, favourable to that State. Yet it must be stressed that this aspect of the term interest is not inherent in the term discussed. If, as observed above, an interest manifests itself in relation to a certain course of conduct, then that course of conduct need not be favourable to the State advancing it, and nor need it entail advantages for it.[13] The only desire for the State advancing an interest is that a certain course of conduct will be realized, and only in the latter sense can one claim that any interest advanced inevitably possesses a subjective aspect. The importance of this argument cannot be stressed enough, for it happens all too often that an asserted interest, a desired course of conduct, is confused with the "allegedly" required condition that such course of conduct must also be in the interest of the person demanding the realization of that course of conduct.

1.2.2. THE DISTINCTION BETWEEN INTERESTS *PUR SANG* AND INTERESTS PROTECTED BY INTERNATIONAL LAW

There can be no doubt that since there are so many individuals and States, there exist an enormous variety of interests in national communities and within the international community. Yet this does not mean that each and every interest is protected by law. Indeed, it seems to be a function of law to separate interests worthy of protection from those which are not to benefit from such protection. This is of course not to say that at a certain point in time all interests worthy of protection are indeed protected by law. For law is not so much a static process, but a dynamic one, and the development of the law is as such very much dependent upon the social circumstances prevailing within the community. While therefore law as a social phenomenon may emerge as a result of the commonly felt needs within a community, nevertheless the progressing complexities of a community will necessitate the institutionalized development of law, with the consequent institution of law as a legal phenomenon. As a counterpart of these developments the law will tend to become more rigid, and less sensitive to the changing social circumstances. For it will become bound to those legal techniques established in the course of time for changing the law, and in the meanwhile the law as it stands will have to be applied.[14] Naturally such divergences may have been foreseen, and may have been addressed by some special legal technique for settling conflicts in case of any such divergence occurring.[15] But, in the absence of such special legal techniques, interests will only be protected by law to the extent that they have found expression in that law through some legal technique.

In international law the dichotomy between interests *pur sang* and interests protected by law has been particularly underlined by the Court in the 1966 South West Africa Cases, where it held:[16]

> "49. The Court must now turn to certain questions of a wider character. Throughout this case it has been suggested, directly or indirectly, that humanitarian considerations are sufficient in themselves to generate legal rights and obligations, and that the Court can and should proceed accordingly. The Court does not think so. It is a court of law, and can take account of moral principles only in so far as these are given a sufficient expression in legal form. Law exists, it is said, to serve a social need; but precisely for that reason it can do so only through and within the limits of its own discipline. Otherwise, it is not a legal service that would be rendered.
>
> 50. Humanitarian considerations may constitute the inspirational basis for rules of law, just as, for instance, the preambular parts of the United Nations Charter constitute the moral and political basis for the specific legal provisions thereafter set out. Such considerations do not, however, in themselves amount to rules of law. All States are interested – have an interest – in such matters. But the existence of an 'interest' does not of itself entail that this interest is specifically juridical in character.
>
> 51. (...) The sacred trust, it is said, is a 'sacred trust of civilization'. Hence all civilized nations have an interest in seeing that it is carried out. An interest, no doubt; – but in order that this interest may take on a specifically legal character, the sacred trust itself must be or become something more than a moral or humanitarian ideal. In order to generate legal rights and obligations, it must be given juridical expression and be clothed in legal form."

The validity of these statements as such – irrespective of the legal consequences attached to this position by the Court – seems to be self-evident. Once law as a legal phenomenon has emerged within a certain community (that is to say once the legal techniques applicable for the creation of legal rules and their enforcement have been determined in an exclusive manner), an institute or organ charged with applying the law cannot, or at least should not, venture to do what is outside its competence. Thus if a certain interest has so far not been accorded the protection by law through the applicable procedures, then such an interest cannot be granted legal protection by those charged with the application or enforcement of law. Eventually such legal protection may come to be accorded through the law creating process.

Although the above mentioned quotation is concerned with humanitarian interests, the division between interests *pur sang* and interests protected by law may be generalized. In the Barcelona Traction Case the Court held in the context of the institute of diplomatic protection:[17]

> "86. Hence the Belgian Government would be entitled to bring a claim if it could show that one of its rights had been infringed and that the acts complained of involved the breach of an international obligation arising out of a treaty or a general rule of law. The opinion has been expressed that a claim can

accordingly be made when investments by a State's nationals abroad are thus prejudicially affected, and that since such investments are part of a State's national economic resources, any prejudice to them directly involves the economic interests of the State.

87. Governments have been known to intervene in such circumstances not only when their interests were affected, but also when they were threatened. However, it must be stressed that this type of action is quite different from and outside the field of diplomatic protection. When a State admits into its territory foreign investments or foreign nationals it is, as indicated in paragraph 33, bound to extend to them the protection of the law. However, it does not thereby become an insurer of that part of another State's wealth which these interests represents. Every investment of this kind carries certain risks. The real question is whether a right has been violated, which right could only be the right of the State to have its nationals enjoy a certain treatment guaranteed by general international law, in the absence of any treaty applicable to the particular case."

And earlier it had observed:[18]

"46. It has also been contended that the measures complained of, although taken with respect to Barcelona Traction and causing it direct damage, constituted an unlawful act vis-à-vis Belgium, because they also, though indirectly, caused damage to the Belgian shareholders in Barcelona Traction. This again is merely a different way of presenting the distinction between injury in respect of a right and injury to a simple interest. But, as the Court has indicated, evidence that damage was suffered does not *ipso facto* justify a diplomatic claim. Persons suffer damage or harm in most varied circumstances. This in itself does not involve the obligation to make reparation. Not a mere interest affected, but solely a right infringed involves responsibility, so that an act directed against and infringing only the company's rights does not involve responsibility towards the shareholders, even if their interests are affected."

The latter part of this quotation, however, appears to reflect, more properly speaking, upon the distinction between interests and rights arising under municipal law.

The review of the distinction between interests *pur sang* and interests protected by international law cannot be complete without some attention being devoted to the Lac Lanoux Award, in which the Tribunal observed:[19]

"Il faut d'abord déterminer quels sont les «intérêts» qui doivent être saufgardés. L'interprétation stricte de l'article 11 permettrait de soutenir qu'il ne sagit que des intérêts correspondant à un droit des riverains. Cependant, diverses considérations déjà dégagées par le Tribunal conduisent à une interprétation plus large. Il faut tenir compte, quelle qu'en soit la nature, de tous les intérêts qui risquent d'être affectés par les travaux enterpris, même s'ils ne correspondent pas à un droit, seule cette solution correspond aux termes de l'article 16, à l'esprit des traités pyrénéens, aux tendances qui se manifestent en matière d'aménagements hydroelectriques dans la pratique internationale actuelle."

Gervais appears inclined, on the basis of this passage, to introduce a generalized differentiation to the effect that there would be interests ("intérêts simples"), legitimate interests ("intérêts légitimes") and rights ("droits"). Such legitimate interests, in contradistinction to simple interests, would enjoy a certain protection, even if not as complete as rights.[20] And he notes that on this score the Tribunal claimed as regards the measure of protection to be afforded to such legitimate interests:[21]

> "Le Tribunal est d'avis que l'Etat d'amont a, d'après les règles de la bonne foi, l'obligation de prendre en considération les différents intérêts en présence, de chercher à leur donner toutes les satisfactions compatibles avec la poursuite de ses propres intérêts et de montrer qu'il a à ce sujet un souci réel de concilier les intérêts des autres riverains avec les siens propres."

The difference, according to Gervais, between rights and legitimate interests is to be found in the fact that the interest protected by a right is specified ("nommé") and is accorded absolute protection, whereas what is concerned in the case of legitimate interests are unspecified interests that are only accorded the safeguard of having to be taken into consideration by another State for the purpose of trying, in good faith, to reconcile them with its own interests.[22]

While the said distinction is not entirely without merits, especially if applied to the process of determining whether or not a certain interest is protected by international law, it seems nevertheless that it cannot be generalized.[23] First of all because it derives from the interpretation of a provision of a treaty which explicitly mentions the protection of interests.[24] Moreover, the Tribunal places this construction upon the provision in question with reference to developments taking place in practice. Such practice relates, amongst others, to the specific subject of liability for acts not prohibited by international law.[25] Since conduct relating to this area is not always regulated by international law, one can only measure the interest of one State against that of another.[26] Furthermore, one may note that this issue is as such connected with the view one takes with regard to the role to be played by rules of international law that regulate the conduct of States. It was held for instance, by the Permanent Court, that restrictions on the independence of States cannot be presumed.[27] Yet does that mean that in the absence of any rule restrictive of a State's freedom it can do anything it wants? The least that can be demanded from States is that they show some regard for the interests of other States.[28] This flows from the sovereign equality of States (since the freedom of one State restricts the freedom of another),[29] and from the principle of good faith.

1.2.3. INTERESTS AND THEIR PROTECTION BY MEANS OF ELABORATION OF PRIMARY RULES OF INTERNATIONAL LAW: THE COMMON INTEREST

After having reached the conclusion that not all interests are protected by international law one is led to the question: which are the legal techniques by means of which interests come to be protected by international law? This concerns a somewhat different aspect than the matter of sources of international law.[30] For the question of sources relates to the manner in which international law is created (formal technique), whereas the means of protection relate to the manner in which such protection is legally effected (material technique). The way in which international law primarily protects interests is through the elaboration of rules. As has been observed above, in subsection 1.2.1, an interest manifests itself in a desired course of conduct, whose realization is sought to be achieved by a State or another subject of international law. But it is obvious that such desired courses of conduct, subjectively appreciated, need not be shared by all the States making up the international community.[31] States may of course hold parallel interests with regard to a certain subject-matter, and may even agree upon the course of conduct to be followed therewith.[32] Yet that does not suffice to make it the common interest, for, as long as these parallel interests have not been established in accordance with the formal sources of international law, any State may legitimately decide to withdraw from its earlier held position with regard to the desired course of conduct. But, once these parallel interests have found expression through some formal source of international law, no State can escape the legal effects resulting therefrom (unless other legal rules provide for opting out of such legal effects). From that moment on the course of conduct laid down in a rule of international law constitutes the common interest for those subjects obligated or favoured by the rule.[33] The consequence is that, though subjective interests are predominant in the phase of formulating and creating the rule,[34] they lose much of their potence as soon as the rule actually comes into existence. From that moment on it is the expressed intention, the expressed course of conduct, and, more particularly, the expressed common interest that prevails over existing subjective interests.[35]

At this point it has to be observed that the interests put forward by States participating in the creation of a certain rule need not necessarily coincide fully with the interests which eventually come to be protected by the rule in question. Judge Altamira, in his separate opinion to the Case concerning Diversion of Water from the Meuse, observed:[36]

> "(...) there is the fact – entirely natural since we are dealing with a treaty – that the Treaty of May 12th, 1863, involves obligations and that these obligations must be fulfilled. The fact that the Treaty is chiefly concerned with the adjustment of the Parties' interests and not with differences of a really legal nature does not mean that no legal relationship is established as regards the fulfilment of the agreement in regard to interests. These interests may have been the reason for the conclusion of the Treaty, but once the Treaty has come into existence, the rights and obligations which it expressly or implicitly creates take precedence. The interests remain in the background and can only be taken into account in so far as is permitted by the legal provisions embodied in the agreement between the Parties. They can never take the place of these provisions or impede their execution."

As may be recalled an interest, as it relates to a certain subject-matter, has as its objective the realization of a certain course of conduct (maintenance or change of the status quo), and only an interpretation of the rule in question may show whether or not it protects the interest of a certain State. However, for the most part, as may be deduced from the quotation, rules do not even refer to the interest protected, let alone to the interests of the States participating in its creation. Mostly they are drafted in prescriptive terms, and if that is the case they approximate the grammatical meaning of the law's obliging character, and thus refer directly towards the status quo or at least to the objective to be attained in relation therewith. If one takes for instance the prohibitory rule "States shall refrain, in their international relations, from the use force", it is clear that it may either relate to a situation in which States are in the habit of using force and such practice is henceforth prohibited, or to a situation in which they do not use force and, since it is desirable that they should abstain from using force for the future, such practice shall become prohibited. In the first case the rule is intended to change the prevailing status quo, whereas in the second it has as objective the maintenance of the status quo. Notwithstanding that it is the status quo to which the formulation of a rule directly refers, or at least to its maintenance or its change, it is nevertheless more correct, in this example, to state that a rule prescribes a certain course of conduct, consisting of either acts or omissions. Unless the rule in question is permissive in character, in which case the course of conduct mentioned in the rule may be followed.

The protection of interests has, generally speaking, taken place by means of the elaboration of primary rules of international law. Those may either prescribe a certain course of conduct, prohibit it, or, to the contrary, permit it.[37] A prescriptive rule of international law can be said to lay down an obligation to adopt particular conduct for those States subjected to the rule. A prohibitive rule lays down an obligation of abstention regarding particular conduct for those States subjected to the rule. And a permissive rule creates rights for the States to which the rule applies. Obligations and rights will be discussed in the following section, but apart from these some correlations between the two will be addressed.

1.3. Obligations, rights and their correlation in international law

The late judge Ago, then special rapporteur, discussing how to formulate the objective element as a condition for the existence of an internationally wrongful act (article 3, Part One, of the ILC-draft),[38] reflected upon the nature of rules, and what springs from them, obligations and rights, in the following manner:[39]

> "The rule is law in the objective sense. Its function is to attribute in certain conditions subjective legal situations – rights, faculties, powers and obligations – to those to whom it is addressed. It is these situations which, as their global appellation indicates, constitute law in the subjective sense; it is in relation to these situations that the subject's conduct operates. The subject freely exercises or refrains from exercising its subjective right, faculty or power, and freely fulfils or violates its obligation, but it does not 'exercise' the rule and likewise does not 'violate' it. It is its duty which it fails to carry out and not the principle of objective law from which that duty flows. This does not mean that the obligation whose breach is the constituent element of an internationally wrongful act must necessarily flow from a rule, at least in the proper meaning of that term. The obligation in question may very well have been created and imposed upon a subject by a particular legal act, a decision of a judicial or arbitral tribunal, a decision of an international organization, etc."

An example may be in order to clarify the difference between the rule, as objective law, and the obligation, as the concrete emanation ensuing therefrom. A well-established rule of customary international law, also laid down in conventional law, provides that a State must grant immunity to persons accredited as diplomatic agents.[40] That rule is binding on all States, and thus States are under the obligation to grant immunity to diplomatic agents. Let us suppose that a certain national X of State A enters into State B, breaches a rule (or obligation maybe) of the criminal code and is apprehended by the police authorities of State B. X is then brought before a judge, and at that moment claims to be a diplomatic agent. The judge, as an organ of State B, is clearly bound under the relevant rule of customary international law to grant immunity to such agents. But immediately the question rises whether the rule applies to X. Is X really a diplomatic agent? Because if he is not, State B will not be under any obligation to grant X the immunity that is claimed. To determine whether or not a person is a diplomatic agent it is necessary to define what is meant by a diplomatic agent, the conditions to be fulfilled, and whether those have been complied with (primarily articles 1 and 7 of the Vienna Convention Diplomatic Relations). So if X is not covered by the definition of diplomatic agents, or if additional requirements have not been met, State B will not be under the obligation to grant immunity to X. Obviously State B is bound by the rule to grant immunity to diplomatic agents, but in the concrete circumstances at hand no obligation will exist to adopt conduct in conformity with that rule.

It follows from these observations that the formulation of a rule of international law[41] presupposes the use of generalized or abstract terms,[42] and this may very well be explained on the basis of the particular circumstances prevailing at the time of its creation, as well as the, most of the time conflicting, interests held by the subjects participating in such creation. Having indicated the relation of rules to obligations and rights, some elaboration of the latter is called for.

1.3.1. OBLIGATIONS

The first and foremost manner of legal protection provided by international law to interests is that it is binding for those subjected to it.[43] Thus it imposes upon its subjects respect for its rules. In a general sense the absence of law means that any State is free to do as it wills, and the primary function of law, qualitatively speaking, lies in the restrictive character it possesses once it exists.[44] Thus law obliges, and from this, grammatically speaking, derives the term "obligation". The subjective nature of obligations, as opposed to the objective nature of rules,[45] leads to the conclusion that it is not sufficient to prove that a rule exists, what it prescribes and to whom it applies, but that it is also necessary, having regard to the particular circumstances prevailing at the time of its application, to specify to what extent the rule obligates States to follow a certain course of conduct in those circumstances. An additional argument for using the term "obligation" may be mentioned in that a rule of international law need not be binding on every individual subject of international law. For treaties are considered to be binding only for those States which have expressed their consent to be bound, and a rule of customary international law may, at the time of its creation, be persistently opposed to by a certain State. If one were to mention the breach of a rule as a constituent element of an internationally wrongful act one would still have to determine whether or not that rule is binding for the State concerned, and whether or not it imposes some obligation on that State. The Commission, in phrasing article 3, Part One, therefore correctly opted for the use of the term "obligation" instead of "rule":[46]

"There is an internationally wrongful act of a State when:

(a) conduct consisting of an action or omission is attributable to the State under international law; and

(b) that conduct constitutes a breach of an international obligation of the State."

A few words may be in order regarding the use by the Commission of the term "breach of an obligation" in article 3 of the ILC-draft. Preceding observations make it clear that, although the choice for the term "obligation" is correct, it is not proper to speak of the breach or violation of an obligation. For what a State must do according to a certain rule is to adopt the conduct prescribed by that rule.[47] What happens therefore in reality in case of a breach of an obligation is that the status quo is maintained where it should have been changed, or is changed where it should have been maintained.[48] Article 3, Part One, of the ILC-draft therefore incorrectly mentions that certain conduct attributable to a State may constitute the "breach" of an international obligation. This preference for the word "breach" may probably be explained by the wish to accentuate the normative character of law, since conduct inconsistent with an obligation results in a situation contrary to what is prescribed by the legal system. Thus the "breach" of an obligation stresses the fact that conduct contravening the law is generally disapproved of. Yet although law is not neutral with regard to such conduct, nevertheless it is better not to prejudge the application of the law to that conduct. Accordingly, it would be better to use the phrase "non-fulfilment of an international obligation", or "the adoption of conduct inconsistent with what is required of a State under an international obligation".[49] That is more or less how article 16, Part One, of the ILC-draft coins it:[50]

"There is a breach of an international obligation by a State when an act of that State is not in conformity with what is required of it by that obligation."

However, in order to conform to prevailing legal terminology reference will be made hereafter to "breach of an obligation", as well as, naturally, the phrase "internationally wrongful act".

1.3.2. RIGHTS

While the first and foremost means of protecting interests lies in restricting the otherwise existing freedom of States to do as they will by means of rules creating obligations, rules of international law may, instead of being drafted in prescriptive or prohibitive terms, be coined in permissive terms. If such is the case the rule in question confers upon its subjects an entitlement to engage in the conduct specified in the rule. This construction concerns, typically, what are called "rights".[51] What is permitted by the rule in question and what it contemplates is, for the most part, not legal action, but physical action. Thus the rule which establishes a right legitimizes conduct that would otherwise have been illegal, conduct that arguably had been considered to be illegal, or conduct that had not been regulated before by any rule of international law.[52]

Of old the juridical meaning of the word "right" has been defined as a "legally protected interest".[53] But one may note that Bilge observes:[54]

"(...) la violation d'une obligation est, toujours, en même temps, une lésion de l'intérêt qu'elle protège."

It is for this reason that it is incorrect to describe a right as a legally protected interest, for rules, whether permissive (laying down rights) or prescriptive and prohibitive (laying down obligations), always protect certain interests. But it does not make much sense to describe an obligation as a legally protected interest, for the immediate reaction to such a statement would be "whose interest"? The basis for the confused definition of a right as a legally protected interest may be found in the more or less automatic allocation of a right to a certain subject of law. For the interests which are thus legally protected – protection offered by a permissive rule to the subjects to which it applies, who are consequently entitled to engage in a certain course of conduct – appear to coincide with the interests of particular subjects of law.[55] But it is obvious that the same does not apply in case of obligations. It is immediately clear that when a subject is exercising a right it is at the same time protecting its interests. But when a subject conforms its conduct to what is required of it by an obligation, then it is still not clear (unless it is specified in the rule who is to benefit from conduct in conformity with an obligation, or if this results from the factual circumstances) in whose interest such conduct is considered to be.

At this point some attention needs to be devoted towards the meaning of the adjective "subjective", which is at times attached to the notion of rights.[56] Rights are of necessity to be described as "subjective", since the course of conduct which the law authorizes a subject to engage in is intimately related to the subject's sphere of action. It would of course make no sense if a permissive rule of international law were to confer rights on those subjects favoured by the rule, without at the same time making it possible for them to engage in the course of conduct to which they are entitled.[57] To coin it differently: the course of conduct specified in the rule must be capable of being realized by the subjects to which the rule applies.[58] From this point of view there is no difference whatsoever between permissive and prescriptive rules, between rights and obligations. Both are subjective in nature, both stem from an objective rule, and both must be capable, at least potentially, of being realized in real life. In the following no use will be made, regarding either rights or obligations, of the adjective "subjective".

1.3.3. OBLIGATIONS CORRELATIVE TO RIGHTS

It has been mentioned before that a right confers upon a subject of law an entitlement to engage in a specified course of conduct, and it has been added that the possibility of realizing such course of action must lie within that subject's sphere of action. Yet naturally this cannot be the only protection offered by law to a right-holder. It is relevant in this regard to refer to the Case concerning the Right of Passage, in which the Court held:[59]

> "The Court sees no reason why long continued practice between two States accepted by them as regulating their relations should not form the basis of mutual rights and obligations between the two States."

And it went on to say on the next page:[60]

> "(...), the Court is, in view of all the circumstances of the case, satisfied that that practice was accepted as law by the parties and has given rise to a right and a correlative obligation."

While the formulations of this principle, that a right must be accompanied by a correlative obligation,[61] differ, nevertheless the ratio for it is clear. Because in the absence of such a correlative obligation on the part of some other subject of international law the right itself might become meaningless. For if any such other subject were not under the obligation to respect another subject's exercise of a right, lawfully and validly conferred by a rule of international law, then any subject could legitimately impede the exercise of such right without being held responsible for such impediment. If therefore a subject acts in disregard of its obligation established correlative to the right conferred upon another subject by a permissive rule of international law, then it may be held responsible for the breach of that obligation. Naturally such obligation to respect the exercise of a right only exists with regard to subjects to which the permissive rule in question applies.[62] It may be stressed here that although seemingly the restrictive character of international law lies mainly in prescriptive and prohibitive rules, that, as may be seen from what has been observed just now, is only partly true.

1.3.4. RIGHTS CORRELATIVE TO OBLIGATIONS

On one occasion the late judge Ago, then special rapporteur, contended:[63]

> "The term 'right' ('droit' in the subjective sense) indicates a 'claim' which the law ('droit' in the objective sense), invoking the legal order, accords to a subject vis-à-vis other subjects, of whom he may rightfully require a specific performance or a specific conduct."

For reasons which will become clear hereafter this definition of "right" was not discussed above in subsection 1.3.2. The definition does fit in with the one entertained above, because Ago's definition does no more than specify the course of conduct (which is to require some subject to perform an obligation) to which a subject may have an entitlement. It should nonetheless be noted that the right mentioned before, and what it has been considered to stand for, namely the entitlement of a subject to engage in a certain course of conduct, differs somewhat from the right as dealt with by special rapporteur Ago.[64] For while, in principle, the exercise of the right spoken of, and the realization of the course of conduct to which that right relates, depends upon some action to be resorted to by the subject that holds the right, Ago defines his right in such a way that the holder of the right is entitled to engage in a certain course of conduct to the effect that it may require some other subject to perform its obligation. Thus the realization of the course of conduct which a prescriptive or prohibitive rule aims at (by means of laying down an obligation, to which corresponds a rule laying down the right to demand performance) is, in principle, dependent upon some subject other than the (subject) holder of the right.

The distinction between primary and secondary rules of international law becomes relevant at this junction. For the Commission, at the instigation of the then special rapporteur Ago, held:[65]

> "It should be noted that in international law the idea of breach of an obligation can be regarded as the exact equivalent of the idea of infringement of the subjective rights of others. (...) The correlation between legal obligation on the one hand and subjective right on the other admits of no exception;"

While not disputing the existence of rights correlative to obligations,[66] the conception here uttered is nevertheless to be criticized. The correlation that is in issue here is the one between an obligation (a prescribed course of conduct, consisting of either acts or omissions, to be realized by a subject of international law) and a right which consists of the entitlement to demand performance of that obligation. The fact is that such a corresponding right will, and can, only be exercised on the occasion of (imminent) non-performance of the obligation concerned. Thus it seems strange to contend that the breach of an obligation by a subject is to be considered equivalent to the breach of a subjective right of another, when it is exactly on the occasion of such an (alleged) breach of obligation that such a right has to be exercised. As long as the obligation is performed there will be no need to resort to the exercise of the right to demand performance of that obligation.[67] The correlative right already exists at the time of performance of the obligation, but can only be exercised upon (imminent) non-performance of that obligation.[68] Furthermore, even though a subject may be in possession of a correlative right to demand performance of a certain obligation, that does not mean that it is necessarily in a position to exercise its right.[69] The exercise of any correlative right to demand the performance of another subject's obligation is intimately connected with the law of international responsibility, and therefore with what has been called secondary rules of international law.

1.4. The necessity of correlative rights, their sources, and the requirement of a legal interest

1.4.1. THE POSSESSION OF A CORRELATIVE RIGHT AS A PREREQUISITE FOR THE COMPETENCE TO DEMAND PERFORMANCE OF OTHER SUBJECTS' OBLIGATIONS

The fact that another subject has the right to demand performance of an obligation presents a limit to the normally existing power of a State to determine its legal position vis-à-vis other States in accordance with canons of auto-interpretation. While usually a State will interpret its conduct as being consistent with rules of international law, that interpretation may be subjected to scrutinization by other States, or by the international community at large (see chapter two). Riphagen asserts:[70]

> "Actually, in most cases, a State will deny, on the grounds of the facts or of the interpretation of the applicable primary rules, that there has been on its side a non-conformity with a legal rule, an internationally wrongful act for which it bears responsibility. Obviously other States are not bound to leave the matter there. They can maintain their interpretation of fact and law and act accordingly."

The notion of rights correlative to obligations is necessary to avoid the creation of a legal vacuum.[71] The Court observed, in the South West Africa Cases of 1966, on this account:[72]

"In the international field, the existence of obligations that cannot in the last resort be enforced by any legal process, has always been the rule rather than the exception, (...)."

If the Court had meant to say that, considering the consensual character of its jurisdiction under international law, the observance of obligations might not always be effected through the means of judicial process, that conclusion would have been unassailable.[73] But ten pages earlier it had also stated:[74]

"Another argument which requires consideration is that in so far as the Court's view leads to the conclusion that there is now no entity entitled to claim the due performance of the Mandate, it must be unacceptable. Without attempting in any way to pronounce on the various implications involved in this argument, the Court thinks the inference sought to be drawn from it is inadmissible. If, on a correct legal reading of a given situation, certain alleged rights are found to be non-existent, the consequences of this must be accepted. The Court cannot properly postulate the existence of such rights in order to avert those consequences."

While not denying that the Court cannot postulate rights which are absent, it nevertheless should have pronounced on the various implications of the argument thus advanced. Because the Ethiopian and Liberian governments had also claimed that South West Africa was a territory under Mandate and that South Africa continued to have obligations thereunder.[75] If the individual member States of the League of Nations had no legal right or interest in the performance, by South Africa, of obligations under the so-called conduct provisions of the Mandate for South West Africa;[76] if the League of Nations could no longer exercise its right to demand performance of the obligations under such conduct provisions due to its disappearance; and if the United Nations could not do so because it could not be considered to be the successor in law to the League of Nations,[77] then the only consequence to be drawn therefrom is that the Mandate for South West Africa had lapsed altogether.[78] The conduct provisions related to the object and purpose of the Mandate, that is, the well-being of the original inhabitants, and with the absence of any subject entitled to invoke the obligations under such provisions the inadmissible conclusion would have to be drawn that South Africa was solely entitled to interpret its obligations, and whether or not its conduct was in conformity with such obligations. If, consequent upon the Court's decision that Ethiopia and Liberia did not have any legal right or interest in the subject-matter of their claims, no subject left in possession of a right to claim observance of South Africa's obligations under the Mandate could be found, then the obligations concerned would have disappeared, since they would have turned potestative in character.[79]

If a State can determine for itself whether an obligation exists, whether or not it has breached that obligation, and whether or not it is responsible and in consequence ought to provide reparation, then the provisions on the breach of an obligation, internationally wrongful acts and responsibility laid down in the ILC-draft could not find any application.[80] The Commission held, fundamentally, in article 1, Part One, of the ILC-draft:[81]

"Every internationally wrongful act of a State entails the international responsibility of that State."

And it stated, equally fundamentally, in article 1, Part Two, of the draft:[82]

> "The international responsibility of a State which, pursuant to the provisions of part 1, arises from an internationally wrongful act committed by that State, entails legal consequences as set out in the present part."

Yet if there is no subject entitled to invoke the responsibility resulting therefrom, that is, if one cannot identify any injured State in the sense of article 5, Part Two, of the ILC-draft,[83] then the concept of law itself becomes futile. Articles 1, Parts One and Two, both postulate the principle of responsibility for wrongful acts in objective terms: responsibility is incurred, and consequences entail, whether or not such responsibility is invoked by another subject.[84] However, if the discharge of responsibility could only follow upon the voluntary act of the State whose responsibility is incurred, and not upon demand, the objective nature of responsibility would wither away. It is surely for that reason that the commentary to article 5, Part Two, stated:[85]

> "Part 1 of the draft articles defines an internationally wrongful act solely in terms of obligations, not of rights. This was done on the assumption that to each and any obligation corresponds *per definitionem* a right of at least one other State."

By postulating the principle of obligations with correlative rights to demand performance of such obligations, one must assume therefore that the complementary rules laying down such rights are conceived,[86] at least theoretically, to cover all breaches of obligations that could occur in practice. Thus it is to be presumed that the law leaves no lacunae in this regard, and provides for the exercise of a right to demand performance of obligations in each and every possible case of breaches thereof.[87]

1.4.2. THE SOURCES OF THE COMPLEMENTARY RULES LAYING DOWN CORRELATIVE RIGHTS

As to the sources of correlative rights established by complementary rules, it is submitted that those lie in the general principles of law,[88] combined with rules of customary international law. The Court observed in the Barcelona Traction Case with regard to obligations *erga omnes*:[89]

> "Some of the corresponding rights of protection have entered into the body of general international law (...); others are conferred by international instruments of a universal or quasi-universal character."

The Court appears to make a distinction between the rules laying down the obligations, and the rules laying down the corresponding rights. Indeed, in most cases the rules laid down in a treaty, establishing obligations or rights (the latter in the sense as discussed in subsection 1.3.2, with the corresponding obligation to respect such rights), do not expressly, or even impliedly, provide for correlative rights. And, in the absence of such provisions, it must be concluded that such rights, and especially the conditions for their exercise, are to be found in those rules of customary international law that relate to State responsibility. A similar line of argument was upheld by the Permanent Court in the Chorzów Factory Case, where it held:[90]

> "It is a principle of international law that the breach of an engagement involves an obligation to make reparation in an adequate form. Reparation therefore is

the indispensable complement of a failure to apply a convention and there is no necessity for this to be stated in the convention itself."

As it is a principle of international law that the breach of an obligation entails the obligation to repair that breach even in the absence of any conventional provision to that effect, so it must also be considered to be a principle of international law that there will always be a subject of international law which possesses the right to demand the performance of obligations.

1.4.3. THE EXERCISE OF CORRELATIVE RIGHTS AND THE REQUIREMENT OF A LEGAL INTEREST

Having established the necessity and principle of the existence of rights correlative to obligations, it now becomes necessary to determine which rules condition the exercise of such rights. It may seem strange that there could exist rights whose exercise is dependent upon further permissive rules. The latter moreover laying down criteria more stringent than seem to be inherent in the terms of the right itself. Yet the correlative rights concerned are but conceived in theory, and are established irrespective of either the nature of the rules which lay them down, or the actual circumstances in which the obligations may be breached. It may seem paradoxical, and perhaps even contradictory, to hold that a subject should have a right which, however, it cannot exercise. Yet such rights are of indeterminate character, and have to filled in by complementary rules that determine under which conditions they can be exercised. What counts is that, as with obligations, rights have to be exercised in relation to concrete circumstances, and, in the case of correlative rights, in relation to the nature of the rules that gave birth to them. Determining which subject(s) may exercise the right to demand the performance of obligations depends ultimately upon the interest which, by means of allocation through legal rules, accrues to a certain subject (or subjects): the legal interest.

This process, typically, determines what has been called the "legal interest" of a subject. What is meant by "legal interest" may be best made clear through this quote of Weil, who observes:[91]

> "For a state to enjoy a right implies its possession of legal standing to claim performance of the corresponding obligation and, in default, to bring to book the person or persons owing that obligation. (...) Thus, not just any state may be regarded as possessing a 'legal interest', *i.e.*, a right, in the observance of any international obligation by the state or states on which it is incumbent;"

The possession of a legal interest by a State therefore relates to nothing other than the correlative right to demand the performance of an international obligation. Obviously such correlative right, or legal interest is not, and cannot be, of subjective character, and whether or not it is present depends upon the criteria laid down, objectively, in the rules complementary to the rule that lays down the primary obligations. That is not to say that the actual circumstances in which (allegedly) a breach of obligation takes place have no role to play. The complementary rules which lay down the correlative right to demand performance only prima facie determine the existence of a legal interest. In actual circumstances the exercise of the right may be dependent upon further conditions.

A short comment may be made here regarding the way in which to establish the existence of a legal interest on the part of other States consequent upon an alleged internationally wrongful act. The proof of the existence of an internationally wrongful act can of course only take place in the course of an examination of the merits of a dispute. The alleged existence of a legal interest makes no sense unless it is found that such an internationally wrongful act has taken place. Yet generally the question of whether or not such legal interest exists is examined before the merits of a dispute is investigated.[92] Thus it is obvious that the existence of a legal interest can only be affirmed on the assumption that certain conduct could be considered to be wrongful under international law, and that it could be considered attributable to a certain State. If afterwards the investigation of the merits of the dispute would show that either of these findings could not be made, the legal interest, that is the possibility to exercise a correlative right, affirmed on the basis of such assumptions, would prove to have never existed. These remarks make clear that one speaks only of the "legal interest" of a State or another subject of international law in those circumstances where a subject is actually exercising its right to demand the performance of (allegedly) breached obligations.

The reason why legal interests are many times identified by reference to the subjective interests of the States in possession of such interest, may derive from the circumstance that States are, generally, free either to exercise their right to performance, or not. Being under no obligation to exercise their rights,[93] the considerations for States in determining whether or not to exercise such rights will mostly turn upon an evaluation of their own individual (subjective) interests.[94] But the existence of a legal interest can only be determined objectively, which, as such, seems to be implied in the adjective "legal" that is added to the term "interest".

1.5. The criteria to determine the existence of a legal interest in the performance of obligations

1.5.1. STATES AND THE GENERAL INTEREST IN THE PERFORMANCE OF OBLIGATIONS

Each and any State has an interest in the performance of other States' obligations. This is why Riphagen observes:[95]

> "Whether a particular State has an interest in the performance of its international obligations by another State is a matter of fact. In the long run every State has an interest in the observance of any rule of international law, including the rule of pacta sunt servanda. But this by no means authorizes – let alone obliges – every State to demand the performance by every other State of its international obligations, let alone to take countermeasures in case of non-performance of those obligations."

Thus for a State to act upon the breach of obligation it will have to show that it has a legal interest, that is, a right allocated to it by the relevant rules of international law. Or to put it more clearly, a right which can be exercised once it is established that the conditions set for such exercise are met in actual fact.

Initially, the reason why there has never crystallized a rule recognizing the legal interest with regard to no matter which obligation imposed by a rule of international law is to avoid chaos in international relations. If any State could legitimately concern itself with each and every breach of an obligation, and in the absence of independent verification of the existence of such breaches and control over reactions to such breaches, a multiplication of inter-State disputes could be expected, which would go hand in hand with instability in the international community.

Another argument may be derived from the sovereignty of States. For what reason could a State concern itself with a breach of an obligation, if such breach had no effect whatsoever on its own relations with the State breaching the obligation.[96] In view of the juxtaposition of independent sovereign States,[97] every State is free under international law to condone a breach of an obligation that concerns it: either afterwards by way of agreement or acquiescence, or beforehand by way of consent (in which case there is not, according to article 29, Part One, of the ILC-draft, an internationally wrongful act, since there is no breach of an obligation; however, nowadays under the limits established by *jus cogens* rules, laid down in article 29, paragraph 2, Part One, of the ILC-draft).

A third argument against conferring a legal interest on States generally with regard to any breach of an obligation lies in the way in which rules of international law are created, that is, to a large extent, through the consent of States. For this reason it would seem to be impossible to grant a State a legal interest with regard to the breach of an obligation imposed by a rule if it were not also itself obligated by the rule in question. Clearly, where a State is not bound to a rule, it cannot be considered to have an interest in breaches of obligations imposed under that rule.[98] And it is this latter remark that leads us to the next subsection.

1.5.2. STATES AND THE COMMON INTEREST IN THE PERFORMANCE OF OBLIGATIONS UNDER RULES OF INTERNATIONAL LAW

As with the foregoing it would appear that according a legal interest to each and every State obligated by a particular rule of international law is apt to overstep the purpose for which international law is created, namely to regulate relations between States. For rules of customary international law are increasingly becoming universal in character, and with the growing interdependency in international relations the number of (States bound by) multilateral treaties has also increased. Thus, to establish as a criterion for the existence of a legal interest, the binding force of a rule for a State, does not enhance stability in international relations. Riphagen reflected upon this aspect as follows:[99]

> "In many cases of internationally wrongful acts there is no problem in legally identifying the injured State. The States which are parties to the creation of the rule of international law (...) are also parties to the primary legal relationships under that rule and, at the same time, parties to the breach, i.e. parties to the new, secondary, legal relationships; the three 'levels' coincide."

While this would seem to speak against the argument here made, it is but necessary to read the sentence immediately after to see why this is not so:[100]

"This is normally the case with obligations imposed in a bilateral treaty."

Clearly if the obligation is derived from a bilateral treaty there would be no problem identifying the State in possession of a legal interest. But with the expansion of customary and conventional international law matters are not as simple any more.

Although it is not possible to use the binding character of a rule for States as a positive criterion to determine whether they are in possession of a legal interest resulting from the breach of an obligation, nevertheless it is possible to find in such circumstance a negative criterion.[101] Only States that are subjected to, or favoured by, a certain rule of international law could potentially be in possession of a legal interest. States that have not consented to the rule (since they did not ratify the multilateral treaty, or because they claimed to be a "persistent objector") do not acquire a legal interest consequent upon a breach of obligation established thereunder.[102]

However, there are some particular interests which have been considered worthy of protection. One of the most prominent concerns the form of intervention laid down in article 63 of the Statute,[103] which provides for the right to intervene in a case whenever the interpretation of a multilateral treaty is in issue between two parties before the Court.[104] Another concerns the right to protest which appears possible in all cases of breaches of obligations. A fine example of this latter interest appears to be provided by the judgment of the Court in the Wimbledon Case:[105]

> "It will suffice to observe for the purposes of this case that each of the four Applicant Powers has a clear interest in the execution of the provisions relating to the Kiel Canal, since they all possess fleets and merchant vessels flying their respective flags. They are therefore, even though they may be unable to adduce a prejudice to any pecuniary interest, covered by the terms of Article 386 (...)."

Of course the article referred to in the quote contains a broad criterion that provides for a cause of action to "any interested Power".[106] It is further to be noted that such protection is not the result of the existence of a legal interest, but a means for safeguarding the integrity of the rules in question. And such rights are provided because of the perceived effect that a breach of obligations, or a disputed interpretation of a rule, may have on the obligations and rights of a State intervening or protesting.[107]

1.5.3. PERFORMANCE OF OBLIGATIONS TOWARDS SPECIFIC STATES

Could it be said then that the criterion to be employed lies with the performance of obligations towards certain, or all, States subjected to the rule? For instance Riphagen mentioned in relation to international delicts:[108]

> "Normally, international obligations (...) are obligations towards a specific State. Even if more than one other specific State is involved, the bilateral relationships created by a rule of international law can normally be treated separately."

And he is followed in this view by Sachariew who holds:[109]

> "In dieser Beziehung bilden die völkerrechtlichen Verbotsnormen keine Ausnahme. Sie erzeugen ebenfalls konkrete Rechte und Pflichte, und zwar schon vor einer eventuellen Verletzung, da auch bei Verbotsnormen konkrete Rechte-Pflichte-Beziehungen entstehen. Die Normverletzung vollzieht sich im Rahmen

> dieser Rechtsverhältnisse in Gestalt einer Pflichtverletzung gegenüber bestimmten Subjekten. Eine Völkerrechtsverletzung außerhalb von Rechtsverhältnissen ist ebensowenig möglich wie eine Anwendung von Völkerrechtsnormen außerhalb von konkreten, korrenspondierenden Rechten und Pflichten. Im Völkerrecht kann die Norm als solche weder verletzt noch erfüllt werden."

It is submitted that such a conception is doubtful. For either the obligation is performed by a certain State, in which case it is obviously being performed towards all the States obligated by the rule. If one takes as example the rule prohibiting the threat or use of force against States, clearly a State refraining from such threat or use of force performs its obligation towards all the States bound by the rule. If it breaches its obligation, it will incur responsibility. It could be asserted that such responsibility is entailed objectively, and towards all the States bound by the rule. It would follow that responsibility will be incurred upon the breach of an obligation irrespective of the exercise by another State of its right to demand performance of that obligation.[110] Generally speaking it is only after the occurrence of a breach of obligation (which makes it dependent upon an interpretation of the rule and the actual circumstances) that it becomes possible to determine the State(s) in possession of a legal interest entitling it (them) to demand the performance of the breached obligation.[111] Indeed, Riphagen appears to acknowledge as much when he observes:[112]

> "Whether the interest of a State is adversely affected by the act of another State is a matter of fact. For State responsibility – i.e. new legal relationships between States – to arise, it is obviously necessary to qualify both the act and the interest; in other words, to determine the parties to the breach. Parties to the breach can only be those States between which the primary relationship exists. The question therefore is a matter of interpretation of primary rules: whose interests a given primary rule is intended to protect? But even if it is established that a given primary rule is – possibly also – intended to protect the interests of a given State, that State is not necessarily a party to the breach."

Indeed, it has to be admitted that a legal relationship exists between the States subjected to a certain rule even before the breach of an obligation by one of them. But such relationships do not as such determine which State(s) is (are) in possession of a legal interest after a breach of obligation has occurred by another State. And all that can be said is that a State obligated or favoured by a rule may acquire a legal interest pursuant to the breach of an obligation established under that rule.

1.5.4. THE EFFECTS OF AN INTERNATIONALLY WRONGFUL ACT AS CRITERION TO DETERMINE THE EXISTENCE OF LEGAL INTERESTS OF STATES

Material and moral damage

It may be asked whether the criterion to determine the legal interest of a State should lie with (the proven or assumed existence of) damage. As is well known the Commission, following its then special rapporteur Ago, considered damage not to be a constituent element of an internationally wrongful act.[113] If one takes the word "damage" to mean material injury, there can be little doubt that the Commission's exclusion of damage from article 3 is correct. Not all internationally wrongful acts entail the occurrence of material damage to either individuals or States.[114] One may ask oneself what purpose a condition of damage could usefully serve, unless it were to determine the State(s) in possession of a legal interest consequent upon an internationally wrongful act. The commentary to article 3 posed the question whether there existed a third constituent element, namely damage caused to the detriment of the subject *whose subjective right had been impaired.*[115] Apparently an extra link is thought to be necessary in order to consider material damage a condition, namely the impairment of a subjective right. Seemingly then damage is used to determine the State(s) in possession of a legal interest, but as such it will fail in its purpose in cases where there is, or would be, no material damage.

To illustrate these thoughts through means of examples, one may refer to the detention of a diplomat contrary to the rules regarding immunity. Clearly the sending State does not suffer any material damage as a result of the receiving State's breach of obligation under such rules.[116] Though the sending State will of course be deprived of the diplomat's services in such a case. Perhaps a better example may then be found by reference to a situation in which the police officers of a State, in pursuit of suspects of a criminal offence, (un)knowingly cross the border with another State, fail to capture the suspects, and then return to their State. In such a case no damage will have been done to the other State. Authors have been wont to speak of moral damage in such cases.[117]

The term "moral damage" is not, as has been noted by the Commission, altogether free from ambiguity.[118] It appears to be used in such cases of internationally wrongful acts where there is no material damage, although of course the typical examples are those referred to above, and those constituting an insult to the honour or dignity of a State.[119] The assertion that there exist moral damages derives from the conception that in the absence of material damage reparation is still possible, mostly in the nature of satisfaction. Yet how can moral damages arise from anything other than breaches of moral demands. Indeed satisfaction is provided by one State to another on the occasion of an (admitted) internationally wrongful act. It is accorded, in other words, on legal grounds. Therefore any damage, whether one wants to call it material, moral, political, or other, constitutes legal damage because of its reparable character under the relevant rules of State responsibility.[120] Indeed, the confusion becomes complete if one considers that the reasons for using the term "damage" lie with the reparable character of acts. Yet the term implies disadvantageous consequences for the State suffering from an internationally wrongful act. As has been pointed out, an internationally wrongful act need not constitute, or entail, a damage, in the ordinary meaning of the word, to another State. Similar arguments seem to apply to so-called legal damages, to be discussed next, which also are not based on prejudicial consequences for other States.

Legal damage

The Commission observed in relation to the breach of human rights obligations:[121]

> "Yet it manifestly constitutes an internationally wrongful act, so that if we maintain at all costs that 'damage' is an element in any internationally wrongful act, we are forced to the conclusion that any breach of an international obligation towards another State involves some kind of 'injury' to that other State.

> But this is tantamount to saying that the 'damage' which is inherent in any internationally wrongful act is the damage which is at the same time inherent in any breach of an international obligation."

One cannot but note the circular reasoning which seems to underlie this argument. Is damage an element of an internationally wrongful act? The Commission claims it is not. Because where there is no damage consequent upon the commission of an internationally wrongful act, it must be considered inherent in such acts. The basis of such argument may be found also in a statement by Anzilotti to the effect that:[122]

> "Le dommage se trouve compris implicitement dans le caractère anti-juridique de l'acte."

While not denying that any international wrongful act is of a nature to undermine the edifice of law (and especially its binding character), still by putting it this way one creates the impression that consequently any State has a legal interest in the performance of other States' obligations. For any law-abiding State will thus suffer a damage due to the anti-juridical character of non-performance of any international obligation, and will therefore be affected by such non-performances.[123] Yet that conclusion is rejected on good grounds by everyone (subsection 1.5.1).

Of course it cannot be denied that the existence of damage, causally flowing from an internationally wrongful act,[124] may, and to a certain extent does, function as a hard and fast rule to determine which State is in possession of a legal interest.[125] But this recognition does not entail the consequence that when there is no damage there is no internationally wrongful act, or even that there would not be any State in possession of a legal interest.[126] In case of breaches of human rights obligations there is damage, but not to another State. The damage is done to the nationals of the State breaching such obligations, and the problem is that no other State will be touched by the said breaches. Ironically, if one were to consider damage to States in the factual sense to constitute the criterion for determining the State(s) in possession of a legal interest, this would identify the State breaching its human rights obligations as the State in possession of the requisite legal interest. That is surely an unacceptable and unreasonable result.

The quotation at the head of this subsection leads in fact to the issue of legal damage. Yet if any internationally wrongful act "towards another State" involves some kind of injury to that other State, or that damage is inherent in any breach of an international obligation,[127] then one can only conclude that such lines are devoid of any substance. Because the damage that is inherent in any breach of an obligation will have been inflicted upon all States of the international community. Only by reference to a further criterion, that injury is done to another State, does one escape that conclusion.[128] Yet even this does not save the Commission from ambiguity. Because it had stated, precisely by reference to the breach of human rights obligations, that:[129]

> "(...) the breach thus committed does not normally cause any economic injury to the other States parties to the convention, or even a slight to their honour or dignity."

While generally injury to another State could be said to include material and moral damage (in the sense explained above), breaches of human rights obligations evade the phrase itself: "injury to another State". One could of course, superficially, apply the theory of diplomatic protection of nationals analogously and hold the damage to the other State's nationals as damage to the protector State. But the ratio for holding damage to citizens abroad as damage to the State has always been the bond of nationality between the State and its citizens. Hence the elaborate rules regarding the nationality of claims. However, to apply such a theory to breaches of human rights obligations does not do justice to the nature of such obligations.

It follows that one has to resort to a more generic term than damage to determine the States entitled to demand performance of another State's obligations. Injury is the word that comes to mind, and which is being used most of the time nowadays. Originally this word "injury" was intended to be understood in purely factual sense. But along the way it seems that it was identified more and more often with "injury to rights", which resulted on its turn in the phrase "infringement of rights". The present writer fails to see how rights can be infringed. Rights exist to be exercised, and clearly a holder of a right may be obstructed in the exercise of its right. But that as such does not indicate that its right is infringed, because generally the right does not become extinct, or even suspended, on the breach of the obligation to respect the right in question. Terminologically speaking also the more correct expression in this regard would be that the correlative obligation is not "to respect the right", but "to respect the exercise of the right". And, as has been pointed out several times already, not all rights are capable of being obstructed by the mere breach of an obligation by another State. Thus where a State in the exercise of a right calls upon another State to fulfil an obligation, then the breach of an obligation is in fact a precondition to be fulfilled before that right can exercised.

To come back now to the issue of injury, the factual intonation of this term was expressly stressed by Pinto (in the discussion by the Commission of Ago's proposed draft article on consent), in reaction to a statement by Reuter to the effect that:[130]

> "(...) the title of the article: 'Consent of the injured State'. In reality, the State was not injured, since it had given its consent."

And to this Pinto in turn observed:[131]

> "(...), he had no difficulty with that term, since, (...), it was used in its factual, as opposed to its legal, sense to refer to a State that had been injured in fact but might not be held to have been injured in law."

And Ago subsequently explained with regard to his terminology:[132]

> "Actually, the State was not 'injured' in the legal sense of the term. The State that gave its consent agreed not to exercise its subjective right to require the other State to act in conformity with an obligation. The legal nature of the act of that State was changed, since it was no longer wrongful, but the physical act remained, and could entail physical injury to the State subjected to it. The expression 'injured State' was a practical expression used to designate the State which by virtue of an international obligation, would have had the right to require that certain conduct was not adopted with respect to it."

And again it appears from this quote that the term "injured State" is used in a somewhat ambiguous manner. First, in the sense that a State may be factually affected by the breach of an obligation. And secondly, to denote the State which is in possession of the right to require another State to fulfil an obligation. The existence of the first element can obviously only be determined after a breach of an obligation has taken place.

The second element, however, presupposes that the determination of the "injured State" may take place even before the breach (or threat of breach) of an obligation. Riphagen also appears to have been caught between these two approaches, as he states:[133]

> "Obviously, this determination cannot be made independently of the origin and content of the obligation breached (the 'primary rule'); indeed, that obligation is an obligation towards another State, or States, or towards the international community of States as a whole (*erga omnes*)."

Immediately after he then refers to the correlation of obligations to rights,[134] yet in a later paragraph he observes:[135]

> "In two other cases it is not so much the facts which indicate the answer to the question which is (or are) the injured State (or States), but rather the 'law'. Indeed, modern treaty practice increasingly recognizes the existence – and provides for the protection – of interests which are not allocated to particular individual States parties."

Only one comment on the part of Jagota could be found which solely focuses on injury and injured States, and he observes:[136]

> "The question whether that term should be defined in general terms, to provide simply that an injured State was a State which had suffered injury because of the breach of an international obligation, or whether it was necessary to elaborate the sources of the primary obligation the breach of which constituted injury."

Eventually Riphagen explicitly rejected injury, and with good cause, as sole criterion to determine which States should be considered injured States.[137]

Effects of an internationally wrongful act upon (a) State(s) as generalized criterion to determine the existence of a legal interest

The latter remarks lead to the conclusion that any criterion to determine the legal interest of a State depends upon the perceived, experienced, or potential, (lack of) effects of the breach of an obligation upon States or the international community. Two observations are in place here. First, the effects of any breach of an international obligation depend in turn on the scope of the rule that lays down the obligation, or more accurately on the course of conduct it prescribes or prohibits.[138] Secondly, the question whether those effects are present will have to be verified in real life, that is, it has to be ascertained which State suffers the effects of an internationally wrongful act.

At this point the question needs to be raised what should be understood by "effects", and more particularly so because those must be distinguished from "damage" or even "injury".

That this distinction is imperative, generally speaking, may be seen from the categories of rights of suspension or termination laid down in article 60 of the Vienna Convention, as well as the categories of the infringement of rights inserted in article 5, Part Two, of the ILC-draft. The first refers to the way in which a material breach of a multilateral treaty affects the other parties to the treaty. The second criterion, infringement of rights,[139] seems to be based on the notion of injury.[140] The fact that these two texts refer to more concrete criteria than the general criterion here advanced, that is, the effects of a breach of an obligation, does not belie the correctness of such criterion. For the different categories laid down in those articles do not all reflect the concrete criteria that they are supposed to represent.

Article 60 of the Vienna Convention has laid down the circumstances in which States may invoke the material breach of a treaty for suspending or terminating the same treaty:[141]

> "1. A material breach of a bilateral treaty by one of the parties entitles the other to invoke the breach as a ground for terminating the treaty or suspending its operation in whole or in part.
>
> 2. A material breach of a multilateral treaty by one of the parties entitles:
>
> (a) the other parties by unanimous agreement to suspend the operation of the treaty in whole or in part or to terminate it either:
>
> (i) in the relations between themselves and the defaulting State, or
>
> (ii) as between all the parties;
>
> (b) a party specially affected by the breach to invoke it as a ground for suspending the operation of the treaty in whole or in part in the relations between itself and the defaulting State;
>
> (c) any other party other than the defaulting State to invoke the breach as a ground for suspending the operation of the treaty in whole or in part with respect to itself if the treaty is of such character that a material breach of its provisions by one party radically changes the position of every party with respect to the further performance of its obligations under the treaty.
>
> (...)
>
> 5. Paragraphs 1 to 3 do not apply to provisions relating to the protection of the human person contained in treaties of a humanitarian character, in particular to provisions prohibiting any form of reprisals against persons protected by such treaties."

The provisions of article 60 are generally interpreted to constitute the basis for concluding that there exist differing categories of treaties, or at least differing categories of treaty obligations.[142] Of course the distinction between bilateral and multilateral treaties is not, as such, in question here. Yet it is precisely the appearance of multilateral treaties in international relations,[143] as well as the changing subject-matter of such treaties, which has militated in favour of the recognition of differing categories of treaties, and of different consequences in case such treaties are breached. The most important differentiation that has taken place in this regard concerns the recognition that there exist multilateral treaties whose breach only affects one party to the treaty, and multilateral treaties whose breach will affect all parties to the treaty. That distinction may be illustrated by reference to the provisions of article 60, paragraphs 2 (b) and 2 (c).[144] A further category may be mentioned in that article 60, paragraph 5, excludes suspension or termination of treaties of a humanitarian character.

The Commission in turn takes a somewhat different terminological course in article 5, Part Two of the ILC-draft, by referring to the concept of injured State and the infringement of its rights:[145]

> "1. For the purposes of the present articles, 'injured State' means any State a

right of which is infringed by the act of another State, if that act constitutes, in accordance with Part One of the present articles an internationally wrongful act of that State.

2. In particular, 'injured State' means:
   (a) if the right infringed by the act of a State arises from a bilateral treaty, the other State party to the treaty;
   (b) if the right infringed by the act of a State arises from a judgment or other binding dispute settlement decision of an international court or tribunal, the other State or States parties to the dispute and entitled to benefit of that right;
   (c) if the right infringed by the act of a State arises from a binding decision of an international organ other than an international court or tribunal, the State or States which, in accordance with the constituent instrument of the international organization concerned, are entitled to the benefit of that right;
   (d) if the right infringed by the act of a State arises from a treaty provision for a third State, that third State;
   (e) if the right infringed by the act of a State arises from a multilateral treaty or from a rule of customary international law, any other State party to the multilateral treaty or bound by the relevant rule of customary international law, if it is established that:
      (i) the right has been created or is established in its favour;
      (ii) the infringement of the right by the act of a State necessarily affects the enjoyment of the rights or performance of the obligations of the other States parties to the multilateral treaty or bound by the rule of customary international law; or
      (iii) the right has been created or is established for the protection of human rights and fundamental freedoms;
   (f) if the right infringed by the act of a State arises from a multilateral treaty, any other State party to the multilateral treaty, if it is established that the right has been expressly stipulated in that treaty for the protection of the collective interests of the State parties thereto.

3. (...)."

Although the article pays lip-service to the idea of injury by referring to "injured State", nevertheless it defines such a State not in relation to the factual effects of an internationally wrongful act, but in relation to the infringement of the right(s) of the injured State as a consequence of the internationally wrongful act of another State. On that account Riphagen, in his commentary on article 5, stated:[146]

> "In many cases the obligation of a State is merely the counterpart or mirror-image of a right of another State; the obligation is not to infringe that right."

Yet as has been explained in subsection 1.3.4 the substantive goal a right aims at may be achieved in two ways. First, by allowing a State to engage in a course of conduct that consists of actions or omissions. Or secondly, by allowing a State to engage into a course of conduct that consists of requiring another State to fulfil its obligations. Only in the first case can the substantive goal that a right aims at be achieved directly by the

State holder of the right, and only in that case could one speak of an infringement of a right if another State breaches its obligation to respect that right.[147] Thus the correlation envisaged in paragraph 1 of article 5 between the breach of an obligation (an internationally wrongful act) and the infringement of a right cannot, generally, be regarded as a sufficient answer to the question which criteria should be used to identify the States entitled to consider themselves injured by an internationally wrongful act. For in many cases a rule of international law will be coined in terms of obligations of States, and leave open the question which States would be in possession of the right to insist upon the performance of such obligations. The use of the general criterion of the infringement of a right renders the reasoning circular. Because if a rule speaks of an obligation of a State, without making reference to a (criterion to determine the existence of a) correlative right, then one will have to determine which State is in possession of such right first.[148] It is only after that that one can determine whether that right has been infringed.

While it is submitted that the basis of rules laying down the criteria to determine the existence of a State's legal interest lies generally with the effect a breach of an obligation causes upon other States, that is not to say that such rule always adopts the consequences of a breach as criterion. For adopting such criterion would lead to the conclusion that it is only after a breach of an obligation that a legal interest comes into existence.[149] But that is not necessarily so. A point in question concerns the Court's opinion regarding the PLO Observers Mission.[150] In that case the Court observed that certain decisions by United States' authorities, contested by the United Nations, could give rise to a dispute between the United Nations and the United States, notwithstanding that no measures of execution had been taken pursuant to such decisions.[151] The Court expressed the opinion that the United States was under an obligation to arbitrate the dispute, and this shows that the United Nations had an interest, and arguably even a legal interest, regarding conduct by United States authorities that only potentially could be considered a breach of obligation.[152]

Since the effects upon States consequent upon a breach of obligations are to determine the legal interests of States, a more tangible term will be used to describe those effects: prejudice. Traditionally the rules laying down the conditions under which States can be considered to be in possession of a legal interest have been concerned with the prejudice which a State directly or indirectly sustains as the result of the breach of an obligation by another State. Technically speaking this amounts to a facts-related and rule contents-related criterion.[153] For whether or not some prejudice to a certain State is present will depend on the factual circumstances, and whether or not it is the result of the breach of an obligation by another State must be determined by an evaluation of the (allegedly wrongful) conduct in relation to the rule laying down the obligation that prescribes a certain course of conduct.[154] It is further obvious that the prejudice suffered must causally result from the breach of the obligation.[155]

It is to be noted that this criterion by referring to prejudice does not refer to the subjective interests of the State that suffers it. Whether or not there is a breach of an obligation depends on the content of the obligation (which is dependent on the scope of the rule) and the conduct of the State alleged to have breached it, and both can be objectively determined. The same goes for the prejudice sustained as the result of a breach, and the legal interest subsequently conferred on a State derives not from the subjectively appreciated prejudice resulting from a breach, but from the rule which names prejudice as a condition for exercising the right to invoke the responsibility of the State that breached an obligation.

An *a priori* categorization may be expounded on this basis, which may be found in the following section. Those categories are based on a generalized view of certain specific primary rules of international law, which, in case obligations established thereunder are breached, produce effects peculiar to their own subdivision. Although these categories, with two exceptions, are based upon the effects a breach of an obligation produces (or might produce), nevertheless differences of a quantitative and qualitative nature may be registered. These differences originate from the content of the rules of each subdivision, and, consequently, from the effects a breach of an obligation established thereunder (perceivably) produce.

1.6. Categories of legal interests of States

1.6.1. NON-PROBLEMATICAL CATEGORIES OF LEGAL INTERESTS

A preliminary remark has to be made concerning the non-problematic position of binding decisions of international tribunals, unilateral declarations and bilateral treaties.

Considering that judgments or awards of international tribunals are almost inevitably confined to those States that have initiated the proceedings,[156] it comes as no surprise that only a State in whose favour a judgment or award has been given possesses a legal interest if the obligation resulting from such judgment or award is breached by another State. Riphagen admits that article 94 of the Charter points to an interest of all member States in the compliance with the decisions of the Court, but he correctly observes that this does not as such leads to the conclusion that third States are in possession of a legal interest in the execution of any decision by the Court.[157] Indeed, as paragraph 2 of the said article states, the other party to the judgment, and not just any State, may have recourse to the Security Council (the latter may then decide upon recommendations or measures to give effect to the judgment). This category of legal interests pursuant to the breach by a State of obligations imposed by a court or tribunal has found its recognition in article 5, paragraph 2 (b), Part Two of the ILC-draft.

Unilateral declarations have been considered by the Court to be able to create an obligation for the State making it.[158] And as a counterpart other States could rely on such declarations, and invoke them to demand performance of the obligation thus constituted. Although in the Nuclear Tests Case the Court considered the French declarations to have been made *erga omnes*, the more normal situation will be that a declaration is made towards (a) specified State(s).[159] In such a case determining the State in possession of a legal interest will also present no difficulty.

With regard to the third unproblematic category it may be noted that determining the State in possession of a legal interest after a breach of an obligation contained in a bilateral treaty presents no difficulties.[160] Only the other State to the bilateral treaty, in contradistinction to the State breaching an obligation thereunder, can be so held.[161] The existence of that category is of course witnessed by article 60, paragraph 1, of the Vienna Convention. This category of legal interests is in fact one of the more important ones, and may also be established by reference to article 5, paragraph 2 (a), Part Two, of the ILC-draft.

1.6.2. LEGAL INTERESTS, PREJUDICE AND THE INDIVIDUAL INTEREST OF STATES

As Riphagen correctly holds, it is only when the breach concerns an obligation contained in a multilateral treaty that determining the injured State(s) may present problems. Thus he observes:[162]

> "But (...) the bulk of international obligations are formulated in abstract terms, and then the question of identifying the injured State arises. This is particularly the case if a multilateral treaty is the source of the obligation breached."

Yet that remark, and his proposed article 5 (a), Part Two, failed to appreciate the role to be played by obligations established under rules of customary international law, whose breach may also give rise to problems concerning the identification of injured States. The Commission however remedied this, and took due account of rules of customary international law, in framing article 5, paragraph 2 (e).[163] What follows hereafter will consequently concern only an examination of the concept of legal interest with regard to the breach of obligations established under rules of customary international law and multilateral treaties.

That the effect of the breach of an obligation determines the legal interest of a State is most clearly established by reference to the criterion laid down in article 60, paragraph 2 (b), which grants a party "specially affected" by a material breach of a multilateral treaty the right to invoke such breach as a ground for suspending in whole or in part the operation of the treaty in the relations between itself and the defaulting State.[164] Originally the right under article 60, paragraph 2 (b), was granted to any other party to the multilateral treaty.[165] Yet eventually it was recognized by the Commission that if it could be said that only one party to the multilateral treaty was affected by the breach concerned, then only that party should be granted a unilateral right of suspension.[166]

The first category relates to rules that lay down obligations whose breach causes effects upon (a) particular State(s). Thus the consequences of a State breaching such obligations are strictly limited, and the legal interest with regard to such breaches accrues only to States which suffer those consequences. And on this account one may read with Riphagen:[167]

> "Bilateral treaties normally give rise to bilateral legal relationships only, i.e. to reciprocal rights and obligations as between the two States parties to the treaty. Multilateral treaties often have the same effect; i.e. even if the content of the obligations imposed is uniform towards all other States parties, the legal relationships remain bilateral ones as between each pair of States parties, and the legal relationship between one pair is quite separate from the legal relationship between another pair of States parties. This may be the case even if the

uniformity of the content of the bilateral legal relationships is itself founded upon an interest common to several States parties which are in the same position, defined in the multilateral treaty itself, or even common to all States parties. (...) A breach of an obligation imposed by a multilateral treaty does not, therefore, necessarily injure each other State party to the treaty individually."

It may well be, as Riphagen stresses,[168] that the multilateral treaty itself contains criteria to determine the State in possession of a legal interest. Examples of such criteria are for instance the terms "coastal State" and "flag-State".[169] Apart from this, obligations established under a rule of customary international law or a multilateral treaty may result, when breached, in a bilateral relationship between the author State and the State in possession of a legal interest.[170]

Generally a distinction can be made in this category between breaches of obligations that cause direct effects upon a certain State, and breaches of obligations that cause indirect effects upon a State.[171]

Legal interests and direct effects upon individual States

Breaches of obligations that cause direct effects upon a particular State generally have to do with rules emanating from the principle of sovereignty.[172] Thus where a State obstructs the exercise of rights, laid down by a permissive rule of international law, which entitle another sovereign State to engage in some specific course of conduct, the effect of this instantly determines the legal interest of the State obstructed in the exercise of its rights. Examples of such rules concern the freedom to exercise jurisdiction within its territory, and freedom of the high seas. Other rules, which are more or less derivative from the principle of sovereignty, and prohibitive in character, that come to mind instantly, concern the prohibition of the use of force against, and of the prohibition of intervention within the internal affairs of, another State. Also all rules related to immunities come within this subdivision (diplomatic and consular immunities, jurisdictional immunities, and immunities of warships).

Legal interests and indirect effects upon individual States

The second subdivision relates to rules concerning the protection of nationals abroad. In this respect the exact content of, and terms used by, the primary rule establishing such protection is irrelevant.[173] Because what matters here is that determining the legal interest depends on the rules relating to claims. And one may recall here the dictum of the Permanent Court in the Mavrommatis Case to the effect that:[174]

"It is an elementary principle of international law that a State is entitled to protect its subjects, when injured by acts contrary to international law committed by another State, from whom they have been unable to obtain satisfaction through the ordinary channels. By taking up the case of one of its subjects and by resorting to diplomatic action or international judicial proceedings on his behalf, a State is in reality asserting its own rights – its right to ensure, in the person of its subjects, respect for rules of international law."

Respect for the rules of international law in this respect of course refers to the rules concerning the protection of aliens.[175] While the existence of the right of diplomatic protection is generally admitted, it is typical for this category that further limitations are imposed for exercising the right in question. The most important are the rules concerning the nationality of claims and the exhaustion of local remedies.[176]

1.6.3. LEGAL INTERESTS, PREJUDICE AND THE COLLECTIVE INTEREST OF STATES

Prejudice resulting from the commission of an internationally wrongful act need not always be, as exemplified in the previous subsection, restricted to certain specific States. Indeed it may happen that a primary rule of international law imposes obligations the breach of which will involve the infliction of prejudice to all States obligated or favoured by that rule, or, to the contrary, will result in no prejudice at all for such States. In such cases each and every State will be in possession of a legal interest. Therefore one can generally distinguish two categories in which there is a collective interest in the performance of obligations.

Legal interests and collective prejudice to States

The first category to be discussed is connected to the concept of collective prejudice. The content of the rule of international law from which an obligation springs may concern a subject-matter in which all States are equally concerned. Examples may be found with the obligations prohibiting the stationing of nuclear weapons on the deep sea bed,[177] and in space,[178] as well as the prohibition of testing nuclear weapons.[179] If such an obligation is breached the prejudice resulting therefrom will fall equally upon all States, for such prejudice concerns the growth of the threat of employment, be it intentionally or not, of such weapons.

This category may be established also by reference to the differing categories of treaties laid down in article 60 of the Vienna Convention. That there may be "specially affected" parties in case of a breach of a multilateral treaty (article 60, paragraph 2 (a)) already leads to the inference that there may be cases in which the breach affects (equally) all the parties to the treaty. More explicit in this sense is article 60, paragraph 2 (c), which grants any party to a multilateral treaty the right to suspend the treaty, if that treaty is of such character that a material breach radically changes the position of every party with respect to the further performance of its obligations under the treaty.[180] As examples of this category the Commission mentioned disarmament treaties. Breaches of obligations under such treaties will affect all the parties to the treaty, and for that reason a right of unilateral suspension is granted to all the parties.[181]

In a very clear manner this category of legal interests has been laid down in article 5, paragraph 2 (e) (ii). Admittedly the right of unilateral suspension of a multilateral treaty arises only in case of a material breach of that treaty, and in the exceptional circumstance that such breach "radically changes the position of every party with respect to the further performance of its obligations under the treaty". However article 5, paragraph 2 (e) (ii) is obviously of wider character, and it is to be remembered that the concern here is State responsibility in its broadest sense. The measures possible under a future convention on State responsibility will go beyond a temporary (or even final) right of suspension of a multilateral treaty. Also, of course, minor breaches do give rise to the responsibility of the author State, and may entail the right of injured States to respond thereto.

Legal interests and prejudice to extra-State interests
One may divide the second category into obligations intended for the protection of a specified subject-matter, or obligations intended for the protection of individuals irrespective of their nationality. In both these cases prejudice resulting from the breach of such obligations will not be detrimental to particular States, but to the subject-matter with which the obligation is concerned, or to individuals. It is for this reason that the legal interest accruing to States as the result of the breach of such obligations may be allocated to all of them, that is to say to all those States obligated by the rule.

Legal interests and the protection of the environment in areas outside national jurisdiction. With regard to the first sub-category, the obligations are related mostly to the protection of the environment. To make clear why all States will be in possession of a legal interest consequent upon the breach of an obligation intended to protect the environment one may refer to Brunnée, who states:[182]

> "The contracting states' benefit lies in the protection of environmental or other values and thus in an interest common to the international community."

One may also read with Lefeber:[183]

> "(...) no individual State has a special individual interest in the preservation of the environment of international areas or in the equitable use of their natural resources. The members of the international community have, one and all, a common interest in the maintenance of the state of international areas."

And somewhat later he claims:[184]

> "Having regard to their content and purpose, these obligations primarily have to be looked upon as instruments protecting the interests of the international community as a whole. Hence, these obligations are *ipso facto* not, at least not exclusively, applicable vis-à-vis another State. In as far as they are employed to protect common interests, they must be considered to be valid *erga omnes*."

While it appears that he confuses the existence of a collective legal interest with the legal interest deriving from obligations *erga omnes*, to be discussed in section 1.8, nevertheless these quotes show an awareness of the fact that no State will generally be individually concerned in case of the breach of an obligation intended to protect the environment in areas outside national jurisdiction. It must be noted however that he refers to the protection of the environment in international areas, and it hardly needs to be stressed that whenever prejudice affecting the environment is inflicted within the national boundaries of a State there is no need to have recourse to this category of legal interests.[185]

Legal interests and the protection of individuals irrespective of nationality. It is this category that causes unrest within the system set out above. For it concerns the legal interest regarding obligations the purpose of which is to prescribe a course of conduct with respect to the nationals of the author State. On account of this feature the generalized criterion of prejudice (effects) sheds little light on the issue of determining the

States in possession of a legal interest in consequence of a breach of such obligations. Because no State will be subjected to disadvantageous consequences as a result of the breach of human rights obligations. The conclusion to be drawn from such a state of affairs is that, in case of the breach of such obligations, every State to which a certain rule applies will acquire a legal interest. And an early dictum of the Court in the Genocide Opinion may serve to support this argument:[186]

> "The Convention was manifestly adopted for a purely humanitarian and civilizing purpose. (...) In such a convention the contracting States do not have any interests of their own; they merely have, one and all, a common interest, namely, the accomplishment of those high purposes which are the *raison d'être* of the convention. Consequently, in a convention of this type one cannot speak of individual advantages or disadvantages to States, or the maintenance of a perfect contractual balance between rights and duties."

And such argument is strengthened by the inclusion in the Genocide Convention of a provision providing for compulsory jurisdiction of the Court with regard to disputes touching on the international responsibility of States parties for breaches of obligation contained in the Convention.[187] This conclusion is not contradicted by the much quoted passage in the Barcelona Traction Case, where the Court observed:[188]

> "91. With regard more particularly to human rights, to which reference has already been made in paragraph 34 of this Judgment, it should be noted that these also include protection against denial of justice. However, on the universal level, the instruments which embody human rights do not confer on States the capacity to protect the victims of infringements of such rights irrespective of their nationality. It is therefore still on the regional level that a solution to this problem has had to be sought; thus, within the Council of Europe, of which Spain is not a member, the problem of admissibility encountered by the claim in the present case has been resolved by the European Convention on Human Rights, which entitles each State which is a party to the Convention to lodge a complaint against any other contracting State for violation of the Convention, irrespective of the nationality of the victim."

If read superficially, the Court here seems to deny Belgium a legal interest with respect to breaches of the human rights obligation that prohibits denial of justice. For instance Smith observes:[189]

> "As to standing to protect the community interest in human rights protection, however, the Court concluded that the instruments setting forth human rights obligations *erga omnes* conferred standing to invoke responsibility for breach only on the state of the victim's nationality."

A first comment, somewhat prematurely since the subject is discussed more fully in section 1.8, concerns his apparent identification of human rights obligations with obligations *erga omnes*. Human rights obligations do not confer standing on each and every State of the international community, but only on such States that are bound to a specific rule laying down a human right. Thus only States that have consented to become a party to a human rights treaty will be in possession of a legal interest in consequence of a breach of an obligation established thereunder. The only exception to such position of principle of course concerns the case in which it can be established that a certain rule laying down a human rights obligation has also its legal basis in customary law. Assuming such a rule to be universal that will mean that all States have a legal interest in calling on the observance of the rule in question. Now obviously the rule that prohibits denial of justice is of more limited scope in so far as it exists in customary international law, since the complementary rule laying down the correlative right to demand observance of the rule is granted only on the basis of nationality. The reference in paragraph 91 of the Barcelona Traction Case to paragraph 34 therefore should not be read as referring to obligations *erga omnes*, and not even to the basic human rights mentioned there, but to human rights in general.

The phrase "on the universal level, the instruments which embody human rights do not confer on States *the capacity to protect* the victims of infringements of such rights irrespective of their nationality" furthermore ought to be viewed with the issue of jurisdiction in mind. The Covenant on Civil and Political Rights does not provide for compulsory jurisdiction of the Court regarding breaches of the obligations contained therein,[190] but does that mean that no State party is entitled to claim the performance by another State party of its obligations under the Convention? If such were the case the conclusion would have to be reached that the performance of obligations under the Convention could not be demanded, and, as has already been argued above in subsection 1.4.1, such a conclusion is inadmissible.

A category of treaties, bearing testimony of this category of legal interests, may be identified in that article 60, paragraph 5, of the Vienna Convention, refuses any right of suspension, let alone termination, whenever such suspension or termination would relate to treaty provisions concerning the protection of the human person contained in treaties of a humanitarian character, in particular to provisions prohibiting any form of reprisals against persons protected by such treaties.[191] It is to be noted that this category includes all provisions intended for the protection of the human person, and not merely those which prohibit reprisals with regard to protected persons.

Article 5, paragraph 2 (e) (iii), Part Two confirms this category of legal interests, in that any State party, or State bound by the relevant rule of customary international law, is injured in case of the breach of obligations created for the protection of human rights or fundamental freedoms.[192]

1.6.4. LEGAL INTERESTS AND THE POSITED COLLECTIVE INTEREST

A penultimate category of legal interests is dominated by the will of States. It may properly be called the posited collective interest of States, insofar as it is within their (legislative) power to extend the legal interest of a State specially affected to other States not so affected. In such a case it is either the recognized importance of the obligation concerned, or of the régime instituted, that dictates the grant of a right to demand the performance of obligations to States other than those States directly affected or injured as a result of a particular breach of obligation.

This category may be considered to lie at the basis of article 60, paragraph 2 (a) of the Vienna Convention. That provision authorizes States parties to a certain multilateral treaty, by unanimous agreement, to suspend or terminate the treaty as a reaction to a material breach of that treaty.[193] That right may even go so far as to amount to a termination *tout court* of the treaty, not only in the relations between the States parties and the defaulting State, but even as between all parties. Clearly this indicates the interest that the States parties to any multilateral treaty have with regard to the due performance of obligations established by such treaties.

Article 5, paragraph 2 (f), Part Two, of the ILC-draft takes account of such a possible interest, as it stipulates that any State party to a multilateral treaty will be injured in case of the breach of obligations established for the protection of the collective interests of the States parties to the treaty. The commentary to article 5 illustrates that this category of legal interests comes into play only if States parties to a multilateral treaty have agreed to consider a breach of obligation as an infringement of their collective interest.[194] Again it may be observed that the provision of article 5, paragraph 2 (f) seems wider than its counterpart in the Vienna Convention, since it does not speak of any unanimity to be resorted to by States parties for determining the requisite measures to react to a breach. And again one should be reminded that the ILC-draft has a wider scope and needs to address all kinds of breaches of obligation, and not merely material breaches. In the commentary only one example is given, namely that of the common heritage of mankind in respect of the mineral resources of the seabed and subsoil beyond national jurisdiction. Other examples come to mind, such as the interest of States in the collective defence against aggression, as witnessed by the rights laid down in article 51 of the Charter, and the interest of States parties to the treaties establishing the European Communities in the due performance of obligations laid down by the treaties, *e.g.* as evidenced by article 170.[195]

1.7. The concept of *jus cogens*

Finally, a last category of legal interest is constituted by reference to the content, or subject-matter, of a certain rule, as well as its recognized importance for the international community: obligations *erga omnes*. However, for a proper understanding of the scope of such category, it is first necessary to refer to, and discuss, the emergence of a concept that triggered the institution of this category: the concept of *jus cogens*. Article 53 of the Vienna Convention, headed "*jus cogens*", runs:[196]

> "A treaty is void if, at the time of its conclusion, it conflicts with a peremptory norm of general international law. For the purposes of the present Convention, a peremptory norm of general international law is a norm accepted and recognized by the international community of States as a whole as a norm from which no derogation is permitted and which can be modified only by a subsequent norm of general international law having the same character."

It would go too far to deal with all the problems and ambiguities that the idea of peremptory norms may pose.[197] The present writer will therefore restrict the discussion to the following topics: the object, purpose, and basis of the concept of *jus cogens*; acceptance and recognition of peremptory norms by the international community of States as a whole; peremptory norms and the international responsibility of States.

1.7.1. THE OBJECT, PURPOSE, AND BASIS OF THE CONCEPT OF *JUS COGENS*

To go to the heart of the matter, a recurrent feature of peremptory norms is that they are referred to as being intended for the protection of the fundamental interests, community interests, common interests, general interests of the (world) community,[198] overriding or vital interests and values of the international community of States.[199] But the problem with all these terms is that the term "interests" is never defined, and indeed, taking into account the discussion of "interest" in subsection 1.2.1, it cannot be defined. For it has been considered to stand for a certain desired course of conduct, the realization of which is sought to be achieved by States. It is therefore clear that the course of conduct to be realized has to be sought in the text of article 53 as it stands. Thus a peremptory norm is a "norm from which no derogation is permitted". On that score the notion of *jus cogens* has to be interpreted in relation to the otherwise existing freedom of two or more States to replace, in so far as it concerns their *inter se* relations, any rule of international law by another rule.[200] That freedom makes it possible for States to legalize conduct, for themselves, which would otherwise be prohibited to them under a pre-existing prohibitive rule of international law. If one considers the rule of article 53 of the Vienna Convention from this perspective, it becomes clear that it establishes a distinction between primary rules of international law which may be changed by States in their *inter se* relations and primary rules of international law which cannot so be changed. If nevertheless such a change is attempted by States through the treaty instrument, article 53 renders the said treaty void.[201]

Reference has been made to "replacing a rule of international law" and "changing a primary rule of international law". Article 53 however makes reference to treaties that "conflict" with a peremptory norm of international law, and it is therefore useful to consider somewhat more closely what this stands for. It is essential to acknowledge that peremptory norms have their roots in ordinary primary rules of international law. Although it could be considered possible that a peremptory norm would be created instantly by States, the way in which the existence of peremptory norms is to be verified appears to prevent this from happening: a certain norm has to be "accepted and recognized by the international community of States as whole". The conclusion to be drawn must be that normally the emergence of a peremptory norm will be preceded by the creation of a rule of customary international law. The formation of peremptory norms thus takes place in two stages: first, the emergence of a rule of customary international law; and secondly, the recognition and acceptance of that rule as a peremptory norm of general international law.[202] The content of the primary rule of international law is decisive in this context, and it is to be noted that most of the primary rules ever mentioned as credible candidates for promotion to the category of peremptory norms are prohibitive rules: they prohibit States to engage upon a certain course of conduct. It is on this account that one should interpret the conflict of a treaty with a peremptory norm as meaning that the treaty concerned would purport either to lay down an obligation for the States concerned to engage upon a course of conduct prohibited by a rule of peremptory character, or a right to do so.

The criterion that a peremptory norm must be "a norm from which no derogation is permitted", although sometimes claimed to be of tautological character in connection to the criterion of "conflict", is not quite superfluous. For it refers to a certain element of will of the international community of States as a whole, and this element will be discussed next.

1.7.2. ACCEPTANCE AND RECOGNITION OF PEREMPTORY NORMS BY THE INTERNATIONAL COMMUNITY OF STATES AS A WHOLE

The question needs to raised what is meant by "international community of States as a whole". A first observation seems to be in order in that "international community" appears to be qualified by the phrase "of States". Clearly predominance is given to States as subjects of international law, of old the main actors within the international community, in determining the peremptory character of norms. Apparently this disqualifies other subjects of international law, at least formally, in participating in the acceptance and recognition phase of the peremptory character of norms.[203]

Apart from this preliminary point the question arises what has been meant by this phrase the international community of States "as a whole". It may be observed that this phrase did not appear in the proposed text of the Commission, and was eventually inserted by the Conference on the proposal of Finland, Greece and Spain. The president of the "Comité de rédaction", Yasseen, after a question by Barros (Chile), explained the meaning of "as a whole" in the following way:[204]

> "(...), le Comité a entendu souligner qu'il ne s'agit pas d'exiger qu'une règle soit acceptée et reconnue comme impérative par l'unanimité des Etats. Il suffit d'une très large majorité, ce qui signifie que, si un Etat refuse isolément de reconnaître la nature impérative d'une règle, ou s'il est soutenue par un très petit nombre d'Etats, cela ne peut affecter l'acceptation et la reconnaissance du caractère impératif de cette règle par la communauté internationale dans son ensemble."

If one proceeds, as one should, from the notion that a peremptory norm must be modelled on a universal rule of customary international law, the goal of the expression "international community of States as a whole" appears to be to bring forward the acceptance and recognition phase, and at the same time safeguard the universality of peremptory norms.

Another argument that has to be made concerns the link between the acceptance and recognition by the international community and the criterion of non-derogation. Non-derogation has at times been mentioned as criterion to determine the peremptory character of norms. Yet as some delegates at the Conference on the Law of Treaties indicated, it is not non-derogation as such which exclusively determines such character.[205] What is determinative in this regard is the explicit acceptance and recognition of a norm as peremptory, and not the mere acceptance of a rule as binding in the sense of article 38, paragraph 1 (b).[206] The acceptance and recognition must therefore be explicit, and directed towards establishing the peremptory character of a rule.[207]

Which rules ought to be considered accepted and recognized as peremptory norms? That is a difficult question, and many have been the answers. In the commentary to then article 50 the Commission pointed out that:[208] "(...) the law of the Charter concerning the prohibition of the use of force in itself constitutes a conspicuous example of a rule in international law having the character of *jus cogens*." However, the Commission did not list any other "conspicuous" examples of treaties void for conflict with *jus cogens*, but limited itself to naming some of the examples suggested. Among those were treaties contemplating the performance of acts criminal under international law, and acts, such as trade in slaves, piracy or genocide, in the suppression of which every State is called to co-operate.[209] Other examples mentioned, not at that time constituting crimes under international law, included treaties contemplating violating human rights, the equality of States and the principle of self-determination.[210] As the Commission apparently could not agree on more conspicuous examples, it provided that the exact content of the rule, that treaties are void if they conflict with a rule of *jus cogens*, would have to be worked out in State practice and in the jurisprudence of international tribunals.[211] At this time those have not provided much guidance. Some arbitral awards have examined whether the rule on permanent sovereignty over natural resources could be considered a peremptory norm, but came to a negative conclusion.[212] The Court has referred to *jus cogens* at times, but has abstained from making any positive conclusions as to its existence.[213] There is no need to attempt to examine exactly which rules of international law are peremptory norms, though at appropriate places arguments will be devoted to issues of *jus cogens*.

1.7.3. PEREMPTORY NORMS AND STATE RESPONSIBILITY

Although the Vienna Convention disclaims any intention of prejudging questions that may arise with regard to the international responsibility of States (article 73), nonetheless such questions, though not explicitly dealt with, are not wholly absent from the text of the Vienna Convention itself.[214] Indeed, especially the consequences of treaties being considered invalid or void, laid down in articles 69 and 71 of the Vienna Convention, betray certain elements inherently connected to the law of State responsibility.[215] Thus with regard to a treaty being considered void under article 53 of the Vienna Convention, article 71, paragraph 1 (a) only requires that the consequences of acts performed in reliance on provisions that conflict with a peremptory norm shall be eliminated.[216] This consequence, as well as that of article 71, paragraph 1 (b) which requires States to bring their mutual relations into conformity with the peremptory norm, more or less resembles what is called *restitutio in integrum*.

Apart from this disguised application of the law of State responsibility certain implications flow from the findings in subsection 1.7.1 concerning the basis of peremptory norms. It has been found that peremptory norms had their basis in primary rules of international law of a prohibitive character, and the conclusion to be drawn is that States which conclude a treaty in conflict with a peremptory norm would also be subject to the rules on State responsibility. At the moment one State party, some, or all States parties to the treaty, execute the treaty, *e.g.* actually engage upon the course of conduct prohibited by a primary rule of international law (considered to be of peremptory character), their responsibility will be engaged. Another implication is that the categories of legal interest described in section 1.6 are all applicable in the event of a breach of obligation under a peremptory norm. The question may be raised then whether the States in possession of a legal interest will be entitled to invoke article 53 and have a treaty declared void even if they are not a party to such a treaty.

The question is acute because reading articles 65 and 66 of the Vienna Convention together leads to the conclusion that only a State which is a party to a treaty conflicting with a peremptory norm can challenge the validity of such a treaty. Article 66 provides that any one of the parties to a dispute concerning the interpretation or application of articles 53 or 64 may submit the dispute to the Court if a solution has not been reached under paragraph 3 of article 65. The latter provision concerns the making of objections if a party, under paragraph 1 of article 65, invokes a ground for impeaching the validity of the treaty. Clearly the "party" which invokes a ground for impeaching the validity of the treaty becomes a "party to a dispute", in the sense of article 66 (a), only after an objection has been raised by any other "party". Both the invoking party and the objecting party therefore must be parties to the disputed treaty if they want to invoke the jurisdiction of the Court under article 66 (a). Most delegates at the Conference on the Law of Treaties seemed to think that any State would be entitled to invoke the principle contained in article 53 (then article 50) that treaties in conflict with a peremptory norm are void.[217] Yet obviously such beliefs, insofar as the application of articles 65 and 66 is concerned, cannot be accorded precedence in view of the ordinary meaning of the terms employed.

However, as noted in subsection 1.7.2, the concept of *jus cogens* starts from the premise that peremptory norms will be grafted upon universal rules of customary international law. The conclusion drawn from articles 65 and 66 of the Vienna Convention, that only parties to the challenged treaty can invoke its invalidity,[218] appears to efface any effectivity the application article 53 might entail. And the essence of peremptory norms is that a treaty in conflict therewith should be declared void irrespective of the will of the individual States parties.[219] The question then is whether the same conclusion should be reached if a State were to rely on the customary law of treaties for claiming the invalidity of a treaty due to conflict with a peremptory norm. What should count is that a peremptory norm is of inherently universal scope. To deny non-parties the right to challenge the validity of a treaty conflicting with a peremptory norm would minimize the possibilities of applying the concept of *jus cogens*. Furthermore, if the object and purpose of the concept of *jus cogens* is to introduce a restriction to the otherwise existing freedom of States to conclude any kind of treaty, the interpretation, that only States which are parties to the disputed treaty can challenge its validity, renders the concept largely inoperative. For the same States to which the restriction applies, States which conclude a treaty that conflicts with a peremptory norm, would be the only ones which could invoke its invalidity. The better interpretation then, under the customary law of treaties, is to consider any State entitled to invoke the invalidity of a treaty conflicting with a peremptory norm. That conclusion is bolstered also by reference to the way in which the existence of a peremptory norm is to be ascertained: through the acceptance and recognition of the international community of States as a whole. It appears contradictory to give any State a say in the acceptance and recognition phase, but to deny any involvement at the stage of the concrete application of the concept of *jus cogens*.

A final question is whether the consequences attached to peremptory norms apply also to unilateral acts. That question is somewhat superfluous, although it can be raised, because the basis of peremptory norms lies with primary rules of international law. These rules at the basis of peremptory norms, for the most part, are prohibitive in character, and if a State engages upon a course of conduct contrary to the rule concerned, then those acts will generate international responsibility. The right question to ask then is: considering that some rules have transformed to peremptory norms, should that also have consequences beyond the law of treaties, that is, in the law of State responsibility. That question has been answered in the positive by the Commission, which, at the instigation of then special rapporteur Ago, adopted article 19 on the distinction between international delicts and international crimes. Before turning to that distinction, however, it is necessary to dwell on the idea of obligations *erga omnes*. This idea, in a chronological sense, preceded the proposal on international delicts and international crimes, and was used to argue in favour of that distinction.

1.8. The Court's dictum on obligations *erga omnes*

At a point in time where article 53 of the Vienna Convention had already adopted the idea of peremptory norms, the Court announced, in the Barcelona Traction Case, the following:[220]

> "33. When a State admits into its territory foreign investments or foreign nationals, whether natural or juristic persons, it is bound to extend to them the protection of law and assumes obligations concerning the treatment to be afforded them. These obligations, however, are neither absolute nor unqualified. In particular, an essential distinction should be drawn between the obligations of a State towards the international community as a whole, and those arising vis-à-vis another State in the field of diplomatic protection. By their very nature the former are the concern of all States. In view of the importance of the rights involved, all States can be held to have a legal interest in their protection; they are obligations *erga omnes*.
> 34. Such obligations derive, for example, in contemporary international law, from the outlawing of acts of aggression, and of genocide, as also from the principles and rules concerning the basic rights of the human person, including protection from slavery and racial discrimination. Some of the corresponding rights of protection have entered into the body of general international law (*Reservations to the Convention on the Prevention and Punishment of the Crime of Genocide, Advisory Opinion, I.C.J. Reports 1951*, p. 23); others are conferred by international instruments of a universal or quasi-universal character."

This dictum, by some considered to have been made obiter, constituted the starting-point of this thesis.[221] Yet at present no more need be done than to discuss some of the elements contained in this statement by the Court. It is proposed therefore to discuss the following two subjects: paragraphs 33 and 34 in the context of the Barcelona

Traction Case; and the scope of obligations *erga omnes* and the relation to the concept of *jus cogens*.

1.8.1. PARAGRAPHS 33 AND 34 IN THE CONTEXT OF THE BARCELONA TRACTION CASE

The Court on this occasion proclaimed "an essential distinction" between two different kinds of obligations, namely obligations arising vis-à-vis another State in the field of diplomatic protection and obligations towards the international community as a whole. What is of paramount importance here is to note the consequences attached by the Court to obligations towards the international community as a whole. First of all it states that considering their very nature they are the concern of all States. That does not help us very much, because, as has been reflected above (subsection 1.5.1), all States have a general interest in the observance of international law. It is the additional sentence that clarifies what kind of concern is envisaged as it stipulates that: "In view of the importance of the rights involved all States can be held to have a legal interest in their protection;" Now the question of legal interest is intimately connected to the subjects entitled to invoke the responsibility of another State, and thus demand the performance of (breached) obligations. In the following paragraphs, which will be quoted in full considering their importance, the Court acknowledges as much when it holds:[222]

> "35. Obligations the performance of which is the subject of diplomatic protection are not of the same category. It cannot be held, when one such obligation in particular is in question, that all States have a legal interest in its observance. In order to bring a claim in respect of the breach of such an obligation, a State must first establish its right to do so, for the rules on the subject rest on two suppositions:
>
> > 'The first is that the defendant State has broken an obligation towards the national State in respect of its nationals. The second is that only the party to which an international obligation is due can bring a claim in respect of its breach.' (*Reparation for Injuries Suffered in the Service of the United Nations, Advisory Opinion, I.C.J. Reports 1949*, pp. 181-182.)
>
> In the present case it is therefore essential to establish whether the losses allegedly suffered by Belgian shareholders in Barcelona Traction were the consequence of the violation of obligations of which they were the beneficiaries. In other words: has a right of Belgium been violated on account of its nationals' having suffered infringement of their rights as shareholders in a company not of Belgian nationality?
>
> 36. Thus it is the existence or absence of a right, belonging to Belgium and recognized as such by international law, which is decisive for the problem of Belgium's capacity.
>
> > 'This right is necessarily limited to intervention [by a State] on behalf of its own nationals because, in the absence of a special agreement, it is the bond of nationality between the State and the individual which alone confers upon the State the right of diplomatic protection, and it is as a part of the function of diplomatic protection that the right to take up a claim and to

> ensure respect for the rules of international law must be envisaged.' (*Panevezys-Saldutiskis Railway, Judgment, 1939, P.C.I.J., Series A/B, No. 76*, p. 16.)
>
> It follows that the same question is determinant in respect of Spain's responsibility towards Belgium. Responsibility is the necessary corollary of a right."

This last remark is not entirely correct if it meant to say that responsibility is only incurred if a State decides to exercise its right to demand performance of (breached) obligations.[223] Yet this quote serves to illustrate the nature of the distinction made by the Court, for Belgium could only exercise a right based on injury done to itself,[224] or to its nationals. The Court, however, correctly observed that it is not injury that confers the right:[225]

> "Every investment of this kind carries certain risks. The real question is whether a right has been violated, which right could only be the right of the State to have its nationals enjoy a certain treatment guaranteed by general international law, in the absence of a treaty applicable to the particular case."

The complication in the Barcelona Traction Case of course was that the criterion of nationality could be applied to either natural persons, or legal persons. The injury, in consequence of (allegedly wrongful) acts by Spain, was done directly to the Barcelona Traction, a corporation established under the laws of Canada, and only indirectly to the Belgian shareholders of that company. Canada could have exercised, and for some time indeed did exercise, its right of diplomatic protection, but refrained from doing so any longer.

Although therefore all these observations seem to lead to the conclusion that States need not be in possession of a right to demand the performance of obligations *erga omnes*, the more correct view is that the Court considers that the rights may be in possession of other States than those which may certainly claim the performance of the correlative obligations because they have suffered from an infringement of their rights (in the current legal terminology), or because they suffer the consequences of the internationally wrongful act (in the writer's terminology). Because if one scrutinizes the text of paragraph 33 more closely, one may notice that the "protection" in the sentence "In view of the importance of the rights involved, all States can be held to have a legal interest in their protection;" does not refer to the protection of the obligations *erga omnes*, but to the protection of the rights involved.[226] This is brought out by the French text: "Vu l'importance des droits en cause, tous les Etats peuvent être considérés comme ayant un intérêt juridique à ce que ces droits soient protégés." If we make the connection with the examples the Court mentions in paragraph 34 (the prohibitions of aggression, genocide, slavery and racial discrimination), then it is obvious that those "rights involved" are in possession first of the victim of aggression and secondly of the peoples or individuals suffering from genocide, slavery or racial discrimination.

The legal interest of a State suffering from aggression is well established in international law, and the legal interest attributed by the Court to other States, over and above the legal interest of the victim State and even if they are not affected by the aggression, also. Indeed the reference by the Court to "the corresponding rights of protection" may be read to mean the rights of States other than the "injured State" (and those exist only where the obligation breached is of *erga omnes* character), and in respect to the example of the prohibition of aggression may be considered to refer to the right of collective self-defence.

In the case of the examples of the prohibitions on genocide, slavery and racial discrimination, however, it is the rights of the populations and individuals concerned, generally speaking, which are at stake, and no other State will be affected through violations of the prohibitions.[227] Thus the observation of the Court, in paragraph 35, to the effect that Belgium would have to establish its right, should be read to mean, not that other States need not establish their right to engage in the protection of obligations *erga omnes*, but that they need not suffer any direct injury (to their rights),[228] in consequence of an internationally wrongful act, in order to be in possession of a legal interest.

Now paragraph 91 of the same judgment has been interpreted in the sense that on the universal level a State can only take up the protection of individuals suffering from the breach of human rights obligations if and when those are of the nationality of the protecting State.[229] That conclusion cannot be shared by the present writer. In view of the importance of paragraph 91 it seems appropriate to quote it once more:[230]

> "With regard more particularly to human rights, to which reference has already been made in paragraph 34 of this Judgment, it should be noted that these also include protection against denial of justice. However, on the universal level, the instruments which embody human rights do not confer on States the capacity to protect the victims of infringements of such rights irrespective of their nationality. It is therefore still on the regional level that a solution to this problem has had to be sought; thus, within the Council of Europe, of which Spain is not a member, the problem of admissibility encountered by the claim in the present case has been resolved by the European Convention on Human Rights, which entitles each State which is a party to the Convention to lodge a complaint against any other contracting State for violation of the Convention, irrespective of the nationality of the victim."

A remark on this score relates to the observation that while the Court in paragraphs 33 and 34 proclaims legal interests for all States with regard to the basic rights of the human person (protection from slavery and racial discrimination, to which may in fact be added protection from genocide), in paragraph 91 the Court merely adopts the general formula of human rights.[231] The Court refers to "instruments" on the universal level, and this may be considered a reference to the 1966 Covenants.[232] It may be suggested that such reference was somewhat inappropriate since none of the instruments referred to had, at that time, entered into force. Furthermore, one may point to the customary origin of the human rights obligations enumerated in paragraph 34, whereas the same cannot be said without qualification with regard to the obligation prohibiting denial of justice on which paragraph 91 turns. Although a rule prohibiting denial of justice does exist in customary international law, that rule has developed within the field of treatment of aliens. The corresponding rights of protection were only established for the State of the same nationality as the alien (allegedly) suffering from maltreatment. Thus the dictum of the Court would have made sense if it had related to the position under customary law. Yet with regard to human rights obligations under treaties, whether universal or regional, and whether or not expressly providing for a right to institute proceedings or initiate claims, all States parties to the treaties concerned will be in possession of a legal interest consequent upon the breach of obligations under such treaties.[233] Nevertheless, there is a need not to confuse the issues here, for the legal interest relating to (breached) human rights obligations is not based on any idea of obligations *erga omnes*. A remark which leads us to the next subsection.

1.8.2. THE SCOPE OF OBLIGATIONS *ERGA OMNES* AND THE RELATION TO THE CONCEPT OF *JUS COGENS*

A preliminary observation concerns the status of obligations *erga omnes* within the structure of primary and secondary rules of international law. The Court has created some confusion in speaking of "corresponding rights of protection". Now if obligations *erga omnes* were to have an independent status within the category of primary rules of international law, then such reference would have made sense. As it is, no indication can be found that they existed in customary or conventional international law before the Court so confirmed. If the corresponding rights of protection existed already, either in customary or conventional international law, what then is the innovation that the Court introduced? What is important to recognize is that obligations *erga omnes* are most intimately connected to the realm of secondary rules of international law, in that "all States can be held to have a legal interest" is the consequence of the characterization of an obligation as *erga omnes* only if and when such an obligation is breached. On that score Meron correctly observed:[234] "Moreover, being *erga omnes* is a consequence, not the cause, of a right's fundamental character."

On that account, to develop somewhat further the terminology involved, it may be noted that the expression "obligations" *erga omnes* is, apparently, a misnomer. The late judge Ago, commenting, explained:[235]

> "In my opinion, the expression is misleading. In reality, almost all obligations of customary international law are obligations *erga omnes* in the sense that they are towards each and all States."

And as illustration of that thought he then referred to the obligation to respect the immunity of diplomats which States owe to all other States. Yet if that obligation was breached, he added, a bilateral relationship resulted between the breaching State and the State suffering from the breach.[236] It follows that when speaking of obligations *erga omnes* the essential idea is not that the obligations are owed to all States, but that in case of the breach of such an obligation the corresponding rights of protection are in possession of each and every State. The Court, in the Barcelona Traction Case, acknowledged this in holding that "all States can be held to have a legal interest in their protection". And commenting Gaja held that:[237]

> "This entails all States being able to put forward a claim that the obligation should be respected and that any act constituting an infringement should be discontinued."

If, as has been held in the previous subsection, this means that the corresponding rights of protection may be in possession of all States besides the State suffering from the breach of the obligation, then the reference by the Court to "corresponding rights of protection" must be considered to be of superfluous character. Indeed a legal interest in possession of a State has been considered to stand for a right of protection, that is, a right to demand the performance of (breached) obligations. Thus if a breach of an obligation *erga omnes* entails for every State a legal interest in its protection, that *ipso jure* means that they are in possession of a corresponding or correlative right of protection. The reference to corresponding rights of protection may then best be understood as evidence of the existence of obligations *erga omnes*, rather than that the establishment of a right should be considered to constitute a condition for a State's reliance on its legal interest resulting from the breach of an obligation *erga omnes*.

Turning now to a more dire question, on the basis of what criterion, or criteria, should one consider that a certain obligation is of *erga omnes* character? It is of course clear that the Court considers the obligations established under the rules prohibiting aggression, genocide, slavery and racial discrimination, to be of *erga omnes* character. Yet it seems that one cannot extract any criterion from those examples. If, for instance, the Court would have omitted the reference to aggression, one could have thought that the criterion sought was that of the human rights character of the obligations concerned.

Annacker has claimed that the essential feature of obligations *erga omnes* is that they are performed towards a community of States and not towards one or more singular States. As such obligations *erga omnes* would be obligations towards all the parties of a multilateral treaty, towards all the States bound by a regional or universal rule of customary international law, or towards the international community. The distinguishing feature, in her words, is their non-bilateralizable structure, that is, they are performed or breached *vis-à-vis* all the States of the community.[238] The argument underlying this construction fails if one considers the example of the prohibition of aggression mentioned by the Court. Clearly a State which violates the prohibition breaches its obligations towards one or more singular States. Annacker appears to attempt to avoid that conclusion by pointing to the fact there are two kinds of *erga omnes* violations: a group which never violates subjective interests (human rights violations), and violations which injure at the same time subjective and objective interests (aggression).[239] Yet she does not make clear why aggression would injure objective interests. Certainly the mere fact that the violation of the prohibition of aggression injures one or more singular States conflicts with her starting-point, namely that obligations *erga omnes* can *only* be fulfilled or breached towards the community of States.[240] To say, as she does, that "the same conduct may well infringe upon the subjective interests of a certain State",[241] is to reverse cause and effect. The commission of aggression is inherently directed towards a particular State. The latter State is not incidentally or marginally affected, it is the target of aggression. That all other States would be affected in their objective interests results only from the recognized importance of the prohibition of aggression, not from the fact that a violation of the prohibition necessarily amounts to a breach of an obligation towards all States.[242]

Leaving aside for the moment the considerations laid down in paragraph 91 of the judgment, the argument that one would have to look, to decide on any criterion, to the human rights character of the obligations, is denied also with reference to the argument made above (subsection 1.6.3) with regard to the legal interest resulting from the breach of human rights obligations. Any State bound by the relevant rule will be in possession of such a legal interest if the obligation established thereunder is breached. The idea of obligations *erga omnes* would not add anything to that conclusion, unless of course the Court would consider every State in possession of a legal interest irrespective of whether or not the State concerned would be bound by the relevant rule. However, that result would seem to be manifestly absurd, or even unreasonable, to use article 32 Vienna Convention terminology. Of course a legal interest for all States would be considered established if the rule concerned would be a rule under universal customary international law (which is the case with regard to the examples of human rights obligations mentioned in paragraph 34). Where there is no such rule of universal customary international law a State not obligated to adopt a specific course of conduct regarding its nationals could not insist that another State should indeed adopt that course of conduct.

The example of aggression, though intimately related to the most important human rights obligation, that of the right to life, is of a different category. The consequences of the violation of the prohibition of aggression are felt, most directly, by the individuals within the State suffering from the aggression. As such the legal interest resulting from such violation is, technically speaking, confined to the State injured thereby. Extending the legal interest of that State to all other States therefore makes perfect sense.[243] The other specific examples mentioned by the Court, genocide, slavery and racial discrimination, have all their basis in human rights obligations. One could argue that obligations *erga omnes* extend the protection of the rights concerned, of the direct victim(s) (individuals or the population), to all other States. Yet such extension of protection is unnecessary. The victims concerned, peoples or individuals, do not have any standing in international law.[244] For that reason the legal interests resulting from a breach of obligation established for their protection must of necessity accrue to those States bound by the same rule. Due to the differing character of the examples given by the Court, however, one cannot determine any criterion on which to base the *erga omnes* character of an obligation.

Now the other phrases and terms mentioned in paragraph 33 also do not seem to offer any definite answer to this question. The "importance" of the rights involved may be subject to differing claims, and only the appellation of obligations as "*erga omnes*" and their being incurred "towards the international community as a whole" would seem to present some form of guide-line. At the time of judgment in the Barcelona Traction Case the latter phrase had only just turned up in article 53 of the Vienna Convention, though it spoke of the international community "of States" as a whole. Although the Court nowhere refers to the concept of *jus cogens*, nevertheless the Court's use of terms has been interpreted to imply a link between the two concepts.[245] On the other hand it may be noted that Ammoun's separate opinion does refer to the concept of *jus cogens*, indeed links it to the notion of legal interest, and mentions:[246]

> "(...) an action brought in defence of a collective or general interest, the objective being to safeguard legality or the respect due to principles of an international or humane nature, translated into imperative legal norms (*jus cogens*)."

Another indication that the Court had the concept of *jus cogens* in mind when speaking of obligations *erga omnes* may be found in the examples it refers to. Those were at the time most often mentioned as candidates for promotion to peremptory norm, or as existing peremptory norms.[247] Thus the prohibitions concerned are, and were, regarded as being related to the fundamental interests in need of protection by every State, and this to the extent of prohibiting any derogation by means of concluding treaties.

A major advantage in combining the concepts lies in the way in which it is to be ascertained that a norm is to be characterized as peremptory, and therefore constitutive of obligations owed *erga omnes*. Because, as has been seen in subsection 1.7.2, whether or not a peremptory norm exists has to be verified by reference to its acceptance and recognition by the international community of States as a whole. Although it is, of course, the subject-matter of a certain rule that makes it a candidate for promotion to peremptory ranks, yet whether or not it actually is a peremptory norm depends on the element of will inherent in the notion of "acceptance and recognition by the international community of States". Thus the concepts move away from the notion of subject-matter, and rely instead on the objective determination by the international community of States. The Commission itself, in its commentary on article 19, Part One, indicated that the breach of an obligation established under a peremptory norm should entail *erga omnes* character:[248]

> "Similarly, it would seem contradictory if, in the case of a breach of a rule so important to the entire international community as to be described as a 'peremptory' rule, the relationship of responsibility was established solely between the State which committed the breach and the State directly injured by it."

1.9. The theory of international crimes

Paragraphs 2 and 3 of article 19, Part One, of the ILC-draft on State responsibility, lay down that:[249]

> "2. An internationally wrongful act which results from the breach by a State of an international obligation so essential for the protection of fundamental interests of the international community that its breach is recognized as a crime by that community as a whole constitutes an international crime.
>
> 3. Subject to paragraph 2, and on the basis of the rules of international law in force, an international crime may result, *inter alia*, from:
>
> (a) a serious breach of an international obligation of essential importance for the maintenance of international peace and security, such as that prohibiting aggression;
>
> (b) a serious breach of an international obligation of essential importance for safeguarding the right of self-determination of peoples, such as that prohibiting the establishment or maintenance by force of colonial domination;
>
> (c) a serious breach on a widespread scale of an international obligation of essential importance for safeguarding the human being, such as those prohibiting slavery, genocide and *apartheid*;
>
> (d) a serious breach of an international obligation of essential importance for the safeguarding and preservation of the human environment, such as those

> prohibiting massive pollution of the atmosphere or of the seas."

The Commission placed international crimes in contradistinction to international delicts, and it provided in article 19, paragraph 4:[250]

> "Any internationally wrongful act which is not an international crime in accordance with paragraph 2 constitutes an international delict."

Thus a distinction was introduced within the law of State responsibility that resembles the dichotomy established within the law of treaties between ordinary norms and peremptory norms.[251] Again it would go too far, at this point, to discuss the theory of international crimes in its entirety,[252] and the following topics are therefore singled out: the object, purpose, and basis of the theory of international crimes; the criteria to determine the existence of an international crime; recognition of crimes by the international community as a whole; consequences of the distinction between international delicts and international crimes; and the relationship between international crimes and obligations *erga omnes*, and their embodiment in article 5, paragraph 3, Part Two, of the ILC-draft.

1.9.1. THE OBJECT, PURPOSE, AND BASIS OF THE THEORY OF INTERNATIONAL CRIMES

Whereas article 53 of the Vienna Convention at least is clear with regard to the sanction to be applied with regard to treaties conflicting with a peremptory norm, the same cannot be said regarding article 19 of the ILC-draft. Indeed it is completely silent on the purpose of a distinction between international delicts and international crimes. There can be no doubt, as article 19, paragraph 1, puts it, that, regardless of the subject-matter of an obligation, any breach of an obligation constitutes an internationally wrongful act. But what the difference is between an international delict and an international crime, both internationally wrongful acts under article 19, paragraph 1, is not at all clear. Indeed, Part One of the ILC-draft is silent on the consequences of all internationally wrongful acts, and not just on those of international crimes.[253] The basic purpose underlying the theory of international crimes seems to be the attachment of additional consequences to internationally wrongful acts that are recognized by the international community as crimes. If that is the case the whole philosophy behind the theory of international crimes appears to be a shift to more law observance, and, in case the law is not observed, to more effective law enforcement.

As in the case of peremptory norms it is essential to recognize that the basis of an international crime lies with the breach of ordinary obligations (internationally wrongful acts), and this leads to the conclusion that all the legal consequences normally attached to an international delict are also applicable to a committed international crime.[254]

In the terminology of Part Two of the ILC-draft this means that a State committing an international crime will be subject to the obligation to repair its internationally wrongful act by all the appropriate means. A State in possession of a legal interest in consequence of the internationally wrongful act will correspondingly be endowed with the right to require the State committing the international crime to repair its internationally wrongful act. Furthermore, a State in possession of a legal interest may, under

certain circumstances, be accorded the right to resort to countermeasures or to use armed force. In such a case, however, the State resorting to countermeasures or force will be subject to the requirements set for the exercise of the right to resort to countermeasures or to armed force (*infra* chapters four and five).
One other aspect of these considerations must be mentioned in that the categories of legal interest, discussed in section 1.6, are applicable to all instances of international crimes. As a consequence it may happen that a certain accumulation of legal interests takes place for particular States in consequence of an internationally wrongful act by another State.

1.9.2. THE CRITERIA TO DETERMINE THE EXISTENCE OF AN INTERNATIONAL CRIME

The basic criterion to decide whether or not breaches of certain obligations constitute international crimes lies, according to the Commission, in the notion that the obligation breached must:[255] "(...) by virtue of its content, be essential for the protection of the fundamental interests of the international community;" As a safeguard for the correct application of this criterion the Commission stipulated a complementary criterion which:[256]

> "(...) makes the international community as a whole responsible for judging whether the obligation is essential and, accordingly, whether its breach is of a 'criminal' nature."

The Commission, so as to highlight these criteria, in paragraph 3 of article 19, went on to provide examples, but "subject to paragraph 2" and "on the basis of rules of international law in force".[257] It continued furthermore, as a matter of drafting technique, to indicate that the examples of paragraph 3, subs (a) to (d) must concern breaches of obligations that are of "essential importance" to a certain general sphere of obligations.[258]

Of far more importance, however, is the Commission's inclusion in all the examples mentioned, again as a matter of drafting technique, that there must be a "serious" breach of obligation in order to conclude to the existence of an international crime, and it added in the commentary:[259]

> "Moreover, even the breach of an obligation of essential importance may not assume proportions sufficient to warrant it being characterized as a crime. This can be done only if the seriousness of the breach is established."

In addition to this more general reference to the seriousness of the breach it qualified one example by adding a quantitative criterion. Thus the serious breach of obligation for safeguarding the human being, laid down in paragraph 3 (c), must take place "on a widespread scale", which in the words of the commentary meant that it ought to take "the form of a large-scale or systematic practice adopted in contempt of the rights and dignity of the human being".[260]
Furthermore, some of the specific examples mentioned implicitly contain quantitative dimensions. The prohibition of aggression in paragraph 3 (a), for instance, may be taken to refer not just to any kind of use of armed force by a State, but to those uses of armed force constituting an act of aggression in the sense of article 39. It may be noted

that the Commission had earlier, in relation to the criterion of seriousness, referred to the fact that:[261]

> "The Charter itself makes a distinction between 'threats to the peace', 'breaches of the peace', and 'acts of aggression'."

One would think that in pointing to the term aggression as displayed in article 39, that is at the top of the list of illegal uses of armed force, the Commission is thinking in terms of armed attacks in the sense of article 51 of the Charter rather than all the different kinds of uses of armed force put down in resolution 3314 (XXIX).[262] The maintenance or establishment of colonial domination, in paragraph 3 (b) on self-determination, is to take place "by force", even if the commentary makes clear that "by force" is intended to mean no more than "against the will of the subject population".[263] And the example of paragraph 3 (d), on the safeguarding of the human environment, stipulates that the serious breach of obligation must concern the prohibition of "massive" pollution.

With regard to the criterion of seriousness it has to be noted that this applies to the general categories of obligations of essential importance, and not to the specific examples mentioned.[264] Although admittedly the phrases "such as that prohibiting" linguistically can only refer back to the obligation,[265] it may be submitted that this would not accord with the intention underlying paragraph 3. For instance if there is a breach "on a widespread scale" of the obligations prohibiting genocide or *apartheid*, can one still argue that there must be a "serious" breach before there is an international crime? Is it possible to deny the existence of an international crime, notwithstanding that there is a breach of the obligation prohibiting "massive" pollution?

It may be suggested, in this latter regard, that the drafting of paragraph 3 is deficient, and that a second reading of article 19 could improve the text as it stands.[266] At present no more need be said about the criterion of a serious breach, though it will be discussed further at appropriate places.

However, there is one aspect, which was not discussed by the Commission in relation to the proposed distinction on delicts and crimes, which deserves attention. That concerns the question of fault. It does not seem, in view of the phrasing of article 3, Part One, that the Commission considered the existence of fault, that is, negligence, (wilful) intent, or premeditation, a condition for the existence of an internationally wrongful act. But as special rapporteur Arangio-Ruiz has noted, questions of fault must be taken into account in matters of reparation.[267] Irrespective of the relevance of fault for deciding on specific forms of reparation, resort to countermeasures or the use of force, one would think that in making a distinction between delicts and "crimes" there ought to be at least some reference in the commentary to the element of will present with the author State of an international crime.[268]

There can be no doubt that an international crime cannot be committed through negligent behaviour. Almost all of the crimes mentioned as examples in article 19, paragraph 3, are characterized by the fact that they can only be committed with wilful intent or premeditation. Any State committing aggression, establishing or maintaining by force colonial domination, engaging in slavery, committing genocide, or engaging in *apartheid*, displays its animus to do what it is doing. If it had had no such animus, one would expect it to act to suppress the conduct of its organs. In fact, none of the breaches characterized as crimes in article 19, paragraph 3, subs (a) to (c), can be committed without the active co-operation of high placed State organs, such as top government officials and high-up police and military officers.

In this respect some remarks by Palmisano, on the crime of aggression, are highly relevant:[269]

> "(...) l'élément subjectif constitué par l'*animus* de l'Etat auteur du fait illicite, joue aussi un certain rôle pour déterminer la gravité «circonstancielle» de l'agression. En disant cela, nous ne nous référons pas simplement au fait – du reste évident – qu'un acte d'agression est toujours réalisé intentionellement par un Etat avec la participation de tous ses organes, mais nous désirons surtout souligner que l'«intention agressive» représente, du moins dans quelques cas, l'élément qui aggrave certains comportements étatiques internationalement illicites jusqu'au niveau requis par la notion de «crime» envisagé dans l'article 19."

In his opinion the aggressive intent of an author State in engaging upon certain acts is sufficient to elevate such conduct to the level of a crime. He goes on to illustrate that point by reference article 3, subs (f) and (g) of General Assembly resolution 3314 (XXIX), neither of which, in his opinion, involve, as such, a use of force by the State.[270] With regard to the first it may be said that a State, allowing its territory, placed at the disposal of another State, to be used for the commission of an act of aggression against a third State, does in fact use force against the third State. The determining factor, it would seem, is that such a State has placed its territory at the disposal of another State *knowing that that State would commit aggression*. Since the act of aggression could not have taken place without its co-operation, it is not too farfetched to claim that the first State has equally used force against the third State. The second example, the sending by or on behalf of a State of armed bands, groups, irregulars or mercenaries, which carry out acts of armed force against another State, similarly involves an actual use of force by the State concerned. The phrase "by or on behalf of a State" signifies the element of attribution necessary for the existence of any internationally wrongful act of a State (article 3 (a), Part One, of the ILC-draft). If a State knows of the existence of such bands and fails to put an end to their activities, it does not breach its obligation to refrain from the use force against another State, but breaches its obligation not to allow its territory to be used for the commission of injurious acts against another State.[271]

The other examples of crimes provided in article 19, paragraph 3, subs (b) and (c), similarly bear witness to the existence, of necessity, of wilful intent or premeditation on the part of the author State. The crime of denial of self-determination cannot occur through sheer negligence, if only because the formulation of the right, that a people "freely" determines its status, must imply action impeding the exercise of that right.[272] The more specific example under sub (b), the establishment or maintenance by force of colonial domination more clearly brings out this aspect, since the Commission claims that "by force" in this context means "against the will of the subject population".[273] In the same vein the breaches of obligations for safeguarding the human being, under paragraph 3 (c), can only be committed through wilful intent or premeditation, since a crime in this respect exists only if the breaches occur "on a widespread scale". And the

Commission added to this, in the commentary, that a crime required breaches on a widespread scale so that it took "the form of a large-scale or systematic practice".[274] Obviously the existence of a large-scale practice in denial of human rights alone would suffice to establish the wilful intent or premeditation on the part of the author State. And the same can be said if it can be shown that certain practices are systematic in character. It may be noted that the specific examples of paragraph 3 (c), slavery, genocide and *apartheid*, constituting serious breaches of obligations on a widespread scale, could hardly be committed otherwise than through wilful intent or premeditation. The specific treaties in this context also make references to elements of intent. The Genocide Convention, in article 2, stipulates that: "(...) genocide means any of the following acts committed with intent to destroy, in whole or in part, a national, ethnical, racial or religious group, (...)." The *Apartheid* Convention, defines in a like manner, in article 2, the crime of *apartheid* as:[275] "(...) acts committed for the purpose of establishing and maintaining domination by one racial group of persons over any other racial group of persons and systematically oppressing them (...)."

In conclusion it may be observed that the existence of wilful intent and premeditation on the part of an author State not merely constitutes an aggravating circumstance generally, but ought to be considered inherent in, and a constituent element of, the commission of any international crime.

1.9.3. RECOGNITION BY THE INTERNATIONAL COMMUNITY AS A WHOLE

The process by which certain internationally wrongful acts are recognized as crimes coincides to a large extent with that laid down in article 53 of the Vienna Convention regarding peremptory norms. Indeed, the Commission observed in this regard in the commentary:[276]

> "Moreover, it is clear what is meant by this reference to the international community as a whole. It certainly does not mean the requirement of unanimous recognition by all the members of that community, which would give each State an inconceivable right of veto. What it is intended to ensure is that a given internationally wrongful act shall be recognized as an 'international crime', not only by some particular group of States, even if it constitutes a majority, but by all the essential components of the international community."

Yet some additional questions remain to be answered.

A first one concerns the observation that article 53 of the Vienna Convention mentions the "international community *of States* as a whole", whereas article 19, paragraph 2, makes reference to the "international community as a whole". If we take as a starting-point the inclusion of States and international organizations (and possibly other subjects of international law) within the notion of "international community", then it needs to be asked whether the latter have some function with regard to the recognition phase of certain breaches of obligation as international crimes. One may take a look at the Vienna Convention on the Law of Treaties between States and International Organizations or between International Organizations, which in article 53 has adopted the same text as that contained in article 53 of the Vienna Convention. It would seem strange that in this treaty where treaties concluded with an international organization are declared subject to the concept of *jus cogens*, and thus void if they conflict with a peremptory norm, still the phrase is adopted "For the purposes of the present Convention, a peremptory norm of general international law is a norm accepted and recognized by the international community *of States* as a whole". If therefore in a treaty so essential to the functioning of international organizations all standing is denied for those organizations in the recognition phase of the peremptory character of norms, then the conclusion seems justified that such standing is also denied with regard to the law of *State* responsibility.

Another aspect which needs to be underlined is that the way in which it has to be ascertained that certain internationally wrongful acts constitute international crimes merely concerns the recognition, in the abstract, that certain breaches of obligation *will* constitute international crimes. Thus article 19, paragraph 2, has nothing to do with the evaluation of whether certain conduct, in the concrete circumstances of the case, amounts to an international crime. That evaluation hinges upon the question who is to determine that an international crime has taken, or is taking, place, and that consequently more severe consequences will attach to the conduct in question. On that issue Arangio-Ruiz has proposed, in article 19, Part Two, to leave the determination of the existence of an international crime to the Court.[277] Any State party to a future convention on State responsibility would be entitled to unilaterally seize the Court if the General Assembly or the Security Council had previously resolved, by qualified majority, that the allegation was sufficiently substantiated as to justify the grave concern of the international community. If the Court determined that a crime had been, or was being, committed, the injured States would be entitled to invoke the special, supplementary consequences as contemplated by his proposed articles 16, 17 and 18, Part Two (discussed mainly *infra* chapters three to five)

Finally, it is necessary to account for the lack of attention paid, in the previous subsection, to the fourth sphere of essential obligations regarding the protection of the human environment as laid down in article 19, paragraph 3 (d).[278] The reason for that lies with the doubts one may entertain as to whether it is possible to say, on the basis of the rules of international law in force, that the international community has recognized obligations for the protection of the human environment as essential for the protection of the fundamental interests of the international community. Or in other words, one may doubt whether the international community has recognized breaches of obligation for the protection of the environment as international crimes. Taking a good look at former special rapporteur Ago's report shows a minimum of argument devoted to the protection of the environment,[279] and the commentary to article 19 does not significantly improve on that score.[280] Of course one could argue that the protection of the environment has, in recent times, received much attention, and has led to a number of extremely important treaties.[281] However, none of those treaties provides any indication that the international community would consider breaches of obligation for the protection of the environment as international crimes.

Furthermore, if one considers the examples of pollution nowadays, one is confronted with the fact that in many cases the pollution finds its origin in many different States, and with the fact that the relatively recent example of Chernobyl has not in any way been treated as a crime. The main reason for the moderate reaction of the international community in that instance may be traced back simply to the absence of any wilful intent, let alone premeditation, to cause pollution.[282] Of course this does not signify that no responsibility had been incurred in this case. That one cannot conclude to the existence of a crime does not mean that there was no internationally wrongful act. Also there can be little doubt that a State which wilfully and with premeditation pollutes the atmosphere or the seas on a large scale will be considered to have committed an international crime.

Certain conduct engaged in by Iraq during its occupation of Kuwait could be considered, at present, to constitute the only example of the international crime of pollution of the atmosphere and the seas. That concerned the spilling of oil into the Persian Gulf in order to prevent or hamper a potential amphibian landing by Coalition forces, and the setting on fire of Kuwaiti oil wells just before and during the Iraqi retreat from Kuwait.[283] In paragraph 16 of resolution 687 the Security Council affirmed that Iraq was: "(...) liable under international law for any direct loss, damage, including environmental damage and the depletion of natural resources, (...);" The Council, so as to implement Iraq's responsibility, has set up a Compensation Commission, but the latter's activities relate to damage caused "as a result of Iraq's unlawful invasion and occupation of Kuwait". One cannot, consequently, regard the Security Council's action with regard to the Iraqi precedent as an example of the implementation of responsibility for the crime of pollution.[284]

Since then the Council, by way of presidential statement, has noted that:[285]

> "The absence of war and military conflicts amongst States does not in itself ensure international peace and security. The non-military sources of instability in the economic, social, humanitarian and ecological fields have become threats to peace and security."

This statement certainly does not qualify as a determination of the Council under article 39 of the Charter. Yet it shows the Council's intention to act under that provision in relation to ecological crises if the circumstances so require. That might be the case if a State wilfully and with premeditation would pollute the atmosphere or seas so as to cause damage to a particular State or people. But certainly it is very unlikely that a State would wilfully and with premeditation massively pollute areas outside national jurisdiction.

In conclusion it may be said that the international community has not, at present, recognized obligations for the protection of the environment as obligations essential for the protection of its fundamental interests. Nor has it determined their breach to constitute an international crime. In view of the rarity of precedents, and the improbability of their recurrence, the crime of pollution will not be discussed separately in the following chapters.

1.9.4. THE CONSEQUENCES ATTACHED TO INTERNATIONAL CRIMES

Over and above the consequences applicable in case of international delicts, there must be other additional consequences which are applicable only in case of international crimes. These may be divided into two broad categories: the imposition upon a State which has committed an international crime of more severe consequences than

applicable in case of international delicts; and the broadening of the category of subjects of international law entitled to invoke the responsibility of a State in case an internationally wrongful act constitutes an international crime.
The former are considered in articles 14 and 15 Part Two of the ILC-draft proposed by the previous special rapporteur Riphagen, yet they have not been adopted by the Commission. Article 14, paragraph 2, provided for obligations on all other States: (a) not to recognize as legal the situation created by such crime; (b) not to render aid or assistance to the State which has committed such crime in maintaining the situation created by such crime; (c) and to join other States in affording mutual assistance in carrying out the obligations under subparagraphs (a) and (b). The present special rapporteur Arangio-Ruiz recently has come up with his own proposals regarding possible consequences of international crimes.[286] Since the additional consequences of international crimes will be discussed mainly in chapters three to five, no more need be said of them here.

The latter category, broadening the category of subjects entitled to invoke the responsibility of a State if the internationally wrongful act constitutes an international crime, leads us to the next subsection.

1.9.5. INTERNATIONAL CRIMES, ARTICLE 5, PARAGRAPH 3, PART TWO OF THE ILC-DRAFT ON STATE RESPONSIBILITY, AND OBLIGATIONS *ERGA OMNES*

The Commission, at different points in its commentary on article 19, already envisaged the possibility that there might be subjects other than the directly injured State entitled to invoke the responsibility of another State which committed an international crime.[287] However, since the Commission at that moment was committed only to the construction of Part One, it did not probe further with regard to the question whether there might be States other than the directly injured State entitled to invoke the responsibility in such cases, and if so what those States could actually do consequent upon their right to invoke that responsibility. Whether they could demand reparation or decide upon countermeasures or the use of force was left to be determined in Part Two of the draft.
The Commission, on the basis of Riphagen's proposal, reached agreement on the *erga omnes* character of international crimes, as it adopted article 5, paragraph 3, Part Two of the ILC-draft:[288]

> "In addition, 'injured State' means, if the internationally wrongful act constitutes an international crime [and in the context of the rights and obligations of States under articles 14 and 15], all other States."

The commentary on this article makes clear that, in principle, all other States are to be considered "injured State" in case of an international crime.[289] But it is added that:[290]

> "In particular, the question arises whether all other States, individually, are entitled to respond to an international crime in the same manner as if their individual rights were infringed by the commission of the international crime."

The answer to that question depends to a large degree upon the progressive institutionalization, as well as the establishment of collective procedures, and will be reflected upon in chapter two. However, the Commission did make clear that individual States will be entitled to invoke some of the legal consequences normally at the disposal of an injured State.[291] The Commission then mentioned, uniquely (for it did not give other examples), the "entitlement to require the author State to stop the breach".[292] Still, some ambiguity remains as regards the theoretical and terminological underpinnings of the adopted text.

Among these a first point to be raised is the fact that contrary to the definition of paragraph 1, the phrase "if the right infringed", featuring in all the examples laid down in paragraph 2, does not have a place within the text of paragraph 3. No explanation for this divergence is offered either in the relevant proposals of Riphagen,[293] or the commentary on article 5. Now by definition "injured State" means a State whose rights have been infringed, and it may be wondered whether that definition applies also to the case of international crimes.[294] If the phrase "In addition" in paragraph 3 is meant to indicate that the definition of paragraph 1 does not apply in case of international crimes, that would provide a satisfactory explanation. If it does not carry that meaning, that would seem strange. Because the legal interest accruing to States consequent upon the commission of an international crime depends upon their being a member of the international community, and not upon any injury they suffer as a result of that crime. The Court, in the Barcelona Traction Case, equated obligations *erga omnes* to obligations towards the international community, and only from that identification resulted legal interests for all States. To refer to rights possessed by "injured" States and infringed in case of international crimes would present a misnomer, and the reference to the "infringement of rights" has therefore rightly been omitted from the text of article 5, paragraph 3.

Another issue in need of attention, though not directly connected to the text of article 5, paragraph 3, is the relationship between peremptory norms, international crimes and obligations *erga omnes*. Now as may be recalled, the Commission has observed, in its commentary on article 19,[295] that in case of the breach of obligations established under a peremptory norm responsibility was to be incurred also towards not-directly injured States. That remark by the Commission appeared to pave the way for the recognition that any State would be entitled to demand the performance of an obligation laid down by a peremptory norm. Yet at the same time the Commission created some confusion, as it observed:[296]

> "It would be simply wrong to conclude that any breach of an obligation deriving from a peremptory norm of international law is an international crime and that only the breach of an obligation having this origin can constitute such a crime. It can be accepted that obligations whose breach is a crime will 'normally' be those deriving from rules of *jus cogens*, though this conclusion cannot be absolute. But above all, although it may be true that failure to fulfil an obligation established by a rule of *jus cogens* will often constitute an international crime, it cannot be denied that the category of international obligations admitting of no derogation is much broader than the category of obligations whose breach is necessarily an international crime."

Taking into account the remarks made in the commentary to article 19, two conclusions seem warranted. First, that all States have a legal interest in case of the breach of an obligation laid down by a peremptory norm. And secondly, since there may exist obligations under peremptory norms whose breach is not an international crime, that peremptory norms are to attain an independent status within the ILC-draft. Consistent arguing, therefore, would lead to the conclusion that one might expect to find a provision in article 5, Part Two, to the effect that in case of a breach of an obligation established under a peremptory norm all States are injured.[297] But one searches in vain to find any. There are of course other provisions within the ILC-draft that are concerned with peremptory norms,[298] but those do not touch upon any question of legal interest.[299] Under this hypothesis it flows from the (absence of any provision in the) ILC-draft that the legal interest accruing to States following the breach of an obligation laid down by a peremptory norm must be determined by application of the categories of article 5, paragraph 2. That conclusion, however is in contradiction to the text of the commentary on article 19, as illustrated above (at the end of subsection 1.8.2).

No problem would have existed if the categories of peremptory norms and international crimes had been considered to overlap completely. And it is to be noted that a number of members of the Commission commented upon the proposed article 18 (later article 19) in the sense of identifying the category of peremptory norms to that of international crimes.[300] If such complete identification had been established, the only thing to do was to find criteria by which to determine when and how the breach of an obligation under a peremptory norm could be considered an international crime. The basic criterion in this respect constitutes the "seriousness" of the breach.[301] That criterion seems to have been endorsed by the Commission, since in all the examples mentioned in article 19, paragraph 3, Part One, it inserted the phrase "a serious breach", although of course it must be admitted that after that phrase they also all add the line "of an international obligation of essential importance for". That additional line appears to reflect more the basic criterion laid down in paragraph 2, for whether an obligation is of essential importance must surely be determined by the international community as a whole, and the essential importance of an obligation therefore does not appear to deserve any independent status as criterion. The commentary, however, makes clear, and indeed it stresses this aspect, that the criteria in order to determine whether an international crime has been committed, as referred to in paragraph 3, must be read in the light of the criterion adopted in paragraph 2: only when the international community has recognized acts to be contrary to an obligation for the protection of the fundamental interests of that community can one consider such acts to constitute crimes.[302] Nevertheless, the commentary was explicit in its conviction that:[303]

> "(...) even the breach of an obligation of essential importance may not assume proportions sufficient to warrant it being characterized as a crime."

In view of article 5, paragraph 2 (e) (iii), however, the conclusion would have to be that conduct constituting a denial of self-determination and human rights violations would imply injured State status for all the States bound by the conventional or customary law rule. As the rules regarding self-determination and basic human rights are established under universal rules of customary international law, all States are in possession of injured State status independent of the gravity of the breaches. Under article 5, paragraph 2 (e) (i) an unlawful use of force will either lead to the injured State status for the directly injured State, or under article 5, paragraph 3, to injured State status for all the other States if the unlawful use of force constitutes the international crime of aggression.

1.10. Summary

It has been found that an interest stands for a desired course of conduct, the realization of which is sought to be achieved by a State or another subject of international law. A prime function of law in general is to accord protection to interests which are worthy of protection. However, not all interests worthy of protection are necessarily protected at any given point in time. For those charged with the application and enforcement of law may grant protection only to the extent that the law has granted an interest protection through the applicable legal procedures. It has been argued by some that a distinction has developed, in international law, between simple interests, legitimate interests and rights, by which the second category, though not the first, would benefit from some protection. However, one cannot say that such a distinction has developed in international law. In international law interests come to be protected through the elaboration of primary rules of international law. Those may prescribe a certain course of conduct, prohibit a particular course of conduct or to the contrary permit it. Prescriptive and prohibitive rules lay down obligations, whereas permissive rules provide for rights.

Law is binding for those subjected to it and imposes respect for its rules. In the absence of law subjects could act as they pleased, and the quality of law consists of its restrictive character once it exists. The law therefore obliges and from this derives, grammatically, the word "obligation". Obligations may be created through the elaboration of prescriptive and prohibitive primary rules. However, the law may instead safeguard the freedom of States by creating a permissive primary rule establishing a right, that is, an entitlement to engage in certain conduct (mostly physical action). If a right has been validly conferred by a permissive rule, a correlative obligation must be seen to exist not to impede the exercise of such a right.

At the same time there exists a correlative right to demand the performance of other subjects' obligations. The basis of that right does not lie with the idea that the breach of an obligation constitutes the equivalent of an infringement of a subjective right: it is precisely on the occasion of a breach of obligation that a correlative right must be exercised. The necessity of correlative rights is postulated on the basis that there must always be, at least theoretically and to begin with, another subject of international law entitled to demand the performance of an obligation. Because if there would not be any such subject, the subject under obligation could itself, and exclusively, determine whether or not it was performing its obligation. The sources of correlative rights lie with the general principles of law and the rules of customary international law related to the law of State responsibility. The actual circumstances and the nature of the rules determine whether a State can exercise a correlative right, that is, whether a subject can be considered to possess a legal interest.

The examination of criteria to determine the legal interests of States has shown that neither the general interest in the observance of international law, nor the common interest under rules of international law, gives rise to a legal interest. Though the latter provides a negative criterion in that States not bound by any particular rule are most certainly not in possession of a legal interest. Considering performance towards specific States also provides no useful criterion to determine the legal interest: only at the occurrence of a breach of obligation is it possible to determine which States are in possession of a legal interest. The criterion to determine the existence of a legal interest does not, however, lie with the existence of material, moral, or legal damage. For the former two would not explain questions of legal interests pursuant to breaches of human rights obligations, whereas the latter would entail the possession of a legal interest for all States. The general criterion to determine the legal interests of States must be the (lack of) effects of an internationally wrongful act upon other States or the international community. The effects of a breach of obligation generally affect particular or all States, and the more tangible term prejudice has been chosen to describe such effects upon States.

Apart from certain non-problematical categories of legal interests, prejudice may be suffered by individual States, by a collectivity of States, or the effects of a breach may not affect any particular State. The prejudice suffered by individual States may be caused directly, for instance by way of obstruction of the exercise of rights of jurisdiction, or it may be caused indirectly to a State to the detriment of its nationals. Prejudice caused to a collectivity of States may come about because a breach of obligation affects all States equally, as is the case for instance with the prohibitions of the stationing of nuclear weapons on the seabed or in space. Where a breach of obligation under a rule would not affect any State specifically, the legal interest will accrue to all States bound by the rule. Such is the case with obligations for the protection of the environment in areas outside national jurisdiction, and obligations for the protection of the human rights of individuals irrespective of nationality. A penultimate category of legal interests of States is constituted by reference to the will of States, and may be coined the posited collective interest. In such a case States have agreed to extend the legal interest of States directly injured or affected to all the States bound by the rule. Examples of this category are collective self-defence provisions and the collective interest of members to the European Union in the due performance of obligations under the treaties, *e.g.* article 170.

A final category of legal interests is constituted by reference to the content, or subject-matter, of a certain rule, and its recognized importance for the international community. Article 53 of the Vienna Convention introduced the concept of *jus cogens* into positive international law, and stipulates that a treaty is void if it conflicts with a peremptory norm. Existing peremptory norms, and credible candidates, are all based on prohibitive primary rules of international law. The object and purpose of the concept of *jus cogens* is to provide a restriction to the otherwise existing freedom of States to conclude any kind of treaty derogating from such rules. The existence of peremptory norms must be established through the acceptance and recognition by the international community of States as a whole. In such a case any State can challenge the validity of a treaty conflicting with a peremptory norm under the customary law of treaties, even if it is not a party to the disputed treaty.

The idea of obligations *erga omnes*, or obligations towards the international community, conveys the idea that all States have a legal interest regarding breaches of such obligations. With regard to the example of the prohibition of aggression this means that all States other than the direct victim are in possession of a legal interest even if they are not affected by the violation of that prohibition. The examples of the prohibitions on genocide, slavery and racial discrimination similarly testify to the possession of a legal interest for all States even if they are not affected by violations of those prohibitions. The observations of the Court in paragraph 91 of the Barcelona Traction Case furthermore cannot be taken to restrict the scope of its statements on obligations *erga omnes*. The criterion to establish whether an obligation possesses *erga omnes* character does not lie with the human rights character of the obligations, but with the fact that they are established under rules accepted and recognized by the international community of States as a whole as peremptory norms.

International crimes are, just like peremptory norms, based on prohibitive primary rules of international law. Accordingly all the legal consequences applicable to an internationally wrongful act will apply also to international crimes. The criteria to determine, in the abstract, whether certain conduct constitutes an international crime, are: the assessment by the international community that the obligation breached is essential for the protection of its fundamental interests; the seriousness of breaches of essential obligations; and the existence of wilful intent and premeditation on the part of a State committing an international crime. In view of those criteria it cannot be said that the international community has recognized environmental obligations as essential for the protection of its fundamental interests, nor has it recognized, so far, that the breach of such obligations would constitute an international crime.

The determination that certain conduct by a State constitutes an international crime may lead to additional consequences for that State (to be discussed in chapters three, four and five), and to the broadening of the subjects entitled to invoke the responsibility of the author State. The phrase "if the right infringed", featuring in all the categories of article 5, paragraph 2, Part Two, of the ILC-draft, has been rightfully omitted from the text of paragraph 3. The status of injured State accruing to all States in case of international crimes comes to them due to their membership in the international community, and not from any prejudice done to them individually.

Although the commentary to article 19 hinted at an injured State status for all States in case of breaches of obligations under peremptory norms, article 5, Part Two, has not followed up on this. To the extent that obligations under peremptory norms are based on primary rules regarding the right of self-determination of peoples or for the protection of human rights, injured State status will accrue to all States, under article 5, paragraph 2 (e) (iii), even if the obligation concerned is not breached in a serious manner. If the obligation to refrain from the use of force, conspicuously considered to be established under a peremptory norm, is not breached in a serious manner, this does not entail injured State status for all States under article 5, Part Two. Consequently, the only special or supplementary consequence under a régime of crimes, in relation to legal interests, would be the status of injured State for all States if the internationally wrongful act constitutes the international crime of aggression.

An issue left in abeyance has been the role to be played by the international community regarding the protection of community interests. If obligations *erga omnes* would truly constitute obligations towards the international community, one would expect that community to be in possession of a corresponding right to demand the performance of those obligations, and to be in possession of a legal interest if such obligations are breached (in a serious manner). An international community would not be able to contribute much to the protection of community interests unless it were organized. Any discussion of the role of the international community in these matters must, for that reason, look to international organizations, and most notably to the United Nations.

NOTES

[1] Text and Commentary Article 1, Part One, YBILC 1973, Volume II, pp. 173-176, 175.

[2] Primary rules of international law will be taken to mean substantive rules of international law, and the secondary rules will be taken to mean those rules which involve the determination, implementation and enforcement of the international responsibility of States. For a more broad perception of secondary rules see Hart, H., The Concept of Law, Second Edition, Clarendon Press, Oxford, 1994, 79-99; and Wellens, K., Diversity in Secondary Rules and the Unity of International Law: Some Reflections on Current Trends, 25 NYIL 1994, pp. 3-37, 6-8.

[3] The 1969 Vienna Convention on the Law of Treaties, 63 AJIL 1969, pp. 875-903.

[4] Barcelona Traction, Light and Power Company, Limited, Judgment, ICJ Reports 1970, p. 3, 32.

[5] Text and Commentary Article 19, Part One, YBILC 1976, Volume II, Part Two, pp. 95-122.

[6] Gervais, A., L'affaire du Lac Lanoux, Étude critique de la sentence du Tribunal arbitral, 6 AFDI 1960, pp. 372-434, 426. Emphasis in the original.

[7] Arató, S., Die völkerrechtliche Haftung, Nyomatott Taizs József könyvnyomdában, Pécs, 1937, 11-12. Consider also this observation of Kraus: "Unter Interesse verstehen wir dabei zunächst Wertvorstellung und sodann Werterhaltungs- und Wertverwirklichungswillen." Kraus, H., Interesse und zwischenstaatliche Ordnung, 49 NZIR 1934, pp. 22-65, 23.

[8] Kraus, Interesse, 41-42. These actions or omissions either have to be undertaken by another State, or by the State advancing the interest in question (*ibid.*).

[9] Union Académique Internationale, Dictionnaire de la terminologie du droit international, Sirey, Paris, 1960, 342.

[10] Kraus, Interesse, 34, observes: "Jedes Interesse ist notwendig auf ein Objekt gerichtet." And, at 35, he holds: "Um sie zu verwirklichen müssen sie sich notwendig in bestimmte konkrete Richtungen auf konkret bestimmte Interessenobjekten, Gegner und Inhalte konkretisieren."

[11] Brunnée, J., "Common Interest" – Echoes from an Empty Shell?, Some Thoughts on Common Interest and International Environmental Law, 49 ZAORV 1989, pp. 791-808, 793. Two footnotes omitted.

[12] Or, in the alternative, an interest may be claimed to exist on the part of another natural or legal person. The claim "to have an interest in something" may therefore either originate from a personal view, or from a view other than the person in whose interest something is asserted to be. The latter claim thus advanced may be phrased to the effect that something "is to your interest".

[13] Kraus, Interesse, 38, states: "Dabei ist es dem Staat auch unbenommen, Zielstrebungen in seinen Interessenbereich einzubeziehen, die ihm nicht nützlich sind. Die Begriffe Interesse und Nutzen decken sich durchaus nicht immer."

[14] Law tends to provide protection with regard to a certain status quo prevailing at a certain time, and changed circumstances may or may not urge for a change in the law. Thus either the law will be upheld or it will be challenged.

[15] García-Amador, F., Sohn, L., and Baxter, R., Recent Codification of the Law of State Responsibility for Injury to Aliens, Oceana Publications, Inc., Dobbs Ferry, New York, 1974, 11-12, mention that in order for law to overcome lacunae and gaps, which arise as the result of the equivocal or unprecise wording of rules, recourse is had, especially in municipal law, to general principles of law, analogy, interpretation of the applicable standard, and equity. In the context of international responsibility, however, they claim that it is the principle which forbids the abuse of rights which is especially important. Note also articles 61 and 62 of the Vienna Convention on supervening impossibility of performance and fundamental change of circumstances respectively.

[16] South West Africa, Second Phase, Judgment, ICJ Reports 1966, p. 6, 34. For comments see among others Reisman, W., Revision of the South West Africa Case, An Analysis of the Grounds of Nullity in the Decision of July 18th 1966 and Methods of Revision, 7 VJIL 1966, pp. 3-90; Verzijl, J., The South West Africa Cases (Second Phase), IR 1966, pp. 87-97; Chandrasekhara Rao, P., South West Africa Cases: Inconsistent Judgments from the International Court of Justice, 6 IJIL 1966, pp. 383-394; Gross, E., The South West Africa Case: What Happened?, 45 FA 1966-1967, pp. 36-48; Falk, R., The South West Africa Cases: An Appraisal, 21 IO 1967, pp. 1-23; Bastid, S., L'affaire du Sud-Ouest africain devant la Cour internationale de justice, 94 JDI 1967, pp. 571-583; Cheng, B., The 1966 South-West Africa Judgment of the World Court, 5 ACSIL 1968, pp. 4-31.

[17] Barcelona Traction Case, Judgment, 46. The Court also observed, at 38, regarding the said distinction in treaties: "Part of the Belgian argument is founded on an attempt to assimilate interests to rights, relying on the use in many treaties and other instruments of such expressions as property, rights and interests. This is not, however, conclusive. Property is normally protected by law. Rights are *ex hypothesi* protected by law, otherwise they would not be rights. According to the Belgian Government, interests, although distinct from rights, are also protected by the aforementioned conventional rules. The Court is of the opinion that, for the purpose of interpreting the general rule of international law concerning diplomatic protection, which is its task, it has no need to determine the meaning of the term interests in the conventional rules, in other words to determine whether by this term the conventional rules refer to rights rather than simple interests." This quotation, and others following, all concern the distinction between rights and interests. The author has, for reasons of consistency, abstained from discussing that distinction here, and all that is written in this section is without prejudice to the discussion of the term "right" in section 1.3.

[18] Barcelona Traction Case, Judgment, 36.

[19] Sentence du tribunal arbitral Franco-Espagnol en date du 16 novembre 1957 dans l'affaire de l'utilisation des eaux du Lac Lanoux, 62 RGDIP 1958, pp. 79-119. For comments Duléry, F., L'affaire du Lac Lanoux, 62 RGDIP 1958, pp. 469-516; Mestre, A., Quelques remarques sur l'affaire du lac Lanoux, in Mélanges offerts à Jacques Maury, volume I, Droit international privé et public, Librairie Dalloz & Sirey, Paris, 1960, pp. 261-271; and Gervais, L'affaire du Lac Lanoux, 372-434. The articles mentioned by the Tribunal are contained in the Acte additionnel aux Traités de délimitation conclus le 2 décembre 1856, 14 avril 1862 et 28 mai 1866, signé a Bayonne, le 26 mai 1866, 62 RGDIP 1958, pp. 84-86.

[20] Gervais, L'affaire du Lac Lanoux, 423-424. He has elaborated his proposed distinction in a later contribution. See Gervais, A., Quelques reflexions a propos de la distinction des «droits» et des «interets», in Mélanges en l'honneur de Paul Roubier, volume 1, Théorie générale du droit et droit transitoires, Librairies Dalloz & Sirey, Paris, 1961, pp. 241-252.

[21] Lac Lanoux Award, 116.

[22] And Gervais concludes, L'affaire du Lac Lanoux, 423-424, that this implies the possibility of a legitimate interest partially being sacrificed to other interests, and if this actually happens that a certain price may have to be paid.

[23] For an author who also rejects this innovation see Bollecker Stern, B., Le préjudice dans la théorie de la responsabilité internationale, Éditions A. Pedone, Paris, 1973, 26. See also Mahiou in YBILC 1985, Volume I, 128; and Arangio-Ruiz, *ibid.*, 149.

[24] Article 11 L'acte additionnel (62 RGDIP 1958, 85): "Lorsque, dans l'un des deux Etats, on se proposera de faire des travaux ou de nouvelles concessions susceptible de changer le régime ou le volume d'un cours d'eau dont la partie inférieure ou opposée est à l'usage des riverains de l'autre Pays, il en sera donné préalablement avis à l'autorité administrative supérieure du département ou de la province de qui ces riverains dépendent par l'autorité correspondante dans la juridiction de laquelle on se propose de tels projets, afin que, s'ils doivent porter atteinte aux droits de riverains de la Souveraineté limitrophe, on puisse réclamer en temps utile à qui de droit, et sauvegarder ainsi tous les intérêts qui pourraient se trouver engagé de part et d'autre."

[25] For the Commission's project on "Liability for Injurious Consequences Arising out of Acts not Prohibited by International Law, see Report of the International Law Commission on the work of its forty-sixth session, 2 May – 22 July 1994, General Assembly, Official Records, Forty-ninth Session, Supplement No. 10 (A/49/10), pp. 367-437.

[26] Apparently in this sense Tammes, in YBILC 1970, Volume I, 185.

[27] The Case of the S.S. Lotus, Publications PCIJ, 1927, Series A, No. 10, p. 4, 18.

[28] See Dissenting Opinion Fernandes, Case concerning the Right of Passage over Indian Territory (Merits), Judgment, ICJ Reports 1960, p. 6, 137. Article 24 of the Charter of Economic Rights and Duties of States, General Assembly resolution 3281 (XXIX), provides: "All States have the duty to conduct their mutual economic relations in a manner which takes into account the interests of other countries. In particular all States should avoid prejudicing the interests of developing countries."

[29] Note the following remark: "(...) no State has the right to use or permit the use of its territory in such a manner as to cause injury by fumes in or to the territory of another or the properties or persons therein, when the case is of serious consequence and the injury established by clear and convincing evidence (...)." Trail Smelter Arbitration (U.S. *v.* Canada), (Hostie, Warren, Greenfields, Arbitrators), 16 April 1938, 9 ILR 1938-1940, pp. 315-333, 317.

[30] Traditionally the sources of international law are enumerated in article 38 of the Statute. The 1945 Statute of the International Court of Justice, 39 AJIL 1945, Supplement, pp. 215-229. While these are the sources the Court has to apply when adjudicating upon disputes between States, it has not hesitated to find that there are bases of obligation other than those enumerated in article 38. In the Nuclear Tests Case for instance it held that unilateral statements made on behalf of a State by responsible officials could lead to an obligation to act in accordance with the course of conduct indicated in the statements. Nuclear Tests (Australia *v.* France), Judgment, ICJ Reports 1974, p. 253, 266-271. For comments Dupuy, P.-M., L'affaire des essais nucléaires français et le contentieux de la responsabilité internationale publique, 20 GYIL 1977, pp. 375-405; Falsafi, H., L'affaire des Essais nucléaires devant la Cour Internationale de Justice, Imprimerie H. Messeiller S.A., Neuchatel (Suisse), 1978; Verma, D., The Nuclear Tests Cases: an Inquiry into the Judicial Response of the International Court of Justice, 8 SAYIL 1982, pp. 20-57. Also Fitzmaurice, G., Fifth Report on the Law of Treaties, YBILC 1960, Volume II, pp. 69-107, 81 and 105.

[31] In which case there may occur either a conflict of interests between States, or other States remain neutral regarding the subject-matter to which the interests concerned relate. See Kraus, Interesse, 49-50, concerning the distinction between parallel and conflicting interests. Birkás further observes: "Beim dasein bestimmter Bedingungen folgen schon aus dem primitiven Nebeneinanderleben notwendige gemeinsame Interessen und ihnen entsprechende Regeln." Birkás, Das Staatsinteresse als Grundlage des Völkerrechts, Carl Heymanns Verlag, Berlin, 1933, 68. See also Higgins, R., Conflict of Interests, International Law in a Divided World, A Background Book, The Bodley Head, London, 1965, 7-8; and Geffcken, H., Das Gesamtinteresse als Grundlage des Staats- und Völkerrecht, Prolegomena eines Systems, A. Deichert'sche Verlagsbuchhandlung Nachf. (Georg Böhme), Leipzig, 1908.

[32] Such parallel interests need not be in the interest of, be favourable to, all States which adhere to a certain course of conduct. For international law is not only based upon perceived identical interests, but also on the exchange of advantages that results from compromise. (Do ut des; reciprocity etc.) Birkás, Das Staatsinteresse, 95-96. Simma, B., Das Reziprozitätselement im Zustandekommen völkerrechtliche Verträge, Duncker & Humblot, Berlin, 1972, 82, observes: "Ein völkerrechtlicher Vertrag kan jedenfalls sowohl gemeinsame Interessen seiner Partner im gerade geklärten Sinn als auch einen ausgleich zwischen *entgegengesetzten* Interessen auf dem Wege gegenseitiger Konzessionen, also durch einen diplomatischen Kompromiß, verkörpern." Footnote omitted; emphasis in the original. Apart from that all States hold one general interest, which relates to the maintenance of international order under the umbrella of law. Kraus, Interesse, 46 and 57-58; and Birkás, Das Staatsinteresse, 76 (who states that this interest is only of secondary importance). However, that is not to say that States do not tend to let their short term interests take precedence over this paramount structural and long term interest. Still, the need for regulating social relations is the driving force behind the creation of all law.

[33] As Kraus, Interesse, 52, correctly points out the interests of States leading up to the creation of a rule of international law may be either parallel, or conflicting. In the latter case there will normally be some exchange of advantages. Nevertheless, the compromise thus reached means that parallel interests come into existence through such barter (*ibid.*, 55-56), and will constitute the common interest for the States concerned once the rule thus created becomes binding for them (*ibid.*, 61-63). It may of course also happen that it is not so much an exchange of advantages which leads a State to abandon a certain desired course of conduct, but that such abandonment results from the sociological power structure between the States concerned, in which case the rules created will mostly reflect the interests of particular States (see Kraus, Interesse, 54-55). Birkás, Das Staatsinteresse, 77, on this account states that international law is either created out of the common interest, or out of legal imperialism (and here he refers to peace treaties and protectorates).

[34] Note this remark by Brunnée, Common Interest, 792-793: "Starting point of all common or shared interest, it is important to note, are the individual interests of the States concerned. From this perspective 'common interest' is the result of coinciding rather than altruistic interests. It does, therefore, have egocentric rather than altruistic features." Two footnotes omitted.

[35] See Birkás, Das Staatsinteresse, 59. Kraus, Interesse, 24, states that interests have a role to play with regard to the interpretation of international law. But he also claims that they are the subjective force of all social life (22-23). The subjective nature of interests probably explains the hesitancy to accord too large a role to the *travaux préparatoires* of treaties. For though it may be said that such subjective interests play a major role at the time of creation of rules of international law, they no longer ought to do so at the time of their interpretation, application or enforcement. Too much attention paid towards the subjective interests of the States which

participated in the creation of a certain rule of international law distracts unjustifiably from the objective nature of that rule.

[36] Separate Opinion Altamira, The Diversion of Water from the Meuse, Judgment, Publications PCIJ, 1937, Series A/B, No. 70, p. 4, 39.

[37] For instance Lefeber refers to permissive and prohibitive rules with respect to the exercise of jurisdiction by individual States. Lefeber, R., The Exercise of Jurisdiction in the Antarctic Region and the Changing Structure of International Law, The International Community and Common Interests, 21 NYIL 1990, pp. 81-137, 89.

[38] Text and Commentary Article 3, Part One, YBILC 1973, Volume II, pp. 179-184.

[39] Ago, R., Second report on State responsibility, YBILC 1970, Volume II, pp. 177-197, 192; and Commentary Article 3, Part One, 184.

[40] Article 29 read together with article 1 (e) of the 1961 Vienna Convention on Diplomatic Relations, 55 AJIL 1961, pp. 1064-1077.

[41] Under the heading of "règle de droit" Union Académique Internationale, Dictionnaire, 521, mentions as a synonym "norme juridique". And it further quotes Roubier, 521-522, to the effect that: "La règle de droit est une règle de conduite qui s'impose aux hommes vivant en société, et dont le respect est assuré par l'autorité publique."

[42] Ago, in YBILC 1970, Volume I, 223, observes: "Every legal rule was necessarily formulated in abstract terms: (...) The purpose of using that concept was to express synthetically an indefinite number of concrete situations. But it was only the formulation of the rule that was abstract; the rule itself had a very concrete content. Nothing could be more concrete than the statement that a State was internationally answerable for any illicit act it committed."

[43] And article 19, paragraph 1, Part One of the ILC-draft puts it in slightly different terms as it recollects that any breach of an obligation, regardless of the subject-matter of that obligation, constitutes an internationally wrongful act. Commentary Article 19, Part One, 95 and 96-97. Article 1, Part One, constitutes the corollary to this statement in that it observes that every internationally wrongful act by a State entails the international responsibility of that State. Commentary Article 1, Part One, 173-176.

[44] Birkás, Das Staatsinteresse, 57, paraphrasing Nelson (Rechtswissenschaft ohne Recht, Leipzig, 1917, 181) states: "Das Völkerrecht sollte in dem Mass als Recht betrachtet werden, wieweit es auch gegen die Staatsinteressen gilt. Das Völkerrecht sei nur dann auf den Interesse begründbar, wenn es auch Interessen beschränkt. Ein Vökerrecht, das Handlungen verbietet, an denen niemand ein Interesse hat, dürfte selbst kein Gegenstand des Interesses sein." Footnote omitted.

[45] Ago, Second Report, 192.

[46] Commentary Article 3, Part One, 184.

[47] Ago, Second Report, 192.

[48] Ago expressed this idea as follows (YBILC 1970, Volume I, 225): "The intention was to say in the clearest possible way that responsibility must be attributed to a State which had not done what it ought to have done or which had done what it ought not to have done." Riphagen, W., Fourth report on the content, forms and degrees of international responsibility (part 2 of the draft articles), YBILC 1983, Volume II, Part One, pp. 3-24, 8, stated in similar terms: "Every single legal rule expresses an 'ought to be'. As such, it cannot escape the question what should happen in case of non-conformity with the legal rule, nor the question how what should happen in that case is to be realized in actual fact."

[49] Thus Ruda, in YBILC 1970, Volume I, 183, observes: "It was better, he thought, to use the words 'non-fulfilment' of an obligation than to speak of its violation." In the same sense Reuter, *ibid.*, 188. Although he adds that: "(...) every failure to comply with a rule did not constitute an illicit act (...)." Alcívar, *ibid.*, 216, remarks: "The legal rule commanded, prohibited or protected and it included the establishment of obligations and rights. It was therefore the non-fulfilment of those obligations – and possibly the exercise of rights going beyond the limits established in the rule – which constituted the illicit act." Contrary Tammes, *ibid.*, 185, who holds that one may use the words "violation of international law", or "violation of a rule of international law". Bilge, A., La Responsabilité Internationale des Etats et son Application en Matière d'Actes Legislatifs, Imprimerie Tsitouris Frères, Istanbul, 1950, 55, claims: "C'est une erreur assez répandu que de considérer comme donnant lieu à une responsabilité internationale toute violation des règles internationales. Toute violation des régles de l'ordre juridique international, (...), ne fait pas naître une responsabilité entraînant l'obligation de réparer. Selon l'intérêt visé par la règle, la violation de celle-ci peut produire une autre conséquence juridique que la responsabilité." And he then refers to article 102 of the Charter which provides that in case a member of the United Nations does not register a treaty with the Secretariat it cannot invoke that treaty before the United Nations. From this he deduces that a distinction has to be made according to whether the violation of a rule entails international responsibility or not. He can only come to such conclusions by taking a very restrictive stand on the consequences of international responsibility, since in his view

responsibility means the obligation to repair. But article 102 does impose the obligation to register treaties in paragraph 1, and the only conclusion to be drawn from its breach is that it carries with it its own exclusive sanction in paragraph 2. The 1945 Charter of the United Nations, 39 AJIL 1945, Supplement, pp. 190-215.

[50] Text and Commentary Article 16, Part One, YBILC 1976, Volume II, Part Two, pp. 78-79.

[51] In many cases authors have the word "right" preceded by the adjective "subjective". *E.g.* Bleckmann, A., The Subjective Right in Public International Law, 28 GYIL 1985, pp. 144-162. This author will not do so for the reasons indicated in the final paragraph of this subsection.

[52] The course of conduct envisaged by a right should always be possible of being realized by the subject-holder of the right. Yet the result aimed at by a rule (the maintenance or change of the status quo) that lays down a right could come about by the action of the holder of the right, or by another subject which is obligated by a prescriptive or prohibitive rule. See for this distinction subsection 1.3.4 of this chapter.

[53] Fritzemeyer traces this to Ihering. Fritzemeyer, W., Die Intervention vor dem Internationalen Gerichtshof, Eine international-verfahrensrechtliche Untersuchung auf rechtsvergleichender Grundlage, Nomos Verlagsgesellschaft, Baden-Baden, 1984, 114. Also Separate Opinion Ammoun, Barcelona Traction Case, Judgment, 324-327; and Gervais, L'affaire du Lac Lanoux, 423. Union Académique Internationale, Dictionnaire, 226, mentions under "droit": "Dans un sens subjectif, une prérogative, un intérêt, un pouvoir d'agir juridiquement protégé, reconnu par le droit objectif."

[54] Bilge, La responsabilité, 55. And Buxbaum, H., Das völkerrechtliche Delikt, Druck der Universitäts-Buchdruckerei von E.Th. Jacob, Erlangen, 1915, 7, observes: "Dass durch Gewohnheits- wie Vertragsrecht nicht nur subjekte Rechte, sondern blosse Interessen geschützt werden können, liegt auf der Hand. Somit ist die rechtswidrige Verletzung eines völkerrechtlich geschützten Interesses völkerrechtliches Delikt." Footnote omitted. One cannot but note that if one wants to define a right as a legally protected interest, it is insensible at the same time to hold that rights and interests may both be protected by international law. See also *ibid.*, 8.

[55] Though of course it would here be more correct to speak of the common interest thus legally protected, since the separate parallel subjective interests are not as such legally protected.

[56] Note also the arguments by judge Ranjeva who refers to objective and subjective rights. Separate Opinion Ranjeva, Case concerning East Timor, Judgment, 30 June 1995, under II.

[57] For instance Dissenting Opinion Armand-Ugon, Right of Passage Case, Judgment, 79, remarks: "One cannot accept an obligation and then withhold the means of performing the obligation." And also (80): "It is not to be supposed that the Maratha Government decided to concede certain rights to Portugal, and at the same time to reserve the power to adopt special measures to defeat the purpose for which those rights had been granted."

[58] An application of this principle may be found in the provision of article 61 of the Vienna Convention concerning supervening impossibility of performance. Nevertheless it may be said that this article has a very restricted scope since it only relates to the disappearance or destruction of an object indispensable for the execution of the treaty. It may be noted that it speaks of *supervening* impossibility of performance, but when the impossibility of performance was built in in the treaty from the start, then a State could probably not be held responsible for the non-performance of such an obligation. See Fitzmaurice, G., Third Report on the Law of Treaties, YBILC 1958, Volume II, pp. 20-46, 26 and 39.

[59] Right of Passage Case, Judgment, 39.

[60] Right of Passage Case, Judgment, 40. Also *ibid.*, 43. And Separate Opinion Wellington Koo, *ibid.*, 63: "It means that with the right on each side there also exists an obligation – that of India to accord passage and that of Portugal to respect the rules of procedure respecting the application for, and grant of, passage. In other words, the rights and obligations of both sides are concomitant and correlative." Also *ibid.*, 66. For similar observations see Dissenting Opinion Armand-Ugon, *ibid.*, 83; Dissenting Opinion Moreno Quintana, *ibid.*, 89; Dissenting Opinion Fernandes, *ibid.*, 138; and Dissenting Opinion Weeramantry, East Timor Case, Judgment, Part D, A (i), and especially Part D, C (i), and Conclusions.

[61] To this principle there are only few exceptions, one of which will be discussed in chapter four concerning the right to resort to countermeasures.

[62] Whether or not other subjects not bound by the rule in question have to respect the exercise of the right may be considered to be in dispute. See Fitzmaurice, Fifth Report, 80-81.

[63] Ago, R., Addendum to the eighth report on State responsibility, YBILC 1980, Volume II, Part One, pp. 1-70, 18. See also Ago, R., Sixth report on State responsibility, YBILC 1977, Volume II, Part One, pp. 3-43, 22, where he observes: "A right, in the subjective meaning of the term, is essentially a faculty to require from someone else a particular conduct or service."

[64] A few pages later (Eighth Report, Addendum, 20) Ago seems to mention a subjective right in the traditional sense of a legally protected interest, as he states: "The interest protected by the subjective right vested in the foreign State, (...)." With regard to self-help (which he mentions in relation to self-defence as the only form of forcible self-help still open to States) Ago seems to envisage the distinction here made, between right as an

entitlement to engage in a certain course of conduct and right as an entitlement to require a certain course of conduct of some other subject, as he states (*ibid.*, 56): "The term accurately reflects the fact that in international law – in any case, in general international law – it is the rightful holder of a particular subjective right who is at the same time given the faculty of taking measures for the purpose of safeguarding the right in question, to see to it that the right is respected and to exercise it." And again (*ibid.*, 56-57): "'Self-protection' or 'self-help' should be construed to mean what legal theory describes as, and comprises under, all the different forms taken by the system which in principle grants to the State, as the holder of a subjective right, the faculty of acting in order to protect and safeguard that right in certain circumstances."

[65] Commentary Article 3, Part One, 182; and originally Ago, Second Report, 192-193.

[66] Such correlation is accepted without much discussion by Smith, B., State Responsibility and the Marine Environment, The Rules of Decision, Clarendon Press, Oxford, 1988, 9; and Hafner, G., Bemerkungen zur Funktion und Bestimmung der Betroffenheit im Völkerrecht anhand des Binnenstaates, 31 GYIL 1989, pp. 187-229, 205. Critically examined in relation to obligations *erga omnes* and international crimes by Willisch, J., State Responsibility for Technological Damage in International Law, Duncker & Humblot, Berlin, 1987, 37-42; and explicitly confirmed with regard to treaty obligations and rights by Simma, Das Reziprozitätselement, 51 (see also 52-54); Sachariew, K., State Responsibility for Multilateral Treaty Violations: Identifying the "Injured State" and its Legal Status, 35 NILR 1988, pp. 273-289, 275-276; and Sachariew, K., Norm und Rechtsverhältnis im Völkerrecht, 37 SR 1988, pp. 495-501, 496. In Aegean Continental Shelf, Interim Protection, Order, ICJ Reports 1976, p. 3, 11, the Court paraphrased a Greek claim in that the Greek Government: "(...) invoked its right to performance by Turkey of the latter's obligations under Article 2, paragraph 4, and Article 33 of the Charter of the United Nations (...)."

[67] Compare the text of article 5, paragraph 1 (a) proposed by Fitzmaurice: "A party to a treaty has a duty towards the other party, or parties to carry it out, irrespective of whether any direct benefits to such other party or parties will accrue therefrom; and correspondingly, any party to a treaty has, as the counterpart of its own obligation, the right to require due performance by any other party of its obligations under the treaty, irrespective of any such factor;" Fitzmaurice, G., Fourth Report on the Law of Treaties, YBILC 1959, Volume II, pp. 37-81, 42 (see also 54).

[68] Technically speaking a correlative right can already be exercised in cases where the breach of an obligation is imminent. Probably more is needed for a State to exercise a correlative right than mere potentiality of breach, since any obligation can be breached. If it could not be breached it would not be an obligation, or it would cease to be one. It seems right to require that there must be certain indications that the obligation is going to be breached.

[69] Union Académique Internationale, Dictionnaire, 352 and 276, respectively mentions both the possession ("Jouissance d'un droit") and the exercise ("Exercise d'un droit") of rights. The first is described as: "Expression (...) qui (...) désigne (...) le fait, pour un état, d'être titulaire d'un droit, qu'il ait ou non la possibilité de le mettre en oeuvre." The latter stands for: "Expression (...) qui (...) désigne (...) la mise en action par un état, d'un droit dont lui-même ou un autre état est titulaire."

[70] Riphagen, Fourth Report, 8-9.

[71] The Court stated in the Barcelona Traction Case, Judgment, 44-45, regarding the discretionary nature of the power to exercise diplomatic protection, and especially when such right is not exercised by the right-holder: "This cannot be regarded as amounting to a situation where a violation of law remains without remedy: in short, a legal vacuum. There is no obligation upon the possessors of rights to exercise them. Sometimes no remedy is sought, though rights are infringed. To equate this with the creation of a vacuum would be to equate a right with an obligation." It may be observed that this argument of the Court does not deal with the absence of correlative rights, but with their non-exercise.

[72] South West Africa Cases, Second Phase, 46. Dissenting Opinion Fitzmaurice, Legal Consequences for States of the Continued Presence of South Africa in Namibia (South West Africa) notwithstanding Security Council Resolution 276 (1970), Advisory Opinion, ICJ Reports 1971, p. 16, 224: "Here again, statements to the effect that certain results cannot be accepted because this would be tantamount to admitting that given rights were in their nature imperfect and unenforceable, do not carry conviction as a matter of international law since, at the present stage of its development, this is precisely what that system itself in large measure is, and will, pending changes not at present foreseeable, continue to be."

[73] And in the Barcelona Traction Case, Judgment, 45, the Court observed: "International judicial proceedings are but one of the means available to States in pursuit of their right to exercise diplomatic protection (...). The lack of a jurisdictional link cannot be regarded either in this or in other fields of international law as entailing the non-existence of a right."

[74] South West Africa Cases, Second Phase, 36.

[75] South West Africa Cases, Second Phase, 10, 12 and 15. South Africa claimed that the Mandate Agreement was no longer in force, and that in any case there was no longer any member of the League of Nations due to the latter's demise. For discussion of these objections against the Court's jurisdiction see South West Africa Cases (Ethiopia *v.* South Africa; Liberia *v.* South Africa), Preliminary Objections, Judgment, ICJ Reports 1962, p. 319, 330-342.

[76] Note the Joint Dissenting Opinion Spender/Fitzmaurice, South West Africa Cases, Preliminary Objections, 547-560, in which they argued that South Africa's third preliminary objection should have been upheld by the Court. For discussion by the Court see *ibid.*, 342-344.

[77] Dissenting Opinion Fitzmaurice, Namibia Opinion, 227-263.

[78] Fitzmaurice hinted so much at this solution, but refrained from adopting it. Dissenting Opinion Fitzmaurice, Namibia Opinion, 267, footnote 45. The conclusion that the Mandate had lapsed leads to the further conclusion that South Africa had no legal title whatsoever with regard to South West African territory, and that the principle of self-determination had to be given effect. For as the Court had earlier observed (though it did not adopt this view as a solution): "The authority which the Union Government exercises over the Territory is based on the Mandate. If the Mandate lapsed, as the Union Government contends, the latter's authority would equally have lapsed. To retain rights derived from the Mandate and to deny the obligations thereunder could not be justified." International Status of South-West Africa, Advisory Opinion, ICJ Reports 1950, p. 128, 133.

[79] See Separate Opinion Lauterpacht, Case of Certain Norwegian Loans, Judgment, ICJ Reports 1957, p. 9, 49-50, where he referred to so-called potestative conditions dependent upon the will of the debtor.

[80] Ko Swan Sik, De Verplichting in het Volkenrecht, T.M.C. Asser Instituut, 's-Gravenhage, 1991, 5, observes: "(...) dat in geval een eenzijdige rechtshandeling bron is van een verplichting, deze slechts reële betekenis heeft als één van de twee polen in een tweezijdige verhouding, en wel tegenover het subjectieve recht dat een ander subject heeft op de vervulling van de verplichting." [Translation by the author: "(...) should a unilateral legal act constitute the source of an obligation, the latter will have real meaning only as one of the poles in a bilateral relationship, and then in relation to the subjective right possessed by another subject to the performance of the obligation."] It is somewhat strange that he mentions the correlation of obligations and rights only by reference to the case where the source of the obligation lies with a unilateral declaration. Gaja, G., Obligations *Erga Omnes*, International Crimes and *Jus Cogens*: A Tentative Analysis of Three Related Concepts, in Weiler, J., Cassese, A., and Spinedi, M. (Eds.), International Crimes of State: A Critical Analysis of the ILC's Draft Article 19 on State Responsibility, Walter de Gruyter, Berlin, 1989, pp. 151-160, 154-155, holds: "Whether a judicial remedy exists or not, it would be inconsistent with the existence of an obligation under a rule of international law if no State could put forward a claim for ensuring that the State having an obligation complies with it and that in case of infringement this is discontinued." Footnote omitted.

[81] Commentary Article 1, Part One, 179-184.

[82] Text and Commentary Article 1, Part Two, YBILC 1983, Volume II, Part Two, pp. 42-43, 42.

[83] Text and Commentary Article 5, Part Two, YBILC 1985, Volume II, Part Two, pp. 25-27.

[84] And this reminisces of the argument to be found in Separate Opinion Fitzmaurice, Barcelona Traction Case, Judgment, 65-66, to the effect that: "In particular I do not base myself as does the Judgment to some extent (...), on any consideration turning on the question of to whom, or to what entity, was the obligation owed in this case, not to act in a manner contrary to international law. This does not seem to me to be the right question to ask where the issue involved is not one of treaty or other particular obligations, but of general international law obligations in the sphere of the treatment of foreigners. If in the latter area a State, (...), acts illicitly, it stands in breach of international law irrespective of whether any other State is qualified to take the matter up. For instance if an individual was concerned, he might be stateless. If in the present case there have been contraventions of international law, they are in no way legitimized, nor do they become any the less illicit, because Canada has not (or even possibly could not) pursue the matter, and because Belgium is held to possess no *locus standi in judicio* for doing so." Footnote omitted. While generally agreeing with this statement it should be noted that international law, on the theoretical level, does postulate the existence of rights correlative to obligations.

[85] Commentary Article 5, Part Two, 25.

[86] The phrase "complementary rules laying down correlative rights" refers to those rules of State responsibility (thus they are secondary rules of international law) defining which States are deemed to be in possession of a correlative right to demand performance of breached obligations. These are being codified by the Commission in article 5, Part Two, of the ILC-draft (on injured States).

[87] In Separate Opinion Fitzmaurice, Barcelona Traction Case, Judgment, 66, one may read regarding the treatment of aliens: "If in the latter area a State, (...), acts illicitly, it stands in breach of international law irrespective of whether any other State is qualified to take the matter up. For instance if an individual was concerned,

he might be stateless." The implication of this statement is unacceptable. If no State is entitled, under international law, to extend its protection to stateless individuals, then it must be concluded that the rule which provides for certain treatment to foreigners only relates to individuals in possession of the nationality of another State (to this effect Dickson Wheel Car Company, 6 ILR 1931-1932, pp. 228-231, 230, footnote 1). If one considers the rule in question also to relate to stateless individuals, then all States must be considered qualified to take the matter up. The latter view is to be preferred, especially considering the quantitatively low number of stateless individuals.

88 Which, according to article 38, paragraph 1 (c) of the Statute, may be applied by the Court to inter-State disputes. The Commission, following Ago, observed in Commentary Article 3, Part One, 182, that: "(...) unlike the situation in municipal law, there are no obligations on a subject which are not matched by an international subjective right of another subject or subjects, (...)." It is submitted that this argument as to municipal law is irrelevant for the issue under consideration here. If under municipal law an obligation of one subject is not matched by a right of another, such a construction will have resulted from explicit provisions, or because the preparatory works, which are much more important in municipal law due to their authoritative character, so indicate.

89 Barcelona Traction Case, Judgment, 32.

90 Case concerning the Factory at Chorzów (Claim for Indemnity) (Jurisdiction), Publications PCIJ, 1927, Series A, No. 8, p. 4, 21. Ehrlich's dissent on this point was directed towards the Permanent Court assuming jurisdiction to determine the nature and extent of such reparation, not towards the principle itself. Dissenting Opinion Ehrlich, *ibid.*, 37-38.

91 Weil, P., Towards Relative Normativity in International Law?, 77 AJIL 1983, pp. 413-442, 431. Footnotes omitted.

92 Morelli explains that the use of terms such as "qualité pour agir" and "*jus standi*", although appearing to relate to some procedural capacity or a right to apply to court, should be understood to relate to substantive capacity or right. Separate Opinion Morelli, Barcelona Traction Case, Judgment, 226. Here he states: "The hypothesis of the existence of a certain obligation on the part of a given State (the respondent State) is assumed, and the question is which State possesses the corresponding hypothetical right; in particular whether or not that right pertains to the applicant State." And again (228): "The point is that any question of capacity can only be raised in relation to a rule of law which is either undisputed or assumed to exist." He further holds, 227, that the possession by an applicant State of a substantive right need not be examined before other questions pertaining to the merits have been investigated.

93 Barcelona Traction Case, Judgment, 44-45.

94 See Separate Opinion Jessup, Barcelona Traction Case, Judgment, 195.

95 Riphagen, Fourth Report, 21. In the same sense Sinclair, YBILC 1983, Volume I, 130. See the broad discussion of this topic by Bollecker Stern, Le préjudice, 50-90, which culminates in the conclusion (89-90) that States do not generally have a legal interest in the observance of any rule of international law. In the same sense Graefrath, B., Responsibility and Damages Caused: Relationship between Responsibility and Damages, 185 RDC ADI 1984-II, pp. 9-150, 50-51; also McCaffrey, S., *Lex Lata* or the Continuum of State Responsibility, in Weiler *et al*, International Crimes, pp. 242-244, 243.

96 Note also Laïs, R., Die Rechtsfolgen völkerrechtliche Delikte, Verlag von Georg Stilke, Berlin, 1932, 140.

97 Dupuy, P.-M., Action publique et crime international de l'état: A propos de l'article 19 du projet de la Commission du Droit International sur la responsabilite des états, 25 AFDI 1979, pp. 539-554, 543.

98 Consider this remark by Hafner, Bemerkungen, 195: "(...) ein aus einer norm des allgemeinen Völkergewohnheitsrechts nicht Berechtigter oder Verpflichteter kann zur Änderung, Durchsetzung oder Geltendmachung dieser Norm nicht berufen sein."

99 Riphagen, Fourth Report, 14.

100 Riphagen, Fourth Report, 14.

101 Consider Reuter, P., Le dommage comme condition de la responsabilité internationale, in Homenaja al profesor Miaja de la Muela, volume II, 1979, pp. 837-846, 845: "Déjà la Cour internationale de Justice avait, sous l'angle particulier du droit à mettre en mouvement une action judiciaire, été amenée à définir l'intérêt à agir d'Etats liés par la même règle de droit que l'Etat coupable mais n'invoquant pas un préjudice spécial du fait de sa violation." Footnote omitted. In his note he refers to the South West Africa Cases of 1962 and 1966, but one may note here that Liberia and Ethiopia were not bound by any rule binding also upon South Africa. Indeed they were not even parties to the Mandate Agreement for South West Africa, as was noted aptly in the Dissenting Opinion Spender/Fitzmaurice, South West Africa Cases, Preliminary Objections, 548.

102 Sachariew, State Responsibility, 275.

[103] Article 63 of the Statute runs:
1. Whenever the construction of a convention to which States other than those concerned in the case are parties is in question, the Registrar shall notify all such States forthwith.
2. Every State so notified has the right to intervene in the proceedings; but if it uses this right, the construction given by the judgment will be equally binding upon it.

[104] Intervention is even more restricted than that since it has to relate to the principal proceedings: "In regard to that question, the Court observes that every intervention is incidental to the proceedings in a case; it follows that a declaration filed as an intervention only acquires that character, in law, if it actually relates to the subject-matter of the pending proceedings." Haya de la Torre Case, Judgment, ICJ Reports 1951, p. 71, 76.

[105] The S.S. Wimbledon, Publications PCIJ, 1923, Series A, No. 1, p. 6, 20.

[106] The 1919 Treaty of Peace with Germany, 13 AJIL 1919, Supplement, pp. 151-386.

[107] Arangio-Ruiz, G., Preliminary Report on State Responsibility, 18 May 1988, A/CN.4/416, 34 pp., 12; and Arangio-Ruiz, YBILC 1988, Volume I, 264-265.

[108] Riphagen, Fourth Report, 13. He does express the opinion (*ibid.*) that: "There are, however, exceptions to the separability of the bilateral relationships." Footnote omitted.

[109] Sachariew, Norm, 496.

[110] Contrary Ushakov, YBILC 1984, Volume I, 277: "In that respect, he endorsed the approach (...), namely that the responsibility of the author State was not engaged until the injured State so requested." In the same sense Ogiso, YBILC 1984, *ibid.*, 309; Riphagen, YBILC 1985, Volume I, 158.

[111] Hafner, Bemerkungen, 191 and 195-196.

[112] Riphagen, Fourth Report, 14. Relevant footnote omitted.

[113] Commentary Article 3, Part One, 183-184; Originally Ago, Second Report, 193-194. For a contrary position see Delbez, L., Les principes généraux du contentieux international, Librairie Générale de Droit et de Jurisprudence, Paris, 1962, 160.

[114] That conclusion appears warranted also by reference to South West Africa Cases, Second Phase, 32.

[115] Commentary Article 3, Part One, 183.

[116] Example mentioned by Koroma, YBILC 1990, Volume I, 193.

[117] For instance Bollecker Stern, 33, with regard to illegal border crossings; Reuter, Le dommage, 845; Graefrath, Responsibility and Damages, 30 and 35.

[118] Commentary Article 3, Part One, 183.

[119] Commentary Article 3, Part One, 183; Bollecker Stern, 31-35.

[120] Note that Pellet claimed: "(...) he did not believe it was possible to speak of 'legal' injury. Any injury arising from an internationally wrongful act must, assuming that there was responsibility, have a 'legal' element." Pellet, YBILC 1990, Volume I, 180.

[121] Commentary Article 3, Part One, 183; Originally Ago, R., Third report on State responsibility, YBILC 1971, Volume II, Part One, pp. 199-274, 223.

[122] Anzilotti, D., La responsabilité internationale des états a raison des dommages soufferts par des étrangers, 13 RGDIP 1906, pp. 5-29, 13.

[123] See comment by the French government on article 3, as quoted by Tanzi, A., Is Damage a Distinct Condition for the Existence of an Internationally Wrongful Act?, in Spinedi, M., and Simma, B. (Eds.), United Nations Codification of State Responsibility, Oceana Publications, Inc., New York, 1987, pp. 1-33, 6-7.

[124] Graefrath, Responsibility and Damages, 35.

[125] For a comment on such function of damage see Graefrath, Responsibility and Damages, 42-47.

[126] Commentary Article 3, Part One, 83, footnote 97.

[127] Commentary Article 3, Part One, 83. See especially Tanzi, Is Damage, 8-10.

[128] One can agree with: "Ou bien l'on arrive à prétendre que, pour l'Etat, toute atteinte à ses droits, c'est-à-dire toute violation du droit international dont il est victime, engendre un préjudice moral. Celui-ci, dans ce cas, est inhérent à tout acte illicite international, il n'est pas un élément distinct, identifiable, et la notion n'a plus de sens." Dominicé, C., La satisfaction en droit des gens, in Dutoit, B., and Grisel, E. (Eds.), Mélanges Georges Perrin, Diffusion Payot, Lausanne, 1984, pp. 91-121, 116. Also 117-118.

[129] Commentary Article 3, Part One, 83.

[130] Reuter, in YBILC 1979, Volume I, 35. And he was supported in this by Verosta, *ibid.*, 40, who called for deletion of "injured State" from the draft article and commentary.

[131] Pinto, in YBILC, 1979, Volume I, 44.

[132] Ago, in YBILC 1979, Volume I, 51.

[133] Riphagen, W., Sixth report on the content, forms and degrees of international responsibility (part 2 of the draft articles); and "Implementation" (*mise en oeuvre*) of international responsibility and the settlement of disputes (part 3 of the draft articles), YBILC 1985, Volume II, Part One, pp. 3-19, 6.

[134] Riphagen, Sixth Report, 6.

[135] Riphagen, Sixth Report, 8. Footnote omitted. When introducing his Sixth Report to the Commission he made the following remarks (YBILC 1985, Volume I, 87), which again illustrates the confusion: "The situation was the complete reverse under international law, which was typically bilateral in that its norms created only bilateral relationships as between the State committing an internationally wrongful act and the State legally affected by such an act. It was surely the progressive development of international law that had brought into being real norms of international law, norms that in principle entailed legal consequences beyond the bilateral legal relationship between the author State and the State directly affected by its acts or omissions." See especially the remarks by Ushakov (YBILC 1985, Volume I, 119), to the effect that: "Just as the author State was the State which had committed an internationally wrongful act – whether a delict or a crime – the injured State was the State with respect to which the act had been committed. Nevertheless it was impossible to determine in any concrete fashion which was the author State and which was the injured State: everything depended on the actual circumstances in which the internationally wrongful act occurred."

[136] Jagota, in YBILC 1985, Volume I, 155.

[137] Riphagen, in YBILC 1985, Volume I, 162.

[138] Riphagen claims correctly (YBILC 1984, Volume I, 262): "When thus defining the 'injured State', it was inevitable to refer to the character of the primary obligation which had been breached."

[139] Although the criterion of "affected" is frequently referred to in the work of the Commission on State responsibility. *E.g.* Ushakov, YBILC 1984, Volume I, 277.

[140] Riphagen, Fourth Report, 8, observes that part 2 of the ILC-draft has to focus on injury to a particular State, to several States, or to the community of States. Ushakov remarks (YBILC 1983, Volume I, 125): "It was precisely the injury suffered as a result of a wrongful act that established a legal relationship between the victim and the author." In the same sense Ni, *ibid.*, 132.

[141] Text and Commentary Article 57, Law of Treaties, YBILC 1966, Volume II, pp. 253-255. Simma, B., Reflections on Article 60 of the Vienna Convention on the Law of Treaties and Its Background in General International Law, 20 OZOR 1970, pp. 5-83, 22 and 56, criticizes article 60 for not enabling a State injured by a material breach of a treaty to suspend or terminate another treaty which is of interdependent character with the first treaty. Yet it may be noted that in fact the Vienna Convention in article 60 does not address the question whether, in case of the breach of a treaty, another interdependent treaty could be suspended or terminated. An analogous argument, allowing the suspension or termination of the interdependent treaty, could be made by reference to the law of State responsibility which allows the non-performance of obligations (as a countermeasure) consequent upon the breach of some other obligation. Zoller, E., Peacetime Unilateral Remedies: An Analysis of Countermeasures, Transnational Publishers, Dobbs Ferry, Inc., New York, 1984, 85-93. See also Arangio-Ruiz, G., Fifth Report, 12 May 1993, A/CN.4/453, 63 pp., 30, footnote 74.

[142] Dehaussy, J., Le problème de la classification des traités et le projet de convention établi par la Commission du Droit International des Nations Unies, in Recueil d'études de droit international en hommage à Paul Guggenheim, Imprimerie de la Tribune de Genève, Genève, 1968, pp. 305-326; Virally, M., Sur la classification des traites, A propos du projet d'articles de la Commission du Droit International, in Comunicazioni e Studi, volume 13, 1969, pp. 17-35; Simma, Article 60, 70-75; Bleckmann, A., Probleme der Anwendung multilateraler Verträge, Gegenseitigkeit und Anwendbarkeit der Vertragspartner, Duncker & Humblot, Berlin, 1974, 47-50, 57-59, and 66-78; Barile, G., The Protection of Human Rights in Article 60, Paragraph 5 of the Vienna Convention of the Law of Treaties, in Etudes en l'honneur de Roberto Ago, Le droit international à l'heure de sa codification, volume II, Giuffrè, Milano, 1987, pp. 3-14. See also Schwelb, E., Termination or Suspension of the Operation of a Treaty as a Consequence of its Breach, 7 IJIL 1967, pp. 309-334; Rosenne, S., Bilateralism and Community Interest in the Codified Law of Treaties, in Friedmann, W., Henkin, L., and Lissitzyn, O. (Eds.), Transnational Law in a Changing Society, Essays in honor of Philip C. Jessup, Columbia University Press, New York, 1972, pp. 202-227; Duckwitz, E., Rechtsfolgen bei Verletzung völkerrechtlicher Verträge, Duncker & Humblot, Berlin, 1975, 62-65; Mazzeschi, R., Termination and Suspension of Treaties for Breach in the ILC Works on State Responsibility, in Spinedi and Simma, United Nations Codification, pp. 57-94; Hutchinson, D., Solidarity and Breaches of Multilateral Treaties, 59 BYBIL 1988, pp. 151-215.

[143] Although reference is made here to the case of multilateral treaties, the same problems arise with regard to rules of customary international law that bind more than two States. The criteria to determine the existence of a legal interest consequent upon the breach of an obligation established under customary international law are, to the mind of this author, identical to those relating to obligations under multilateral treaties.

[144] The distinction in question may also be illustrated by reference to article 20, paragraphs 1 and 2. See Dehaussy, Classification, 312-313.

[145] Commentary Article 5, Part Two, 25-27. Original proposal by Riphagen, Sixth Report, 5-8. Discussed by Commission in YBILC 1985, Volume I, 84-163. Commented upon by Graefrath, B., Das Verantwortlichkeitsverhältnis im Völkerrecht und die Definition des "Verletzten Staates", in Graefrath, B., Probleme des Völkerrechts, Akademie-Verlag, Berlin, 1987, pp. 107-138; and Simma, B., Bilateralism and Community Interest in the Law of State Responsibility, in Dinstein, Y. (Ed.), Essays in Honour of Shabtai Rosenne, International Law at a Time of Perplexity, Martinus Nijhoff Publishers, Dordrecht, 1989, pp. 821-844.

[146] Riphagen, Sixth Report, 6; also Riphagen, YBILC 1985, Volume I, 162.

[147] Although it would be better anyway to refer to an infringement of a right as an obstruction of the exercise of a right. See also Riphagen, W., Third report on the content, forms and degrees of international responsibility (part 2 of the draft articles), YBILC 1982, Volume II, Part One, pp. 22-50, 35, footnote 68.

[148] See also the comments of Tomuschat (YBILC 1985, Volume I, 125), Yankov (*ibid.*, 145), Arangio-Ruiz (*ibid.*, 149), and Koroma (*ibid.*, 152), which are supportive to Riphagen's approach with regard to defining the injured State as a State whose rights had been infringed (or violated). At this point one may note that to rely on such correlation between primary rights and primary obligations is to present reasoning circular in character, for as Fitzmaurice held (Separate Opinion, Barcelona Traction Case, Judgment, 66): "Nor is the question of the entity to which the obligation is due helpful even for the purpose of identifying the party entitled to claim, for such entity would itself previously need to be identified, and the discussion would turn in a circle."

[149] For instance Riphagen observes (Fourth Report, 13): "Such *démarches* or appeals may be made even before the internationally wrongful act has actually been committed."

[150] Applicability of the Obligation to Arbitrate under Section 21 of the United Nations Headquarters Agreement of 26 June 1947, Advisory Opinion, ICJ Reports 1988, p. 12.

[151] Headquarters Agreement Opinion, 30.

[152] The opinion turned on the issue of interpretation of the Headquarters Agreement, since no conduct contrary to its provisions had as yet been given effect by the United States. See Separate Opinion Schwebel, Headquarters Agreement Opinion, 51.

[153] Riphagen, Third Report, 36.

[154] Hafner, Bemerkungen, 213, mentions in relation to the function of "Betroffenheit" that; "Für diese Zwecke muß die Betroffenheit individualisierbar sein, der entsprechende Staat muß in der auf eine rationale Weise ihm zurechenbaren, völkerrechtskonformen Interessenentfaltung selbst bedroht sein, wobei Gegenstand des Interesses Regelungsobjekt von primären Normen sein muß. Den nur dann ist eine anderen Staaten auferlegte Verpflichtung als zu seinem Vorteil bestehend anzusehen oder ihm 'material' Interessen zu bescheinigen."

[155] Arangio-Ruiz, G., Second Report on State Responsibility, 9 June 1989, A/CN.4/425, 125 pp., 27-39. See also Reuter, Le dommage, 837.

[156] The principle of *res judicata*, *e.g.* article 59 Statute.

[157] YBILC 1984, Volume I, 262.

[158] Nuclear Tests Case, Judgment, 267-270.

[159] Ko Swan Sik, De Verplichting, 5.

[160] Hafner, Bemerkungen, 204.

[161] Riphagen, Fourth Report, 14; and Sixth Report, 7. Leaving aside here any question regarding stipulations for third States and objective régimes. See also in this respect articles 35 and 36 of the Vienna Convention.

[162] Riphagen, Fourth Report, 14.

[163] Commentary Article 5, Part Two, 26.

[164] Simma, Article 60, 67-70.

[165] Article 20 and Commentary, in Waldock, H., Second Report on the Law of Treaties, YBILC 1962, Volume II, pp. 27-80, 72-77. Discussion by Commission in YBILC 1963, Volume I, 120-132, 245-247 and 294-295. Adopted in first reading as article 42, YBILC 1963, Volume II, 204-206; see Simma, Article 60, 68-70.

[166] This recognition occurred after comments by the governments of the Netherlands and the United States to the effect that the provision as it stood would allow any party to suspend the treaty and not just the party whose interests were affected. See Waldock, H., Fifth Report on the Law of Treaties, YBILC 1966, Volume II, pp. 1-50, 34-37. Discussion by Commission in YBILC 1966, Volume I, Part I, 59-67 and 127-129. Adopted in second reading as article 57, YBILC 1966, Volume II, 253-255.

[167] Riphagen, Sixth Report, 7. Three footnotes omitted.

[168] Riphagen, Sixth Report, 7.

[169] Sachariew, Norm, 498.

[170] Sachariew, Norm, 498. As examples he mentions treaties concerning diplomatic and consular relations, parts of the treaties on the law of the sea, and the Vienna Convention. Also Sachariew, State Responsibility, 277-278.

171 The Commission has indicated with regard to the article on compensation that damage may be caused directly (to the State's territory or organization in a broad sense) or indirectly (to its physical or juridical nationals or agents). Text and Commentary Article 8, Part Two, in Report of the International Law Commission on the work of its forty-fifth session, 3 May – 23 July 1993, General Assembly, Official Records, Forty-eighth Session, Supplement No.10 (A/48/10), pp. 168-193, 180-181.

172 Riphagen, Fourth Report, 21, states: "While the rule or obligation may be in abstract terms, the breach is always concrete and the injury is therefore easily allocated to a particular State. Thus most obligations under general customary international law are simply a reflection of the right of sovereignty of another State (...)." Also YBILC 1983, Volume I, 101. Also Riphagen, Sixth Report, 6.

173 Especially the question whether aliens are to be accorded national treatment, or have to be treated in accordance with the international minimum standard has no influence on determining the legal interest of a State.

174 The Mavrommatis Palestine Concessions, Publications PCIJ, 1924, Series A, No. 2, p. 6, 12.

175 Barcelona Traction Case, Judgment, 32.

176 Riphagen, Fourth Report, 14, states: "Actually, if the direct victim of the act is not a State but another entity, one still has to establish a link between that entity and a State in order to identify the injured State. Such a link may be established by another (primary) rule of international law, such as the rules relating to what is often called 'the nationality of claims'." Text and Commentary Article 22, Part One, YBILC 1977, Volume II, Part Two, pp. 30-50.

177 Article 1 of the 1971 Traité interdisant des armes nucléaires et d'autres armes de destruction massive sur le fond des mers et des océans ainsi que dans leur sous-sol, adopted by way of General Assembly resolution 2660, in Resolutions adoptées par l'Assemblée générale au cours de sa vingt-cinquime session, 15 septembre-17 décembre 1970, Documents Officiel, Supplement No. 10 (A/8028), pp. 13-15.

178 Article 4 of the 1967 Treaty on Principles Governing the Activities of States in the Exploration and Use of Outer Space, including the Moon and other Celestial Bodies, 61 AJIL 1967, pp. 644-649. See also Sachariew, Norm, 498-499. A further category mentioned by him concerns obligations performed or breached towards an international organization. *Ibid.*, 499; and Sachariew, State Responsibility, 277.

179 Article 1 of the 1963 Treaty Banning Nuclear Weapons Tests in the Atmosphere, in Outer Space and Under Water, 57 AJIL 1963, pp. 1026-1028. See also Sachariew, State Responsibility, 281.

180 Simma, Article 60, 75-77. See also the proposed article 63 with regard to treaties providing for objective régimes, which did not make its way into the draft. Waldock, H., Third Report on the Law of Treaties, YBILC 1964, Volume II, pp. 5-65, 26-34. Discussed and eventually deleted by Commission in YBILC 1964, Volume I, 96-109. See also Dehaussy, Classification, 324-325.

181 Commentary Article 57, Law of Treaties, 255. See also Dehaussy, Classification, 323-324.

182 Brunnée, Common Interest, 797. He makes this statement in relation to an argument on reciprocity.

183 Lefeber, The Exercise of Jurisdiction, 91. Footnote omitted.

184 Lefeber, The Exercise of Jurisdiction, 91.

185 Trail Smelter Award, 317. Smith envisages a distinction with regard to areas outside national jurisdiction between harm done to the high seas environment (or to put it differently: harm to common interests), and harm to the interests of (a) particular State(s). Smith, State Responsibility, 86-87.

186 Reservations to the Convention on Genocide, Advisory Opinion, ICJ Reports 1951, p. 15, 23. Admittedly the Court in a later judgment denied the existence of a legal interest on the part of Ethiopia and Liberia in respect of certain human rights obligations allegedly breached by South Africa under the Mandate Agreement for South West Africa. South West Africa Cases, Second Phase, 51. It is submitted that the said judgment provides little support against the argument here made, because in that case the legal situation was very much complicated by the disappearance of the League of Nations.

187 Article 9 of the 1948 Convention on the Prevention and Punishment of the Crime of Genocide, adopted by way of General Assembly resolution 260 (III), reprinted in 45 AJIL 1951, Supplement, pp. 7-10.

188 Barcelona Traction Case, Judgment, 47. For the many contradictory interpretations see Bollecker Stern, Le préjudice, 84-86; Simma, B., Zur bilateralen Durchsetzung vertraglich verankerter Menschenrechte: Aktivlegitimation und zulässige Mittel nach allgemeinem Völkerrecht, in Schreuer, C. (Ed.), Autorität und internationale Ordnung, Duncker & Humblot, Berlin, 1979, pp. 129-154, 144; Simma, B., Fragen der zwischenstaatlichen Durchsetzung vertraglich vereinbarter Menschenrechte, in Staatsrecht – Völkerrecht – Europarecht, Festschrift für Hans-Jürgen Schlochauer, Walter de Gruyter, Berlin, 1981, pp. 635-648, 642-643; Frowein, J., Die Verpflichtungen *erga omnes* im Völkerrecht und ihre Durchsetzung, in Bernhardt, R. (Ed.), Völkerrecht als Rechtsordnung, Internationale Gerichtsbarkeit, Menschenrechte, Festschrift für Hermann Mosler, Springer-Verlag, Berlin, 1983, pp. 241-262, 245-246; Quigley, J., The International Law Commission's Crime-Delict Distinction: A Toothless Tiger?, 66 RDISDP 1988, pp. 117-161, 130-132; MBaye, K., L'interêt pour agir devant la Cour internationale de Justice, 209 RDC ADI 1988-II, pp. 223-345,

307-308; Kamminga, M., Inter-State Accountability for Violations of Human Rights, 1990, 154-156. Note also Genugten, W. van, Mensenrechten tussen staatssoevereiniteit en internationale jurisdictie, 21 NTRR 1992, pp. 204-223, 215-216.

189 Smith, State Responsibility, 95. He appears to correct his position somewhat when he refers to the idea that (97): "This is quite distinct from an obligation directed only to the community such as human rights obligations *vis-à-vis* the state's own nationals. No individual state has a right or interest in such cases other than as a member of the community." He recognized, earlier on the same page, that: "When an obligation logically may be defined as directed only to the 'community', it is patent that only an *actio popularis* will support an action by any member state based on the breach of such obligation." On the next page (98) he then comes to the conclusion that: "(...) the *actio popularis* now enjoys no more than inchoate status as a functional principle of customary law." Gaja, G., *Jus Cogens* Beyond the Vienna Convention, 172 RDC ADI 1981-III, pp. 271-316, 280, to the contrary states: "There are also some norms which create obligations towards States irrespective of the existence of a direct interest on their part. For instance, multilateral treaties concerning human rights impose on each contracting State obligations which exist in any specific situation towards all the other contracting States."

190 See however articles 41 and 42 of the 1966 International Covenant on Civil and Political Rights, 61 AJIL 1967, pp. 870-887.

191 The amendment which led to article 60, paragraph 5, was introduced by Switzerland, and finally adopted by the Conference. See respectively Conférence des Nations Unies sur le droit des traités, Première session, A/CONF.39/11, Vienne, 1968, Publications des Nations Unies, New York, 1969, 385; and *ibid.*, Deuxième session, A/CONF.39/11/Add.1, Vienne, 1969, Publications des Nations Unies, New York, 1970, 178. For further comments see *ibid.*, Première session, 386, 388-391, and *ibid.*, Deuxième session, 119-123; and Simma, Article 60, 72-75.

192 Note however this statement by the Commission in relation to human rights instruments: "(...) it is clear that not every one of the rights enumerated in these instruments, nor every single act or omission attributable to a State which could be considered incompatible with the respect of such rights even if an isolated act or mission (which might not even be intentional), must necessarily be qualified as giving rise to the application of the present provision." Commentary Article 5, Part Two, 27.

193 One may note that, contrary to the text of the other provisions of that article, it omits the words "to invoke it as a ground for" from its text. An amendment by the United Kingdom to insert that phrase into it was defeated.

194 Commentary Article 5, Part Two, 27. Riphagen appeared to have this in mind when he discussed the issue of "constructive injury". Riphagen, Third Report, 36-38, and 43. See especially Zoller, E., Enforcing International Law through U.S. Legislation, Transnational Publishers, Inc., Dobbs Ferry, New York, 1985, 64-72.

195 The 1957 Treaty establishing the European Economic Community, 51 AJIL 1957, pp. 865-937.

196 For earlier drafts Lauterpacht, H., First Report on the Law of Treaties, YBILC 1953, Volume II, pp. 90-162, 154 (article 15). For comment Yepes, Mémoire, YBILC 1953, Volume II, 163-166, 165-166; Fitzmaurice, G., Third Report on the Law of Treaties, YBILC 1958, Volume II, pp. 20-46, 26-27 (articles 16, paragraph 2, and 17); Waldock, Second Report, 39 (articles 1 (c) and 13, paragraph 1). Drafting Committee, YBILC 1963, Volume I, 213; Commission, YBILC 1963, Volume II, 198 (article 37); Commission, YBILC 1966, Volume II, 247 (article 50).

197 On *jus cogens* see among others Mann, F., The Doctrine of *Jus Cogens* in International Law, in Ehmke, H. (Ed.), Festschrift für Ulrich Scheuner, Duncker & Humblot, Berlin, 1973, pp. 399-418; Sztucki, J., *Jus Cogens* and the Vienna Convention on the Law of Treaties, A Critical Appraisal, Springer-Verlag, Wien, 1974, especially 164-194; Whiteman, M., *Jus Cogens* in International Law, With a Projected List, 7 GJICL 1977, pp. 609-626; Gros Espiel, H., Self-Determination and *Jus Cogens*, in Cassesse, A. (Ed.), UN Law/Fundamental Rights, Two Topics in International Law, Sijthoff and Noordhoff, Alphen aan den Rijn, 1979, pp. 167-173; Gangle, W., The *Jus Cogens* Dimensions of Nuclear Technology, 13 CJIL 1980, pp. 63-87; Minagawa, T., Essentiality and Reality of International *Jus Cogens*, 12 HJLP 1984, pp. 1-15; Sinclair, I., The Vienna Convention on the Law of Treaties, Second Edition, Manchester University Press, Manchester, 1984, 203-241; Frowein, J., *Jus Cogens*, in Bernhardt, R. (Ed.), EPIL, Instalment 7, Elsevier Science Publishers B.V., Amsterdam, 1984, pp. 327-330; Bedjaoui, M., Droit au developpement et *jus cogens*, 54/55/56 YAAA 1984/85/86, pp. 275-299; Christenson, G., The World Court and *Jus Cogens*, 81 AJIL 1987, pp. 93-101; Saulle, M., *Jus Cogens* and Human Rights, in Etudes en l'honneur de Roberto Ago, volume II, pp. 385-396; Janis, M., The Nature of *Jus Cogens*, 3 ConnJIL 1988, pp. 359-363 and 370; Turpel, M., and Sands, P., Peremptory International Law and Sovereignty: Some Questions, 3 ConnJIL 1988, pp. 364-369 and 371; Rosenne, S., Developments in the Law Treaties 1945-1986, Cambridge University Press, Cambridge, 1989, 281-288; Strydom, H., *Ius Cogens*: Peremptory Norm or Totalitarian Instrument?, 14 SAYIL 1988-1989, pp. 42-58; D'Amato, A., It's a Bird, It's a Plane, It's *Jus Cogens*!, 6 CJIL 1990, pp. 1-6;

Kadelbach, S., Zwingendes Völkerrecht, Duncker & Humblot, Berlin, 1992; Charlesworth, H., and Chinkin, C., The Gender of *Jus Cogens*, 15 HRQ 1993, pp. 63-76.

198 Minagawa, T., *Jus Cogens* in Public International Law, 6 HJLP 1968, pp. 16-28, 24.

199 Hannikainen, L., Peremptory Norms (*Jus Cogens*) in International Law, Historical Development, Criteria, Present Status, Finnish Lawyers' Publishing Company, Helsinki, 1988, 4-5. He also uses terms such as vital common interests and common interests of States (55-56).

200 The Commission observed, Commentary Article 50, Law of Treaties, 247, that: "The view that in the last analysis there is no rule from which States cannot contract out has become increasingly difficult to sustain, (...)." See also Fitzmaurice, Third Report, 27 and 39-41. As Minagawa, *Jus Cogens*, 17, points out, this freedom is based on the assumption that the consent of other States may be obtained. In so far as the action of States in creating a new rule of treaty law would purport to legalize conduct, prohibited by another rule of international law, with regard to States the consent of which has not been obtained, or with regard to States that had not taken part in the earlier treaty from the start, the treaty would lack legal effect due to the application of the rule of *pacta tertius nec prosunt nec nocent* and the principle that treaties are *res inter alios acta* for third States. See articles 30 and 34 to 38 Vienna Convention. If the States concerned would in effect give application to the treaty in their relations with other States this might lead to the engagement of international responsibility on their part. Minagawa, *Jus Cogens*, 17; Lauterpacht, First Report, 154.

201 Yasseen (Irak), Conférence des Nations Unies, Deuxième session, 110, observed: "Personne ne conteste de nos jours qu'un traité qui vise à rendre légitime l'esclavage (...) est nul *ab initio*." It is also for this reason that the concept of *jus cogens* is looked upon as a limit to the freedom of States to conclude treaties. See Bresson (France), Conférence des Nations Unies, Première session, 335. But it has to be noted that such limit does not actually inhibit States from concluding treaties that conflict with peremptory norms. It is therefore also possible to view the provision of article 53 as laying down a prohibition to conclude a specified category of treaties, whose breach by two or more States carries with it its own exclusive sanction: the voidness of the legal act thus performed.

202 This concerns the idea of what Gómez Robledo, A., Le *jus cogens* international: sa genèse, sa nature, ses fonctions, 172 RDC ADI 1981-III, pp. 9-217, 104-108, calls "le double consentement".

203 In the same sense Ruegger (Suisse), Conférence des Nations Unies, Première session, 110, who observes: "Avec tout le respect du à l'Assemblée générale des Nations Unies, [M. Ruegger] ne saurait admettre qu'une résolution de cet organe, parfois adoptée à une très faible majorité, puisse établir du *jus cogens*." Apparently of contrary conviction Rosenne (Israel), *ibid.*, 337, who indicates that a void treaty could be declared so by any State and any international organization. And it is for this reason that, *a fortiori*, there is no real need to refer to the convictions in this respect of "the teachings of the most qualified publicists of the various nations" (article 38 Statute). One may note that the 1986 Vienna Convention on the Law of Treaties between States and International Organizations or between International Organizations in its article 53 does not envisage a role for international organizations in the acceptance and recognition phase. Text in 25 ILM 1986, pp. 543-589. See also Text and Commentary Article 53, Law of Treaties, International Organizations, YBILC 1982, Volume II, Part Two, p. 56, 56.

204 Conférence des Nations Unies, Première session, 514.

205 Yasseen (Irak), Conférence des Nations Unies, Première session, 321; implicitly Jagota (Inde), *ibid.*, 334. The former observed: "Toutefois, les règles auxquelles aucune dérogation n'est possible ne relèvent pas toutes de *jus cogens*. Lorsqu'un certain nombre d'Etats conviennent dans un traité, que les parties ne pourront pas conclure de conventions contraires à certaines clauses du traité, la violation de cette interdiction dans un traité ulterieur ne rend pas celui-ci nul; elle met simplement en jeu la responsabilité de l'Etat qui a commis une telle violation." For an example of a clause prohibiting the conclusion of a later treaty by only some of the parties to the former treaty see article 36 of the General Act of Berlin, text in Separate Opinion van Eysinga, The Oscar Chinn Case, Publications PCIJ, 1934, Series A/B, No. 63, p. 65, 133 (see 133-136); and Separate Opinion Schücking, *ibid.*, 148-150, who links the article to the notions of nullity, *jus cogens* and public morality.

206 Note that Ariff (Malaisie), Conférence des Nations Unies, Première session, 354 proposed the following phrase: "reconnue en tant que telle par la communauté internationale". Yasseen, as president of the Drafting Committee, referred to article 38 in explaining the term "acceptée et reconnue".

207 Note that van Hoof observes: "The point of departure, as was said, is that the *opinio juris cogentis* has to be expressed through the same manifestations of consent or acceptance in the sense of *opinio juris*." Hoof, G. van, Rethinking the Sources of International Law, Kluwer, Deventer, 1983, 162 (more broadly 156-166). As an example of acceptance or recognition one may mention the statements of Nicaragua and the United States, noted by the Court, to the effect that the rule prohibiting the use of armed force constitutes a peremptory norm.

Military and Paramilitary Activities in and against Nicaragua (Nicaragua *v.* United States of America), Merits, Judgment, ICJ Reports 1986, p. 14, 100-101.

[208] Commentary Article 50, Law of Treaties, 247.

[209] Commentary Article 50, Law of Treaties, 248.

[210] Commentary Article 50, Law of Treaties, 248.

[211] Commentary Article 50, Law of Treaties, 248.

[212] Texaco Overseas Petroleum Company and California Asiatic Oil Company *v.* The Government of the Libyan Arab Republic, Dupuy, Sole Arbitrator, Preliminary Award, 27 November 1975, and Award on the Merits, 19 January 1977, 53 ILR 1979, pp. 389-511, 479-483; Government of Kuwait *v.* American Independent Oil Company Aminoil), Arbitration Tribunal (Reuter, Sultan, Fitzmaurice), 24 March 1982, 66 ILR 1984, pp. 518-627, 587-588.

[213] North Sea Continental Shelf, Judgment, ICJ Reports 1969, p. 3, 42; Nicaragua Case, Merits, 100-101. For further references see Separate Opinion Padilla Nervo, North Sea Continental Shelf Case, 97; Dissenting Opinion Tanaka, *ibid.*, 182; Dissenting Opinion Lachs, *ibid.*, 229; Dissenting Opinion Sørensen, *ibid.*, 248; Separate Opinion Ammoun, Barcelona Traction Case, Judgment, 304, 311 (footnote 56), 312, and 325; Separate Opinion Ranjeva, East Timor Case, Judgment, under I; Dissenting Opinion Weeramantry, *ibid.*, in Part C, under (vii); and Dissenting Opinion Skubiszewski, *ibid.*, paragraph 135.

[214] Especially Fitzmaurice discussed issues of State responsibility. Fitzmaurice, Fourth Report, 37-81. Under the heading of "Limits of the Treaty Obligation (Circumstances Justifying Non-Performance)" (*ibid.*, 43-46) he included articles on self-defence and reprisals. And under the heading of "Consequences of Breach of Treaty", *ibid.*, 49-50, he included an article on cessation and reparation, which followed a paragraph that stated: "Where there is a breach of treaty, it gives rise to international responsibility, (...)." For his commentary see *ibid.*, 62-70 and 80-81.

[215] Sinclair (Royaume-Uni), Conférence des Nations Unies, Première session, 488; Maresca (Italie), *ibid.*, 489; see also Castro (Espagne), *ibid.*, 490.

[216] And one may note that this provision drastically mitigates the fact that treaties which are void under article 53 are void in total (article 44, paragraph 5, of the Vienna Convention), and not merely the provisions in conflict with the peremptory norm. See Schwelb, E., Some Aspects of International *Jus Cogens* as Formulated by the International Law Commission, 61 AJIL 1967, pp. 946-975, 971-972.

[217] Barros (Chili), Conférence des Nations Unies, Première session, 325; Eek (Suède), *ibid.*, 333; Rosenne (Israël), *ibid.*, 337; Kebreth (Ethiopie), *ibid.*, 341; Ruegger (Suisse), *ibid.*, 352, although he only speaks of making protests; Fujisaki (Japon), *ibid.*, 437-438; Bresson (France), *ibid.*, 438; Truckenbrodt (République fédérale d'Allemagne), *ibid.*, 445; implicitly Vallat (Royaume-Uni), *ibid.*, 457; Wershof (Canada), *ibid.*, 459; Pinto (Ceylan), *ibid.*, Deuxième session, 131. Although he observed: "Ceylan considère donc que tout Etat, ou du moins tout Etat partie à la convention, doit avoir le droit de contester la validité d'un traité en faisant valoir qu'il tombe sous le coup des articles 50 et 61, (...)." In its context, since he supports a right for any State to invoke article 50, "convention" appears to indicate the future Vienna Convention on the Law of Treaties, and not the convention thought to be void due to conflict with a peremptory norm; Guardia (Argentine), *ibid.*, 132; implicitly Haraszti (Hongrie), *ibid.*, 133; Bikoutha (Congo-Brazzaville), *ibid.* Some delegates observed that article 50 was silent with regard to the question by which States it could be invoked. Dons (Norvège), *ibid.*, 353; Truckenbrodt (République fédérale d'Allemagne), *ibid.*, 445. Of apparently different opinion Warioba (République-Unie de Tanzanie), *ibid.*, Première session, 468; and Ramani (Malaisie), *ibid.*, Deuxième session, 112; seemingly Castro (Espagne), *ibid.*, 132.

[218] The Vienna Convention on the Law of Treaties between States and International Organizations or between International Organizations has adopted similar provisions in articles 65 and 66.

[219] The Commentary Article 50, Law of Treaties, 248, states that: "(...) nullity attaches to a treaty under the article only if the rule with which it conflicts is a peremptory norm of general international law from which no derogation is permitted, even by agreement of particular States."

[220] Barcelona Traction Case, Judgment, 32. References to obligations *erga omnes* in international jurisprudence include Separate Opinion Ammoun, *ibid.*, 324-327. Judge Ammoun does not mention obligations *erga omnes*, but his remarks seem to flow from paragraphs 33 and 34; Dissenting Opinion Riphagen, *ibid.*, 338-340 and 354; especially Dissenting Opinion Schwebel, Military and Paramilitary Activities in and against Nicaragua (Nicaragua *v.* United States of America), Provisional Measures, Order, ICJ Reports 1984, p. 169, 195-198. On rights or obligations *erga omnes* (on self-determination) see Separate Opinion Ranjeva, East Timor Case, Judgment, under I; Dissenting Opinion Weeramantry, *ibid.*, especially Part A, 3 (iii), Part B (x), Part C (vi), Part D, A (i), C (i) and (iii), and Conclusions. Regarding the Barcelona Traction Case see Charpentier, J., Affaire de la Barcelona Traction, Arrêt du 5 février 1970, 16 AFDI 1970, pp. 307-328; Higgins, R., Aspects of the Case Concerning the Barcelona Traction, Light and Power Company, Ltd., 11 VJIL 1970, pp. 327-343;

Francescakis, Ph., Lueurs sur le droit international des sociétés: L'arrêt «Barcelona» de la Cour internationale de justice, 59 RCDIP 1970, pp. 609-664; Grisel, E., L'arrêt de la Cour internationale de justice dans l'affaire de la Barcelona Traction (Seconde Phase): Problèmes de procédure et de fond, 27 SJIR 1971, pp. 31-48; Seidl-Hohenveldern, I., Der Barcelona Traction-Fall, 22 OZOR 1971, pp. 255-309; Briggs, H., Barcelona Traction: The *Jus Standi* of Belgium, 65 AJIL 1971, pp. 327-345.

221 On obligations *erga omnes* see Frowein, Die Verpflichtungen *erga omnes*, 241-262; Meron, T., Human Rights and Humanitarian Norms as Customary Law, Clarendon Press, Oxford, 1989, 188-201; Meron, T., Common Rights of Mankind in Gentili, Grotius and Suárez, 85 AJIL 1991, pp. 110-116; Simma, B., Does the UN Charter Provide an Adequate Legal Basis for Individual or Collective Responses to Violations of Obligations *Erga Omnes*?, in Delbrück, J. (Ed.), The Future of International Law Enforcement, New Scenarios – New Law?, Duncker & Humblot, Berlin, 1993, pp. 125-146; Annacker, C., The Legal Régime of *Erga Omnes* Obligations in International Law, 46 AJPIL 1994, pp. 131-166; and Annacker, C., Die Durchsetzung von *erga omnes* Verpflichtungen vor dem Internationalen Gerichtshof, Verlag Dr. Kovac, Hamburg, 1994. See also Sperduti, G., Les obligations solidaires en droit international, in Makarczyk, J. (Ed.), Essays in International Law in Honour of Judge Manfred Lachs, Martinus Nijhoff Publishers, The Hague, 1984, pp. 271-275; Charney, J., Third State Remedies in International Law, 10 MJIL 1989, pp. 57-110; Thirlway, H., The Law and Procedure of the International Court of Justice 1960-1989 (Part One), 60 BYBIL 1989, pp. 1-157, 92-102; and Lachs, M., Slavery: The Past and the Present, in Delissen, A., and Tanja, G. (Eds.), Humanitarian Law of Armed Conflict, Essays in Honour of Fritz Kalshoven, Martinus Nijhoff Publishers, Dordrecht, 1991, pp. 613-625.

222 Barcelona Traction Case, Judgment, 32-33.

223 The French text, which is authoritative, runs slightly different: "La responsabilité est le corollaire nécessaire du droit." Barcelona Traction Case, Judgment, 33. In view of this formulation one would have expected the English text to read, as a literal translation, that responsibility is the necessary corollary of *law*.

224 The Court observed later on: "Hence the Belgian Government would be entitled to bring a claim if it could show that one of its rights had been infringed and the acts complained of involved the breach of an international obligation arising out of a treaty or a general rule of law." Barcelona Traction Case, Judgment, 46.

225 Barcelona Traction Case, Judgment, 46.

226 Barcelona Traction Case, Judgment, 32.

227 The Court has held, relatively recently, that: "In the Court's view, Portugal's assertion that the right of peoples to self-determination, as it evolved from the Charter and from United Nations practice, has an *erga omnes* character, is irreproachable." East Timor Case, paragraph 29. It observed furthermore that, for the parties, the territory of East Timor remains a non-self-governing territory and that its people has the right to self-determination. *Ibid.*, paragraphs 31 and 37.

228 Gaja, Obligations *Erga Omnes*, 151, observes in regard to an analysis of the concepts of obligations *erga omnes*, international crimes and *jus cogens*: "The necessary starting-point for an analysis appears to be the distinction between legal rules that impose on States obligations whose breach in a concrete case only concerns one or more specifically affected States, on the one hand, and, on the other, those rules whose violation in a concrete case affects a number of States, irrespective of the existence of a specific interest on their part."

229 *E.g.* Seidl-Hohenveldern, I., *Actio Popularis* im Völkerrecht?, in Il processo internationale, Studi in onore di Gaetano Morelli, Comunicazioni e Studi, volume 14, Giuffrè, Milano, 1975, pp. 803-813, 804-806 and 813. For the contrary view see Schwelb, E., The *Actio Popularis* and International Law, 2 IYHR 1972, pp. 46-56.

230 Barcelona Traction Case, Judgment, 47.

231 For a view that such a distinction could possibly be made see Meron, T., On a Hierarchy of International Human Rights, 80 AJIL 1986, pp. 1-23, 10-11; and Meron, Human Rights, 192-194.

232 The 1966 International Covenant on Civil and Political Rights; and the 1966 International Covenant on Economic, Social and Cultural Rights, 61 AJIL 1967, pp. 861-870.

233 For a view tending to the same conclusion see Meron, Human Rights, 196-200.

234 Meron, On a Hierarchy, 9. See also Meron, Human Rights, 192.

235 Ago, R., Obligations *Erga Omnes* and the International Community, in Weiler *et al*, International Crimes, pp. 237-239, 237. Also in this sense Annacker, The Legal Régime, 135-136.

236 Ago, Obligations *Erga Omnes*, 237-238.

237 Gaja, Obligations *Erga Omnes*, 154.

238 Annacker, The Legal Régime, 135-137 and 149-150.

239 Annacker, The Legal Régime, 149-150. For similar observations see Dupuy, P.-M., The International Law of State Responsibility: Revolution or Evolution?, 11 MJIL 1990, pp. 105-128, 120-123; Dupuy, P.-M., Responsabilite et legalite, in SFDI, Colloque Du Mans, La responsabilité dans le système international, Editions A. Pedone, Paris, 1991, pp. 263-297, 289-290.

[240] Annacker, The Legal Régime, 136 and 149.

[241] Annacker, The Legal Régime, 149.

[242] C.f. Simma, Does the UN Charter, 132-133, who observes: "First, I suggest that we maintain the distinction between obligations *erga omnes* in the Barcelona Traction sense and rules of general international or multilateral treaty law whose structure of application (...) is such that they cannot be split up into a number of parallel bilateral relationships. Certain uses of the high seas, for instance, cannot be agreed upon by pairs of states without encroaching upon the rights and interests of others. But this does not necessarily mean that obligations of such integral structure will also constitute genuine obligations *erga omnes.* I submit that the factor distinguishing the latter can only be seen in a particular value judgment according to which the international community as a whole considers observance of certain obligations as imperative. From this perspective, the core provisions of the great human rights or humanitarian conventions also referred to by the Barcelona Traction dictum might be taken as examples where integral treaty and truly *erga omnes* obligations coincide."

[243] Then special rapporteur Ago, commenting upon the Barcelona Traction Case, noted: "It follows, the Court held, that the responsibility flowing from a breach of those obligations is entailed not only with regard to the State that has been the direct victim of the breach (*e.g.* a State which has suffered an act of aggression in its territory); it is also entailed with regard to all the other members of the international community. Every State, even if it is not immediately and directly affected by the breach, should therefore be considered justified in invoking the responsibility of the State committing the internationally wrongful act." Ago, R., Fifth report on State responsibility, YBILC 1976, Volume II, Part One, pp. 3-54, 29. Footnote omitted. Note the somewhat different text in Commentary Article 19, Part One, 99.

[244] Note that Jenks argues in favour of an *actio popularis* when two conditions are met: that the beneficiary of substantive rights is not in a position to act on his own behalf; and that this situation was foreseen and explicit provision was made for it. Jenks, C., The General Welfare as a Legal Interest, in Wilner, G. (Ed.), *Jus et Societas,* Essays in Tribute to Wolfgang Friedmann, Martinus Nijhoff Publishers, The Hague, 1979, pp. 151-158, 154-158.

[245] See further Simma, Durchsetzung, 142; Silagi, M., Die Popularklage als Fremdkörper im Völkerrecht, 4 SAYIL 1978, pp. 10-28, 13-14; Mann, The Doctrine, 406; Macdonald, R., Fundamental Norms in Contemporary International Law, 25 CYIL 1987, pp. 115-149, 136-139; Brunnée, Common Interest, 801; Meron, Human Rights, 194; Sinclair, The Vienna Convention, 213; Gómez Robledo, Le *jus cogens* international, 171; implicitly Bollecker Stern, Le préjudice, 87-88; Nagy, K., Forms of Legal Relationship in International Responsibility, in Haraszti, G. (Ed.), Questions of International Law, volume 2, Sijthoff and Noordhoff International Publishers, Alphen a/d Rijn, 1981, pp. 129-145, 135-140.

[246] Separate Opinion Ammoun, Barcelona Traction Case, Judgment, 325. See also 304, 311 (footnote 56) and 312 for references to *jus cogens* not linked to the idea of legal interests.

[247] Note the examples in Commentary Article 50, Law of Treaties, 248. And also Dupuy, P.-M., Observations sur la pratique des "sanctions" de l'illicite, 87 RGDIP 1983, pp. 505-548, 536-537; Macdonald, Fundamental Norms, 36.

[248] Commentary Article 19, Part One, 102. See also *ibid.*, 116.

[249] Commentary Article 19, Part One, 95-96. Special rapporteur Ago's draft (Fifth Report, 54) on article 18, paragraphs 2 and 3 (renumbered 19) read:
"2. The breach by a State of an international obligation established for the purpose of maintaining international peace and security, and in particular the breach by a State of the prohibition of any resort to the threat or use of force against the territorial integrity or political independence of another State, is an 'international crime'.
3. The serious breach by a State of an international obligation established by a norm of general international law accepted and recognized as essential by the international community as a whole and having as its purpose:
(a) respect for the principle of the equal rights of all peoples and of their right of self-determination; or
(b) respect for human rights and fundamental freedoms for all, without distinction based on race, sex, language or religion; or
(c) the conservation and the free enjoyment for everyone of a resource common to all mankind is also an 'international crime'."

[250] On the distinction see Graefrath, B., Oeser, E., and Steiniger, P., Internationale Verbrechen – Internationale Delikte, 22 DA 1977, pp. 90-101; Hofmann, R., Zur Unterscheidung Verbrechen und Delikt im Bereich der Staatenverantwortlichkeit, 45 ZAORV 1985, pp. 195-231; Mohr, M., The ILC's Distinction between "International Crimes" and "International Delicts" and its Implications, in Spinedi and Simma, United Nations Codification, pp. 115-141; Quigley, The International Law Commission's Crime-Delict Distinction, 117-161; Palmisano, G., Les causes d'aggravation de la responsabilite des etats et la distinction entre «crimes» et «delits» internationaux, 98 RGDIP 1994, pp. 629-673.

[251] On the relationship between the two concepts Gaja, Obligations *Erga Omnes*, 151-160; Hoogh, A. de, The Relationship between *Jus Cogens*, Obligations *Erga Omnes* and International Crimes: Peremptory Norms in Perspective, 42 AJPIL 1991, pp. 183-214. It may be noted here that the first comments by Commission members focused on the idea of international crimes constituting breaches of obligations established under peremptory norms. See Tammes, YBILC 1976, Volume I, 64; Hambro, *ibid.*, 65; Sette Camara, *ibid.*, 68; Vallat, *ibid.*, 68-69; Sahovic, *ibid.*, 70; Martinez Moreno, *ibid.*; Rossides, *ibid.*, 83.

[252] On crimes see among others Marek, K., Criminalizing State Responsibility, 14 RBDI 1978-1979, pp. 460-485; Dominicé, C., Die internationalen Verbrechen und deren rechtliches Regime, in Fischer, P., Koeck, H., and Verdross, A. (Eds.), Völkerrecht und Rechtsphilosophie, Internationale Festschrift für Stephan Verosta zum 70. Geburstag, Duncker & Humblot, Berlin, 1980, pp. 227-248; Green, L., New Trends in International Criminal Law, 11 IYHR 1981, pp. 9-40; Gounelle, M., Quelques remarques sur la notion de «crime international» et sur l'évolution de la responsabilité internationale de l'état, in Le droit international: unité et diversité, Mélanges offerts à Paul Reuter, Pedone, Paris, 1981, pp. 315-326; Bindschedler, R., Völkerrechtliche Verantwortlichkeit als Verbrechen, in Dutoit and Grisel, Mélanges Georges Perrin, pp. 51-61; Graefrath, B., Völkerrechtliche Verantwortlichkeit für internationale Verbrechen, in Graefrath, B. (Ed.), Probleme des Völkerrechts, Akademie-Verlag, Berlin, 1985, pp. 89-110; Malekian, F., International Criminal Responsibility of States, Borgstroms Trycker AB, Stockholm, 1985, especially 168-197; Graefrath, B., and Mohr, M., Völkerrechtliche und strafrechtliche Verantwortlichkeit für internationale Verbrechen, 35 SR 1986, pp. 29-40; Cassese, A., Remarks on the Present Legal Regulation of Crimes of State, in Etudes en l'honneur de Roberto Ago, volume III, pp. 49-64; Rigaux, F., Le crime d'etat, Reflexions sur l'article 19 du projet d'articles sur la responsabilite des etats, in Etudes, *ibid.*, pp. 301-325; Sahovic, M., Le concept du crime international de l'etat et le developpement du droit international, in Etudes, *ibid.*, pp. 363-369; Napel, H.-M. ten, The Concept of International Crimes of States: Walking the Thin Line between Progressive Development and Disintegration of the International Legal Order, 1 LJIL 1988, pp. 149-169; Gilbert, G., The Criminal Responsibility of States, 39 ICLQ 1990, pp. 345-369; and Dekker, I., Criminal Responsibility and the Gulf War of 1980-1988: The Crime of Aggression, in Dekker, I., and Post, H. (Eds.), The Gulf War of 1980-1988, The Iran-Iraq War in International Legal Perspective, Martinus Nijhoff Publishers, Dordrecht, 1992, pp. 249-268.

[253] Commentary Article 19, Part One, 117.

[254] C.f. article 14, paragraph 1, Part Two, proposed by Riphagen, W., Fifth report on the content, forms and degrees of international responsibility (part 2 of the draft articles), YBILC 1984, Volume II, Part One, pp. 1-4, 4, which ran: "An international crime entails all the legal consequences of an internationally wrongful act and, in addition, such rights and obligations as are determined by the applicable rules accepted by the international community as a whole." Contrary Commentary Article 19, Part One, 117-118.

[255] Commentary Article 19, Part One, 119.

[256] Commentary Article 19, Part One, 119.

[257] Commentary Article 19, Part One, 120.

[258] Commentary Article 19, Part One, 120.

[259] Commentary Article 19, Part One, 120. Mohr expressed doubts as to the criterion of seriousness, since it would leave too much room for subjectivism. See Mohr, The ILC's Distinction, 123.

[260] Commentary Article 19, Part One, 121.

[261] Commentary Article 19, Part One, 110. A member of the Commission asked the question: "(...) why a 'small aggression' which caused relatively minor destruction of property and the death of a few innocent people should entail additional consequences in terms of authorized armed countermeasures when such countermeasures would presumably not be allowed in the case of a wide-scale genocide." See Commission Report 1994, 338. Note also Napel, The Concept of International Crimes, 157.

[262] Note Dupuy, P.-M., Observations sur le "crime international de l'etat", 84 RGDIP 1980, pp. 449-486, 463-464. Apparently contrary Graefrath, B., Oeser, E., and Steiniger, P., Internationale Verbrechen, 96. See also Yokota, K., War as an International Crime, in Constantopoulos, D., Eustathiades, C., and Fragistas, C. (Eds.), Grundprobleme des internationalen Recht, Festschrift für Jean Spiropoulos, Schimmelbusch & Co., Bonn, 1957, pp. 453-460; Mazov, V., Responsibility for Aggression in International Law, 6 IA (Moscow) 1972, pp. 43-48; Sucharitkul, S., Terrorism as an International Crime: Questions of Responsibility and Complicity, 19 IYHR 1989, pp. 247-258; Graefrath, B., and Mohr, M., Legal Consequences of an Act of Aggression: The Case of the Iraqi Invasion and Occupation of Kuwait, 43 AJPIL 1992, pp. 109-138.

[263] Commentary Article 19, Part One, 121.

[264] Contrary Palmisano, Les causes d'aggravation, 641-642: "En effet, l'agression est menionnée dans le paragraphe non pas comme contenu d'une interdiction posée par «une obligation internationale d'importance essentielle», obligation dont la grave violation représenterait un crime. Autrement dit, on définit comme un

crime, non pas l'agression tout court, mais la violation grave de l'interdiction d'agression (ainsi que la violation grave de l'interdiction de domination coloniale, de génocide, etc.)." Two footnotes omitted. At the next page he indicates his adherence to the opposite stance, which, though less faithful to the text, corresponds to the intentions of the Commission.

265 See Palmisano, Les causes d'aggravation, 642, footnote 29.

266 C.f. Palmisano, Les causes d'aggravation, 643.

267 Arangio-Ruiz, G., State Fault and the Forms and Degrees of International Responsibility: Questions of Attribution and Relevance, in Le droit au service de la paix, de la justice et du développement, Mélanges Michel Virally, Éditions A. Pedone, Paris, 1991, pp. 25-41.

268 Some members of the Commission have pointed to the fact, in the 1994 discussion, that the concept of fault was inseparable from the concept of crime. See Report 1994, 337. Arangio-Ruiz stated: "There is hardly any question that wilful intent (dolus as the gravest degree of fault) is an essential, sine qua non feature of a crime." Arangio-Ruiz, G., Seventh Report on State Responsibility, 9 May 1995, A/CN.4/469, 49 pp., 19. In a similar sense Tunkin, G., International Law, A Textbook, Progress Publishers, Moscow, 1986, 229.

269 Palmisano, Les causes d'aggravation, 645. Emphasis in the original. Note also Ago, R., Remarks on Some Classes of Crimes by States, in Weiler *et al*, International Crimes, p. 215, 215; and generally Salmon, J., L'intention en matiere de responsabilite internationale, in Le droit au service de la paix, pp. 413-422.

270 Palmisano, Les causes d'aggravation, 645-647.

271 Note Trail Smelter Award, 317; Corfu Channel case, Judgment, ICJ Reports 1949, p. 4, 18; and Nicaragua Case, Merits, 83-85.

272 Palmisano, Les causes d'aggravation, 648, noted in this regard: "Il est impensable que l'instauration d'un régime politique, économique, social ou culturel contraire à la volonté du peuple – d'un peuple d'une colonie, aussi bien que d'un peuple «métropolitain», ou encore d'un peuple d'une race ou d'une foi différente par rapport à celle du groupe sociale qui constitue la classe dominante – se réalise «par hasard», soit «par négligence». Il faut toujours un projet prémédité de la part de l'Etat qui l'effectue." More generally *ibid.*, 647-652.

273 Commentary Article 19, Part One, 121. The phrase mentioned in the text constitutes only part of a sentence, and the Commission continued that sentence by adding: "(...), even if that will has not been manifested, or has not yet been manifested, by armed opposition."

274 Commentary Article 19, Part One, 121. Note especially G.P.R., Torture and Other Violations of Human Rights as International Crimes, 17 RICJ 1976, pp. 41-50, 46-50; Medina Quiroga, C., The Battle of Human Rights, Gross, Systematic Violations and the Inter-American System, Martinus Nijhoff Publishers, Dordrecht, 1988, 7-19; and Palmisano, Les causes d'aggravation, 653-659.

275 The 1973 International Convention on the Suppression and Punishment of the Crime of *Apartheid*, adopted by way of General Assembly resolution 3068 (XXVIII), reprinted in 13 ILM 1974, pp. 50-57. See also the 1966 International Convention on the Elimination of All Forms of Racial Discrimination, 60 AJIL 1966, pp. 650-661. See Booysen, H., Convention on the Crime of *Apartheid*, 2 SAYIL 1976, pp. 56-96, 91-92, who claims that the Convention is void due to conflict with a peremptory norm, since the object of the Convention, the suppression of *apartheid*, could only be accomplished by way of aggression. See also Wellens, K., *Apartheid*, An International Crime, in Heyde, L., Leijten, J., Mertens, Th., and Vermeulen, B. (Eds.), Begrensde Vrijheid, Opstellen over mensenrechten aangeboden aan Prof. Dr. D.F. Scheltens bij zijn afscheid als hoogleraar aan de Katholieke Universiteit Nijmegen, Tjeenk Willink, Zwolle, 1989, pp. 288-311.

276 Commentary Article 19, Part One, 119. Note also Ago, R., The Concept of "International Community as a Whole": A Guarantee to the Notion of State Crimes, in Weiler *et al*, International Crimes, pp. 252-253; and Palmisano, Les causes d'aggravation, 638.

277 Text in Arangio-Ruiz, Seventh Report on State Responsibility, 24 May 1995, A/CN.4/469/Add.1, 4 pp., 4. Arguments in Seventh Report, 25-49. He has also proposed an article 7, Part Three, which would provide jurisdiction for the Court to decide disputes over the implementation of the consequences of crimes, that is reparation and countermeasures. See Arangio-Ruiz, G., Seventh Report on State Responsibility, 29 May 1995, A/CN.4/469/Add.2, 3 pp., 3.

278 On which generally Brunnée, Common Interest, 791-808; Lefeber, The Exercise of Jurisdiction, 81-137; Gormley, W., The Legal Obligation of the International Community to Guarantee a Pure and Decent Environment: The Expansion of Human Rights Norms, 3 GIELR 1990, pp. 85-116; Wolfrum, R., Purposes and Principles of International Environmental Law, 33 GYIL 1990, pp. 308-330; Boyle, A., State Responsibility for Breach of Obligations to Protect the Environment, in Butler, W. (Ed.), Control over Compliance with International Law, Martinus Nijhoff Publishers, Dordrecht, 1991, pp. 69-81; Kiss, Mazzeschi, Spinedi, Dupuy (P.-M.), Charney, Conforti, and the late judge Ago, in Francioni, F., and Scovazzi, T. (Eds.), International Responsibility for Environmental Harm, Graham & Trotman, London, 1991, at respectively pp. 3, 15, 75, 125, 149, 179, and 493; and Palmisano, Les causes d'aggravation, 659-664.

[279] Ago, Fifth Report, 32 (footnote 148), 48 (footnote 262), 49 (footnote 270), 52, and 53.
[280] Commentary Article 19, Part One, 101, 108-109, 115 (footnotes 542 and 546), and 120-121.
[281] Note among others the 1972 Convention on the Dumping of Wastes At Sea, 11 ILM 1972, pp. 1291-1309; the 1973 International Convention for the Prevention of Pollution from Ships, 12 ILM 1973, pp. 1319-1335; the 1974 Convention for the Prevention of Marine Pollution from Land-Based Sources, 13 ILM 1974, pp. 352-368; the 1979 Convention on the Long-Range Transboundary Air Pollution, 18 ILM 1979, pp. 1442-1450; the 1985 Vienna Convention for the Protection of the Ozone Layer, 26 ILM 1987, pp. 1529-1540; the 1987 Montreal Protocol on Substances that Deplete the Ozone Layer, 26 ILM 1987, pp. 1551-1561; the 1992 Convention on Biological Diversity, 31 ILM 1992, pp. 822-841; and the 1992 United Nations Framework Convention on Climate Change, 31 ILM 1992, pp. 851-873.
[282] Palmisano, Les causes d'aggravation, 662: "(...) s'il est vrai que les obligations «d'importance essentielle» pour la protection de l'environnement concernent uniquement les activités étatiques polluant considérablement la planète, l'on peut croire que la gravité «circonstancielle» depend justement de la plus grande intensité anti-juridique de l'«attitude psychologique» de l'Etat responsable. En d'autres termes, ce qui qualifierait un fait illicite de «crime écologique» serait non pas tellement la dimension du dommage causé, mais le dol spécifique de l'Etat qui pollue." See generally *ibid.*, 659-664. Also Quigley, The International Law Commission's Crime-Delict Distinction, 135.
[283] See Dupuy, P.-M., Apres la guerre du Golfe..., 95 RGDIP 1991, pp. 621-638, 632-634.
[284] C.f. Palmisano, Les causes d'aggravation, 659-660, and 660, footnote 69.
[285] Statement by the President of the Security Council made on behalf of the members of the Security Council, 3046th meeting, 31 January 1992.
[286] For texts of proposed articles see Arangio-Ruiz, Seventh Report, Addendum 1, 1-4; and Arangio-Ruiz, G., Seventh Report on State Responsibility, 29 May 1995, A/CN.4/469/Add.2, 3 pp., 3.
[287] Commentary Article 19, Part One, 99-100 and especially 102. References to authors are to be found at 111-116.
[288] Commentary Article 5, Part Two, 25 and 27. For the proposals see Riphagen, Fifth Report, 1-4; and Fourth Report, 10-15, and 21-23. At page 13 he claimed: "But it would seem that, beyond the case of international crimes, there are no internationally wrongful acts having an *erga omnes* character." Note also Brown Weiss, E., In Fairness to Future Generations, International Law, Common Patrimony and Intergenerational Equity, The United Nations University Press, Tokyo, 1989, 90.
[289] Commentary Article 5, Part Two, 27. Riphagen had observed regarding his proposed draft on the *erga omnes* character of international crimes (Sixth Report, 8): "It cannot be concluded, again, from the absence of determination of such particular secondary and/or tertiary rules that, in the case of an international crime having been committed, there is no injured State at all. The alternative is to consider every other State, in principle, an injured State."
[290] Commentary Article 5, Part Two, 27. Riphagen had expressed himself in a similar manner (Sixth Report, 8): "Obviously, this does not necessarily imply that, for every State individually, the commission of an international crime entails the same 'new rights'." Footnote omitted. The *erga omnes* character of international crimes was supported by members of the Commission, although doubts were voiced regarding the scope of any right of unilateral action in reaction against a crime committed. Sinclair, YBILC 1985, Volume I, 89; McCaffrey, *ibid.*, 96-98; Flitan, *ibid.*, 102-103; Huang, *ibid.*, 109; Francis, *ibid.*, 110; Balanda, *ibid.*, 115; Ogiso, *ibid.*, 122; Njenga, *ibid.*, 124; Tomutschat, *ibid.*, 125-126; Mahiou, *ibid.*, 128; Barboza, *ibid.*, 130-131; Razafindralambo, *ibid.*, 135; Akinjide, *ibid.*, 139; Lacleta Munoz, *ibid.*, 144; Yankov, *ibid.*, 145; Arangio-Ruiz, *ibid.*, 150, expressed doubts whether crimes other than aggression should be mentioned in article 5; implicitly Rasheed Mohamed Ahmed, *ibid.*, 151; Koroma, *ibid.*, 153, expressed thoughts similar to those of Arangio-Ruiz; Jagota, *ibid.*, 154; Riphagen, *ibid.*, 157.
[291] Commentary Article 5, Part Two, 27.
[292] Commentary Article 5, Part Two, 27.
[293] Indeed, in his proposed article 5 Riphagen (Fifth Report, 3) did not offer any definition of "injured State", and only under sub (a) mentioned the infringement of a right. All the other examples laid down were modelled on the phrase "if the internationally wrongful act constitutes a breach of an obligation imposed by". Article 5, sub (e), on international crimes, ran: "if the internationally wrongful act constitutes an international crime, all other States."
[294] For a comment on this aspect see Hoogh, The Relationship, 204-205.
[295] Commentary Article 19, Part One, 102. See also *ibid.*, 116.
[296] Commentary Article 19, Part One, 119-120. It may be noted that Ago, commenting upon his proposed article 18 (later article 19), even did not rule out the possibility that the breach of an obligation established under a rule not of peremptory character could constitute an international crime. YBILC 1976, Volume I, 57. And

later on he observed (*ibid.*, 74): "Only the breach of certain imperative rules could be considered an international crime." Hofmann in turn claims that, in view of the criterion of seriousness, not every breach of an obligation *erga omnes* constitutes an international crime. Hofmann, Zur Unterscheidung, 220.

297 Only Ushakov appeared to envisage a legal interest for all States consequent upon the breach of an obligation incumbent under a peremptory norm, and he stated (*ibid.*, 119): "But perhaps it should be provided that, when the internationally wrongful act had been committed in violation of a peremptory norm of general international law, it was the international community of States and the States composing it that were directly or indirectly injured."

298 See adopted articles 18, paragraph 2; 29, paragraph 2; and 33, paragraph 2 (a), Part One. Proposed articles 12 (b), Part Two; and 4 (b), Part Three. Díaz González (YBILC 1985, Volume I, 134) interpreted article 14, paragraph 1, Part Two proposed by Riphagen as a reference to the concept of *jus cogens*.

299 Although article 4 (b), Part Three, of the ILC-draft proposed by Riphagen in a limited way seems to relate to the issue of legal interest with regard to obligations laid down under peremptory norms. Riphagen, W., Seventh Report on State Responsibility, 4 March 1986, A/CN.4/397, 29 pp., 9-10.

300 Tammes, YBILC 1976, Volume I, 64; Calle y Calle, *ibid.*, 65 and 75; Sette Camara, *ibid.*, 68; Vallat, *ibid.*, 68-69; Sahovic, *ibid.*, 70; Martínez Moreno, *ibid.*; Rossides, *ibid.*, 83. Contrary Ustor, *ibid.*, 84; and Ago, *ibid.*, 90. For instance Ushakov, YBILC 1976, Volume I, 71, reflected: "(...), whereas an international crime always constituted a breach of an obligation *erga omnes*, it could not be said that the breach of an obligation *erga omnes* always constituted an international crime. For example, the current rules of the law of the sea were obligations *erga omnes*, but a breach of those obligations was not necessarily an international crime. The same was true of peremptory rules: whereas an international crime was always a breach of a peremptory rule, the breach of such a rule was not necessarily an international crime."

301 Noted earlier in Hoogh, The Relationship, 202 and 206.

302 Commentary Article 19, Part One, 120.

303 *Ibid.* Ushakov, commenting upon article 18 (later article 19), was of the contrary opinion, and he held (YBILC 1976, Volume I, 73): "Thus, a serious breach of a minor obligation was not an international crime, whereas even a minor breach of an essential obligation was." (see also *ibid.*, 72). And he elaborated this by stating that any breach of the obligation to refrain from the use of force against the territorial integrity or political independence of another State constituted the crime of aggression (*ibid.*). In his opinion (*ibid.*, 71) the criterion to decide whether the breach of an obligation constituted a crime lay with "the importance for mankind of the right safeguarded by the obligation". Or it depended, in other words, on (*ibid.*, 72) "the interests protected by the obligation". Nevertheless he somewhat inconsistently observed (*ibid.*, 73): "Again, an isolated act of discrimination constituted a violation of human rights, but that did not make it an international crime. *Apartheid* and genocide, however, were international crimes since they imperilled the existence of an entire people." His remarks seem more to have been directed against the text adopted by Ago, than against the criterion of seriousness as such.

CHAPTER 2

OBLIGATIONS *ERGA OMNES*, INTERNATIONAL CRIMES, AND THE LEGAL INTERESTS OF THE INTERNATIONAL COMMUNITY AND THE UNITED NATIONS

2.1. Introduction

Up to this point the present writer has deliberately abstained from undue reference to the phrases "international community" and "community interest". There can be no doubt as to the reason: if there is a community interest in the performance of State obligations, then it must be the community that is in possession of a correlative right to demand performance, and a legal interest if obligations are breached. Whatever may be thought of the use in article 53 of the Vienna Convention of the phrase "international community *of States* as a whole", it cannot be understood to incorporate the community interest with regard to treaties void for conflict with a peremptory norm.[1] Only the reference (article 66 of the Vienna Convention) of disputes concerning articles 53 and 64 to the Court may, in a limited way, be considered to stand for community involvement.[2]

Article 19, Part One, of the ILC-draft has not made any significant change in this respect, notwithstanding its deletion of the reference to States after "international community" as a determining factor in the manner of recognition of internationally wrongful acts as international crimes.[3] The sole origin of the idea of a legal interest for the international community lies therefore with the notion of obligations *erga omnes*, which, by word of the Court, are "obligations towards the international community as a whole".[4] Now that language closely resembles the similar phrase in article 53 of the Vienna Convention. But although there appears to be a close identification between the notions of obligations *erga omnes* and of *jus cogens*, one cannot assume both of them to convey the same meaning of international community. Because "international community" regarding the concept of *jus cogens* refers to the creation of law – admittedly a special kind of law – , whereas with regard to obligations *erga omnes* it concerns, more properly speaking, the enforcement of law.

Within the State communities making up the international community, the enforcement of law is generally centralized in community organs. Exceptions to this monopoly of community enforcement of law exist only as clearly circumscribed provisions in special laws, and then always under control by the courts. On the international level the first question to ask is "which are the community organs designed to enforce the laws within the international community"? There is a theory claiming that States besides creating the law also enforce the law, and that in doing so they are to be considered to be acting in dual capacity. The capacity conferred by law to resort to unilateral enforcement of one's rights, and the capacity to act as a community organ to enforce the law.[5] It may be submitted that the theory is based on false premises. One cannot equate decentralized enforcement by States acting individually to centralized enforcement through community organs. Nor can one claim that decentralized enforcement constitutes at the same time community enforcement (exception made with regard to the European Union).[6] Community enforcement generally exists only by means of centralizing the enforcement function in community organs. If that is the case it becomes clear that for community enforcement one has to look, not to States, but to international organizations.

In its commentary to article 1, Part One, the Commission noted that "responsibility" would cover the new relations resulting from an internationally wrongful act whether or not those were:[7] "(...) limited to the offending State and the directly injured State or extend also to other subjects of international law, (...)." At this stage of the development of international relations therefore the role to be played by international organizations as subjects of international law, and especially the United Nations, regarding community enforcement cannot be neglected. In the past international organizations have had much to do with the performance, or non-performance, of the obligations States had accepted by becoming a party to an organization's constituent instrument. Provisions in constituent treaties are for the most part concerned with the organization's power of suspension of membership, or expulsion from the organization. Some of those treaties also provide for coercive measures against States decided upon by the organization, and which are to be implemented by the members. Generally such provisions do not state in any outright manner that the organization has the right to claim the performance of the obligations accepted by States under the constituent instrument, or that the obligations concerned are performed towards the organization.

Arangio-Ruiz has proposed, in article 18, paragraph 2, Part Two, to confer jurisdiction on the Court to determine the existence of a crime.[8] The right to seize, unilaterally, the Court would be vested in every State, subject to the condition that either the General Assembly or the Security Council would have resolved, by qualified majority, that an allegation of the commission of a crime was sufficiently substantiated to justify the serious concern of the international community. The question is of course to what extent the international community already has a role to play regarding international crimes, that is whether the community possesses the right to invoke the responsibility of a State committing a crime. This chapter will consequently investigate under which circumstances the community, as personified by the United Nations, can be considered to be in possession of a legal interest consequent upon the commission of an internationally wrongful act.

This chapter will first of all discuss, in section 2.2, the phrase "obligations towards the international community as a whole". Certain arguments on the international legal personality of the United Nations will be examined in section 2.3. Next, in section 2.4, the criteria to determine the legal interest of States examined in chapter one (section 1.5) will be discussed from the angle of determining the legal interest of the United Nations. Section 2.5 will follow up on this by examining the legal bases of the United Nations' legal interest. Finally section 2.6 will focus on the legal interest of the United Nations consequent upon the commission of an international crime, and on the question whether a committed international crime vests *ipso facto* the competence of the

Security Council under article 39 of the Charter.[9] The Security Council, however, may not be able to come to any decision, measures, or action under Chapter VII of the Charter. For that reason it will also be investigated in this section which effects accrue to recommendations of the General Assembly or the Security Council.

2.2. Obligations towards the international community as a whole

When discussing the concept of obligations *erga omnes*, in connection to international crimes, the late judge Ago commented upon the notion of the international community as follows:[10]

> "When *erga omnes* was used in the *obiter dictum* of the *Barcelona Traction* decision, the Court had something else in mind: obligations towards the international community. We then began to see the emergence of something which already exists to some extent today and we hope will go on growing; namely that the entity called the international community, distinct from its members who have rights and obligations, is able to enter into legal relationships with its members. That is a very great advance, and very probably notions like that of *jus cogens* or of international crimes will be able truly to take form only once that phenomenon has become a reality. I do not believe that one can say "if there is an internationally wrongful act a little more serious than another one, or than other ones, we shall call it a 'crime', and all States will legitimately be able to intervene". Not at all. It is not all States, but rather the international community that is envisaged as the possible bearer of a right of reaction to this particularly serious form of internationally wrongful act. Accordingly, the whole idea of obligations *erga omnes* is bound up not only with the fact of recognition of the existence of that community as such, but also with the fact of more advanced institutionalization of that community. (...) That was the intention, and that is why I believe that it is extremely important for institutions to be established through which progress can be achieved in this area."

As a comment on late judge Ago's identification of obligations *erga omnes* to obligations towards the international community, it has to be noted that his conception is not borne out by the terms of paragraph 33 of the Barcelona Traction Case. Superficially the Court appears to use the phrases "obligations towards the international community" and "obligations *erga omnes*" in an interchangeable fashion. However, the Court observes that the obligations towards the international community are by their very nature "the concern of all States"; and that "in view of the importance of the rights involved, all States can be held to have a legal interest in their protection".[11] These sentences illustrate that by mentioning obligations towards the international community, in the sense of obligations *erga omnes*, the Court did not have in mind a personified (or even abstract) international community, but States. Whatever the Court may have thought, or may think, with regard to the international community, it appears thus to have kept within the traditional bilateral concepts of inter-State relations.

Furthermore, one may note that the Court uses the expression "international community *as a whole*", and that refers back to the concept of *jus cogens* as laid down in article 53 of the Vienna Convention. Indeed, it would seem strange if the Court, in the context of contentious proceedings, would have had anything else in mind but States. Especially so since it used paragraph 33, in which appears the idea of obligations *erga omnes* as obligations towards the international community, as an argument for denying Belgium any *jus standi* with regard to the denial of justice (allegedly) committed by Spain:[12]

> "Obligations the performance of which is the subject of diplomatic protection are not of the same category. It cannot be held, when one such obligation is in question, in a specific case, that all States have a legal interest in its observance."

Obviously one may draw the inference that if Belgium had pointed to a(n) (breached) obligation of Spain towards the international community, then it would also have had a legal interest in its observance.

Does all this mean that there is no room for obligations whose breach gives rise to a legal interest on the part of the international community? That would be a hasty conclusion, although Ago, then special rapporteur, argued in his second report:[13]

> "In spite of the divergence of the views described above, the different conceptions of responsibility nevertheless coincide in agreeing that every internationally wrongful act creates new legal relations between the State committing the act and the injured State. As has already been pointed out, this in no way precludes the establishment of other relations between the former State and other subjects of international law. What must be ruled out, it appears, at least at the present stage of international relations, is the idea that as a result of an internationally wrongful act general international law can create a legal relationship between the guilty State and the international community as such, just as municipal law creates a relationship between the person committing an offence and the State itself. International law can have no such effect, so long as it does not recognize a personification of the international community as such. But this situation has certainly not prevented international treaty law from providing that in certain cases a particular internationally wrongful act may be the source of new legal relations, not only between the guilty State and the injured State, but also between the former State and other States or, especially, between the former State and organizations of States. The development of international organization, as early as the League of Nations but more particularly with the United Nations, has led to consideration of the possibility that a State committing an internationally wrongful act of a certain kind and of a certain importance might be placed in a new legal relationship not only with the injured State, but also with the Organization."

Now these two displayed comments by the late judge Ago are highly revealing, because they show that he considers it possible to envisage a personified international community, although of course in 1970 he denied the presence of such a community. His later comment on international crimes, framed in rather more positive terms, is not inconsistent *per se* with his earlier comment contained in his second report. In both comments he links the personification of the international community to the then present degree of institutionalization of international relations.

In this last passage it appears that then special rapporteur Ago makes a distinction between treaty régimes and general international law. If one takes general international law to stand for customary international law, an argument could be made that the personified international community is not likely to be established by customary international law. That argument is bolstered by his references, in both instances, to the United Nations, even if in his 1970 views on the matter the personified international community and the United Nations do not quite coincide. The inevitably intricate character of the relations between a personified international community and its members leads to the conclusion that the basis for such a community must be a treaty régime. And his rejection, in 1970, of the existence of a personified international community should perhaps be considered to be somewhat hasty in view of his scant examination of the question.

However, the comprehensively universalized character of the relations between any community and its members further leads one to observe that the requirement of consent by members of the international community to the establishment of treaty relations with one another to a certain degree hampers the establishment of a personified community. The reference by the Court, in paragraph 34 of the Barcelona Traction Case, to corresponding rights of protection laid down in general international law or in international instruments of a universal or quasi-universal character, even if apparently only in the context of legal interests of States, must be seen to lend credibility to the universal character of rules laying down obligations *erga omnes*. Universal character of the rules in question is not ensured solely by reference to relevant instruments of a universal or quasi-universal character, but also by reference to general international law.[14] The personified international community, to be established through universal membership in an organization established by way of treaty, may have to rely on customary international law to the extent that certain members of the community decline to take up membership in the intended universal organization.[15] Substantive rules of customary international law, co-existent and in a general sense identical to the treaty rules,[16] may make up for the lack of universal membership of an organization.

However, the fact that rules of customary international law apply to States irrespective of their being bound by similar or identical treaty rules accepted through their membership in an international organization, cannot *ipso jure* lead to the conclusion that the organization itself has the right to demand the performance of the obligations under the relevant rules of customary international law.

And this same observation goes for rules contained in treaties other than the organization's constituent instrument or treaties drafted by the organization itself. Not even the case of rules contained in treaties concluded under the organization's auspices provides as clear-cut a case as some would make one believe. Considering these uncertainties it becomes clear that the organization's legal interest with regard to breaches of obligations ought to be examined within a broad context, and that a mere superficial glance at the organization's constituent instrument does not suffice. International personality appears, to this writer, to be the perfect starting-point for examining questions concerning an organization's legal interests. And since the United Nations is the only organization that could be said to represent the personified international community,[17] it appears fully justified to limit the following analysis to the United Nations.

2.3. The international legal personality of the United Nations

That a personified international community, taking the form of an international organization, must have international personality flows from the use of the term "personified". A community or organization that does not take any distinct form compared to its members could at the most be considered to represent the members' interests (whatever these may be). The Court already early in its existence proclaimed by way of general principle, insofar as the United Nations is concerned, the international personality of that organization.[18] It decided that issue in its reply to the request by the General Assembly whether the United Nations could bring an international claim, and the Court deduced international personality first and foremost from the fact this was indispensable to achieve the ends for which the United Nations had been founded.[19] The Court then, indirectly, pointed to a number of provisions in the Charter which endorsed its conclusion: article 2, paragraph 5, article 25; articles 10, 11, 13, and 14; articles 104 and 105; and articles 43, 75, 77, and 105, paragraph 3.[20]

More important perhaps was the definition adopted by the Court on international personality, if only for the purposes of its opinion, to the effect that:[21]

> "(...) if the Organization is recognized as having that personality, it is an entity capable of availing itself of obligations incumbent upon its Members."

Here the Court finds that the essence of international personality lies in the capability to avail oneself of other persons' obligations. This, as such, appears to be somewhat ambiguous phrasing, but the French text more strikingly refers to:[22] "(...) une entité capable d'être bénéficiaire d'obligations incombant à ses Membres." Later the Court reached the conclusion that the United Nations is an international person, which in the words of the Court meant:[23]

> "(...) that it is a subject of international law and capable of possessing international rights and duties, and that it has the capacity to maintain its rights by bringing international claims."

The Court elaborated on that statement in its discussion of the institute of diplomatic protection, and held:[24] "(...) that only the party to whom an international obligation is due can bring a claim in respect of its breach." It is essential to observe that these quotes are all of the same order in implying that State responsibility can be invoked not only by States, but also by the United Nations.[25] The Charter provisions referred to by the Court, however, do not explicitly point to breaches of obligations by States or incurred State responsibility towards the United Nations.[26]

An important aspect of the Court's opinion concerns the fact that it upholds the United Nations' legal personality, and capacity to bring claims, not only in regard to members of the United Nations, but also towards non-members:[27]

> "On this point, the Court's opinion is that fifty States, representing the vast majority of the members of the international community, had the power, in conformity with international law, to bring into being an entity possessing objective international personality, and not merely personality recognized by them alone, together with capacity to bring international claims."

The argument made here is certainly valid to the extent that it concerns the possibility for States to create an organization in possession of objective international personality.

But that is not the point! Either an organization can bring claims, or it cannot. If it can proceed to bring claims against members, it will also be in possession of the international competence to do so with regard to non-members. No, the essential question is whether the organization can, in the words of the Court, avail itself of the obligations of the non-member; whether the non-member State has any obligation with regard to the agents of the organization; and whether that obligation is in any way distinct from any obligation the specific non-member State may have under the rules of customary international law regarding the protection of aliens. These questions were not answered by the Court since they had not been submitted to it. The question was phrased in abstract terms and assumed that State responsibility had been incurred.[28] The Court on a number of occasions referred to injury caused by the breach of obligations towards the United Nations,[29] and it had no problem in finding:[30]

> "The question lies within the limits already established; that is to say it presupposes that the injury for which reparation is demanded arises from a breach of an obligation designed to help an agent of the Organization in the performance of his duties."

In relation to members of the United Nations that obligation can hardly be denied in view of the obligation contained in article 2, paragraph 5, of the Charter, and the Court pointed this out.[31] But the matter is more complicated with regard to non-members. The Court's only answer to the question whether the United Nations could make claims against non-members was that:[32]

> "(...) fifty States, representing the vast majority of the members of the international community, had the power (...) to bring into being an entity possessing objective international personality, and not merely personality recognized by them alone, together with capacity to bring international claims."

This does not provide a satisfactory answer to the question which obligation, owed to the United Nations, could be breached by a non-member. The Court denied that there existed any analogy between the United Nations' right to functional protection and the right of diplomatic protection of States with regard to their nationals.[33] Though of course that analogy could have provided the necessary basis of obligation for non-members.[34] Notwithstanding article 2, paragraph 6, obligations for non-members cannot be founded on the Charter, since that cannot create obligations for them.[35] The only remaining basis would then have to be sought in the analogous application of rules of customary international law regarding the immunities to be accorded to diplomatic or consular agents. The analogy can certainly be made, but one would have expected the Court to come up with more of an argument on the specific basis of obligation of non-members than it did.

One further question must be addressed, which concerns the potential scope of the legal interests considered to be in possession of the United Nations. In concluding that the United Nations is an international person (and can bring claims against States), the Court observed:[36]

> "That is not the same thing as saying that it is a State, which it certainly is not, or that its legal personality and rights and duties are the same as those of a State. Still less is it the same thing as saying that it is a 'super-State', whatever that expression may mean."

The United Nations should therefore not be considered – fortunately so – a State, nor for that matter – perhaps unfortunately so – a super-State. What the Court significantly indicates here is that the United Nations need not be in possession of the same rights and obligations as States are. To put it otherwise, the United Nations cannot *ipso jure* claim the possession of rights enjoyed by States under customary international law, or be considered to be obligated the same way as States are under customary international law. But if that is the case, how then to decide under which circumstances the United Nations will be entitled to demand the performance of obligations by States? The Court, in a follow-up to its observation concluded with the important remark that:[37]

> "Whereas a State possesses the totality of international rights and duties recognized by international law, the rights and duties of an entity such as the Organization must depend on the purposes and functions as specified or implied in its constituent documents and developed in practice. (...), the Court concludes that the Members have endowed the Organization with capacity to bring international claims *when necessitated by the discharge of its functions.*"

While not denying that the United Nations' exercise of rights (or performance of obligations) should be in some relation to the constituent instrument's purposes and functions, nevertheless one could find arguments militating in favour of a broader view towards the existence of rights than a capacity to bring international claims on the basis of a necessity for discharging its functions.

The (non-) exercise of rights generally takes place on the basis of a weighing of interests, and the consequent decision may just as well lead to exercise, as not. The argument of necessity for discharge of functions cannot be upheld, since any subject is generally free to exercise or fail to exercise rights. Furthermore, it can hardly be denied that the scope of functions of the United Nations is so broad as to bring almost any activity, whether in the exercise of rights or not, in relation to the discharge of functions. Yet the mere fact that certain activities could be said to be necessitated by the discharge of functions by the United Nations cannot alone be considered sufficient argument to conclude that a right exists.

On the other side of the scale, that of obligations, it is obvious that the United Nations cannot undertake activities which States, whether or not members, are not allowed to engage in their individual capacity. That conclusion is based of course on the argument that States cannot create a collectivity in order to do what they cannot do individually.[38] It is well known however that States are not to the same extent bound by obligations. The United Nations therefore can only be bound to international law insofar as obligations exist universally, that is, for all States. This leads to the conclusion that the United Nations is bound, if circumstances so require, by universal customary international law.

However, States are free, subject to considerations of *jus cogens*, to alter the rules applicable in their *inter se* relations. An illustration of this is provided by the regulation of the use of force in the United Nations Charter. Members are under the obligation to refrain from the threat or use of force against other States, and may only react to uses of force that come under the heading of an armed attack. That means effectively that members are under the obligation to refrain from using force in reaction to another State's use of force if that other State's force could not be considered an armed attack.

The Security Council could be said to be obligated, under the argument that it is prevented from doing what individual members are not allowed to do, not to use force against States. However, the criterion to determine whether or not the Security Council is entitled to resort to force in reaction to a certain situation, or certain acts, is not the criterion of armed attack, but the criterion of threat to the peace. Thus in so far as the use of force is concerned it is allowed to do what members are not allowed to do.

2.4. Criteria to determine the United Nations' legal interest

The starting-point regarding the search for criteria determining the legal interest of the United Nations lies with a discussion of the criteria, either rejected or adopted in chapter one, that determine the legal interests of States. Thus it will be examined in this section whether such criteria would apply in determining the United Nations' legal interest.

2.4.1. THE UNITED NATIONS AND THE GENERAL INTEREST IN THE PERFORMANCE OF OBLIGATIONS

That the United Nations has an interest regarding the performance of international obligations cannot be doubted. Indeed there are references in the Charter that witness such interest. Thus the preamble of the Charter affirms the determination of the peoples of the United Nations to "establish conditions under which justice and respect for obligations arising from treaties and other sources of international law can be maintained";[39] article 1, paragraph 1, witnesses that the primary goal of the United Nations is "to bring about by peaceful means, and in conformity with the principles of justice and international law, the adjustment or settlement of international disputes or situations which might lead to a breach of the peace"; and article 13, paragraph 1 (a), ordains that the General Assembly "shall initiate studies and make recommendations for the purpose of (...) encouraging the progressive development of international law and its codification".[40]

But in order for an interest to generate legal rights and obligations, as the Court indicated in the 1966 South West Africa Cases, it must be given juridical expression and be clothed in legal form.[41] In this regard it may be noted that the most firm of these texts is contained in the preamble, which, as was noted by the Court, constitutes only "the moral and political basis for the legal provisions thereafter set out."[42] Of the two legal provisions mentioned just now, article 13, paragraph 1 (a) is rather more concerned with the abstract or theoretical development of international law than with the application of that law in the field of State responsibility. Only article 1, paragraph 1, appears to provide some indication that the United Nations would be in possession of a general legal interest with regard to the performance of obligations by States. Yet that indication is at the same time weakened by the fact that the United Nations' purpose, to bring about settlement of disputes, or adjustment of situations, in accordance with international law and justice, only operates insofar as the dispute or situation concerned could lead to a breach of the peace. Generally speaking of course any dispute or

situation may lead to a breach of the peace, but in concreto most of them will not. It would not seem right therefore to deduce from this a general legal interest in the performance of obligations.
That conclusion is strengthened by certain arguments regarding other provisions of the Charter, namely articles 5, 6, 14, 39 in conjunction to 41 and 42, and article 94, paragraphs 1 and 2.[43]

Before embarking upon the arguments concerned there is need to reflect upon a rather important argument. It concerns the finding that where there is a power or competence to resort to sanctions for the breach of obligations by a member there is also the necessary implication of the possession of a competence to determine that a member has breached its obligations.[44] This in fact amounts to saying that a legal interest exists for an organization entitled to resort to sanctions against members. Now that is clearly a correct way of phrasing, because there is an unbreakable connection in the chain obligation – breach of that obligation – obligation to repair the breach (right to reparation) – and the right to resort to sanctions or to use force.[45] The Charter in fact does include references to breaches of obligation and/or to resort to sanctions or force in consequence of such breaches.
The only provision in which a direct link can be said to exist between the breach of obligations (though in rather unsatisfactory terms) and a consequent resort to sanctions is article 6 of the Charter. In that article is said that a member of the United Nations may be expelled from the organization if it has persistently violated the principles of the Charter. On the other hand that means that a member could not be expelled on the mere ground that it has (allegedly) breached obligations other than those contained in article 2 regarding the principles. The basic obligations of article 2 are those in paragraph 3 on the peaceful settlement of disputes, and paragraph 4 on the prohibition of the use of force.
In article 5 no reference is made to any breach of obligation on the part of a member. It stipulates however that a member may be suspended from the exercise of the right of privileges of membership if preventive or enforcement action has been taken against that member. Preventive or enforcement action is generally interpreted as meaning measures under article 41, or action under article 42 of the Charter,[46] and those are in turn dependent on the application by the Security Council of its power, expressed in article 39, to determine a threat to the peace, breach of the peace, or act of aggression.

The interpretation of article 39 is in fact decisive for the issue here at stake, that is, the general interest in the performance of obligations. In this context it may be observed, preliminary, that there are authors who deny the necessity of any breach of obligation by a member of the United Nations in order to provide a basis for Security Council action under article 39, and thus consequent action under articles 41 and 42.[47] Apparently the main argument in support of this stance concerns the observation that threats to the peace encompass acts and situations which do not constitute threats or uses of force. For some there is no question of any correlation between threats to the peace and threats of force, which for them implies that no obligation need be violated in order to provide a basis of Security Council action.[48] To a limited extent this appears acceptable. A determination by the Security Council under article 39 need not entail direct consequences for the State at the origin of the threat to the peace.

The picture changes if the Security Council proceeds, on the basis of such a determination, to edict measures under article 41, to take action under article 42, or authorizes action (*infra* chapters four and five), as against a specific (member) State. Under customary international law a State can only be subjected to certain measures involving a breach of obligation by the State(s) inflicting them if it has committed a prior breach of obligation. Taking into account that the measures of articles 41 or 42 may involve, for the States implementing the decision of the Security Council, breaches of their obligations towards the target State, that means, under the theory that a threat to the peace need not involve any breach of obligation, that they would be justified (and of course obligated under article 25) to apply those measures notwithstanding that the target State had not committed any prior breach of obligation. An interpretation of the powers of the Security Council under articles 39, 41 and 42 in that sense would amount to an unacceptable derogation from one of the most fundamental conditions attached to the enforcement of the responsibility of States, namely that countermeasures or the use of force can only be resorted to in response to a prior internationally wrongful act.

Hereafter it will be assumed that where the Security Council makes a determination under article 39, and resorts to measures under article 41, action under article 42, or authorizes action, it enforces the responsibility of a (member) State, and more particularly that State/s reparation obligations.

The argument in the previous paragraphs was that the imposition of measures under articles 41 and 42, to the extent that they could not be considered to amount to retortions, requires a prior breach of obligation by the targeted State. Another argument sometimes put forward relates to an alleged absolute discretionary power possessed by the Security Council in determining whether or not certain facts constitute a threat to the peace, breach of the peace, or act of aggression. Gowlland-Debbas argues that regarding:[49]

> "(...) the question of what constitutes a threat to the peace, it is evident that in accordance with **Charter** requirements the determination of its existence entails a factual and political judgement and not a legal one."

And a few sentences later she asserts:[50]

> "A determination by the Council is not for instance the sort of question that could be reviewed by the International Court of Justice as some have proposed."

If a decision of the Security Council as to the existence of a threat to the peace is really of political character, and does not have any legal component, or if such a decision could not be reviewed by the Court as to its compatibility with Charter requirements or international law in general, then the answer to the question – whether the United Nations is in possession of a general interest in the performance of obligations by members – would be devoid of interest. For in both cases the Security Council/s freedom of action would be absolute. If its decision is to be considered of political character, no legal rules or requirements could be held against it, since no objective meaning could be adduced to "threats to the peace".[51] If its decision could not be reviewed by the Court, then no other organ (and certainly not an individual State) could be said to obtain that possibility, the General Assembly/s powers of appreciation being restricted to the making of recommendations. Questions of review of Security Council resolutions by the Court stand postponed, however, to chapter six.

The statement that the determination of threats to the peace by the Security Council involves no legal pronouncements is unfounded. The Court had stated as early as 1948, in its Admission Opinion, that:[52]

> "The political character of an organ cannot release it from the observance of the treaty provisions established by the Charter when they constitute limitations on its powers or criteria for its judgment."

The Admission Opinion of course concerned the interpretation of the word "peace-loving" in article 4, paragraph 1, of the Charter. It cannot be gainsaid, however, that the phrase "threat to the peace, breach of the peace or act of aggression", featuring in article 39, does provide limitations on the Security Council/s powers and criteria for its judgment. Because the power of the Council to resort to measures under article 41, or action under article 42, is grafted upon a determination under article 39 to the effect that, as a minimum, a threat to the peace exists. And in its Expenses Opinion the Court had ample opportunity to note:[53]

> "It has been argued that the question put to the Court is intertwined with political questions, and that for this reason the Court should refuse to give an opinion. It is true that most interpretations of the Charter of the United Nations will have political significance, great or small. In the nature of things it could not be otherwise. The Court, however, cannot attribute a political character to a request which invites it to undertake an essentially judicial task, namely, the interpretation of a treaty provision."

This observation of the Court was made in the context of a request for an advisory opinion, and one may wonder whether the same could be held to apply in regard to its contentious jurisdiction. The Nicaragua Case shows some insight in this issue. In that case the United States had argued, in an attempt to show that Nicaragua/s claims were inadmissible, that:[54]

> "(...) a claim of unlawful use of armed force is a matter committed by the United Nations Charter and by practice to the exclusive competence of other organs, in particular the Security Council;"

The Court noted on the basis of this argument that the United States had not advanced the more radical stance that the dispute was not legal in character, and that the United States itself had emphasized that the argument did not mean that international law was not relevant.[55]

Furthermore, the Court, in order to decide on the legitimacy of the exercise of a right of self-defence by the United States, proceeded in that same judgment with the interpretation of the decisive condition of armed attack.[56] Admittedly that interpretation was not made in relation to article 51 of the Charter, since the Court had somewhat earlier decided that it had to apply the multilateral treaty reservation and hence could only apply customary international law.[57] However, in interpreting the condition of armed attack the Court drew upon both the Charter and General Assembly resolution 3314 which defined aggression. If the phrase "armed attack" is subject to legal interpretation, then why not also the phrase "threat to the peace, breach of the peace or act of aggression"?

In this respect the phrases "breach of the peace" and "act of aggression" clearly refer to situations in which force is actually being used.[58] The phrase "threat to the peace" moreover implies the idea that a situation exists that may lead to a breach of the peace or an act of aggression. This can be deduced from the prime purpose of the United Nations, laid down in article 1, paragraph 1, of the Charter, which is:

> "To maintain international peace and security, and to that end: to take effective collective measures for the prevention and removal of threats to the peace, and for the suppression of acts of aggression or other breaches of the peace, and to bring about by peaceful means, and in conformity with the principles of justice and international law, adjustment or settlement of international disputes or situations which might lead to a breach of the peace;"

Of course the Charter does not contain any definition of the phrases of article 39,[59] and this must mean that the Security Council enjoys a very wide margin of appreciation as to the exercise of its power under article 39. Yet even the Security Council may venture outside such margin, and thus determine the existence of a threat to the peace where there actually is none.

In sum, the Security Council is limited in determining a threat to the peace by the consideration that a situation lying at the basis of such a threat could, at least arguably, lead to a breach of the peace.[60] There does not seem to be any compelling reason for considering the question which situations or acts would come under the heading of a threat to the peace to be a political rather than a legal one. These arguments are complemented by another one concerning article 94, paragraph 2, of the Charter.

Article 94, paragraph 1, of the Charter states that members of the United Nations undertake to comply with decisions of the Court to which they are a party. Paragraph 2 then stipulates:

> "If any party to a case fails to perform the obligations incumbent upon it under a judgment rendered by the Court, the other party may have recourse to the Security Council, which may, if it deems necessary, make recommendations or decide upon measures to be taken to give effect to the judgment."

The measures referred to are generally considered to encompass measures similar to those of article 41, or even those of article 42. Now assuming for the sake of argument that the Security Council is completely free to determine that a situation constitutes a threat to the peace, irrespective of whether that situation would involve a breach of obligation by a member, then one would wonder why article 94, paragraph 2, had been inserted at all. For that provision would be completely superfluous, and certainly there would be no need to envisage the possibility of resorting to sanctions in case of failure to abide by a judgment of the Court. Applying the well known interpretation rule that an interpretation of a provision ought not to lead to the result of making it devoid of effect, one should also reject the idea that failure to abide by the obligations under a judgment of the Court should *ipso jure* be considered a threat to the peace.[61]
Furthermore, it is possible, on the basis of an *a contrario* argument, to assert that if the Security Council has the power to enforce the breach of obligations in the specific case

of failure to abide by a judgment of the Court, then it should be denied that power with regard to the enforcement of the breach of obligations generally.[62] Contrary to what has been claimed before the Senate of the United States, the provision of article 94, paragraph 2, indeed envisages that the Security Council will function as sort of a sheriff, and will enforce the judgment of the Court.[63] A difference with the position under certain national legal systems is that the Security Council is not under any obligation to enforce obligations contained in the judgment of the Court, since the Security Council will do so only "if it deems necessary" and can also not be ordered to do so. But the fact that the Security Council/s power to decide on measures to ensure the fulfilment of the Court/s judgment is discretionary in nature cannot be seen to justify the stance that the Security Council could also resort to measures to enforce obligations in general. Indeed the Security Council/s power under article 94, paragraph 2, to react to the failure by one party to fulfil its obligations under the judgment is dependent on the other party deciding to have recourse to the Security Council. In the absence of a request by the other party the Security Council could not resort to the recommendations or measures envisaged in article 94, paragraph 2.[64]

On the basis of the above interpretations it is safe to say that the United Nations is not in possession of a general interest with regard to the performance of obligations by its members. *A fortiori* that will mean that it also possesses no general interest in the performance of obligations by non-members. To the extent that the Security Council may, under article 39, concern itself with the non-performance of obligations, this finds a limit in that a breach of obligation could only be considered a threat to the peace, as a minimum, if it could lead to a breach of the peace.

2.4.2. THE UNITED NATIONS AND THE COMMON INTEREST IN THE PERFORMANCE OF OBLIGATIONS UNDER RULES OF INTERNATIONAL LAW

In chapter one the question was discussed whether or not States could be considered to be in possession of a legal interest with regard to the performance of obligations under a certain rule on the basis of the mere fact that they are bound by that rule. The same question may be asked in regard to the United Nations. And it would seem, as was the case in chapter one, that the answer has to be in the negative.

If we take as a starting-point the observation made above that the United Nations cannot do collectively what a State taken by itself is not allowed to do individually,[65] the conclusion imposes itself that the United Nations is also bound by the rules of universal customary international law. Nevertheless, this does not lead us to the further conclusion that it can also demand the performance of obligations by members whenever those obligations are breached. First of all it has to be remembered that in view of the correlation between obligations and rights there is always another State which is in possession of a legal interest. The fact that the United Nations is considered also to be bound by the rule under which allegedly an obligation has been breached does not suffice to provide the United Nations with a legal interest regarding such alleged breach. If for instance an exclusively bilateral relationship is established in consequence of the breach of an obligation under the rules laying down the correlative right (article 5, Part Two, of the ILC-draft), other States also bound by the rule in question would not have any right to involve themselves in that relationship. The fact that the United Nations should be considered bound by the rule in question, based on the assumption that it is universal in character, therefore has no relevance. If the other States bound by the rule may not, individually, interfere with the relationship between the author State and the injured State, then the collective membership of the United Nations may likewise not interfere. This conclusion may of course also be based on the well known principle that one cannot transfer more rights to another than one oneself possesses.

In this context one may note that Meng mentions the situation in which a breach of obligation would be directed against one of the members of the EEC, that is, not against all of them, and then gives the example of an expropriation of German corporations by a commercial partner of the EEC. He quite correctly acknowledges that only the Federal Republic of Germany would be entitled to resort to reprisals against the State in breach of its obligations under the rules regarding the protection of aliens. But he proceeds with the surprising observation that:[66]

> "(...) nach der im Völkerrecht für internationale Organisationen geltenden konstitutiven Anerkennungstheorie nur solche Staaten Rechte gegen die Gemeinschaft erwerben können – die dann im Repressalienfall wieder entzogen werden können – , welche die Gemeinschaft als Völkerrechtsubjekt anerkannt haben. Mit dieser Anerkennung wird aber auch der Integrationsstand und auch der Bestand an übergangenen Gemeinschaftskompetenzen anerkannt. Wer also die Rechte eines Mitgliedstaat verletzt, muß mit dem Kompetenzübergang und damit rechnen, daß die Gemeinschaft mit Sanktionen antwörtet. Durch die Anerkennung dürfte die kollektive Antwort rechtmäßig werden."

Now that is a big step. Imagine that one member of the EEC has under international law the right to resort to reprisals consequent upon the breach of an obligation. Because it has, under the EEC-treaty no longer any competence to resort to certain specific measures of reprisal, since that competence has passed on to the EEC, the EEC itself becomes the bearer of the right of reprisal. If States outside the EEC had realized that by entering into relations with the EEC they would run the risk of having to face economic sanctions by the EEC every time they were in breach of an obligation that has nothing to do with the EEC, they undoubtedly would have thought twice before entering in such relations. The application of some sort of constitutive recognition theory appears not to overcome the rule that a State cannot transfer more rights than it possesses.

One may legitimately wonder whether (and the question logically flows from the argument that the United Nations cannot engage in conduct which States individually cannot engage in) the United Nations is entitled to act where States are individually, or in concert, entitled to act. If one looks at the rules laying down the correlative rights for States, it becomes clear that in a number of cases legal interests will accrue to each and every State of the international community. Does this then mean that the United Nations is in possession of a legal interest, since each and every one of its members is in possession of a legal interest with regard to a certain breach of obligation? The above mentioned principle, that one cannot transfer more rights than one possesses, does not stand in the way of considering the United Nations in possession of a legal interest if that is held in common among its members. Yet something more is needed, or so it would seem, than the mere fact that all members are individually in possession of a legal interest. A transfer of legal interest from the members to the United Nations would appear to be required. That transfer cannot be said to be present on the basis of the mere fact that all the members of the United Nations should be considered bound by a certain rule of international law, and may, in case of a specific breach of obligation under the rule, exercise their rights to demand the performance of that obligation. If one were to hold that the existence of rights for the entire membership of an organization would lead to an independent legal interest on the part of the organization itself, that would mean that organizations which had no interest (in the subjective sense) in the particular rule would be entitled to demand the performance of obligations under the rule. An organization established for the promotion of the economic welfare of its members would thus be able to demand the performance of its members/ obligations under, for instance, a treaty providing for the protection of human rights. Clearly that would be a rather unsatisfactory state of affairs, and the fact that all the members of a certain organization, or the United Nations, are in possession of a legal interest with regard to a certain breach of obligation cannot be considered sufficient ground to conclude upon the existence of an additional and separate legal interest of the organization, or the United Nations, itself. Limitations of a functional nature, flowing from the constitutional instrument, apply to all international organizations, even to the United Nations.

2.4.3. PERFORMANCE OF OBLIGATIONS TOWARDS THE UNITED NATIONS

In chapter one, subsection 1.5.3, was discussed whether the criterion to determine the legal interests of States should lie with the performance of obligations towards specific States. In that context an argument by Sachariew was discussed to the effect that prohibitive rules would give rise to concrete rights and obligations even before any breach would take place. That stance was rejected by reference to the example of the rule prohibiting the threat or use of force against other States. For if a State performs its obligations in this respect, and abstains from the threat or use of force, it cannot be said that the State in possession of a correlative right to demand performance could be identified before an actual or imminent breach took place. The question in this subsection is whether one could consider that obligations imposed on States are performed *ipso jure* towards the United Nations irrespective of the circumstances surrounding any actual or imminent breach.

Although universal rules of customary law should be considered binding on the United Nations, that does not mean that the obligations imposed on States by the rule are *ipso jure* also performed towards the United Nations as such. Rules of customary international law, for instance, have, to a considerable degree, been created without the participation of the United Nations. They are created through means of a process of crystallization of State practice and the conviction of the States participating in the practice that the said practice is binding upon them as a matter of law. Obligations under those rules are generally performed by States in their relations with other States, and a breach of obligations could not therefore be considered a breach towards the United Nations. Furthermore, if a State acquires a legal interest in consequence of the breach of an obligation by another State, there does not appear to be any reason why it should be possible for the United Nations to interfere with the relationship of responsibility established between the author State and the injured State.

An independent legal interest for the United Nations, moreover, could not be based on the argument that the obligation concerned was performed or breached towards the collectivity of States, and therefore also performed or breached towards the United Nations. Applying the fiction involved, to the effect that obligations were being performed not only towards States but also towards the United Nations, would appear to be stretching reality a little bit too far. Even though it is possible to envisage the realization of the collective (or even common) interest by means of organizational action intended to supplement or provide a substitute for State action, an independent legal interest for an organization cannot be said to accrue to it from the mere fact that an obligation is breached towards its members. In that sense the above mentioned argument on functional restrictions applies equally to the criterion under discussion.

2.4.4. THE EFFECTS OF AN INTERNATIONALLY WRONGFUL ACT AS CRITERION TO DETERMINE THE EXISTENCE OF A LEGAL INTEREST OF THE UNITED NATIONS

The conclusion of the previous subsection would not hold, of course, if the United Nations could point to an interest of its own regarding the performance of the obligations concerned. Obligations and rights have to be performed and exercised in concrete circumstances, and it is only when certain circumstances occur that rules can be invoked or applied. If the United Nations were to engage in certain activities which, when carried out by individual States, would trigger the applicability of the rules in question, then obligations normally performed by States in relation to other States must also be performed by them in their relations with the United Nations. Of course the Court expressly denied, in its Reparation Opinion, that it analogously applied rules regarding the diplomatic protection of aliens to agents of the United Nations.[67] It based the United Nations/ capacity to make claims for reparation on the basis that an obligation had been breached towards the United Nations. While not in itself implausible, the argument fails due to the fact, as argued above, that the Court did not establish the existence of any obligation of non-members to treat agents of the United Nations in a certain way. Such an obligation appears to exist only insofar as it is possible to apply in an analogous manner the rules regarding the treatment of aliens. It is therefore submitted that analogous application of rules to the relations between the United Nations and States is not only feasible, but in certain cases even required.

That rules may at times be analogously applied to the relations between the United Nations and States does not lead to the conclusion that the prejudice done to the United Nations in consequence of breaches of obligations by States, whether or not members, will constitute the only basis or criterion for considering the United Nations in possession of a legal interest. Indeed a number of provisions in the Charter bears witness to the existence of a legal interest on the part of the United Nations, irrespective of any injury having been suffered by the United Nations. It will furthermore be found that the existence of a legal interest on the part of the United Nations is not even restricted to breaches of obligations by members, and that on some occasions it extends beyond the individual and or collective legal interests possessed by States themselves.

2.5. Legal bases of the United Nations' legal interest

2.5.1. THE UNITED NATIONS/ LEGAL INTEREST REGARDING BREACHES OF OBLIGATION UNDER THE CHARTER

As noted above, in subsection 2.4.1, there is an unbreakable link in the chain obligation – breach of that obligation – obligation to repair the breach (right to reparation) – and the right to resort to sanctions or to use force. As also noted there, this means that a legal interest exists for the United Nations in those cases where it may resort to sanctions. That this is so follows most clearly from the provision of article 6 which authorizes the United Nations to expel a member which has consistently violated the principles of the United Nations. The most important of those principles are of course paragraphs 3 and 4 of article 2, which prescribe that members shall settle their disputes peacefully and that they shall refrain from the threat or use of force against the territorial integrity or political independence of any State, or in any manner inconsistent with the purposes of the United Nations.

The provision regarding suspension, article 5, makes a cross-reference in that it allows suspension of members against which preventive or enforcement action has been taken by the Security Council. Thus suspension of a member can only take place if the Security Council has determined a threat to the peace, breach of the peace, or act of aggression, and has singled out a particular member against which measures are taken under articles 41 or 42. The legal interest of the United Nations is most clearly present with regard to situations constituting a threat to the peace, breach of the peace, or act of aggression.

In subsection 2.4.1 it was argued that that there is, or should, always be a breach of obligation at the basis of the Security Council/s resort to the measures of articles 41 or 42. The question arises whether any breach of obligation would suffice to establish the Security Council/s competence under Chapter VII. It has already been asserted (subsections 2.4.1 and 2.4.2) that the United Nations is not in possession of a general or common interest regarding breaches of obligations. Determinations of a breach of the peace or act of aggression by the Security Council under article 39 should be seen in relation to the obligations of members to settle their disputes peacefully, and to refrain from the threat or use of force, as laid down in article 2, paragraphs 3 and 4, of the Charter. Obviously any use of military force across international frontiers, or against the armed forces of another State, will be considered not merely a threat to the peace, but a breach of the peace or even an act of aggression.

Nobody will deny, more generally speaking, that the United Nations is allowed to discuss violations of the Charter.[68] Article 10 grants the General Assembly the power to discuss any questions or any matters within the scope of the Charter. Article 14 more specifically mentions that the General Assembly may recommend measures for the peaceful adjustment of any situation which it deems likely to impair the general welfare or friendly relations among nations, including situations resulting from the violation of the provisions of the Charter setting forth the purposes and the principles of the United Nations. It is clear from the broad scope of the provisions laying down the purposes and principles (articles 1 and 2) that any subject contained in the Charter may thus be discussed. Article 11, paragraph 2, furthermore envisages the General Assembly discussing questions relating to the maintenance of international peace and security and making recommendations to the State(s) concerned or to the Security Council.[69]

The provisions of Chapter VI of the Charter on the other hand bear witness to the competence of the Security Council with regard to disputes that could endanger the maintenance of international peace and security, and it would certainly not be far-fetched to consider certain violations of the Charter giving rise to such disputes. Article 34 stipulates that the Security Council may investigate any dispute in order to determine whether or not it is likely to endanger the maintenance of international peace and security. It is worth mentioning moreover that apart from the provisions dealing with procedures or methods of peaceful settlement (articles 33, 36 and 38) article 37 offers the possibility to the Security Council of recommending "such terms of settlement as it may consider appropriate".[70]

2.5.2. THE UNITED NATIONS/ LEGAL INTEREST REGARDING BREACHES OF OBLIGATION UNDER TREATIES BETWEEN THE UNITED NATIONS AND STATES

In the Reparation Opinion the Court not only declared the United Nations to be in possession of international legal personality, but it also pointed to the treaty making capacity of the United Nations as evidence of such personality.[71] Indeed the Court observed that:[72]

> "The 'Convention on the Privileges and Immunities of the United Nations/ creates rights and duties between each of the signatories and the Organization."

It is clear that if and when a signatory of that treaty were to deny agents privileges and immunities due to them because of that treaty, the United Nations would be the only party entitled under the treaty to demand the performance of the obligations imposed, and compensation in case cessation or restitution would no longer be possible. Obviously it would be possible for States (whether parties to the treaty or third States) to make complaints regarding the treatment of agents of the United Nations possessing their nationality. The basis of such complaints would not however be a breach of obligation under such treaty, but a breach of obligation regarding the treatment due to aliens.[73] That such concurrence of legal interests may take place follows from the Reparation Opinion, in which the Court also decided that there is no rule assigning priority to either the rights of the United Nations, or to the rights of the national State.[74]

That such a legal interest exists for the United Nations with regard to breaches of obligations under any treaty to which it is a party may also be seen from the

Headquarters Agreement Opinion.[75] In that opinion the Court determined that the United States was under an obligation to arbitrate a dispute which existed between itself and the United Nations. The United Nations had initiated the arbitration procedure on the basis that there existed a dispute regarding the interpretation or application of the Headquarters Agreement. The United States agreed with the interpretation advanced by the United Nations, and denied that it had, as yet, breached its obligations under the agreement. The Court noted that a concurrence on the view that there existed a breach of obligation, or that certain conduct to be adopted would constitute a breach of obligation, did not mean that no dispute regarding the interpretation or application of the agreement existed.[76] It has to be admitted of course that the Court was not concerned here to determine whether or not the United States had breached its obligations under the Headquarters Agreement, but that the question was whether the United Nations had sufficient grounds to insist that the United States was under the obligation to participate in the arbitration process. Naturally the Court could not have endorsed the United Nations/ stance that there existed a dispute regarding the interpretation or application of the Headquarters Agreement if the United Nations could not establish any legal interest regarding breaches of obligation thereunder.

The situation described above is typical in the sense that both treaties referred to in this subsection concern bipolar treaties, meaning that the rights and obligations contained in such treaties operate between United Nations, as one party, and a number of States, as other parties. Or to put it differently the rights and obligations contained in the treaty do not operate between the *States* parties, but between the United Nations and States parties. The case would of course be different if the United Nations would become a party to a certain treaty on an equal basis with States. In such a case, or so one could assert, the question of a legal interest for the United Nations, upon consequent breaches of obligations under such a treaty, would have to be decided analogously to the rules applicable to States (*infra* chapter one).

2.5.3. THE UNITED NATIONS/ LEGAL INTEREST REGARDING BREACHES OF OBLIGATION UNDER TREATIES SPONSORED BY THE UNITED NATIONS

One may note that the Charter envisages in article 13, paragraph 1 (a), that the General Assembly will promote the progressive development and codification of international law. It is well known of course that the General Assembly instituted the International Law Commission in furtherance of the function ascribed to it,[77] and that it has since, sometimes on the basis of texts prepared by the Commission, convened international conferences in pursuit of the conclusion of highly important treaties. The question arises what role, if any, the United Nations can play with regard to the treaties concluded upon its initiative and under its organization. And more particularly, can the United Nations claim a legal interest with regard to States breaching their obligations under such treaties?

A first remark regarding the question at hand concerns the observation that the function assigned to the General Assembly under article 13 of the Charter does not modify, nor takes away, and nor takes the place of, the treaty making capacity of

United Nations members. They clearly remain free to conclude treaties as they see fit (leaving aside any question of *jus cogens*), and they are under no obligation to involve the General Assembly in the preparation of any treaty that they would wish to come to life. The argument could be made that in situations where States accept the role of the United Nations in preparing such treaties they can no longer be heard to deny the existence of a legal interest on the part of the United Nations in case of breaches of obligations under those treaties.[78]

It must be asserted nevertheless that the United Nations is in need of a provision enabling it to exercise functions in respect of such treaties. One of the few discussing this issue in terms of legal interest, Morgenstern, appears to envisage a legal interest for international organizations only to the extent that those are involved in the supervision or enforcement procedures established in such a treaty. She seems to deny international organizations any legal interest regarding breaches of obligation under the treaty if the body destined to discuss implementation reports is composed of nationals elected by the States parties.[79] That argument is bolstered moreover by another one concerning article 36, paragraph 2, of the Vienna Convention on the Law of Treaties between States and International Organizations or between International Organizations.[80] That provision stipulates that a provision of a treaty does not give rise to rights for third organizations (meaning an organization that is not a party to the treaty in question, article 2 (h)). This rule, applied analogously,[81] would prevent any right arising for the United Nations unless an express provision of the treaty were so to stipulate.

An argument in support of this stance may be derived from the Court/s opinion on the Genocide Convention, in which it observed that:[82]

> "(...) there can be no doubt that the precise determination of the conditions for participation in the Convention constitutes a permanent interest of direct concern to the United Nations which has not disappeared with the entry into force of the Convention."

This position was taken up by the Court in response to an objection made to the effect that the Assembly/s request for an opinion constituted an inadmissible interference in the interpretation of the convention. To counter that claim the Court pointed out that it had been the Assembly which took the initiative in respect of the Genocide Convention, drew up the provisions, and opened it for signature and accession.[83] In one breath the Court also mentioned the two articles which connected the General Assembly with the life of the Genocide Convention.[84] But the provisions in question, articles XI and XVI, merely deal with the role of the General Assembly regarding signatures and revision requests. It is quite noteworthy that the Court did not refer to article VIII which envisages States parties having recourse to the competent organs of the United Nations. Such a provision could of course be considered to be connected to questions of supervision or implementation. Yet the Court apparently saw no need, in the context of a request for an opinion regarding reservations, to make a reference to article VIII. Indeed, the text of article VIII itself militates against the existence of an independent legal interest of the United Nations.[85] It stipulates that the States parties may call upon the competent organs of the United Nations to take such action *under the Charter* as they consider appropriate for the prevention and suppression of acts of genocide. This would seem to indicate that the competent organs do not act on their own accord under the Genocide Convention.[86] For any action appropriate for the prevention or suppression of acts of genocide must be taken on the basis of the Charter, not on the basis of the Genocide Convention.

2.5.4. THE UNITED NATIONS/ LEGAL INTEREST REGARDING BREACHES OF OBLIGATION UNDER TREATIES EXTRANEOUS TO THE CHARTER AND UNITED NATIONS ACTIVITIES

A fortiori, of course, it would seem that the United Nations also cannot claim any legal interest with regard to breaches of obligations under treaties to which it is not a party, with regard to which it has not participated in the preparation, and with regard to which it has not been accorded any supervisory functions.[87] On this account it has quite correctly been claimed by Sur:[88]

> "De facon plus générale, le Conseil de sécurité serait sans doute dans une position juridiquement délicate pour constater la violation de traités auxquels il n/est pas partie, ni l/Organisation dont il est une organe, et qui sont conclus en dehors du cadre de l/ONU. Constater une telle violation relève de la compétence exclusive des parties, et la constatation est subordonnée aux procédures acceptées par elles. Le Conseil n/a pas de compétence à cette fin. Lorsqu/il est habilité à intervenir dans le cadre d/un traité, celui-ci doit le prévoir expressément, et cette compétence doit en outre être compatible avec la Charte. C/est ainsi que, aux termes de l/article 94 de la Charte, le Conseil est autorisé à intervenir pour assurer le respect des arrêts de la Cour internationale, à la demande d/une partie au litige, et à réagir le cas échéant contre les violations du Statut de la Cour. Mais la Charte ne lui attribue pas une compétence générale à l/égard de l/ensemble des traités, même lorsqu/ils sont relatifs à la paix et à la sécurité internationale. En pareil cas, il ne peut que se fonder sur ses propres compétences, établir directement les obligations des membres et les mesures d/exécution qu/elles appellent, sans s/appuyer sur aucun traité particulier."

The key words in this context are "qui sont conclus en dehors du cadre de l/ONU". Sur nowhere explains what should be understood by these words, but one may guess that treaties drawn up by the General Assembly would qualify as treaties concluded in the United Nations sphere. It is not clear whether he would consider the Security Council competent to determine a breach of obligations under such treaties. But certainly his conclusions with regard to treaties otherwise unrelated to the United Nations are correct.

2.5.5. THE UNITED NATIONS/ LEGAL INTEREST REGARDING BREACHES OF OBLIGATION UNDER CUSTOMARY INTERNATIONAL LAW

As has been argued above the United Nations is bound by universal rules of customary international law,[89] and thus may either derive rights from those rules, or may be placed under obligations through those rules. It may furthermore be asserted that the rules of customary international law regarding international responsibility are also applicable to international organizations.[90] It follows that the United Nations may incur international responsibility for acts attributable to it, if and when those acts are inconsistent with its international obligations. Additionally that means that the United Nations can invoke the international responsibility of other subjects of international law whenever it is affected by such other subjects/ breaches of obligations.

This possibility of the United Nations acquiring the right to invoke responsibility for breaches of obligation is not restricted to invoking the responsibility of its own members, but also extends to non-member States and to other international organizations. This latter option, invoking the responsibility of other international organizations, may be thought to be quite logical in view of the possibility of the conclusion of treaties between international organizations. If such a treaty is concluded and only organizations may become parties to it, then only organizations that have become a party to it may acquire the right to demand performance of the obligations contained in the treaty. In such a case the decision to exercise the organization/s rights under the treaty will of course be subjected to the constituent instrument/s procedures.

The first possibility, invoking the responsibility of non-member States, may be thought to have been conspicuously approved by the Court in its Reparation Opinion. What is most important about that opinion is the fact that the Court envisaged a right to demand the performance of obligation of non-member States, thus implying that the United Nations could acquire rights, and eventually exercise them, under rules of customary international law. Of course the Court did not indicate any basis of obligation for the non-member State in question, and expressly denied any analogy to rules of customary international law regarding the treatment of aliens. But the fact is that the basis of obligation for non-member States could not be found in any treaty, which only left a basis of obligation under rules of customary international law.

As to the exact limits of the possibility of the United Nations to invoke rights under rules of customary international law, it may first of all be pointed out that the United Nations is not in possession of a general or common interest regarding the performance of obligations by its members or by non-members. It would seem to follow that the United Nations could only claim a legal interest if it, as an organization, was (or would be) affected by a particular breach of obligation. The United Nations being affected by a particular breach of obligation could only happen in a situation in which the United Nations in fact engaged in activities covered by the subject-matter of the particular rule laying down the obligation. As examples of rules being applicable to the United Nations, and which consequently could give rise to rights for the United Nations, one could mention the customary rules of humanitarian law. But that is not where it ends. One could, for instance, envisage the United Nations owning boats or ships, and registering them at the United Nations Headquarters. In such a case the United Nations could provide diplomatic protection to ships under its flag in instances where those ships engage in activities on the high seas on an equal footing with States. In all such situations the rules laying down the correlative rights of States, discussed in chapter one, ought to be applied analogously to the United Nations.

2.6. The United Nations, obligations *erga omnes* and the distinction between international delicts and international crimes

In the introduction to this chapter the present writer has indicated the belief that if obligations *erga omnes* are to be considered obligations towards the international community, then obligations towards the community ought not only be seen in terms of obligations towards States, but in terms of obligations towards an international organization, that is, towards the United Nations.[91] Before that it had been found, in chapter one, that the serious breach of obligations laid down by peremptory norms may entail the label of international crime, which, according to article 5, paragraph 3, Part Two, of the ILC-draft, entails injured State status for all States.[92] In that line of thought it would follow that a legal interest pursuant to the commission of an international crime would not only accrue to all States, but also to the United Nations. It has been claimed in the past that the United Nations has jurisdiction over international crimes,[93] and more particularly that:[94]

> "Under article 19 (...) an international crime would involve the breach of an obligation towards the international community as represented by the United Nations."

Thus an obligation *erga omnes*, which in the words of the Court entails a legal interest for all States, would also entail a legal interest for the United Nations. However, that conclusion is not as clear-cut as could be thought. Now Riphagen quite correctly observes:[95]

> "Article 19 of part 1 of the draft also seems to presume that an international crime, in the sense of para. 2 of that article, may not be at the same time 'a serious breach of an international obligation of essential importance for the maintenance of international peace and security/ in the sense of para. 3, under (a)."

He then gives a follow-up to this remark by stating his inclination to a positive answer to the question whether or not the international community as a whole, by recognizing certain conduct as a crime, should be considered to have declared applicable the procedures contained in the Charter for collective decision making.[96] Since the possibility for collective *decision* making in the Charter is, generally speaking, the competence of the Security Council (article 25), one may assume that Riphagen/s stance boils down to the, in his report unsubstantiated, assertion that each and any international crime amounts, at the very least, to a threat to the peace. That assertion warrants, indeed requires, further scrutinization.

First of all it may be said that the competence of the Security Council in the field of peace and security is not determined by customary international law, nor generally by conventional sources, but by the Charter. Thus Riphagen/s remark that, *unless a contrary intention is clearly established*, the international community in recognizing particular conduct as a crime should be considered to have declared applicable Security Council procedures, fails to convince.[97] In analogy to existing rules regarding the creation of rights for third States or international organizations (articles 36 of the Vienna Conventions) it would seem rather that parties to a particular treaty (in this case a future convention on State responsibility) should express their intention to establish Security Council competence regarding international crimes.[98] Given the absence of a convention on State responsibility at present, the applicability of Security Council procedures regarding threats to the peace to international crimes could only be based on customary international law. It would seem to be required therefore to establish the existence of a general practice, accepted as law, to the effect that certain breaches of obligations by States which, in abstracto, are recognized as international crimes will generally be considered threats to the peace by the Security Council.

In subsections 2.4.1 and 2.4.2 the conclusion was reached that the United Nations in general, and the Security Council in particular, could not be considered to be in possession of a general or common interest in the performance of obligations by members or non-members. This means that the United Nations cannot claim to possess a legal interest regarding just any breach of obligation by its members. The more specific question needs to be raised if a serious breach of an obligation essential for the protection of the fundamental interests of the international community gives rise to an independent legal interest on the part of the United Nations. The connected question to be answered also is whether a committed international crime vests, *ipso facto*, the competence of the Security Council under article 39 of the Charter. The Security Council may, for one reason or another, refrain from adopting any decision under Chapter VII. In the second place will be discussed therefore which effects accrue to recommendations adopted by either the General Assembly or the Security Council.

2.6.1. THE UNITED NATIONS/ LEGAL INTEREST CONSEQUENT UPON THE COMMISSION OF AN INTERNATIONAL CRIME AND THE COMPETENCE OF THE SECURITY COUNCIL UNDER ARTICLE 39 OF THE CHARTER

The United Nations' legal interest regarding the maintenance of international peace and security and the competence of the Security Council under article 39 of the Charter

That the General Assembly may act in relation to situations in which States threaten or use force may be seen from the texts of articles 10, 11 and 14 of the Charter. Thus it may discuss and make recommendations regarding any matter within the scope of the Charter and regarding questions related to the maintenance of international peace and security brought before it by States or the Security Council, and it may recommend the adjustment of situations resulting from violations of articles 1 and 2 of the Charter. It has, furthermore, considered itself competent, by way of resolution 377 (V), to recommend measures, including the use of armed force in relation to situations constituting breaches of the peace or acts of aggression, if the Security Council, due to the lack of unanimity among permanent members, fails to exercise its primary responsibility.[99] The Security Council has accepted such competence, since in accordance with the terms of article 12, paragraph 1, of the Charter, it has called for emergency sessions of the Assembly, as provided in resolution 377, in order to make the appropriate recommendations.[100]

There can be no doubt as to the competence of the Security Council in the field of maintenance of international peace and security. The Charter is first of all focused on the peaceful settlement of disputes between States, and secondly, should peaceful settlement have failed, on the maintenance or restoration of international peace and security. In order to achieve the latter the Security Council has been endowed with the competence, under article 39 of the Charter, to determine the existence of a threat to the peace, breach of the peace, or act of aggression.[101] Should such threats to the peace, breaches of the peace, or acts of aggression not be brought to an end through the voluntary action of those capable of doing so, the Security Council has been given the power to call upon its members to apply the measures of article 41,[102] to take military action under article 42,[103] or as has been the case lately to authorize the use of armed force.[104] In addition it may be noted that decisions of the Security Council under articles 39, 41 and 42 (insofar as the Security Council has at its disposal the military means to resort to action under article 42) are binding on members, since they have agreed, under article 25, to accept them and carry them out.

Taking a look now at article 19, paragraph 3 (a), Part One, of the ILC-draft, it is to be noted that an international crime may result from *a serious breach* of an obligation essential to the maintenance of international peace and security, *such as that prohibiting aggression.* Comparing that provision with the competence of the Security Council under article 39, one cannot but acknowledge that the competence of the Security Council is not restricted to serious threats to the peace, serious breaches of the peace, or serious acts of aggression. On the assumption that a serious breach of an obligation essential for the maintenance of international peace and security means a breach of obligation under article 2, paragraphs 3 and 4, of the Charter, one could assert that there is not even a perfect correlation between threats of States to use force and threats to the peace. Apparently there may be threats to the peace without there even being a State using, or threatening to use, force against another State.

The reference to the rule prohibiting aggression should furthermore not be understood to be a reference to "aggression" in a general sense, as in the General Assembly resolution on the Definition of Aggression, but to the idea of aggression as an international crime, *e.g.* aggression as an armed attack. Indeed the Commission observed in relation to the criterion of seriousness that article 39 of the Charter differentiates between threats to the peace, breaches of the peace, and acts of aggression.[105] The Court, in the Nicaragua Case, furthermore distinguished:[106] "(...) the most grave forms of the use of force (*those constituting an armed attack*) from other less grave forms." Certainly minor breaches, such as clashes along the borders, cannot be considered to constitute the crime of aggression. It may be recalled that intent and premeditation should be considered a constituent element of any international crime (chapter one, subsection 1.9.2).

In view of the above arguments it is clear that the competence of the Security Council is beyond doubt with regard to international crimes involving the use of force, and that it is not limited to armed attacks as the most serious breaches possible under article 2, paragraphs 3 or 4.

The United Nations' legal interest regarding the safeguarding of the right of self-determination of peoples and the competence of the Security Council under article 39 of the Charter

The principle of self-determination of peoples does have a place within the Charter. Thus article 1, paragraph 2, of the Charter states one of the purposes of the Charter to be the development of friendly relations among nations based on respect for the principle of self-determination of peoples. This phrase then reappears in article 55 of the Charter, with regard to which article 56 provides that members pledge to take joint and separate action in co-operation with the United Nations for the achievement of the purposes of article 55. Though these two provisions would not seem to lay down any specific competence of the United Nations to concern itself with issues of self-determination, Chapters XI and XII of the Charter clearly envisage a substantial role of the United Nations in regard to the principle involved.

Article 76 (b) provides that one of the objectives of the Trusteeship System is to promote self-government or independence for territories placed under trust. The move towards the progressive development of self-government or independence is to be attained in accordance with the freely expressed wishes of the peoples concerned.

Chapter XI of the Charter, headed "Declaration regarding Non-Self-Governing Territories", provides in article 75 that members which are responsible for such a territory shall promote the well-being of the inhabitants, and that to that end they are to develop self-government and to assist them in the progressive development of their free political institutions. While not making any express reference to the "freely expressed wishes of the peoples concerned", one may assume that the provision, by mentioning free political institutions, intended the territories concerned to also attain, possibly, independence.

The General Assembly eventually adopted resolution 1514 (XV) in which it declared that:[107] "All peoples have the right to self-determination; by virtue of that right they freely determine their political status and freely pursue their economic, social and cultural development." It continued by declaring that immediate steps were to be taken to transfer all powers to the peoples living in Trust Territories and Non-Self-Governing Territories. As a follow-up the 1966 Covenants on Civil and Political Rights and on Economic, Social and Cultural Rights, drawn up by the Assembly, both copied the formulation of resolution 1514 (XV) in their common article 1.[108]

The Security Council has concerned itself with issues of self-determination when discussing certain situations or disputes. In this context it has made references to self-determination in a number of resolutions,[109] and to elections and the like in others. In some cases it has determined a threat to the peace under article 39 of the Charter.[110]

As to these resolutions it may be noted that in five cases the Security Council resorted to the indication of measures under article 41 of the Charter,[111] and in five others it called upon or authorized the use of armed force.[112] However, some of the resolutions related to tense relations between certain specific States. One may note that the situation regarding Jammu and Kashmir relates to a dispute between India and Pakistan. Whereas the situation regarding the Western Sahara concerned Spain, Morocco and Mauritania. And the situation in Cyprus relates to the United Kingdom, Greece and Turkey. In none of these situations did the Council decide on measures. The situations

in the Congo, the former Yugoslavia, Somalia, Rwanda and Angola are all complicated by civil war and widespread human suffering. The cases of Rhodesia, South Africa, and Haiti would seem to be the only ones where the Council has acted upon some notion of self-determination. The first two situations were accompanied by armed acts, the second moreover by institutionalized racial discrimination, whereas the latter involved a refugee flow to the United States thus causing tension. The Security Council decided on a broad range of measures against Rhodesia, including a limited use of force, on a broad arms embargo against South Africa, and a broad range of measures against Haiti followed by an authorization to use force.
Though the Security Council has clearly felt itself empowered to discuss the situations concerned, one cannot escape the conclusion that a denial by one State of the right of self-determination of a people living in a territory under its administration will not inevitably result in the existence of a threat to the peace. The most that can be said is that the competence of the Security Council under article 39 will probably be established if the denial of self-determination coincides with actual fighting going on within the territory concerned or tense relations between specific States.

The Commission may have realized as much, because it did not merely provide that a serious breach of an obligation essential for the safeguarding of the right of self-determination constituted an international crime. On the contrary. It added, in the sentence mentioning the examples, that the establishment or maintenance of colonial domination should be "by force". However, in its commentary on article 19 the Commission explained:[113]

> "The expression 'by force/ should be understood as meaning against the will of the subject population, even if that will is not manifested, or has not yet been manifested, by armed opposition."

By using the expression "by force", while in the commentary adding that this is to mean against the will of the population, the Commission somewhat creates confusion. In the minds of most scholars the term "force" is nowadays closely identified to that contained in article 2, paragraph 4, of the Charter. In that provision it is generally interpreted as meaning armed or military force. When using the expression in article 19, paragraph 3 (b), of Part One of the draft, the Commission appears to suggest that for an international crime to be present there must be a use of armed force against either the population or the liberation movement of the territory under control. Following up on this line of thought it may be said that such a use of force, while technically speaking not of international character, could lead to the existence of a threat to the peace.[114] It may be noted in this connection that the Security Council has, on occasion, called upon a certain State to cease colonial wars,[115] and has recognized, in that context, the legitimacy of the struggles of peoples or liberation movements.[116] Indeed, the Security Council has gone even further than that, urging members:[117]

> "(...) to render moral and material support to the people of Southern Rhodesia in their struggle to achieve their freedom and independence."

But although the Security Council has called upon States to implement the right of self-determination with regard to peoples under their domination, it has generally refrained from determining the existence of a threat to the peace followed by mandatory sanctions under article 41 of the Charter or the use of force (with the obvious exception of Rhodesia, the less obvious example of South Africa, and the clear case of Haiti). The call for material support to peoples struggling for independence cannot, as such, be interpreted as an absolute call for military support for liberation movements.[118]

In the absence of any military confrontation between the colonizing State and a liberation movement, or forceful repression of the population itself, or tense relations between certain interested States, the competence of the Security Council under article 39 will not *ipso facto* be established regarding the crime of denial of self-determination of peoples.

The United Nations' legal interest regarding the safeguarding of the human being and the competence of the Security Council under article 39 of the Charter

The expression "human rights", as is the case with the phrase "self-determination of peoples", is mentioned a number of times in the Charter. Thus the preamble affirms "faith in fundamental human rights, in the dignity of the human person, in the equal rights of men and women (...)." Article 1, paragraph 1, of the Charter, as one of the purposes of the United Nations, then mentions the need to "achieve international co-operation (...) in promoting and encouraging respect for human rights and for fundamental freedoms for all without distinction as to race, sex, language, or religion;" And in Chapter IX the Charter provides in article 55, under (c), that the United Nations shall promote "universal respect for, and observance of, human rights and fundamental freedoms for all without any distinction as to race, sex, language, or religion." Article 56 is again relevant, since it provides that all members "pledge to take joint and separate action in co-operation with the Organization for the achievement of the purposes set forth in Article 55." Responsibility for the discharge of the functions under Chapter IX lies with the General Assembly and, under the authority of the General Assembly, with the Economic and Social Council (article 60). And finally,[119] article 62, paragraph 2, observes that the Economic and Social Council may make "recommendations for the purpose of promoting respect for, and observance of, human rights and fundamental freedoms for all."[120]

A milestone in the development of the field of human rights constituted the adoption, by the General Assembly, of the 1948 Universal Declaration of Human Rights.[121] Considering the legally non-binding nature of recommendations, irrespective of the names given to them, of the General Assembly, the logical follow-up was the preparation of a draft convention on human rights. That follow-up was realized in 1966, at which time the General Assembly adopted the International Covenant on Civil and Political Rights, and the International Covenant on Economic, Social and Cultural Rights. Apart from these general conventions on human rights the General Assembly has adopted a number of conventions related to the protection of specific groups of persons,[122] or with regard to protection against violations of specific human rights.[123]

Regarding the protection of human rights it may also be noted that the Economic and Social Council adopted resolution 1235, in 1967, which authorized the Human Rights Commission and its Sub-Commission on Prevention of Discrimination and Protection of Minorities to "examine information relevant to gross violations of human rights and fundamental freedoms, as exemplified by the policy of *apartheid* as practised in the Republic of South Africa (...) and racial discrimination as practised notably in Southern Rhodesia, (...)." Later on it decided, in resolution 1503 of 1970, to authorize the Sub-Commission on Prevention of Discrimination and Protection of Minorities to institute a working group that was to examine communications, including replies by governments, that apparently revealed a consistent pattern of gross and reliably attested violations of human rights.

The Security Council has, in a number of resolutions, issued certain demands or calls regarding (violations of) human rights, and in that context has made references to instruments for the protection of human rights. In some of the relevant resolutions the Security Council has considered certain acts or situations capable of endangering the peace, disturbing the peace (etc.). In regard to a number of cases the Security Council has actually determined, under article 39 of the Charter, the existence of a threat to the peace, or referred to Chapter VII.[124]

First of all it may be noted, with regard to the resolutions determining the existence of a threat to the peace, that they were increasingly followed by measures under article 41, especially arms embargoes, and authorizations to use force. Taking a closer look at the situations underlying the particular resolutions, one has to come to the conclusion that in most of them the human rights performance was not of primary concern to the Security Council.

Thus the situation in Congo was marked by the occurrence of a civil war, interference by certain States, and the absence of rule of law, generally, in Congo.[125]

In regard to Rhodesia there can be no doubt that what was at stake was its people/s right to self-determination.[126] Indeed the resolution in which the Security Council censured human rights violations in Rhodesia was not the first to determine a threat to the peace in that regard.[127] It may furthermore be observed that a denial of self-determination will almost inevitably lead to a situation in which the civil and political rights of individuals will be violated.

The determination of a threat to the peace with regard to the situation prevailing in and around South Africa was focused on the military build-up by South Africa and its repeated acts of aggression against neighbouring States.[128] Even if one were to consider the aggression aspects subordinate to the context of human rights violations,[129] still it may be pointed out that these human rights violations could be considered incidental to South Africa/s refusal to allow the South African people to decide freely its own future. Thus the issue would be reduced to one of self-determination (as is not too unlikely in the light of some Security Council resolutions to that effect).[130]

The situation regarding Iraq/s repression of Kurds in the northern parts of its territory appears to present a more plausible example of the Security Council/s involvement with human rights violations. Yet the way in which the issue was phrased in the preambular parts of resolution 688 may raise doubts as to such involvement:

> "*Gravely concerned* by the repression of the Iraqi civilian population in many parts of Iraq, including most recently in Kurdish populated areas which led to a massive flow of refugees towards and across international frontiers and to cross border incursions, which threaten international peace and security in the region,"

And in the first paragraph the Security Council condemned Iraq/s repression of its population, including the Kurds, the *consequences* of which threatened international peace and security. Arguably it was not Iraq/s repression of its population that threatened international peace and security, but the fact that such repression led to a cross-border flow of refugees and cross-border incursions.

Insofar as the situation in the former Yugoslavia is concerned, the main origin of the human rights violations taking place there lie with the occurrence of the civil war. That civil war, in turn, was due to the revival of the national (and nationalistic) aspirations of the peoples living within the former Yugoslavia. While a large part of the Security Council/s attention has been devoted to the inhuman practices of some (or all) of the parties concerned, one has to acknowledge that its main concern has been to ensure the cessation of fighting and the achievement of peaceful solutions to the crisis.[131] In the same vein it may be observed that the Security Council/s resolution determining the existence of a threat to the peace was adopted over seven months earlier than its resolution calling upon parties to ensure cessation of forcible expulsions and attempts to alter the demographic circumstances of particular areas in the former Yugoslavia.[132]

The situations of Somalia, Liberia, Georgia, Angola and Rwanda, may all be characterized as civil wars. The Security Council/s concern with the cases of Liberia, Angola, and Georgia cannot be said to be based on human rights issues.[133] The examples of Somalia and Rwanda on the other hand are based on human rights concerns. However, though the Council eventually took effective action for humanitarian relief in Somalia,[134] it failed to take effective action in regard to the genocide in Rwanda.[135]

That leaves the situation in Haiti which has effectively been dealt with. Yet there the human rights at stake were the civil and political rights of the Haitian people. Though the *de facto* régime engaged in repression of the population, it would rather seem that the issue at stake was one of ongoing self-determination, that is, exclusion of an elected government, rather than human rights.[136]

As to the works of the Commission, it cannot be ignored that it seems to take as a basis the distinction between certain classes of human rights obligations.[137] Indeed, in the Barcelona Traction Case the Court observed that obligations *erga omnes* derive, among others, from the principles and rules concerning the "basic" rights of the human person.[138] Which rights were to be considered basic was not exactly specified by the Court, though it mentioned that they included protection from slavery and racial discrimination (before its mention of basic rights of the human person it had made a reference to the prohibition of genocide). Thus the main core of human rights obligations would lie with the right to life (and probably the right not to be subjected to torture and cruel, inhuman or degrading treatment), the right not to held in slavery, and the right to equality before the law.

An interesting feature of article 19, paragraph 3 (c), that ought to be discussed, concerns the fact that it derogates from the usual formula adopted with regard to the other examples. Thus it specifies that the serious breaches must not only concern obligations essential for the safeguarding of the human being, but that they must be committed *on a widespread scale*. In its commentary on article 19 the Commission observed that this phrase should be read to mean that:[139]

> "(...) for a breach to be characterized as an international crime, (...), it must take the form of a large-scale or systematic practice adopted in contempt of the rights and dignity of the human being."

The Commission further explained that the purpose of the qualification was not to extend beyond what was reasonable the category of international crimes, and to keep in line with the rules of international law then in force.[140] Although one could imagine this addition to reflect a quantitative standard, it appears rather to represent a qualitative condition. For especially if the breaches of human rights obligations may be said to constitute systematic practices perpetrated by the government responsible for law and order within the State, it becomes clear that the acts and omissions of that government are not merely attributable to the State, but that such acts or omissions are engaged in with intent. It would be well to relate this issue to article 56 of the Charter, in which members pledge to take joint and separate action, in co-operation with the United Nations, for the achievement of the purposes laid down in article 55. One of the purposes of article 55 is universal respect, and observance of, human rights and fundamental freedoms. Any member that engages in systematic practices of human rights violations cannot be considered to have lived up to its obligation under article 56 of the Charter.

By way of conclusion it cannot be said that the Security Council has taken breaches of obligations for the protection of human rights as the decisive or sole basis of its decisions under article 39. However, the possibility of the Security Council determining the existence of a threat to the peace on the ground of systematic human rights violations cannot wholly be discarded. The practice of the Security Council up to date, with regard to human rights violations, does bear witness to an increased vigilance on its part, but its action has not exactly been effective.

In sum it may be said that the United Nations will be in possession of a legal interest consequent upon the commission of an international crime. It cannot be said however that the practice of the Security Council shows the consistency necessary to conclude to the existence of a rule of customary international law indicating that an international crime will *ipso facto* be considered a threat to the peace under article 39 of the Charter.

2.6.2. THE EFFECTS OF RECOMMENDATIONS ADOPTED BY THE GENERAL ASSEMBLY AND THE SECURITY COUNCIL

Another question to be asked, and this brings us in fact to the issue of consequences, is what the effect is that may be brought about by resolutions of the General Assembly or Security Council, pursuant to the United Nations/ legal interest, phrased by way of recommendation. On that account it may be noted, preliminary, that the Court, in its Namibia Opinion, took a broad stance with regard to the General Assembly/s powers:[141]

> "This is not a finding on facts, but the formulation of a legal situation. For it would not be correct to assume that, because the General Assembly is in principle vested with recommendatory powers, it is debarred from adopting, in specific cases within the framework of its competence, resolutions which make determinations or have operative design."

Although eventually the Court proceeded with its opinion on the basis of its assessment that the Security Council had made an article 24 binding declaration of illegality, it may be observed that the opinion is also based on the finding that the General Assembly had legitimately terminated the Mandate. And the above quotation appears to lead

to the conclusion that such termination by the General Assembly had binding effect for United Nations members.[142] The observations of the Court are furthermore based on the premise that the United Nations was in law the successor of the League in respect of the Mandate agreement for South West Africa, and that therefore the General Assembly, when faced with breaches of a fundamental character by South Africa, acted as a party in terminating the Mandate agreement.[143] As such one ought to take as a guideline, as the Court did, the provisions of the 1969 Vienna Convention on the Law of Treaties in regard to material breaches of treaties.[144]
Article 60 makes provision for a State party to invoke a material breach of a treaty as a ground for suspending or terminating it in whole or in part. If a party actually invokes article 60 it has to, in accordance with article 65, send a notification to all the other parties stating the measures to be adopted and the reasons therefor. If no other party objects, within three months, to the adoption of such measures those can be carried out. If any objection is raised within that period the parties concerned must seek, within twelve months, a peaceful solution to their dispute in accordance with article 33 of the Charter of the United Nations. And finally article 66 provides, if the attempt to arrive at a peaceful solution fails, that an obligatory conciliation procedure will be utilized. The outcome of that procedure, as the Annex states in its sixth paragraph, is not binding on the parties and conclusions drawn by the conciliation commission are to be considered of recommendatory character only.
It follows from these procedures that eventually any party wishing to invoke a material breach as a ground for terminating a treaty will not be bound by any conclusions as to facts or law established by the Conciliation Commission. It also shows that ultimately a party terminating a treaty does so without any judicial determination having been made regarding the existence of an (alleged) material breach.[145]

Since in this case the United Nations, and not its members as such, was considered to be a party to the mandate agreement, the United Nations naturally could act as a party on the subject of treaty termination. And because the United Nations may avail itself, in certain circumstances, of the right of terminating a treaty, the obvious conclusion must be that, once exercised, the individual United Nations members will become bound by the act of treaty termination. The Court, in its Namibia Opinion, laid down the consequences (obligations) for United Nations members (and in this particular case even for non-members) of a binding declaration of illegality by the United Nations. Basically those could be said to reflect a duty of non-recognition, and a duty to abstain from support or assistance, with regard to South Africa/s illegal occupation of Namibia.[146]

Generally speaking the powers which the General Assembly possesses are of recommendatory character only. There are but few examples that witness a power of the General Assembly to issue resolutions that will bind United Nations members. As such the question may be asked whether the consequences that are normally attached to a declaration of illegality contained in a binding resolution of the General Assembly or Security Council will ensue also if the resolution concerned cannot be considered to contain decisions, but recommendations of those organs only. Recommendations of the General Assembly, or even the Security Council, so it is recognized, do not create obligations for United Nations members. And though it might be said that United Nations members are under an obligation to consider, in good faith, whether or not to take the action recommended by one of those organs, still they would not be obliged, in law, to act in accordance with the recommendation.[147] To the extent however that the General Assembly and the Security Council would not be acting in their capacity of representing the organization, that is as an independent subject of international law, the conclusion cannot be the same. Even if the United Nations would be acting in the exercise of a right to demand performance of certain specific obligations, and in furtherance of that cause determines the existence of a breach of obligations by members or non-members,[148] that alone would not make it a decision of the United Nations binding the members. Thus the fact that the United Nations would authoritatively determine the existence of a breach of obligation by a member or non-member would not entail the obligation for members or non-members to recognize the illegality of the acts or situation concerned and to refrain from support or assistance in respect of those acts. As recommendatory resolutions of the General Assembly or the Security Council do not create obligations to act in accordance with them, mere declarations of illegality, which do not require any further action, also do not acquire binding force.

At this junction it may be noted that the Court not only justifies its conclusions regarding non-recognition by reference to the Charter, but also by reference to general international law.[149] It may be doubted whether general international law, customary international law that is, contains a general obligation for States not recognize certain (allegedly illegal) acts or situations. Since most of international law is dispositive in character States may eradicate the illegality of certain acts or situations by concluding a treaty to that effect, or by not invoking and executing the responsibility of the author State. That circumstance is fortunately mitigated because of the existence of the well known maxim that nobody can transfer more rights than it possesses. Thus a decision of a State not to invoke the responsibility of another State will only affect its own right to demand the performance of the obligations breached, and will obviously not affect other States/ rights. To put it in more concrete terms, one State/s recognition does not, indeed cannot, wipe out the illegality of the acts or situation concerned.[150] There does exist an obligation not to recognize any acquisition of territory effected through the use of force.[151] Furthermore, Arangio-Ruiz has proposed in relation to crimes to stipulate an obligation for States, subject to a prior determination of the existence of a crime by the Court, not to recognize as legal a situation created by a crime.[152]

The picture is somewhat different insofar as aid or assistance is concerned. The common yardstick in this regard would appear to be article 27, Part One, of the ILC-draft on State Responsibility, which provides:[153]

> "Aid or assistance by a State to another State, if it is established that it is rendered for the commission of an internationally wrongful act carried out by the latter, itself constitutes an internationally wrongful act, even if, taken alone, such aid or assistance would not constitute the breach of an international obligation."

Although this provision appears to narrow down the options open to States for rendering aid or assistance to States committing internationally wrongful acts, the commentary to article 27 offers certain clarifications that limit considerably its impact. The Commission explains that the sentence "if it is established that it is rendered for the commission of an internationally wrongful act" lays down the condition of intent on the part of the providing State.[154] Intent in this context means that the aid or assistance must have been rendered so as to facilitate the commission of the internationally wrongful act.[155] This in turn means that it is not enough that a State providing aid or assistance is aware that it could be used (eventually) for unlawful purposes,[156] but rather that it should have knowledge of the intention of the receiving State to use such aid or assistance for the commission of an internationally wrongful act. Furthermore, as the commentary points out, intent on the part of the providing State must be established and cannot be presumed.[157] Arangio-Ruiz has quite rightly proposed, in his latest report, an article 18, paragraph 1 (b), Part Two, to place States under the obligation, subject to a prior determination of the existence of a crime by the Court, to abstain from any act or omission which may assist the wrongdoing State in maintaining the situation created by a crime.[158]

To come back now to the issue under consideration, the legal effect of General Assembly or Security Council recommendations, if a declaration of illegality is contained in a non-binding resolution States will generally have to consider in good faith whether or not that declaration is justified in fact and law. It may be assumed that both facts and law will be (well) documented, and that therefore no State will be able to assert ignorance as to the essentials. In the light of such knowledge all States will have to determine their position with regard to the allegations made, and if they find the allegations to have been true they will have to draw the consequences. They will have to refrain from giving aid or assistance for the purpose of facilitating the commission of further internationally wrongful acts. That is of course not to say that a State which finds the allegations to be unfounded can legitimately provide aid or assistance in support of the acts concerned. In the absence of binding decisions by competent organs each State determines for itself its legal position. But whether or not such position is correct must be evaluated in the light of the facts of the case and the law applicable to such facts. A State that finds certain acts of another State to be lawful may be found wrong in its evaluation, and if it has given aid or assistance to that other State in support of future acts (pursuant to its perception that previous acts had been lawful), it will be found to have committed its very own internationally wrongful act.

2.7. Summary

The reference in the Barcelona Traction Case to obligations towards the international community as a whole must be read in the light of the Court/s other claims, namely that they are the concern of all States and that all States can be held to have a legal interest in their protection. The question whether there exists a personified international community depends on the degree of institutionalization of international relations. Due to the intricate and complex character of the relations between any community and its members, a personified international community must be based on a treaty régime intended to form the basis of a universal international organization. To the extent that certain members of the international community decline to take up membership in the organization, a personified international community may have to rely on those universal rules of customary international law substantially identical to the treaty rules. However, the fact that non-members are bound by such universal rules of customary international law does not mean that the organization can *ipso jure* claim the performance of obligations under such rules. The United Nations is the only organization that could credibly make a claim to constitute a personified community, and its international personality constitutes the key to the investigation of its legal interests.

As a subject of international law the United Nations possesses international legal personality. This means that it may possess the right to demand the performance of obligations by both members and non-members. However, the United Nations, as it is not a State, cannot *ipso jure* be considered to claim rights under customary international law. However, it can also not be considered bound to customary international law in the same way. On the basis of the argument that an organization cannot do what the members cannot do individually, the United Nations is bound by universal rules of customary international law. States are however free, generally, to change international legal rules in their *inter se* relations. An illustration of this is constituted by the prohibition of the use of force in the Charter, because States can only use force lawfully in case of defence against an armed attack, whereas the Security Council can use force if it determines the existence of a threat to the peace.

As to the criteria to determine the United Nations/ legal interest in the performance of obligations by States, it cannot be said that the United Nations, and more particularly the Security Council, is in possession of a general interest to that effect. Though the latter can claim the performance of obligations through its powers under article 39 of the Charter, it can do so only if it determines the existence of a threat to the peace. That phrase can be interpreted objectively in the sense that a threat to the peace must concern a situation that could lead to a breach of the peace. The United Nations also cannot be considered to possess a common interest in the performance of obligations. Although it is bound by the universal rules of customary international law, limitations of a functional nature prevent it, generally, from claiming the performance of obligations under such rules. For analogous reasons such obligations cannot be said to be performed towards the United Nations. However, if the United Nations engages in activities ordinarily engaged in by States, and suffers prejudice as a result of breaches of obligation by States, it will be in possession of a legal interest in relation to the author State.

Other bases of legal interests exist for the United Nations. In circumstances in which the Charter envisages sanctions, basically articles 5, 6 and 39 to 42, the United Nations must be considered to possess a legal interest regarding breaches of obligation by members. The United Nations may further possess a legal interest regarding breaches of obligations under treaties to which it is a party. A legal interest must generally be denied to the United Nations regarding breaches of obligations under treaties to which it is not a party. Only if the treaty concerned envisages specific rights for the United Nations regarding the supervision or the implementation of the treaty could any question of legal interest arise. To the extent that the United Nations is affected by breaches of obligations under rules of customary international law, it will possess a legal interest regarding such breaches. In this light the United Nations may be entitled to claim the performance of obligations even in respect of other international organizations and non-member States.

The United Nations is necessarily in possession of a legal interest regarding the crime of aggression. Furthermore, the competence of the Security Council under article 39 of the Charter is present regarding any situation involving a threat or use of force contrary to article 2, paragraphs 3 and 4.

The United Nations is in possession of a legal interest regarding the crime of denial of self-determination. However, the Commission has explained that the phrase "by force" applicable to the example of colonial domination mentioned in article 19, paragraph 3 (b), Part One, means against the will of the population even if that will is not manifested by armed opposition. Viewed also in that light, it cannot be said that the Security Council has generally considered itself competent under article 39 of the Charter regarding the crime of denial of self-determination. To the extent that the crime of denial of self-determination is accompanied by military confrontation between a government and armed opposition, by forceful repression of the population, or by tense relations between interested States, Security Council competence under article 39 will be established.

The United Nations is in possession of a legal interest consequent upon the commission of the crime of widespread breaches of basic human rights obligations. The resolutions in which the Security Council has concerned itself with the crime of widespread breaches of basic human rights obligations do not reveal, however, that it will inevitably consider that crime a threat to the peace.

Resolutions of the General Assembly or the Security Council phrased by way of recommendation do not carry with them any obligation to act in accordance with them. However, if one of those organs determines a breach of obligation, and demands the performance of obligations by an author State, other States are put on guard and cannot claim ignorance regarding the factual and legal situation. Should States on their own evaluation of the facts and the law provide aid or assistance to the author State with a view to facilitating the commission of further (wrongful) acts, they will commit their own internationally wrongful acts.

NOTES

[1] The 1969 Vienna Convention on the Law of Treaties, 63 AJIL 1969, pp. 875-903.

[2] Even this is qualified to a large degree by the finding, in chapter one, that the texts of articles 65 and 66 of the Vienna Convention, read in conjunction, lead to the conclusion that only the States parties to the disputed treaty may bring the dispute before the Court. Apparently the States parties to the Vienna Convention themselves cannot do so, which limits of course considerably the scope of article 66.

[3] Text and Commentary Article 19, Part One, YBILC 1976, Volume II, Part Two, pp. 95-122.

[4] Barcelona Traction, Light and Power Company, Limited, Judgment, ICJ Reports 1970, p. 3, 32.

[5] Kelsen asserts that States resorting to decentralized enforcement measures may be considered to be acting as organs of the international community constituted by international law. See Kelsen, H., Principles of International Law, Rinehart & Company Inc., New York, 1952 (Third Printing 1959), 13-14 and 25.

[6] Article 190 of the 1957 Treaty establishing the European Economic Community, 51 AJIL 1957, pp. 865-937.

[7] Text and Commentary Article 1, Part One, YBILC 1973, Volume II, pp. 173-176, 175.

[8] Arangio-Ruiz, G., Seventh Report on State Responsibility, 24 May 1995, A/CN.4/469/Add.1, 4 pp., 4. Arguments and motivation in Seventh Report on State Responsibility, 9 May 1995, A/CN.4/469, 49 pp., 25-49.

In favour of such course of action Dupuy, P.-M., Observations sur le "crime international de l'etat", 84 RGDIP 1980, pp. 449-486, 484-485.

[9] The 1945 Charter of the United Nations, 39 AJIL 1945, Supplement, pp. 190-215.

[10] Ago, R., Obligations *Erga Omnes* and the International Community, in Weiler, J., Spinedi, M., and Cassese, A. (Eds.), International Crimes of State: A Critical Analysis of the ILC's Draft Article 19 on State Responsibility, Walter de Gruyter, Berlin, 1989, pp. 237-239, 238. Also Ago, R., The International Community and International Organizations, in Dupuy, R.-J. (Ed.), Handbook on International Organizations, Martinus Nijhoff Publishers, Dordrecht, 1988, pp. 3-12.

[11] As noted in chapter one, subsection 1.8.1, considering the French text, the protection to be granted refers back to the rights mentioned, not to obligations *erga omnes*.

[12] Barcelona Traction Case, Judgment, 32.

[13] Ago, R., Second report on State responsibility, YBILC 1970, Volume II, pp. 177-197, 184. Footnote omitted.

[14] It is to be noted that the Court in paragraph 34 of the Barcelona Traction Case after mentioning general international law makes a reference to its opinion on the Genocide Convention. The reference is to Reservations to the Convention on Genocide, Advisory Opinion, ICJ Reports 1951, p. 15, at 23. One may assume that the Court therefore wanted to refer to the phrase that the obligations contained in the Genocide Convention were binding on States even in the absence of any conventional undertaking.

[15] Note Seidl-Hohenveldern, I., Das Recht der Internationalen Organisationen einschließlich der Supranationalen Gemeinschaften, Dritte, vermehrte Auflage, Carl Heymanns Verlag KG, Köln, 1979, 87-88. One may note that Riphagen observes that an organized international community need not be a universal one. Riphagen, W., Third report on the content, forms and degrees of international responsibility (part 2 of the draft articles), YBILC 1982, Volume II, Part One, pp. 22-50, 39.

[16] Reference may be made here to the findings of the Court in the Nicaragua Case to the effect that the rules of customary international law on the use of force are not fully identical to those contained in the United Nations Charter. Military and Paramilitary Activities in and against Nicaragua (Nicaragua *v.* United States of America), Merits, Judgment, ICJ Reports 1986, p. 14, 93-94. It argued, furthermore, that the respective rules of customary and treaty origin applied autonomously, and that the inapplicability of the treaty rule does not have as effect that the customary rule also becomes inapplicable. *Ibid.*, 94-96. The autonomous application of rules of customary international law, assuming these to be universally binding on the members of the international community, thus remedies the lack of universal membership.

[17] C.f. Annacker, C., The Legal Régime of *Erga Omnes* Obligations in International Law, 46 AJPIL 1994, pp. 131-166, 157.

[18] Reparation for injuries suffered in the service of the United Nations, Advisory Opinion, ICJ Reports 1949, p. 174, 178-179.

[19] Reparation Opinion, 178.

[20] Reparation Opinion, 178-179.

[21] Reparation Opinion, 178. Just before this sentence the Court posed the question: "(...) whether the Charter has given the Organization such a position that it possesses, in regard to its Members, rights which it is entitled to ask them to respect."

[22] Reparation Opinion, 178.

[23] Reparation Opinion, 179.

[24] Reparation Opinion, 181-182.

[25] On organizations and responsibility see Eagleton, C., International Organization and the Law of Responsibility, 76 RDC ADI 1950-I, pp. 319-425; Butkiewicz, E., The Premisses of International Responsibility of Inter-Governmental Organizations, 11 PYIL 1981-1982, pp. 117-140; Meng, W., Internationale Organisationen im völkerrechtlichen Deliktsrecht, 45 ZAORV 1985, pp. 324-357; Perez Gonzalez, M., Les organisations internationales et le droit de la responsabilité, 92 RGDIP 1988, pp. 63-102; and Zacklin, R., Responsabilite des organisations internationales, in SFDI, Colloque Du Mans, La responsabilité dans le système international, Editions A. Pedone, Paris, 1991, pp. 91-100. Generally on international organizations Riphagen, W., Over concentratie en delegatie bij internationale instellingen, in *Varia Juris Gentium*, Questions of International Law, Liber Amicorum presented to Jean Pierre Adrien François, A.W. Sijthoff, Leyden, 1959, pp. 229-253; Schermers, H., Inleiding tot het Internationale Institutionele Recht, Kluwer, Deventer, 1983; Lukashuk, I., International Organizations and the Functioning of International Law, 24 IJIL 1984, pp. 68-76; Morgenstern, F., Legal Problems of International Organizations, Grotius Publications Limited, Cambridge, 1986.

[26] Articles 2, paragraph 2, 6, and 14 mention respect for obligations under the Charter and the violation of provisions setting forth the purposes or principles of the Charter. It is noticeable further that the Court did not refer directly to these articles, and furthermore failed to point to articles 39, 41, 42 and 51 which could be considered, at the least implicitly, to touch on questions of responsibility.

[27] Reparation Opinion, 185.

[28] Question One posed to the Court ran: "In the event of an agent of the United Nations in the performance of his duties suffering injury in circumstances involving the responsibility of a State, has the United Nations, as an Organization, the capacity to bring an international claim against the responsible *de jure* or *de facto* government with a view to obtaining the reparation due in respect of the damage caused (*a*) to the United Nations, (*b*) to the victim or to the persons entitled through him?" Reparation Opinion, 176-177.

[29] Reparation Opinion, 180, 181-182.

[30] Reparation Opinion, 182.

[31] Reparation Opinion, 183. The Court also referred to the fact that some of the undertakings of the members had been made in complementary agreements.

[32] Reparation Opinion, 185.

[33] Reparation Opinion, 181-182.

[34] Bleckmann, A., Zur Verbindlichkeit des allgemeinen Völkerrecht für internationale Organisationen, 37 ZAORV 1977, pp. 107-121, 113-116, claims that the binding character of rules of customary international law for international organizations could be based on analogies with rules binding on States insofar as the circumstances under which those rules apply are pertinent. Also Tunkin, G., The Legal Bases of International Organization Action, in Dupuy, R.-J., A Handbook on International Organizations, pp. 261-276.

[35] See articles 34 and 35 of the Vienna Convention. Judge Krylov observed that in order for non-member States to be bound by a legal obligation (even if such States could not fail to recognize the existence of the United Nations as an objective fact), the United Nations and those States ought to have concluded a general or special agreement. Dissenting Opinion Krylov, Reparation Opinion, 217 and 218-219.

[36] Reparation Opinion, 179.

[37] Reparation Opinion, 180. Emphasis added. Judge Hackworth endorsed the Court's view that the United Nations could bring claims for damage suffered by the organization. He criticized the Court for assuming the existence of an implied power with regard to the espousal of private claims, since he considered that power not to be necessary to the exercise of powers expressly granted. Dissenting Opinion Hackworth, *ibid.*, 198. Judge Badawi Pasha observed that international persons are deemed to exist only for the benefit of States that signed and ratified or acceded to its constitutions. Dissenting Opinion Badawi Pasha, *ibid.*, 205. He also denied the United Nations the possibility of endorsement of private claims. *Ibid.*, 213-216.

[38] Argument to be found with Morgenstern, Legal Problems, 32. One may note that Bleckmann observes (Zur Verbindlichkeit, 118), discussing the question whether any difference exists between organizations with or without legal personality, that: "Die Mitgliedstaaten, die durch eine internationale Organisation mit eigener Rechtspersönlichkeit handeln, dürfen aber vom Völkerrecht nicht anders gestellt sein, als wenn sie außerhalb der internationalen Organisation oder innerhalb einer internationalen Organisation ohne Rechtspersönlichkeit handeln. Der »Schleier« der juristischen Person muß insoweit durchstoßen werden. Die »Flucht in die internationale Organisation« zur Umgehung des Völkerrechts muß verbaut werden."

[39] Only references in the Charter to international law are discussed and the references to justice will not. That is because justice is in fact not a legal concept and may stand in opposition to international law. Kelsen, H., The Law of the United Nations, A Critical Analysis of Its Fundamental Problems, Stevens & Sons Limited, London, 1951, 15-18; Fitzmaurice, G., The Foundations of the Authority of International Law and the Problem of Enforcement, 19 MLR 1956, pp. 1-13, 12-13; and Aulagnon, L., Aperçus sur la force dans la regle de droit, in Mélanges en l'honneur de Paul Roubier, volume 1, Théorie générale du droit et droit transitoire, Librairies Dalloz & Sirey, Paris, 1961, pp. 29-37, 35-37.

[40] It is of course well known that the Assembly, in order to implement this latter provision, has initiated the establishment of the International Law Commission as one of its subsidiary organs. And this study largely focuses on the outcome produced by that Commission. See United Nations, The Work of the International Law Commission, Fourth Edition, New York, 1988.

[41] South West Africa, Second Phase, Judgment, ICJ Reports 1966, p. 6, 34.

[42] South West Africa Cases, Second Phase, 34. Kelsen's view is that a preamble may contain obligations insofar as sanctions would be attached to the violation of such obligations. He agrees however on the non-binding nature of the preamble of the Charter. Kelsen, The Law of the United Nations, 9-10.

[43] The provision of article 19 regarding the loss of the right to vote in case of failure to pay the contribution due to the United Nations will not be discussed separately, since the sanction of the loss of the right to vote is foreseen as the sanction for the violation of a specific kind of obligation and therefore has no relevance for the

question of a general legal interest in possession of the United Nations. The same argument furthermore counts for the provision of article 102, paragraphs 1 and 2. On these issues Kelsen, The Law of the United Nations, respectively 717-720 and 721-724.

[44] Note also the arguments found in Schermers, Inleiding, 58.

[45] The term sanction is used in the most general way, and encompasses, here, both measures by States and international organizations. See *infra* chapter four.

[46] Schütz, H.-J., Article 5, in Simma, B. (Ed.), The Charter of the United Nations, A Commentary, Oxford University Press, Oxford, 1994, pp. 175-185, 177-181. Though he states that in some cases it seems justified to accept a recommendation as "action" within the meaning of article 5. *Ibid.*, 180.

[47] Notably Gowlland-Debbas, V., Collective Responses to Illegal Acts in International Law, United Nations Action in the Question of Southern Rhodesia, Martinus Nijhoff Publishers, Dordrecht, 1990, 452; Sur, S., La résolution 687 (3 avril 1991) du Conseil de Securité dans l'affaire du Golfe: Problèmes de rétablissement et de garantie de la paix, 37 AFDI 1991, pp. 25-97, 41; and Combacau, J., Le pouvoir de sanction de l'O.N.U., Étude théorique de la coercition non militaire, Editions A. Pedone, Paris, 1974, 93. The latter notes that in practice the United Nations has always justified resort to the measures under article 41 by reference to the violation of a pre-existing obligation.

[48] Gowlland-Debbas, Collective Responses, 452; Sur, La résolution, 41. Gowlland-Debbas has stated in a later publication that insofar as the determination of an internationally wrongful act forms a constituent part of the Council's determination of a threat to the peace it could be reviewed as to its factual and legal basis. Gowlland-Debbas, V., Security Council Enforcement Action and Issues of State Responsibility, 43 ICLQ 1994, pp. 55-98, 97-98.

[49] Gowlland-Debbas, Collective Responses, 451-452. Boldness in the original; footnote omitted. Repeated in Gowlland-Debbas, Security Council Enforcement, 61 and 71-72. In the same sense McDougal, M., and Reisman, W., Rhodesia and the United Nations: The Lawfulness of International Concern, 62 AJIL 1968, pp. 1-19, 8; Ruzié, D., Organisations internationales et sanctions internationales, Librairie Armand Colin, Paris, 1971, 87; and Sinclair, I., State Responsibility and the Concept of Crimes of States, in Weiler *et al*, International Crimes of State, pp. 223-225, 224. This was also the stance taken by the United States in the Nicaragua Case, Merits, 27. Annacker, The Legal Régime, 157, claims that the determination of threats to the peace is left to the discretion of the Security Council, and that any situation so characterized by the Council must be considered a threat to the peace.

[50] Gowlland-Debbas, Collective Responses, 452. See also Gowlland-Debbas, Security Council Enforcement, 72, 74, and 97-98.

[51] Gaja, G., Reflexions sur le role du Conseil de Securite dans le nouvel ordre mondial, A propos des rapports entre maintien de la paix et crimes internationaux des Etats, 97 RGDIP 1993, pp. 297-320, 315 claims, as a first hypothesis, that a determination that a threat to the peace exists poses questions of an essentially political order, and that the Court could only exercise any control if it qualifies the determination as arbitrary. A second hypothesis concerns the situation where the Security Council would determine the existence of a violation of an obligation, in which case the Court could exercise full control and declare, on the basis of legal and factual considerations, that the violation does not exist. In agreement, as to the second hypothesis, Gowlland-Debbas, Security Council Enforcement, 97-98.

[52] Admission of a State to the United Nations (Charter, Art. 4), Advisory Opinion, ICJ Reports 1948, p. 57, 64.

[53] Certain expenses of the United Nations (Article 17, paragraph 2, of the Charter), Advisory Opinion, ICJ Reports 1962, p. 151, 155. See also Admission Opinion, 61.

[54] Nicaragua Case, Merits, 26.

[55] Nicaragua Case, Merits, 27.

[56] Nicaragua Case, Merits, 103-104 and 110-111.

[57] Nicaragua Case, Merits, 29-38.

[58] C.f. Frowein, J., Article 39, in Simma, The Charter, pp. 605-616, 609-610.

[59] Article 1 of General Assembly resolution 3314 (XXIX) defines aggression as follows: "Aggression is the use of armed force by a State against the sovereignty, territorial integrity or political independence of another State, or in any manner inconsistent with the Charter of the United Nations, as set out in this Definition."

[60] C.f. Halderman, J., Some Legal Aspects of Sanctions in the Rhodesian Case, 17 ICLQ 1968, pp. 672-705, 692; and Gaja, Reflexions, 301: "Le Chapitre VII n'a pas été écrit pour donner au Conseil de sécurité une compétence dans n'importe quelle matière. Il ne semble pas que la notion de menace à la paix puisse être dissociée de l'existence du risque d'un conflit armé international. (...) Encore faut-il que le risque d'un conflit soit véritablement pris en considération par le Conseil et qu'il ne soit pas un prétexte invoqué pour lui permettre d'exercer des pouvoirs qui ne lui auraient pas été attribués." However, after examining the practice of the Security Council (302-307), he concludes (307): "Il semble toutefois que les résolutions du Conseil

s'inscrivent dans la tendance à utiliser en fait une notion de menace contre la paix qui, (...), n'a pas un rapport étroit avec le risque d'un conflit armé international. Cette tendance trouve surtout sa raison d'être dans l'exigence de répondre à des violations d'obligations essentielles pour la société internationale."

[61] See the discussion of the issue of whether article 94, paragraph 2, enlarges the competence of the Security Council in Goodrich, L., and Hambro, E., Charter of the United Nations, Commentary and Documents, Second and Revised Edition, Stevens & Sons Limited, London, 1949, 486-487; Kelsen, The Law of the United Nations, 540-544 and 721; Pillepich, A., Article 94, in Cot, J.-P., and Pellet, A. (Eds.), La Charte des Nations Unies, Commentaire article par article, 2e édition, revue et augmentée, Economica, Paris, 1991, pp. 1275-1285, 1276; and Mosler, H., Article 94, in Simma, The Charter, pp. 1003-1007, 1005-1007. All four appear to be of the view that article 39 need not be applied by the Security Council before resorting to the measures envisaged in article 94.

[62] Argument referred to by Giraud, E., Le droit international public et la politique, 110 RDC ADI 1963-III, pp. 419-809, 682.

[63] Argument of Pasvolsky, quoted by Goodrich and Hambro, Charter of the United Nations, 486.

[64] And contrary to what has been asserted by Kelsen the Security Council cannot endorse the position of the party that fails to honour its obligations under the judgment. Kelsen, The Law of the United Nations, 539-541. In agreement on the position taken here Klein, E., Paralleles Tätigwerden von Sicherheitsrat und Internationalem Gerichtshof bei Friedensbedrohenden Streitigkeiten, Zu Fragen der Zuständigkeit und Organtreue, in Bernhardt, R. (Ed.), Völkerrecht als Rechtsordnung – Internationale Gerichtsbarkeit – Menschenrechte, Festschrift für Hermann Mosler, Springer-Verlag, Berlin, 1983, pp. 468-491, 489-490.

[65] But note the example of the use of force discussed in the final paragraph of section 2.3.

[66] Meng, W., Die Kompetenz der EWG zur Verhängung von Wirtschaftssanktionen gegen Drittländer, 42 ZAORV 1982, pp. 780-803, 795-796.

[67] Reparation Opinion, 182.

[68] See generally Schachter, O., The Quasi-Judicial Role of the Security Council and the General Assembly, 58 AJIL 1964, pp. 960-965; and Higgins, R., The Place of International Law in the Settlement of Disputes by the Security Council, 64 AJIL 1970, pp. 1-18.

[69] The competence of the General Assembly under article 11 is however restricted by the fact that: "Any such question on which action is necessary shall be referred to the Security Council by the General Assembly either before or after discussion." Article 12, paragraph 1, furthermore provides that: "While the Security Council is exercising in respect of any dispute or situation the functions assigned to it in the present Charter, the General Assembly shall not make any recommendation with regard to that dispute or situation unless the Security Council so requests."

[70] Terms of settlement in this context may be taken to mean that the Security Council may propose that a specific solution be adopted for the settlement of the dispute in question. Higgins, The Place of International Law, 8-9, 11-13, and 16. Note that she envisages the Security Council recommendation as to the terms of settlement of a dispute to be in conformity with international law principles.

[71] Reparation Opinion, 179.

[72] Reparation Opinion, 179.

[73] That the bases of claims were different was acknowledged by the Court. Reparation Opinion, 186.

[74] Reparation Opinion, 185.

[75] Although it may be noted in relation to that opinion that the right of the United Nations to invoke the arbitration clause rested upon a potential breach of obligations rather than on an actual breach of obligations by the United States. Applicability of the Obligation to Arbitrate under Section 21 of the United Nations Headquarters Agreement of 26 June 1947, Advisory Opinion, ICJ Reports 1988, p. 12, 28-30. On the relation between breaches of obligations and disputes regarding the interpretation or application of the agreement see Separate Opinion Schwebel, *ibid.*, 51.

[76] Headquarters Agreement Opinion, 28.

[77] See generally United Nations, The Work of the International Law Commission.

[78] Confirmed rather implicitly by Sur, La résolution, 59.

[79] The fact that such a body may function within the system of the United Nations appears not to influence her stance that the organization has no legal interest. Morgenstern, Legal Problems, 115-117.

[80] The 1986 Vienna Convention on the Law of Treaties between States and International Organizations or between International Organizations, 25 ILM 1986, pp. 543-589.

[81] And it can only be applied analogously since the situation discussed here, a right arising for the United Nations with regard to a treaty between States, is not covered by the convention. It only applies to treaties between States and international organizations or to treaties between international organizations (article 1 (a)).

[82] Genocide Convention Opinion, 20. It also observed on page 19: "It is indeed beyond dispute that the General Assembly, which drafted and adopted the Genocide Convention, and the Secretary-General, who is the depositary of the instruments of ratification and accession, have an interest in knowing the legal effects of reservations to that Convention and more particularly the legal effect of objections to such reservations."

[83] Genocide Convention Opinion, 19.

[84] Genocide Convention Opinion, 19.

[85] Note also for instance article 10 of the Non-Proliferation Treaty which provides that notice of a withdrawal shall be communicated to the States parties and to the Security Council. See the 1968 Traité sur la non-prolifération des armes nucléaires, 73 RGDIP 1969, pp. 248-253.

[86] C.f. Cassese, A., La communaute internationale et le genocide, in Le droit au service de la paix, de la justice et du développement, Mélanges Michel Virally, Éditions A. Pedone, Paris, 1991, pp. 183-194, 185, who notes that military measures against a responsible State can only be adopted by the Security Council if the genocide constitutes a threat to the peace, act of aggression, or breach of the peace.

[87] Contrary to what has been claimed the registration of a treaty in accordance with article 102, paragraph 1, of the Charter does not lead to a competence of the Security Council to impose respect of the treaty. Weckel, P., Le Chapitre VII de la Charte et son application par le Conseil de Sécurité, 37 AFDI 1991, pp. 165-202, 182, footnote 54.

[88] Sur, La résolution, 59. Footnote omitted.

[89] Tunkin, The Legal Bases, 261-262.

[90] Butkiewicz, The Premisses, 117-122.

[91] Note the remark made by a member of the Commission, in the 1994 discussion, to the effect that: "(...) in the case of an international crime, the victim was the community of States as a distinct legal entity and that the concept of international crimes helped to promote the international community to the status of, as it were, a quasi-public legal authority." See Report of the International Law Commission on the work of its forty-sixth session, 2 May – 22 July 1994, General Assembly, Official Records, Forty-ninth Session, Supplement No. 10 (A/49/10), 335. Note also the opinions expressed at 340-341, 346, 349-354, 359-362.

[92] One has to keep in mind here that a certain breach of obligation is not an international crime because the obligation concerned is of *erga omnes* character, but because the obligation concerns the fundamental interests of the international community and is recognized as such by States. For a reversal of cause and effect in this context see Ushakov, YBILC 1981, Volume I, 142.

[93] Riphagen, W., Fourth report on the content, forms and degrees of international responsibility (part 2 of the draft articles), YBILC 1983, Volume II, Part One, pp. 3-24, 11. He adds that this does not necessarily mean that an international crime constitutes a threat to the peace, breach of the peace, or act of aggression under article 39 of the Charter. *Ibid.*, 11-12. In Riphagen's opinion one consequence of jurisdiction of the United Nations over international crimes is that the commission of an international crime cannot constitute a matter essentially within the domestic jurisdiction of a State under article 2, paragraph 7, of the Charter. *Ibid.*, 12. It is difficult to see any ratio for the consideration that the essence of United Nations jurisdiction over international crimes means that the acts concerned are not within the domestic jurisdiction of a State. Difficult to see because what is, and what is not, within the domestic jurisdiction of a State depends on whether or not the acts in question are covered by existing rules of international law. Thus any breach of an international obligation means that the conduct in question is not within the domestic jurisdiction of States. Most members did not express any opinion on United Nations jurisdiction over international crimes. The American member of the Commission adopted Riphagen's position regarding United Nations jurisdiction over international crimes, and indeed envisaged the applicability of Chapter VII to all international crimes. McCaffrey, YBILC 1983, Volume I, 142-143. Only one member doubted Riphagen's position of United Nations jurisdiction over all the international crimes listed in article 19. Sinclair, *ibid.*, 131. See also the critical observations regarding the Security Council functioning on the basis of a veto power for only a few States. Díaz González, *ibid.*, 148. In relation to Riphagen's next report the Soviet member expressed the view that all international crimes should be regarded as detrimental to international peace and security, and claimed that only the international community could take measures. Ushakov, YBILC 1984, Volume I, 277-278. See also Quentin-Baxter, *ibid.*, 306; Malek, *ibid.*, 310-311; McCaffrey, *ibid.*, 313; Balanda, *ibid.*, 315; and Riphagen, *ibid.*, 317. In his commentary on article 14 Riphagen insists on the exercise of rights, in case of international crimes, by injured States in the context of the organized international community. Riphagen, W., Sixth report on the content, forms and degrees of international responsibility (part 2 of the draft articles); and "Implementation" (*mise en oeuvre*) of international responsibility and settlement of disputes (part 3 of the draft articles), YBILC 1985, Volume II, Part One, pp. 3-19, 14. Reuter asserts that the phrases "organized international community" (the United Nations) and "international community as a whole" do not quite coincide. Reuter, YBILC 1985,

Volume I, 94. See also McCaffrey, *ibid.*, 96 and 98; Ogiso, *ibid.*, 122; Tomuschat, *ibid.*, 127; Barboza, *ibid.*, 132; Díaz González, *ibid.*, 133; Malek, *ibid.*, 147-148; Arango-Ruiz, *ibid.*, 150.

[94] Calle y Calle, YBILC 1980, Volume I, 87. Other references to obligations towards the international community are Schwebel, YBILC 1980, Volume I, 92; Evensen, *ibid.*, 94. See also Riphagen, *ibid.*, 81 and 97. In agreement with Calle y Calle, Graefrath, B., Völkerrechtliche Verantwortlichkeit für internationale Verbrechen, in Graefrath, B. (Ed.), Probleme des Völkerrechts, Akademie-Verlag, Berlin, 1985, pp. 89-110, 104; Mohr, M., The ILC's Distinction between "International Crimes" and "International Delicts" and its Implications, in Spinedi, M., and Simma, B. (Eds.), United Nations Codification of State Responsibility, Oceana Publications, Inc., New York, 1987, pp. 115-141, 126-127; and Quigley, J., The International Law Commission's Crime-Delict Distinction: A Toothless Tiger?, 66 RDISDP 1988, pp. 117-161, 134-137.

[95] Riphagen, Third Report, 45. Similarly Bindschedler, R., Völkerrechtliche Verantwortlichkeit als Verbrechen, in Dutoit, B., and Grisel, E. (Eds.), Mélanges Georges Perrin, Diffusion Payot, Lausanne, 1984, pp. 51-61, 60, who claims that the Charter would have to be amended to cover the other international crimes.

[96] Riphagen, Third Report, 45. In a footnote (142) he adds that in this respect there is no need for formal amendment of the Charter. In the commentary on his proposed article 6 he mentions that one cannot exclude the occurrence of situations in which an international crime will not involve the maintenance of international peace and security. After that he claims: "The definition of 'international crime' in article 19, paragraph 3, part 1 of the draft articles implies that the international community as a whole is injured by such wrongful act. It may therefore be presumed that the organized international community, that is, the United Nations Organization, has a role to play in determining the special legal consequences entailed by such act, even if the maintenance of international peace and security is not considered to be involved." Riphagen, Third Report, 48. One may note that he nowhere explains in detail what kind of other role could be played by the United Nations in determining the special legal consequences of an international crime that does not involve the maintenance of international peace and security. On page 49 he merely mentions that States, by recognizing certain breaches of obligation as crimes, accept a role of the organized international community, and that the United Nations has been involved in some way or another with all the examples mentioned in article 19, paragraph 3. An important remark on his count is that such role of the United Nations need not be based on the Charter, and he mentions the case of Namibia as an example for that position.

[97] Riphagen, Third Report, 45.

[98] A perfect example of such conferred, extra-Charter, competence may be found in article 11 of the 1958 Convention on Fishing and Conservation of the Living Resources of the High Seas, in which the powers of the Security Council under article 94, paragraph 2, are declared applicable to decisions of a special commission established under articles 9 and 10 of the aforementioned Convention. Text in 52 AJIL 1958, pp. 851-858.

[99] General Assembly resolution 377 (V), Uniting for Peace.

[100] See Security Council resolutions 119, 120, 129, 157, 303, 462, 500, 571, 572, 573, 577, 580, and 612.

[101] See the following resolutions of the Council making initial determinations regarding the use of armed force (reaffirmations omitted): 54 (Palestine); 82 (Koreas); 502 (Argentina-United Kingdom); 598 (Iraq-Iran); 660 (Iraq-Kuwait); arguably 713 (Yugoslavia); arguably 733 (Somalia); 748 (Libya); 757 (former Yugoslavia); 788 (Liberia); arguably 858 (Georgia); 864 (Angola); and arguably 918 (Rwanda).

[102] Note the following resolutions on measures under article 41 in response to situations involving recourse to armed force: arguably 418 (South Africa); 661 (Iraq-Kuwait); 670 (Iraq-Kuwait); 687 (Iraq-Kuwait); 713 (Yugoslavia); 748 (Libya); 787 (former Yugoslavia); 788 (Liberia); 820 (former Yugoslavia); 864 (Angola); 883 (Libya); arguably 918 (Rwanda); and 942 (former Yugoslavia).

[103] Arguably resolution 161 (Congo).

[104] See the following resolutions: arguably 665 (Iraq-Kuwait); 678 (Iraq-Kuwait); arguably 787 (former Yugoslavia); arguably 794 (Somalia); 817 (former Yugoslavia); 836 (former Yugoslavia); 908 (former Yugoslavia); arguably 929 (Rwanda); 958 (former Yugoslavia); and 981 (former Yugoslavia).

[105] Commentary Article 19 Part One, 121.

[106] Nicaragua Case, Merits, 101.

[107] General Assembly resolution 1514 (XV), Declaration on the granting of independence to colonial countries and peoples.

[108] The 1966 International Covenant on Civil and Political Right, 61 AJIL 1967, pp. 870-887; and the 1966 International Covenant on Economic, Social and Cultural Rights, 61 AJIL 1967, pp. 861-870.

[109] See the following resolutions (reaffirmations omitted): 163, 180, 290, 302, and 322 (Portuguese domination over certain (specific) African territories); 202 (Rhodesia); 246 (Namibia); 377 (Western Sahara); 384 (East Timor); 417 (South Africa); 668 (Cambodia), 956 (Palau). Note also the vaguely phrased resolutions 713 and 724 regarding the situation in the former Yugoslavia.

[110] Resolutions: 161 (Congo); 221 (Rhodesia); 353 (Cyprus); 713 (former Yugoslavia); arguably 733 (Somalia); 864 (Angola); 886 (Somalia); 917 (Haiti). Arguably it did so with regard to certain Portuguese actions in Africa (resolutions 290 and 302).

[111] Resolutions: 232 (Rhodesia); 713 (Yugoslavia); 733 (Somalia); 864 (Angola); 917 (Haiti). As the Security Council terminated, in resolution 919, the arms embargo against South Africa, it referred to the establishment of a united, democratic, non-racial government.

[112] See the following resolutions: 221 (Rhodesia); 794 (Somalia); 816 (former Yugoslavia); 836 (former Yugoslavia); 908 (former Yugoslavia); arguably 917 (Haiti); 929 (Rwanda); 940 (Haiti); 958 (former Yugoslavia); 981 (former Yugoslavia). A salient detail regarding resolution 221 may be found in that, at that moment, the Security Council had not yet imposed mandatory sanctions with regard to the territory of Southern Rhodesia.

[113] Commentary Article 19, Part One, 121.

[114] If one were to consider the dominated territory and its people to constitute a new or incipient State, one might even consider the use of force by the colonial State an international use of force. See particularly Ago, R., Fifth report on State responsibility, YBILC 1976, Volume II, Part One, pp. 3-54, 35 (footnote 171) and 37. In resolution 290 the Security Council came no further than a declaration that Portuguese colonialism on the African continent was a serious threat to the peace and security of *independent* African States.

[115] *E.g.* resolution 312.

[116] Resolution 312 regarding Portuguese colonies (reaffirmed in resolution 322); resolution 232 regarding Southern Rhodesia (reaffirmed in resolutions 253, 328, 386, 403, 411, 424, 445 and 448); resolution 269 regarding Namibia (reaffirmed in resolutions 301, 428, 447 and 566); resolution 282 regarding South Africa (reaffirmed in resolutions 417, 473, 554, 556 and 591).

[117] Resolution 253 (reaffirmed in resolutions 277 and 411). With regard to the people of Namibia see resolution 269 (reaffirmed in resolution 566).

[118] Cassese discusses the issue from a somewhat different angle, and observes that liberation movements have the right to use force in search for the implementation of the right to self-determination since such use of force would not constitute a breach of the international prohibition on the use of force. As regards the support which may be lent to liberation movements he then claims that third States can only give various forms of support and that they cannot use force themselves (he adds that third States have the right to resort to peaceful countermeasures). Cassese, A., Remarks on the Present Legal Regulation of Crimes of States, in Etudes en l'honneur de Roberto Ago, Le droit international à l'heure de sa codification, volume III, Giuffrè, Milano, 1987, pp. 49-64, 51-54, and especially note 1.

[119] A further reference to human rights may be found in article 76, sub (c), of the Charter, regarding the objectives of the trusteeship system.

[120] Article 62 does not state with regard to which entity the recommendations may be made, but paragraph 1 of the article also provides that recommendations may be directed towards members. Paragraph 3 on the other hand provides that the Economic and Social Council may prepare draft conventions for submission to the General Assembly.

[121] Universal Declaration of Human Rights, General Assembly resolution 217 (III). It may be noted that a number of European States took the initiative, as a follow-up, of concluding the 1950 Convention for the Protection of Human Rights and Fundamental Freedoms, 45 AJIL 1951, Supplement, pp. 24-39. More slowly the American States adopted the 1969 American Convention on Human Rights, 65 AJIL 1971, pp. 679-701; and some time after that the African States adopted the 1981 African Charter on Human and Peoples' Rights, 21 ILM 1982, pp. 59-68.

[122] The 1951 Convention relating to the Status of Refugees, 63 AJIL 1969, pp. 389-407; the 1979 Convention on the Elimination of All Forms of Discrimination against Women, adopted by way of General Assembly resolution A/RES/34/180, reprinted in 19 ILM 1980, pp. 34-45; and the 1989 Convention on the Rights of the Child, adopted by way of General Assembly resolution A/RES/44/25, reprinted in 28 ILM 1989, pp. 1456-1476.

[123] The 1948 Convention on the Prevention and Punishment of the Crime of Genocide, adopted by way of General Assembly resolution 260 (III), reprinted in 45 AJIL 1951, Supplement, pp. 7-10; the 1956 Convention supplémentaire relative à l'abolition de l'esclavage, de la traite des esclaves, et des institutions et pratiques analogues à l'esclavage, 61 RGDIP 1957, pp. 137-142; the 1966 International Convention on the Elimination of All Forms of Racial Discrimination, adopted by way of General Assembly resolution 2106 (XX), reprinted in 60 AJIL 1966, pp. 650-661; the 1973 International Convention on the Suppression and Punishment of the Crime of *Apartheid*, adopted by way of General Assembly resolution 3068 (XXVIII), reprinted in 13 ILM 1974, pp. 51-57; and the 1984 Convention against Torture and Other Cruel, Inhuman or Degrading

Treatment or Punishment, adopted by way of General Assembly resolution A/RES/39/46, reprinted in 23 ILM 1984, pp. 1027-1037, and 24 ILM 1985, pp. 535-536.

[124] Resolutions: 161 B (Congo); 253 (Rhodesia); 418 (South Africa); arguably 688 (Iraq); 733 (Somalia); 757 (former Yugoslavia); 788 (Liberia); 841 (Haiti); arguably 858 (Georgia); arguably 864 (Angola); 918 (Rwanda).

[125] In resolution 161 B the Security Council called for the convening of the Congolese parliament. Note especially resolutions 145 and 146 which respectively call upon the government of Belgium to withdraw its troops from Congo, and from the province of Katanga in particular. The latter resolution is intriguing in that it makes a reference to articles 25 and 49 without determining a threat to the peace under article 39. A further reference to article 25 without determining a threat to the peace concerns resolution 269.

[126] Note especially resolutions 202, 216 and 217 regarding the potential and actual unilateral declaration of independence.

[127] See especially earlier resolutions 221 and 232.

[128] The first paragraph of resolution 418 states that: "(...) the acquisition by South Africa of arms and related *matériel* constitutes a threat to the maintenance of international peace and security;"

[129] Which is arguable since the acts of aggression committed by South Africa were to some degree the result of operations carried out by liberation movements from the territory of neighbouring States.

[130] Resolutions 417 and 556.

[131] See particularly resolutions 713, 724 and 743.

[132] See resolution 713 adopted on 25 September 1991 and resolution 752 adopted on 15 May 1992.

[133] Resolutions 788 (Liberia); 858 (Georgia); 864 (Angola).

[134] Resolutions 733 and 794 (Somalia).

[135] Resolutions 918 and 929 (Rwanda).

[136] Resolutions 841, 873, 875, 917 and 940 (Haiti).

[137] Generally Meron, T., On a Hierarchy of International Human Rights, 80 AJIL 1986, pp. 1-23.

[138] Barcelona Traction Case, Judgment, 32.

[139] Commentary Article 19, Part One, 121.

[140] Commentary Article 19, Part One, 121.

[141] Namibia Opinion, 50. The first sentence of the quotation refers to the declaration of the General Assembly to the effect that the Mandate had been terminated, and that South Africa had no other right to administer the Territory. Note further that in the French text the word "determinations" is translated as "décisions" (the English text is authoritative though).

[142] On this account the Court observed that the United Nations, as a successor to the League, had the right to act in respect of serious breaches of the mandatory's obligations, and that the mandatory's consent to termination could not be required. Namibia Opinion, 49.

[143] See Namibia Opinion, 45-51.

[144] The Court stated: "The rules laid down by the Vienna Convention on the Law of Treaties concerning termination of a treaty relationship on account of breach (...) may in many respects be considered a codification of existing customary law on the subject. Namibia Opinion, 47.

[145] Riphagen notes that the Court, in the Namibia Opinion, fails to take into account the existence of the procedural requirements of the Vienna Convention. Riphagen, W., The Legal Consequences of Illegal Acts under Public International Law (Advisory Opinion I.C.J. of June 21, 1971), 20 NTIR 1973, pp. 27-36, 29. He is undoubtedly correct on that score. But the procedural requirements do not alter the conclusion that the termination of a treaty rests upon some unilateral decision to that effect. Whether or not termination is legitimately resorted to depends on whether or not substantive rules (article 60 Vienna Convention) have been complied with (especially the material breach condition). The provisions of the Vienna Convention on the Law of Treaties between States and International Organizations or between International Organizations, which provides for (in article 66) resort to the advisory jurisdiction of the Court (the opinion to be accepted as decisive by the parties), had, at the time of rendering of the Namibia Opinion, not even come into existence.

[146] The Court first stated that States were under the obligation to recognize the illegality and invalidity of South Africa's presence in Namibia. Secondly, it laid down the obligation to refrain from support or assistance to South Africa regarding such occupation. A third obligation concerned the duty not to enter into treaty relations with South Africa in so far as it purported to act on behalf of Namibia, and to abstain from applying treaties which involve active inter-governmental co-operation in regard to Namibia. Fourthly, it deduced the obligation not to send diplomatic and consular missions to Namibia, and to make clear that maintenance of diplomatic or consular relations with South Africa did not involve recognition of South Africa's authority over Namibia. Finally the Court concluded that States were under the obligation to abstain from entering into

economic and other forms of relationship that could affirm South Africa's authority over Namibia. Namibia Opinion, 54-55.

[147] Separate Opinion Klaestad, South West Africa-Voting Procedure, Advisory Opinion, p. 67, 88. See also Separate Opinion Lauterpacht, *ibid.*, 115-121 (especially 118-119).

[148] Note Zoller, E., Peacetime Unilateral Remedies: An Analysis of Countermeasures, Transnational Publishers, Inc., Dobbs Ferry, New York, 1984, 112 (more broadly 110-112).

[149] Namibia Opinion, 55.

[150] C.f. Dissenting Opinion Skubiszewski, Case concerning East Timor, Judgment, 30 June 1995, paragraphs 116 and 122-133.

[151] C.f. Dissenting Opinion Skubiszewski, East Timor Case, paragraphs 122-133 and 163; and certain opinions expressed within the Commission, in Commission Report 1994, 355.

[152] Article 18, paragraph 1 (a), Part Two, in Arangio-Ruiz, Seventh Report, Addendum 1, 3; commented upon in Arangio-Ruiz, Seventh Report, 23-24.

[153] Text and Commentary Article 27, Part One, YBILC 1978, Volume II, Part Two, pp. 98-105. Originally Ago, R., Seventh report on State responsibility, YBILC 1978, Volume II, Part One, pp. 31-60, 52-60. Generally Klein, E., Beihilfe zum Völkerrechtsdelikt, in Münch, I. von (Ed.), Staatsrecht – Völkerrecht – Europarecht, Festschrift für Hans-Jürgen Schlochauer, Walter de Gruyter, Berlin, 1981, pp. 425-438; and Quigley, J., Complicity in International Law: A New Direction in the Law of State Responsibility, 57 BYBIL 1986, pp. 77-131.

[154] Commentary Article 27, Part One, 104. For exactly this reason rightly criticized by Graefrath in relation to the crime of *apartheid*. Graefrath, B., Verantwortlichkeit und Wiedergutmachung bei Apartheidverbrechen, 35 NJ 1981, pp. 115-117, 115-116.

[155] Commentary Article 27, Part One, 104.

[156] Commentary Article 27, Part One, 104.

[157] Commentary Article 27, Part One, 104.

[158] Arangio-Ruiz, Seventh Report, Addendum 1, 3. Based partly on Riphagen's proposed article 14, paragraph 2, Part Two. Riphagen, W., Fifth report on the content, forms and degrees of international responsibility (part 2 of the draft articles), YBILC 1984, Volume II, Part One, pp. 1-4, 4. Note further Arangio-Ruiz' proposals (*ibid.*) to insert obligations in article 18, Part Two, to the effect that States should: assist each other regarding non-recognition and abstention from assistance to the author State (paragraph 1 (c)); refrain from hindering the exercise of rights under articles 16 or 17 (paragraph 1 (d)); fully implement the prosecute or extradite principle (paragraph 1 (e)); take part in any lawful measure decided or recommended by an international organization of which they are members (paragraph 1 (f)); facilitate the adoption and implementation of any lawful measure intended to remedy any emergency situations caused by the crime (paragraph 1 (g)).

CHAPTER 3

THE OBLIGATION OF AN AUTHOR STATE TO PROVIDE REPARATION, AND THE CORRESPONDING RIGHT OF (AN) INJURED STATE(S) AND THE UNITED NATIONS TO DEMAND SUCH REPARATION, IN CASE OF INTERNATIONAL CRIMES

3.1. Introduction

The Commission, commenting on the use of the term "international responsibility" in article 1, Part One, of its draft, indicated that this was intended:[1]

> "(...) to cover every kind of new relations which may arise, in international law, from the internationally wrongful act of a State, whether such relations are limited to the offending State and the directly injured State or extend also to other subjects of international law, and whether they are centred on the duty of the guilty State to restore the injured State in its rights and repair the damage caused, (...)."

The first two chapters of this thesis have been devoted to issues concerning the determination of the subjects of international law entitled to invoke the responsibility of a State for having committed an internationally wrongful act. Or to put it in other words, in determining the subjects involved, besides the author State, in the new relationship established on the basis of incurred responsibility. The question then arises what that new relationship amounts to. What does it mean to be responsible? And what is it injured States or the United Nations can demand of the author State in order for the latter to absolve itself of all responsibility? The Commission answered these questions by noting that:[2]

> "A State discharges its responsibility incumbent on it for breach of an international obligation by making good, that is to say, by making reparation for the injury caused."

It is further necessary to determine the existence of an obligation on the part of the author State to provide reparation to the injured State(s) or the United Nations, as well as the determination of which forms of reparation ought to be granted to such State(s) or the United Nations. In view of the opinions expressed in chapter one on the correlation between obligations and rights, it may be pointed out that any obligation to provide reparation corresponds to the right(s) of the injured State(s) or the United Nations to demand and receive such reparation.

Article 19, Part One, devoted largely to the distinction between international delicts and international crimes, constitutes a break with tradition. The commentary specifies that the importance of the subject-matter of certain obligations and the seriousness of their breach should lead to a difference in characterization of internationally wrongful acts.[3] And it is at this point that the Commission acknowledges that:[4]

> "(...) having differentiated between internationally wrongful acts, it will inevitably be compelled to go on and differentiate between the régimes of responsibility applicable."

Answering the question as to what would be the content of the régime applicable to international crimes was postponed until the consideration of Part Two of the draft articles.[5] Yet it was indicated in the commentary that, since the acts in question are more serious than others, they should entail more severe legal consequences.[6] While attention has been devoted mainly to the subjects entitled to act and the kind of measures they could resort to, it was recognized later on that the area of reparation also lent itself to the forwarding of more demanding claims by injured subjects.[7]

The Permanent Court has held in the past that:[8]

> "*It is a principle of international law that the breach of an engagement involves an obligation to make reparation in an adequate form.*"

The reparation provided by an author State should always be adequate to remedy the internationally wrongful act. Since the distinction established by the Commission is intended to be of normative character, the consequences of crimes should be more severe than those of delicts. Meaning of course that the new, more far-reaching, obligations which are, in addition, imposed on an author State of a crime cannot also be imposed on the author State of a delict. That is not to say that the general forms of reparation ought to be different, but rather that the scope of the obligations imposed under the rules of a specific form of reparation will be more extensive. The special or supplementary consequences that attach to international crimes in the field of reparation constitute the subject-matter of this chapter.

This chapter will first, in section 3.2, devote arguments to the basis and nature of reparation. It will continue to examine the various forms of reparation in sections 3.3 to 3.7, namely cessation, restitution, compensation, satisfaction, and guarantees against repetition. Section 3.8 finally will focus on a number of restrictions that may, or may not, apply regarding the exercise of rights of reparation.

3.2. The basis and nature of reparation

3.2.1. THE BASIS OF REPARATION: OBLIGATION AND/OR RIGHT

What is the essence of reparation and on what basis does one conclude to the existence of an obligation to provide reparation? The fundamental answer to these questions seems to lie with that so often quoted dictum of the Permanent Court in the Chorzów Factory Case:[9]

> "The essential principle contained in the actual notion of an illegal act – a principle which seems to be established by international practice and in particular by the decisions of arbitral tribunals – is that reparation must, as far as possible, wipe out all the consequences of the illegal act and re-establish the situation which would, in all probability, have existed if that act had not been committed. Restitution in kind, or, if this is not possible, payment of a sum corresponding to the value which a restitution in kind would bear; the award, if

need be, of damages for loss sustained which would not be covered by restitution in kind or payment in place of it – such are the principles which should serve to determine the amount of compensation due for an act contrary to international law."

The Permanent Court here observes that the essential principle of reparation is that it "must, as far as possible, wipe out all the consequences of the illegal act and re-establish the situation which would, in all probability, have existed if that act had not been committed". Indeed it considers this principle to be "contained in the actual notion of an illegal act". If we relate this stance to some of the opinions expressed in chapter one, it may be said that law always desires that a certain specified situation exists, and that a certain course of conduct is followed by those subjected to the law. Thus the existence of an act not in conformity with what is required of a subject of law under an obligation of that subject leads to the conclusion that the course of conduct desired by the law is not realized in actual fact and that an illegal act, or in international law an internationally wrongful act, has taken place.[10] The law, of course, cannot remain indifferent to illegal acts, and consequently contemplates a strategy in order that the objective desired by it shall nevertheless be accomplished. Since law in general is focused on the peaceful settlement of disputes (such settlement to be proceeded with in accordance with the substantial rules applicable to the dispute), it does not resort immediately to the enforcement procedures at its disposal, but first interposes an obligation on the author of the illegal act to redress the wrong committed. And if such redress by the author is provided on an expedient basis, the author of an illegal act may prevent the occurrence of further consequences contemplated by law. One may note on this account that for instance Arangio-Ruiz remarked, in the context of the obligation to discontinue an internationally wrongful act, that:[11]

> "(...) there is a chance that the wrongdoer will realize the illegality of its behaviour and the obligation to correct it;"

Having reached this point it becomes necessary to reflect a bit more on the choice of the Commission to opt for (as a matter of drafting technique) coaching the issue of reparation in terms of rights of the injured State.[12] The Commission of course recognizes that the rights of the injured State stand against the obligations of the author State. However, though recognizing the correlation that exists in this respect, it seems that the Commission tends to conceal a fundamental misconception regarding the basis of responsibility, as well as that of reparation. The Commission observed in its commentary to the provision on cessation of wrongful conduct:[13]

> "Whereas, as far as the various forms of reparation are concerned, the preference for a formulation in terms of rights of the injured State is justified in view of the fact that it is by decision of the injured State that a secondary set of legal relations is set in motion."

While it is clear that through the decision of an injured State to press a claim against the author State secondary legal machinery may be set into motion (although that might also result from the initiative of the author State), that is not exactly the same thing as saying that the secondary legal relationship would not come into existence if the injured State were not to press any claim. And that is exactly what the Commission is saying here.

Considering article 1, Part One, of the ILC-draft, it seems somewhat strange to insist that the secondary relationship between an author State and injured State (or organization) would not come into existence in the absence of a claim for reparation on the part of the injured State. Article 1, Part One, stipulates that:

> "Every internationally wrongful act of a State entails the international responsibility of that State."

Thus it is premised on the idea that where there is an internationally wrongful act, there will also be, on the part of the author State, *ipso jure*, incurred international responsibility.[14] Taking the construction proposed by the Commission as a starting-point, that would lead to the conclusion that a State would be responsible, but would nevertheless not be obliged to do anything in response to that responsibility unless an injured subject would press a claim. Indeed secondary obligations would not come into existence on the basis of the legal rules on responsibility, but on the basis of the voluntary decision of an injured subject. One may ask however on what basis an injured subject would be entitled to claim reparation if not on the basis of a pre-existing right to demand such reparation. Otherwise one would have to say that an injured subject would have the power to unilaterally create its own right. Yet rights are ordinarily created through the operation of rules of law. And if one concludes to the existence of a pre-existing right to demand reparation, one also has to conclude to the existence of a corresponding obligation on the part of the author State to provide such reparation. Thus there would come into existence secondary legal relationships, meaning new correlated obligations and rights, even before any injured subject would press a claim for reparation.[15]

Now article 1, Part Two, of the ILC-draft adds to the premise of article 1, Part One, that:

> "The international responsibility of a State which, pursuant to the provisions of part 1, arises from an internationally wrongful act committed by that State, entails legal consequences as set out in the present part."

Again terminology in this article leads to a conclusion opposite to that of the Commission. The international responsibility of a State entails legal consequences for that State. Again the rule is phrased in objective terms. The article does not say that the legal consequences entail because of the decision of an injured subject to press a claim for reparation. It merely states that legal consequences ensue from the fact that a State has incurred international responsibility.[16] The same findings may be deduced from the articles provisionally adopted by the Commission so far. One may read in articles 6 *bis* to 10 *bis* the phrase "the injured State is entitled to obtain".[17] It seems somewhat circular to state that a State is entitled to obtain, while at the same time asserting that making a claim creates the entitlement.

All these arguments are buttressed especially by considerations related to the issue of interest. In his second report Arangio-Ruiz discussed the question as from which date (*dies a quo*) interest should be paid by the author State to the injured State.[18] In determining the *dies a quo* he discussed three possible positions: interest to be paid as from the date of damage; interest to be paid as from the date a claim was made; and interest to be paid from the date of the award of the principal damage. At the end of his discussion he supports the view that interest should be paid as from the date of the damage, and he quotes Brownlie in support:[19]

> "(...) the dies a quo is the date of the commission of the wrong."

If that is really the case, it becomes clear that secondary legal relationships come into existence, not at the will of the injured State, but from the operation of the law on the date at which the internationally wrongful act is committed. How could there be an obligation on the part of the author State to pay interest to the injured State if the two States do not stand in some relation to each other. Secondary legal relationships must have come into existence on the date of the commission of the internationally wrongful act, and not on the date of a claim by the injured State. Otherwise this would amount to saying that an obligation is imposed on the author State (since it is under an obligation to pay interest as from the day of the internationally wrongful act), even though secondary legal relationships (based on a claim by the injured State that the author State has committed an internationally wrongful act) have not yet come into existence.

An injured State under article 5, Part Two, will be entitled to invoke the responsibility of the author State and demand reparation. That position is adequately reflected in article 6 *bis*, paragraph 1, Part Two, on delicts, as adopted by the Commission:[20]

> "The injured State is entitled to obtain from the State which has committed an internationally wrongful act full reparation in the form of restitution in kind, compensation, satisfaction and assurances and guarantees on non-repetition, as provided in articles 7, 8, 10 and 10 bis, either singly or in combination."

Under article 5, paragraph 3, Part Two, all States are injured States if the internationally wrongful act constitutes an international crime. Arangio-Ruiz has followed up on this, and posited the right of all States to demand reparation, by proposing an article 16, paragraph 1, Part Two, on crimes:[21]

> "Where an internationally wrongful act of a State is an international crime, every State is entitled, subject to the condition set forth in paragraph 5 of article 19 below, to demand that the State which is committing or has committed the crime should cease its wrongful conduct and provide full reparation in conformity with articles 6 to 10 bis, as modified by paragraphs 2 and 3 below."

The reference to article 19, paragraph 5, Part Two, subjects cessation and reparation demands to a decision of the Court that a crime is, or has been, committed. The modifications proposed in paragraphs 2 and 3 concern the partial relaxation of certain restrictions applicable to restitution in kind, satisfaction, and guarantees against repetition. Under this proposal the only safeguard left for an author State of an international crime would be the preservation of its existence as an independent member of the international community, its territorial integrity, and the vital needs of its people. While fully agreeing with the right of every State to demand reparation in case of crimes, one would have to object, as a matter of legal principle, to the implications deriving from this text. It may be noted that the right of States to demand reparation is subjected to a prior determination of the existence of a crime under article 19, paragraph 5, Part Two. In effect this means that injured States cannot exercise their right to demand reparation until after the Court's determination. While the right to resort to countermeasures in case of delicts will most likely be subjected, in one way or another, to dispute settlement procedures, the right of an injured State to demand reparation exists and can be exercised in case of delicts as soon as an internationally wrongful act has been committed. The idea of differentiating two régimes of responsibility applicable to respectively delicts and crimes is grafted upon the idea that aggravated consequences for the author State will be instituted under the latter. If the right to demand reparation in case of crimes is subordinated to a prior determination by the Court, this amounts to imposing more stringent conditions for injured States in case of crimes than are applicable in case of delicts.

Furthermore, the proposed article 19, paragraph 5, Part Two, states that the Court's determination will fulfil the condition for implementation of the special or supplementary legal consequences as contemplated in articles 16 to 18. Yet article 16, paragraph 1, provides that after that determination States will be entitled to demand cessation and reparation. Yet, as will be seen hereafter, not all the forms of reparation constitute aggravated consequences of the commission of a crime. There is thus a discrepancy between the texts of article 16, paragraph 1, and article 19, paragraph 5, Part Two.

From a practical point of view, moreover, this means that the exercise of the right to demand reparation will be possible only after the termination of full-fledged contentious proceedings before the Court.[22] Taking into account the length of such proceedings generally, this might imply that the exercise of the right to demand reparation could take place only after a period of time ranging between, probably, one to five years. However, the purpose of attaching aggravated consequences to international crimes lies with the need for more effective suppression of the crime. Certainly that purpose cannot be accomplished by subordinating the exercise of the right to demand reparation to a prior determination of the existence of a crime by the Court.

It may be observed, in conclusion, that a State which has committed an internationally wrongful act will incur international responsibility. In order to absolve itself from that responsibility it will have to provide reparation to the injured State(s). Any injured State in the sense of article 5, Part Two, should have the right to demand reparation, whether in case of delicts or in case of crimes, as from the moment the wrongful act was committed.

3.2.2. THE NATURE OF REPARATION: REPARATORY AND/OR PUNITIVE TRAITS

Another important issue to be discussed concerns the hotly debated question whether reparation is of reparatory character or whether it also has punitive character. Although the question is ordinarily asked more in connection to the question whether countermeasures or sanctions should be seen as punitive measures, the question nevertheless has to be raised also in regard to the subject of reparation.

The preliminary question, however, is what should be understood by the reparatory character of reparation and what should be understood by the punitive character of reparation. It does not fully make sense to assert that anything going beyond repairing the wrongful act should be considered to constitute punishment. Because at this point one defines the one element only in connection to the other, without giving a definition

of that other element. So in order to determine the character of reparation one has to define what is meant by reparatory traits as well as punitive traits of reparation.
As to this preliminary question it seems that its answer must lie with the object pursued by reparation in a temporal sense. The Permanent Court observed in the Chorzów Factory Case that reparation must "wipe out all the consequences of the illegal act and re-establish the situation which would, in all probability, have existed if that act had not been committed." As may be noted from this formulation, the object of reparation, according to the Permanent Court, is to eliminate all those consequences which flow from a wrongful act, that is to say to eliminate all those consequences which flow from an act committed in the past. *The goal of reparation, in the strict sense, is to undo what has been done.* Indeed, the Permanent Court after having defined the forms which were to implement this basic premise, specified that reparation should consist of "Restitution in kind, or, if this is not possible, payment of a sum corresponding to the value which a restitution in kind would bear; the award, if need be, of damages for loss sustained which would not be covered by restitution in kind or payment in place of it – ". It cannot but be noted that there is no mention whatsoever of those forms of reparation which are commonly understood to fall under the category of satisfaction. And especially those forms could be said to be directed, not towards past acts and any consequences flowing therefrom, but towards the potential commission, in the future, of similar or identical internationally wrongful acts.
However, one would be simplifying matters unduly by claiming that punishment could not be directed at past acts. Punishment is directed at the past, even if it would ordinarily take away the existence or restrict the freedom of an author of a wrongful act, or compel it to make a financial contribution in the near or distant future. But the essential characteristic of reparation in the strict sense is that its goal consists of establishing the situation that would have existed had the wrongful act not taken place. The measures ordinarily resorted to under the heading of punishment do not in any way contribute to that goal, and hence are to be considered as retribution for wrongful conduct. It is on that basis one has to view statements to the effect that anything going beyond restitution and compensation would constitute punishment. It is therefore proper to discuss here in more detail those forms of reparation called satisfaction, in particular punitive damages, and guarantees against repetition.

The frequent use of the phrase punitive damages was commented upon as follows in the Lusitania Award:[23]

> "The words 'exemplary,' 'vindictive' or 'punitive' as applied to damages were misnomers. The fundamental concept of 'damages' is satisfaction, reparation for a loss suffered; a judicially ascertained compensation for wrong. The remedy should be commensurate with the loss. The superimposing of a penalty in addition to full compensation and naming it damages, with the qualifying word exemplary, vindictive or punitive, was a confusion of terms, inevitably leading to confusion of thought."

The confusion of thought to which the mixed commission refers appears to be the link made between the concepts of punishment and of damages. As follows from this quote damages are intended to provide redress to an injured party as a consequence of a wrongful act, whereas penalties are conceived either as retribution for the wrongful act

in question or as means to prevent, generally or specifically, the commission of similar wrongful acts. While the grant of compensation presupposes the existence of ascertainable damage, the grant of punitive damages would amount to compensation for non-existent damage, that is, really a penalty.
It is on this account that the mixed commission stated that:[24]

> "(...) as between sovereign nations the question of the right and power to impose penalties, unlimited in amount, is political rather than legal in its nature, and therefore not a subject within the jurisdiction of this Commission."

The reason that the imposition of penalties would not be subject to the jurisdiction of the commission is that the question of right and power to do so involves a political question, meaning of course that there did not exist any legal rule at the time providing for so-called punitive damages.[25] The fact, however, that there is, or was, no such rule of international law providing for the imposition of penalties on States should not obscure the additional fact that there has been a trend to grant compensatory relief to injured States in excess of the ascertainable damages resulting from the internationally wrongful act of another State.[26] The circumstance that the amount of compensatory relief granted is not reasoned by way of specified categories of damages likewise should not lead one to believe that therefore the idea of imposing a penalty in some sense is totally absent from the minds of those deciding the case.

It may be noted that a certain inconsistency appeared in the text of Arangio-Ruiz' proposed article 10, paragraph 1, on satisfaction, which runs:[27]

> "In the measure in which an internationally wrongful act caused to the injured State a moral or legal injury not susceptible of remedy by restitution in kind or pecuniary compensation, the State which committed the wrongful act is under the obligation to provide the injured State with adequate satisfaction in the form of apologies, nominal or punitive damages, punishment of the responsible individuals or assurances against repetition, or any combination thereof."

Is it not strange that there would exist a moral or legal injury "not susceptible of (...) pecuniary compensation", but even more so that such injury would have to be remedied through the payment by the author State of "nominal or punitive damages"? Thus the award of punitive damages would apparently not be based on the existence of ascertainable damage, and also would not be susceptible of pecuniary compensation, but would nevertheless lead to the payment of money to the injured State(s).[28] The situation becomes even more confusing if one would consider the possibility of an author State having to pay punitive damages to an injured State by reason of the breach of obligations for the protection of human rights. Such a breach does not inflict any material damage on any State, and one would venture to say that payment of punitive damages to one injured State ought to lead then also to the payment of punitive damages to all injured States (all those States bound by a multilateral treaty or by the rule of customary international law; article 5, paragraph 2 (e) (iii), Part Two of the ILC-draft). That however appears to be an untenable proposition. The Commission appears to have avoided such a far-reaching position by stipulating that in cases of gross infringement of the rights of the injured State satisfaction may take the form of damages reflecting the gravity of the infringement.[29] Before concluding the arguments regarding the alleged punitive traits of reparation some attention has to be devoted to guarantees against repetition.

Often it is asserted that satisfaction serves to provide a remedy for the moral, political or juridical injury done to a State.[30] If that is really the case there would be no sufficient argument for saying that reparation would involve punitive traits. For the redress offered through the method of satisfaction would be directed towards the elimination of the wrongful act itself or its consequences, *e.g.* to the elimination of that which had happened in the past and which affected another State. Therefore one would be justified in claiming that reparation in the broad sense would only encompass functions of reparatory character.

However, that would be jumping to conclusions. First of all it may be noted that most of the forms of reparation thus placed under the heading of satisfaction do not seem to address the issue of elimination of past actions and its consequences, but are rather intended to secure the performance of obligations in the future.[31] Thus it may be said that the declaration of illegality, whether or not by the author State's acknowledgement of responsibility or by an independent organ, and the expression of regrets or apologies by the author State, are clearly intended to strengthen the rule in the relations between the author State and the injured State. As to the prosecution and punishment of those nationals or agents of the State involved in the commission of the internationally wrongful act, that would seem to present another example of deterrence of similar acts, rather than to undo the consequences of the wrongful act or to compensate the damage suffered by the injured State. While it may be admitted that on the level of domestic criminal law the prosecution and punishment of those agents must be seen as retribution for their past actions, the same cannot be said for the international sphere where the measures are rather directed towards prevention of similar acts by the nationals or agents concerned.

A second line of argument is the following. It is claimed that the purpose of satisfaction is to provide redress for the injured State's moral, political and legal damage.[32] At the same time the claim is made that guarantees against repetition form part of the category of satisfaction,[33] and a very specific example is quoted by Arangio-Ruiz from the practice of the human rights committee.[34] It is on that account that one may observe that in case of breaches of obligations for the protection of human rights no ascertainable damage is suffered by any of the injured States, nor is there for that matter any moral and political damage inflicted upon the injured States. What seems to be left is the statement by Anzilotti, and followed by Ago and the Commission, that:[35]

> "Le dommage se trouve compris implicitement dans le caractère anti-juridique de l'acte."

If therefore guarantees against repetition are to be given or taken in the context of breaches of obligations for the protection of human rights, those could only be based on the notion of so-called legal damage. Such damage would exist rather on the basis of the existence of an internationally wrongful act (with no perceptible difference as to which States would be affected by the act) than on the basis that any damage would have been done to any specific State (leaving aside the case that nationals of other States would suffer from the act). The more natural meaning to be attached to the phrase "guarantees against repetition" is of course that they are intended to present a safeguard against future commissions of internationally wrongful acts. In the broad sense they are to be considered a consequence of an internationally wrongful act, since guarantees could not be demanded in the absence of such an act. This should not deceive us however. Just like in domestic law acts may have both criminal law and civil law consequences,[36] acts in international law can produce consequences of reparatory nature and consequences of a deterrent nature.

It is for the above reasons that whenever there is question of the awarding of compensation going beyond the actually suffered material damage, it would be quite correct to speak of penalties, and thus of punishment, rather than to term them punitive damages. Furthermore, guarantees against repetition should not be seen as a remedy for undoing the moral, political or legal damage done, but rather as a form of reparation intended to prevent the commission of future wrongful acts, and therefore endowed with deterrent character.

3.3. Cessation of internationally wrongful acts

The first form of reparation to be discussed concerns that of cessation of the internationally wrongful act. In this context some arguments will first be devoted to the role of protest.

3.3.1. THE ROLE OF PROTEST

The Commission, arguing that cessation should be phrased by way of obligation for the author State, noted:[37]

> "Given the inorganic structure of inter-State society, the norms of international law developed by States themselves are vulnerable, being exposed to destruction as a result of breaches of those norms by States. The significance of cessation of a wrongful act goes beyond the level of bilateral relations to the level of relations between wrongdoers and all the other States and members of the international community."

As has been observed in chapter one, all States have an interest in the performance of obligations by other States, though, as has also been indicated, such an interest cannot provide the basis for concluding that they are also in possession of a legal interest. Nevertheless it may be asserted that it is possible for each and every State to protest against any conduct considered by it to amount to an internationally wrongful act.[38] Indeed, as is made clear by McCaffrey, such a protest may be imperative in two senses:[39]

> "Satisfaction was a remedy against moral damage, but its most significant purpose was to reaffirm respect for the rule of law which had been breached. It should be remembered that such a breach could be constitutive of practice. In the absence of any protest it could ripen into permission or ultimately even into a custom. It was therefore essential for it to be challenged by another State. In that situation, satisfaction reaffirmed the existence of the obligation which had been breached and ruled out acquiescence."

First, it may be deduced that protesting certain behaviour will prevent the establishment or modification of a rule of customary international law. By protesting States indicate their belief that there is no legal ground for considering the act to be part of a general practice accepted as a law. Secondly, protest by a certain State may prevent a situation arising in which the author State could claim that that (injured) State had concurred in or accepted the act. Thus protesting would prevent an injured State from any possible loss of right to demand reparation from the author State of an internationally wrongful act. A distinction, however, has to be made as to whether the protesting State is an injured State under the relevant rules of State responsibility, or whether it does not possess that capacity.[40]

Whenever a State is not an injured State, a protest by that State can only serve as a reminder to the author State of the state of international law as perceived by it.
Arangio-Ruiz appears to take a broader view, as he states that cessation:[41]

> "(...) serves the interest of putting an end to a violation of international law which is in progress. Such an interest is not confined to the injured State or States and it acquires not infrequently, considering the organic structure of inter-State society, a very considerable dimension. (...) It increases, as shown by current examples, with the gravity of the delict or crime in progress."

One could say, as far as delicts are concerned, that he apparently considers all States to have an interest, but perhaps even a right to demand cessation notwithstanding that they are not injured States. No State, which is not an injured State in respect of the same internationally wrongful act, may involve itself in the relationship that exists between the author State and the injured State. Therefore the protest should only be phrased in such a manner that it adequately reflects the position of the protesting State on the existence, application or interpretation of the rule of international law at stake. A non-injured State's protest should not, moreover, amount to support for, or repudiation of, the demand, or lack of demand, for reparation made by any injured State. That would be tantamount to a prohibited intervention in the external affairs of the author and injured States, for the latter are free, subject to any consideration of *jus cogens*, to decide on any settlement diverging from the general régime of State responsibility.[42]
The situation is different whenever the protest originates from an injured State. In that case the protest serves, first of all, to allege the existence of an internationally wrongful act on the part of the author State. Naturally such a protest by the injured State, taken in isolation, would suffice to establish its position as to the existence, application or interpretation of any relevant rule of international law. It would stand to logic that an injured State would have its protest accompanied also by a demand for reparation. Whether or not the injured State merely protests against the commission of an internationally wrongful act, or has such protest accompanied by a demand for reparation, makes no difference as to the existence of a right to demand reparation. Because the right to demand reparation, as is in fact the obligation to provide reparation, is created automatically on the basis of the secondary rules of State responsibility. The protest alone serves to reaffirm such a right, which, as has been pointed out above, comes into existence as soon as an internationally wrongful act is committed. Only with the passing of a considerable amount of time after the protest, and coupled to inaction on the part of the injured State, could one conclude to any loss of right for the injured State.

While the foregoing holds insofar as international delicts are concerned, a different situation obtains whenever an international crime is committed.[43] Since all States are injured States in case an international crime is committed, it follows that their protests will also reaffirm their right to demand reparation. Apart from that their status of injured States means that they are under no strain to restrict themselves to merely stating their position as to the existence, application or interpretation of the rule in question. They can support any claim for reparation made by another State (especially a directly injured State) and repudiate the lack of claims by other States. Although it may be said that there is no rule of international law providing that States are under an obligation to exercise certain rights (leaving aside decisions of the Security Council; article 25 of the Charter),[44] still other States may urge upon the exercise of such rights. Such action would not constitute a prohibited intervention in the external affairs of the author State or other injured States. Indeed, the obligation that is breached in case of an international crime flows from a peremptory norm of general international law, and that means that States cannot beforehand consent to such a breach (article 29, paragraph 2, Part One, of the ILC-draft), and nor can they acquiesce in such a breach.[45]

3.3.2. THE OBLIGATION TO DISCONTINUE INTERNATIONALLY WRONGFUL ACTS

Any protest by an injured State will most likely be accompanied or followed by a demand to discontinue the internationally wrongful act in those circumstances where it persists in time. The Commission has adopted article 6, Part Two, on "cessation of wrongful conduct":[46]

> "A State whose conduct constitutes an internationally wrongful act having a continuing character is under the obligation to cease that conduct without prejudice to the responsibility it has already occurred."

With regard to this obligation the Commission has claimed that:[47]

> "(...) cessation is not a form of reparation but rather the object of an obligation stemming from the combination of wrongful conduct in progress and the normative strength of the primary rule of which the wrongful conduct is held in breach. (...) the obligation to discontinue the wrongful conduct is to be considered not only existent but in actual operation on the mere strength of the primary rule, quite independently of any representation or claim on the part of the injured State."

While being in full agreement with the Commission's assessment that no claim by an injured State is needed so that the author State is under the obligation to cease the wrongful conduct in question, the same cannot be said with regard to its opinion that the obligation to discontinue such conduct is based on the primary rule. Although it is true that in the strict sense the obligation to cease the wrongful conduct is not apt to "wipe out all the consequences of the illegal act", still it is possible to assert its basic reparatory character by pointing to the fact that it prevents further harm being done. While of course, in the light of the aim of preventing further harm, cessation of wrongful conduct operates in regard to the future, it cannot but be acknowledged that its immediate concern lies with the present. Clearly the return to legality by the author

State means a renewed performance of the primary obligation, but its direct and immediate effect is the end of ongoing wrongful conduct. Contrary therefore to what has been claimed the object of cessation is not a return to legality, but an end to illegality.[48] The return to legality marked by the performance of the obligation to discontinue by the author State constitutes nothing more than a side-effect, or mirror-effect, of the prime object of the obligation to discontinue: prevention of further damage by stopping to act wrongfully.[49]

That there is a marked difference between the two obligations may be shown also by reference to the differing object to be achieved by performing the obligation to cease the wrongful conduct. For instance, if one takes the rule which provides that diplomats are to be immune from any interference by the receiving State, it is clear that it imposes on the receiving State the obligation not to do something, that is, to abstain from engaging in certain conduct. Now if that obligation is breached by the receiving State through the arrest and detention of a diplomat for a longer period of time, it becomes subject to the obligation to cease its wrongful conduct. As long as the diplomat is detained the receiving State is in breach of its obligation not to interfere with the immunity enjoyed by diplomats, but it is also in breach of the obligation to cease any interference. But while the first breach is brought about by action of the receiving State (detention of the diplomat), the second breach is brought about by inaction of the receiving State (non-release of the diplomat). Therefore the obligation to discontinue internationally wrongful acts is not based on the prolonged operation of any primary rule of international law, but on the basis of the secondary rules of State responsibility.

Arangio-Ruiz has indicated that the provision on cessation in case of delicts does not need to be altered to accommodate the régime of crimes.[50] The obligation to discontinue internationally wrongful acts appears to take on importance especially if the internationally wrongful act constitutes an international crime.[51] That is so because, as has been noted in chapter one, subsection 1.9.2, the commission of an international crime always implies the existence of wilful intent on the part of the author State. Due to such intent an author State mostly will not be willing to depart from its wrongful behaviour, and will tend to choose a recalcitrant stance with regard to those States protesting the behaviour and demanding a stop to it.[52] Clear examples of such a trend are the attitudes of Rhodesia and South Africa,[53] but also that of Iraq after its invasion of Kuwait.[54] In such cases the States in question would appear to be in breach of their obligations under the primary rule, as well as their obligations under the secondary rule to discontinue their first breach of obligation.

It might be objected that in cases of international crimes the acts in question do not constitute continuing internationally wrongful acts, but at the most represent a sequence of internationally wrongful acts which, although they have to be seen in relation to each other, nevertheless remain distinct.

Such an argument could especially be made as regards the rule prohibiting a State to commit aggression, as indicated in article 19, paragraph 3, sub (a), Part One of the ILC-draft, or to use military force against the territorial integrity and/or political independence of another State. The breach of obligation would then be consumed as soon as a military attack by one State did no longer encounter any forceful opposition by the other State, even though the military forces of the first State controlled part or the whole territory of the second State. Since it would no longer be *using* force against the other State, its breach of obligation would have come to an end.[55] The occupation that follows does not then constitute a breach of obligation of the primary rule prohibiting the use of force against the territorial integrity and/or political independence of States,[56] but would rather represent a breach of the obligation to provide reparation to the injured State.[57] The occupation constitutes a failure to "wipe out all the consequences of the illegal act and re-establish the situation which would, in all probability, have existed if that act had not been committed." It is in fact this failure which would seem to trigger the right of an injured State to demand an end to, and obligation of the author State to cease, the illegal occupation. This right of the injured State (and the correlative obligation of the author State) is not grafted upon the obligation to discontinue internationally wrongful acts, but rests upon the secondary rule that stipulates the right of the injured State to claim (and the correlative obligation of the author State to provide) restitution in kind. Only if one were to consider the failure to provide restitution in kind as a separate internationally wrongful act could one claim a renewed obligation to cease wrongful conduct.[58] At the same time it cannot but be noted that that same argument then may be made on and on again (*ad infinitum*).

The situation is somewhat different with the other international crimes mentioned in article 19, paragraph 3. Whether one follows the same argument as in the preceding paragraph really depends on the formulation of the primary rule of international law: does the rule prohibit a State from breaching its obligations to respect certain specific human rights of its citizens, or does it prohibit a State from engaging in a policy of breaching its obligations to respect such rights. It is clear that it is the systematic and wilful character inherent in the commission of particular internationally wrongful acts which qualifies them as international crimes. To some extent the gravity of the internationally wrongful acts is only marginal to that intent. But it is submitted that in judging whether a breach of obligation must be discontinued one has to look not to the policy maintained by a State, but to the occurrence of actual conduct contrary to the primary rule.

Taking a look at the specific formulations adopted by the Commission, it cannot but be noted that a breach of the rule providing for self-determination of peoples, according to article 19, paragraph 3, sub (b), may come about also when colonial domination is maintained by force. And as the commentary makes clear the term "by force" means against the will of the people in question.[59] Clearly therefore the breach of the obligation under the rule providing for self-determination of peoples is continuing in character, and is consequently capable of being discontinued.

A further criterion lies with the basic human rights character of some of the primary rules concerned. Only when the human rights denial involves a permanent condition for the individuals concerned is there a possibility of discontinuance. As to the examples mentioned in article 19, paragraph 3, sub (c), it is to be noted that slavery implies a permanent condition for the individual subjected to it, and therefore the obligation to cease the wrongful conduct would apply to any situation in which a State would breach the prohibition. The same cannot be said with regard to the example of genocide which is based on the denial of the right to life. Once that right is taken away from an individual the breach is consumed. The same argument goes with regard to the rule prohibiting *apartheid*, which is based on the right of individuals to be free from discrimination on the basis of race.

One issue needs to be discussed, and it concerns the observation of Arangio-Ruiz to the effect that:[60]

> "(...) any more or less timely discontinuance of a wrongful conduct will have a bearing on the quality and quantity of reparation to be made in favour of the injured State."

From this remark one may deduce that an author State which does not cease acting wrongfully will not necessarily aggravate its responsibility. But how about the limitation of responsibility due to discontinuance? There can be no doubt that ceasing the wrongful act will limit the quantity of reparation extant upon the commission of an internationally wrongful act, basically because of non-occurrence of damage.[61] But the question is whether discontinuance also has some bearing upon the quality of reparation to be provided by the author State. Insofar as some forms of reparation are typically intended to restore international legality, to undo what has been done, it may be noted that there can be no mitigation of responsibility. Thus the reparation forms restitution and compensation may in no way be reduced because of cessation by the author State. It makes sense however to allow the other forms of reparation, satisfaction and guarantees against repetition, to be less strictly applied in case the author State in a more or less timely fashion recognizes the wrongfulness of its conduct, ceases it, and recognizes that it ought to make good for it. Nevertheless it would seem that there is no letting up with regard to the author State's obligation, based on the rule to provide satisfaction, to prosecute and try those responsible for acts which constitute crimes under the domestic laws involved.

The obligation to cease wrongful conduct appears to gain importance in case such conduct constitutes an international crime. Yet that is not really so,[62] since such belief is based on the confusion between the breach of the obligation under the primary rule and the breach of the obligation under the secondary rule which stipulates a return to the situation that would have existed had the wrongful act not taken place. This brings us to the next section regarding restitution.

3.4. Restitution

The second form of reparation to be discussed is restitution, or restitution in kind,[63] regarding which the Commission adopted article 7, Part Two:[64]

> "The injured State is entitled to obtain from the State which has committed an internationally wrongful act restitution in kind, that is, the re-establishment of the situation that existed before the wrongful act was committed, (...)."

The first question concerns the scope of the concept. There is a tendency to equate the idea of restitution to that certain part of the dictum of the Permanent Court in the Chorzów Factory Case which stated that reparation must "wipe out all the consequences of the illegal act and re-establish the situation which would, in all probability, have existed if that act had not been committed." That tendency has culminated in the two definitions, formulated by the Commission, as proposed by Arangio-Ruiz, of restitution in kind. The first focuses on the so-called status quo *ante*:[65]

> "(...) restitution in kind would consist in re-establishing the status quo ante, namely the situation that existed prior to the occurrence of the wrongful act in order to bring the parties' relationship back to its original state."

The second one is grafted completely on the dictum of the Permanent Court, and would:[66]

> "(...) understand restitution in kind (...) as the establishment or re-establishment of the situation that would exist, or would have existed, if the wrongful act had not been committed."

This second formulation is more closely drafted on the terms used by the Permanent Court.[67] However, those terms were not in the first place concerned with the definition of restitution in kind, but with the content of the obligation to provide reparation. It was reparation which had to be apt to wipe out all the consequences of the wrongful act, not restitution in kind as such. This may be demonstrated by quoting once more (the remainder of) the text of that dictum:[68]

> "(...) reparation must, as far as possible, wipe out all the consequences of the illegal act and re-establish the situation which would, in all probability, have existed if that act had not been committed. Restitution in kind, or, if this is not possible, payment of a sum corresponding to the value which a restitution in kind would bear; the award, if need be, of damages for loss sustained which would not be covered by restitution in kind or payment in place of it (...)."

It may be noted that payment of compensation is envisaged not only as a substitute for restitution in kind, but also in case restitution in kind would not cover loss sustained. Apparently restitution in kind would constitute only a first attempt to eliminate the consequences of the wrongful act and to establish the situation that would have existed had the wrongful act not taken place. If that first attempt has been made and yet not all consequences of wrongful act have been eliminated as a result, the second step would be to provide pecuniary compensation for those consequences not eliminated as a result of restitution in kind to the injured State. On this basis it may be safe to say that the first definition is in fact better suited to represent the gist of the Permanent Court's view of the matter.[69] The Commission's text of article 7, Part Two, on restitution in kind, appears in line with that view.

An essential question to be answered is whether there exists any discretion, on the part of the author State or injured State, as to the choice of forms of reparation. To put it differently, is it possible for either of them to opt either for restitution or compensation? Which one of them could exercise such a right of option, and would the other State in the responsibility relationship be bound by it?

Some of these questions were addressed by Arangio-Ruiz in his preliminary report.[70] He restricted himself to a discussion of the question whether the injured State could exercise a right of option between restitution and compensation. The ratio for such a restriction would seem to be obvious, though it would not be superfluous to state it explicitly rather than leave it to implication. If a right of option were given to the author State of an internationally wrongful act, it would of course choose that form of reparation which suited best its own interests.[71] To some extent already the idea of any new substantial right for the author State would be contrary to logic, considering that the secondary rules are generally intended to provide for rules laying down new rights of the injured States and new obligations for the author State. As Arangio-Ruiz pointed out,[72] the normal course of events has been changed by the author State, and it would not seem right if it were to benefit from its illegal behaviour (*ex injuria jus non oritur*). In its final remarks on the issue discussed here the Commission quite rightly points to the fact that:[73]

> "Restitution in kind is the form of reparation which most closely conforms to the general principle of the law of responsibility according to which the author State is bound to 'wipe out' all the legal and material consequences of its wrongful act by re-establishing the situation that would exist if that act had not been committed; as such it comes foremost before any other form of reparation lato sensu and particularly before reparation by equivalent."

While acknowledging the importance of restitution in the scheme of the forms of reparation, and stating that it "comes foremost before any other form of reparation", nevertheless the Commission does not grant it any precedence over the other forms of reparation. It has claimed that it is unnecessary:[74] (...) to expressly provide for the injured State's freedom to choose between restitution in kind and compensation." The text of article 8, Part Two, quoted *infra* at the beginning of section 3.5, does not appear to lay down a right to choose. Indeed, such a right would seem to be in contradiction to the Permanent Court's stance in the Chorzów Factory Case,[75] where it observed that reparation had to consist of "restitution in kind, or, *if this is not possible*, payment of a sum corresponding to the value which a restitution in kind would bear;" Apparently the Permanent Court envisaged compensation only if restitution would not be possible.[76]

Arguing in favour of a right of choice for the injured State Arangio-Ruiz had pointed out furthermore that compensation is always possible, and that only the amount of damages to be paid might constitute a problem for the author State.[77] Contrary to what has been claimed by Grotius,[78] money is not the common measure of valuable things. Why admit that the injured State could opt for compensation over restitution if the latter is perfectly possible, and the author State is willing, or at least not unwilling, to conform to an obligation in that respect. In the scheme of things such a rule would also provide security as to the order of forms of reparation to be accorded by the author State. Thus it would be liable to pay compensation only to the extent that restitution would not be possible, or not adequate, to provide full reparation to the injured State.[79]

Another matter for discussion lies with the notion that the obligation to provide restitution in kind would not only involve material restitution but also legal restitution.[80] The Commission observed that:[81]

> "(...) one can hardly conceive a restitution to be effected by a State – whether of territory, persons or movable objects – which would involve purely material operations. To return an unlawfully occupied or annexed territory, to withdraw a customs line unlawfully advanced, to restore to freedom a person unlawfully arrested and detained, or to re-establish in their homeland a group of persons

> unlawfully expelled and expropriated, legal provision must be made at the constitutional, legislative, judicial and/or administrative level. From that viewpoint restitutio will be essentially 'legal'. Material restitutio will merely be in such cases a translation into facts of legal provisions. (...) In practice, any international restitution in kind will be an essentially juridical restitutio within the legal system of the author State, accompanying or preceding material restitutio."

However, the fact that an author State will, for purely domestic reasons, be compelled to undertake certain changes in its domestic legal system in order that it be possible for it to comply with an obligation to release and return persons,[82] property,[83] or territory,[84] is irrelevant from the international point of view. As the Commission and Arangio-Ruiz point out, from the viewpoint of international law domestic legal provisions or decisions are considered to be mere facts.[85] They conclude from this that the distinction between material and legal restitution stresses no more than:[86]

> "(...) the different kinds of operations which the organs of the author State should carry out in order to achieve restitution in kind. (...) It follows that, as a rule, material and legal restitutio should be viewed not so much as different remedies but as distinct aspects of one and the same remedy."

The point to be made here is that while it may be true that it is, or may be, practically impossible for an author State to provide restitution without some legal provision or decision in its domestic legal system, that does not mean that consequently there is a rule of international law to the effect that material restitution should necessarily be accompanied by legal restitution.

This may be illustrated by the example, also mentioned by the Commission and Arangio-Ruiz, of the restitution of territory. After Iraq's invasion of Kuwait the Security Council demanded, by way of resolution 660, the withdrawal of Iraqi troops to the positions held at 1 August 1990. No reference can be found in that resolution to the need of any legal decision or provision under Iraq's domestic legal system. Only after Iraq's decision to establish a "comprehensive and eternal merger" with Kuwait did the Security Council, through resolution 662, decide that any annexation of Kuwait had no legal validity, and was considered null and void. Only on that basis, international invalidity it seems, did the Security Council then demand that "Iraq rescind its actions purporting to annex Kuwait".[87]

There can be little doubt that it is perfectly possible to engage in the restitution of persons, property or territory without any effectuation of so-called legal restitution.

Indeed, the argument can be made more forcefully to the extent that the commission of internationally wrongful acts need not be based on any legal provision within the domestic system. If one looks at the rules of attribution laid down in Part One of the draft articles on State responsibility, it cannot be overlooked that a number of them concern the commission of acts by agents acting *ultra vires* their competence, or even the commission of acts by individuals acting on behalf of the State. If acts by such agents or individuals would involve the detention of nationals of other States,[88] no domestic legal provision would justify the conduct in question (there may even exist rules of criminal law prohibiting the conduct in question) and no legal provision would need to be changed on account of such acts. Thus the so-called legal restitution should rather be seen in the light of guarantees against the repetition of wrongful acts (on which more in section 3.7). For if a legal provision were to remain into force, unmodified, even though it constituted the constitutive basis for the commission of an internationally wrongful act, repetition of the wrongful conduct in question could not be ruled out. Indeed, the domestic legal system of the author State might not even be such as to prevent its nationals or citizens from enforcing such legal provisions as against the injured State or its nationals.[89]

As to the régime of international crimes Arangio-Ruiz has proposed the deletion of some of the restrictions applicable to restitution in case of delicts.[90] Those will be discussed in section 3.8, and at appropriate places. It may be convenient to start off here with the preceding subject, that of the question of choice by the injured State. For at this point it may be noted that Arangio-Ruiz claims, also as regards international delicts, that:[91]

> "Whenever restitutio was due by the author State for a violation of an imperative rule or, more generally, of a rule setting forth an erga omnes obligation, it could not be renounced (in favour of pecuniary compensation) by the directly injured State or States. In such a situation the only proper response should be to place upon the author State the obligation to provide full restitution in kind."

It is not quite clear why it should not be possible for the directly injured State to opt for compensation in such cases. It is obvious that only a State which suffers any kind of damage or loss will be in a position to claim either restitution or compensation. The other (non-directly) injured States do not have any interest of their own, as such, in restitution or compensation, since they will not benefit in any way from either. The only interest they have, at that point, will be the restoration of legality through discontinuance of the wrongful act(s), as well as guarantees against repetition. Any interest they have as regards restitution, compensation or satisfaction boils down to the author State's performance of its obligations in that respect towards the directly injured State and the reaffirmation of the rule as a consequence of that performance. It is hard to see why the (directly) injured State would ordinarily have a free choice, but not so in cases of breaches of obligations under peremptory norms or breaches of obligations *erga omnes*. Of course it is hard to see anyway why it should have a free choice between restitution and compensation to begin with. The fact that restitution in kind has in actual practice mostly been displaced by compensation in favour of the injured State does not mean that the injured State would not have the option of insisting on restitution in kind, and correspondingly that the injured State could refuse an offer of restitution in kind by the author State.[92] An exception could at the most be made with regard to the restitution of property to the extent that such property would have been considerably reduced in value since the time the internationally wrongful act had been committed.[93] But where restitution is possible without any significant decrease in value, it should be considered the basic obligation imposed on the author State as a consequence of its wrongful act.

While there would not seem to be any reason for claiming a different rule as to restitution applicable in case of international delicts, the situation mainly differs because of the magnitude inherent in the commission of an international crime and the importance of the rules concerned.[94] It is on that basis that one would insist, as a matter of principle, on an absolute obligation for the author State to release and/or return persons, property or territory.[95] That restitution in kind should be given precedence over compensation may be demonstrated especially with reference to the international crime of aggression. If hostilities cease and the State initiating the attack remains in control over (part of) the territory of the other State, all injured States obtain the right to claim a return of the territory concerned to the directly injured State. Any settlement between the directly injured State and the author State providing for a transfer of territory from the first to the second thus would seem to come up against the rights of the other injured States. Generally such a transfer would be unacceptable also on the basis of the maxim *ex injuria jus non oritur*, and even an agreed amount of compensation between the two States, as a sort of *quid pro quo*, would not seem to be satisfactory considering that such an agreement would most likely fall under article 52 of the Vienna Convention.

As to the crime of aggression one may note that in the past peace treaties between the (previously) warring States have tended to include provisions on restitution.[96] However, generally such treaties have been imposed by the victor State on the defeated State.[97] For that reason one cannot regard them, at least not without hesitation, as an implementation of the responsibility of the aggressor State. Furthermore, the aggressor State may have been victorious in battle, and have imposed the treaty on the injured State. To a large extent this possibility explains the creation in international law of the rule prohibiting recourse to the use of armed force, as well as the corollary rule that imposes the obligation to settle international disputes by peaceful means only. And equally for such reasons a collective peace and security system has been agreed to in the Charter, so that the military more powerful State could not impose its will on a weaker State.

A perfect example of the recent past may illustrate the point regarding restitution and it concerns the Iraq-Kuwait crisis. In relation to that crisis the Security Council has taken the opportunity to claim restitution from Iraq as to territory, Kuwaiti nationals, third State nationals, Kuwaiti property, prisoners of war, as well as the remains of deceased Kuwaiti or third State nationals and prisoners of war.[98]

With regard to the crime constituting a denial of self-determination, the primary goal of restitution will be the transfer of power, control or sovereignty to the people concerned. Any transfer of power (and territory) should of course be complete. In this regard complications are bound to occur and as an example one may mention the way in which the people living in that part of the territory of Cameroon under British administration exercised its right. While the people living in the southern part of the territory voted in favour of joining the Republic of Cameroon, the people of the northern part later on voted to join Nigeria. The General Assembly finalized these elections by terminating the Trusteeship Agreement with the United Kingdom in resolution 1608 (XV). The Republic of Cameroon, voting against said resolution, then brought a case against the United Kingdom before the Court, claiming that the latter had breached the Trusteeship Agreement by administering the northern part of the territory as a part of the British Protectorate of Nigeria.[99] Due to the fact that the breaches claimed to exist had been consummated, so observes Cameroon, it could not claim *restitutio in integrum*. For that reason it restricted itself to claim a finding by the Court that the Administering Authority had committed breaches of the Trusteeship Agreement.[100] The Court found however that any judgment it might pronounce would be without object, since the only relief asked of the Court was a declaratory judgment. It therefore held that it could not adjudicate upon the merits of the claim.[101]

The crimes of slavery, genocide and *apartheid* are generally not committed in any way within a bilateral relationship of States. The factual victims of the crimes are the population and individuals of a State, and a claim for restitution will focus on the individuals suffering from the wrongful conduct. In the case of slavery clearly the remedy of restitution is inapplicable, since remedying the situation involves a release of the individuals so held and constitutes cessation. However, it is obvious that genocide involves irreparable damage for the individual, since a life taken away can never be returned. As to the crime of *apartheid*, restitution may take on a multitude of forms, depending on the kind of human rights obligation breached. But again it is clear that some breaches cannot be remedied by restitution, such as those constituting the wrongful killing of individuals for their opposition to the policies of the State.

In conclusion it may be said that restitution constitutes the primary form of reparation for any kind of internationally wrongful act, and as such takes precedence over compensation. With regard to international crimes, it may be said that it can be effected most easily in relation to the crimes taking place within a bilateral context. As to the crimes based on breaches of human rights obligations, it may observed that the possibility of restitution depends on the nature of the human right involved.

3.5. Compensation

The Commission has adopted article 8, Part Two, on compensation:[102]

> " 1. The injured State is entitled to obtain from the State which has committed an internationally wrongful act compensation for the damage caused by that act, if and to the extent that the damage is not made good by restitution in kind.
>
> 2. For the purposes of the present article, compensation covers any economically assessable damage sustained by the injured State, and may include interest and, where appropriate, loss of profits."

It may be opportune, first of all, to start off by repeating the stance taken in the previous section, and which appears to be enshrined in the text, to the effect that the compensation form of reparation ought only to be seen as a complement to, or substitute of, restitution. Thus, as a matter of legal principle, compensation is due to the injured State only if restitution is not possible (or only partially so).[103] On the other hand it may be noted that restitution need not adequately remedy all of the damage done by an internationally wrongful act. For that reason, as paragraph 2 shows, the author State may also be under an obligation to pay compensation for *lucrum cessans*,[104] and to pay interest on the sum due for reparation.[105]

The only viable exception to the primacy of restitution in the scheme of reparation forms is when both the author State and injured State come to agree on a settlement involving compensation rather than restitution. In such a scheme neither State can impose its will on the other. The injured State can insist on restitution, which then could not be refused by the author State. But the author State could make an offer of restitution, which the injured State in turn could not refuse. Only their combined will then can result in a choice for compensation as a means to put an end to the responsibility of the author State.

Regarding the definition and function of compensation the Commission has stated that the phrase "economically assessable damage" covers:[106]

> "(i) damage caused to the State's territory in general, to its organization in a broad sense, its property at home and abroad, its military installations, diplomatic premises, ships, aircraft, spacecraft, etc.
> (so-called 'direct' damage to the State); and
> (ii) damage caused to the State through the persons, physical or juridical, of its nationals or agents (so-called 'indirect' damage to the State)."

And the Commission specified later on:[107]

> "The role of compensation is to fill in any gaps, large, small or minimal which may be left in full reparation by the noted frequent inadequacy of restitution in kind."

At this point it becomes necessary to discuss the question whether injured States, in the presence of a directly injured State, can claim any form of reparation, notably compensation, or whether they can only claim cessation, restitution, satisfaction or guarantees against repetition.[108]

Insofar as there exists a directly injured State this would seem to indicate that non-directly injured States are all entitled to support the claims of the directly injured State. But even if the directly injured State does not press any claim, they could still claim from the author State that it provide reparation to the directly injured State. Even a directly injured State's opposition would not suffice to take away the basis, their injured State status, for their claims of reparation.[109] The argument for that stance may be found with the already noted principle (subsection 3.3.1) that no State can consent to the breach of obligations under a peremptory norm, nor acquiesce in it. It is not to be expected, however, that a directly injured State will object to the support given by non-directly injured States as against the author State.

The situation is somewhat different when the breach of obligations does not lead to any State being specifically affected by it. The absence of any directly injured State is particularly obvious in case of breaches of human rights obligations. In such cases it might be said that the interest of the injured States lies with discontinuance of ongoing breaches, restitution in some instances, as well as with the prevention of future breaches. The question then is whether injured States are also in a position to claim substitute or complementary compensation, or satisfaction, in those cases where the breach has already been consumed, or where restitution would not be possible or sufficient to provide complete reparation. Again the answer appears to lie with the pronouncement of the Permanent Court to the effect that reparation "must wipe out all the consequences of the illegal act", and further that reparation ought to consist of "restitution in kind, or, if this is not possible, payment of a sum corresponding to the value which a restitution in kind would bear". On this basis it is safe to say that the author State cannot escape its responsibility by merely discontinuing its wrongful conduct and the release, as a kind of restitution, of individuals. It will also be under the obligation, insofar as irreparable harm has been done, to provide compensation in case of breaches of human rights obligations.[110] The same example of arbitrary detention may be mentioned. In such a case compensation ought to be granted for the time spent by an individual arbitrarily detained. Damage may include loss of labour pay, physical abuse, etc. Such compensation should be paid, not to the injured States, but to the victims. It would be unnecessarily cumbersome to redirect any compensation through the injured States to the nationals of the author State.

As a general observation regarding the compensation régime applicable to international crimes it may be noted that Arangio-Ruiz does not envisage any modifications of the consequences applicable to delicts.[111]

With regard to the specific crimes it may be mentioned first of all that the crime of aggression may eventually lead to the conclusion of a peace treaty settling among others the amount of, or the procedures for determining the extent of, compensation to be paid. In principle the obligation to compensate encompasses all damages caused as a result of the aggression, and not merely damages caused by internationally wrongful acts after the beginning of the armed conflict.[112] Thus responsibility is incurred principally on the basis of the original internationally wrongful act, the crime of aggression, and it is extended to cover breaches of humanitarian law. But although an armed conflict may end with the conclusion of a peace treaty, that is by no means to say that a peace treaty is necessary in order to conclude to the existence of an obligation to compensate.[113] But in general it can be said that some agreement would seem to be required for the determination of the scope and extent of the obligation to compensate.

At this point attention needs to be drawn to a re-orientation[114] with regard to the application of the rules on reparation as a result of the Iraq-Kuwait conflict. Indeed, by now it has become clear that the Security Council is in position to determine, by way of binding resolution,[115] that reparation is due as the result of aggression.

Thus the Security Council, in resolution 687, operative paragraph 16, made the following statement:

> "*Reaffirms* that Iraq, (...), is liable under international law for any direct loss, damage, including environmental damage and the depletion of natural resources, or injury to foreign Governments, nationals and corporations, as a result of Iraq's unlawful invasion and occupation of Kuwait;"

This statement as such does not present any novel feature with regard to the obligation to provide compensation. But the Security Council went on, in resolution 692, to create a Fund for compensation purposes and a Compensation Commission to administer that Fund.[116] The novelty of all this lies with the manner in which the Fund is to be financed. In order to ensure proper financing the Security Council determined that Iraq was to contribute to the Fund a certain percentage of its petroleum (products) export value.[117] And in resolution 706 the Security Council authorized the purchase by States of petroleum or petroleum products from Iraq up to an amount of 1.6 billion dollars, the amount of such purchases to be paid, directly, into an escrow account of the United Nations. In this manner the Security Council ensured that no evasion of paying the required percentage was possible, since payment into the account will be effectuated through the States in which the purchases are made.[118] Clearly such a procedure sets a powerful precedent for the effective enforcement of any compensation claim as a result of a committed crime of aggression. Resolution 687 will clearly be binding upon members of the United Nations generally, since it constitutes a decision in the sense of article 25 of the Charter. Consequently Iraq is also bound by the Security Council's decisions. Of course the Security Council, in its determination of Iraq's responsibility, acts, not as a judicial organ, but as a party to the dispute or at least, to some extent, as a champion for Kuwait and other States.[119] Paraphrasing the Permanent Court's wording in the Mavrommatis Case,[120] the Security Council, by taking up the claims of its members, is in reality asserting its right to ensure, in the person of its members, respect for the rules of international law. It may be noted that at the end of resolution 687, the Council conditioned the entry into force of a cease-fire between Iraq and the Coalition forces on Iraq's acceptance of the provisions of resolution 687. Already earlier, in resolution 686, the Security Council had demanded that Iraq should:

> "Accept in principle its liability under international law for any loss, damage, or injury arising in regard to Kuwait and third States, and their nationals and corporations, as a result of the invasion and illegal occupation of Kuwait by Iraq;"

Nevertheless it is to be noted that the way in which the Fund is to be financed, though not directly imposed on Iraq, testifies to a highly creative and innovative manner of enforcement of compensation claims.

Insofar as the other international crimes are concerned, their end does not seem to be followed by any agreement on the settlement of compensation claims.[121] Apparently greater importance is attached to the cessation of the internationally wrongful acts concerned, restitution and guarantees against their repetition. One issue that arises in this respect is the claim of Graefrath that some States are under the obligation to provide compensation to the peoples of South Africa and Namibia for having been the accomplices of the *apartheid* régime.[122] It is certainly undeniable that States committing an international crime are under an obligation to provide reparation to the injured subject. But such an obligation is in fact an impossibility when the international crime concerned escapes the bilateralism of inter-State relations, and consists of breaches of human rights obligations pure and simple. The acts of genocide committed in Cambodia gave rise to the responsibility of that State. At the most one could defend the view that other States could insist on the establishment of some fund to compensate the victims. It is more complicated to assert responsibility for complicity. In article 27, Part One, of the ILC-draft the Commission has laid down the rule that a State rendering aid or assistance to another State which is acting wrongfully shall commit its own wrongful act only if such aid or support is rendered for the commission of the wrongful act. And it specified in the commentary that:[123]

> "(...) the participation referred to in this article does not relate to cases in which the conduct of a State takes the form, not of actions or omissions intended to make it possible or easier for another State to commit an internationally wrongful act, but rather of action specifically intended to effect, with another State or other States, the breach of a given international obligation."

The burden of proof inherent in this stance would seem to require then that it is established that aid or assistance was rendered to another State with intent to commit a breach of a specific obligation.[124] Considering the notoriety inherent in the commission of international crimes, one would have to say that the criteria set by the Commission are too strict.[125] One should establish therefore (especially with regard to those crimes which of necessity are committed through the use of armed force against another State or against the population, whether or not there is opposition to such acts) that aid or assistance in the form of arms or military *materiel* rendered to a State committing an international crime will constitute an act of complicity and may entail a complementary obligation to provide compensation to the injured subject(s).

3.6. Satisfaction

Of old there has been a tendency to describe satisfaction as reparation for the moral, political or legal damage caused as a result of an internationally wrongful act.[126] At times it has also been considered to be apt to remedy breaches of obligation committed against the honour, dignity or prestige of States.[127] As observed in chapter one, subsection 1.5.4, the terms moral and legal damage are quite inapt to be used as criteria to determine the legal interests of States. For the same reasons they are inapt to explain the existence of that category of reparation named satisfaction. Because in reality moral damage can only result from the breach of moral demands, and legal damage, since it is considered to be present upon the commission of any breach of obligation, cannot be distinguished from the illegal act itself. Also anything which is reparable in character and for which specific forms of reparation exist (chapter one, subsection 1.5.4) could be seen to constitute legal damage. Thus the ratio for the existence of the category of satisfaction is that an injured State will be gratified by acknowledgement of the wrongfulness of an act, the expression of regrets or apologies, saluting of flags, by seeing culprits punished, or by receiving money in excess of compensation due for the material damages. But of course such satisfaction may result already from the fact that an author State discontinues its wrongful act, returns persons, property or territory, or provides compensation.[128] In all those cases there is some form of acknowledgement, if only implicitly, of the wrongfulness of the acts.[129] It would therefore be more accurate to adhere to the stance that all the specific manifestations of satisfaction, in one way or the other, serve as a guarantee against repetition. In a somewhat more limited way Graefrath explains with regard to satisfaction:[130]

> "I tend not to relate satisfaction only to moral or political damage. It seems to me that it would be more precise to understand as satisfaction all measures taken by the author State of an internationally wrongful act to affirm the existence of the affected obligation and to prevent continuation or repetition of the wrongful act."

The argument here may be extended to cover not only satisfaction, but also the other forms of reparation, restitution in kind and compensation. In the event the author State provides reparation, leaving aside here the question of *ex gratia* payments, this tends to affirm the existence of the obligation and thus offers a guarantee against repetition.

Nevertheless the idea of the provision of guarantees against repetition warrants separate discussion, especially in the light of their importance in case of international crimes.

Generally speaking three specific manifestations of satisfaction are known to exist. First of all the acknowledgement of the wrongfulness of the acts, the expression of regrets or apologies in their regard, and sometimes salutes to the flag. In the second place has been mentioned the investigation as to the culprits of the acts, their prosecution and eventual conviction and punishment. Thirdly, of course, the highly controversial concept of punitive damages ought to be discussed. These manifestations have been laid down in article 10, Part Two, on satisfaction in case of delicts, adopted by the Commission:[131]

> "1. The injured State is entitled to obtain from the State which has committed an internationally wrongful act satisfaction for the damage, in particular moral damage, caused by that act, if and to the extent necessary to provide full reparation.
>
> 2. Satisfaction may take the form of one or more of the following:
> (a) an apology;
> (b) nominal damages;
> (c) in cases of gross infringement of the rights of the injured State, damages reflecting the gravity of the infringement;
> (d) in cases where the internationally wrongful act arose from the serious misconduct of officials or from criminal conduct of officials or private parties, disciplinary action against, or punishment of, those responsible.
>
> 3. The right of the injured State to obtain satisfaction does not justify demands which would impair the dignity of the State which has committed the internationally wrongful act."

The phrase "if and to the extent necessary to provide full reparation" is meant by the Commission to express the exceptional character of the remedy of satisfaction, since there may be circumstances in which there exists no basis for granting satisfaction.[132] With regard to international crimes Arangio-Ruiz has proposed, in a future article 16, paragraph 3, that the author State would not be entitled to benefit from the restriction envisaged in article 10, paragraph 3.[133]

3.6.1. ACKNOWLEDGEMENT OF RESPONSIBILITY AND EXPRESSION OF REGRETS OR APOLOGIES

Primarily the obligation to express regrets or provide apologies is based on the notion that the author State of an internationally wrongful act ought to recognize the illegality of its conduct.[134] That notion presents, in ordinary circumstances, the prerequisite for fulfilling all other obligations of reparation, because the recognition of illegality by the author State usually precedes the conclusion of an agreement settling on restitution in kind or the payment of substitute or complementary compensation. Performance of the obligation to provide apologies may not lead to explicit recognition of the wrongfulness of the acts, since apologies may be phrased very generally. It is possible to apologize, for instance, by saying that one regrets the occurrence of the acts. One may wonder therefore if the draft article should not rather be based on an obligation of the author State to recognize that its acts were wrongful. That would seem to be in accordance with the often quoted dictum of the Court in the Corfu Channel Case to the effect that its declaration, that the acts of the British Navy violated Albania's sovereignty, constituted "in itself appropriate satisfaction."[135]

As to the obligation of the author State to apologize, it may be noted that such an obligation only makes sense insofar as the internationally wrongful act affects a specific State or its nationals. Because in case of breaches of human right obligations the injured States would not seem to be interested as such in apologies. Furthermore, it might be more appropriate to speak of the expression of regrets or apologies, depending on the question whether or not the internationally wrongful act involved intent on the part of the agents of the author State. Such a distinction could well be made if regard is had to paragraph 2 of article 10, Part Two, originally proposed by Arangio-Ruiz:[136]

> "The choice of form or forms of satisfaction shall be made taking into account the importance of the obligation breached and the existence or degree of wilful intent or negligence of the State which has committed the wrongful act."

Thus apologies would be in order if there was such intent, while the mere expression of regrets would suffice in those cases where no such intent could be inferred, or where the acts concerned were committed by individuals in no way representing the State (though could engage in their activities through a lack of diligence on the part of the State authorities).

With regard to international crimes recognition of illegality of the conduct in question does not seem to have played a major role. A quick look, for instance, through Security Council resolutions indicates that it rather relies on declaring the illegality, and the consequent responsibility of the author State, itself. Its primary objective after that is to obtain for the injured State or subject cessation of the wrongful conduct, restitution of persons, property or territory, compensation, and possible guarantees against repetition.

3.6.2. PUNISHMENT OF RESPONSIBLE INDIVIDUALS

The second possible means of satisfying an injured State consists of the prosecution, conviction and punishment of the persons, whether they be State agents or private individuals, responsible for the acts committed. It would seem to be inherent in the idea of punishment that individuals will be tried or disciplined only for conduct constituting violations under criminal or administrative law.[137] At this point a distinction will have to be made according to whether the individuals responsible for the acts were agents of the State and acted within their capacity as State organs, or whether they were private individuals. In the latter case the punishment of the individuals may be proceeded with by the author State, but also by the injured State should the individuals concerned come within its territorial jurisdiction (in that case it will still need to be in possession of an accepted basis of criminal jurisdiction). As much was established through the Lotus Case, in which the Permanent Court judged Turkey justified in prosecuting a French national for negligence during his watch duties on board a ship in international waters.[138] The situation is different insofar as agents of the State are concerned, for their punishment by the injured State will conflict with the general rule that a State cannot punish the organs of another State.[139] Their disciplinary sanctioning or punishment as a form of satisfaction therefore can be demanded by the injured State, but will have to be effected by the author State.[140] On the rule that State organs cannot be punished by another State there is only one exception, and that concerns the issue of crimes under international law.

In cases of crimes under international law individuals may be punished by each and any State for those acts found to be criminal by a rule of international law. Ordinarily an individual within the territorial jurisdiction of a State could only be prosecuted if an accepted basis of criminal jurisdiction was extant. Basically such a basis of criminal jurisdiction may be constituted by the link of nationality between the prosecuting State and either the culprit or the victim of the criminal act, or because the criminal act had taken place on the territory of the prosecuting State. In case of crimes under international law such a link between the prosecuting State and the individual culprit or victim, or its territory, is not required. What this in effect means is that universal jurisdiction has been established for crimes under international law. Thus any State is authorized to proceed with the prosecution, conviction and punishment of individuals engaging in piracy and slavery, notwithstanding the lack of a traditional basis of criminal jurisdiction. It is to be noted of course that such crimes under international law could be committed by individuals of a certain State either with or without the knowledge of their national State. If the national State was indeed involved in the acts, that would mean that it acted wrongfully and had incurred responsibility. Yet in the absence of such responsibility of the national State all the other States could still proceed with the punishment of the individuals. Thus universal jurisdiction of States is not a consequence of the international responsibility of a State, that is on the basis of a secondary rule, but is based on primary rules. The ratio for the rules on crimes under international law therefore lies with the punishment of individuals for acts universally condemned, irrespective of the status of the individuals within the organization of their national State.

A connected development, but of far greater importance, has occurred after the first and second world wars. It concerns the possibility of the prosecution by States of individuals which committed criminal acts in their capacity as State organs.[141] It is this development, which led to the Nuremberg and Tokyo trials after World War II,[142] that was invoked by the Commission as one of the prime arguments in favour of recognizing the distinction between delicts and crimes.[143] Yet the Commission at the same time indicated:[144]

> "(...) that it would be wrong to identify the right-duty of certain States to punish individuals who have committed such crimes with the 'special form' of international responsibility applicable to the State in cases of this kind. The obligation to punish individuals who are organs of the State and are guilty of crimes against the peace, against humanity, and so on does not, in the Commission's view, constitute a form of international responsibility of the State, and such punishment certainly does not exhaust the prosecution of the international responsibility incumbent upon the State for internationally wrongful acts which

> are attributed to it in such cases by reason of the conduct of its organs. Punishment of those in charge of the State machinery who have started a war of aggression or organized an act of genocide does not *per se* release the State itself from its own international responsibility for such acts."

Obviously it is correct to assert that the punishment of individuals, which committed criminal acts in their capacity of State organs, does not release the State from all responsibility. Clearly the author State will still be bound to provide restitution in kind or compensation to the injured State, at least where bilateral relations are involved. But that is not exactly the same as saying that the punishment of such individuals would not constitute, for the author State, a form of responsibility. To some extent it may be asserted that the punishment of culprits by the author State is necessary to have it perform its obligation to "re-establish the situation which would, in all probability, have existed if that act had not been committed". The object desired by any prohibitive primary rule of international law is that certain acts would not take place. And the object sought to be achieved by the obligation to provide reparation (re-establishment of the situation that would have existed had the acts not been committed), the secondary rule, is that the acts would not have taken place in the first place. Yet the latter involves an apparent impossibility. Yet in order to pretend that the situation has in fact been re-established, punishment of the culprits would seem to be in order.

With regard to international crimes such punishment serves the additional, and in fact far more important, purpose of providing a guarantee against repetition of the criminal acts. The Commission recognized as much when it stated:[145]

> "The need to prevent the breach of obligations which are so essential would indeed appear to warrant both that the individual-organ committing such a breach should be held personally liable to punishment, and that concurrently the State to which the organ belongs should be subject to a special régime of 'international responsibility'."

Thus the prosecution, conviction and punishment of those responsible for the commission of an international crime constitutes an imperative as a kind of measure against repetition. For what is to prevent the responsible officials or organs of the State from repeating their acts if they are not subjected to individual scrutinization for their role during the commission of the crime? As such, as will be seen in section 3.7, it has a close relation to another form of guarantee, that is, change of government.

Since the obligations concerned are of fundamental importance to the international community, this not only gives rise to a rule endowing each and every State with so-called universal jurisdiction.[146] It also provides States with the possibility to set up an international tribunal for the prosecution, conviction and punishment of the individuals. The first examples of that kind were the Nuremberg and Tokyo tribunals, and the precedent has been slow to be repeated. Recently however the Security Council decided on the creation of an International Tribunal that is to prosecute persons responsible for serious violations of international humanitarian law committed in the territory of the former Yugoslavia after 1 January 1991, and on the creation of the International Tribunal for the sole purpose of prosecuting persons responsible for genocide and other serious violations of international humanitarian law committed in the territory of Rwanda and Rwandan citizens responsible for genocide and other such violations committed in the territory of neighbouring States, between 1 January 1994 and 31 December 1994.[147] Again one may point to the innovative character of the measures decided upon by the Security Council. For even though the full implementation of such measures may be obstructed by the States concerned (especially Serbia and Montenegro, Croatia, Bosnia and Herzegovina, and Rwanda) in that they may refuse to surrender suspects, at the moment such suspects would leave their country they become liable to arrest and surrender to the jurisdiction of the tribunal.[148] Although superficially one might conclude that what is concerned is the prosecution of war crimes, that is clearly not the case. Articles 2 to 5 of the Statute of the International Tribunal has laid down the jurisdiction of the International Tribunal over grave breaches of the Geneva Conventions of 1949, violations of the laws or customs of war, genocidal acts, and crimes against humanity. Aside from acts contained in the second category (which mostly concern the so-called Hague Law), all the other acts concern the denial or violation of fundamental human rights. And as we all know such acts have taken place on such a terrifying scale and on such an organized basis, that their characterization as international crime under article 19, paragraph 3 (c), Part One, cannot be called in question.

3.6.3. PUNITIVE DAMAGES

Thirdly, as may be seen from the quoted article 10, Part Two, in the first paragraph of this section, the Commission supports the right of an injured State, in case of delicts, to claim from the author State damages reflecting the gravity of the infringement.[149] The Commission has pointed to the exceptional nature of such damages by noting that they are only to be awarded in cases of gross infringement of the injured State's rights, and that:[150]

> "They are given to the injured party over and above the actual loss, when the wrong done was aggravated by circumstances of violence, oppression, malice, fraud or wicked conduct on the part of the wrongdoing party."

It is to be expected that the payment of punitive damages will be envisaged also in case of international crimes. Arangio-Ruiz' proposal to delete the restriction contained in paragraph 3 of article 10 seems to head in this direction.[151] There are however grounds to deny the existence of any rule of State responsibility, even in case of delicts, stipulating the right to claim punitive damages. Primarily the argument to be made is that the State practice in this respect is confused, that there is no *opinio juris* that States are bound to pay punitive damages, that the jurisprudence does not unambiguously show support for them, and that authors tend to be against, or reluctant in recognizing, the institute of punitive damages. But there are more fundamental arguments against recognition of punitive damages as a form of satisfaction.

First of all there is the matter that not all internationally wrongful acts necessarily cause moral or legal injury to another State. Breaches of human rights obligations by a State for instance do not affect any other State, and consequently cannot be said to cause even a moral or legal injury to those States. It may be admitted of course that the proposed article 10 has been skilfully worded, as it provides that damages only have to be forwarded to the injured State in case of gross infringement of the rights of the injured State. However, if regard is had to article 5, Part Two, it is to be noted that paragraph 1 defines an injured State as a State whose rights are infringed by an act of another State, and all the categories established under paragraph 2 head off by mentioning "if the right infringed". Should damages be paid then to all the injured States in case of human rights violations, even when it cannot be said that they suffer any moral or other damage? Considering that certain human rights are protected by universal rules of customary international law, the provision of article 10 implies an obligation of the author State to pay damages to each and every State.

A second argument against punitive damages lies in the indisputable fact that it does not function in any way to remedy the internationally wrongful act since it is not reparatory in character.[152] What the payment of punitive damages by the author State amounts to in reality is an unjust enrichment of the injured State.[153] Under domestic law there is of course always the possibility of imposing financial burdens on subjects which violate criminal law provisions. But the penalties so inflicted generally do not benefit the victims of the violations, but flow into the public financial funds of the State and are to be used for public purposes. In international law that option could be envisaged,[154] but the payment of punitive damages will ordinarily constitute an unwarranted financial benefit for the injured State.

Thirdly, it may be noted that some internationally wrongful acts may entail large scale damages, leading to substantial compensation claims. The typical example of these are of course international crimes. To the extent that an author State would already be under an obligation to pay a large amount of compensation to the injured State, the award of punitive damages would not favour equality among States. An obligation to pay money as punitive damages can be more easily met by the economically sound or powerful States than by developing States. But it would not be just to impose larger amounts of money as punitive damages on the first category of States than on the second.

Insofar as international crimes are concerned, there has been a tendency to deny the possibility of introducing into the draft articles any criminal responsibility or to attach any penal connotation to civil law orientated concepts such as reparation. Punitive intent is denied, sometimes, even in the case of satisfaction and guarantees against repetition.[155] Aside from that, punitive damages would not seem to be appropriate for the crime of widespread breaches of basic human rights obligations, because there simply would not be any damage to other States.

3.7. Guarantees against repetition

Traditionally it has been the custom for the author State to provide the injured State with assurances that the wrongful act would not occur again. But a verbal guarantee might not always be completely satisfactory. For that reason it has also been accustomed for the author State, on demand of the injured State, to take certain measures to assure non-repetition. In most cases such measures might include no more than the forwarding, through administrative channels, of appropriate instructions to officials in the lower or higher levels of the State's organization. They might also be directed towards those working for the government, or even to those politically responsible in the governmental echelons. Sometimes the demand of the injured State concerns the repeal of a domestic court judgment. The more extreme case of measures against repetition, one would say, involves demands by the injured State that specific legislation be modified or repealed. Measures falling within the latter two categories normally require the co-operation of parliament. Ordinarily the executive branch of the State is responsible for foreign relations, and one can easily see the political difficulties that may arise from such demands. Nevertheless such measures have been demanded by injured States, and have been implemented by author States.[156] The Commission consequently adopted the following article 10 *bis*, Part Two, on assurances or guarantees against repetition:[157]

> "The injured State is entitled, where appropriate, to obtain from the State which has committed an internationally wrongful act assurances or guarantees of non-repetition of the wrongful act."

According to the Commission the phrase "where appropriate" is meant to indicate that assurances or guarantees constitute an exceptional remedy, to be granted only in circumstances to be determined by a third party. Such circumstances are the real risk of repetition and the seriousness of the injury.[158] The function of such assurances or guarantees lies, in the words of the Commission, with the prevention of future wrongful acts, and presupposes a risk of repetition of the wrongful acts.[159] Obviously such a risk will be present especially, to use the words of the Commission, in circumstances where a wrong is aggravated by violence, oppression, malice, fraud or wicked conduct on the part of the author State. Such will be the case especially if the internationally wrongful act committed constitutes an international crime.

The issue of guarantees against repetition in case of international crimes is of paramount importance, yet at the same time their implementation presents huge problems. Before going into these, there is the preliminary question who is to decide on the kind of measures adequate to prevent recurrence of a crime. Ideally such a decision on the adequacy of measures to prevent repetition would fall to the Court, but this would not seem likely to happen in present day realities. At the same time it cannot but be noticed that in case of delicts any decision on reparation is subject to an agreement between the injured and author States.[160] Considering however the far-reaching measures necessary in case of crimes, to be discussed in the following subsections, the adequacy of such measures certainly should not be a matter of discretion to be decided by the injured State(s). In the past there have been numerous instances in which measures against repetition were laid down in a peace treaty, the most notable examples being the peace treaties after the end of the first and second world wars.[161] Yet though there can be no doubt regarding Germany's responsibility for starting World War II, not to mention the genocidal and other horrific acts, it can hardly be considered satisfactory that a limited number of States decided on the fate of an up till then sovereign State. Even the fact that such (peace) treaties were based on unconditional surrenders, and to some limited extent may be considered consensual in character, really cannot and does not change their essentially imposed nature.[162]

Some progress has been made in that the recent act of aggression by Iraq against has led, at least initially, to a Security Council response and eventually to the adoption of cease-fire resolution 687.[163] That resolution can in many respects be considered the contemporary equivalent of a peace treaty, and will be used as a basis of discussion, if not exclusively, for the following subsections.

Another preliminary issue concerns the question whether the Security Council possesses any legislative competencies. The question needs to be answered especially in the light of resolution 687, since that imposes a number of obligations on Iraq which go far beyond what it was bound to under conventional or customary law rules. In this respect reference must be made to the matters discussed in chapter two as to the meaning and scope of the threat to the peace, and the competence of the Security Council thereto. As stated the notion threat to peace must be interpreted objectively and in a legal manner. Also article 39 does not lay down any independent obligation not to threaten the peace, and must be read in the light of existing obligations and their breach by members. The Security Council's action must therefore be directed towards the *mise en oeuvre* of a member State's responsibility. Any action it takes must be geared towards the fulfilment by the author State of its obligations to provide reparation. If the Security Council must remain faithful already to the rules on responsibility and cannot go beyond the scope of such rules, one would say that *a fortiori*, since there would be no wrongful conduct by a member, it cannot impose conduct on a member which is not also prescribed by a primary rule of international law.

In first instance the Security Council will of necessity be laying emphasis on the author State's obligation to cease its wrongful conduct and will try to make it comply with its obligation to return territory, persons and property. But it is not restricted to the more reparatory obligations, and may also involve itself with the author State's obligations to provide satisfaction and guarantees against repetition. There is however one operative condition for the Security Council's competence in this matter, and that lies with the necessity of a continued threat to the peace. The Security Council's competence does not amount to an unlimited power to enforce member States' obligations in whatever circumstances it thinks fit.[164] Where the non-performance of specific reparation obligations would not lead to a threat to the peace, the Security Council should retreat and abstain from enforcement regarding such breaches. Whether such will be the case of course will depend on the specific circumstances of any particular situation. Additionally, measures desired of, or imposed on, an author State have to be scrutinized as to whether they are adequate to prevent repetition of similar wrongful acts. If they are not, such measures cannot be demanded or imposed.

At this point it may be noted that Arangio-Ruiz has proposed, by way of an article 16, paragraph 3, Part Two, to delete the restriction applicable to satisfaction and guarantees against repetition to the effect that demands by injured States could not be made to the extent that they would conflict with the author State's dignity, or with rules protecting the author State's sovereignty and liberty.[165] The deletion of that restriction would make it possible to demand "disarmament, demilitarization, dismantling of war industry, destruction of weapons, acceptance of observation teams, or change to a form of government not incompatible with fundamental freedoms, civil and political rights and self-determination" (mentioned in the context of the crime of aggression);[166] as well as the "abrogation of discriminatory, racial or segregational legislation, popular consular consultations such as free elections or plebiscites, restoration of fundamental rights and freedoms, dismantling of environmentally dangerous plants and compliance with the aut dedere aut iudicare principle with regard to individuals accused of delicta iuris gentium." (in the context of the other crimes of article 19, paragraph 3, Part One).[167] A number of these measures, and others, will be discussed in the following subsections.

3.7.1. GUARANTEES REGARDING DISPUTES LYING AT THE BASIS OF THE CRIME

The Security Council, in paragraphs 2 to 4 of resolution 687, put down the following:

> "2. Demands that Iraq and Kuwait respect the inviolability of the international boundary and the allocation of islands set out in the "Agreed Minutes Between the State of Kuwait and the Republic of Iraq Regarding the Restoration of Friendly Relations, Recognition and Related Matters", signed by them in the exercise of their sovereignty at Baghdad on 4 October 1963 and registered with the United Nations and published by the United Nations in document 7063, United Nations, Treaty Series, 1964;
> 3. Calls upon the Secretary-General to lend his assistance to make arrangements with Iraq and Kuwait to demarcate the boundary between Iraq and Kuwait, drawing on appropriate material, including the map transmitted by Security Council document S/22412 and to report back to the Security Council within one month;
> 4. Decides to guarantee the inviolability of the above-mentioned international boundary and to take as appropriate all necessary measures to that end in accordance with the Charter of the United Nations;"

That the Security Council is entitled to guarantee the inviolability of the international boundary between Iraq and Kuwait cannot be called in question. Although article 2, paragraph 4, of the Charter would seem to prohibit the threat or use of force against the territorial integrity of States only, it may be argued, and will be (chapter five), that the prescription of article 2, paragraph 3, of the Charter implies a prohibition of all cross-border uses of force. Of course Iraq's actions fell squarely under article 2, paragraph 4, since it claimed Kuwait to be part of its territory and used force on the whole of Kuwait's territory. Iraq's action was intentionally aimed at the destruction of the continued territorial existence of Kuwait, and therefore also at its very political independence.

However, the Security Council's intention was not merely to ensure inviolability of Kuwait's frontiers, but also to have that frontier demarcated as between Iraq and Kuwait.[168] Now we all know that initially Iraq claimed part of Kuwait's territory. Yet at the same time we know this claim, and others, to have been no more than a pretext for Iraq's aggressive and expansionist action. To view the lack of demarcation as a, or the, cause of Iraq's crime would appear to be an unjustified exaggeration. Especially so since by effecting the demarcation not only the factual status quo *ante* was changed to the benefit of Kuwait.[169] Admittedly, it is possible to argue that the fixation of the border could function as a guarantee to prevent future aggressive acts. Clearly Iraq will no longer be in a position to claim parts of Kuwait's territory as its own. However, the demarcation of the border has, to some extent, changed the territorial status quo as it existed before Iraq's aggression. The fact that this change is in conformity with the, naturally desired, legal status quo would not seem to justify treating Iraq's continuing non-performance of its obligations under the 1963 Agreed Minutes as a threat to the peace.[170] Indeed, by making these changes in the factual border line tensions are more likely to be perpetuated and may constitute a more severe threat to the peace.[171] As a guarantee against repetition of the act of aggression it seems to fail in its purpose, since it is implemented in the face of Iraqi opposition to the demarcation. A far better alternative would have been to recommend any dispute regarding the frontier to be settled through arbitration or judicial channels. That would have been in accordance also with article 36, paragraph 3, of the Charter, since territorial disputes in essence are legal in character. In that way Iraq could have had its day in Court, and in the event of a negative decision might have given way gracefully.[172] In this respect one may also point to the fact that the Security Council is not a judicial body, and though it has to apply legal rules at times this does not give it *carte blanche* to decide disputes between members. Its powers under Chapter VI are of recommendatory character only, and its powers under Chapter VII are to be exercised only for the maintenance or restoration of international peace and security. As a guideline the Security Council should therefore not concern itself with any unsettled disputes dating from before the commission of a crime.

In the same line of thought one should reject any attempt to impose upon the author State of a crime disadvantages of any kind. Any change in contracts or agreements (between States, States and foreign nationals, or private individuals among themselves) validly concluded and/or executed before the commission of the crime is off-limits. In past peace treaties one may deduce a trend to impose modifications or abrogations.[173] Basically the imposition of such burdens on the author State are in conflict with the obligation not to go beyond what is adequate to wipe out the consequences of the wrongful act and to re-establish the situation that would have existed without it. Being utterly unconnected to the commission of a crime such burdens should be abjured as being inconsistent with the principle of sovereign equality of States as laid down in article 2, paragraph 1, of the Charter. And since they are unconnected to the crime such burdens are clearly not apt to prevent the recurrence of the crime concerned and cannot be justified on that count.

It has to be underlined, by way of conclusion, that by committing a crime an author State does not place itself outside the community of States. In this context a provision suggested by Riphagen could be considered a most valuable contribution, as it ran:[174]

> "A breach of an international obligation does not, in itself, deprive that State of its rights under international law."

It is submitted that an author State generally retains all of its rights, even if for the moment it would not be in a position to exercise them. That ought to be the case even when an internationally wrongful act constitutes a crime. Although some rights of the author State may be put on hold, as it were, they will be revived once the basic goals of reparation are met.

3.7.2. GUARANTEES REGARDING THE COMMISSION OF, OR CONDUCT DURING, THE CRIME

The Security Council elaborated quite extensively, in resolution 687, the specific measures which it expected Iraq to implement in the area of disarmament.[175] This was done in order to restore international peace and security in the area, apparently on the consideration that there existed a threat to the peace even after the end of hostilities. As it was put in the preamble, the Security Council needed "to be assured of Iraq's peaceful intentions in the light of its unlawful invasion and occupation of Kuwait". When reading however the specific provisions of section C of resolution 687 (paragraphs 7 to 14) one is struck by the fact that none of the measures recorded relates directly to reducing the size of Iraq's army or to disarming members of its armed forces.[176] Rather they are all directed towards the destruction of weapons of mass-destruction and related materials (including ballistic missiles with a reach of more than 150 kilometres). The disarmament measures set forth in resolution 687 in fact relate not so much to the commission of the crime, but rather to Iraq's conduct during the crime. This conduct, as the Security Council records, mainly consisted of making threats to use chemical weapons. It did include, however, the actual use of ballistic missiles against targets in Saudi Arabia and Israel. While Saudi Arabia had joined the Coalition and could be considered a belligerent, the same could not be said as regards Israel. The Security Council further took note of reports by members that Iraq had obtained materials for the development of nuclear weapons. In addition to its breaches of obligations by invading Kuwait, Iraq apparently had already previously breached its obligations under the Treaty on Non-Proliferation of Nuclear Weapons,[177] and subsequently breached its obligation not to use force against a non-belligerent State. While it did not actually use chemical weapons against Coalition members, the Security Council observed that this would have entailed a breach of Iraq's obligations under the 1925 Geneva Protocol.[178] It also noted Iraq's earlier uses of chemical weapons, without denouncing those as breaches of obligations under the 1925 Geneva Protocol.

It comes as no surprise then that the Security Council required Iraq to co-operate in the destruction of all its chemical and biological weapons, ballistic missiles with a reach of more than 150 kilometres, and manufacturing facilities regarding the foregoing (paragraph 9). Additionally it required Iraq to place all its nuclear-weapons-usable materials under exclusive control, for custody and removal, of the International Atomic Energy Agency (paragraph 12). Some of the obligations thus created go far beyond anything Iraq had been obligated to under treaty or customary law.[179] Especially the obligation to allow the destruction of its chemical and biological weapons, as well as its ballistic missiles, did not exist previously under any primary rule of international law. Clearly therefore their formulation in resolution 687 can be justified only to the extent that they can be seen as measures against the repetition of wrongful acts. The aim of the disarmament obligations in resolution 687 envisages the prevention of further wrongful acts unrelated, as such, to the crime of aggression. The question is then whether these new obligations can at all be justified, since they appear all to be based on Iraq's unlawful invasion of Kuwait. The answer must be affirmative.

First may be mentioned that ballistic missiles have in fact been used, and their further use will, in all likelihood, only take place during a situation of armed conflict. As such the destruction of such missiles appears justified, especially if one considers that they were aimed at areas with a dense civilian population. The same argument goes for the destruction of Iraq's chemical weapons potential, considering its earlier use, albeit in a previous armed conflict, of chemical weapons. The argument, of doubtful character in itself, that the use of chemical weapons could lawfully be resorted to in situations of internal armed conflict, fails basically because such use by Iraq in the past amounted to an attempted genocide on its Kurdish minority. While Iraq cannot be considered bound by a conventional rule prohibiting the use of biological weapons,[180] actual use can be said to conflict with well-established principles of humanitarian law. Those principles prohibit the use of weapons in circumstances where such use would cause superfluous suffering or where they could not be used indiscriminately (that is, when they could not be used without substantially affecting non-combatants). On that basis one would have to say that there is hardly any situation in which biological weapons could lawfully be used. As to the obligations regarding nuclear-weapons-usable materials, they are all based on Iraq's obligations under the Non-Proliferation Treaty. Their goals are not therefore to be seen in relation to the prevention of future wrongful acts, but rather in relation to Iraq's obligation to cease its wrongful conduct. There can also be little doubt that Iraq's possession of chemical, biological or nuclear weapons could create tension in the region, especially considering its previously exposed willingness to use such weapons. On that basis alone there are sufficient grounds to conclude to the existence of a threat to the peace.

With regard to international crimes other than aggression, disarmament obligations as a means to prevent repetition of the wrongful acts do not necessarily provide a complete answer. Regarding the crime of denial of self-determination the adequate response would appear to be the transfer of authority, alongside the withdrawal of any foreign troops. To the extent that the arms of such foreign troops would have been financed out of the separate budget of the territory held in bondage, they would have to be transferred to the new State. As to the crime of breaches, on a widespread scale, of basic human rights obligations, the remedy to be provided as a means to prevent recurrence lies with the re-organization of the police, paramilitary, and armed forces. If regard is had to quite a number of recent agreements between governments and its (armed) opposition, one will see that frequently provisions are made for the re-organization of the police, paramilitary, and armed forces.[181] Sometimes the agreement even stipulates the integration, in one way or another, of the oppositional armed forces within the governmental armed forces. In some circumstances there may of course be a need to disband specific organizational units of the police, paramilitary, and armed forces.

In conclusion it may be said that all kinds of measures related to the police, paramilitary, and armed forces may be demanded and imposed regarding international crimes in order to prevent repetition of wrongful acts. The proposals of Arangio-Ruiz in his seventh report support this.[182] Yet whatever the specific measures envisaged in order to prevent the repetition of wrongful acts, they probably will all be ineffectual to the extent that they do not uproot the causes of the illegal conduct when the individuals engaging in specific criminal acts are not held accountable for their action or inaction. This leads us to the following subsection.

3.7.3. GUARANTEES AFFECTING OR CHANGING THE STATE ORGANIZATION

At the end of World War II,[183] and afterwards, legal and factual action was taken in order to ensure that those responsible for the commission of war crimes, crimes against the peace, and crimes against humanity, would be brought to justice.[184] Eventually a number of the individuals concerned were prosecuted, tried and convicted by the International Military Tribunals of Nuremberg and Tokyo. Though the trials constituted a moral and legal imperative, they cannot be seen in isolation from their essential objective: to prevent the defeated States from ever again committing acts of aggression against peace-loving States.[185] They were not restricted to the prosecution of individuals for war crimes and crimes against humanity, but were concurrently directed towards the prosecution of individuals for crimes against the peace. Defendants at Nuremberg were consequently accused of the "planning, preparation, initiation, or waging of a war of aggression, or a war in violation of international treaties, agreements, or assurances". Their capability to commit the original crime (planning and initiating the war of aggression), and the connected crimes during the war (war crimes and crimes against humanity), had come from the high-ranking positions they had held in the government of their country. Apart from the unbearable thought of seeing these individuals walking around freely as if they had done nothing wrong,[186] the Allies (the United Nations) quite rightly saw that nothing but a complete turnabout would suffice in order to prevent recurrence of the crimes. In that line of thought they ordered the arrest and surrender of all the principal Nazi political heavy weights.[187] In the same vein they inserted into the Charter for the International Military Tribunal the possibility of the Tribunal declaring certain groups or organizations to be criminal organizations.[188] Previously a number of armistice agreements provided for the dissolution of fascist organizations, and the prohibition of such organizations was established in peace treaties. Article 17 of the Peace Treaty with Italy may be quoted as typical in this respect:

> "Italy, which, in accordance with Article 30 of the Armistice Agreement, has taken measures to dissolve the Fascist organizations in Italy, shall not permit the resurgence on Italian territory of such organizations, whether political, military or semi-military, whose purpose it is to deprive the people of their democratic rights."

This provision steps beyond the mere suppression of criminal acts and organizations, but concerns the political structure of the State.

Not being content with the prosecution of those politically responsible as such, the allied powers adopted article 13 (b) of the 1945 Declaration regarding the Defeat of Germany:

> "The Allied Representatives will impose on Germany additional political, administrative, economic, financial, military and other requirements arising from the complete defeat of Germany."

By this they opened the possibility of imposing on Germany not merely a change of government, but a veritable power to dictate even constitutional requirements. That such powers existed and could be exercised at the will of the occupying States may be seen from the 1949 Washington Accords,[189] which determined the powers and responsibilities of the governments of the United States, the United Kingdom and France from the moment of creation of the Federal Republic of Germany. Indeed such powers amounted to a *de facto* veto power on constitutional changes, as may be seen from article 5 of the 1949 "Statut d'occupation":[190]

> "Tout amandement de la loi fondamentale devra être approuvé par les Autorités d'occupation avant d'entrer en vigeur."

The "Statut d'occupation" was abrogated through article 1, paragraph 2, of the Convention on Relations between the Three Powers and the Federal Republic of Germany.[191] These States reserved, in article 2, paragraph 1, their rights regarding the stationing of troops and their protection in Germany; regarding Berlin; and regarding Germany as a whole (including the unification of Germany and a peace treaty).[192]

The Security Council did not in any way stipulate a change of government within Iraq,[193] or even the prosecution of those responsible for the unleashing of the war. Could such far-reaching provisions nevertheless be adopted in a contemporary (peace) treaty? The question needs to be answered, because article 2, paragraphs 3 and 4, of the Charter are designed to protect the political independence of States. It may be admitted that such protection is envisaged through the stipulated peaceful settlement of disputes, and that such political independence is safeguarded only by prohibiting the use of military force. Indeed, the rule prohibiting the use of military force against the territorial integrity and political independence of States has been presented as the prime example of a peremptory norm. The Court, for instance, noted the concurrence of views in that regard on the part of the United States and Nicaragua.[194] Could a treaty then be imposed, through the use of force, on a State that had committed aggression, considering that such a treaty might conflict with a rule of *jus cogens*? A first observation could be that the prohibition contained in article 2, paragraph 4, only relates to the first use of force and not to a reactive use of force. The problem with this argument is that it does not take into account that there are many ways in which a State can breach the prohibition. Clearly a minor violation could not justify an all out responsive use of force, and for that reason could also not justify an imposed treaty. Some observations of the Court in the Nicaragua Case lend credibility to this argument:[195]

> "In the view of the Court, under international law in force today – whether customary international law or that of the United Nations system – States do not have a right of 'collective' armed response to acts which do not constitute an 'armed attack'."

Since it is not possible for States collectively to lawfully use force in reaction to acts not constituting an armed attack, a treaty imposed in such circumstances must logically be deemed invalid.

The situation would seem to be different when there is Security Council involvement. The Security Council can take action with regard to acts that do not constitute an armed attack by one State against another. In appropriate circumstances it could even resort to the use of force on the basis of the (mere) existence of a threat to the peace.

Yet could it impose a treaty on a State that had done no more than stress certain claims it makes on the territory of another State, publish maps showing part of the territory of another State as its territory, or showing some symbol on its flag claimed by another State to be its historical and cultural heritage? By doing all these things Macedonia certainly has caused tension with Greece and contributed to the existence of a threat to the peace, but could, or ought, the Security Council for that reason determine the outcome of this dispute by making Macedonia back down through threatening the use of force? Not likely, not really. Yet could it have used force, or authorized the use of force, to oust the government of Iraq on account of Iraq's act of aggression? Yes it could, and in fact did, given the broad goals contained in resolution 678, paragraph 2, which included the restoration of peace and security in the area. The continued reign of Saddam Hussein in Iraq prevents the institution of a more peaceable government. Account has to be taken, furthermore, of Iraq's earlier act of aggression, under the same leadership, against Iran. There is just cause to believe that there is a chance of repetition of Iraq's aggressive behaviour. The Security Council would have been fully justified in determining an Iraq with an unaltered leadership to constitute a threat to the peace.[196] In circumstances where the use of force (authorized) by the Security Council is justified, the imposition of a treaty to accomplish the goals of reparation consequent upon a wrongful act will also be justified.

By arguing on this issue account has to be taken, naturally, of the Court's ruling in the Nicaragua Case on the principle of non-intervention:[197]

> "A prohibited intervention must accordingly be one bearing on matters in which each State is permitted, by the principle of State sovereignty, to decide freely. One of these is the choice of a political, economic, social and cultural system, and the formulation of foreign policy. Intervention is wrongful when it uses methods of coercion in regard to such choices, which must remain free ones. The element of coercion, which defines, and indeed forms the very essence of, prohibited intervention, is particularly obvious in the case of an intervention which uses force, either in the direct form of military action, or in the indirect form of support for subversive or terrorist armed activities within another State."

These observations on the freedom of choice regarding a State's political system may be said adequately to reflect the position under existing primary rules of customary international law.[198] But do they reflect the content of customary law with respect to the secondary rules on State responsibility? It is submitted that they do so only partially. First of all it may be noted that the Court apparently would have validated the actions of the United States if those could have been considered as an exercise of a right of self-defence, and it held:[199]

> "In the Court's view, however, if Nicaragua has been giving support to the armed opposition in El Salvador, and if this constitutes an armed attack on El Salvador and the other appropriate conditions are met, collective self-defence could be legally invoked by the United States, even though there may be the possibility of an additional motive, one perhaps even more decisive for the United States, drawn from the political orientation of the present Nicaraguan

> Government. The existence of an additional motive, other than that proclaimed by the United States, could not deprive the latter of its right to resort to collective self-defence."

In the event the Court found that the acts attributed to Nicaragua could not be considered an armed attack on El Salvador, or Honduras and Costa Rica.[200] Yet these remarks by the Court seem to indicate that the American support for the *contras*, whose avowed aim was to overthrow the government of Nicaragua,[201] might have been justified if there had been an armed attack. Furthermore, applying the maxim "qui peut le plus, peut le moins", it is possible to argue that a State, which may use direct military force in defence, could also resort to the indirect uses of military force. Judge Schwebel, in his dissenting opinion to the Nicaragua Case, commented on the argument, put forward by Nicaragua, that the exercise of self-defence and the overthrow of the government of the attacking State were incompatible, as follows:[202]

> "(...) if, *arguendo*, one assumes that the purpose of United States military and paramilitary activities in and against Nicaragua is the overthrow of its Government, it does not follow that that necessarily is incompatible with, and constitutes an abandonment of, the argument of self-defence. In some, indeed most, instances, overthrow of the aggressor government might be an unnecessary and disproportionate act of self-defence, but in others it may be necessary and proportionate. It depends on the facts (...)."

On the assumption that the indeterminate phrase "aggressor government" is meant to designate governments resorting to an illegal use of force, it does indeed depend on the facts whether or not they would justify the overthrow of a government. Judge Schwebel's reliance on the facts is dictated by his far more extensive interpretation of the concept of armed attack, which in his opinion includes aid to irregulars.[203] It is on that count that one ought to read his stance that the overthrow of the aggressor government may be a(n) (un)necessary and (dis)proportionate reaction to the armed attack. He seems to gradually scale down on the ladder of armed attacks. All out invasions establishing a right to necessary and proportionate overthrows of government, and aid to armed opposition against which one could not attempt the overthrow of the aggressor government. In contrast to judge Schwebel's construction, it might be more appropriate to uphold the Court's view which amounts to distinguishing between "the most grave forms of use of force (those constituting an armed attack) from other less grave forms".[204] Most grave uses of force are, according to the Court, armed attacks by regular forces, as well as the acts laid down in article 3 (g) of the Definition of Aggression (the sending by or on behalf of a State of armed bands, groups, irregulars or mercenaries, which carry out acts of armed force against another State) to the extent that these amount to "an actual armed attack conducted by regular forces".[205] Such are the acts which ought to be considered to amount to an international crime under article 19, paragraph 3 (a), Part One of the ILC-draft on State responsibility.

Where a State has not initially engaged in the crime of aggression, but rather became the accomplice, after or before the act, the specific form of political guarantee of neutrality comes into play. That is in fact the measure imposed on Austria after World War II. Nevertheless, generally speaking, imposed neutrality would seem to miss its mark as a measure against repetition. It would be rather more prudent to try and promote the integration of such a State into the wider community of peace-loving States.[206] Additionally it may be said that imposed neutrality may hinder the State concerned in applying for membership in the United Nations. Thus a gap may be, and was, created insofar as participation in sanctions ordered by the Security Council is concerned. As non-members such States are not bound by decisions of the Security Council. They are inhibited from providing aid or assistance to an author State by virtue of the rule laid down in article 27, Part One, of the ILC-draft. But sanctions imposed by the Security Council may be of significantly wider scope than what a State would be under an obligation not to do under article 27. Luckily non-members have tended to adopt the same kind of measures as those ordered by the Security Council, while generally affirming their autonomy in doing so.[207]

International crimes generally ought to give rise to the additional obligation for the author State to change its government as a guarantee against repetition.[208] An obligation like that could not be imposed in case of international delicts. With respect to crimes other than acts of aggression there may be some difference regarding the extent of the obligation.

In the past the crime of denial of self-determination did not generally lead to the imposition of an obligation to change the government of the colonizing State. That was so especially because the colonizing of territories, and all kinds of dominating structures, had not been considered unlawful in the past. Rather a government engaging in colonization had to put an end to its domination and surrender its authority to the people of the colonized territory. By now there are of course not that many territories left under the rule of a foreign State, and the peoples of such territories appear not to want to become independent. Since the entry into force of the United Nations Charter colonization or foreign domination can only come about through the threat or use of force. The crime of denial of self-determination will then inevitably be coupled to an illegal threat or use of force, and the Security Council will be competent regarding such acts.

An interesting example, though by far not the only one,[209] is presented by the Indonesian intervention in East Timor. At the time the Security Council adopted resolutions 384 and 389, deploring the Indonesian invasion, stressing the territorial integrity of East Timor and the right to self-determination of its people, and called upon Indonesia to withdraw from the territory.[210] It may not be too farfetched to say that the Security Council could have insisted on Indonesia to effect a change of government, considering the risk of possible repetition of similar acts on the part of Indonesia. And since the acts concerned imply a use of force, continued governance of Indonesia by the régime responsible for committing the international crime may be said to amount to a threat to the peace.

However, foreign domination may perhaps also come about through infiltration, instigation of *coup d'états*, or support for armed opposition. Such acts need not involve a threat or use of force. To the extent that such acts were supported or initiated by the government of a State, an obligation to reconstitute the government may be necessary so as to prevent repetition.

The crimes based on the breach, on a widespread scale, of basic human rights obligations certainly imply the need for an obligation to resort to a change or reconstitution of the government. Either the government will be instigating the breaches, adopting a policy to that effect, or it has lost control and cannot prevent other State organs (the police, paramilitary, or armed forces) from committing the breaches. Examples of the first category, among others, have been the massacres in Cambodia during the rule of the *Khmer Rouge*, and the imposition of *apartheid* in South Africa. In the second category one may find the situation(s) of lawlessness occurring in Somalia (and Rwanda). Many (more or less recent) agreements between governments and oppositional movements or forces in countries with a poor record on the protection of human rights have shown the relation between government implication in human rights violations and the absence of democratic rule.[211] On that account they have provided for certain changes in the constitution and the holding of completely free and democratic elections.[212] Going back into the more distant past, one may point to the provisions on human rights in the peace treaties with Italy, Bulgaria, Finland, Romania and Hungary.[213] Apparently a relationship was seen to exist between the protection of such human rights as freedom of thought and expression and the prevention of acts of aggression. But the basic premise of such an approach is that the human rights concerned will be guaranteed by the government. Yet it may be seriously doubted whether any government not established through democratic procedures will ensure implementation of those rights. And it is submitted that disregard for these political rights by a State could easily lead to the breach of its obligation to respect fundamental human rights. Consequently a State which has been guilty of an international crime consisting of human rights violations may be required to reconstitute its government through the holding of free and democratic elections.[214] If necessary a State may be required to insert into its constitution safeguards regarding the implementation of human rights on the domestic plane.

The conclusion must be that the arrest, prosecution, conviction, and punishment of those individuals responsible for the commission of the crime may be demanded and imposed on a State which has committed an international crime. That State will further be under an obligation to change its government, to change its constitution to the extent necessary, and to hold free elections so as to prevent the recurrence of criminal acts. The only limit to such measures constitutes, as rightly proposed by Arangio-Ruiz in his article 16, paragraph 3, Part Two, the continued existence of the author State as an independent member of the international community.

3.7.4. GUARANTEES AND TERRITORIAL ISSUES

Primarily one has to ask whether it is possible to impose, as a measure against repetition, an obligation on a State which committed aggression to agree, or acquiesce, to a complete loss of territory.[215] Ordinarily, it has to be noted, this implies not merely a loss of sovereignty over territory or a loss of political independence, but the wiping out of existence of the entire State. A further remark may be made in that such a measure is not likely to be agreed to by any State, and would of necessity have to be imposed by the threat or, more likely, the use of military force. Naturally annexation would be accompanied by physical control over the subjugated territory. By its nature, therefore, annexation presents the most perfect example of a measure that is adequate to achieve the desired goal: prevention of further internationally wrongful acts.

In a preliminary fashion it may observed that annexation, or indeed any acquisition of territory, could not be recognized or validated if it resulted from the first use of military force. That rule, which would seem to follow from the maxim *ex injuria jus non oritur*, has been affirmed time after time by the Security Council and the General Assembly.[216] Their reliance on the rule may in turn be traced back to the Charter's basic article 2, paragraph 4, which prohibits the use of force against the territorial integrity of States. That article, though it does not say so expressly, intends only to prohibit the first use of force by States. That is so because Charter articles 42 (principally)[217] and 51 clearly envisage reactions by the use of force against a first use of force. It is not entirely clear whether statements by the Council and Assembly on the inadmissibility of the acquisition of territory by force intend also to cover responsive uses of force, but precedents support an interpretation to that effect.

Reference may be made to two precedents. The first concerns the Declaration regarding the Defeat of Germany which stated, in the preamble, that the assumption of supreme authority over Germany would not have the effect of annexing Germany.[218] Logically this declaration can be taken to mean that Germany, as a State, would not be annihilated. Neither through complete or partial allocation of its territory to one or another State, nor through the dividing up of its territory among neighbouring States. The second precedent relates to Iraq. The Security Council, after Iraq's defeat by Coalition forces, affirmed:[219]

> "(...) the commitment of all Member States to the independence, sovereignty and territorial integrity of Iraq and Kuwait, and *noting* the intention expressed by the Member States co-operating under paragraph 2 of Security Council resolution 678 (1990) to bring their military presence in Iraq to an end as soon as possible consistent with achieving the objectives of the resolution,"

The argument which has to be addressed is whether a lawful use of force by States could lead to the annexation of another State. The lawful use of force can only be force in the exercise of a right of self-defence, since a use of force by one State against another can only be justified if the latter had initiated an armed attack against the first.[220] First of all one has to note the purpose of self-defence, which consists of repelling the attack. If the attack is repelled there would not seem to be any cause for "defence".[221] That argument, though not entirely persuasive in itself, is buttressed by considerations regarding potential misuse of the right of self-defence. While generally there does not appear to be any doctrine of abuse of rights in this respect, it may be pointed out that uses of force below the threshold of an armed attack do not give any right to self-defence. A State desiring to conquer another State's territory could try to provoke an armed attack through uses of force falling below the scale required for self-defence. The State thus provoked might be tempted to consider an all out invasion, and if it went on with it would trigger the right of self-defence of the provoking State.

More importantly, General Assembly resolution 2625 contains some phrases which would suggest that States can never resort to annexation. First of all it contains the earlier mentioned rule on the inadmissibility of the acquisition of territory by the threat or use of force.[222] The relevant paragraph ends with the observation that the foregoing shall not be construed to affect the provisions of the Charter,[223] or the powers of the Security Council under the Charter. Apparently the principle is not susceptible of derogation by States. The same conclusion results from the rules in the resolution regarding the sovereign equality of States. It states the obligation that "each State has the duty to respect the personality of other States" and in absolute terms the rule that "the territorial integrity and political independence of the State are inviolable". Reference may be made in this regard to the German precedent. If the commission of the ultimate international crime, aggressive war, of this century did not lead to extinction of the German State, which other international crime could justify such extinction?

These arguments are supported by reference to the concept of *jus cogens*. The most conspicuous example of a peremptory norm is the rule prohibiting the use of force.[224] Any treaty derogating from that rule, according to article 53 of the Vienna Convention on the Law of Treaties and its commentary, is void. One might say of course that the Charter of the United Nations provides for derogations, since it envisages the use of force by the Security Council in article 42, and by States in article 51. On the basis of such an argument one would either have to conclude that the peremptory norm prohibiting the use of force is not as absolute as one might think, or that because of the existence of articles 42 and 51 the Charter is void. This latter construction obviously would lead to an absurd result.[225] The matter could be resolved if one were to assert that the peremptory norm enshrined in article 2, paragraph 4, of the Charter, does not simply prohibit the use of force, but the use of force against the territorial integrity or political independence of States. One could claim then that the lawful uses of force in the Charter are in fact enforcement measures, whose object is the protection of the territorial integrity and political independence of States. At the same time the implication must be made that such enforcement measures should not only protect the territorial integrity of the defending or injured State, but also the territorial integrity and political independence of the attacking or author State. This interpretation would have to be supplemented so as to avoid inconsistency with the position taken in the previous subsection. It was said there that one could demand a change of government, or even the introduction of constitutional safeguards on human rights and democratic rule. Why should these be possible as a guarantee against repetition, and not the annexation of a State? It is submitted that the protection afforded to the political independence of States lies not with the possibility to determine one's own political system *stricto sensu*, but rather ought be read in relation to the rules on self-determination and the prohibition of foreign domination. For so long as the people of a State is in a position to determine itself the government it wants and the status of the territory, the political independence of a State will not be compromised. The contrary will only be the case if it is ruled by a foreign State and the people is not free to determine its own political (and legal) status within the international community.

Could the Security Council decide upon, or force, an annexation in favour of another State or by imposing an international régime, with exclusive international control, for the territory of the vanquished State? It is submitted that it could not, and reference may be made here to the Vienna Convention on the Law of Treaties between States and International Organizations or between International Organizations.[226] In articles 52 and 53 the basic rules have been laid down that a treaty imposed by threat or use of force inconsistent with the principles of the Charter is void, and that a treaty is void if it conflicts with a peremptory norm. By adopting these provisions the Commission observed that there existed the distinct possibility that an international organization would resort to an illegal threat or use of force, and that it might do so in order to coerce the conclusion of a treaty.[227] By virtue of the same argument this entails the conclusion that an international organization is capable of concluding a treaty that conflicts with a peremptory norm.[228] In applying the construction adopted in the previous paragraph, this means that it could not conclude any treaty imposed through the threat or use of force when such a treaty would result in the loss of territorial sovereignty and/or political independence of a State.[229] And if an organization is prevented from achieving that result by imposing a treaty, it follows that it also cannot obtain the desired result by forcefully imposing it upon the State committing aggression. The claim might furthermore be made that by annexing a State, without providing its people with the possibility of choosing their political status, one would be committing a breach of the (peremptory) norm of self-determination.

Up till now the question was one of annexation of a complete State. But what about taking away part of the territory of a State as a guarantee against repetition? Tunkin for instance supported this by reference to the amputation effected at the end of World War II:[230]

> "L'amputation de certains territoires de l'Allemagne et du Japon à la suite de cette guerre se distingue radicalement des usurpations antérieures opérées en vertu de droit du vainqueur: l'action des Alliés à l'égard de l'Allemagne et du Japon se fondait sur le principe de la responsabilité internationale de l'Etat pour l'agression commise par lui (...)."

At the end of many a war parts of the territory of the vanquished State have been severed from it and been ceded to another State,[231] provided with an international status,[232] placed under the authority of other States by virtue of mandate or trust agreements,[233] or have become independent.[234]

The question whether colonies or non self-governing territories may be taken away from the author State of an international crime need not bother us nowadays. In the past it was possible to sever the ties between the mother country and the colonized territory, because there did not exist rules laying down the right of peoples to self-determination. Through the enunciation of these rules after World War II, it has become impossible to lawfully acquire colonies. By virtue of the rules on self-determination the people of any non self-governing territory still existent has the right to determine its future, and it would seem that among its choices there should be one concerning the continuation of its ties with the mother country. The international community might insist on independence for such territories, but it is hard to see how the choice would be free if they could not also freely determine the available options.

Regarding territory forming an integral part, in the contiguous sense, of the author State itself, the guiding principles are those described above. No part of the territory of a State committing aggression can be taken away from it. The basic provision of the Charter on the prohibition of the threat or use of force is not merely concerned with attempts to annex complete States, but also with attempts to disrupt the territorial "integrity" of the State. Thus the disengagement of any part of the territory of a State that has committed an international crime, whatever the size of it, should be rejected as being in conflict with the (peremptory) norm prohibiting the use of force against the territorial integrity of States.

While there can be no question of any disruption of the territorial integrity of a State, that is not to say that certain specific measures against repetition could not take the place of a loss of territory. Especially where parts of the territory have been used to commit specific acts of aggression, the imposition of complete or partial demilitarization may be in order. That would appear to be the case especially where overseas non self-governing territories are concerned. But the same goes for frontier strips that may present ample opportunities for border incidents or acts of aggression,[235] or for instance militarily strategic islands.[236]

If the international crime concerned related to acts of genocide against that part of the population of different ethnic origin and concentrated in specific areas, measures of demilitarization may be appropriate. Where the suppression of separatist activities involves direct intimidation and extermination of an ethnic people more drastic action may be required. In such a case it may be appropriate to afford the people afflicted to exercise (once more) its right of self-determination. The situation regarding the Kurds in Northern Iraq may be mentioned as an example of this kind.

Lastly in this subsection on guarantees and territorial issues there is the matter of partial or complete occupation of the territory of an author State of an international crime. Precedents may be found in the occupation of Germany and Japan at the end of World War II,[237] and the partial and temporary occupation of Iraq after being defeated.[238]

Although occupation could be considered a completely autonomous form of guarantees against repetition, one ought rather see it as a kind of forced execution of obligations. As such it relates not to measures of self-defence or Security Council enforcement by the use of force, which both aim at the cessation of wrongful acts or prevention of future wrongful acts, but constitutes some sort of imposed performance of the other reparation obligations incumbent upon the author State. By occupying the author State of an international crime the most effective means of ensuring performance of obligations is resorted to. This means in effect that the regular options of the State, to freely determine whether to perform or not to perform its obligations, are taken away from it. Ordinarily, that is, in case of delicts, such freedom could not be taken away from a State. Yet in case of international crimes, especially the crimes of aggression and genocide,[239] such measure could be resorted to. The crime of denial of self-determination would not seem to lend itself to such a measure, since it would involve occupying the mother country. Possible occupation of the dominated territory would appear to be possible only to the extent that the crime has been accompanied by the international crime of aggression. Measures implying supervision by the international community of the dominated territory may be resorted to in order to achieve a free exercise of the right to self-determination.

In conclusion it may be said that the commission of an international crime should, in general, not lead to any disruption of the territorial integrity of the author State.

Arangio-Ruiz consequently correctly proposes that a future article 16, paragraph 3, Part Two, ought to safeguard the territorial integrity of a State committing an international crime. The only exception to this would be the case where the crime involves the targeting of a specific ethnic people, in which case the appropriate remedy would be to allow the people concerned to exercise its right to self-determination.

3.8. Restrictions regarding the exercise of rights of reparation

The restrictions applicable to the exercise of rights to demand reparation are of diverse dimensions. In the light of the topics under discussion, obligations *erga omnes* and international crimes, it is possible to envisage restrictions that would flow from the multiplicity of injured States or a legal interest on the part of an organization (subsection 3.8.1). Thus the absence of affected States, the presence of a directly injured State, and the influence of an organization's competence, need to be discussed. Others restrictions may flow from general concepts (subsection 3.8.2), such as the exclusion of specific forms of reparation on the basis of a treaty régime and *jus cogens*. Further restrictions are those which specifically apply only to the right to demand reparation (subsection 3.8.3). Among these one may find the restrictions, proposed by Arangio-Ruiz, of excessive onerousness and the impossibility of performance. Considering the arguments put forward in favour of those restrictions, the principle of proportionality will be discussed alongside that of excessive onerousness, and the concept of domestic jurisdiction alongside that of impossibility of performance.

3.8.1. RESTRICTIONS REGARDING REPARATION, MULTIPLICITY OF INJURED STATES, AND THE ORGANIZATIONAL INTEREST IN REPARATION

Restrictions based on the absence of specially affected States

As may be seen from the categories covered by article 5, paragraph 2 (e) (ii) and (iii), Part Two of the ILC-draft, *e.g.* human rights, it may happen that a breach of obligation does not affect any State in particular.[240] That is the case if a breach of obligation results in damage that is non-allocable, does not produce any damage at all, or leads to damage that is allocable to the author State.

The first category involves damage that is done to that part of the environment not under any State jurisdiction. Damage in such a case produces multilateral injury to the States parties or the States bound by the customary rule.

The middle hypothesis may occur, for instance, when a State does not introduce legislative provisions it was bound to under a multilateral treaty, or stations nuclear weapons on the deep sea-bed or in outer-space.[241]

The third category concerns an author State doing damage to its own nationals. This may involve breaches of its obligations under a multilateral treaty or a customary rule to respect the human rights of its nationals. Where these breaches flow from a universal rule of customary law, all other States are injured States. Thus they all have the right to demand reparation of the author State. This may be deduced especially from Arangio-Ruiz' proposal to add an article 5 *bis*, Part Two:[242]

> "Whenever there is more than one injured State, each one of them is entitled to exercise its legal rights under the rules set forth in the following articles."

Contrary to what has been claimed,[243] this means that all injured States can claim reparation,[244] if not necessarily for themselves.

The third category just mentioned is of special importance for international crimes. Besides the direct reference to protection of the human being in article 19, paragraph 3 (c), Part One, denial of self-determination, *apartheid*, slavery, and genocide likewise involve breaches of human rights obligations. The only limit that applies to the rights of injured States to demand reparation for these breaches flows from the nature of the obligations. The obligations laid down by these rules impose on States the duty to treat all those under their jurisdiction, but especially their nationals, in a certain way. If such obligations are breached the basic damage will have been done to the author State's nationals. Consequently compensation cannot be claimed by injured States for themselves. At most injured States can claim that the author State provides compensation, or an effective remedy at the domestic level, to the injured nationals.

Restrictions based on the presence of a directly injured State

Three possible hypotheses may involve a breach of obligation giving rise to a situation where there is a specially affected injured State and all the other injured States.

The first one concerns a breach of obligations that causes damage to the environment. The consequent multilateral injury to other States may be accompanied by specific injury to one of them. That is the case when the pollution reaches an injured State's national jurisdiction or affects its economic position.

The second hypothesis covers the situation where a State's breach of human rights obligations not only affects the nationals of the author State, but also those of the injured States. It might be objected of course that such acts constitute separate internationally wrongful acts. These two hypotheses might be viewed respectively as breaches based on the Trail Smelter criterion,[245] or as breaches regarding the protection to be afforded to aliens. That argument is to be rejected, since the specific damage results only incidentally from the original wrongful act. A specially affected injured State may of course claim cessation, restitution in kind, and compensation to the extent of the injury. That claim may be espoused by the other injured States. But claims for satisfaction and measures against repetition can only be based on the wrongful act itself.

There is a third possibility of the existence a specially affected injured State among all injured States. That radically different hypothesis concerns a State being the victim of an armed attack. In such a case the status of directly injured State is not the result of it incidentally suffering damage, but because it was the target of the international crime of aggression. The status of injured State enjoyed by other States does not result from their being affected or being the victim. It results from the fact that aggression amounts to the breach of an obligation *erga omnes*.[246] The status of injured State under article 5, paragraph 3, Part Two, comes to them as members of the international community.

Now Graefrath and Mohr note in respect to the distinction:[247]

> "Die abstrakte Mitteilung, bei internationalen Verbrechen gälten alle Staaten als verletzte Staaten, hebt zwar einen wichtigen Unterschied zu den internationalen Delikten hervor; zugleich aber verwischt sie, daß nicht alle Staaten gleichmäßig betroffen sind und keineswegs gleiche Rechte gegenüber dem Rechtsverletzer oder unabhängig von dem unmittelbar verletzten Staat geltend machen können."

At this point they make clear that the difference lies with the claim for compensation, which accrues only to those States that suffer any material damage.[248] All other possible claims for reparation (cessation, restitution, satisfaction, and guarantees) may be formulated by all the other injured States.[249] Injured States' support for a claim to compensation by the directly injured State is of dependent nature.[250] That is witnessed by the fact that they cannot insist on the payment of compensation once the directly injured State declares itself satisfied with the amount granted (subject of course to the appreciation that the directly injured State was not in any way coerced to accept a particular amount of compensation). The other rights of reparation are not at the discretionary disposal of the directly injured State, and it cannot renounce them in favour of the author State unless the other injured States agree or acquiesce.

Restrictions based on an organization's competence

There are no inherent objections to international organizations invoking the responsibility of a State for breaches of international law. A limitation applies in that their exercise of rights of reparation must fall within the scope of their functions as delimited by the constitutive treaty. As to the United Nations, the General Assembly can claim reparation on the basis of breaches of obligations under the Charter, but in doing so it acts as the representative organ of a subject of international law. By making a claim it may become a party to a dispute with a State, and naturally it cannot impose its will on the other party. Since it is invested with recommendatory powers only,[251] it also cannot direct other members to adopt specific measures other than non-recognition of the wrongful act.[252] The situation that obtains with regard to the Security Council is not essentially different. In shaping its recommendations it also cannot decide on countermeasures to be adopted by members towards the defaulting State. That changes only where it determines the existence of a threat to the peace, breach of the peace, or act of aggression.[253] Yet at the same time this constitutes the basic limit to its powers. Where there is no such determination it is doomed to exercise its recommendatory powers only.

Even where it does determine a threat to the peace, the measures it directs members to adopt in regard to the author State must be geared towards the elimination of the threat to the peace. If measures for the enforcement of reparation claims cannot be said to contribute to the elimination of the threat, they ought not to have been taken. Some of the measures that the Security Council directed members to adopt in the wake of the Iraq-Kuwait conflict come under that heading. One may seriously doubt whether the forced demarcation and the establishment of the Compensation Commission are apt to lessen the threat Iraq poses to neighbouring States. Especially so since the most efficacious means to destroy the threat would have been to topple the Iraqi régime, and to implement the individual responsibility of its main leaders. After that Kuwait's claim to stable borders and the satisfaction of compensation claims could have led to negotiations with Iraq on a less politicized basis.

The question is whether Security Council's competence in the matter affects the individual exercise of rights of reparation by (directly) injured States. A statement by Gowlland-Debbas may be taken as indicative:[254]

> "The Council in reacting to violations of fundamental norms of international law is not acting as an impartial arbitrator or third party, but in lieu and place of the injured States in matters which affect the interests of the international community as a whole."

Previously the present writer took the statement of the Permanent Court in the Mavrommatis Case (section 3.5) and observed that the Security Council by taking up the claim of its members, on their behalf, asserted its right to ensure respect for the rules of international law. That analogy, however, cannot be drawn to its full conclusion. An injured State not only may espouse the claims of its nationals, it can in fact waive their claims against foreign States or decide not to pursue them. In such a case the injured individual, not being a subject of international law, is left without a remedy at the international level. The Security Council, on the other hand, cannot avail itself of a similar prerogative. It cannot do away with the rights of its members, since it is bound by virtue of articles 1, paragraph 1, and 24, paragraph 2, of the Charter to act in accordance with principles of justice and international law.

3.8.2. RESTRICTIONS REGARDING REPARATION BASED ON GENERAL CONCEPTS

The exclusion of specific forms of reparation due to the existence of a treaty régime

In the Diplomatic Staff Case the Court depicted the rules of diplomatic law as a self-contained régime which:[255]

> "(...) on the one hand, lays down the receiving State's obligations regarding the facilities, privileges and immunities to be accorded to diplomatic missions and, on the other, foresees their possible abuse by members of the mission and specifies the means at the disposal of the receiving State to counter any such abuse. These means are by their nature entirely efficacious (...)."

These observations of the Court were directed against the argument of the Iranian government that the Court could not address the taking of hostages independently from the history of interference, by the United States, in the internal affairs of Iran.[256] Iran's argument, although somewhat vaguely worded, amounted to a claim that its disregard of the American staff's immunities was justified, as a countermeasure, by the American breach of obligation not to intervene in the Iranian internal affairs.[257] Riphagen took on the issue and claimed the existence of subsystems which could, to the extent that they elaborated secondary legal consequences tailored to the subsystem, exclude the application of the general rules on State responsibility.[258] And especially the faculty to resort to countermeasures in response to an internationally wrongful act might be excluded in such a case (on which more in chapter four). Yet the issue could be relevant also in regard to reparation.[259] Especially so if one would exclude certain forms of reparation from the claims of States or organizations on the basis that they had not been regulated in an applicable treaty.

Non-application of the secondary rules on reparation may be argued in three ways. First, the treaty does not provide for any rules on reparation and therefore the general rules would not apply at all. Secondly, the treaty provides special rules so that the general rules are excluded. Thirdly, the treaty rules on reparation, which are not complete, must be considered exhaustive and preclude the application of the general rules.

As regards the first hypothesis, that a treaty does not provide any rules regarding reparation, one should adhere to the view of the Permanent Court in the Chorzów Factory Case that:[260]

> "It is a principle of international law that the breach of an engagement involves an obligation to make reparation in an adequate form. Reparation is therefore the indispensable complement of a failure to apply a convention *and there is no necessity for this to be stated in the convention itself.*"

By now there is a long standing practice that when a jurisdictional clause provides for the settlement of disputes regarding the interpretation or application of a treaty, the latter also includes jurisdiction to settle disputes over the responsibility for non-application of the treaty.

The second argument is entirely persuasive and is based on the well-known maxim *lex specialis derogat legi generalis* (the special rule takes precedence over the general rule). Its principle has been laid down in article 2, Part Two, of the ILC-draft:[261]

> "Without prejudice to the provisions of articles [4] and 5, the provisions of this Part govern the legal consequences of any internationally wrongful act, except where and to the extent that those legal consequences have been determined by other rules of international law relating specifically to the internationally wrongful act in question."

Only one remarks has to be made. The special rule must concern the same subject-matter and scope, if not the same content, as the general rule. Only where the two rules would both apply could one give precedence to the special rule. Naturally the maxim takes on meaning only if the two rules are different in content. That could be so, for instance, if the special rule would pose restrictions which the general rule would not.

Thirdly a problem may arise if a treaty establishes an organ that is to settle disputes between the States parties, but at the same time fails to specify the remedies, or specifies only some, that may be applied by it. In the first case one would expect that the organ charged with settling disputes may apply all the remedies available under the secondary rules of State responsibility.[262] As to the second one would think that it could only apply such remedies as are expressly provided.

The issue is relevant for the relationship between the specific international crimes and treaties on their subject-matter.[263] In the opinion of the Commission the international community of States as a whole is to designate (having regard to the importance of the rules and the kind of interests they protect) the specific conduct to be considered crimes, and the legal consequences flowing therefrom. Would it not be strange that a treaty, with a limited number of States parties, could prevent the application of the secondary rules on crimes established by the whole international community. Apart from that the question to be answered is whether the States concluding the treaty concerned intended to provide for a completely autonomous régime of responsibility.

Taking a look at the Charter shows us that it is completely silent on issues of reparation. It is hard to imagine that the States, in concluding the Charter, would have wanted to deny any possibility of reparation for breaches of obligation under the Charter. The Security Council itself has on numerous occasions, as has been seen in previous sections, stressed the obligation of members to provide reparation for violations of the Charter. And the Court held that the United States had breached its obligation not to use force as against Nicaragua, and stipulated the former's duty to provide compensation therefor. Its decision was based on the customary rules on the use of force. Yet would the Court have given a different decision if it had had the chance of applying Charter rules? One thinks not.

As to the crimes other than aggression it cannot but be noted that all the relevant treaties provide for nothing more than supervision procedures and procedures for complaints by individuals. The latter are subject however to the general consent of the State party concerned. The organs established for such purposes are not intended to give binding decisions for the State party (allegedly) in breach of its obligations under the treaty. They can only investigate on the basis of State reports and non-governmental organization's reports, and on that basis can only note the existence of breaches and recommend the appropriate remedies. Since that is the case an injured State would be hard put to it if it had to accept that no more could be done than that in the matter of reparation. Furthermore, it is suggested that the lack of provisions on sanctions in case of breaches of obligations under the treaty indicates that the treaty is intended to function only with regard to breaches that are committed by State organs without any wilful intent or premeditation on their part. The latter kind of breaches, for that reason alone, could not be considered international crimes. Thus jurisdiction over a crime ordinarily falling to the treaty organ would be transferred to the international community.

Peremptory norms and human rights

Not much more need be said about the restrictions imposed by existing peremptory norms. Especially the section on guarantees against repetition has shown that a State cannot be subjected to involuntary loss of territory or foreign domination. To that may be added that the population may not be held collectively accountable for the crime of the State,[264] and only persons that are individually responsible for (ordering or not preventing) specific acts could be punished. Clearly States could not, due to an international crime committed, take it on themselves to commit another crime towards the population or people of a State. A State committing the crime of aggression or genocide could not be punished by its population being subjected to genocide. Nor could the nationals of a State be deprived of their human rights, and they could not be discriminated against on the basis of their State's crime. Generally the restriction regarding the exercise of rights of reparation to be imposed on the basis of respect for human rights must be that reparation must not affect the vital needs of the population of the author State. On that basis too mitigation of compensation payments ought to be envisaged.

3.8.3. SPECIFIC RESTRICTIONS REGARDING REPARATION

Excessive onerousness and proportionality

With regard to international delicts Arangio-Ruiz proposed the following restriction: an injured State can only claim restitution in kind to the extent it "would not be excessively onerous for the State which has committed the internationally wrongful act."[265] The Commission followed up on this by posing the restriction that restitution in kind should not involve "a burden out of all proportion to the benefit which the injured State would gain from obtaining restitution in kind instead of compensation;" The Commission explains that this is based on:[266] "(...) equity and reasonableness and seeks to achieve an equitable balance between the onus to be sustained by the author State and the benefit which the injured State would gain from obtaining reparation in that specific form rather than compensation." However, the Commission claimed, with reference to the distinction between delicts and crimes, that:[267]

> "(...) the limit of excessive onerousness would assume a different weight according to the qualitative and quantitative dimension of the wrongful act for which reparation is sought. Indeed in the case of the most serious wrongful acts such as aggression and genocide, it would be inequitable for the effort of reparation incumbent upon the author State – including the fullest restitution in kind – to be considered excessive in proportion to the violation committed by that State."

On the basis of the agreement within the Commission Arangio-Ruiz has gone on to propose, by way of article 16, paragraph 2, Part Two, that the restriction of article 7 (c), Part Two, would not apply in case of crimes.[268]

Since it is a general rule that reparation must adequately wipe out the wrongful act and its consequences, there seems to be no letting up on the basic obligations of the author State to provide restitution in kind and substitute or complementary compensation. Nevertheless, it may strike one as odd that the burden of reparation (restitution in kind) may be disproportional to the wrongful act and the injury sustained in the case of delicts.[269] Yet at the same time the Commission and Arangio-Ruiz claim that there can be no question of excessive onerousness (disproportionality) in case of crimes. It is hard to see where the difference lies. The author State of an internationally wrongful act, whether that be a delict or a crime, has complete jurisdiction over its territory. It is perfectly capable of returning persons, property, or territory, if it would want to. Certainly no injured State could waive its right to demand the release of persons wrongfully held prisoner, and therefore it could not claim substitute compensation. With regard to property the question is perhaps more complicated, since the title to it may have passed into private hands. But should that stand in the way of restitution? Even if the property concerned had come into the hands of private individuals that acted in good faith, one would still have to insist on restitution. Because in claiming that it could not be returned, due to domestic legal obstacles, one would be placing the domestic legal order above the international legal order. In regard to territory the matter is even more straightforward. In that case what is at stake is transfer of factual control over the territory. This requires no more than timetables for withdrawal by the author State and the corresponding taking of control by the injured State.

Concluding it may said that there should be no possibility at all to refuse restitution in kind, not in case of crimes and not in case of delicts.[270]

The same conclusion is not valid for compensation. Since restitution in kind and compensation are both reparatory in character, the principle of proportionality cannot operate in respect of these forms of reparation. They are of necessity strictly proportional to the wrong committed. The amount of compensation to be paid by the author State of an international crime, however, should be mitigated. Not because paying compensation might amount to any disproportional burden for the author State. The reason for insisting on an extenuation of responsibility is that the consequences of crimes may be of such gravity that they would inequitably burden the population of the author State. As Graefrath puts it, the obligation to pay compensation should not jeopardize the existence of a people.[271] That the amount to be paid as compensation could be reduced, on this ground, was already recognized by article 232 of the Treaty of Peace with Germany, in which the Allied and Associated Governments recognized that Germany's resources would not be adequate to make complete reparation.[272] Article 14 of the Peace Treaty with Japan after World War II, while stipulating Japan's duty to pay compensation, recognized that:

> "(...) the resources of Japan are not presently sufficient, if it is to maintain a viable economy, to make complete reparation for all such damage and suffering and at the same time meet its other obligations."

As to the modalities of mitigation, it is submitted that two should be considered. First, regarding all the crimes mentioned in article 19, paragraph 3, Part One, the costs incurred for the suppression of the crime should be excluded from the amount of compensation. Examples regarding such limitation may be found in the past.[273] But the Security Council, far from excluding anything from the amount, has decided, in resolution 706, that Iraq ought to pay, in addition, for the costs incurred for the implementation of its disarmament obligations, the costs for the facilitation of return of Kuwaiti property, and half the costs of the demarcation of the boundary. Apparently the Security Council intends to have Iraq pay everything related to its unlawful invasion and occupation of Kuwait. Nevertheless, it would be proper to insist that all losses suffered as a result of the Security Council imposed sanctions and the eventual use of force by Coalition forces against Iraq ought not to be compensated by the latter.[274]

That is what has been decided by the Governing Council of the Compensation Commission. It has excluded the possibility of compensation in cases where the damage resulted *solely* from the trade embargo and related measures imposed upon Iraq.[275] It has also excluded damage suffered by members of the Allied Coalition Armed Forces arising out of their involvement in Coalition military operations against Iraq unless the following three conditions were met: compensation is awarded in accordance with the general criteria already adopted; the claimants were prisoners of war as a consequence of their involvement in Coalition military operations against Iraq in response to its unlawful invasion and occupation of Kuwait; and the loss or injury resulted from mistreatment in violation of international humanitarian law (including the 1949 Geneva Conventions).[276] In the light of the formulation of these exclusions it had not been clear whether this allowed the possibility of compensation for war damage, *e.g.* the destruction of weapons, the use of ammunition, etc. After certain requests by

governments the Governing Council put the matter beyond doubt:[277] "The Governing Council confirms that the costs of the Allied Coalition Forces including those of military operations against Iraq, are not eligible for compensation.
Another way of reducing the amount of compensation could lie with the setting of limits on compensation claims put forward by individuals and corporations. Thus a minimum might be set on the basis of the maxim *de minimis non curat praetor*. A maximum should be set on the basis that paying full compensation inequitably burdens the author State of an international crime.[278] The Governing Council has adopted fixed amounts with regard to certain categories of claims, namely those relating to: departures from Iraq or Kuwait during the period of 2 August 1990 to 2 March 1991; serious personal injury; the death of a spouse, child or parent.[279] Claims to that effect will be upheld upon simple documentation of the facts. But if the losses concerned were greater than the fixed amounts, claims may be submitted under other categories established by the Governing Council. With regard to mental pain and anguish, however, the Governing Council has established ceilings.[280] While paying *lucrum cessans* and interest does not as such amount to unjustifiable enrichment, one might consider these not to be appropriate in case of crimes.[281] Further mitigation could be imposed if the claiming individual is well-off, or if the claiming corporation has the necessary funds for dealing with set-backs. A final obstacle for claiming compensation ought to be that the damage was covered by insurance.[282]

Impossibility of performance and domestic jurisdiction
In his preliminary report Arangio-Ruiz discussed whether an author State would be relieved of its obligation to provide restitution in kind in case of impossibility of performance thereof.[283] Such would be the case when there was factual or material impossibility, for instance if the persons concerned had been killed or the property had been destroyed.[284] In general territory would not seem to be subject to destruction,[285] and thus may be left out in the discussion. The Commission has provided, by way of article 7 (a), Part Two, that restitution would have to be provided only to the extent that it would not be materially impossible.[286]

Real difficulties arise in regard to so-called legal impossibility of performance. In this respect the Commission has stated:[287]

> "Any State which is well aware of its international obligations – secondary as well as primary – is bound to see to it that its legal system, not being opposable to the application of international legal rules, is adapted or adaptable to any exigencies deriving from such rules."

As the Commission observes a State's legal system is not opposable to the application of international legal rules. That is so because by virtue of such rules the domestic jurisdiction of a State has been restricted. What remains, or not, under a State's domestic jurisdiction is dependent upon the existence and operation of international rules. Where the conduct of States is regulated by prohibitive and prescriptive rules they can no longer on the basis of their sovereignty claim any remaining domestic jurisdiction. Any State of course ought to be aware of its obligations under primary rules of international law. And to the extent that there is a clash between rules of the domestic legal system and such primary obligations the latter must prevail. The same can be said in case of conflict between domestic legal rules and the secondary rules on restitution in kind. But this cannot be said of all secondary rules on reparation. Legal impossibility should be considered also in relation to satisfaction and guarantees against repetition.

In respect to the claim for punishment of individuals a problem may arise to the extent that the criminal law of the injured State would not have prohibited the acts deemed to be internationally wrongful. In such a case *post facto* modification of the law will inevitably be insufficient, since prosecution of the individual will come up against the fundamental principle of *nullum crimen sine lege*. And it would seem that this problem can be generalized, since an individual could not be sanctioned or punished for an act that is not in any way covered by the prohibitive rules of the injured State's administrative or criminal law. Since criminal laws are always published, indeed generally the operation of laws within the domestic legal system is dependent upon publication, any lacuna with respect to the prohibition of certain acts could have been known to the injured State. For these reasons demands by the injured State for the punishment of individuals would seem to come up against the obstacle of legal impossibility, and since it might have known of this the injured State would have to restrict itself to claiming, as a guarantee against repetition, the introduction of legal provisions prohibiting the conduct in question. It might be objected of course that a State cannot invoke its legal system in order to escape performing an international obligation. That argument is entirely persuasive with regard to a conflict between obligations under primary rules of international law and domestic legal provisions. But the same cannot be said if obligations under secondary rules conflict with the domestic legal system. Unless the primary rules could, of necessity, not be observed without the introduction of criminal prohibitions, one would have to say that the legal impossibility thus emerged falls within the injured State's domestic jurisdiction. The provision of article 6 *bis*, paragraph 3, adopted by the Commission thus has been phrased too rigorously.[288]

These issues are relevant for international crimes also. If acts of the author State come under the heading of international delicts, its domestic legal system should be respected if it presents obstacles to the prosecution of the suspects. Where the acts amount to international crimes, impossibility of performance due to domestic legal obstacles cannot be recognized. While one could not expect a State to adopt legislation derogating from the maxim *nullum crimen sine lege*, international law requires that suspects should be brought under international jurisdiction. Where there is the possibility of prosecution under the author State's criminal law, international law offers an author State the option of either prosecuting or extraditing the suspects. However, if such prosecution is impossible, or not likely to be implemented in a serious way, international jurisdiction may well have to be asserted. Such jurisdiction could consist of demands for extradition, execution of universal jurisdiction, or the setting up of an international tribunal. In the past some specialized international tribunals have been set up, *e.g.* the Nuremberg and Tokyo Military Tribunals, and the International Tribunals for the former Yugoslavia and Rwanda. The creation of a general tribunal is under discussion by the Commission. Punishment of individuals, as a form of satisfaction, would thus be taken away from the author State in case of international crimes.

The domestic jurisdiction of States generally ought to be preserved as much as possible. Guarantees against repetition in case of international delicts therefore should not include demands for modification or repeal of legislation unless such legislation provided the constitutive basis for the internationally wrongful act. If that is the case the author State perhaps would have to change legislation already because of an injured State's claim for restitution. The situation is entirely different where international crimes are concerned. The limit just mentioned does not apply,[289] and a demand for guarantees may involve the modification or repeal of legislation unrelated to the wrongful act. But the matter does not stop there. As has been elaborated in section 3.7, in case of crimes it is possible to demand a wide span of measures affecting the organization of the State itself. These include the re-organization of the police, paramilitary or armed forces, a change of government, but also the introduction of specific provisions in the constitution. The latter may relate to the observance of human rights, adherence to democratic principles, peaceful settlement of disputes and non-aggressive policies, and neutrality. All these measures therefore touch upon the very sovereignty of the State and could clearly only be justifiably imposed on States which committed an international crime.[290]

3.9. Summary

Performance of the obligation(s) to provide reparation, including cessation, constitutes the means for the author State to discharge the responsibility incumbent upon it as a result of its internationally wrongful act. Such reparation must be adequate to wipe out the consequences of the illegal act and re-establish the situation which, in all probability, would have existed if that act had not been committed. The obligation to provide reparation finds its basis in the responsibility incurred upon the commission of an internationally wrongful act. Consequently it is established *ipso jure* upon the commission of the wrongful act, and a claim by the injured State is not necessary to establish the secondary legal relationships. Generally reparation is, as the word indicates, of reparatory character only. That goes especially for cessation of wrongful conduct, restitution in kind, and compensation. The expression of regrets or apologies, the conviction and punishment of responsible individuals, and guarantees against repetition in general, do not constitute punishment, but are to be considered of deterrent character. Only the payment of compensation over and above the actual loss sustained must be considered to constitute punishment.

Since under article 5, paragraph 3, Part Two, all States are injured States in case an international crimes is committed, this means that all States can protest the behaviour of the author State. A protest will serve to reaffirm an injured State's right to demand reparation. Injured States can claim reparation and support, or repudiate the lack of, claims for reparation by other (directly) injured States. Such action will not constitute a prohibited intervention in the external affairs of the author State and/or other injured States. Similarly all States can demand the cessation of wrongful conduct if that constitutes an international crime. This as such does not constitute a special or supplementary consequence of the régime of crimes. However, more or less timely discontinuance of wrongful conduct must be taken into account in regard to matters of satisfaction and guarantees against repetition.

Restitution in kind constitutes the form of reparation which is most apt to wipe out the consequences of a wrongful act and to re-establish the situation that existed before it had taken place. As such, regarding both delicts and crimes, no right of choice exists for either the injured State or the author State to opt for compensation instead of restitution. Only an agreement between the injured and author States can constitute the basis for a choice for compensation if restitution is perfectly possible. Furthermore, the author State's performance of its obligation to provide restitution, that is, the return of persons, property, or territory, can be effected without there being any need to change the author State's legal system. To the extent that such a change is demanded by the injured State it will function as a guarantee against repetition. No special or supplementary consequences of crimes need to be envisaged as to restitution in kind.

Similarly no special or supplementary consequences apply in the field of compensation. However, recently the Security Council has taken it upon itself to ensure the payment of compensation by Iraq to all those States and their nationals which suffered damage due to its unlawful invasion and occupation of Kuwait. For that purpose it has created a Fund to which Iraq must contribute a percentage of its petroleum export value. In order to ensure the liquidity of that fund the Security Council has further decided that Iraq may sell oil, subject to the proviso that the buying States will pay the amount of the purchases into a United Nations' escrow account. By setting up these arrangements the Security Council has designed a highly innovating and creative manner to enforce compensation claims.

The first manifestation of satisfaction, the expression of regrets or apologies, does not play any distinct role in case of international crimes. The second manifestation of satisfaction, the prosecution, conviction, and punishment of individuals responsible for the commission of the crime, constitutes an imperative in order to prevent recurrence of the crime. In case of delicts the implementation of individual responsibility is left to the discretion of the author State. In case of crimes it may be taken on by States, individually, and by the Security Council. If such is the case the setting up of an international tribunal functions both as a deterrent and as a guarantee against repetition. The third manifestation of satisfaction, damages reflecting the gravity of the infringement of rights of the injured State or punitive damages, does not, and should not, have any place at all in international law.

The scope of guarantees against repetition to be provided or implemented by the author State ought to be extended in case of international crimes, and this must be seen to constitute special or supplementary consequences of the régime of crimes. The two main categories of guarantees are those related to the police, paramilitary and armed forces, and those related to the State organization. Appropriate guarantees within the first category may include obligations regarding disarmament, dismantling of war industries, destruction of weapons, re-organization of the police, paramilitary or armed forces, and the admission of observation teams. Appropriate guarantees related to the State organization may include obligations for the prosecution and punishment of those responsible for the commission of the crime, the prohibition of specific political groups or parties, a change of government, constitutional changes, the holding of free elections, and respect for human rights. Guarantees against repetition which are either demanded or imposed should not amount, generally, to an imposed settlement of disputes or to the loss of territory or political independence. An exception regarding this latter position would be constituted by a situation in which the author State of an international crime targeted a specific ethnic people. In such a case the people concerned should be allowed, as a guarantee against repetition, to exercise its right of self-determination.

With regard to restrictions to the exercise of rights of reparation it may be said that the absence of specially affected States leads to the conclusion that all the injured States can claim reparation. If there is a directly injured State, that is, in case of the crime of aggression, all the other injured States may demand cessation, restitution, satisfaction and guarantees. Claims for compensation, however, are of dependent nature, and the directly injured State may put an end to them. The Security Council may take up the case of one of its members regarding rights of reparation. However, it cannot do away with such rights, since it is bound by virtue of article 1, paragraph 1, of the Charter, to bring about the settlement of disputes in conformity with principles of justice and international law.

No restriction regarding the exercise of rights of reparation exists on the basis of a treaty régime unless it can be established that the rules contained on that subject in the treaty are exclusive. Neither the Charter, nor specific treaties in the field of human rights, testify to any intention to that effect.

Demands for reparation should not conflict with peremptory norms of general international law. Consequently demands for guarantees against repetition should not lead to a complete loss of independence for the author State, nor should they, generally, affect its territorial integrity. Demands for compensation should not impose such a burden on the population of the author State as to put in jeopardy its vital needs.

The restriction of excessive onerousness proposed by the Commission in regard to restitution should certainly not apply in case of international crimes, and Arangio-Ruiz has rightly proposed its deletion. However, that restriction should apply to compensation, since the population of the author State may be inequitably burdened due to the extensive nature of the damage. Again, the vital needs of the population must not be put in jeopardy.

Impossibility of performance in a factual sense will certainly constitute an obstacle to provide restitution, but the same cannot be said regarding the so-called legal impossibility. Any State ought to be aware of its obligations under primary and secondary rules of international law. However, one ought to respect as much as possible the domestic jurisdiction of the author State with regard to satisfaction and guarantees in case of delicts. Changes in legislation should be demanded only if it formed the constitutive basis for the internationally wrongful act. In case the internationally wrongful act constitutes an international crime the limit of domestic jurisdiction will not apply in the same way, since guarantees demanded or imposed in such a case may involve changes in the State organization itself.

It has been stated a number of times that specific forms of reparation may be demanded or imposed. Clearly a mere demand for reparation by an injured State or the United Nations does not amount to imposing reparation. True, imposition of reparation demands, though exceptional, may come about if injured States take, or if the United Nations orders members to take, measures within their territorial jurisdiction regarding the funds, property, or nationals of the author State which satisfy the demands directly. The ordinary and more likely scenario is that injured States or the United Nations (threaten to) impose or resort to measures detrimental to the author State or its nationals and so coerce it to perform its reparation obligations. Such measures may amount to non-military countermeasures or to the actual use of armed force against the author State. The following chapter is therefore devoted to the right of injured States or the United Nations to resort to non-military countermeasures in response to international crimes.

NOTES

[1] Text and Commentary Article 1, Part One, YBILC 1973, Volume II, pp. 173-176, 175.

[2] Text and Commentary Article 6 *bis*, Part Two, in Report of the International Law Commission on the work of its forty-fifth session, 3 May – 23 July 1993, General Assembly, Official Records, Forty-eighth Session, Supplement No. 10 (A/48/10), pp. 142-151, 143. The Commission went on: "The word 'reparation' is the generic term which describes the various methods available to a State for discharging, or releasing itself from, such responsibility." *Ibid.* See also Haasdijk, S., The Lack of Uniformity in the Terminology of the International Law of Remedies, 5 LJIL 1992, pp. 245-263, 246.

[3] Text and Commentary Article 19, Part One, YBILC 1976, Volume II, Part Two, pp. 95-122, 117.

[4] Commentary Article 19, Part One, 117.

[5] Commentary Article 19, Part One, 117.

[6] Commentary Article 19, Part One, 109. Arangio-Ruiz recently proposed the following article: "Without prejudice [In addition] to the legal consequences entailed by an international delict under articles 6 to 14 of the present Part, an international crime as defined in article 19 Part One entails the special or supplementary consequences set forth in articles 16 to 19 below." Arangio-Ruiz, G., Seventh Report on State Responsibility, 24 May 1995, A/CN.4/469/Add.1, 4 pp., 2.

[7] See Arangio-Ruiz, G., Fifth Report on State Responsibility, 8 June 1993, A/CN.4/453/Add.2, 35 pp., 11, 20, 22-24; Fifth Report on State Responsibility, 24 June 1993, A/CN.4/453/Add.3, 36 pp., 3-7, 10 and footnote 117; Sixth Report on State Responsibility, 26 April 1994, A/CN.4/461/Add.1, 7 pp., 5; and Seventh Report on State Responsibility, 9 May 1995, A/CN.4/469, 49 pp., 7-14.

[8] Case concerning the Factory at Chorzów (Claim for Indemnity) (Jurisdiction), Publications PCIJ, 1927, Series A, No. 8, p. 4, 21. Emphasis added.

[9] Case concerning the Factory at Chorzów (Claim for Indemnity) (The Merits), Publications PCIJ, 1928, Series A, No. 17, p. 4, 47.

[10] Note Personnaz, J., La Réparation du Préjudice en Droit International Public, Librairie du Recueil Sirey, Paris, 1939, 53-59.

[11] Arangio-Ruiz, G., Preliminary Report on State Responsibility, 18 May 1988, A/CN.4/416, 34 pp., 12. Note this similar observation on satisfaction: "Although the demand for satisfaction will normally come – unless felicitously preceded by the offending State's own initiative – from the injured State, the satisfaction to be given consists of actions to be taken by the offender itself." Arangio-Ruiz, G., Second Report on State Responsibility, 9 June 1989, A/CN.4/425, 125 pp., 111.

[12] The Commission makes one exception to the formulation in terms of rights and stipulated the obligation of the author State to cease the wrongful conduct. The reason for the exception, so the Commission claims, is that cessation should be seen to result from the persisting operation of the primary legal relationship. Text and Commentary Article 6, Part Two, in Commission Report 1993, pp. 132-142, 132, and 140-141. Originally Arangio-Ruiz, Preliminary Report, 21-22. He also drafted his proposed article 10, on satisfaction, in terms of obligations. Arangio-Ruiz, G., Second Report on State Responsibility, 22 June 1989, A/CN.4/425/Add.1, 25 pp., 25. Also Arangio-Ruiz, Fifth Report, Addendum 3, 5, in the context of international crimes.

[13] Commentary Article 6, Part Two, 141. Originally Arangio-Ruiz, Preliminary Report, 21-22. He added (21): "Were the injured State not to put forward any claim for reparation, the 'secondary' legal relationship might not emerge."

[14] C.f. Cheng, B., General Principles of Law as applied by International Courts and Tribunals, Stevens & Sons Limited, London, 1953, 168-170 (more broadly 163-177).

[15] C.f. Mann, F., The Consequences of an International Wrong in International and National Law, 48 BYBIL 1976-1977, pp. 1-65, 14.

[16] C.f. Cepelka, C., Les conséquences juridiques du délit en droit international contemporain, Universita Karlova, Praha, 1965, 36.

[17] For texts see Report 1993, 130-132. Arangio-Ruiz used such expressions as "the right to claim" and "entitled to claim". See Arangio-Ruiz, G., Preliminary Report on State Responsibility, 27 May 1988, A/CN.4/416/Add.1, 53 pp., 33; Arangio-Ruiz, Second Report, Addendum 1, 24.

[18] Arangio-Ruiz, Second Report, 61-73. The Commission did not take up any position in this regard, and stated that questions of interest had to be solved on a case-by-case basis. It stressed that one had to bear in mind the overriding principle of "full reparation". Text and Commentary Article 8, Part Two, in Commission Report 1993, pp. 168-193, 185.

[19] Brownlie, I., State Responsibility, System of the Law of Nations, Part I, Clarendon Press, Oxford, 1983, 229. See Arangio-Ruiz, Second Report, 72.

[20] Commentary Article 6 *bis*, Part Two, 142-151.

[21] Arangio-Ruiz, Seventh Report, Addendum 1, 2. Texts of the other articles run from 2 to 4. For arguments on his choice made in respect of reparation see Seventh Report, 7-14.

[22] Note however that his proposed article 17, paragraph 2, Part Two, which would allow the adoption of urgent, interim measures required to protect the rights of the injured State or limit the damage caused by the crime. It may be assumed that such measures would be aimed at coercing the author State of a crime to cease its wrongful conduct and to provide restitution in kind. Arangio-Ruiz, Seventh Report, Addendum 1, 3; and Seventh Report, 17, where he points out that such measures are aimed at: "(...) securing immediate access to the victims for purposes of rescue and/or aid or preventing the continuation of a genocide, measures concerning humanitarian convoys, anti-pollution action, passage facilities, etc."

[23] The Lusitania, United States and Germany: Mixed Claims Commission (Parker, Anderson, Kiesselbach), 1 November 1923, 2 ILR 1923-1924, pp. 193-194, 202-203, 209-211, 339, and 340, at 209.

[24] Lusitania Award, 194.

[25] Contrary Arangio-Ruiz, Second Report, 89-90, who claims that the ratio for the Mixed Claims Commission arguing the political nature of questions regarding penalties lies with the fact that the imposition of punitive damages would not fall within the ambit of arbitration, and that punitive damages concerned a matter rather to be dealt with at the diplomatic level. But see Title 2, article 171, paragraph 2, of the 1992 Treaty on European Union, 31 ILM 1992, pp. 253-330, providing for the imposition of penalties, on demand of the European Commission, on member States in case of non-compliance with a judgment of the European Court.

[26] An example of this trend, mentioned in Arangio-Ruiz, Second Report, 105 and 108, concerns the case decided by the Secretary-General regarding the Rainbow Warrior incident. See Ruling Pertaining to Differences between France and New Zealand arising from the Rainbow Warrior Affair, New Zealand *v.* France, Secretary-General (United Nations), 6 July 1986, 74 ILR 1987, pp. 241-274.

[27] Arangio-Ruiz, Second Report, Addendum 1, 25.

[28] Note the reference by the Commission to Grotius' statement that: "money is the common measure of valuable things". Commentary Article 8, Part Two, 179. Also Pellet, YBILC 1990, Volume I, 180.

[29] Text and Commentary Article 10, Part Two, in Commission Report 1993, pp. 193-209.

[30] Commentary Article 10, Part Two, 195-196; Arangio-Ruiz, Second Report, 87. Also Nagy, K., The Problem of Reparation in International Law, in Bokor-Szego, H. (Ed.), Questions of International Law, volume 3, Martinus Nijhoff Publishers, Dordrecht, 1986, pp. 173-190, 185; Dominicé, C., La satisfaction en droit des gens, in Dutoit, B., and Grisel, E. (Eds.), Mélanges Georges Perrin, Diffusion Payot, Lausanne, 1984, pp. 91-121, 92.

[31] Note that Arangio-Ruiz places the idea of guarantees against repetition under the heading of satisfaction, but at the same time seems to acknowledge that they are intended to prevent the commission of future internationally wrongful acts. Arangio-Ruiz, Second Report, 113-115, and 123-125.

[32] See particularly Arangio-Ruiz, Second Report, 7-16, 79-80, 87, 93, 101-102, 106-108 and 111.

[33] Implicitly Arangio-Ruiz, Second Report, 124; rather explicit Arangio-Ruiz, YBILC 1990, Volume I, 142, where he states: "Guarantees of non-repetition, though dealt with separately in chapter IV of the report, were a particular form of satisfaction."

[34] Arangio-Ruiz, Second Report, 124.

[35] Anzilotti, D., La responsabilité internationale des états a raison des dommages soufferts par des étrangers, 13 RGDIP 1906, pp. 5-29, 13. Note that he adds: "La violation de la règle est effectivement toujours un dérangement de l'intérêt qu'elle protège, et, par voie de conséquence, aussi du droit subjectif de la personne à

laquelle l'intérêt appartient; il en est d'autant plus ainsi que dans les rapports internationaux le dommage est en principe plutôt un dommage moral (méconnaissance de la valeur et de la dignité de l'État en tant que personne du droit des gens) qu'un dommage matériel (dommage économique ou patrimonial au vrai sens du mot)." *Ibid*, 13-14. Also Ago, R., Second report on State responsibility, YBILC 1970, Volume II, pp. 177-197, 195; Third report on State responsibility, Volume II, Part One, pp. 199-274, 223; Text and Commentary Article 3, Part One, YBILC 1973, Volume II, pp. 179-184, 183. Of course this position follows from their view that there is an absolute correlation between obligations and subjective rights (in the sense as indicated in chapter one), and that therefore any violation of an obligation constitutes at the same time a violation of the subjective right of another State.

[36] The examples of libel and slander mentioned by Thiam, YBILC 1990, Volume I, 183.

[37] Commentary Article 6, Part Two, 141. More broadly *ibid.*, 134-136 and 140-141. Originally Arangio-Ruiz, Preliminary Report, 12; and YBILC 1988, Volume I, 265-266.

[38] Abi-Saab, G., The Concept of "International Crimes" and its Place in Contemporary International Law, in Weiler, J., Spinedi, M., and Cassese, A. (Eds.), International Crimes of State: A Critical Analysis of the ILC's Draft Article 19 on State Responsibility, Walter de Gruyter, Berlin, 1989, pp. 141-150, 149.

[39] McCaffrey, YBILC 1990, Volume I, 189.

[40] An intermediate position concerns an impending internationally wrongful act, on which the Commission states: "Indeed, in the presence of conduct of another State which manifestly appears to constitute the initial phase of a course of action (or omission) likely to lead to a wrongful act, the State could, with all the necessary precaution, take the appropriate steps, with due respect for the principle of non-intervention in the other party's domestic affairs, to suggest in an amicable manner an adjustment of the former State's conduct which might avert liability." Commentary Article 6, Part Two, 140. Originally Arangio-Ruiz, Preliminary Report, 15.

[41] Arangio-Ruiz, Preliminary Report, 12. Also Commentary Article 6, Part Two, 141.

[42] Note Abi-Saab's remark that: "Violations of international law are clearly matters of 'international concern', and protests against them cannot be considered as acts of 'intervention'." Abi-Saab, The Concept of International Crimes, 149.

[43] Detter De Lupis, I., The Concept of International Law, Norstedts Förlag, Stockholm, 1987, 127, observes that all States can protest conduct constituting the breach of fundamental rules.

[44] The 1945 Charter of the United Nations, 39 AJIL 1945, Supplement, pp. 190-215.

[45] Generally Ronzitti, N., Use of Force, *Jus Cogens* and State Consent, in Cassese, A. (Ed.), The Current Legal Regulation of the Use of Force, Martinus Nijhoff Publishers, Dordrecht, 1986, pp. 147-166. Note also this observation by Condorelli: "Thus, it is established that the responsibility of a State guilty of serious breaches of humanitarian law cannot be set aside whether by consent of the people who were victims of such breaches or by an exoneration agreement among States. The logic underlying these provisions is understandable: since the act is wrongful *erga omnes*, its wrongfulness cannot be assuaged by the consent of the direct victims (individuals or States)." Condorelli, L., The Continuity between certain Principles of Humanitarian Law and the Concept of Crimes of State, in Weiler *et al*, International Crimes, pp. 233-237, 236.

[46] Commentary Article 6, Part Two, 132-142. Note also article 1, paragraph 2, Part Two, adopted at the same session: "The legal consequences referred to in paragraph 1 are without prejudice to the continued duty of the State which has committed the internationally wrongful act to perform the obligation it has breached." Text and Commentary Article 1, paragraph 2, Part Two, in Commission Report 1993, p. 132, 132.

[47] Commentary Article 6, Part Two, 140-141. The Commission had stated earlier (*ibid.*, 134) that cessation is situated in between the categories of primary and secondary rules. It may be noted that the Commission on this basis has positioned the provision on cessation before the provision on reparation. Also Arangio-Ruiz, YBILC 1988, Volume I, 266. Of the same opinion Dominicé, La satisfaction, 97 and 108-109; and Deman, C., La cessation de l'acte illicite, 23 RBDI 1990, pp. 476-495, 477-480.

[48] Deman, La cessation, 477 and especially 484.

[49] Deman, La cessation, 478, points to this goal of cessation.

[50] Arangio-Ruiz, Seventh Report, 8. And note his proposed article 16, paragraph 1, Part Two. Seventh Report, Addendum 1, 2.

[51] The Commission stated in Commentary Article 6, Part Two, 135: "It should be recalled in this connection that cessation is the remedy which is most frequently resorted to by organs of international organizations, particularly the General Assembly and the Security Council of the United Nations, in the presence of the most serious breaches of international law." Also Deman, La cessation, 478 and 484.

[52] The situation is naturally different where defeat is imminent or an armistice is desirable. See article 1 of the 1940 Treaty of Peace between Finland and the Union of Soviet Socialist Republics, 34 AJIL 1940, Supplement, pp. 127-131; article 1 of the 1940 Armistice between France and Germany, 34 AJIL 1940, Supplement, pp. 173-178; article 1 of the 1940 Armistice between France and Italy, 34 AJIL 1940, Supplement, pp. 178-

183; paragraph 2 of the 1945 Unconditional Surrender of German Forces at Rheims, 39 AJIL 1945, Supplement, pp. 169-170; paragraph 2 of the 1945 Unconditional Surrender of German Forces at Berlin, 39 AJIL 1945, Supplement, pp. 170-171; and article 2 of the 1945 Declaration regarding the Defeat of Germany, 39 AJIL 1945, Supplement, pp. 171-178.

[53] With respect to the latter see Arangio-Ruiz, Fifth Report, Addendum 3, 3-4.

[54] Arangio-Ruiz, Fifth Report on State Responsibility, Addendum 3, 4.

[55] Note Condorelli's remark that: "It must nevertheless be clarified that the crime has to be regarded as still continuing as long as there is still any one of its consequences not eliminated. In other words, one cannot say that the wrongful act has really ceased while its effects are still present." Condorelli, L., Measures Available to Third States Reacting to Crimes of State, in Weiler *et al*, International Crimes, pp. 264-266, 265. This argument may be countered of course by pointing to the fact that it is the goal of reparation to "wipe out all the consequences of the illegal act". Thus it may be said that although the crime continues (since the author State has not fulfilled its obligation to provide reparation under the secondary rules), the breach of obligation under the primary rule may have come to an end. On the other hand it may be granted that where the crime constitutes a denial of self-determination, the breach of obligation under the primary rule is continuous in character and thus must be stopped through cessation. *Ibid.*

[56] Leaving aside here the argument that such occupation amounts to exercising governmental control over the territory of another State, and therefore conflicts with another primary rule of international law which provides for exclusive jurisdiction by States over their territory.

[57] The Security Council demanded, in resolution 660, that: "(...) Iraq withdraw immediately and unconditionally all its forces to the positions in which they were located on 1 August 1990;" Graefrath, B., and Mohr, M., Legal Consequences of an Act of Aggression: The Case of the Iraqi Invasion and Occupation of Kuwait, 43 AJPIL 1992, pp. 109-138, 113, primarily claim that this constituted an application of the legal consequence of cessation, although they add that it also amounted to: "(...) the first elements of a claim for restitution in kind." *Ibid.* Gowlland-Debbas also ranges the demand for withdrawal of Iraqi troops under the subject of cessation. Gowlland-Debbas, V., Security Council Enforcement Action and Issues of State Responsibility, 43 ICLQ 1994, pp. 55-98, 79.

[58] Note Dominicé's remark that the breach of an obligation to provide reparation in turn constitutes a wrongful act. Dominicé, La satisfaction, 102. Also *ibid.*, 106.

[59] Commentary Article 19, Part One, 121.

[60] Arangio-Ruiz, Preliminary Report, 12. Note also in a similar, but less clear, sense Commentary Article 6, Part Two, 134.

[61] Deman, La cessation, 478.

[62] Arangio-Ruiz observes that: "As far as cessation of the breach is concerned, it does not seem that crimes present any special character in comparison with 'ordinary' wrongful acts (whether or not erga omnes)." Arangio-Ruiz, Fifth Report, Addendum 3, 3. He does not, in his latest report, provide any substantive arguments on cessation in case of crimes. Arangio-Ruiz, Seventh Report, 8.

[63] Generally Arangio-Ruiz, Preliminary Report, Addendum 1, 3-33; and Thomsen, S., Restitution, in Bernhardt, R. (Ed.), EPIL, Instalment 10, Elsevier Science Publishers B.V., Amsterdam, 1987, pp. 375-378.

[64] Text and Commentary Article 7, Part Two, in Commission Report 1993, pp. 151-168.

[65] Commentary Article 7, Part Two, 151-152. Footnote omitted. Originally Arangio-Ruiz, Preliminary Report, Addendum 1, 3.

[66] Commentary Article 7, Part Two, 152. Footnote omitted. Originally Arangio-Ruiz, Preliminary Report, Addendum 1, 3.

[67] Thomsen, Restitution, 376.

[68] Chorzów Factory Case, Merits, 47.

[69] See also Arangio-Ruiz, Preliminary Report, Addendum 1, 3-5.

[70] Arangio-Ruiz, Preliminary Report, Addendum 1, 25-27.

[71] Mann, The Consequences, 3.

[72] Arangio-Ruiz, Preliminary Report, Addendum 1, 26.

[73] Commentary Article 7, Part Two, 153. Footnote omitted. More broadly *ibid.*, 153-155. Originally Arangio-Ruiz, Preliminary Report, Addendum 1, 27.

[74] See Commentary Article 8, Part Two, 178.

[75] Chorzów Factory Case, Merits, 47. Emphasis added.

[76] Contrary Arangio-Ruiz, Preliminary Report, Addendum 1, 25, who claims that the case supports a right of choice. He comes to that conclusion on the basis of Germany's change in claim, during the proceedings, from restitution to compensation. That change was intimated by Germany's consideration that: "the Chorzow factory, in its present condition, no longer corresponded to the factory as it was before the taking over in 1922."

Ibid. The Permanent Court's dictum then can be conciliated with such change of claim only if one holds that the Permanent Court held Germany's change to constitute a plea to the effect that restitution was no longer possible. Admittedly the Permanent Court had earlier observed (Chorzów Factory Case, Merits, 27-28): "It is a principle of international law that the reparation of a wrong may consist in an indemnity corresponding to the damage which the nationals of an injured State have suffered as a result of the act which is contrary to international law. This is even the most usual form of reparation; it is the form selected by Germany in this case and the admissibility of it has not been disputed." Although the use of the word "selected" would seem to indicate a choice for the injured State, it is submitted that such use is in fact conditioned by the fact that there had been no objection to a claim of compensation by the author State.

[77] Arangio-Ruiz, Preliminary Report, Addendum 1, 26.

[78] Quoted in Commentary Article 8, Part Two, 179. Also Pellet, YBILC 1990, Volume I, 180.

[79] In favour Nagy, The Problem of Reparation, 176-177. Contrary Mann, The Consequences, 4-5.

[80] Commentary Article 7, Part Two, 156-163. Arangio-Ruiz, Preliminary Report, Addendum 1, 6-13.

[81] Commentary Article 7, Part Two, 159-160. Originally Arangio-Ruiz, Preliminary Report, Addendum 1, 11.

[82] United States Diplomatic and Consular Staff in Tehran, Judgment, ICJ Reports 1980, p. 3, 44-45.

[83] Case concerning the Temple of Preah Vihear (Cambodia *v.* Thailand), Merits, Judgment, ICJ Reports 1962, p. 6, 37; Diplomatic Staff Case, Judgment, 45.

[84] Temple Case, Merits, 37.

[85] Commentary Article 7, Part Two, 160. Arangio-Ruiz, Preliminary Report, Addendum 1, 11-12. With reference of course to Case concerning certain German Interests in Polish Upper Silesia (The Merits), Publications PCIJ, 1926, Series A, No. 7, p. 4, 19.

[86] Commentary Article 7, Part Two, 161. Arangio-Ruiz, Preliminary Report, Addendum 1, 12.

[87] Eventually affirmed by the Security Council in resolution 686. In resolution 687 the Security Council demanded that "Iraq and Kuwait respect the inviolability of the international boundary".

[88] And one may point to the fact that, during the hostages crisis in Iran, the American diplomats and nationals were originally taken hostage by individuals not connected to the Iranian State. It may be noted of course that Iran was not held responsible in first instance for the acts of the individuals, but for its failure to exercise due diligence in preventing and repressing the acts in question. Diplomatic Staff Case, Judgment, 29-33.

[89] Article 4, Part One, and article 6 *bis*, paragraph 3, Part Two, of the draft of course lie down the rule for such an eventuality. Text and Commentary Article 4, Part One, YBILC 1973, Volume II, pp. 184-188.

[90] Arangio-Ruiz, Seventh Report, 8-11; and Arangio-Ruiz, Seventh Report, Addendum 1, 2.

[91] Arangio-Ruiz, Preliminary Report, Addendum 1, 26. Footnote omitted. Also Arangio-Ruiz, Fifth Report, Addendum 2, 23 and especially footnote 58 (23-24).

[92] The fact that many agreements between an author State and an injured State envisage compensation rather than restitution would not seem to have led to a rule of customary law leaving a choice between the two remedies to the injured State.

[93] Note Arangio-Ruiz' observations on the German claims regarding the Chorzów factory. Arangio-Ruiz, Preliminary Report, Addendum 1, 25. As to the contrary case, that of an increase of value, Nagy appears to envisage only an obligation to pay compensation for the author State. It may be added though that he does so on the basis that restitution in kind would be: "(...) greatly disproportionate to the loss suffered." Nagy, The Problem of Reparation, 177. Footnote omitted.

[94] Also Arangio-Ruiz, Fifth Report, Addendum 3, 5.

[95] Graefrath and Mohr, Legal Consequences, 121, have argued that the obligation to provide reparation (including restitution), which rests upon the author State, is non-negotiable. Also Graefrath, B., Völkerrechtliche Verantwortlichkeit für internationale Verbrechen, in Graefrath, B. (Ed.), Probleme des Völkerrechts, Akademie-Verlag, Berlin, 1985, pp. 89-110, 105-106.

[96] *E.g.* articles 245 to 247 of the 1919 Treaty of Peace with Germany, 13 AJIL 1919, Supplement, pp. 151-386. See also Thomsen, Restitution, 376. Clearly such provisions would not cover the return of territory (since that could be taken by one or the other of the States parties, though the treaty might constitute a legal basis), but rather the return of property and persons.

[97] Especially Stone, J., *De Victoribus Victis*: The International Law Commission and Imposed Treaties of Peace, 8 VJIL 1968, pp. 356-373; and Jennings, R., The Acquisition of Territory in International Law, Manchester University Press, Manchester, 1963, 56-61.

[98] Respectively resolutions 660, 662; 674, 686; 664, 667, 674, 686; and for the latter three 687. Note also that resolution 674 calls on States to collect information regarding possible claims for restitution or financial compensation by Iraq; and the examples of claims of restitution mentioned by Arangio-Ruiz, Fifth Report, Addendum 3, 6.

[99] See Case concerning the Northern Cameroons (Cameroon *v.* United Kingdom), Preliminary Objections, Judgment, ICJ Reports 1963, p. 15, 21-26.

[100] Northern Cameroons Case, Preliminary Objections, 31.

[101] Northern Cameroons Case, Preliminary Objections, 38.

[102] Commentary Article 8, Part Two, 168-193.

[103] Riedel observes: "The award of damages thus presupposes that restitution (*restitutio in integrum*) or satisfaction are not possible or not sufficient means of reparation." Riedel, E., Damages, in Bernhardt, EPIL, Instalment 10, pp. 68-73, 68. Arangio-Ruiz notes on the other hand: "Notwithstanding the 'primacy' of restitution in kind as a matter of equity and legal principle, reparation by equivalent is the most frequent and quantitatively the most important among the forms of reparation. This is the consequence of the fact that restitution in kind is very frequently inapt to ensure a complete reparation." Arangio-Ruiz, Second Report, 17.

[104] Commentary Article 8, Part Two, 185-193. Originally Arangio-Ruiz, Second Report, 44-56.

[105] Commentary Article 8, Part Two, 183-185. Originally Arangio-Ruiz, Second Report, 57-78.

[106] Commentary Article 8, Part Two, 180-181 (generally 178-183). Two footnotes omitted. Originally Arangio-Ruiz, Second Report, 5 and 17-19. On direct and indirect damage see also *ibid.*, 27-29, where he appears to discard the distinction. But also *ibid.*, 40 and footnote 101, where he observes that indirect damage, that is damage to the nationals of a State, should really be seen to constitute direct damage.

[107] Commentary Article 8, Part Two, 177. Originally Arangio-Ruiz, Second Report, 17.

[108] Spinedi claims as much: "Those who maintain that in case of international crime all States have the right to claim reparation for the wrong, certainly do not pretend that all States can claim compensation for the material damage. What they are asserting is the right for every State, whether directly injured or not, to claim through diplomatic channels or before an international tribunal, should the State have *jus standi*, the cessation of the wrongful act, the *restitutio in pristinum* (when possible), and the adoption of measures apt to prevent the repetition of the breach." Spinedi, M., Convergences and Divergencies on the Legal Consequences of International Crimes of States: With Whom Should Lie the Right of Response?, in Weiler *et al*, International Crimes, pp. 244-249, 247. See also her International Crimes of State, The Legislative History, *ibid.*, pp. 7-138, 119-120.

[109] Graefrath, B., International Crimes – A Specific Regime of International Responsibility of States and its Legal Consequences, in Weiler *et al*, International Crimes, pp. 161-169, 165.

[110] An additional argument may be made in this respect. If there is not one single injured State entitled to claim that compensation be paid to the individual victims, then there is in fact no remedy at all. For the victims generally do not have any standing on the international level (leaving aside the available conventional remedies), and only when there is a national State other than the author State involved would there be a right to claim compensation.

[111] Arangio-Ruiz, Seventh Report, 11.

[112] Graefrath, B., Responsibility and Damages Caused: Relationship between Responsibility and Damages, 185 RDC ADI 1984-II, pp. 9-150, 91-92.

[113] Graefrath, Responsibility and Damages, 92-93.

[114] Before 1990 the Security Council had restricted itself to asserting the right to compensation of certain States or entities. See resolutions 262, 387, 455, 475, 487, 527, 545, 546, 567, and 568.

[115] Resolution 687 was adopted under Chapter VII of the Charter and in accordance with article 25 decisions contained therein are binding on members of the United Nations.

[116] Graefrath and Mohr, Legal Consequences, 123-127; Gowlland-Debbas, Security Council Enforcement, 81-82.

[117] That percentage was to be based on an evaluation of the needs of Iraq's population, its economy, and its payment capacity as related to its external debt servicing. Eventually the Security Council, in resolution 705, set the percentage of compensation to be paid to the Fund at 30 per cent of the annual exports.

[118] Iraq's only possible means of obstructing the functioning of the Compensation Commission, which it has indeed resorted to, is not to effect any purchases at all. That unfortunate circumstance was noted by the Security Council in resolution 778. See also resolution 986 which renewed the offer of the Council to Iraq to export petroleum or petroleum products.

[119] Note the observations by Gowlland-Debbas, Security Council Enforcement, 73, to the effect that: "The Council in reacting to violations of fundamental norms of international law is not acting as an impartial arbitrator or third party, but in lieu and place of the injured States in matters which affect the interests of the international community as a whole."

[120] The Mavrommatis Palestine Concessions, Publications PCIJ, 1924, Series A, No. 2, p. 6, 12.

[121] Note from a general angle the 1978 Rhodesian Constitutional Agreement, 17 ILM 1978, pp. 261-264, and the 1979 Independence Constitution, 19 ILM 1980, pp. 388-402; the 1991 Agreement on a Comprehensive

Political Settlement of the Cambodia Conflict, 31 ILM 1992, pp. 183-188; the 1992 General Peace Agreement for Mozambique, S/24635; the 1993 Agreement Liberia, S/26272 (Cotonou Agreement); the proposed 1993 Agreement relating to Bosnia and Herzegovina, S/26377/Add.1; see also the 1994 Framework agreement for the Federation (Croatia/Bosnia and Herzegovina), S/1994/255.

[122] Graefrath, Responsibility and Damages, 93. See also Wellens, K., *Apartheid*, An International Crime, in Heyde, L., Leijten, J., Mertens, Th., and Vermeulen, B. (Eds.), Begrensde Vrijheid, Opstellen over mensenrechten aangeboden aan Prof. Dr. D.F. Scheltens bij zijn afscheid als hoogleraar aan de Katholieke Universiteit Nijmegen, Tjeenk Willink, Zwolle, 1989, pp. 288-311, 297-298. Past denials of self-determination may also give rise to the obligation of the author State to provide compensation for specific wrongs committed towards individuals during the period of domination. Note Graefrath, Völkerrechtliche Verantwortlichkeit, 106-107.

[123] Text and Commentary Article 27, Part One, YBILC 1978, Volume II, Part Two, pp. 99-105, 99.

[124] See chapter two, subsection 2.6.2, where reference was made to the observation of the Commission that such intent could not be presumed.

[125] C.f. Graefrath, B., Verantwortlichkeit und Wiedergutmachung bei Apartheidverbrechen, 35 NJ 1981, pp. 115-117, 115-116.

[126] Generally Commentary Article 10, Part Two, 195-196. Originally Arangio-Ruiz, Second Report, 5, 10-16, 79-82, 87. See also Przetacznik, F., La responsabilité internationale de l'état a raison des préjudices de caractère moral et politique causés a un autre état, 78 RGDIP 1974, pp. 917-974.

[127] Arangio-Ruiz, Second Report, 5, 11, and 79.

[128] See Dominicé, La satisfaction, 94.

[129] Especially Dominicé, La satisfaction, 112-116, and 120-121.

[130] Graefrath, Responsibility and Damages, 85-86.

[131] Commentary Article 10, Part Two, 193-209. Originally Arangio-Ruiz, Second Report, Addendum 1, 25. See also Gilbert, G., The Criminal Responsibility of States, 39 ICLQ 1990, pp. 345-369, 352-354.

[132] Commentary Article 10, Part Two, 197.

[133] Arangio-Ruiz, Seventh Report, 11-14; and Seventh Report, Addendum 1, 2. Subject of course, as noted earlier, to the safeguard of the author State's independent existence, its territorial integrity, and the vital needs of its people.

[134] Riedel, E., Satisfaction, in Bernhardt, EPIL, Instalment 10, pp. 383-384, 383.

[135] Corfu Channel case, Judgment, ICJ Reports 1949, p. 4, 35.

[136] Arangio-Ruiz, Second Report, Addendum 1, 25.

[137] Arangio-Ruiz' proposal appeared not to include disciplinary action against officials, as it only spoke of *punishment* of responsible individuals. See Arangio-Ruiz, Second Report, Addendum 1, 25.

[138] The Case of the S.S. Lotus, Publications PCIJ, 1927, Series A, No. 10, p. 4, 22-32.

[139] *E.g.* Spinedi, The Legislative History, 138.

[140] Note the opinion expressed within the Commission that: "(...) in case of crimes, prosecution should be possible, (...), without the consent of the author State." See Report of the International Law Commission on the work of its forty-sixth session, 2 May – 22 July 1994, General Assembly, Official Records, Forty-ninth Session, Supplement No. 10 (A/49/10), 342.

[141] Graefrath, B., and Mohr, M., Völkerrechtliche und strafrechtliche Verantwortlichkeit für internationale Verbrechen, 35 SR 1986, pp. 29-40, 31, 34, and 36, note that State organs cannot claim immunity on the basis that they acted on behalf of the State. See also Drost, P., The Crime of State, volume 1, Humanicide, A.W. Sijthoff, Leyden, 1959, 290-297, on the necessity of avoiding the punishment of individuals for crimes committed by legal persons.

[142] Charter of the Nuremberg Tribunal to be found in the 1945 Agreement for the Prosecution and Punishment of the Major War Criminals of the European Axis, 39 AJIL 1945, Supplement, pp. 257-264. Judgment of the Nuremberg Tribunal, 41 AJIL 1947, pp. 172-333.

[143] Commentary Article 19, Part One, 102-104.

[144] Commentary Article 19, Part One, 103-104. Graefrath, Völkerrechtliche Verantwortlichkeit, 100-103, views the implementation of individual responsibility as a specific sanction regarding serious violations of international law. Also Hofmann, R., Zur Unterscheidung Verbrechen und Delikt im Bereich der Staatenverantwortlichkeit, 45 ZAORV 1985, pp. 195-231, 208.

[145] Commentary Article 19, Part One, 104.

[146] Which in fact is endowed on States more and more often with regard to all kinds of related criminal acts, such as terrorism, drugs connected crimes, torture, etc.

[147] Resolution 827 and 955. The establishment of the first tribunal was envisaged by the Security Council in resolution 808 in which it requested a report on the matter by the Secretary-General, and effected by means of

resolution 827. Report containing the Statute of the International Tribunal to be found in 32 ILM 1993, pp. 1159-1205.

[148] Resolution 827, operative paragraph 4 in combination with articles 29 and 19, paragraph 2, of the Statute of the International Tribunal.

[149] Arangio-Ruiz' proposal was far more straightforward, as he proposed a provision on "punitive" damages, when compared to the Commission's diplomatic phrasing. Generally Arangio-Ruiz, Second Report, 79-112; and Arangio-Ruiz, Second Report, Addendum 1, 21-23, and 25.

[150] Commentary Article 10, Part Two, 205. Footnote omitted.

[151] Arangio-Ruiz, Seventh Report, 11-14; Arangio-Ruiz, Seventh Report, Addendum 1, 2. See also Arangio-Ruiz, Fifth Report, Addendum 2, 20-21, footnote 51; and Fifth Report, Addendum 3, 5, where he investigates the question as to whether reparation should be more burdensome in case of crimes, and where he states: "A second derogation might concern the prohibition of 'punitive damages', (...)." It is not quite clear why he speaks of a prohibition on punitive damages considering that he envisages that possibility in case of delicts. Note also the opinion by some members that punitive damages were a necessary element of any régime of crimes, reported in Commission Report 1994, 343.

[152] C.f. Jiménez de Aréchaga, E., and Tanzi, A., International State Responsibility, in Bedjaoui, M. (Ed.), International Law: Achievement and Prospects, Martinus Nijhoff Publishers, Dordrecht, and UNESCO, Paris, 1991, pp. 347-380, 369.

[153] C.f. Annacker, C., The Legal Régime of *Erga Omnes* Obligations in International Law, 46 AJPIL 1994, pp. 131-166, 154, in the context of breaches of human rights obligations.

[154] Although one may note the initiative taken by the arbitral tribunal in the second Rainbow Warrior Award, in which it recommended that the French government should pay some 2 million US dollars into a fund for the promotion of friendly relations between the peoples of New Zealand and France. Rainbow Warrior (New Zealand *v.* France), France-New Zealand Arbitration Tribunal (Jiménez de Aréchaga, Keith, Bredin), 30 April 1990, 82 ILR 1990, pp. 500-590, 578.

[155] The Commission observed, in Commentary Article 10, Part Two, 208, that it: "(...) did not find it necessary to pronounce itself on the question whether an afflictive nature should be attributed to satisfaction as a form of reparation." Note also Arangio-Ruiz, Fifth Report, Addendum 3, 29, footnote 147, who observed, after noting that the majority of the Commission did not ascribe any punitive function to reparation, that: "Rather contradictorily, in our view, a punitive function would have to be excluded (in the form of punitive damages or otherwise) even from such obviously sanctioning forms of reparation as the various kinds of satisfaction and guarantees of non repetition."

[156] Arangio-Ruiz, Second Report, 113-125.

[157] Text and Commentary Article 10 *bis*, Part Two, in Commission Report 1993, pp. 210-215.

[158] Commentary Article 10 *bis*, Part Two, 215.

[159] Commentary Article 10 *bis*, Part Two, 210-211.

[160] C.f. Marek, K., Criminalizing State Responsibility, 14 RBDI 1978-1979, pp. 460-485, 478.

[161] Part V (military matters: demobilization, reduction of army, arms embargo, no compulsory military service, mobilization prohibited, dismantling fortified works, no warships or submarines, no military or naval air force) and Part XIV (guarantees: occupation and withdrawal of German troops) of the 1919 Treaty of Peace with Germany. Provisions similar, though not always as far-reaching, to Part V may be found in the 1919 Treaty of Peace between the Allied and Associated Powers and Austria, 14 AJIL 1920, Supplement, pp. 1-183; the 1919 Treaty of Peace between the Allied and Associated Powers and Bulgaria, and Protocol, 14 AJIL 1920, Supplement, pp. 185-309; the 1920 Treaty of Peace between the Allied and Associated Powers and Hungary, and Protocol and Declaration, 15 AJIL 1921, Supplement, pp. 23-151; the 1920 Treaty of Peace between the Allied Powers and Turkey, 15 AJIL 1921, Supplement, pp. 179-295; the 1947 Treaty of Peace between the Allied and Associated Powers and Italy, 42 AJIL 1948, Supplement, pp. 47-142; the 1947 Treaty of Peace with Bulgaria, 42 AJIL 1948, Supplement, pp. 179-202; the 1947 Treaty of Peace with Finland, 42 AJIL 1948, Supplement, pp. 203-223; the 1947 Treaty of Peace with Hungary, 42 AJIL 1948, Supplement, pp. 225-251; the 1947 Treaty of Peace with Roumania, 42 AJIL 1948, Supplement, pp. 252-277; and the 1955 State Treaty for the Re-Establishment of an Independent and Democratic Austria, 49 AJIL 1955, Supplement, pp. 162-191. See further the 1919 Treaty of Peace between the Principal Allied and Associated Powers and Czecho-Slovakia, 14 AJIL 1920, Supplement, pp. 311-323; the 1919 Treaty between the Principal Allied and Associated Powers and Roumania, 14 AJIL 1920, Supplement, pp. 325-332; the 1919 Treaty of Peace between the Principal Allied and Associated Powers and the Serb-Croat-Slovene State, 14 AJIL 1920, Supplement, pp. 333-342; and the 1951 Treaty of Peace between the Allied Powers and Japan, 46 AJIL 1952, Supplement, pp. 71-86.

[162] See for instance Jennings, The Acquisition of Territory, 56-61.

[163] Generally Sur, S., La résolution 687 (3 avril 1991) du Conseil de Securité dans l'affaire du Golfe: Problèmes de rétablissement et de garantie de la paix, 37 AFDI 1991, pp. 25-97; Cottereau, G., De la responsabilité de l'Iraq selon la résolution 687 du Conseil de Sécurité, 37 AFDI 1991, pp. 99-117.

[164] Which may be deduced also on the basis of an *a contrario* interpretation of article 94, paragraph 2, of the Charter (chapter two, subsection 2.4.1).

[165] Arangio-Ruiz, Seventh Report, Addendum 1, 2. On guarantees in the context of aggression, colonialism and *apartheid* see Graefrath, B., Oeser, E., and Steiniger, P., Völkerrechtliche Verantwortlichkeit der Staaten, Staatsverlag der DDR, Berlin, 1977, 132-137 and 151-152.

[166] Arangio-Ruiz, Seventh Report, 12. Relevant footnote omitted.

[167] Arangio-Ruiz, Seventh Report, 12-13. Two relevant footnotes omitted.

[168] A number of peace treaties have recorded the determination of boundaries and the renunciation of territory. With regard to the Germany one may note that the following paragraph in the preamble of the 1945 Declaration regarding the Defeat of Germany stated that the Four Powers would: "(...) hereafter determine the boundaries of Germany or any part thereof and the status of Germany or of any area at present being a part of German territory."

[169] One should be well aware that due to this demarcation a substantial part of Um Quasr now lies on Kuwaiti territory. C.f. Mendelson, M., and Hulton, S., The Iraq-Kuwait Boundary, 64 BYBIL 1993, pp. 135-195, 192-195. Note especially resolution 833.

[170] In the preamble of resolution 773 the Security Council claimed: "Recalling in this connection that through the demarcation process the Commission is not reallocating territory between Kuwait and Iraq, but it is simply carrying out the technical task necessary to demarcate for the first time the precise co-ordinates of the boundary set out in the Agreed Minutes between the State of Kuwait and the Republic of Iraq regarding the restoration of Friendly Relations, Recognition and Related Matters signed by them on 4 October 1963, and that this task is being carried out in the special circumstances following Iraq's invasion of Kuwait (...)." Repeated in the preamble of resolution 833.

[171] Note the mention, in the preamble of resolution 806, of border incidents involving UNIKOM.

[172] The Libyan leader Khadaffi has accepted his loss regarding the Aouzou strip, after a judgment by the Court in favour of Chad. See Territorial Dispute (Libyan Arab Jamahiriya/Chad), Judgment, ICJ Reports 1994, p. 6.

[173] *E.g.* articles 21, 23 to 26, 29, 40 and 43 of the 1947 Peace Treaty with Italy; and articles 2, 3, 8 (b), and 10 of the 1951 Peace Treaty with Japan.

[174] Riphagen, W., Second report on the content, forms and degrees of international responsibility (part 2 of the draft articles), YBILC 1981, Volume II, Part One, pp. 79-101, 100. The article was placed by Riphagen under the heading of "general principles", and apparently applied also in case the breach of obligation constituted a crime. That may be seen also by his comment to the article: "But the point is that even the most serious 'international crime' (...) does not in itself – i.e. automatically – deprive the author State of its sovereignty as such." Riphagen, Second Report, 86.

[175] Generally Sur, La résolution 687, 50-68; Marauhn, T., The Implementation of Disarmament and Arms Control Obligations Imposed upon Iraq by the Security Council, 52 ZAORV 1992, pp. 781-803, and especially 786. Germany was subjected to complete disarmament after World War II. See articles 2 (a) and 13 (a) of the 1945 Declaration regarding the Defeat of Germany. Note also the French disarmament, imposed by Germany, under the 1940 Armistice Agreement (articles 4 to 9); and similar provisions imposed by Italy under the 1940 Armistice Agreement (articles 9-13 and 15).

[176] Leaving aside here the continued application of the arms embargo against Iraq as laid down in paragraph 24 of resolution 687.

[177] See the 1968 Traité sur la non prolifération des armes nucléaires, 73 RGDIP 1969, pp. 248-253.

[178] The 1925 Geneva Protocol for the Prohibition of the Use in War of Asphyxiating, Poisonous or Other Gases, and of Bacteriological Methods of Warfare, in Roberts, A., and Guelff, R. (Eds.), Documents on the Laws of War, Clarendon Press, Oxford, 1982, pp. 139-140.

[179] The Court noted in Military and Paramilitary Activities in and against Nicaragua (Nicaragua *v.* United States of America), Merits, Judgment, ICJ Reports 1986, p. 14, 135, that: "(...) in international law there are no rules, other than such rules as may be accepted by the State concerned, by treaty or otherwise, whereby the level of armaments of a sovereign State can be limited, and this principle is valid for all States without exception."

[180] Iraq has only signed the 1972 Convention on the Prohibition of the Development, Production and Stockpiling of Bacteriological (Biological) and Toxin Weapons and on Their Destruction, adopted by way of General Assembly resolution 2826 (XXVI), reprinted in 11 ILM 1972, pp. 310-314. The Security Council has only *invited* Iraq to ratify that treaty (paragraph 7, resolution 687).

[181] On El Salvador note the 1991 New York Agreement, reprinted in A/46/502, Annex; the 1991 Mexico Agreements (the Political Agreements Elaborating on the Constitutional Reform), reprinted in A/46/553, Annex; and especially the 1992 Peace Agreement, reprinted in A/46/864, Annex. On Liberia see the 1991 Final Communiqué of the Fourth Meeting of the Committee of Five of the Economic Community of West African States on the Liberian Crisis, reprinted in S/24815, Annex; the 1993 Agreement, reprinted in S/26272, Annex; the 1994 Akosombo Agreement, reprinted in S/1994/1174; the 1994 Agreement on the clarification of the Akosombo Agreement, reprinted in S/1995/7, Annex II. Regarding Angola note Annexes III to V of the 1994 Lusaka Protocol, reprinted in S/1994/1441, Annex. On Haiti see the 1992 Protocol between President Jean-Bertrand Aristide and the Parliamentary Negotiating Commission to find a Definitive Solution to the Haitian Crisis, reprinted in A/46/891, Annex I; the 1992 Protocol between President Jean-Bertrand Aristide and Prime Minister-Designate, Rene Theodore, under the Auspices of the Organization of American States (OAS), reprinted in *ibid.*, Annex II; the 1993 Governors Island Agreement, reprinted in Report of the Secretary-General, A/47/975, 2-3; and the 1993 New York Pact, reprinted in A/47/1000, Annex. And on Rwanda see the 1993 Protocol of Agreement between the Government of the Republic of Rwanda and the Rwandese Patriotic Front on the Integration of the Armed Forces of the Two Parties, reprinted in A/48/824, Annex VI. See also the 1993 Declaration of Principles on Interim Self-Government Arrangements (between Israel and the PLO), reprinted in 32 ILM 1993, pp. 1527-1544, which provides in article 8 that the Council will establish a strong police force on the West Bank and the Gaza Strip. In a similar vein see articles 8 and 9 of the 1994 Agreement on the Gaza Strip and the Jericho Area, reprinted in 33 ILM 1994, pp. 626-640.

[182] Arangio-Ruiz, Seventh Report, 11-14. Note also the conflicting views in Report 1994, 347-349.

[183] In article 227 of the 1919 Treaty of Peace with Germany, provision was made for the prosecution of the German Emperor on the basis of his "supreme offense against international morality and the sanctity of treaties". Note also that the peace treaties tended to lay down obligations for the State concerned to hand over individuals suspected of having violated the laws and customs of war.

[184] C.f. Cassese, A., La communaute internationale et le genocide, in Le droit au service de la paix, de la justice et du développement, Mélanges Michel Virally, Éditions A. Pedone, Paris, 1991, pp. 183-194, 194.

[185] See especially articles 53 and 107 of the Charter. Note also the condition, contained in article 4, paragraph 1, of the Charter, for becoming a member of the United Nations: a State applying for membership must be peace-loving. See also the opinion of the Court on Admission of a State to the United Nations (Charter, Art. 4), Advisory Opinion, ICJ Reports 1948, p. 57, 62-63.

[186] The more likely course of events if the Allies had decided to leave the prosecution of the responsible individuals to German courts.

[187] Article 11 (a) of the 1945 Declaration regarding the Defeat of Germany.

[188] Article 9 of the Charter of the Nuremberg Tribunal. Article 10 of that Charter stipulated the final character of such a declaration. The effect of a declaration was that proven membership of a criminal organization could lead to the imposition of penalties, including the death penalty. In its judgment the Tribunal first clarified that "criminal guilt is personal" and that "mass punishments should be avoided". According to the Tribunal therefore individuals should not be punished for membership of a criminal organization, when they "had no knowledge of the criminal purposes or acts of the organization", nor when they "were drafted by the State for membership, unless they were personally implicated in the commission of acts declared criminal by Article 6 of the Charter (...)." Nuremberg Judgment, 251.

[189] The 1949 Accords de Washington sur l'Allemagne, in Colliard, C., and Manin, A. (Eds.), Droit International et Histoire Diplomatique, Documents choisis, volume II, Europe, Éditions Montchrestien, Paris, 1976, pp. 264-271. See especially articles 1, 3, and 7 of the 1949 Aide-mémoire concernant les principes directeurs qui président a l'exercise des pouvoirs et responsabilités des gouvernements de la France, du Royaume Uni et des États-Unis après l'établissement d'une République Fédérale Allemande, 265; and article 5 of the 1949 Statut d'occupation définissant les pouvoirs devant être conservé par les autorités occupantes, 266-267.

[190] The 1949 "Statut d'occupation", in Colliard and Manin, Droit International, 267.

[191] The 1954 Convention on Relations between the Three Powers and the Federal Republic of Germany, 49 AJIL 1955, pp. 57-69.

[192] Which came about some 35 years later. See the 1990 Agreement on the Settlement of Certain Matters Relating to Berlin, 30 ILM 1991, pp. 446-449; the 1990 Treaty between the Federal Republic of Germany and the German Democratic Republic on the Establishment of German Unity (Unification Treaty), 30 ILM 1991, pp. 463-498; and the 1990 Treaty on the Final Settlement with Respect to Germany, 29 ILM 1990, pp. 1187-1192.

[193] As noted by Kawasaki, K., Crimes of State in International Law, 15 SLR 1993, pp. 27-45, 45.

[194] Nicaragua Case, Merits, 100-101. The Court took those statements as evidence of the validity of the claim that the prohibition exists in customary international law.

[195] Nicaragua Case, Merits, 110.

[196] It is publicly known that the lifting of the sanctions against Iraq is barred to a large extent due to the avowed wish of some permanent members to see Saddam Hussein replaced. See Sur, La résolution 687, 70-71.

[197] Nicaragua Case, Merits, 108. Article 1, paragraph 1, of the 1966 International Covenant on Civil and Political Rights, 61 AJIL 1967, pp. 870-887, stipulates: "All peoples have the right to self-determination. By virtue of that right they freely determine their political status and freely pursue their economic, social and cultural development."

[198] Nicaragua Case, Merits, 130-135. The same cannot be said of conventional instruments. Under certain human rights treaties States commit themselves to grant specific political rights to their citizens and to hold periodical, free, elections. *E.g.* article 10 of the 1950 Convention for the Protection of Human Rights and Fundamental Freedoms, 45 AJIL 1951, Supplement, pp. 24-39; article 3 of the 1952 Protocol I to the Convention for the Protection of Human Rights and Fundamental Freedoms, in Brownlie, I. (Ed.), Basic Documents on Human Rights, Third Edition, Clarendon Press, Oxford, 1992, pp. 341-343; and articles 19 and 25 of the 1966 International Covenant on Civil and Political Rights.

[199] Nicaragua Case, Merits, 71.

[200] Nicaragua Case, Merits, 119-120. The Court observed, in relation to Nicaragua's actions towards El Salvador, that the provision of arms to the armed opposition in another State did not constitute an armed attack. In regard to Honduras and Costa Rica it considered that it was hard to determine whether the cross-border incidents with those States amounted to an armed attack by Nicaragua, and rejected such qualification on the basis that the States concerned had not declared themselves to be under attack. *Ibid.*, 120-121.

[201] Nicaragua Case, Merits, 124. The official policy of the United States was that its actions were not intended to overthrow the Nicaraguan government. *Ibid.*, 56-57 and 123-124. On the latter page the Court argues: "The Court considers that in international law, if one State, with a view to the coercion of another State, supports and assists armed bands in that State whose purpose is to overthrow the government of that State, that amounts to an intervention by one State in the internal affairs of the other, whether or not the political objective of the State giving such support and assistance is equally far-reaching."

[202] Dissenting Opinion Schwebel, Nicaragua Case, Merits, 299-300.

[203] Dissenting Opinion Schwebel, Nicaragua Case, Merits, 332.

[204] Nicaragua Case, Merits, 101.

[205] Nicaragua Case, Merits, 103.

[206] Where Austria is concerned such integration, in this case in the European society, was prevented due to the political animosity current after World War II. Since the bi-polarity in world politics has come to an end, it cannot but be noted that Austria has joined the European Union. Note also article 4 of the 1955 State Treaty for the Re-Establishment of an Independent and Democratic Austria.

[207] Generally Bindschedler, R., Das Problem der Beteiligung der Schweiz an Sanktionen der Vereinten Nationen, besonders im Falle Rhodesiens, 28 ZAORV 1968, pp. 1-15; and Zemanek, K., Das Problem der Beteiligung des immerwährend neutralen Österreich an Sanktionen der Vereinten Nationen, besonders im Falle Rhodesiens, 28 ZAORV 1968, pp. 16-32.

[208] C.f. Schermers, H., The Obligation to Intervene in the Domestic Affairs of States, in Delissen, A., and Tanja, G. (Eds.), Humanitarian Law of Armed Conflict, Essays in Honour of Fritz Kalshoven, Martinus Nijhoff Publishers, Dordrecht, 1991, pp. 583-593, 589-590; and Kawasaki, Crimes of State, 43 and 45, who argues in favour of an obligation to effect a complete change in the governmental structures of the author State of an international crime.

[209] *E.g.* the Vietnamese invasion of Cambodia, which ousted the *Khmer Rouge* government of Cambodia. While that invasion put a stop to one of the worst massacres of this century, Vietnam was outcasted because it installed a Vietnamese controlled government, and remained in occupation of Cambodia for more than ten years.

[210] Observe that the Court has refused to entertain the case brought by Portugal against Australia, but noted that, for the parties, the territory of East Timor remains a non-self-governing territory and that its people has the right to self-determination. Case concerning East Timor, Judgment, 30 June 1995, paragraphs 31 and 37.

[211] Note the 1992 General Peace Agreement of Mozambique. On El Salvador the 1990 Agreement on Human Rights, reprinted in A/44/971, Annex; the 1991 Mexico Agreements (especially the Political Agreements Elaborating on the Constitutional Reform; and the Commission on the Truth); and the 1992 Peace Agreement. On Rwanda the 1993 Protocol of Agreement between the Government of the Republic of Rwanda and the Rwandese Patriotic Front on the Rule of Law, reprinted in A/48/824, Annex III; and the 1993 Protocols of Agreement between the Government of the Republic of Rwanda and the Rwandese Patriotic Front on Power-Sharing within the Framework of a Broad-Based Transitional Government, in *ibid.*, Annex IV. On Guatamala see the 1991 Framework Agreement on Democratization in the Search for Peace by Political Means (Querétaro Agreement), reprinted in A/46/713. On Liberia see the 1993 Agreement; and the 1994 Akosombo

Agreement. On Angola Annexes VI and VII of the 1994 Lusaka Protocol. On Haiti see the 1992 Protocols; the 1993 Governors Island Agreement; and the 1993 New York Pact. Note also on the West Bank and the Gaza Strip the 1993 Declaration of Principles on Interim Self-Government Arrangements (article 3), and its 1993 Protocol on the Mode and Conditions of Elections, reprinted at 32 ILM 1993, p. 1535.

212 See the highly interesting studies of Franck, T., The Emerging Right to Democratic Governance, 86 AJIL 1992, pp. 46-91; and Crawford, J., Democracy and International Law, 64 BYBIL 1993, pp. 113-133.

213 Respectively article 15, article 2, article 6, article 3, and article 2. Attempts by certain Western States to ensure implementation of these provisions in Bulgaria, Romania and Hungary through arbitral channels failed due to the existence of drafting errors in the relevant provisions. See the following opinions in this respect: Interpretation of Peace Treaties, Advisory Opinion, ICJ Reports 1950, p. 65; and Interpretation of Peace Treaties (second phase), Advisory Opinion, ICJ Reports 1950, p. 221.

214 Note that the provision on the prohibition of fascist organizations has been inserted for the express purpose that such organizations should not be permitted to be able to take way the democratic rights of the people.

215 Arangio-Ruiz, Fifth Report, Addendum 3, 9.

216 *E.g.* Security Council resolutions 242, 713; General Assembly resolution 2625 (XXV). Note the remarks of Jennings, The Acquisition of Territory, 54.

217 Article 42 entails the possibility of the Security Council resorting to a first use of force, since such force need not relate to a breach of the peace or act of aggression, but may concern a (mere) threat to the peace.

218 See also Jennings, The Acquisition of Territory, 52.

219 Resolution 686. Repeated in slightly altered form in resolution 687.

220 Nicaragua Case, Merits, 103-104 and 108-111.

221 Consider for example the armed conflict between Iraq and Iran, and the question whether Iran could continue to act in self-defence. Discussed by Kaikobad, K., "*Ius Ad Bellum*": Legal Implications of the Iran-Iraq War, in Dekker, I., and Post, H. (Eds.), The Gulf War of 1980-1988, The Iran-Iraq War in International Legal Perspective, Martinus Nijhoff Publishers, Dordrecht, 1992, pp. 51-70, 64-65; Weller, M., The Use of Force and Collective Security, *ibid.*, pp. 71-90, 86-90; note also Siekmann, R., Comments, *ibid.*, pp. 91-94, 92-93. All three appear to come to the conclusion, although on different grounds, that Iran's right to self-defence had lapsed.

222 Resolution 2625 (XXV), under the principle on the prohibition of the threat or use of force.

223 Nor for that matter "any international agreement prior to the Charter régime and valid under international law;"

224 Text and Commentary Article 50, Law of Treaties, YBILC 1966, Volume II, pp. 247-249.

225 Waldock, Second Report on the Law of Treaties, YBILC 1962, Volume II, pp. 27-80, 39.

226 Text in 25 ILM 1986, pp. 543-589. Commentaries Articles 52 and 53, International Organizations, YBILC 1982, Volume II, Part Two, pp. 55-56.

227 Commentary Article 52, International Organizations, 56. According to the Commission the expression "group of States", used in certain General Assembly resolutions, covers international organizations. International organizations therefore could, in theory (the Commission's language), unlawfully resort to armed force.

228 The Commission held in Commentary Article 53, International Organizations, 56: "(...) it can hardly be maintained that States can avoid compliance with peremptory norms by creating an organization." It hereby implies that an international organization cannot conclude a treaty which the individual States could not conclude due to its conflict with a peremptory norm.

229 Note however McNair who states: "(...) a treaty which is induced by collective armed force exercised on behalf of the international community differs from a treaty induced by coercion for the purpose of securing some national objective, and requires the application of different principles;" McNair, A., The Law of Treaties, Oxford University Press, Oxford, 1961, 210.

230 Tunkin, as quoted by Dupuy, P.-M., Observations sur le "crime international de l'etat", 84 RGDIP 1980, pp. 449-486, 458. Note the interesting remarks by Reuter, P., Trois observations sur la codification de la responsabilite internationale des etats pour fait illicite, in Le droit au service de la paix, pp. 389-398, 392-394.

231 *E.g.* Japanese renunciation of the Kurilles and part of Sakhalin, article 2 (c) of the 1951 Treaty of Peace with Japan.

232 *E.g.* Triest, article 21 of the 1947 Treaty of Peace with Italy.

233 *E.g.* the changing of administering authority regarding the Pacific islands: article 2 (d) of the 1951 Treaty of Peace with Japan.

234 Articles 27 and 33 of the 1947 Treaty of Peace with Italy; and 2 (a) of the 1951 Treaty of Peace with Japan.

235 Articles 42 and 43 of the 1919 Treaty of Peace with Germany. For instance resolution 242 calls for appropriate demilitarized zones. Note also the 1940 French/Italian Armistice Agreement (articles 3-8).

236 *E.g.* Aaland Islands, in Colliard and Manin, Droit International, 26 and 72-75.

[237] Note the protocols on the occupation of Germany, in Colliard and Manin, Droit International, pp. 175-181, 185-186, and 194-196; on Japan see article 6 (a) of the Treaty of Peace with Japan. On the occupation of France after its defeat by Germany, see 1940 German/French Armistice Agreement (articles 2, 3, and 18).

[238] Resolutions 686 and 687.

[239] *E.g.* the administration of Cambodia by UNTAC in accordance with the 1991 Agreement on a Comprehensive Political Settlement of the Cambodia Conflict. See Annex 1, UNTAC Mandate, 31 ILM 1992, pp. 189-192.

[240] See generally Hofmann, Zur Unterscheidung, 223-229; and Arangio-Ruiz, Fifth Report, Addendum 3, 5-7.

[241] Article 4 of the 1973 International Convention on the Suppression and Punishment of the Crime of *Apartheid*, adopted by way of General Assembly resolution 3068 (XXVIII), reprinted in 13 ILM 1974, pp. 50-57; article 1 of the 1970 Traité interdisant des armes nucléaires et d'autres armes de destruction massive sur le fond des mers et des océans ainsi que dans leur sous-sol, adopted by way of General Assembly resolution 2660, in Resolutions adoptées par l'Assemblée générale au cours de sa vingt-cinquime session, 15 septembre – 17 décembre 1970, Documents Officiel, Supplement No. 10 (A/8028), pp. 13-15; and article 4 of the 1967 Treaty on Principles Governing the Activities of States in the Exploration and Use of Outer Space, including the Moon and other Celestial Bodies, 61 AJIL 1967, pp. 644-649.

[242] Arangio-Ruiz, G., Fourth Report on State Responsibility, 1 June 1992, A/CN.4/444/Add.2, 37 pp., 37.

[243] Cassese states that States other than the directly injured one (if any) can only claim cessation in case of massive disregard for human rights. Cassese, A., Remarks on the Present Legal Regulation of Crimes of States, in Etudes en l'honneur de Roberto Ago, Le droit international à l'heure de sa codification, volume III, Giuffrè, Milano, 1987, pp. 49-64, 63. Dominicé, C., Die internationalen Verbrechen und deren rechtliches Regime, in Fischer, P., Koeck, H., and Verdross, A. (Eds.), Völkerrecht und Rechtsphilosophie, Internationale Festschrift für Stephan Verosta zum 70. Geburstag, Duncker & Humblot, Berlin, 1980, pp. 227-248, 243-244, poses the question whether the international community could claim restitution.

[244] C.f. Hofmann, R., Zur Unterscheidung, 224; and Napel, H.-M. ten, The Concept of International Crimes of States: Walking the Thin Line between Progressive Development and Disintegration of the International Legal Order, 1 LJIL 1988, pp. 149-169, 165.

[245] Trail Smelter Arbitration (U.S. *v.* Canada), (Hostie, Warren, Greenfields, Arbitrators), 16 April 1938, 9 ILR 1938-1940, pp. 315-333, 317.

[246] The status of injured State in such cases is not grafted upon the existence of an alleged subjective right to peace. Levin, as referred to by Dupuy, Observations sur le "crime international de l'etat", 457; and Mazov, V., Responsibility for Aggression in International Law, 6 IA (Moscow) 1972, pp. 43-48, 45, mentions that "peace is indivisible". It might be objected that it is only "indivisible" because we have said so.

[247] Graefrath and Mohr, Völkerrechtliche und strafrechtliche verantwortlichkeit, 35.

[248] Graefrath and Mohr, Völkerrechtliche und strafrechtliche verantwortlichkeit, 36.

[249] Wellens, *Apartheid*, An International Crime, 301, observes, as to the crime of *apartheid*, on the rights of injured States: "Accordingly every State has the right to require them to discontinue the act, to release and return the persons and objects held through *apartheid*, to re-establish the situation as it existed before the introduction of *apartheid* and to provide appropriate guarantees against repetition. *All these demands may be formulated by States acting individually or collectively.*" Emphasis added. See also 298-299. Sucharitkul, S., Terrorism as an International Crime: Questions of Responsibility and Complicity, 19 IYHR 1989, pp. 247-258, 255, states that the injured State can claim cessation, compensation, and satisfaction. He does not specify whether third States could equally claim reparation, but only mentions the obligations of such States. Mohr, M., The ILC's Distinction between "International Crimes" and "International Delicts" and its Implications, in Spinedi, M., Simma, B. (Eds.), United Nations Codification of International Responsibility, Oceana Publications, Inc., New York, 1987, pp. 115-141, 129-130, only mentions the claim for cessation of the wrongful conduct and the corresponding duty of non-recognition. Similarly Aréchaga, and Tanzi, International State Responsibility, 357-358. At the latter page they state: "(...) the right to demand cessation of the wrongful act by States not directly injured does not exist in the case of international delicts." That conclusion only goes for the primary rule prohibiting the use of armed force. Note also Arangio-Ruiz, Fifth Report, Addendum 3, 3-4.

[250] C.f. Hofmann, Zur Unterscheidung, 224. Though he appears to claim that all the claims of the other injured States, on cessation and satisfaction, are of dependent nature.

[251] Especially Arangio-Ruiz, Fifth Report, Addendum 3, 13.

[252] Though the members remain subject to the possibility of complicity.

[253] See Arangio-Ruiz, Fifth Report, Addendum 3, 13-15 and 17-18.

[254] Gowlland-Debbas, Security Council Enforcement, 73.

[255] Diplomatic Staff Case, Judgment, 40. The Court had rejected, at 38, the justification claimed by Iran, for the reason that: "(...) diplomatic law itself provides the necessary means of defence against, and sanction for, illicit activities by members of diplomatic or consular missions."

[256] Note article 41, paragraph 1, of the 1963 Vienna Convention on Diplomatic Relations: "Without prejudice to their privileges and immunities, it is the duty of all persons enjoying such privileges and immunities to respect the laws and regulations of the receiving State. They also have a duty not to interfere in the internal affairs of that State." Text in 55 AJIL 1961, pp. 1064-1077.

[257] As such it was considered by the Court. Diplomatic Case, Judgment, 38.

[258] Note Riphagen, W., Third report on the content, forms and degrees of international responsibility (part 2 of the draft articles), YBILC 1982, Volume II, Part One, pp. 22-50, 30-34.

[259] Simma mentions the question of an independent international right to reparation (compensation) for EEC members on account of persistent violations of EEC law only in passing. Simma, B., Self-Contained Regimes, 16 NYIL 1985, pp. 111-136, 126. On whether the GATT system (and the Government Procurement Agreement) excludes resort to the general rules on reparation see Mavroidis, P., Government Procurement Agreement, The Trondheim Case: the Remedies Issue, 48 ASZIW 1993, pp. 77-93, 89-90. For the 1947 General Agreement on Tarifs and Trade see 55 UNTS, pp. 194-285.

[260] Chorzów Factory Case, Jurisdiction, 21. Emphasis added.

[261] Text and Commentary Article 2, Part Two, YBILC 1983, Volume II, Part Two, pp. 42-43.

[262] See Mavroidis, Government Procurement, 85-93, as to a GATT panel's competence to recommend remedies not provided for in the GATT or the Government Procurement Agreement.

[263] The crime of aggression is covered by the rules of the Charter; the crime of genocide in the 1948 Convention on the Suppression and Punishment of the Crime of Genocide, adopted by way of General Assembly resolution 260 (III), reprinted in 49 AJIL 1955, pp. 7-10; the crime of *apartheid* in the 1973 International Convention on the Suppression and Punishment of the Crime of *Apartheid*, adopted by General Assembly resolution 3068 (XXVIII), reprinted in 13 ILM 1974, pp. 50-57; the crime of slavery in among others the 1956 Convention supplémentaire relative à l'abolition de l'esclavage, de la traite des esclaves et des institutions et pratiques analogues à l'esclavage, 61 RGDIP 1957, pp. 137-142. With regard to the crime of widespread breaches of basic human rights obligations see especially the 1966 International Covenant on Civil and Political Rights, but also the 1966 International Covenant on Economic, Social and Cultural Rights, 61 AJIL 1967, pp. 861-870.

[264] C.f. Rigaux, F., Le crime d'etat, Reflexions sur l'article 19 du projet d'articles sur la responsabilite des etats, in Etudes en l'honneur de Roberto Ago, volume III, pp. 301-325, 324.

[265] Arangio-Ruiz, Preliminary Report, Addendum 1, 33.

[266] Commentary Article 7, Part Two, 165. Also Arangio-Ruiz, Preliminary Report, Addendum 1, 22. And note: "(...) the raison d'être of the limit of excessive onerousness resides in the principle of proportionality between the seriousness of the violation and injury on the one hand and the quality and quantity on the other, (...)." *Ibid.*

[267] Commentary Article 7, Part Two, 166. Originally Arangio-Ruiz, Preliminary Report, Addendum 1, 22.

[268] Arangio-Ruiz, Seventh Report, Addendum 1, 2. He also proposes to lift the restriction of article 7 (d), Part Two, which states that restitution in kind should not: "(...) seriously jeopardize the political independence or economic stability of the State which has committed the internationally wrongful act, whereas the injured State would not similarly be affected if it did not obtain restitution in kind." The arguments in this subsection generally apply with regard to the economic stability of an author State. The commentary makes clear that that restriction has been inserted in the draft mostly with the issue of nationalizations in mind. Commentary Article 7, Part Two, 167-168. The restriction regarding the political independence of a State would be lifted in his proposal, but subject to the proviso that the author State would preserve its status as an independent member of the international community.

[269] The Court has denied, in principle, that it could not order *restitutio in integrum*. Denmark had argued, in relation to the Finnish request for provisional measures in the Great Belt Case, that an eventual decision on the merits in favour of Finland could not lead to an order of restitution as that would be excessively onerous. The Court observed: "(...) whereas in principle however if it is established that the construction of works involves an infringement of a legal right, the possibility cannot and should not be excluded *a priori* of a judicial finding that such works should not be continued or must be modified or dismantled." A bit further on it went on to say: "Whereas it is for Denmark, which is informed of the nature of Finland's claim, to consider the impact which a judgment upholding it could have upon the implementation of the Great Belt project, and to decide whether and to what extent it should accordingly delay or modify that project;" Passage through the Great Belt (Finland *v.* Denmark), Provisional Measures, Order, ICJ Reports 1991, p. 12, 19.

[270] C.f. Arangio-Ruiz, Preliminary Report, Addendum 1, 15 and 20-21.

[271] Graefrath, Responsibility and Damages, 92. He bases this limit on the right of self-determination of peoples, and quotes article 1, paragraph 2, last sentence, of the International Covenant on Civil and Political Rights: "In no case may a people be deprived of its own means of subsistence."

[272] The second paragraph of the said article went on to state, however, that Germany was required to make compensation for all the damage done to the civilian population and their property. See also articles 231 and 234.

[273] Article 8 of the treaty between Poland, Russia and the Ukraine provided: "Les deux parties contractantes renoncent réciproquement au remboursement des frais de guerre, c'est-à-dire des dépenses de l'Etat affectées à la guerre, ainsi qu'à l'indemnisation des dommages causés par la guerre, c'est-à-dire pour les dommages causés à eux ou à leurs ressortisants sur le terrain des opérations de guerre par suite de ces opérations et des mesures militaires prises pendant la guerre polono-russo-ukrainienne." Text in Colliard and Manin, Droit International, 71. Article 13 however stipulates payment, by Russia and the Ukraine to Poland, of some 30 million rubles for Poland's participation in the Ancient Russian economy.

[274] Contrary Graefrath, Zur Geschichte der Reparationen, VEB Deutscher Zentralverlag, Berlin, 1954, 137; and Graefrath, International Crimes, 165. In this respect one may point to the fact that the need to substitute destroyed military material offers economic advantages to States in the form of profits and employment.

[275] In S/AC.26/1991/7/Rev.1, reproduced in 31 ILM 1992, pp. 1045-1052, from S/23765, Annex, the Governing Council excluded compensation for losses suffered as a result of the trade embargo and related measures (1046). In S/AC.26/1992/9, reprinted in 31 ILM 1992, pp. 1037-1040, 1038, it extended the exclusion to cover also the economic situation caused by the trade embargo and related measures, and regarding the latter clarified that these referred to the prohibitions of Security Council resolution 661 and subsequent relevant resolutions and the measures taken by States pursuant thereto. It further stated that compensation would be provided to the extent that Iraq's invasion and occupation of Kuwait constituted a cause of direct loss that was separate and distinct from the trade embargo and related measures. In S/AC.26/1992/15, reprinted in 34 ILM 1995, pp. 244-247, 246, the Governing Council indicated that exclusion of compensation for losses due to the trade embargo and related measures, and the economic situation caused thereby, encompasses only such losses resulting *solely* therefrom.

[276] S/AC.26/1992/11, reproduced in 31 ILM 1992, pp. 1067-1068, 1067-1068, from S/24363, Annex II.

[277] S/AC.26/Dec. 19 (1994), reprinted in 34 ILM 1995, p. 253, 253 (note also at 249)

[278] Graefrath and Mohr recommend that compensation claims against Iraq should rather be settled by reaching a lump sum agreement, and leave it to the individual States to satisfy claims of their nationals and corporations. Graefrath, and Mohr, Legal Consequences, 126.

[279] So called decision 1 of the Governing Council, reprinted in 30 ILM 1991, pp. 1712-1714, 1713.

[280] S/AC.26/1992/8, reprinted in 31 ILM 1992, pp. 1036-1037, 1036-1037.

[281] The Compensation Commission has, on the contrary, decided that interest will be awarded from the date the loss occurred until the date of payment. See S/AC.26/1991/16, reprinted in 34 ILM 1995, pp. 247-248, 247.

[282] Apparently contrary The Cysne, 5 ILR 1929-1930, 491: "For this reason the Tribunal could not accept the German contention that there was no occasion for awarding damages seeing that the owners, who were insured, suffered no damage, and that for the insurance company the sinking of the vessel constituted the realisation of a risk the equivalent of which they had received in the form of premiums. In estimating the amount of compensation the Tribunal was bound to consider the fact that the owners of the vessel suffered, at that particular period, a loss which was much in excess of the small sum for which it was insured. There was also the loss of cargo and of profits, and the legal expenses (...)."

[283] Arangio-Ruiz, Preliminary Report, Addendum 1, 13-21.

[284] Arangio-Ruiz, Preliminary Report, Addendum 1, 13-14.

[285] Note however the claims of Nauru against Australia to the effect that the latter had mined the phosphate grounds of Nauru, thus making those grounds uninhabitable for the Nauruan people. On the basis that this constituted a breach of obligations under the trusteeship agreement Nauru claimed that Australia had to pay compensation for the restitution of those grounds to its original state. After the Court's judgment on jurisdiction and admissibility the two parties reached an out of court settlement. See Agreement between Australia and the Republic of Nauru for the Settlement of the Case in the I.C.J. concerning Certain Phosphate Lands in Nauru, 32 ILM 1994, pp. 620-621.

[286] See Commentary Article 7, Part Two, 151, and 163-164.

[287] Commentary Article 6 *bis*, Part Two, 150-151. Originally Arangio-Ruiz, Preliminary Report, Addendum 1, 20-21, in the context of restitution in kind.

[288] See Commentary Article 6 *bis*, Part Two, 142, and 146-151.

[289] C.f. Arangio-Ruiz, Fifth Report, Addendum 3, 5.

[290] Arangio-Ruiz, Fifth Report, Addendum 3, 5 and 9, footnote 117.

CHAPTER 4

THE RIGHT OF (AN) INJURED STATE(S) AND THE UNITED NATIONS TO RESORT TO NON-MILITARY COUNTERMEASURES IN RESPONSE TO INTERNATIONAL CRIMES

4.1. Introduction

The Commission indicated in its commentary to article 1, Part One, that the new relations arising from a State's international responsibility might lead to giving:[1] "(...) the injured State itself or other subjects of international law the right to impose on the offending State a sanction admitted by international law." The issue to discussed in this chapter concerns, in a strict sense, resort to that faculty called reprisals.[2] Then special rapporteur Ago, in his elaboration of the circumstances precluding the wrongfulness of conduct, had decided to name those sanctions.[3] The Commission in turn decided not to use the word "sanction", since there existed a tendency to reserve that word for:[4]

> "(...) reactive measures applied by virtue of a decision taken by an international organization following a breach of an international obligation having serious consequences for the international community as a whole, and in particular for certain measures which the United Nations is empowered to adopt, under the system established by the Charter, with a view to the maintenance of international peace and security."

In phrasing the provision on reprisals, article 30, Part One, the Commission instead resorted to the use of the words countermeasure (in the title) and measure (in the text). That provision consequently runs:[5]

> "The wrongfulness of an act of a State not in conformity with an obligation of that State towards another State is precluded if the act constitutes a measure legitimate under international law against that other State, in consequence of an internationally wrongful act of that other State."

In the commentary no explanation was offered for that choice, but apparently use of the term countermeasures was preferable because of the unfavourable connotations attached to the term reprisal.[6]

The subsequent special rapporteur, Riphagen, in his elaboration of Part Two on the content, forms and degrees of international responsibility, decided to split up the notion of countermeasures into measures adopted by way of reciprocity and measures by way of reprisal.[7] The first would involve the suspension of the performance of obligations identical to those breached by the author State. The second would involve measures that were directed to the suspension of performance of obligations other than those breached by the author State. The present special rapporteur, Arangio-Ruiz, announced his dislike of the term countermeasures and spoke of measures instead.[8]

Later on, as he engaged in the study of countermeasures, though conforming to actual practice by speaking of countermeasures, he expressed a preference for the term reprisals.[9] At the same time he abandoned, and was followed in this by the Drafting Committee and the Commission, the distinction introduced by his predecessor Riphagen between measures by way of reciprocity and measures by way of reprisal.[10]

Over the years, as may be seen from the inclusion of article 30, Part One, into the ILC-draft,[11] and the proposed article 11, Part Two,[12] it has been generally recognized that an injured State may acquire the right to resort to countermeasures. However, disagreement exists with regard to almost all aspects of the unilateral exercise of such a right. Questions regarding the basic requirements for a legitimate resort to decentralized or centralized countermeasures, as well as the restrictions applicable when such measures are implemented, have been extensively examined in the bulky literature on the subject.[13] Such examination has not led to any real consensus on the legality or legitimacy of past or present countermeasures. Controversy will therefore most likely continue to rule with respect to any future resort to unilateral measures. The discussion has not been abated by the fact that some of the measures concerned had been adopted not by States individually but on a concerted basis. Indeed that could hardly have been otherwise considering that the controversies reigned during the Cold War. The measures adopted by the European Economic Community rather than the individual member States did not find general support with other States.[14]

One area as to which the controversy appears to have been lessened somewhat concerns resort to sanctions by the Security Council under Chapter VII of the Charter.[15] The measures of article 41,[16] decided upon pursuant to a determination under article 39 that a threat to the peace, breach of the peace, or act of aggression exists, seem to have escaped the general disapproval reserved for unilateral or group co-ordinated countermeasures. Yet there has been general recognition also of the fact that sanctions imposed by the Security Council, and implemented by member States, fall under the heading of countermeasures.[17] The commentary to article 30 states:[18]

> "As has been seen, the terms 'countermeasures' and 'measure' used in the present article refer both to action by a State within the framework of sanctions ordered by a competent international organization on the basis of the rules by which it is governed and to action that a State is authorized to take, under general international law, in reaction to an internationally wrongful act. In both cases, as the article states, the measures in question must constitute 'a measure legitimate under international law' against the State which has previously committed the internationally wrongful act."

It is obvious then that any reigning controversy regarding the conditions and restrictions applicable to unilateral countermeasures will affect the discussion of sanctions. But the seemingly centralized decision making regarding resort to sanctions creates at least a presumption of legitimacy that appears to be lacking for decentralized resort. The foregoing quotation implies that all the conditions for a legitimate resort to unilateral countermeasures apply also to sanctions ordered by an international organization. But it is added in the commentary, a little bit later on, that:[19]

> "What is more, the conditions governing the various forms of reaction permissible under international law are not necessarily the same in all cases. For

> example, the condition of prior submission of a demand for reparation, and even the principle of proportionality between the offence reacted against and the reaction itself, do not play the same role in the case of reprisals and in the case of sanctions adopted collectively in a competent international organization."

At appropriate places therefore the measures possible under article 41 of the Charter will be discussed alongside countermeasures.

Three subjects will not be addressed in any particular manner in this chapter: measures by way of reciprocity (or reprisals in kind), the suspension and termination of treaties, and countermeasures involving uses of military force.

As to the first subject it may be observed that one of the more noteworthy features of countermeasures is that as a reaction against certain particular breaches of obligations they need not involve suspension of the same or similar obligations towards the author State. To put it differently: there does not exist any rule that requires an injured State to respond in kind.[20]

The second subject that will not be discussed, suspension and termination of treaties, has been codified in article 60 of the Vienna Convention on the Law of Treaties.[21] At this place one may point to article 73 of the Vienna Convention which states that it shall not "prejudge any question that may arise from (...) the international responsibility of a State". Suffice it to say that the only question is whether countermeasures affecting treaty obligations may be adopted in response to breaches of obligations under a treaty which would not amount to material breaches, or in response to breaches of obligations under other treaties, customary international law, or otherwise. The answer must be in the affirmative.[22]

The third subject excluded from this chapter, countermeasures involving the use of military force (armed reprisals), relates especially to the interpretation of Charter provisions and concomitant rules of customary law.[23] Those will be discussed in chapter five and the subject examined here will only concern so called non-military or peaceful countermeasures.

The following topics will be discussed in this chapter. The basis and nature of countermeasures will be discussed in section 4.2. It will examine such issues as the relation to reparation, punishment and punitive intent, coercion, collective responsibility, circumstances precluding wrongfulness, the denial of a right of the author State, and the exceptional or generalized nature of countermeasures. Section 4.3 will investigate possible preconditions for resort to countermeasures, namely the existence of an internationally wrongful act, reparation demands, dispute settlement, and additional requirements regarding Security Council measures under article 41 of the Charter.

Finally section 4.4 will investigate possible restrictions regarding resort to countermeasures. It will focus first on restrictions due to the multiplicity of injured States, or the Security Council's exercise of powers, in case of international crimes. In the second place it will discuss the exclusion of countermeasures due to the existence of certain treaty régimes, peremptory norms, or human rights obligations. Lastly in this section attention will be devoted to questions of necessity and proportionality.

4.2. The function and nature of countermeasures

4.2.1. THE FUNCTION OF COUNTERMEASURES

Relation to reparation

A basic issue with regard to resort to countermeasures concerns the function(s) they are to perform within the responsibility relationship between the author State and injured State(s).[24] Generally any resort to countermeasures by an injured State should be instrumental in the sense of putting pressure on an author State to acknowledge its responsibility and absolve itself therefrom.[25] The first issue to be discussed therefore concerns the relationship between resort to countermeasures and the obligations of the author State in the field of reparation.

If a breach of obligation is committed that is attributable to a State, the conditions for the existence of an internationally wrongful act are met, and such a State will engage its international responsibility. In essence, as the Commission observed, this means that the State internationally responsible will have imposed upon itself new obligations in the field of reparation. To make good for its wrongful act it must perform those reparation obligations, as the Permanent Court put it in the Chorzów Factory Case,[26] suitable to "wipe out all the consequences of the illegal act and re-establish the situation which would, in all probability, have existed if that act had not been committed".

Arangio-Ruiz pointed to the fact, as to the function to be assigned to countermeasures in the draft articles, that:[27]

> "The study of international practice seems to indicate that in resorting to countermeasures injured States affirm that they are seeking and indeed appear to seek cessation of the wrongful conduct (in case of a wrongful act having a continuing character) and/or reparation in a broad sense (possibly inclusive of satisfaction) and/or guarantees of non-repetition."

Although the special rapporteur found it difficult to ascertain whether such a function would be the only admissible one under international law,[28] it is submitted that, in a broad sense, such should be the case. Essentially the régime of responsibility is intended to ensure that the author of a wrongful act makes amends and so ensures an end to its responsibility. Contrary to the basic dichotomy established by domestic legal systems, international law does not know of any separation between the civil and criminal consequences of a wrongful act. There is but the one unitary régime of reparation. Though some of the differing forms of reparation can be attributed with preventive or deterrent character, that does not affect the absence of any division, in international law, between civil and criminal responsibility. This unitary régime establishes the general rule for the author State to provide reparation, and the more explicit rules determining the specific forms, content and conditions for considering reparation granted. As soon as the author State has performed the substitute reparation obligations its responsibility will have come to an end. For that reason the measures resorted to must be reversible in character, since they are justified only for as long as the author State has not performed its reparation obligations.[29] In essence article 11, paragraph 1, Part Two, provisionally adopted by the Commission, reflects the basic goal to be attained by countermeasures:[30]

"As long as the State which has committed an internationally wrongful act has not complied with its obligations under Articles 6 to 10 bis, the injured State is entitled to take countermeasures, that is, subject to the conditions and restrictions set forth in articles 12, 13 and 14, not to comply with one or more of its obligations towards the State which has committed the internationally wrongful act, as necessary in the light of the response to its demands by the State which has committed the internationally wrongful act in order to induce it to comply with its obligations under articles 6 to 10 bis."

That text is also in accordance with Arangio-Ruiz' finding that international practice indicates that countermeasures going beyond the aim of reparation would constitute in themselves unlawful acts.[31]

Questions of punishment and punitive intent

Somewhat surprisingly the commentary to article 30, following Ago in this respect, defined countermeasures as:[32] "measures the object of which is, by definition, to inflict punishment or to secure performance". As stated in the previous subsection the goal to be attained by an injured State imposing countermeasures on an author State should be to obtain reparation. The question may nevertheless be asked whether international law, either in any explicit sense or in disguised manner, authorizes an injured State to inflict punishment on the author State.

It is clear that international law does not know of any explicit power to impose punishment on a State for a breach of obligation. Underlying such absence of powers is the obvious fact that States are corporate personalities and as such cannot be subjected to physical punishment analogous to that existing under domestic systems of laws. That is not to say that international law could not in any way contain rules envisaging specific forms of punishment. However, although forms of punishment may be thought off, they have not, in any explicit manner, been laid down in rules of customary international law.[33]

While explicit rules on punishment do not exist, the rules on reparation contain some disguised forms. As much has been observed by Arangio-Ruiz in his fourth report:

"It is easy to presume, of course, that any State resorting to countermeasures against a law-breaking State does not do so without some measure of punitive intent. In most cases such an intent will be so totally absorbed by the intent to seek cessation/reparation that it will not cross the threshold of distinct legal relevance. The situation may well be different in cases where the main concern of the injured State is to seek satisfaction and/or guarantees of non-repetition. An intent to chastise may become in such cases more pronounced: and although satisfaction will be a self-inflicted penalty, the harm inflicted by the countermeasure aimed at obtaining satisfaction seems to be pretty close to a penalty inflicted by the injured State."

Leaving aside for a moment the question of punitive intent, the obvious conclusion would have to be that some forms of reparation, notably satisfaction (the punishment of responsible individuals) and guarantees against repetition, could be characterized as punishment. However, as may be seen from the discussion in chapter three, subsection

3.2.2, those forms of reparation concern the prevention and deterrence of wrongful acts rather than that they constitute punishment. They also do not go very far, since their implementation is dependent on the consent and co-operation of the author State and any punishment or penalty flowing therefrom is consequently self-imposed. It should be noted though that the obligations of the author State in this respect may be enforced through countermeasures also in case of international delicts. The minimal importance adduced, by the injured State, to most international delicts committed may of course induce it to settle for restitution and/or compensation.

As to the issue whether any punitive intent lies behind an injured State's resort to countermeasures, that would appear to have relevance insofar as the measures resorted to are apt to do more than just put pressure on the author State to provide reparation. The question would remain relevant of course in those instances, noted by Arangio-Ruiz,[34] where an injured State resorts to certain measures but does not demand any reparation. Yet even in those cases one could argue that there is an implied plea, manifested by the disapprobation of the wrongful act, for cessation or prevention of future acts. Arangio-Ruiz rightly comes to the conclusion that:[35] "(...) it would be difficult to conceive the presence of such an intent as more than a factual characterization of the function of countermeasures." Evidence of the existence of punitive intent on the part of the injured State would appear to be present only to the extent that the injured State did not abide by the rules on (dis)proportionality (discussed in subsection 4.4.3).

Coercion distinguished

A necessary preliminary remark on terminology is in order here. Oddly enough the terminology of domestic systems of law and international law has drifted apart as to the meaning to be attached to the word "sanction". In domestic systems of law the imposition of sanctions on a subject of law does not refer to the use of coercion with regard to that subject. Instead sanctions may concern the imposition of any of the specific forms of punishment the system envisages as a possible consequence of the commission of a crime or misdemeanour. Generally sanctions under a domestic criminal system of law consist of such penalties as the death penalty, corporal punishment, imprisonment, and fines. Originally domestic scholars and international arbitrators followed such terminology. Austin already, often enough quoted as to his opinion that international law constituted nothing more than positive international morality,[36] in this regard led the way and pointed out that physical compulsion ought not to be considered a sanction.[37] And the arbitrators in the Cysne Award discussed a Portuguese claim, for a special indemnity as a kind of sanction, as follows:[38]

> "Il résulte très clairement de cela qu'il ne s'agit pas, en réalité, d'une indemnité, de la réparation d'un préjudice matériel ni même moral, mais bien d'une sanction, d'une peine infligée à l'État coupable et inspirée, comme les peines en général, par les idées de rétribution, d'avertissement et d'intimidation."

In international law nowadays, to the contrary, the use of the word sanction should be reserved for the coercion applied in respect of a State that has committed a violation of that law.[39] And it is for that reason that confusion has obtained so as to ascribe to sanctions and countermeasures punitive character.

Ago and the Commission certainly did not help, as the latter stated, in the commentary to article 1, Part One, that:[40]

> "The term 'sanction' is used here to describe a measure which, although not necessarily involving the use of force, is characterized – at least in part – by the fact that its purpose is to inflict punishment. That is not the same purpose as coercion to secure the fulfilment of the obligation, or restoration of the right infringed, or compensation."

The confusion of thought underlying these matters may be traced back to the mistaken notion that the purpose of sanctions is necessarily to inflict punishment. Mistaken because what Ago and the Commission fail to realize is that, under domestic systems of law, specific forms of punishment are sanctions, but sanctions do not necessarily constitute punishment. Forms of punishment naturally are accompanied by the use or threat of physical compulsion. It is applied without any reference to the will of the individual punished. However, physical compulsion is not an end in itself. It is applied only insofar as necessary to ensure that the ordained punishment will be undergone by the responsible individual. Physical compulsion constitutes a means to an end.

Similarly, in international law, coercion must constitute a means to an end. It is conceivable that countermeasures and sanctions would serve, besides constituting an attempt to have the author State perform its reparation obligations, the purpose of forcing an author State to undergo punishment. But the question would remain what the author State would have to do in order to escape the application of coercive measures against it. Ordinarily one would expect a system of law to make clear to its subjects what it is they have to do in order to do away with their responsibility. By saying that the application of countermeasures or sanctions are punitive measures one is really saying that a State must suffer punishment without specifying what kind of punishment, or the manner in which coercion could be avoided by the author State. Coercion becomes punishment. But if one assumes coercion to constitute punishment, the injured State could persist with its measures indefinitely. At one time or another however, an end must come for applied coercion.

An individual which does not oppose punishment under domestic law will not find itself confronted by physical compulsion.[41] It may be noted also that physical compulsion resorted to under domestic systems of law is not reserved for the purpose of imposing punishment alone. It is also resorted to in order to have subjects perform their obligations in the field of reparation under civil laws. If such obligations are performed voluntarily there will be no question of resorting to compulsion towards the responsible individual. That again shows that physical compulsion under domestic law, or coercion in international law, constitutes a means to achieve an end, and not an end in itself. However, performance of reparation obligations or punishment will generally come about under the general threat of resort to coercion (in cases there is no voluntary compliance with these).

This last remark leads to an argument concerning the correlation between rights and obligations. As was argued in chapter one, section 1.3, there exists, generally, a correlation between rights and obligations. At the same time it was indicated that one exception to that correlation would be discussed in chapter four. If a State possesses a right, so it was said, an obligation must exist on the part of other States to respect and not to hinder the exercise of that right. There are two aspects worthy of discussion.

The first and foremost observation is that the right to resort to countermeasures constitutes the exception spoken of. An author State, against which certain measures are taken, is not under any obligation to respect the injured State's exercise of its right to resort to countermeasures. This flows from the fact that coercive measures are applied without any reference to the will of the targeted State. Or, to put it more accurately, coercion is applied because the author State is unwilling to conform with its reparation obligations. It has manifested a will not to conform to the injured State's demands. The object of resort to countermeasures then is to force the will of the author State and have it perform its obligations.[42] For that reason the right to resort to countermeasures is at times referred to as a faculty.[43] Yet since any subject of law is free, in a psychological sense, to engage in breaches of obligations, the implication is that it is under no obligation to endure the application of coercion against it. And since it is under no obligation to co-operate in inflicting coercion upon itself, it can use all such lawful means in order to circumvent coercive measures. While this freedom is substantially limited under domestic laws (through the imposition of additional obligations), the same cannot be said of international law. In the context of the subject under consideration, non-armed countermeasures, this means that a targeted State can evade the application of economic measures by countering them or turning elsewhere. If an injured State for instance acts, as a countermeasure, in breach of its obligation to deliver goods to the author State, the latter can abstain from paying for the goods (if it has not already done so). Furthermore, the author State may, in such circumstances, try to obtain the goods from some other supplier. This latter remark brings us to the next issue, the relative effect of countermeasures.

Since there does not exist any rule imposing an obligation on the author State to suffer under coercive measures, *a fortiori* other States will also not be obliged to respect the injured State's exercise of the right to resort to countermeasures. Such States can undermine the effect of countermeasures, for instance, by providing substitute goods to the author State. The only general limit to circumvention through other States is provided by the provision of article 27, Part One, of the ILC-draft on State responsibility. Only when another State has knowledge of the intention of the author State to use goods for committing a wrongful act should it abstain from delivering such goods. The same goes for services, since article 27 concerns not only aid but also assistance. This situation moreover does not change when circumvention takes place not through third States (a State that is not an injured State under article 5, Part Two), but through other injured States. Since there does not exist any rule obliging States to exercise their rights, other injured States can still support the author State.

As pointed out in chapter three, section 3.5, the conditions for application of article 27, Part One, are too strict in regard to those wrongful acts constituting crimes. The notoriety inherent in the commission of a crime, as witnessed by the scale of the wrongful conduct, should lead to a presumption that certain aid or assistance must necessarily contribute to the commission of the crime. That conclusion goes especially regarding aid or assistance in the form of deliveries of arms or military material, or the training of police, military or other personnel. For that reason injured States, in case of international crimes, are not allowed, for instance, to circumvent another injured State's suspension of military aid or assistance programmes. The basis for such prohibited circumvention is not, however, a general rule stipulating support for other States' countermeasures, but the possibility of becoming the accomplice of the author State in the commission of its international crime.

Regarding international law the question is whether it allows States, as the primary subjects, to enforce the law through application of coercion to other States. That question was discussed at length, and answered affirmatively, by Kelsen.[44] As is well known he took the stand that any system of law must establish a coercive order,[45] and in international law specific coercive measures, reprisals and war, could be resorted to as a consequence of another State committing a wrongful act.[46]
While international law does not know of any criminal sanctions (punishment) in the traditional (domestic) sense, it does contain implicit ones, as discussed earlier, in the form of satisfaction and guarantees against repetition. More fundamentally one might ask whether it is conceivable that a system of law would focus completely on the reparatory consequences of a wrongful act and disregard the punitive ones. That question could be answered affirmatively if the system involved would ensure the effective enforcement of the reparatory consequences of wrongful acts. Effective enforcement encompassing, in this instance, a high improbability of getting away with the commission of wrongful acts. Although such a system can be imagined, it is hard to see it confining itself completely to reparatory consequences. As a minimum the deterring forms assuring satisfaction for the injured party and guarantees against repetition of wrongful acts would be likely to enter such a system. That, at least, is the situation under international law. Furthermore, the more severe consequences that could attach to international crimes primarily relate to those forms of reparation endowed with preventive or deterrent character.

4.2.2. THE NATURE OF COUNTERMEASURES

Collective responsibility
The responsibility incurred consequent upon a breach of an international obligation by a State is collective in character. For that reason the fulfilment of reparation obligations by an author State, although effected by the organs of that State, burdens the entire population of the State. And that is especially the case when reparation has to be provided in the form of compensation. Regarding resort to countermeasures similar issues arise.

There is a basic difference between collective responsibility imposing upon an author State new reparation obligations and collective responsibility as the basis for resort to coercive measures. While the collective character of the responsibility of an author State presses only indirectly upon the population of that State, the same cannot be said of countermeasures. Just as reparation obligations do not bear upon the organs of the State, so imposed countermeasures also do not touch those organs. Kelsen observes in this respect:[47]

> "But the sanction stipulated by this law – (...) – war or reprisals, are not directed against the organs whose function it was to fulfil the obligations of international

> law and who have not done so. (...) The sanctions – war or reprisals – directly or indirectly affect the people of the state, i.e. the individuals belonging to the state, (...). That means that international law establishes collective responsibility for the violation of obligations imposed upon the states."

However, the burden of reparation will generally bear quite evenly upon the population of the author State. But countermeasures tend to be directed at those of the author State's population which are, or come, easily within the injured State's grasp.

Thus countermeasures will first and foremost affect nationals of the author State present within the injured State, or those engaging in commercial activities with the author State or its nationals. As the Court observed in the Barcelona Traction Case,[48] a State is under the obligation to extend the protection of the law, and other obligations, to the foreign investments and aliens it allows into its territory. But those obligations are not immune to breaches by way of countermeasures. Consequently an injured State's resort to countermeasures may involve a change of status of foreign nationals, the annulment of contracts, confiscation of goods, and nationalization of companies. In all such cases nationals of the author State are directly affected and suffer the full brunt of coercive measures.

Yet even when the injured State more generally resorts to the application of coercion directly affecting the State, still the population, and especially the poorer and less well-off parts, will suffer.

An economic boycott, prohibitions of exports and imports, and freezing of assets of the author State will, if not always directly, affect the population. Generally the effects of such measures will not so soon be felt by those well-off or rich. But especially those groups are the ones having influence within the political structures and organs of the State.[49] Naturally these indirect effects will be felt only if the author State is in some way dependent on the injured State,[50] or when the boycott and other measures do not allow for circumvention.

The latter, no possibility of circumvention, will generally only be the case with sanctions imposed by the Security Council. It has ordered sanctions in a number of instances, though generally not to the extent of creating the indirect effects. It is debatable whether indirect effects, on powerful groups, have occurred with regard to Iraq, the Federal Republic of Yugoslavia and Haiti.[51] That is of course not to say that there could be no circumvention in a factual sense. The main difference is that any such factual circumvention by States will constitute breaches of obligation, since members of the United Nations have agreed to accept and carry out decisions of the Security Council (article 25 Charter). At this point one may observe that the collective responsibility of an author State is matched by the mechanism of collective enforcement enshrined in the Charter.

Circumstances precluding wrongfulness

In his examination of the origin of international responsibility former special rapporteur Ago lastly came upon the subject of certain circumstances which would, in his opinion, preclude the wrongfulness of conduct otherwise in breach of an obligation.[52] Among these were consent, countermeasures, *force majeure*, fortuitous events, state of necessity and self-defence.[53] For all these cases, so he says,[54] notwithstanding the "apparent" fulfilment of the two conditions defined in article 3, the inference that an internationally wrongful act exists cannot be made. Although he speaks of the apparent fulfilment of *both* conditions laid down in article 3, it is but the apparent existence of the breach of an obligation which concerns him. Thus there can be no doubt that in all the circumstances laid down in Chapter V of Part One there will in fact be conduct attributable to a State. However, then special rapporteur Ago argued:[55]

> "The conduct in question cannot be characterized as wrongful for the good reason that, owing to the presence in that particular case of a certain circumstance, the State which committed the act was not under any obligation to conduct itself otherwise."

This conception of Ago and the Commission appears debatable. It assumes that in the presence of any one of the circumstances mentioned in articles 29 to 34, Part One, the obligation is not merely set aside,[56] but that it is in fact obliterated: the obligation simply no longer exists. But if that is the case the provision of article 35,[57] that preclusion of wrongfulness under articles 29 and 31 to 33 will not "prejudge any question that may arise in regard to compensation for damage caused by that act", becomes even more difficult to understand. If there is no obligation, and still less therefore any apparent or real breach of an obligation, why then should a State be considered liable to an obligation to pay compensation? This would indeed constitute an arbitrary rule, since it amounts to an assertion that despite the fact that a State has not acted wrongfully at all, it nevertheless is bound to reimburse another State for damages.

But that is not the end of it. A similar argument may be made in so far as resort to countermeasures is concerned. Let us suppose State A has breached its obligation not to nationalize companies without payment of adequate compensation. State B, an injured State under article 5, paragraph 2, sub (e) (i), Part Two, reacts to this internationally wrongful act by liquidating funds held by banks in State A's territory. The dispute between States A and B is eventually settled by the payment of compensation to State B. The liquidation of funds is not to be considered wrongful, since it constitutes a legitimate countermeasure and State B was not under any obligation to refrain from liquidating the funds. But the question is whether State B is entitled to keep the funds so liquidated even in the presence of full compensation by State A for its wrongful acts. In the present draft the answer would have to be in the positive, yet that would seem to be a rather unsatisfactory solution.[58] The answer would not be any different if one was to claim that State B was not entitled to liquidate the funds but could only freeze the accounts. For then the question is whether State B could continue the freezing notwithstanding the agreement on compensation, and the answer, in strict logic, would have to be the same. Nor would it be sufficient to point to an obligation on the part of the injured State to end resort to countermeasures once reparation had been provided, or to the renewed operation of the primary rule as a result therefrom. Logic dictates the same answer.

This example shows that while resort to countermeasures as a reaction to an internationally wrongful act may be considered lawful, their lawfulness does not result from the absence or obliteration of the obligation targeted. Rather their lawfulness ensues from a cause justifying non-performance of obligations towards another State. It was, therefore, not without reason that Riphagen phrased his articles 8 and 9, on respectively measures by way of reciprocity and reprisal, in terms of the suspension of the performance of obligations.[59] And similarly Arangio-Ruiz and the Drafting Committee phrased proposed article 11, Part Two, in a manner that countermeasures would amount to the possibility of the injured State not to comply with its obligations.[60] Such a construction would then amount to a situation in which the injured State could oppose a new right or faculty towards the author State that would entitle it to resort to non-performance of certain obligations. At the same time such a new right would not be opposable to third States, and therefore any non-performance of obligations affecting them would be wrongful. Technically speaking a construction like this would not be inconsistent with the fundamental article 1, Part One, which stipulates that "every internationally wrongful act of a State entails the international responsibility of that State".[61] At the most one could say it conflicts with the opinion of Ago and the Commission that:[62]

> "(...) it is difficult to conceive that international law could characterize an act as wrongful without attaching to it disadvantageous consequences for its author."

Yet it may be countered that while the circumstance would not preclude the wrongfulness, it would also not preclude the responsibility of the injured State. What it would do would be to make it impossible for the author State to invoke the responsibility of the injured State. At the same time that might not preclude other, originally third, States from invoking the injured State's responsibility. The absence of disadvantageous consequences would therefore be relative, not absolute, since States other than the author State would obtain the right to invoke the injured State's responsibility.

An example of such a line of reasoning may be found in judge Schwebel's Dissenting Opinion to the Court's judgment on the merits in the Nicaragua Case. The Court decided, in operative paragraph (8), that the United States had breached its obligations under customary international law by not notifying the existence and location of mines laid by it.[63] Judge Schwebel claimed that the breach of obligation by the United States, to the effect that the latter had not notified the existence and location of mines in the vicinity of Nicaraguan ports, although wrongful in connection to other States, could be opposable to Nicaragua as a self-defence measure.[64] It may be noted that self-defence constitutes a circumstance precluding wrongfulness under Part One of the draft (article 34). The conduct attributable to the United States, failure of notification, is the same in both instances. In the Commission's proposal the same omission (and not merely identical conduct), failure to notify the existence and location of mines, would be both wrongful and lawful at the same time.[65] It would be wrongful towards other States, but fully justified and lawful towards Nicaragua.

The Cysne Award seems to have headed in the right direction as it denied the legality of a measure of reprisal, resorted to by Germany against Portugal, in the following terms:[66]

> "Cette solution est la consequence logique de la règle suivant laquelle les représailles, consistant en un acte en principe contraire au droit des gens, ne peuvent se justifier qu'autant qu'elles ont été provoquées par un autre acte également contraire à ce droit. *Les représailles ne sont admissibles que contre l'État provocateur.*"

In this case the original act contrary to international law which provoked the German reprisal had been committed by Great Britain and not by Portugal. Consequently the German acts could not be considered legitimate as against Portugal. The award did not address the question whether the German acts could have been lawful as against Great Britain.

It is submitted that the proper way would be to define circumstances justifying non-performance of obligations towards the author State. The result would be a loss, in principle, for the author State, of its right to invoke the responsibility of the injured State. That right might be revived to the extent that the injured State oversteps the limits set for the exercise of its right to resort to countermeasures, or breaches obligations that ought not to form the object of any countermeasure. At the same time States other than the author State could invoke the injured States responsibility to the extent that they could be considered injured States under article 5, Part Two, of the ILC-draft.

Measures constituting a denial of a right of the author State

In combination with the definition of countermeasures, stressing their punitive character, the Commission observed that they also were:[67]

> "(...) measures which, under different conditions, would infringe a valid and subjective right of the subject against which the measures are applied."

In connection to this comment it may be noted that it is this essential characteristic which distinguishes a countermeasure from measures of retortion. Arangio-Ruiz noted, in his third report,[68] that the majority of the authors generally defined retortion measures as "reactions of a State to an unlawful, unfriendly act, as are themselves unfriendly but not unlawful." The reactions mentioned would thus cover both measures taken against unlawful acts, as measures responding to unfriendly acts. The correctness of that stance, including permissible reactions to unlawful acts in the notion of retortions, is reflected in the references made by former special rapporteur Ago to the measures under article 41 of the Charter. As he points out, the use of the word sanctions is less strict in the Charter (the word, in fact, does not feature in the Charter), and the measures enumerated in article 41 may amount to both *per se* lawful acts as countermeasures.[69] At the same time one cannot but acknowledge, as Arangio-Ruiz does,[70] that measures of retortion, licit acts by definition, do not have any role to play within a future convention on State responsibility.

The definition offered, or characteristic defined, here is unsatisfactory in the sense that resort is had to the notion of subjective rights. In chapter one, subsection 1.3.4, it was explained that there exists a correlation between rights and obligations. And for the same reason that the Commission considered it expedient to choose for the breach of obligation (and not for the violation of rights) as the basis for the existence of an internationally wrongful act, it would be wise, in other articles and their commentaries, to proceed on the basis of obligations only. As may be seen from the commentary to article 30, Part One, there is no need to refer to corresponding rights:[71]

> "(...) an act of the State, although not in conformity with what is required of it by a binding international obligation towards another State, is not wrongful if it constitutes the application with respect to that other State of a measure

> permissible in international law as a reaction to an international offence which the latter State has committed previously."

In view of the correlation between rights and obligations and the choice for breach of obligation as constitutive criterion for internationally wrongful acts one ought to make reference to breaches of obligations only.

Exceptionally justified or generally applicable measures

The Commission has had occasion to reflect on the notion of circumstances precluding wrongfulness, and considers that:[72]

> "When any one of these circumstances is present in a particular case, the wrongfulness of the act of the State is *exceptionally* precluded (...). The exceptional character lies precisely in the fact that the circumstance found to be present in the specific case in question renders ineffective an international obligation which, in the absence of that circumstance, would be incumbent on the State and would make any conduct that was not in conformity with the requirements of the obligation wrongful. There is an obvious difference between conduct that is generally lawful and conduct that is generally wrongful and will remain so unless there is a special circumstance which, in a specific case, removes its wrongfulness."

The present writer would like to take exception to the proposition that resort to countermeasures would only exceptionally preclude the wrongfulness of conduct in response to an internationally wrongful act. The contrary is in fact the case: legally speaking (the possibility of) resort to countermeasures is the rule, not the exception. Kelsen has correctly formulated the premise that law establishes a coercive order.[73] As such, Kelsen observes, law is based on the idea that in the presence of a delict a sanction ought to be applied with respect to the subject responsible for the illegal conduct.[74] By saying that sanctions "ought to be applied" he only meant to indicate that in case a delict is committed application of the sanction is lawful.[75]

But again that is not the end of it. The observation that the application of sanctions is lawful in cases of committed delicts suggests a large degree of generality. The obvious fact that in actual life a sanction is generally not applied to those responsible for a delict, does not warrant the conclusion that the application of sanctions is only exceptionally permitted. For these non-occurrences are due, not to the fact that the application of the sanction would not, intrinsically, be legally justified, but to circumstances which legally pre-empt the necessity to impose sanctions. Principal among these are the possibility of obtaining reparation through peaceful means and third party settlement of disputes (see generally next section). The Commission appeared to have had this in mind when it observed that there are cases in which:[76]

> "(...) international law, while not in principle ruling out the possibility of applying a sanction against a State which has committed a breach of a particular international obligation, requires the State that is the victim of that breach not to resort to such action until it has first sought adequate reparation."

On that score one could claim, of course, that resort to countermeasures should be considered exceptional, because preconditions for such resort would not have been met.[77] But that would be to ignore the obvious fact that in all those cases where preconditions have been met, there exists the general option, for the injured State, of resort to countermeasures. In the end that option remains available to an injured State whenever it has not been granted adequate reparation by the author State.

What is left is the Commission's argument on the difference between generally lawful and generally unlawful conduct. But that is hardly more convincing. Conduct that is generally lawful certainly does not need any separate special circumstance in order to justify it. On the other hand there is the strict logical necessity that conduct which is generally unlawful must be in need of a special circumstance to justify it. Of essence things could not be otherwise. This concerns, in Kelsen's words,[78] the situation in which the employment of force constitutes either a delict or a sanction. The special circumstance necessary to justify resort to countermeasures by an injured State resides in the earlier committed internationally wrongful act and a State's consequential status as injured State. But the meaning of "special" is not to be considered identical to "exceptional". We are talking categories here (implying generality of application), not incidents. The claim that resort to countermeasures is, or must be, exceptional would have to lead, moreover, to application of the interpretation rule that exceptions must be interpreted restrictively. It is suggested that such application is not warranted as regards the generally accepted, and justified, means of coercion.

4.3. Preconditions for resort to countermeasures

4.3.1. THE COMMISSION OF AN INTERNATIONALLY WRONGFUL ACT

There is one essential condition that must, of necessity, be fulfilled in order to justify an injured State's resort to countermeasures against the author State: the latter's commission of an internationally wrongful act.[79] That position appears the only feasible one, and has been upheld, implicitly, in phrasing article 11, Part Two, by Arangio-Ruiz, the Drafting Committee, members of the Commission, and the Commission itself.[80] Their language is implicit in the sense that a countermeasure will involve non-compliance of obligations by the injured State towards the State which has committed a wrongful act, but only if the latter has not complied with its reparation obligations. Of course only a State which has committed a wrongful act may be confronted by new reparation obligations. The assumption, then, must logically be that countermeasures are not justified in relation to States that have not committed any breach of obligation, whether primary or secondary. That position has, to some extent, formed the substance of article 11, paragraph 2, Part Two, adopted by the Commission:[81]

> "Where a countermeasure against a State which has committed an internationally wrongful act involves a breach of an obligation towards a third State, such a breach cannot be justified as against the third State by reason of paragraph 1."

In phrasing article 11 the Commission has done away with the argument that resort to countermeasures could be justified, against another State, by a State believing in good faith, but mistakenly, that that other State had committed a wrongful act.[82] As has been noted earlier the Commission could not conceive a position where no disadvantageous consequences would be attached to wrongful conduct.[83] Even more difficult to conceive, one may submit, would be disadvantageous consequences (a breach of obligation) directed towards a State that had not acted wrongfully at all.

Since all States are injured States in case an internationally wrongful act constitutes an international crime (article 5, paragraph 3, Part Two), all States possess the right, subject to the conditions discussed below, to resort to countermeasures against the author State of a crime.[84] That is also the position of Arangio-Ruiz, who has in his latest report proposed an article 17, Part Two, stipulating, subject to a determination of the existence of a crime by the Court, that every State will be entitled to resort to countermeasures if its reparation demands are not met with an adequate response from the author State.[85]

As argued in the previous chapter, subsection 3.2.1, subjecting demands of reparation to a prior determination by the Court will amount in fact to unreasonable delays regarding the exercise of rights to invoke the author State's responsibility for an international crime. Such delays would be especially unjust in relation to the right to demand cessation of the crime and restitution.

Although he similarly subjects the right to resort to countermeasures to a determination by the Court, his proposed article 17, paragraph 2, provides that that condition will not apply to:[86] "(...) urgent, interim measures as are required to protect the rights of the injured State or to limit the damage caused by the international crime." Explaining his proposal Arangio-Ruiz indicates that such measures would aim at:[87]

> "(...) securing immediate access to the victims for purposes of rescue and/or aid or preventing the continuation of a genocide, measures concerning humanitarian convoys, anti-pollution action, passage facilities, etc."

By putting it this way the suspension of an injured State's right to resort to countermeasures brought about by article 17, paragraph 1, would prevent the adoption of all kinds of trade, financial, and other measures regarding (nationals of) the author State. However, resort to countermeasures to limit the damage caused by a crime, whether that of aggression, denial of self-determination, or widespread breaches of basic human rights obligations, would involve, and indeed necessitate, far-reaching countermeasures to coerce the author State to discontinue its wrongful acts and effect restitution in kind. Since Arangio-Ruiz has proposed to maintain the prohibition on measures involving the threat or use of armed force,[88] it is not quite clear just how injured States would secure immediate access to victims, prevent the continuation of genocide, etc.

Furthermore, even though it may be admitted that cessation of conduct constituting a crime and restitution constitute imperatives, it has been found, in chapter three, that especially guarantees against repetition amount to special or supplementary consequences of the régime applicable to crimes. An author State of a crime, especially that of aggression, might thus be tempted to discontinue its acts, or to put those on hold as it were, simply to avoid the imposition of the more far-reaching guarantees against repetition.

To deny the immediate enforcement of reparation obligations by way of countermeasures similarly does not reflect the idea that the aggravation of the régime applicable to international crimes is intended to ensure more effective suppression of conduct constituting crimes. For reasons analogous to those expressed in relation to reparation, any enforcement by way of countermeasures should be allowed as soon as, and as long as, the author State of a crime continues, and does not adequately remedy, its wrongful conduct.

Some words are necessary here regarding the so-called "principle" of auto-interpretation or auto-determination.[89] It has been claimed that each State can and may interpret the relevant rules of international law, and thus may determine its own legal situation vis-à-vis other States. Accordingly no State could impose its interpretation on another. For that reason it would not be possible to determine whether an internationally wrongful act had really taken place, since the interpretation of the one would stand against the interpretation of the other.[90] Consequently it would also not be possible to conclude to the existence of new reparation obligations for the State that allegedly had committed the wrongful act.[91] This in turn would imply that, in the absence of any (objective) determination of the existence of an internationally wrongful act by an international organ, no State would be justified in its resort to coercive measures.[92]

A preliminary remark would be that those using the phrase "principle" of auto-interpretation incorrectly attach a legal connotation to something that primarily constitutes a matter of fact. What the idea of auto-interpretation really amounts to is a description of the situation prevailing within an overwhelmingly decentralized and badly organized community of States. It is the absence of international organs endowed with jurisdiction and competence to determine, with binding force for the parties to a dispute, the existence of an internationally wrongful act,[93] that accounts for the phenomenon of auto-interpretation. It certainly cannot be accounted for by reference to the existence of a legal rule or principle of either conventional or customary origin.

It cannot be denied of course that each State tends to adopt some interpretation on the scope and content of a rule of international law. And similarly there can be little doubt that one State's interpretation cannot as such prevail over another State's interpretation. As all States are subjects of international law and equal before that law (note also article 2, paragraph 1, of the Charter), the seemingly inescapable conclusion would have to be drawn that a stalemate exists when there are conflicting interpretations on either the law or the facts. Because of this stalemate the further conclusion would have to be drawn that there exists no possibility whatsoever to determine the existence of an internationally wrongful act.

That however constitutes an unwarranted and unacceptable conclusion. In the absence of an authoritative determination, conduct allegedly in conflict with an international obligation must be assessed in the light of all relevant rules of international law. As to conflicts on the interpretation of the law, it may be said that there are limits to interpretation.

The concrete result of these observations are adequately summed up by Arangio-Ruiz in his fourth report. Correctly he denies, with regard to the existence of an internationally wrongful act, the necessity:[94]

> "(...) that the existence of such an act and the allegedly injured State's right to take countermeasures should have been the object of a prior determination by an arbitral or judicial procedure or subject to any kind of action of a political or fact-finding body. Nor does it seem that the presence of an internationally

> wrongful act should have been the object of a prior agreement between the allegedly injured State and the alleged law-breaker."

A State may of course be wrong in its evaluation of the law or the facts. For that reason countermeasures by a State (allegedly injured) will be resorted to under the presumption of a well-founded claim.[95] Any resort to countermeasures therefore entails the risk of being proved wrong. Should that be the case, the logical consequence will be incurred responsibility for the State resorting to (counter)measures. That is so because any countermeasure by definition concerns conduct in breach of an international obligation. And such a breach can be justified only by virtue of the existence of a previously committed internationally wrongful act. If there is no previously committed wrongful act, there also cannot be any justification for the (counter)measure.[96]
It comes as some surprise then, in view of the quotation in the previous paragraph, that he proposes to subject the exercise of the right to resort to countermeasures in case of international crimes to a prior determination of the existence of a crime by the Court. The main reason for his proposal lies with his assessment, based on the universalization of injured State status in case of crimes, that:[97]

> "The risks of arbitrariness, inconsistencies and conflict involved in deciding on the existence of a crime and its attribution and in subsequently implementing the consequences will be very high."

Although there will certainly be conflicts regarding crimes, it is not quite clear why there would be arbitrariness and inconsistencies. In contrast to delicts the existence of wrongful conduct constituting a crime will be less difficult to ascertain due to the seriousness of the acts involved and the generally uncontroversial status of the rules involved (peremptory norms). The only difficulty would lie with establishing whether the threshold of seriousness had been overstepped so that it would be possible to speak of a crime rather than a delict. Yet, as will be argued later on, if there is the possibility that States will qualify particular conduct of another State as a crime, that other State could either perform its reparation obligations or offer binding dispute settlement so as to prevent the imposition of aggravated measures under the régime of crimes. There does not therefore appear to be any higher risk of arbitrariness in case of crimes than there is in case of delicts.

Here it may be expedient to devote some argument to the basis, in international law, of the measures under article 41 of the Charter. Under that provision the Security Council may order members to take certain measures. Such order generally does not contain any indication as to whether measures would constitute countermeasures, in need of separate justification, or whether they would amount to no more than retortions. Irrespective of their nature is the fact that the decisions of the Council are binding upon members of the United Nations under article 25 of the Charter which imposes an obligation to carry them out. Although article 25 provides that members shall accept and carry out decisions of the Security Council, this does not imply an authorization as such for the latter to have members breach their obligations. Nor can such a conclusion be deduced from article 41.[98]

Consequently there is a need for these articles to be reinforced:[99] hence the inclusion in the Charter of article 103. That article provides that obligations under the Charter prevail over conflicting obligations under other international agreements.[100] The phrase "obligations under the Charter" covers both obligations under provisions of the Charter and obligations imposed by way of Security Council decision. However, article 103 is deficient to the extent that it omits any reference to obligations under customary international law. It is possible to argue that there is no problem where an obligation under a treaty is matched, substantially, by a similar obligation established under rules of customary international law. The decision of the Security Council imposing an obligation to take certain measures would prevail over applicable treaty obligations, and simultaneously over identical customary international law obligations. One might consider it silly to claim that the Charter obligations would prevail over treaty obligations and could not lead to a claim by the author State, but that they would not prevail over the identical customary law obligations and that the author State could press a claim on the basis of their breach.

But though the argument could be considered silly where there is a concurrence of conventional and customary law obligations, it increases its vigour when measures under article 41 affect obligations under customary law solely, or where members are not a party to the relevant treaty and yet are subject to a similar rule of customary law. In these cases article 103 provides no remedy and recourse must be had to some additional ground to vest the authority of the Security Council under article 41.[101] That ground can only reside in the circumstance that measures under article 41 may be considered to constitute countermeasures against internationally wrongful acts.[102] This situation does not appear to have been considered by the Commission, which noted in a footnote:[103]

> "(...) it seems indisputable that under Article 103 of the Charter the Member State called upon to apply the sanctions could not claim to be debarred from doing so by a treaty binding it to the non-member State which was the subject of the sanctions."

Which is true. But while it may be admitted that article 103 would be the basis for members of the United Nations, the justifying effect of sanctions against a non-member could only be based upon it having committed an internationally wrongful act.

A related issue in this section concerns the relationship of the customary rules on international responsibility to the powers of the Security Council under Chapter VII of the Charter. Some have asserted that there exists no such relationship. For them the Security Council only marginally applies or enforces the international responsibility of its members. Such application or enforcement would, however, be incidental to the Security Council's true function, that is, the maintenance of international peace and security.[104] The paramount importance of that function would account for granting it an unfettered discretionary power to determine threats to the peace, breaches of the peace and acts of aggression.[105] The exercise of its power under article 39 of the Charter would not, moreover, be subject to any review whatsoever by the Court (on which more in chapter six).[106] It may be submitted that these stances are inadequate, incorrect, and unacceptable as a matter of law.

In subsection 2.4.1 of chapter two it was noted that there existed an unbreakable link between an obligation, its breach, the obligation to repair, and the right to resort to countermeasures or to use force. And it was observed just then that article 103 could not fully provide justifying effect for measures taken by members pursuant to a Security Council decision regarding breaches of obligation under customary international law or as against non-members. For that reason it was submitted that the power of the Security Council to decide on measures under article 41 of the Charter should be seen as a competence of the Security Council to impose upon member States the obligation to exercise their rights to have resort to countermeasures. These considerations are buttressed by the fundamental postulate that only a breach of obligation may give rise to a justifiable reaction comprising a breach of obligation (sanction or countermeasure). Since the measures of article 41 may involve breaches of obligation by members, the inference ought to be that a breach of obligation by the targeted State must have preceded it.[107]

Arguments against this stance do not really convince. It cannot but be admitted that article 39 of the Charter does not pose any such condition. It merely provides that the Security Council may decide upon the measures of article 41 in the presence of a threat to the peace, breach of the peace, or act of aggression. The latter two qualifications, however, inevitably involve some breach of obligation under article 2, paragraphs 3 or 4, of the Charter. Both of them will in fact amount to a use of force contrary to those paragraphs.[108] The same cannot be said of threats to the peace. A threat to use military force, in contravention of article 2, paragraph 3 or 4, will generally generate a threat to the peace. This does not mean, on the other hand, that there cannot exist a threat to the peace without a threat to use force by either a member or non-member. A threat to the peace does not necessarily involve a breach of obligation under article 2, paragraphs 3 or 4, of the Charter.[109]

Yet a contextual interpretation of the Charter shows that an unremoved or continued threat to the peace must lead to a breach of the peace. Article 1, paragraph 1, states the purpose of the United Nations to maintain international peace and security, through effective collective measures, in order to prevent the occurrence of threats to the peace and to suppress breaches of the peace. And article 24 of the Charter accords the Security Council primary responsibility for the maintenance of international peace and security. It specifies, in paragraph 2, that the powers for the realization of its tasks are laid down in Chapters VI, VII, VIII and XII. One of those specific powers is laid down in article 39 stipulating that the Security Council may determine the existence of a threat to the peace, breach of the peace, or act of aggression. In the presence of any one of these it can then decide upon the measures of articles 41 or 42 to maintain or restore international peace and security. That sentence implies that in a certain situation there is something to maintain or to restore. Where there is a breach of the peace or act of aggression, measures under articles 41 or 42 necessarily aim at the restoration of international peace and security. If there is a threat to the peace the aim of those measures must be to maintain international peace and security, that is, to prevent the occurrence of a situation that would require the restoration of international peace and security. As the preamble underlines, the goal of the United Nations is to save future generations from the scourge of war. Although stipulations contained in a preamble do not possess binding force, one may use their words as a guideline for the interpretation of the treaty. It is submitted that the Security Council could only deal with a specific situation as a threat to the peace if that situation could lead to a breach of the peace.[110] However, some authors claim that the Security Council, acting under article 39, need not determine the State thought to be responsible for the prevailing situation.[111] This fails to convince. A State could, or should, not be considered to contribute to a situation constituting a threat to the peace if it is not acting contrary to its obligations.[112] That argument is enhanced, necessarily, where a State is acting in the exercise of a right.[113] In both these cases measures under article 41 could not be justified as against either members or non-members.

A follow up to the remarks regarding the "principle" of auto-interpretation or auto-determination lies with the effect of so-called "authoritative" interpretation or determination.[114] The Security Council possesses the power, under article 39 of the Charter, to determine threats to the peace, breaches of the peace and acts of aggression, and can decide upon the measures of articles 41 and 42. Such determination and especially the resultant imposition of measures against a State responsible for the situation, are binding upon members of the United Nations by virtue of article 25 of the Charter. A member State against which measures are taken, even though bound by the Charter, will not implement such measures. Though this amounts to a breach of obligation under the Charter, nobody in fact expects it to do so. Such a State can moreover dispute whether other members are really entitled (they are certainly under an obligation to do so) to resort to the measures of article 41 in the absence of a wrongful act on its part. That the Security Council has exercised its powers under article 39 and in that relation, possibly, decided upon the existence of wrongful acts, is not decisive. For the Security Council is not a judicial organ.[115] The object of the measures imposed by the Security Council under article 41 must be to "give effect to its decisions". Those decisions must be instrumental in maintaining or restoring international peace and security.

But the Security Council is no legislator. It cannot create obligations off-hand for purposes other than enforcement under articles 41 or 42. In the exercise of its powers under articles 39 and 41 it can oblige members to impose measures against another member. At that point it has to specify what is required by that other member in order for those measures to be lifted. In deciding on what is required the Security Council cannot create obligations: it can only declare them. Therefore it can only stipulate a course of conduct for the targeted member to the extent that such conduct already constituted the subject-matter of an obligation for that member. Basically two possibilities are open to the Council. One is to require a member to comply with its obligations under primary rules of international law. The other is to require it to fulfil its obligations under the secondary rules of State responsibility. The operational condition for the Security Council's demands in the latter sphere constitutes the existence of an internationally wrongful act. If that condition is not satisfied any Security Council's imposition of sanctions in the form of countermeasures will be illegal and entails the United Nations' responsibility towards the targeted member State. Authoritative as determinations by the Security Council may be, they are not conclusive as to the existence of internationally wrongful acts.[116]

In relation to the subject under consideration, international crimes, this fundamental precondition for resort to countermeasures does not pose any problems. Although States tend to deny the existence of an internationally wrongful act on the basis of legal argument or the facts, such denial is hardly possible for international crimes. That follows first of all from the nature of the rules involved which all concern universally accepted rules elevated to the rank of *jus cogens*. Even though interpretations of such rules may vary, generally speaking their basic content is undisputed. As to the facts related to crimes, generally no evidential problems arise. That is so mainly because of the constitutive criterion of a *serious* breach of obligation. If one takes for instance the crime of aggression, the State guilty of an armed attack can ordinarily easily be identified due to the offensive nature of its actions.[117] Considerations similar to these pertain regarding the other international crimes.

More problematic, in evaluating the consequences of crimes in relation to countermeasures, is Arangio-Ruiz' claim that:[118]

> "No lawyer could fail to note, however, that the Security Council is empowered to assess discretionarily any situation involving a threat to the peace, a breach of the peace or an act of aggression with a view to maintaining or restoring international peace or security. The Council has neither the constitutional function nor the technical means to determine, on the basis of law, the existence, the attribution or the consequences of any wrongful act, whether 'delict' or 'crime'. The Council's competence to decide discretionarily on the existence of one of those situations is in principle confined to the purposes of Articles 39 and following of Chapter VII of the Charter. That Chapter and the other relevant Charter provisions do not seem to cover the assessment of responsibility except for the determination of the existence and attribution of an act of aggression."

Apparently Arangio-Ruiz generally denies to the Security Council the possibility to determine, on legal grounds, the existence of a wrongful act. The result of this must be an incapacity for the Security Council of invoking a State's international responsibility and the consequences arising therefrom. Yet, as may be seen from the last sentence of this quotation, the Security Council does possess the competence to assess responsibility arising from acts of aggression. It is to be noted that examples taken from Security Council practice do not all relate to the main hypotheses covered by article 39 of the Charter, that is, uses of force constituting breaches of the peace or acts of aggression. As noted above the phrases "threat to the peace" and "threat or use of force" are not interchangeable. There need not be a threat or use of force under article 2, paragraphs 3 and 4, for there to be a threat to the peace under article 39. That follows already from the fact that article 2, paragraphs 3 and 4, concern mainly inter-State threats or uses of force. It is clear, however, that purely internal national developments, as for instance civil wars, may have an impact on international peace and security.

It seems rather that Arangio-Ruiz' stance regarding Security Council competence in matters of State responsibility stems, maybe logically and certainly understandably, from this consideration:[119]

> "Be it as it may with regard to aggression, the propriety of relying too much on political bodies for the implementation of liability for State crimes becomes highly questionable with regard to the other hypotheses contemplated in

> paragraph 3 of article 19. The delinquencies of the kind described in subparagraphs (b), (c) and (d) of that paragraph should be met – at least de lege ferenda – by judicial means."

Regarding the undeniable political character of the Security Council's composition, the prime argument must be that there is no difference with States. For ages States have been allowed to press claims and resort to countermeasures on the basis of their allegation that another State had breached international law. And in doing so they have never been induced, as a matter of law, to have prior recourse to a judicial body.[120] So why should we deny the Security Council this possibility of invoking the responsibility of States and having recourse to countermeasures? Just because it is a political body? To say this should sooner be considered an ardent plea for universal compulsory jurisdiction for the Court.[121] Yet even in the presence of a system of universal compulsory jurisdiction one would still need another, executive, body in order to take measures for the prevention of irreparable harm. If there is any risk of irreparable harm, intervention by the Court, through the indication of provisional measures, might still be so tardy as to warrant such a body taking action on its own initiative.[122] For purposes of preventing irreparable harm such a body would have to determine that wrongful acts are being committed.

Arangio-Ruiz substantiated his position on the Security Council by reference to the "essentially political function of the maintenance of the peace".[123] He then points out that the Council does not act necessarily or regularly and that selectiveness results; that it is not bound to use uniform criteria and consequently may treat similar crimes differently; and that the nature of its decisions or its actions seems to rule out a duty to motivate and that its choices are discretionary and possibly arbitrary.[124] It cannot but be admitted that there are, and have been, striking differences of treatment by the Security Council of States (accused of) having committed international crimes. Part of the discrepancies in treatment flow from the degree to which States perceive threats to the peace. Others depend on the question to what extent powerful States or their former colonies are involved. Apart from these the exercise of the veto power by permanent members has, in the past, resulted in inaction. But there is insufficient ground to deny the legitimacy of the application of sanctions by the Security Council if the only argument is that they are not applied also in respect of a similar case. Double standards constitute regrettable recurring, but unavoidable, features in international relations, since States determine courses of action on the basis of political expediency and are also not subjected to continuous legal scrutiny.

4.3.2. REPARATION DEMANDS, DISPUTE SETTLEMENT AND COUNTERMEASURES

It may be opportune to start off this section with the observation that there does not seem to exist an obligation for States to settle each and any of their disputes. That clear-cut position is weakened only to the extent that article 2, paragraph 3, of the Charter stipulates: "Members shall settle their international disputes by peaceful means in such a manner that international peace and security, and justice, are not endangered." It is obvious that the main purpose of this provision is that any settlement of disputes must be effected through peaceful means. It has been argued by Arangio-Ruiz that:[125]

> "If a meaning is to be given to the distinct provision of Article 2, paragraph 3 – namely, a meaning other than that of a mere redundancy of Article 2, paragraph 4 – one should perhaps admit that the Charter's condemnation is not really confined to the prohibition of armed measures (for which Art. 2, para. 4 is sufficient). It would seem to extend, by virtue of the letter and spirit of Article 2, paragraph 3 and the whole of Chapter VI (Arts. 33 to 38), to any unilateral measures which may endanger – if not 'friendly relations' and 'co-operation' – international peace and security and justice."

From these considerations he then went on to deduce the existence of an obligation for the injured State to have recourse to dispute settlement procedures before any resort to countermeasures.[126] Leaving aside here the argument of redundancy (see also chapter five, section 5.2), it seems proper to dispute his claim that resort to countermeasures by an injured State against an author State, without prior recourse to dispute settlement procedures, would in effect amount to an attempt to settle a dispute in a manner that justice would be endangered. First of all it may be noted that before an injured State resorts to countermeasures an injustice had already taken place: an internationally wrongful act by the author State. By saying that an injured State's resort to countermeasures without prior recourse to "peaceful means" could conflict with considerations of justice, Arango-Ruiz is really equating the author State's injustice to the injured State's faculty of doing justice for itself.[127] True, resort to countermeasures amounts to: "(...) authorizing non-compliance with international obligations as a means of coercing a party in a dispute over cessation/reparation for a tort."[128] But that is not the same as saying that for that reason dispute settlement obligations are put, if only indirectly, into question.[129] Those can still be complied with by both the injured and author States. The author State may not like being coerced into compliance with its reparation obligations or to accept dispute settlement procedures. But the fact is that it has brought this upon itself because, and as soon as, it committed an internationally wrongful act. Resort to countermeasures by an injured State has, on the other hand, always been considered lawful under generally accepted legal rules.[130] And if there do exist obligations in the field of dispute settlement, the author and injured States are enjoined to perform such obligations irrespective of whether the injured State has resorted to countermeasures against the author State.

Debatable also is Arangio-Ruiz' observation, in the context of denying any difference between cessation and reparation for the purpose of prior exhaustion of peaceful means, that:[131]

> "It must not be overlooked that although one speaks, for the sake of brevity, of the 'injured State' and the 'State which has committed the internationally wrongful act' it would be more correct always to speak – or at least to think – in terms of allegedly injured and allegedly law-breaking States. As no certainty exists at the outset as to whether a wrongful act has been or is being committed by the allegedly law-breaking State, one should only speak, until the issue is resolved in one way or the other, of an alleged obligation to cease and an alleged obligation to provide reparation."

However persuasive such reasoning may seem, it misses the point. A right to resort to countermeasures by an injured State *exists* only if there has been a previously committed internationally wrongful act by the author State. If there does not exist any such wrongful act, there also does not exist any right to resort to countermeasures. So if a State resorts to certain measures (which in its opinion constitute justifiable countermeasures) in the absence of a wrongful act by the targeted State, it will have incurred responsibility due to a non-justifiable breach of obligation(s). Where there is a wrongful act on the part of the targeted State, resort to countermeasures by an injured State will be justifiable *per se*, unless it has failed to comply with the conditions (obligations) under conventional or customary law. Such a case would exist only if one could point to a rule stipulating an obligation for an injured State not to resort to countermeasures prior to agreed dispute settlement. Article 2, paragraph 3, of the Charter can only be regarded as such in a limited way. The obligation under article 2, paragraph 3, would come into operation only when countermeasures would reach such a scale that an author State might be tempted to end the effect of such measures through the threat or use of armed force. On the other hand it might be said that this obligation would apply also to the author State. One could expect it to do justice, considering it to be the source of an earlier injustice, by offering settlement of the dispute before it reached the proportions just mentioned.

These remarks go a long way towards the position that there need not be any recourse to dispute settlement procedures before an injured State resorts to countermeasures. Yet it is essential to recognize that there must be some attempt, as a minimum, by the injured State to obtain reparation by means of the voluntary compliance by the author State of its obligations in that respect.[132] That conclusion can be based, indirectly, on the findings of subsection 4.2.1 to the effect that any right to resort to countermeasures should be considered obsolete once the author State has complied with its reparation obligations. Voluntary compliance by the author State is possible only if it has been given the opportunity of complying. In other words, it must be presented some leeway in order that it can comply. Such leeway must comprise also of some room for negotiations between the injured and author States on the specific forms, scope and content of the latter's reparation obligations. For the same reason it is necessary to insist that an injured State must give notice to the author State of its reasoned claim. That claim must include an evaluation of the circumstances and the applicable legal rules surrounding the alleged wrongful act, the allegation of incurred responsibility, and demands of reparation which include a specification as to form, scope and content. This position is based also on the argument that what is not claimed by the injured State need not be granted by the author State. That is not the same as saying that the author State would not be under an obligation to provide reparation to the injured State. Rather it reflects the idea that the injured and author States are generally free, subject to considerations of *jus cogens*, to come to any agreement they consider politically expedient. Since the author State must be given the chance to comply voluntarily with its reparation obligations, the further conclusion must be that where there is no claim at all for reparation, there also should not be recognized any right to resort to countermeasures. Arangio-Ruiz has correctly pointed out that article 11, paragraph 1,

Part Two, proposed by the Drafting Committee (which is substantially identical to article 11, paragraph 1, provisionally adopted by the Commission, quoted *supra* subsection 4.2.1), quite inadequately reflects such considerations.[133] It stipulates that an injured State has the right to resort to countermeasures as long as the author State has not complied with its reparation obligations. That would mean that this right could be exercised even where the author State acknowledges its responsibility and expresses its willingness to provide reparation, but disputes the scope and content of its obligations. That constitutes an unacceptable solution, and Arangio-Ruiz rightly insists on improvement there.

To some extent this undesirable effect of the Commission's draft could be avoided if the Drafting Committee's text on article 12, paragraphs 1 and 2, would be adopted:[134]

> " 1. An injured State may not take counter-measures unless:
> (a) it has recourse to a [binding/third party] dispute settlement procedure which both the injured State and the State which has committed the internationally wrongful act are bound to use under any relevant treaty to which they are parties; or
> (b) in the absence of such a treaty, it offers a [binding/third party] dispute settlement procedure to the State which has committed the internationally wrongful act.
>
> 2. The right of the injured State to take counter-measures is suspended when and to the extent that an agreed [binding] dispute settlement procedure is being implemented in good faith by the State which has committed the internationally wrongful act, provided that the internationally wrongful act has ceased."

The combined effect of these paragraphs boils down to the possibility of the author State to have countermeasures suspended. Arangio-Ruiz argues against these proposals mainly because they allow resort to countermeasures *prior* to recourse to dispute settlement procedures.[135] However, to require an injured State to exhaust all possible dispute settlement procedures before resorting to countermeasures would place it under an unacceptable burden. To some extent this appears to have been realized by Arangio-Ruiz, because he has since dropped the criterion of exhaustion of all amicable dispute settlement procedures available under international law. His latest proposal on article 12, Part Two, stipulates in paragraph 1 that:[136]

> "The injured State shall not resort to countermeasures prior to the conclusion of:
> (a) a binding third party settlement procedure to which it is entitled to accede by unilateral initiative under a treaty or other dispute settlement instrument in force;
> (b) failing such title, a binding third party procedure offered to and accepted by the State which has committed the internationally wrongful act;"

As a matter of sound legal drafting technique one would have to object to both the text adopted by the Drafting Committee and by Arangio-Ruiz. The argument against both of them lies with the fact that they place the burden of any resort to, or offer regarding, dispute settlement on the injured State. However, the *onus* should be placed on the author State.[137] Admittedly it is the injured State which might want to resort to countermeasures. But the author State is the cause of the whole situation. By fulfilling its reparation obligations it could prevent the injured State's exercise of a right to resort to countermeasures. By failing to do so it opens the door towards the injured State's exercise of its right. Naturally it may wish to dispute the injured State's version of the facts or its interpretation of the law. Or it may object to specific forms of reparation or their extent. In both cases it should be the author State that ought to bear the burden of initiating dispute settlement procedures and place itself under the scrutiny of a third party.

Another question is whether the author State could limit itself to offering legally non-binding third party dispute settlement, such as mediation or conciliation, and whether in doing so it could bring about a suspension of the injured State's right to resort to countermeasures. The answer to this must be in the negative. The purpose of mediation and conciliation is to bring States together and in that way promote the peaceful settlement of a dispute existing between them. But neither of these settlement methods leads to a legally binding determination of the facts or the law. They are intended to appease the parties rather than to settle the dispute in any decisive way. For that matter, those charged to mediate or conciliate need not be jurists. So there is no guarantee at all for the injured State, or for the author State, that the conclusion they arrive at will conform to legal standards. It is rather clear that there does not yet exist any rule of international law which stipulates that an offer for legally binding dispute settlement, that is recourse to arbitration or an international court, ought to be made before resort to countermeasures. Similarly there is no rule stipulating that any such offer made by either the author or injured State ought to be accepted by the one or the other. One might even wonder, in the light of the Air Services Agreement Award,[138] whether there exists any obligation to refrain from resort to countermeasures during negotiations or during proceedings of a dispute settlement procedure. The proposal by the Drafting Committee and especially Arangio-Ruiz' latest draft both appear to be heading, as a matter of progressive development, towards requiring such an offer, as well as acceptance by the other party to the dispute, in order that recourse to countermeasures may be avoided. The introduction of such a requirement would certainly have to be considered an improvement of the law in this field.

In connection to the above considerations Arangio-Ruiz has proposed a paragraph 3 to article 12:[139]

> "Except in the case of urgent temporary measures envisaged in paragraph 2 (a) of the present article no countermeasures shall be resorted to by the injured State without appropriate and timely communication of its intention to the State which has committed the internationally wrongful act."

A preliminary remark would be that by mentioning the word "intention", apparently the intention to resort to countermeasures is meant. This requirement now, which might be considered appropriate for the purpose of maintaining friendly relations between the injured and author States, is not in line with the nature of any measures contemplated. The whole idea of providing for countermeasures is that they offer an opportunity to coerce the author State into performing its reparation obligations. In some cases that object may be achieved already through an announcement that resort to countermeasures is imminent. Or such object may be achieved indirectly by threatening or preparing for countermeasures unless recourse is had to dispute settlement procedures.[140] The notion of coercion, typical for resort to countermeasures, would be lost somewhat if prior notification had to be given of an injured State's intention to that effect. Any surprise aspect will be lost and the author State will be given the opportunity to circumvent coercive measures, or try to mitigate the disadvantageous effects flowing therefrom.[141] On this basis it is also possible to assert that, *a fortiori*, there need not be any specification of the kind of measures contemplated by the injured State.[142] Thus, whether or not the measures contemplated are of an urgent and temporary character, the injured State can exercise its right to resort to countermeasures without communicating to the author State its intention do so. Such exercise is prevented only where the author State acknowledges its responsibility and offers to provide adequate reparation, or offers to have recourse to binding dispute settlement procedures.

As to these same issues one might wonder whether the Security Council would be bound to stimulate the peaceful settlement of disputes between States before resorting to measures under article 41 of the Charter. From the viewpoint of Charter interpretation the conclusion must be that once the Security Council has determined the existence of a threat to the peace, breach of the peace or act of aggression, the peaceful settlement of disputes is something that belongs to the past.[143] That conclusion does not result from the fact that conditions set for the exercise of unilateral countermeasures necessarily would not apply to measures ordered by the Security Council.[144] Rather it flows from the system of the Charter in which the Security Council possesses a broad discretionary competence to decide whether a certain dispute or situation could still be resolved by making use of its recommendatory powers under Chapter VI (labelled "pacific settlement of disputes"); or whether a certain dispute or situation has escalated to the point that the circumstances of article 39 exist, which call for the exercise of its power to decide on measures under Chapter VII (labelled "action with respect to threats to the peace, breaches of the peace, and acts of aggression"). The Council's exercise of power to decide on the imposition of measures under article 41 does not exclude it from calling upon parties to negotiate on the settlement of their disputes. However, Security Council practice also shows that it does not feel itself bound, for which it has been criticized,[145] to respect recourse by one of the parties to a procedure liable to lead to the settlement of the dispute. Be that as it may, the specially agreed conventional rules of the Charter take precedence over any rule to have recourse to dispute settlement procedures under customary international law. That is mainly so because, in the system of the Charter, the parties to a dispute have proved, or are considered, unable to solve their dispute through peaceful means as soon as the Security Council determines the existence of a threat to the peace, breach of the peace, or act of aggression under article 39. Even then it can still opt for calming the waters through the indication of provisional measures under article 40. But as a matter of law it is not required to have any recourse to that provision.

An instructive example of all this lies with the Lockerbie Case. As is well known the United States and the United Kingdom demand that Libya surrenders two of its nationals accused of having planted a bomb in the aeroplane which later crashed at Lockerbie.[146] Libya refuses to surrender them on the basis that it has the right under the Montreal Convention to opt for the prosecution of accused individuals rather than to extradite them. The Security Council, by way of resolution 731,[147] urged Libya to respond fully and effectively to the requests of the United States and the United Kingdom. Libya then chose to invoke the jurisdiction of the Court under the relevant provision of the Montreal Convention and asked it to settle the dispute over extradition. It also requested the indication of provisional measures to safeguard its right to prosecute under the Montreal Convention.[148] Before the Court delivered an order regarding these requests the Security Council adopted resolution 748 in which it determined that in particular Libya's continued failure to respond fully and effectively to earlier requests for surrender constituted a threat to international peace and security. For that reason, acting under Chapter VII of the Charter, it decided that Libya must comply with the requests for surrender and that until it did comply States had to adopt measures in the fields of air transports, arms, Libya's diplomatic representation, and on the entry of Libyan nationals accused of terrorist activities into their territories. By taking this action the Security Council effectively prevented the Court to exercise its power under article 41 of the Statute.[149] It remains to be seen whether the Court will also consider resolution 748 to constitute an impediment to delivering a judgment on the merits in favour of Libya.

One of the differing consequences that could be attached to crimes, envisaged by Arangio-Ruiz, concerns the lifting of any obligation to suspend resort to countermeasures prior to, or during, recourse to dispute settlement procedures.[150] In his proposed article 17, Part Two, he provides that all States could resort to countermeasures after the Court had determined the existence of a crime (paragraph 1), and before any such determination to the extent that urgent, interim measures are required to protect the rights of an injured State or to limit the damage caused by the crime (paragraph 2).[151] The main reason for dispensing with any such obligation may be found in that an author State of an international crime is acting in a manner which shows the deliberate and intentional character of its acts. Basically it possesses knowledge of what is happening and it wants what is happening to happen: its actions are premeditated. So a first observation must be that the obligations to cease any wrongful conduct and those related to restitution acquire especial importance in case of crimes. Arangio-Ruiz has pointed to the fact, discussing delicts, that there is no essential need to require an author State to cease its wrongful conduct in order for a possible suspension of the injured State's right to resort to countermeasures to come about on the basis of an obligation to have prior recourse to dispute settlement procedures.[152] An (alleged) author State of a delict may have reasons to believe that what it is doing is not wrong (claim of non-breach), it may claim that it was unaware of what was going on (claim of non-attribution), or it may claim that there are circumstances precluding the wrongfulness of its conduct. Similar claims cannot be forwarded by a State committing an international crime: they strain belief.

Secondly, the gravity of the internationally wrongful acts being committed, coupled to the premeditated character of such acts, provides a strong indication that urgent measures are necessary to induce the author State to perform its reparation obligations. The importance of cessation of acts being committed, to have the author State provide restitution in case of aggression, or to make it provide guarantees against repetition cannot be underestimated. Any internationally wrongful act constituting an international crime would give rise to the application of, to use Arangio-Ruiz' formulation of article 17, paragraph 2, "urgent, interim measures as are required to protect the rights of an injured State or to limit the damage caused by the international crime."[153]

Arangio-Ruiz foreshadowed, in his fifth report, and argued in his seventh report, that the aggravated consequences of crimes could lie also with the relaxation of the conditions generally applicable to countermeasures.[154] He agreed not only that there did not need to be any prior exhaustion of dispute settlement mechanisms, but that even the prior notification requirement would not be applicable in case of crimes.[155] Of course he now proposes a prior determination of the existence of a crime by the Court, and he has argued that particularly severe measures which could have adverse effects for the author State's population must be communicated to the author State.[156] He did not fail to notice that the recent Iraq-Kuwait crisis bore witness of such relaxation, since a number of States, on their own initiative, adopted economic measures against Iraq without any attempt at dispute settlement.[157] Having regard, again, to the existence of government policies and to the premeditated nature of crimes, insistence on the necessity of prior communication of claims and recourse to dispute settlement does indeed appear superfluous.[158] That is not to say that no specific demands of reparation should be made. Generally States have their resort to countermeasures accompanied by demands for cessation and reparation in the broad sense.[159]

4.3.3. ADDITIONAL REQUIREMENTS FOR SECURITY COUNCIL MEASURES UNDER ARTICLE 41 OF THE CHARTER

It has been asserted, earlier on, that the power of the Security Council to decide on the application of measures under article 41 should be considered to amount to resort to countermeasures under customary international law. Besides the conditions generally applicable to such resort, the question arises whether the Charter poses any others. Two subjects need to be discussed. The first, on the legal effect of recommendations and decisions, presents a preliminary character. The second, on the relationship between articles 39 and 41 of the Charter, does not present any real difficulties.

General Assembly and Security Council recommendations and decisions: justification for otherwise wrongful acts?

The Commission noted in its commentary on article 30, Part One, regarding countermeasures, that sanctions applied in conformity with the Charter would not be wrongful, and it continued:[160]

> "This view would, moreover, seem to be valid not only in cases where the duly adopted decision of the Organization authorizing the application of a sanction is mandatory for the Member States but also where the taking of such measures is merely recommended."

A few preliminary observations need to be made on this position. First of all it may be noted that the only organ with competence to decide on sanctions mandatory for United Nations members is the Security Council. This follows from article 25 of the Charter which provides that members agree to accept and carry out decisions of the

Security Council. This means, *a contrario*, that members have not generally agreed to accept and carry out decisions of the General Assembly, nor for that matter decisions of the Economic and Social Council, the Trusteeship Council, or the Secretariat. The effect of decisions of the Court is regulated specifically in the Charter. Under article 94, paragraph 1, any member has undertaken to comply with decisions of the Court in any case to which it is a party (see also article 59 of the Statute).

A second remark is that the Commission expresses the view that measures recommended *by the organization* would not be wrongful. The question is which organs could issue recommendations to members that they adopt countermeasures. In the light of articles 39 and 41 of the Charter there can be no doubt as to the Security Council's competence to recommend countermeasures. The position of the General Assembly and the Economic and Social Council is less clear. In view of articles 10, 11 (paragraph 2), and especially 14, of the Charter, one would have to acknowledge the General Assembly's competence in this respect. The Economic and Social Council is authorized, under article 62 (paragraph 2), to make recommendations for the purpose of "promoting respect for, and observance of, human rights and fundamental freedoms for all." It would seem that recommending the application of coercive measures by members goes way beyond the mere "promotion" of respect for, and observance of, human rights. Provisions related to the other organs of the organization, the Trusteeship Council, the Secretariat and the Court, do not contain any reference to a power to make recommendations.

Before entering into discussion of the legal effect of recommendations, it may be asked whether the Assembly's competence is not restricted by virtue of the terms of articles 14, 12 (paragraph 1) and 11 (paragraph 2). Article 14 provides that the Assembly may recommend measures for the peaceful adjustment of situations, including those resulting from the violation of articles 1 and 2. The question is whether countermeasures can be considered peaceful means of dispute settlement. That question should be answered in the affirmative. Although they are certainly not prone to promote friendly relations between States, they are peaceful in the sense that they do not involve resort to inter-State armed force. The competence of the Assembly is obviously restricted by article 12, paragraph 1, which states that it shall not make recommendations with regard to disputes or situations with regard to which the Security Council is exercising its Charter functions. Finally the interpretation of article 11, paragraph 2, shows that the Assembly may recommend to States on issues related to the maintenance of international peace and security. However, the final sentence of that paragraph provides that: "Any such question on which action is necessary shall be referred to the Security Council by the General Assembly either before or after discussion." Does "action" generally encompass countermeasures? It would seem not. Although the Charter makes numerous, seemingly interchangeable, references to "action" or "measures",[161] the action mentioned in article 11, paragraph 2, can only be meant to cover Security Council enforcement action under Chapter VII.[162] That indeed was the position of the Court in its Expenses Opinion:[163]

> "The word 'action' must mean such action as is solely within the province of the Security Council. (...) The 'action' which is solely within the province of the Security Council is that which is indicated by the title of Chapter VII, namely

'Action with respect to threats to the peace, breaches of the peace, and acts of aggression'. (...) Accordingly, the last sentence of Article 11, paragraph 2, has no application where the necessary action is not enforcement action."

Such action can only relate to the maintenance of international peace and security if and to the extent that there exists, as a minimum, a threat to the peace. The Assembly will remain competent to recommend to States resort to countermeasures for so long as the Security Council is not exercising its functions under the Charter.

It may be said, with Kelsen, as to the Assembly's competence, that:[164] "Recommendations, by their very nature, do not constitute a legal obligation to behave in conformity with them." So a State which acts upon an Assembly recommendation to adopt countermeasures could not be said to be under any obligation to do so. The question is whether that State can invoke the General Assembly recommendation and claim that it provides a justification for a breach of obligation towards the targeted State. As with Council decisions under articles 39 and 41 or 94, paragraph 2, any breach of obligation pursuant to a recommendation can be justified only as a reaction against an earlier committed internationally wrongful act. From a purely legal point of view, however, a wrongful act need not give rise to a right of any State to adopt countermeasures. Minor breaches of obligations under the rules prohibiting intervention and the threat or use of military force for instance do not entail injured State status for all States, but only for the State directly affected by those breaches (article 5, Part Two, of the ILC-draft on State responsibility). A decision by the Security Council that all States must impose countermeasures on an author State implies that in cases of minor breaches also States which do not possess injured State status are legally justified in their reaction independently from the customary rules on State responsibility. As States are not under an obligation to comply with any recommendation issued by the Assembly, one would have to conclude also that they cannot derive any rights therefrom.[165] For that reason States acting in response to a recommendation can only claim a justifying effect for their breaches of obligation towards an author State if they possess injured State status under the customary rules on State responsibility.

To the extent that a State is not to be considered so, yet acts upon the recommendation to adopt countermeasures, it will be in breach of its obligation and will have incurred international responsibility for its wrongful acts. Such responsibility cannot be disclaimed by pointing a finger at the Assembly resolution recommending such action. Since, as noted above, a recommendation cannot bind members to act in any specific way, it follows that any measures adopted pursuant thereto also cannot be attributed to the United Nations and, consequently, does not engage its responsibility.[166] This issue is moot insofar as international crimes are concerned. As all States are to be considered injured States, countermeasures adopted pursuant to an Assembly recommendation will be justifiable on the basis of customary international law.

Should these findings be different, in regard to the Security Council, in view of its power under article 41 to decide on mandatory measures, that is, measures which in the light of article 25 must be accepted and carried out by members? Eisemann, for instance, commenting on article 41, states:[167]

"Un Etat qui adopterait, à l'encontre d'un autre, des mesures de sanctions économiques en application d'une invitation de l'Assemblée (ou même du

> Conseil de sécurité n'agissant pas dans le cadre du Chapitre VII) ne ferait juridiquement qu'un acte unilatéral, et il ne pourrait invoquer la Charte pour justifier sa politique de sanctions dans l'hypothèse où elle serait contraire à des engagements internationaux antérieurs."

On the basis of an *a contrario* argument one could assert that he apparently considers that a State could invoke the Charter if the Council had recommended it to adopt economic sanctions under Chapter VII (that is, under article 39 of the Charter). However, in the sentence immediately preceding this stance he quoted the Court's statement in the Expenses Opinion to the effect that:[168] "Seul le Conseil de sécurité peut *prescrire* des mesures d'exécution par une action coercitive contre un agresseur." Now it is precisely this power of the Security Council which ought to lead to a negative answer. Why should one accord justifying effect to countermeasures adopted pursuant to a recommendation of the Council, when the Council could just as easily have *required* members to adopt those measures? If the Council leaves any decision on resort to coercive measures to the members themselves, the conclusion must again be that measures adopted on the invitation of the Security Council under Chapter VII are in need of separate justification under the customary rules on State responsibility. For the above reasons member States of the United Nations can only claim Charter justification for resort to countermeasures against another member, if such measures have been imposed upon them by way of Security Council decision under articles 39 and 41.[169]

Article 41 measures and determinations under article 39

There is general recognition that the Security Council must first determine the existence of a threat to the peace, breach of the peace, or act of aggression, before it can decide upon the measures of article 41.[170] Goodrich and Hambro, for instance, note in regard to article 41:[171]

> "It is clear from the wording of this Article, taken together with that of Article 39, that a decision to use 'measures not involving the use of armed force' can only be taken following a determination, explicit or implicit, that a 'threat to the peace, breach of the peace, or act of aggression' exists."

It is not quite clear how an implicit determination of a threat to the peace, breach of the peace, or act of aggression could be considered sufficient for purposes of application of article 41 of the Charter. If a determination under article 39 constitutes a (pre)condition for possible application of article 41 measures, then explicit wording appears requisite. Mere reference, by the Council, that it is acting under Chapter VII of the Charter certainly cannot be considered adequate. And similarly a mere invocation of article 41 cannot be considered sufficient. The imposition of measures, on the other hand, without any reference to article 41, would leave much to the imagination of the beholder. Admittedly, use of interpretation rules could correct the more unlikely conclusions. However, the Council not only has competence to decide on the measures of articles 41 and 42, but can also engage in the formulation of recommendations and provisional measures. The texts of articles 39 and 40, though, also appear to require a determination under article 39 for the adoption of recommendations and provisional measures.[172] In this light, and since the Security Council only has the power to decide on mandatory measures in relation to articles 41 and 42 (and 94), it would not be too onerous to require it to determine, in an explicit manner, the existence of any threat to the peace, breach of the peace, or act of aggression.

The competence of the Security Council to determine threats to the peace, breaches of the peace, or acts of aggression, should be seen in relation to the fundamental provisions of article 2, paragraphs 3 and 4, of the Charter. In this respect it should be noted that article 2, paragraph 4, not only prohibits members to use force against the territorial integrity or political independence of States, but also to use force inconsistent with the purposes of the United Nations. Article 2, paragraph 4, read in conjunction with article 1 then leads to the conclusion that the threat or use of force by a member in denial of the self-determination of peoples, or against human rights and fundamental freedoms, constitutes a breach of obligation under article 2, paragraph 4.[173] That conclusion would in turn provide a stronger argument for considering international crimes to come under the heading of threats to the peace, breaches of the peace, or even acts of aggression. Thus the competence of the Security Council in taking action under article 41 of the Charter would be established beyond doubt.

Yet these conclusions, and any enthusiasm resulting therefrom, must be tempered. First of all it has to be mentioned that article 2, paragraph 4, only stipulates that members shall refrain from the threat or use of force *in their international relations only*. Uses of force in denial of self-determination need not fall under the heading of international relations. And uses of force constituting violations of human rights and fundamental freedoms would, almost by definition, not take place in the international relations of members.

Secondly, one might wish to stress that the Security Council competence to determine threats to the peace does not require there to be a threat to "international" peace. Reading on in article 39 of the Charter one finds that the Security Council may "decide what measures shall be taken in accordance with Articles 41 and 42, to maintain or restore *international* peace and security." In conformity with interpretation canons the ordinary meaning to be given to these terms then is that the Security Council can only adopt the measures of article 41 if a threat to the peace, perhaps of domestic origin, necessitates measures to maintain or restore international peace and security. In fact international peace or security must already be endangered or disturbed in a concrete sense in that article 37, paragraph 2, states that the Security Council may deem that the continuation of a dispute is "in fact" likely to endanger international peace and security. *A fortiori* there must be a threat to international peace and security that would, if materialized, necessitate the restoration of international peace and security.

A third argument to be discarded relates to article 2, paragraph 7, which provides that: "Nothing contained in the present Charter shall authorize the United Nations to intervene in matters essentially within the domestic jurisdiction of any state or require the Members to submit such matters to settlement under the present Charter." The Security Council would be entitled to intervene in such matters by virtue of the last sentence of article 2, paragraph 7: "(...) but this principle shall not prejudice the application of enforcement measures under Chapter VII." Matters within the domestic jurisdiction of States are by definition not regulated by rules of international law. Yet it is clear that such matters may still give rise to international tension, especially where for instance there are ethnic ties between the population of a State and a minority within another State. Although the Security Council would thus have competence under article 39, especially where there is a threat of armed conflict between the two States, the measures of article 41 could still not be taken against a State that had not in any way committed any breach of obligations. In relation to international crimes the issue is not whether there are internationally wrongful acts, but rather whether there is any threat of armed conflict between the author State and injured State(s). In such a case, and in both respects, the domestic jurisdiction clause really has no relevance at all. First, because the commission of an internationally wrongful act removes the issue from the domestic jurisdiction, and secondly because if there is such a threat of armed conflict there will most likely, as a minimum, also be a breach of obligation under article 2, paragraph 3, of the Charter.

Interpretation of the Charter therefore shows that the measures under article 41, imposed on an author State committing the international crimes of denial of self-determination and widespread breaches of basic human rights obligations, still necessitate a prior determination by the Security Council under article 39 of the Charter. Such determination by the Security Council can only provide the basis for the measures of article 41 if imposition is necessary for the maintenance or restoration of international peace and security.

4.4. Restrictions regarding resort to countermeasures

4.4.1. RESTRICTIONS REGARDING COUNTERMEASURES, MULTIPLICITY OF INJURED STATES, AND THE ORGANIZATIONAL INTEREST IN COUNTERMEASURES

Restrictions based on the absence of specially affected States

Breaches of obligations for the protection of human rights of individuals irrespective of nationality need not affect any State specifically. For that reason injured State status results for all those States bound by the relevant rule of conventional or customary law. To the extent that such breaches of obligations are the result of negligent behaviour of States, there would not seem to be any fears that they refuse to remedy their ways.

Especially in case of breaches of human rights obligations States ought to have recourse to the supervision mechanisms contained in treaties to which they are parties. The same cannot be said where the breaches are intentional or premeditated and of a serious nature. In such cases all injured States can adopt countermeasures towards the author State.

Other restrictions, to be discussed below, also would not seem to place any obstacles in the way of countermeasures. Arangio-Ruiz for instance observed, in the context of delicts, that proportionality constitutes:[174]

> "(...) a general and flexible principle ensuring that the implementation of international responsibility does not lead to inequitable results. Where measures are taken by several States as a consequence of one and the same breach, respect for proportionality should prevent the aggregate effect of the unilateral measures to cause disproportion between the reaction and the breach or its effects."

But proportionality, especially important for delicts, does not play the same role in respect of crimes. The fact that all States would obtain the right to invoke the reparation obligations of the author State, and all such States would exercise their rights to resort to countermeasures towards that State, would still not necessarily result in disproportional action. That is so, basically, because the gravity of the crimes, the severe fault on the part of the author State, and the importance of the rules breached, may all be taken into account in judging (dis)proportionality.

Allegations of wrongfulness, incurred responsibility and demands for reparation still have to be made, but this does not seriously hamper the adoption of countermeasures in case of crimes. On the other hand it could be claimed that injured States ought to respect recourse to dispute settlement procedures by the author State and another injured State. In such a case they may claim the opportunity to be afforded to take part in, either directly or through intervention procedures, the proceedings. Nevertheless the suspension of countermeasures by injured States not taking part in the procedure cannot be demanded in case of international crimes. A final, and the most important, limit on resort to countermeasures by injured States will concern the restriction that basic human rights will be safeguarded. The conclusion, however, must be that no specific restrictions on resort to countermeasures can be posed because there would not be any specially affected State.

Restrictions based on the presence of a directly injured State

Of the international crimes mentioned in article 19, paragraph 3, Part One, only the one under sub (a) on the rule prohibiting aggression can lead to a situation in which there truly is a directly injured State and where there are other injured States. The other examples of crimes could be said to involve more strongly affected States which gives them a more direct interest in the breaches at hand. As noted before, chapter three, subsection 3.8.1, even then their status of specially affected State is incidental to their true status flowing from breaches of obligations affecting all States alike. Questions on directly injured States and other injured States will therefore only be discussed from the angle of the prohibition of aggression.

In chapter one and chapter three it has been noted that not all uses of force give rise to injured State status under article 5, Part Two. Only such uses of force as amount to an armed attack do so. That, as has been noted before, is in accordance with the observations made by the Court in the Nicaragua Case. In the context of the subject under consideration the Court emphatically stated:[175]

> "While an armed attack would give rise to an entitlement to collective self-defence, a use of force of a lesser degree cannot, as the Court has already observed (...), produce any entitlement to take collective counter-measures involving the use of force. The acts of which Nicaragua is accused, even assuming them to have been established and imputable to that State, could only have justified proportionate counter-measures on the part of the State which had been the victim of these acts, namely El Salvador, Honduras or Costa Rica. They could not justify counter-measures taken by a third State, and particularly could not justify intervention involving the use of force."

This conclusion only concerns such uses of force falling below the level of an armed attack. When there is an armed attack by one State against another, all other States will also be considered injured States. Such an armed attack may be countered through the exercise of a right of individual or collective self-defence, and/or by the exercise of a right to have resort to countermeasures. With regard to the exercise of the former right the Court has asserted the existence of two conditions: a declaration by the directly injured State that it is under attack, and a request by the directly injured State to other States calling for action in collective self-defence.[176] The question then is whether these conditions also apply with regard to the exercise of the other injured States' rights to adopt countermeasures. Tomuschat answered in the affirmative, claiming that what applied to self-defence should apply to countermeasures as well.[177] So far the draft articles adopted by the Commission do not embody such conditions. Article 5, Part Two, defines the injured States and, in the context of delicts, those are entitled to demand reparation from the author State or to resort to countermeasures as against the latter if reparation is not forthcoming. Arangio-Ruiz has gone even further and, after a thorough examination,[178] proposed the insertion of an article 5 *bis*, Part Two, which provides that: "Whenever there is more than one injured State, each one of them is entitled to exercise its legal rights under the rules set forth in the following articles." Whether this principled position would apply also to international crimes is not altogether clear. To the extent that injured States' nationals would be wronged by an author State's commission of an international crime, the position proposed by Arangio-Ruiz should be upheld. This would be the case for instance if an injured State's nationals would be caught up in an attempted genocide, denial of self-determination or widespread human rights violations, or if intentional pollution of the atmosphere or the seas would affect its special economic interests or would reach its national jurisdiction.[179] In such cases the injury done to an injured State would provide it with injured State status over and above the status it already enjoyed under article 5, paragraph 3, as a result of an international crime.[180] Yet the other States also enjoy that status notwithstanding that they are not factually damaged by the crime.

Arangio-Ruiz seems to have denied, in regard to the international crime of aggression, any virtue in a distinction between directly injured States and non-directly injured States.[181] He refers in this respect to:[182] "(...) the nature and the gravity of the injury respectively sustained in fact." Proof of that he finds in that there are the target State of the aggression, States bordering the direct victim, States of the region, allies of the victim State, States depending on the victim State's vital exports, States participating in a collective security system, and all other States bound by the rule of general international law prohibiting aggression.[183] Yet all of these examples are but the ratio for the existence of a collective security system. Other States may suffer disadvantageous consequences as a result of an author State's internationally wrongful act towards the injured State. However, it has been generally acknowledged that this does not entail injured State status for all those States affected. The whole point of drafting the rules of article 5, Part Two, is to provide limits to such causation. The idea is to provide which States are "legally" considered to be injured. The stance of the Court in the Nicaragua Case shows that States will not be considered injured States where there is no all out armed attack. Yet the lower levels of uses of force may certainly affect other bordering

States, or impede exports of vital products. Legally speaking such States will still not be injured States.[184]

The crime of aggression provides injured State status to all States by virtue of its status as breach of an obligation *erga omnes*. Were it not for the existence of that concept, all other States would lack such status. The victim of an armed attack on the other hand derives its status as injured State from the fact that in accordance with traditional criteria it is affected by the author State's breach of obligation. The rationale for injured State status for all States in case of an armed attack can only lie with the need to ensure more effective responses to aggression. Whether or not more effective responses are required ought to be left for decision by the directly injured State. For that reason it is necessary to impose the conditions of a declaration and a request also with regard to the exercise of a right to adopt collective countermeasures. The victim State of an armed attack may consider that it is adequately countering the attack and that no further action is necessary. Or it may try to obtain such help through adoption of countermeasures by other injured States as it deems helpful in hampering the author State's military operations. Finally, though not necessarily in last resort, it may call upon other injured States to engage in collective self-defence actions.

Only one exception exists, which goes without saying, with regard to the conditions of a declaration and request. The conditions concerned can only be imposed if the directly injured State is in a position to make a declaration and to issue the request. If as a result of an armed attack the competent officials of the victim State are not in a position to act, *e.g.* because they have all been taken prisoner, then the other injured States can exercise their right to adopt countermeasures without the "requisite" declaration and request. In the case of Kuwait the government fled the country and consequently the conditions of declaration and request had to be fulfilled.

Restrictions based on the exercise of Security Council powers

In subsection 4.4.2 it will be explained that the existence of Security Council competence as such, without any exercise thereof, could not lead to the disappearance of an injured State's right to adopt countermeasures. It has been asserted however, by Pellet,[185] that there would no longer be any right to resort to unilateral countermeasures once the Security Council imposed sanctions, under articles 39 and 41, on the author State. In framing the argument he referred to the, in his mind analogous, provision of article 51 of the Charter, which stipulates that the right of self-defence shall not be impaired until the Security Council has taken measures necessary to maintain international peace and security.

Against this it may be said that the Charter does not contain any such provision limiting the members' rights to adopt countermeasures. The reason for that would seem to be that there is no prohibition on the use economic force in the Charter. Since the Charter does prohibit the use of armed force, under article 2, paragraphs 3 and 4, the provision on self-defence constitutes a necessity. Similarly the limit to the right of self-defence, measures taken by the Security Council, is needed for optimizing responses to armed attacks and for review of the accuracy of the allegation of an armed attack. As economic coercion is not as such prohibited by the Charter, a limit analogous to that of article 51 would have to be spelled out. Why would States give up their right to adopt countermeasures by implication?

Furthermore, article 51 only covers two of the hypotheses of article 39, that is, the commission of an armed attack as a breach of the peace or an act of aggression. Is it conceivable that States have given up their right to adopt countermeasures considering that the Security Council was far less likely to act in cases of lesser gravity? And even if it did act, it might do so only by having resort to less coercive measures. Moreover, the restriction to the right of self-defence seems to have as a further rationale that the Security Council might consider that the situation could be remedied by having recourse to measures under article 41 only, or that action in self-defence should be substituted by action under article 42. The idea then would be to have unilateral or collective armed actions substituted by Security Council action of a lesser degree. That would amount to review by the Security Council of the necessity and proportionality of unilateral or collective exercises of self-defence. Of course the reporting requirement laid down in article 51 of the Charter is meant to enable the Security Council to assess, first, whether an armed attack has occurred, and secondly, whether it ought to substitute the defending State's action by its own.

The argument could be made that there is some inconsistency with regard to the position taken on the GATT and the Charter (*infra* subsection 4.4.2).[186] While States parties to the GATT must seek authorization by the CONTRACTING PARTIES in order to take countermeasures, States parties to the Charter would be able to go ahead with such measures independently from any authorization by the Security Council.

The difference can be explained by reference to article XXIII of the GATT. This provision stipulates that in case of a breach of obligation under the GATT a State party shall make representations or proposals to the party so accused. Should the matter not be satisfactory adjusted it may be referred to the CONTRACTING PARTIES. They in turn could then decide that the situation is serious enough to warrant the suspension of concessions or obligations by the affected State party. The Security Council on the other hand has been given the task to maintain or restore international peace and security. In that context it must determine breaches of obligations by members or non-members. The scope of the Security Council's competence is so general that virtually any breach of obligation might be considered to give rise to a threat to the peace. However, the interpretation of Charter provisions in their context shows that the Security Council was not intended as a general law enforcing body comparable to the police. Rather it was to take on those situations involving members' breaches of obligation which provided a threat to the maintenance of order in international relations. Yet since almost any situation might give rise to the exercise of Security Council powers, it is difficult to assume that States parties by becoming members have renunciated their right to adopt coercive measures under customary international law.

The question as to whether members would be entitled to adopt further or more severe measures than imposed by the Security Council must be answered taking into consideration the injured State status under rules of State responsibility. Under the GATT only a contracting party affected, or liable to be affected, by a breach of obligation, by measures whether or not in conflict with the GATT, or by any other situation, will be authorized to suspend concessions or obligations.[187] In cases involving uses of force not constituting an armed attack the Court has denied any standing for States not affected by such force.[188] Even if the Security Council had taken measures under articles 39 and 41 in such circumstances, other States could not take further or more severe measures due to lack of injured State status. In case of the international crime of aggression, *e.g.* an armed attack by one State against another, all States are injured States and may invoke the responsibility of the author State. To deny them the right to adopt countermeasures going beyond Security Council measures, would be to deny the taking of, supposedly, more effective measures. The Security Council might, for instance, in its first response to an armed attack, impose upon members no more than a duty to sever diplomatic relations. If members could from that moment no longer adopt countermeasures because the interpretation of the Charter should lead to that conclusion, and if the Security Council would not go beyond diplomatic steps, members of the United Nations would be stuck to implementing no more than mere measures of retortion. All this notwithstanding their injured State status under the customary rules of State responsibility, and the need for effective responses to international crimes. It is submitted that States are prevented from having recourse to countermeasures only in the presence of a Security Council resolution imploring them to refrain from adopting any or specific measures.[189]

4.4.2. RESTRICTIONS REGARDING COUNTERMEASURES BASED ON GENERAL CONCEPTS

The exclusion of a right to take countermeasures due to the existence of a treaty régime

The exclusion of countermeasures due to the existence of a treaty régime has been discussed mainly from the angle of self-contained régimes, and has attracted much attention from the two most recent special rapporteurs on State responsibility and authors on international law. As to the former especially Riphagen, on the basis of self-contained régimes, resorted to the idea of so-called subsystems:[190]

> "(...) a system was an ordered set of conduct rules, procedural rules and status provisions, which formed a closed legal circuit for a particular field of factual relationships. A subsystem, then, was the same as a system, but not closed in as much as it had an interrelationship with other subsystems."

Among the latter Simma for instance observed, in reaction to Riphagen, that a self-contained régime would apply to:[191]

> "(...) a certain category of subsystems, namely those embracing, in principle, a full (exhaustive and definite) set of secondary rules. A 'self-contained regime' would then be a subsystem which is intended to exclude more or less totally the application of the general legal consequences of wrongful acts, in particular the application of the countermeasures normally at the disposal of an injured party."

At the outset it should be clear that there are two angles to the question whether States would be prevented from having resort to countermeasures due to the existence of a treaty régime. First there is the possibility that the existence of a treaty régime would exclude the possibility of resort to countermeasures suspending the obligations established under the régime. And secondly there is the possibility that the existence of the régime would exclude any resort to countermeasures outside the régime. Both possibilities will be discussed on the basis of the presumption that States parties to a particular treaty will only have given up the right to resort to countermeasures in an express manner or by way of necessary implication.

An important matter for both categories of régimes is whether the régime involved provides for resort to countermeasures. One may note that Simma claimed that a self-contained régime had to embrace *a full set* of secondary rules.[192] Taking a look at the potential candidates in the field of self-contained régimes, one will see that only the system of the Charter and that of the GATT are so equipped. The Charter envisages Security Council imposition of measures under article 41 with respect to threats to the peace, breaches of the peace, and acts of aggression. The GATT provides, in article XXIII, that the CONTRACTING PARTIES may authorize, if they consider a situation to be serious enough, the suspension of concessions or obligations under the GATT with respect to a breach of obligation under the GATT, any measure whether or not in conflict with provisions of the GATT, or any other situation. The other likely examples of self-contained régimes, the system of diplomatic law and the law of human rights, do not provide for resort to countermeasures. In view of the rather more complex questions arising in this chapter, compared to that of chapter three, separate discussion of potential régimes is necessary, beginning with diplomatic law, continuing with human rights law and Charter law, and ending with GATT law. Any discussion of these issues must primarily be based upon the interpretation of the relevant provisions of the instruments concerned and of the concomitant rules of customary international law.[193]

Exclusion of countermeasures under the régime of diplomatic law? The 1961 Vienna Convention on Diplomatic Relations provides, in article 9, paragraph 1, that the receiving State can declare any person *persona non grata* or unacceptable without stating the reasons for such a decision.[194] The sending State is then under the obligation to recall that person or terminate its functions. Articles 39, paragraph 2, and 44 stipulate that persons enjoying immunities shall be granted facilities and sufficient time, even in case of armed conflict, to leave the country. These provisions seem to provide the basis for the conclusion that a receiving State is not entitled, by way of countermeasure, to disregard the immunities of persons accredited to it.

In arriving at such a conclusion one has to take into account that the receiving State is under the obligation to grant diplomatic staff and their family free passage even in case of armed conflict, that is to say, even if the supreme international crime is being committed against it. So even if the sending State is breaching its obligation not to use force against the territorial integrity or political independence of the receiving State, the latter cannot react by breaching its obligation to respect the immunities of the former State's diplomatic staff. Since that is the case an injured (receiving) State will also not be entitled, by way of countermeasure, to disregard the immunities as a reaction against other breaches of obligation against the author (sending) State. That conclusion was reached also by the Court in the Diplomatic Staff Case,[195] in which it rejected the justification claimed by Iran, namely that the United States had seriously breached its obligation under article 41, paragraph 1, not to interfere in the internal affairs of Iran. Such (alleged) interference, even if proved, could only be countered by way of declaring *persona non grata* those suspected thereof, or by breaking off the diplomatic relations with the sending State. In both cases the interference would stop, and for that reason the Court observed that such means were "entirely efficacious".[196] That observation is certainly accurate, because, under article 9, paragraph 1, the receiving State would have the right to disregard the immunities of any person who had been recalled, or whose functions had been terminated, by the sending State, and who nevertheless had not left the receiving State's territory within a reasonable period of time. It is on that basis that the Commission has formulated the provision of article 14 (c), Part Two, of the ILC-draft, that countermeasures shall not amount to:[197] "(...) any conduct which infringes the inviolability of diplomatic or consular agents, premises, archives and documents;" For the reasons stated any countermeasures affecting an author State's diplomatic or consular personnel are out of the question.

However, would the injured State be entitled to react to an author State's breach of obligation under the régime of diplomatic law by having resort to countermeasures affecting obligations outside that régime? According to the Court the rules of diplomatic law, which constitute a self-contained régime, foresee possible abuses by members of diplomatic missions, and specifies the, entirely efficacious, means to counter those.[198] But the only remedies available under the treaty are the declaration of *persona non grata*, and the breaking off of diplomatic relations. Such action will certainly put a stop to breaches and will also prevent repetition. But that is not the same as saying that in that way full reparation has been granted to the injured State. How about restitution in kind (if abuses would involve theft), compensation (if the abuses involve destruction of property), satisfaction (punishment of culprits), or guarantees against repetition? It may be noted first of all that the optional protocol envisages the compulsory jurisdiction of the Court as to disputes regarding the interpretation or application of the 1961 Vienna Convention.[199] As found in subsection 3.8.2 of chapter three, generally the absence of provisions on reparation must be interpreted to mean that the general rules on State responsibility apply. An injured State under the 1961 Vienna Convention, whether that be the sending or receiving State, is not therefore restricted to claiming cessation, but can also demand other forms of reparation.[200] The observation of the Court that the rules of diplomatic law constitute a self-contained régime only accounts for cessation and non-repetition and a prohibition of countermeasures affecting immunities. The 1961 Vienna Convention, furthermore, does not in any way provide for resort to countermeasures in response to breaches of obligation under the treaty. The claim by the Court that diplomatic law provides the "means of defence against, and sanction for, illicit activities of members" surely cannot be considered fully justified. Declaring members *persona non grata* and the breaking off of diplomatic relations constitute mere measures of retortion and not countermeasures. For such reasons resort to countermeasures in fields other than that of diplomatic law must be considered lawful.[201]

Exclusion of countermeasures under the régime of human rights law? A first examination should be directed towards the question whether a State could resort to countermeasures breaching human rights in response to the breach of human rights obligations in another State. However, for reasons of economy discussion of that question stands postponed to later in this section.

It has been asserted on occasion that the multilateral treaties in the field of human rights provide their own machinery for monitoring, supervision, and implementation. For that reason countermeasures, in reaction to breaches of obligation under such treaties, could not be resorted to.[202] That stance appears to have been supported by the Court in the Nicaragua Case as it discussed the issue of human rights violations:[203]

> "This particular point requires to be studied independently of the question of the existence of a 'legal commitment' by Nicaragua towards the Organization of American States to respect these rights; the absence of such a commitment would not mean that Nicaragua could with impunity violate human rights. However, where human rights are protected by international conventions, that protection takes the form of such arrangements for monitoring or ensuring respect for human rights as are provided for in the conventions themselves."

After noting that Nicaragua had ratified some human rights treaties, and the American Convention on Human Rights in particular,[204] the Court observed that the mechanisms provided therein had functioned, that two reports had been issued, and that therefore the OAS had been in a position to take a decision on the basis of these reports.[205] It then stated:[206]

> "In any event, while the United States might form its own appraisal of the situation as to respect for human rights in Nicaragua, the use of force could not be the appropriate method to monitor or ensure such respect."

The Court's observation that the United States could itself appraise the human rights situation in Nicaragua was indispensable. That is so because the Court was precluded from (interpreting or) applying multilateral treaties by reason of the American reservation to its jurisdiction.[207] Any evaluation of the question whether the United States could take countermeasures against Nicaragua had to be based on customary international law. It is submitted that resort to countermeasures can indeed be an appropriate method to ensure respect for human rights. Basically because such respect might not be forthcoming on the basis of representations alone. Thus demands for reparation regarding breaches of human rights obligations may be enforced by way of countermeasures.

In this relation an examination of the most important treaty in the field, the International Covenant on Civil and Political Rights, allows for no different conclusion. Article 40 places States parties to the Covenant under the obligation to submit reports on measures to give effect to the rights under the Covenant to the Human Rights Committee (paragraph 1). Yet the only course of action open to the Committee is to submit such reports, and its general comments, to the States parties (paragraph 4). A State party may, under article 41, accept the competence of the Committee to receive any complaint that it is breaching obligations under the Covenant. But any such acceptance is subject to a condition of reciprocity. Furthermore, any function the Committee exercises in this respect is limited to the provision of good offices to the States parties in dispute. True, the idea of these provisions is to come to an "amicable solution to the matter on the basis of respect for human rights", but at the same time that is where it ends. If the States parties do not reach an amicable solution to their dispute, the only thing left for the Committee to do is to submit a report containing a brief statement of the facts.[208] Any dispute on the responsibility of a State under the Covenant will then not be settled through any procedure established under the Covenant. Settlement could still be reached of course if the States parties concerned have accepted the jurisdiction of the Court through some general instrument with regard to these kind of disputes. Moreover, the Covenant does not make any reference to possible resort to countermeasures. To the contrary, article 44 stipulates that States parties may settle their disputes in accordance with other agreements. As no reference to customary law is made that would not necessarily mean that injured States under the Covenant could resort to countermeasures. But then again article 44 is concerned with the settlement of disputes only, and does not refer in any way to the enforcement of obligations. Should a dispute between States parties on a breach of obligation under the Covenant and the resulting incurred responsibility reach a stalemate, resort to countermeasures to force the author State to fulfil its reparation obligations will be lawful.

If an international crime would be committed by a State party to the Covenant, the rejection of a right to resort to countermeasures regarding such breaches, on the argument that Covenant procedures take precedence, cannot be accepted. The procedure established under article 41 for instance requires that no communication shall be accepted unless it has been ascertained that all available domestic remedies have been invoked and exhausted. Yet in a State where human rights obligations are being breached on a widespread scale it is hardly likely that the individuals concerned, will attempt, or will have the opportunity to attempt, to have recourse to the legal remedies, if any, that are available to them. It would seem obvious that the effective functioning of the Covenant procedures is fully dependent on the good faith of the States parties. But it is hardly imaginable that "an amicable solution to the matter on the basis of respect for human rights" will or indeed can be arrived at in a situation where a State party is wilfully engaging in premeditated breaches of human rights obligations. Resort to countermeasures in response to the commission of an international crime would therefore, *a fortiori*, be fully justified under both the Covenant and customary international law.[209]

Exclusion of countermeasures under the régime of the Charter? The question may be asked whether an injured State would be entitled to suspend, as against the author State, performance of its obligations under the Charter. Insofar as this would amount to a use of military force under article 2, paragraphs 3 and 4, the issue will be discussed in the next chapter. It might be asked nevertheless whether resort to countermeasures could be considered to be contrary to article 2, paragraph 3, which stipulates that members shall "settle their international disputes by peaceful means in such a manner that international peace and security, and justice, are not endangered." First of all it may be stressed that resort to countermeasures does not as such count as a means of dispute settlement. It should be considered a *peaceful* means inasmuch as its purpose is to coerce an author State into fulfilling its reparation obligations without any actual use of armed force against that State.[210] The argument here is that it is not meant to settle

the dispute. The object of countermeasures is to make the author State want to settle the dispute in the traditional way, that is, by means of negotiation, mediation, conciliation, arbitration or judicial settlement.
As already pointed out, subsection 4.3.2, resort to countermeasures furthermore cannot be said to be contrary to justice. What is unjust is that the author State fails to acknowledge its responsibility and fails to take the necessary steps to absolve itself therefrom. To the extent that an author State would suffer from extensive countermeasures (inclusive measures of retortion) by the injured State, it might be tempted to have recourse to less peaceful means to ensure the survival of its population. Indirectly then countermeasures could endanger international peace and security. This kind of situation appears to be covered by the Commission's proposed draft article 14, sub (b), Part Two, prohibiting countermeasures involving:[211] "(...) extreme economic or political coercion designed to endanger the territorial integrity or political independence of the State which has committed an internationally wrongful act;" Of course such countermeasures could only be resorted to if the internationally wrongful act was of the utmost gravity. Otherwise countermeasures would conflict with the rule of proportionality.[212] It would seem, on the other hand, that the broad competences of the Security Council are adequate to handle tension as a result of such a situation. As Bowett remarked the Security Council can oversee countermeasures and indicate whether it considers them to be disproportionate.[213] For reasons stated non-military countermeasures do not concern breaches of obligation under the Charter.

The other side of the question is whether States would be prevented from taking countermeasures in response to the commission of the international crime of aggression. Preclusion of countermeasures would in such a case have to be based upon the competence of the Security Council to address the issue. This issue is relevant only to the extent that the Security Council has failed to act under articles 39 and 41 (or 42) even though an armed attack is taking place, or has taken place, against a member of the United Nations. The decisive argument should be, in such circumstances, that States are free to act in conformity with existing rules of customary international law. The Court for instance noted, in the Expenses Opinion, regarding the purposes of the United Nations under article 1 of the Charter, that:

> "These purposes are broad indeed, but neither they nor the powers conferred to effectuate them are unlimited. Save as they have entrusted the Organization with the attainment of these common ends, the Member States retain their freedom of action."

As the Security Council would not have acted upon a situation (an armed attack) that clearly calls for action, the interpretation that States would not have the right to take countermeasures against an aggressor State is not acceptable. They might of course act in collective self-defence under article 51 of the Charter. On the interpretation suggested, and in the absence of a Charter provision enabling them to adopt countermeasures, they could not support their legitimate self-defence actions by refusing, for instance, to provide the development aid promised by treaty to the author State. If they choose not to aid the injured State by resorting themselves to armed force against the author State, and if the injured State has already been vanquished, the same interpretation prevents recourse to countermeasures on their part. In such a case, and assuming that the Security Council would remain passive, the result is that the directly injured State would be completely incapable to resort to countermeasures or the use of force. The other injured States, having relinquished their rights to act in collective self-defence, would be precluded from taking countermeasures because an inactive Security Council possesses competence over the situation. Such an interpretation would be both absurd and unreasonable.

Exclusion of countermeasures under the régime of the GATT? Finally the rules of the GATT must be discussed. This issue is especially important due to the wide scope of the obligations accepted by States parties to the GATT. If one were to conclude that the GATT constitutes a régime excluding possible resort to countermeasures, this would imply, for a considerable number of States, the absence of any real power to put pressure on States breaching their obligations.

Important and complicated is the issue whether a contracting party could resort to countermeasures affecting GATT obligations in response to another contracting party's internationally wrongful act in fields other than the GATT.[214] First it may be observed that the CONTRACTING PARTIES do not possess any power to authorize countermeasures with regard to breaches of obligation lying outside the scope of the GATT. Superficially one might form that impression by reading that complaints under article XXIII by a contracting party may concern "any other situation", and that if the situation is serious enough the CONTRACTING PARTIES could authorize the suspension of concessions or obligations under the GATT. However, the complaint by a contracting party must concern a claim that a benefit accruing to it under the GATT is being nullified or impaired, or that the attainment of the objectives of the GATT is being impeded. Any authorization by the CONTRACTING PARTIES therefore can only concern, and respond to, matters coming within the functional scope of the GATT.

The provisions of articles XX and XXI also do not concern any power of the States parties to adopt countermeasures responding to internationally wrongful acts extraneous to the GATT. They constitute general exceptions to the scope of the GATT. The exceptions under article XXI could lead to the adoption of countermeasures under other treaties or customary international law. Yet measures adopted would not involve any breach of obligation under the GATT.[215] It would not be too farfetched to consider measures taken in response to international crimes to relate to an "emergency in international relations" (article XXI (b) (iii)). Any action taken under that heading must, however, be necessary for the protection of essential security interests.[216] Article XXI (b) (iii) expressly mentions action taken in time of war, but an emergency in international relations would probably relate also to lesser grave uses of force, and to breaches of the prohibition on intervention.[217] Other conduct constituting international crimes (genocide, denial of self-determination, and serious human rights violations) cannot be considered, inherently, to relate to essential security interests, though of course the repercussions flowing therefrom might.

The report of a GATT panel on the dispute between Nicaragua and the United States is relevant here.[218] As a result of the situation in Central America the United States imposed a cut in sugar quotas on Nicaragua. The latter took action under GATT procedures and claimed that this constituted a violation of articles II, XI, XIII, paragraph 2, and Part IV, of the GATT. The United States limited itself to claiming that the dispute did not fall within the scope of the GATT. It motivated this by saying that the cut-back in quotas restricted Nicaragua's capability of financing its arms build-up, which, the United States claimed, threatened peace in the region. The panel established that the cut in quotas was incompatible with article XIII, paragraph 2, and noted that the United States had not invoked any exception under GATT rules. United States action was thus considered incompatible with the GATT. A second panel report on the other hand had to refrain from review of United States acts because its mandate did not authorize such review. As Mavroidis points out panels are not courts and their concern is first and foremost to achieve a settlement of the dispute and the balancing of mutual interests.[219] The silence of the GATT on countermeasures affecting it may also be taken into account. Would not States parties, by now, have taken the opportunity to clarify the situation and amended the GATT by introducing a reprisal prohibition?[220] It is submitted that the GATT also cannot be seen as a régime excluding countermeasures, and that consequently the States parties can legitimately claim a right to take unilateral countermeasures affecting obligations thereunder.

Some discussion is necessary whether States parties would be prevented from taking countermeasures affecting obligations outside the GATT in response to a breach of obligation under the GATT. In this respect article XXIII, paragraph 1, of the GATT provides that a contracting party may complain if it considers that any benefit accruing to it under the GATT is being nullified or impaired, or that the attainment of objectives of the GATT is being impeded, as a result of: a breach of obligation by a contracting party, a contracting party's application of measures whether or not those are in conflict with the GATT, any other situation. The CONTRACTING PARTIES may authorize, under paragraph 2 of the same article, a contracting party to suspend concessions or obligations under the GATT towards another contracting party if it considers the situation to be serious enough. The use of the verb "authorize" implies that without authorization of the CONTRACTING PARTIES a State could not resort to countermeasures affecting obligations under the GATT in response to any of the three situations envisaged under article XXIII.

Moreover, one would have to say, in such a case, that a State could also not take countermeasures affecting obligations outside the GATT.[221] First of all because complaints on any of the three situations of article XXIII clearly fall under the exclusive competence of the GATT procedures. Secondly, because the determination whether or not the circumstances are serious enough to warrant resort to countermeasures is subject to a decision of the CONTRACTING PARTIES. Resort to countermeasures affecting obligations outside the GATT without authorization of the CONTRACTING PARTIES prejudges any decision it could make as to whether the circumstances are serious enough. Though measures by one contracting party against another would lie outside the GATT, their cause and rationale may be traced back to the situations envisaged under article XXIII. For those a dispute settlement procedure exists, coupled to a possibility of resort to countermeasures. Any resort to countermeasures without having recourse to the procedure under article XXIII should be considered inadmissible.

The situation changes somewhat if the CONTRACTING PARTIES determine that a situation is serious enough to warrant non-compliance with concessions or obligations under the GATT. Any countermeasures adopted in excess of those authorized could not be said to prejudge the competence of the CONTRACTING PARTIES. For resort to such measures the ordinary conditions and restrictions would have to be obeyed. In the context of international crimes the hypotheses envisaged, conduct falling under GATT competence, are not relevant.

Peremptory norms and human rights

Two prohibitions envisaged by the Commission concern conduct derogating from basic human rights and conduct in contravention of a peremptory norm of general international law. In the light of the more restricted scope of the latter prohibition that one will be discussed first.

Countermeasures in contravention of peremptory norms. In article 14, Part Two, the Commission states that an injured State shall not resort, by way of countermeasures, to:[222] "(e) any other conduct in contravention of a peremptory norm of general international law." It has been asserted, in subsections 3.7.3 and 3.7.4 of chapter three, that the peremptory norm on the use of force only applies if it is directed against the territorial integrity or political independence of a State. Similarly it has been stated, in subsections 1.9.2 of chapter one and 2.6.1 of chapter two, that the crime of aggression can only concern armed attacks. As the subject under consideration in this chapter concerns the faculty of resort to peaceful or non-armed countermeasures, it is hard to see how resort to this faculty could be said to contravene the prohibition of the use of force against the territorial integrity or political independence of the author State. Other considerations might prevail with regard to resort to forceful or armed countermeasures. As such measures concern rather the scope of the prohibitions of the use of force under the Charter and under customary international law, discussion is postponed until chapter five.

The second hypothesis, an injured State's resort to countermeasures contravening the peremptory norm on self-determination of peoples, is also not easily envisaged. The only example that might be considered would lie with the situation sketched in subsection 3.8.2 of chapter three where a State ceded part of its territory, populated by a people claiming the right to self-determination, to another State, with transfer of the territory to be effected at a certain set time and date. If the first State would refuse to effect the transfer, it could be considered to have committed an internationally wrongful act. The latter State, superficially speaking an injured State under article 5, Part Two, might then exercise its right to resort to countermeasures to induce the author State to perform its obligation of restitution in kind (specific performance in this case). The latter State could only superficially be considered an injured State, because the agreement concluded between the two States would be void due to conflict with a peremptory norm. Therefore it would seem that (counter)measures by an "injured" State could not legitimately be resorted to, because there would not be any valid treaty, no valid obligation to effect a cession, nor any valid obligation to provide restitution in kind. As a consequence there could not exist any right to resort to countermeasures and a State having recourse thereto would breach its obligations towards the State refusing transfer. It becomes clear from this example that almost any resort to countermeasures could only indirectly conflict with a peremptory norm.

As to the peremptory norms prohibiting genocide, slavery and *apartheid*, it can be said that those could be breached by way of resort to countermeasures by an injured State. That situation might occur especially when an injured State would take countermeasures, for whatever reasons, against the nationals of the author State, for instance by killing them, imposing forced labour upon them, or by taking action discriminating against them. All these examples concern the breach of (basic) human rights of nationals of the author State. For that reason it may be appropriate to discuss the issue in the next paragraphs.

Countermeasures in contravention of human rights obligations. The Commission has proposed, in article 14, Part Two, to ban countermeasures which would involve:[223] "(d) any conduct which derogates from basic human rights;" That text reflects the observations of Arangio-Ruiz in this respect and the discussion which took place in the Commission.[224]

A first and very general remark must be made here. The whole movement for the protection of human rights started more or less with the reprisal prohibitions in the field of the protection of the victims of war and prisoners of war. Before that an arbitration tribunal had already stated, in the Naulilaa Award,[225] that reprisals are limited by the experiences of humanity. Also the Institute of International Law had laid down, in article 6, paragraph 4, of the 1934 resolution on reprisals, that States must:[226] "(...) s'abstenir de toute mesure de rigeur qui serait contraire aux lois de l'humanité et aux exigences de la conscience publique." After World War II the protection of human rights was enhanced through the Universal Declaration of Human Rights, the (European) Convention for the Protection of Human Rights and Fundamental Freedoms, the International Covenant on Civil and Political Rights, and other instruments. The whole thrust of this development has been devoted to limit the freedom of action of States with regard to their own nationals. Of course the rights contained in such instruments generally apply equally to non-nationals. As to the restriction that countermeasures should not amount to breaches of basic human rights obligations, the observation imposes itself that there is no logic whatsoever to be found in an injured State taking countermeasures affecting its own nationals. It is obvious that an author State will not feel any compulsion as a result of such measures being taken by the injured State. For that reason the question of countermeasures is relevant only to the extent that the injured State would resort to countermeasures affecting the author State's nationals.[227]

Any discussion as to whether countermeasures may affect human rights obligations should take account of the provision of article 4, paragraphs 1 and 2, of the International Covenant on Civil and Political Rights, which stipulates:

> " 1. In time of public emergency which threatens the life of the nation and the existence of which is officially proclaimed, the States Parties to the present Covenant may take measures derogating from their obligations under the present Covenant to the extent strictly required by the exigencies of the

situation, provided that such measures are not inconsistent with their other obligations under international law and do not involve discrimination solely on the ground of race, colour, sex, language, religion or social origin.

2. No derogation from articles 6, 7, 8 (paragraphs 1 and 2), 11 ,15, 16 and 18 may be made under this provision."

Prohibited derogations under paragraph 2 concern the rights to life; not to be subjected to torture or cruel, inhuman or degrading treatment or punishment; not to be held in slavery or servitude; not to be imprisoned solely on the basis of the inability to fulfil contractual obligations; not to be held guilty of acts or omissions that did not constitute criminal offences, under national or international law, at the time they were committed, and not to be imposed heavier punishment than was applicable at the time the offence was committed; to be recognized as a person before the law; and to freedom of thought, conscience and religion. Under paragraph 1 States parties obtain the right to take measures derogating from all the other obligations under the Covenant subject to the proviso that there is an officially proclaimed public emergency that threatens the life of the nation, that the measures are strictly required by reference to the exigencies of the situation, and that they do not involve discrimination. Whatever may be said with regard to countermeasures affecting the human rights of the author State's nationals as to the latter condition, there appears to be no doubt possible that resort to countermeasures would not fulfil the other conditions. Does this mean that an injured State party to the Covenant cannot exercise its right to resort to countermeasures affecting the human rights of another State party's nationals? On the basis of a very formalistic kind of argument one could assert that an injured State would be able to suspend, as a countermeasure, its obligations under article 4, and after that suspend other obligations under the Covenant. However, in light of the object and purpose of the Covenant, that appears a rather extensive interpretation of a State's competence to have recourse to countermeasures under customary international law.

A State may of course be under the obligation to take measures affecting human rights obligations by reason of a Security Council decision. In view of the operation of article 103 of the Charter such obligation of members would necessarily prevail over the obligations of States parties under the Covenant. Whether the Security Council could take just any decision to impose measures infringing the human rights of a targeted State's nationals remains to be seen (*infra* this subsection).

Within the Commission some supported the position that only resort to countermeasures affecting basic human rights would be prohibited.[228] Others were less enthusiastic, and appeared to favour a comprehensive ban on countermeasures affecting human rights.[229] The argument could be made that the Covenant does not include any reprisal prohibition. In contrast the 1949 Geneva Conventions stipulate expressly that States parties are not allowed to take reprisals against the individuals protected under the subject-matter of the Conventions.[230] The silence of the Covenant could then be interpreted to mean that resort to countermeasures affecting the human rights of an author State's nationals would not be prohibited.[231] Also there exists a certain well known interpretation rule that treaty rules may be interpreted in the light of customary international law (or "all relevant rules of international law", as article 31 of the

Vienna Convention puts it). Since there did not exist any reprisal (countermeasure) prohibitions under rules of customary international law (at least no others than those similar to the 1949 Geneva Conventions) at the time the Covenant was adopted, this would indicate the freedom left to States (parties). As the Permanent Court noted in the Lotus Case, restrictions on the independence of States cannot be presumed.[232]

For these reasons it is believed that resort to countermeasures should be possible as regards the author State's nationals. However, such resort should be restricted to human rights that are not of fundamental character. That may be deduced also from the fact that the Covenant specifically stipulates, under article 4, paragraph 2, that some "basic" human rights may not be derogated from. Arangio-Ruiz was obviously aware of this, and he noted, in this third report, as to the specific obligations for the protection of *basic* human rights, that:[233]

> "Whatever the seriousness of the violation involved, the injured State's measures could not be such as to tread upon certain fundamental principles of humanity to the detriment of the offending State's nationals in the injured State's territory: by violating, for example, their right to life, their right not to be subjected to physical or moral violence, notably to torture, slavery or any other dignity."

He also discussed the question which human rights could indeed legitimately be breached by way of countermeasure, and especially the question whether the property of the author State's nationals could be taken away.[234] At that time he did not reach any conclusion on the issue. In his fourth report he took the view that property rights did not fall under the category of basic human rights.[235] He also came to the conclusion that countermeasures could not be resorted to insofar as the core or fundamental human rights were concerned.[236] At the same time he indicated that the draft did not need to enumerate which human rights were so essential that they could not be breached as a countermeasure, since that issue was to be left to the evolution of human rights law.[237] As may be seen from the quoted article 14, sub (d), at the beginning of this subsection, the Commission, quite correctly so, has taken over Arangio-Ruiz' proposals in this respect.

On the basis of this discussion it may be said that basic human rights are: the right to life, the right to physical and psychological integrity (prohibition of torture), the right not to be subjected to cruel and degrading treatment, and possibly also the right to a fair trial. It is also possible to mention, following the Barcelona Traction Case,[238] the right not to be subjected to slavery or racial discrimination. Not to be considered basic human rights are: the right to property and the right to freedom of movement. The latter may lead to entry or leave prohibitions. As to the former, there appears to be a trend, which should be supported, that resort to countermeasures affecting the right to property of the author State's private individuals should only be of temporary character.[239] Noteworthy is that the right to property has been denied protection under both the Covenant on Civil and Political Rights and the Covenant on Economic, Social and Cultural Rights.

One can be very brief as to the question whether the Security Council could impose upon its members disrespect for the basic human rights of a targeted State's nationals. Article 24, paragraph 2, of the Charter stipulates that the Security Council, in the discharged of its duties, shall act in accordance with the purposes and principles of the United Nations. One of the purposes of the United Nations, laid down in article 1, paragraph 3, is to achieve international co-operation in "promoting and encouraging respect for human rights and for fundamental freedoms for all without distinction as to race, sex, language, or religion;" The Security Council must by virtue of these provisions respect the human rights of a targeted State's or entity's nationals. Naturally this does not mean that the Security Council could not impose any measures affecting the human rights of a targeted State's nationals. As an example one may take resolution 942, paragraph 14, in which the Security Council severely restricted the freedom of movement of Bosnian Serbs and others by ordering members not to allow the entry, into their territories, of specific categories of individuals. It may be said, generally, that an international organization can invoke the same rules as States can. The other side of that argument is, as has been noted in chapter two, that an international organization cannot engage in activities which are prohibited to its members. The Security Council, in deciding on measures under article 41, is basically limited in the same way as States are.

It is possible to be even more brief as to the question whether a relaxation of this restriction should be contemplated in case of international crimes. The answer is: certainly not. Arangio-Ruiz has quite rightly indicated that the prohibition on countermeasures involving violations of basic human rights should be applicable also in case of crimes.[240] Considering the essential background of the related developments of *jus cogens*, obligations *erga omnes* and international crimes, it would be surprising if the humanitarian goals underlying those concepts would be deserted with regard to innocent nationals of an author State of an international crime. The only other manner in which nationals of the author State can be affected through countermeasures lies with the exercise of criminal jurisdiction not ordinarily conferred on an injured State by virtue of either national or international law. Examples of such exercise may be found in the Nuremberg and Tokyo trials, and the Yugoslav and Rwandan Tribunals set up by the Security Council.

4.4.3. GENERAL RESTRICTIONS REGARDING COUNTERMEASURES

Under customary international law two conditions have traditionally been imposed regarding the injured State's exercise of its right to resort to countermeasures: the conditions of necessity and proportionality. From the temporal perspective the first condition hinges on an evaluation whether measures were necessary at the point in time at which countermeasures were resorted to. The second condition must concern an evaluation between the two basic elements involved: the internationally wrongful act(s) and the countermeasure(s).

The requirement of necessity

It should be recognized that a State should not exercise its right to resort to countermeasures unless this is necessary to achieve the object intended by such resort. From the purely theoretical point of view the existence of the internationally wrongful act alone already paves the way for the adoption of countermeasures. From the legal point

of view, considering that an author State becomes subject to the obligation to provide reparation instantaneous with the commission of its wrongful act (chapter three, subsection 3.2.1), the adoption of countermeasures would be justified straight away.
The text of article 11, paragraph 1, Part Two, adopted by the Commission perfectly illustrates the point: "As long as the State which has committed an internationally wrongful act has not complied with its obligations under Articles 6 to 10 bis, the injured State is entitled to take countermeasures, that is, subject to the conditions and restrictions set forth in articles 12, 13 and 14, not to comply with one or more of its obligations towards the State which has committed the internationally wrongful act, as necessary in the light of the response to its demands by the State which has committed the internationally wrongful act in order to induce it to comply with its obligations under articles 6 to 10 bis."
Although such non-compliance will most likely be subjected, in one way or the other, to the conditions proposed by the Drafting Committee in article 12, paragraph 1, on dispute settlement, strictly speaking the conditions of that article would seem to constitute progressive development. The arbitrators in the Air Services Agreement Award for instance came down hard in favour of the freedom of the injured State in this respect. They claimed that international law did not prohibit countermeasures during negotiation, nor while arbitral or judicial proceedings were under way.[241] That claim was restricted only by their observation that the injured State's right to initiate countermeasures might disappear if a tribunal possesses the necessary means, that is a power to indicate interim measures of protection, to achieve the objectives justifying countermeasures.[242]
Arguments in favour of an immediate right to adopt countermeasures are apparently warranted by reference to international practice. Compelling reasons nevertheless exist to moderate this doctrinal stance.

Logically one could assert that a necessity to adopt countermeasures can never be said to exist, since States are not under any obligation to exercise their rights (leaving aside Security Council decisions). Moreover, subject to any consideration of *jus cogens*, they are free to waive any right they might possess as the result of an author State's wrongful act. This logical argument fails because the injured State would not get what it wants: reparation. For that reason the requirement of necessity must be seen in relation to this objective sought to be attained by adopting countermeasures. The continued justification and necessity of countermeasures can only lie with the failure of the author State to provide reparation to the injured State(s).
In subsection 4.3.2 it was noted that an injured State should not be allowed to adopt countermeasures without it having attempted to obtain its due from the author State. It was stressed that voluntary compliance is preferable in any system of law, and that therefore the author State should be given the opportunity to comply. This required representations by the injured State regarding the circumstances and applicable legal rules and specific demands of reparation. If the author State would not deny its responsibility this might also require some negotiations. Before any such point in time resort to countermeasures should be considered inadmissible for failure to conform to the rule of necessity. Should the author State prove recalcitrant from the start, denying any responsibility, countermeasures could at once be resorted to. The only exception to

this would be the author State's co-operation, in good faith, in implementing dispute settlement. The principle of good faith in this respect would require its demonstrable genuine wish to solve the substantive dispute with the injured State. Such would not be the case if the author State would, for instance, raise objections to the jurisdiction of the tribunal or to the admissibility of the claim (insofar as those would be manifestly unfounded). As long as, and to the extent that, the author State would partake in good faith in any procedure, any necessity to take countermeasures would ordinarily have vanished.

The discussion of necessity is relevant also in regard to the powers of the Security Council under Chapter VII. The wording of articles 39, 40 and 41 of the Charter indicates a wide measure of discretion for the Security Council in deciding the kind of action necessary for the maintenance or restoration of international peace and security. Article 39, first of all, provides a choice for the Security Council: to recommend or to decide on the measures of articles 41 or 42. Secondly, the location of article 40 between articles 39 and 41 implies a further element of discretion for the Security Council, since the indication of provisional measures is possible if it considers this necessary or desirable. Yet the Security Council is not bound to call upon compliance with such measures, though it will duly take account of any failure to comply (article 40, third sentence). It could just as well go straight on to impose measures under article 41, or take action under article 42. As pointed out (subsection 4.3.2) the Security Council has also resorted to the measures of article 41 in order to put pressure on Libya to surrender two of its nationals to the United States or the United Kingdom. Libya had earlier initiated proceedings against those States before the Court. But as noted earlier the Security Council, once it determines the existence of a threat to the peace under article 39, is no longer bound to the imperative of dispute settlement under Chapter VI of the Charter.

Similarly one could assert that States reacting to international crimes could, and in fact should, not be prevented from taking countermeasures. The element of wilful intent and premeditation on the part of the author State establishes the presumption that it will not be willing either to accept or to implement in good faith any dispute settlement procedure. The example diverging from general experience in this respect constitutes the proceedings of Ethiopia and Liberia against South Africa, on the introduction of *apartheid* in Namibia, before the Court.[243] South Africa, unlike certain other States in later periods, showed up before the Court and pleaded its case fully. None of the objections it raised to the jurisdiction of the Court or the admissibility of the claims could be said to be manifestly unfounded.[244] Though this latter aspect of the cases may be said to reflect the problematical character of the Court's jurisdiction in this particular case, as well as the unfamiliarity with human rights issues at the time of conclusion of the mandate agreements. The only other example seems rather typical for the attitude of (author) States in general towards peaceful dispute settlement: the Nicaragua Case. The United States did its best to have none of its disputes with Nicaragua settled by the Court. Action comprised the filing of a reservation to its declaration under article 36, paragraph 2, of the Statute, some days before Nicaragua instituted proceedings, the filing of preliminary objections, and withdrawal from proceedings after the Court had established its jurisdiction and the admissibility of the Nicaraguan claims.[245] That is not to say that the American objections were manifestly unfounded.

In conclusion, and on the basis of the preceding arguments, it can be said that the requirement of necessity presents few difficulties in case of international crimes.

The requirement of proportionality

That a condition of proportionality applies to countermeasures adopted has been generally recognized.[246] The underlying ratio for this condition lies with the conviction that a committed internationally wrongful act may justify resort to countermeasures, but that it does not justify just any kind, any scope, or any number of measures.[247] In that sense Riphagen's proposal may be quoted, once more, that:[248] "A breach of an international obligation does not, in itself, deprive that State of its rights under international law." It might be possible to assert that countermeasures were sufficiently restricted by means of the express reprisal prohibitions. Yet that would still mean that resort to countermeasures might result in devastating effects for the author State in contrast to none, minor or moderate effects for the injured State. It is on that account that the general legal principle of proportionality is imposed as a condition for resort to countermeasures. And it is on that basis that the Commission has provisionally adopted article 13, Part Two, in the following terms:[249]

> "Any countermeasure taken by an injured State shall not be out of proportion to the degree of gravity of the internationally wrongful act and the effects thereof on the injured State."

As may be shown by this provision the whole idea of proportionality rests on a comparison between two parts of a relationship: the internationally wrongful act and the countermeasures adopted in response thereto. The only question is which elements should be taken into account in judging whether there is proportionality or whether there is disproportionality. As such have been mentioned, by Arangio-Ruiz, the wrongful act committed, the effects thereof, the injury suffered, the importance of rules infringed, and the aim of the measures adopted.[250]

A preliminary remark is that any element inherent in the wrongful act must of necessity be evaluated in relation to the same element contained in the measures adopted. Thus damage done to the injured State by reason of the wrongful act must in first instance be compared to the damage done to the author State by way of countermeasure(s). Similarly the importance of the rule under which an author State has breached its obligation should be put against the importance of the rule(s) affected by the countermeasure(s). And if one takes into account the seriousness of the wrongful acts, then the seriousness of the countermeasures must also be evaluated. Only when an element is not at the same time inherent in both parts, wrongful act and countermeasure, should one compare unequal elements.

Secondly, it may be noted that evaluating the response in relation to the wrongful act may be effected easily if the response affects the same obligations as the wrongful act: that is, when the countermeasures constitute reciprocal measures or reprisals in kind. To the extent that countermeasures concern the suspension of obligations under other rules than those initially put in question, judging the proportionality of the responding measures becomes more complicated. The Commission's formulation that countermeasures should not be "out of proportion to the degree of gravity of the internationally wrongful act and the effects thereof on the injured State" appears to be based on the fact that there often is a lack of symmetry between the wrongful acts of the author State and the measures adopted by the injured State.[251]

As yet there are no commentaries available to this provision. The terms therefore have to interpreted by reference to their natural meaning. Starting with the effects of the wrongful act on the injured State, that seems to refer to the issue of quantifiable damage, or in the words of article 8, paragraph 2, Part Two, to "any economically assessable damage". As countermeasures, in view of their object, ought to be reversible in character, the damage done to the injured State must be compared to the actual or potential damage for the author State. However, the effects of a wrongful act on the injured State need not only consist of economically assessable damage. Should a national of the injured State for instance not get the treatment due to it under international law and die as a result of that, the economically assessable damage lies with the contribution that national provided to its relatives and the injured State's economy. And, as a matter of principle, the degree of fault must be taken into account in judging an injured State's response.[252] Another consideration is that an internationally wrongful act does not necessarily have effects on the injured State. This all leads in fact to the following criterion, the element of the degree of gravity of the internationally wrongful act.

The degree of gravity of the internationally wrongful act provides the basis for two criteria.[253] First of all there may be taken into account the scale on which wrongful acts have taken place.[254] Thus for instance an isolated act of nationalization or expropriation cannot be evaluated in the same way as a full scale nationalization of complete industries. Similarly an isolated act affecting one injured State's national cannot be judged the same way as acts tending to cause damage to all of the injured State's nationals. A second criterion constitutes the degree of fault on the part of the author State. There may exist on the part of the author State mere negligence, wilful intent, or even premeditation.[255] This can be weighed also by reference to the previous criterion, namely the scale on which acts have been committed. Yet the scale is not decisive as such. That may be shown by the response of the Netherlands, suspension of its large scale development aid to Surinam, to the killing of some 15 individuals of the opposition.[256] In suspending such aid the predominant consideration was that the acts of the Surinam government could not have been accidental or negligent, but had been intentional and maybe even premeditated.

A final issue to be discussed as to the elements relevant for judging the proportionality of a response to the original wrongful act concerns the aim of the countermeasures. In that regard Arangio-Ruiz, and apparently also the Drafting Committee, was of the opinion that proportionality should not be measured:[257] "(...) on the basis of the aptness of the reaction to attain a particular aim." Whether the reaction would be apt to accomplish the aim sought to be achieved, obtaining of reparation, is something that can only be ascertained by reference to whether or not the aim is achieved. If the aim is not achieved, the reaction was apparently not apt to achieve it. If the aim is achieved, the reaction clearly was apt to obtain reparation. So judging the proportionality in relation to the aptness of the reaction might lead to a spiral of more numerous or more severe countermeasures. It appears to amount to little less than saying that the end justifies the means.

Taking into account so-called positions of principle similarly does not seem to help. The arbitrators in the Air Services Agreement Award observed that in judging the proportionality of the American response to the French acts account had to be taken of the general air transport policy of the United States as evidenced by agreements concluded by it with numerous other States.[258] There is no indication, however, that they took into account the general air transport policy of France. Surely the importance of positions of principle cannot be established in relation to one party's attitude alone.

The importance of the rules concerned, on the other hand, does provide guidance as to the proportionality of the response.[259] Establishing the importance of rules must be done by pointing to the demonstrable opinions of the international community of States. As such may count the conclusion and widespread ratification of multilateral treaties prohibiting specific conduct or derogations from standards, the elevation of certain rules to peremptory norms of general international law, as well as the recognition of certain State conduct as an international crime.

Under the Charter the Security Council has been empowered, under article 41, to decide that members shall impose measures on a recalcitrant State to give effect to its decisions. The only judge as to whether such measures are necessary, as well as apt to attain the objective of such decisions, would appear to be the Security Council itself. To the extent that it concerns itself with the enforcement of the prohibitions of the use of force, slavery, genocide and racial discrimination, denial of self-determination, and breaches of basic human rights, the criteria for judging proportionality between wrongful acts and responses thereto seem to provide more than enough leeway to justify even the imposition on a State of a complete trade embargo. Although States cannot dispute the judgment of the Security Council as to the necessity and proportionality of such embargoes by refusing to comply with their obligations under article 25, this does not necessarily mean that issues of proportionality could not be reviewed by the Court. One might wonder for instance whether the continued trade embargo towards Iraq has not, by now, reached disproportional features considering that the only remaining alleged breaches of obligation seem to be based on a perception, rather than on proof, that Iraq is not fully performing its disarmament obligations under resolution 687. An even more potent argument is that the effects of the embargo, in view of health reports on the Iraqi population, appears to be leading to intolerable impairment of the basic human rights of that population. The latter argument, however, strictly speaking does not concern proportionality.

In respect to international delicts the Commission has adopted article 14 (b), Part Two, in which it has formulated the prohibition of countermeasures that would involve:[260] "extreme economic or political coercion designed to endanger the territorial integrity or political independence of the State which has committed an internationally wrongful act;" It is not clear what is meant by political coercion and to what extent such coercion could jeopardize the territorial integrity or political independence of States. Resort to extreme economic measures, on the other hand, might have the effect of threatening the territorial integrity or political independence of a State. Yet it is not quite obvious that this prohibition ought to be formulated in the context of international delicts. Because any conduct likely to have such effects, adopted in response to an international delict, will amount to disproportional, and hence unlawful, countermeasures. To the extent that such coercion would not consist of countermeasures but in acts of retortion, it is somewhat doubtful that it would be unlawful. Generally States are not under any obligation to engage in trade with other States, or to continue to provide voluntary development aid to them.[261] Furthermore, a threat to the territorial integrity or political independence of a State could only come about if that State would be almost exclusively dependent on the State resorting to coercion, or if coercion is effectively resorted to by a great number of States. If such coercion consists of acts of retortion and is singularly directed towards the goal of having the target State perform its reparation obligations, there also would not be any breach of the prohibition of intervention.

Could the same, disproportionality, be asserted if extreme economic coercion would be adopted in response to an international crime? Arangio-Ruiz stated that in relation to crimes one might conceive of attenuation regarding the admissibility of extreme economic or political measures, measures affecting the independence, sovereignty, or domestic jurisdiction, measures affecting third States, and punitive measures.[262] In his latest report he indicated that the prohibition of extreme economic coercion should remain applicable in case of crimes.[263] If all such measures could be resorted to, the question would arise whether this would still conform to any traditional conception or applicable standard of proportionality. Obviously extreme economic coercion might be out of proportion, from a quantitative point of view, even in response to an international crime. Yet taking into account the degree of gravity of the wrongful acts, the fault on the part of the author State, and the importance of the rules concerned, which have all been elevated to the rank of *jus cogens*, one would have to claim that even the application of extreme economic coercion would not be disproportional.

Moreover, the formulation of article 14 (b), Part Two, adopted by the Commission stipulates that the coercion must be "designed" to threaten the territorial integrity or political independence of the targeted State. Yet, as shown in chapter three, the general rule is that reparation does not include any obligation to cede territory to other States. Nor should it lead to a loss of political independence in the sense that one or more States would dominate the author State. Countermeasures must, as noted in section 4.2, be instrumental in obtaining reparation. The adoption of countermeasures intended to pressure the author State of an international crime to provide guarantees against repetition, such as the introduction of military, political, and humanitarian safeguards under domestic law, would not be precluded.

4.5. Summary

The goal to be attained by an injured State having resort to countermeasures is to ensure the performance by the author State of its substitute reparation obligations.

Furthermore, international law does not know of any power to impose punishment. Even satisfaction and guarantees against repetition do not constitute punishment, but relate to the prevention and deterrence of wrongful acts generally. Factually a State resorting to countermeasures may do so with an intent to punish. However, such intent can be proved only to the extent that the measures resorted to go beyond that which is necessary to obtain reparation or if they are disproportional to the wrongful act.

Resort to countermeasures is therefore intended to coerce the author State into performing its reparation obligations. However, the author State is not under any obligation, unlike the situation under domestic law, to put up with countermeasures. It is allowed to evade the effect of such measures, for instance through third or other injured States. The latter are only inhibited from providing aid and assistance to the extent that they have knowledge that it will be used for the commission of further wrongful acts. In case of crimes injured States should generally not provide aid or assistance, *e.g.* arms, which can be used to sustain the commission of the crime.

International responsibility is collective in character, and the burden of countermeasures, more than that of reparation, will be felt especially by the nationals of the author State. However, even the most comprehensive trade embargo decided on by the Security Council will affect the well-off and the rich, groups that are influential within the State organization, the least and the latest.

An internationally wrongful act of an author State should not be considered a circumstance precluding the wrongfulness of measures adopted by the injured State. Rather it should be considered to justify the non-performance of obligations and a corresponding impossibility of the author State to invoke the injured State's responsibility. Other States suffering from the breach of obligation could still invoke the responsibility of the original injured State. In view of the correlation between rights and obligations (chapter one), there is also no need to define countermeasures as involving a denial of a right of the author State. It ought to be recognized further that countermeasures do not constitute exceptional measures, but that they can be resorted to, generally, against States that have committed a wrongful act.

The prime precondition for an injured State's or the Security Council's recourse to countermeasures is to be found in the commission of an internationally wrongful act. As all States are injured States in case of the commission of an international crime, all States will be entitled to resort to countermeasures against the author State. Any resort to countermeasures, whether by an injured State or by the Security Council, is based on a presumption that a wrongful act has been committed. If that presumption is rebutted an injured State or the United Nations will have incurred responsibility for a non-justifiable breach of obligation.

Generally an injured State is not under any obligation to resort to dispute settlement procedures prior to any recourse to countermeasures. However, its right to adopt countermeasures will be suspended if the author State acknowledges its responsibility and offers reparation, or if it proposes resort to, and co-operates in good faith with, binding dispute settlement procedures. The Security Council is likewise, as a matter of Charter interpretation, not under any obligation to refrain from adopting measures under article 41 prior to dispute settlement by the parties to the dispute. With regard to international crimes it may be said that an injured State's right to resort to countermeasures will not be suspended upon an author State's verbal recognition of responsibility, nor upon an offer to have recourse to a binding dispute settlement procedure.

Recommendations of the General Assembly or the Security Council cannot justify the adoption of measures which a State could not lawfully take itself as an injured State. The Security Council's recourse to the measures of article 41 of the Charter must furthermore be preceded by a determination of a threat to the peace, breach of the peace, or act of aggression under article 39, and must be aimed at the maintenance or restoration of international peace and security.

No restriction ensues regarding resort to countermeasures because there would not be any specially affected States in case of breaches of human rights obligations. The presence of a directly injured State in case of the crime of aggression entails the restriction that countermeasures by other injured States can only be resorted to if there is a declaration of armed attack and a request to take such measures. The fact that the Security Council has adopted measures under article 41 in response to an international crime does not restrict the injured States from adopting any or more far-reaching countermeasures. Only a decision of the Security Council to refrain from adopting measures impairs the right to adopt countermeasures.

Resort to countermeasures may be excluded due to the existence of a treaty régime. Under diplomatic law countermeasures are excluded which deny the immunity of diplomats, consular agents, or the inviolability of the premises. Under human rights law countermeasures cannot be adopted in denial of fundamental or basic human rights. It is possible, however, under the law of the GATT/WTO to adopt countermeasures affecting obligations under the GATT/WTO. No provision in the Charter prevents States from adopting countermeasures in response to either a delict or a crime.

Due to the existence of wilful intent and premeditation on the part of the author State the requirement of necessity does not present any difficulties in case of international crimes. It is not to be expected that the author State will, in good faith, co-operate with attempts to have any dispute on its responsibility and reparation obligations settled. In the light of the various elements which may be taken into account for judging the proportionality of countermeasures adopted in response to an internationally wrongful act, the requirement of proportionality would not appear to pose any problems in case of crimes. Those elements include the degree of gravity (scale of the acts, effects, damage or injury done), degree of fault (negligence, wilful intent, or premeditation), and the importance of the rules (established by reference to widespread ratifications of multilateral treaties, elevation to the rank of peremptory norm, and recognition of conduct as an international crime).

The Commission in its commentary to article 1, Part One, mentioned the possibility that the new responsibility relationship might give injured States or other subjects the right to apply a sanction to the author State. That possibility has formed the subject of the present chapter. It may be noted that the Commission did not address the issue whether that relationship might also lead to the use of armed force by an injured State or another subject against an author State. However, it is precisely this issue that lies at the basis of article 34, Part One, on self-defence as a circumstance precluding wrongfulness. The following chapter will therefore address the question whether an injured State or the United Nations could resort to armed force against a State which has committed an international crime.

NOTES

[1] Text and Commentary Article 1, Part One, YBILC 1973, volume II, pp. 173-176, 175.

[2] On reprisals see Venezia, J.-C., La notion des représailles en droit international public, 64 RGDIP 1960, pp. 465-498; Akehurst, M., Reprisals by Third States, 44 BYBIL 1970, pp. 1-18; Bowett, D., Economic Coercion and Reprisals by States, 13 VJIL 1972, pp. 1-12; Tomuschat, C., Repressalie und Retorsion, Zu einigen Aspekten ihrer innerstaatlichen Durchführung, 33 ZAORV 1973, pp. 179-222; Onuf, N., Reprisals, Rituals, Rules, Rationales, Center of International Studies, Princeton University, 1974; Malanczuk, P., Zur Repressalie im Entwurf der International Law Commission zur Staatenverantwortlichkeit, 45 ZAORV 1985, pp. 293-323; Doehring, K., Die Selbstdurchsetzung völkerrechtliche Verpflichtungen, Einige Einzelprobleme der Repressalie, 47 ZAORV 1987, pp. 44-55.

[3] Ago, R., Eighth report on State responsibility, YBILC 1979, Volume II, Part One, pp. 3-66, 39-47. He does not offer any explanation for this change of name, though it may be noted that he examines the arbitral practice on reprisals and uses the latter term on a number of occasions.

[4] Text and Commentary Article 30, Part One, YBILC 1979, Volume II, Part Two, pp. 115-122, 121. See on sanctions Ruzié, D., Organisations internationales et sanctions internationales, Librairie Armand Colin, Paris, 1971; Leben, C., Les sanctions privatives de droits ou de qualité dans les organisations internationales spécialisées, Recherches sur les sanctions internationales et l'évolution du droit des gens, Établissements Émile Bruylant, Bruxelles, 1979; Osieke, E., Sanctions in International Law: The Contributions of International Organizations, 31 NILR 1984, pp. 183-198.

[5] Commentary Article 30, Part One, 115.

[6] Stressed also by some members of the Commission participating in the 1992 debate on countermeasures. Bennouna, YBILC 1992, Volume I, 80; implicitly Tomuschat, *ibid.*, 85; Güney, *ibid.*, 132; Al-Baharna, *ibid.*, 168; Mahiou, *ibid.*, 173-174; Razafindralambo, *ibid.*, 176.

[7] Proposed articles 8 and 9, Part Two, in Riphagen, W., Fifth report on the content, forms and degrees of international responsibility (part 2 of the draft articles), YBILC 1984, Volume II, Part One, pp. 1-4, 3; Commentaries, in Sixth report on the content, forms and degrees of international responsibility (part 2 of the draft articles); and "Implementation" (*mise en oeuvre*) of international responsibility and settlement of disputes (part 3 of the draft articles), YBILC 1985, Volume II, Part One, pp. 3-19, 10-11. See also Fourth report on the content, forms and degrees of international responsibility (part 2 of the draft articles), Volume II, Part One, pp. 3-24, 17-21.

[8] Arangio-Ruiz, G., Preliminary Report on State Responsibility, 18 May 1988, A/CN.4/416, 34 pp., 25-26, footnote 8.

[9] Arangio-Ruiz, YBILC 1992, volume I, 69 and 129.

[10] As may be seen from article 11 proposed by Arangio-Ruiz, G., Fourth Report on State Responsibility, 12 May 1992, A/CN.4/444, 40 pp., 40; and article 11 proposed by the Drafting Committee, 5 EJIL 1994, pp. 118-119.

[11] Commentary Article 30, Part One, 115-122.

[12] Arangio-Ruiz, Fourth Report, 40; Drafting Committee, 5 EJIL 1994, 118-119.

[13] Root, E., The Outlook for International Law, 10 AJIL 1916, pp. 1-11; Peaslee, A., The Sanction of International Law, 10 AJIL 1916, pp. 328-336; Morgenthau, H., Theorie des sanctions internationales, 62 RDILC 1935, pp. 474-503 and 809-836; Rousseau, C., L'application des sanctions contre l'Italie et le droit international, 63 RDILC 1936, pp. 5-64; Kunz, J., Sanctions in International Law, 54 AJIL 1960, pp. 324-347; Valki, L., Does International Law Contain Sanctions?, Annales Universitatis Scientiarum Budapestinensis de Rolando Eötvös nominatae, Separatum, Sectio Iuridica, Tomus XXI, 1979, pp. 255-275; Leben, C., Les contre-mesures inter-étatiques et les réactions à l'illicite dans la société internationale, 28 AFDI 1982, pp. 9-77; Zemanek, K., Die völkerrechtliche Verantwortlichkeit und die Sanktionen des Völkerrechts, in Neuhold, H. (Ed.), Österreichisches Handbuch des Völkerrechts, volume 1, Wien, 1983, pp. 368-388; Kooijmans, P., Actie, harde actie: Enkele opmerkingen over de volkenrechtelijke toelaatbaarheid van eenzijdige sanctiemaatregelen, 37 IS 1983, pp. 771-777; Zoller, E., Quelques réflexions sur les contre-mesures en droit international public, in Études offertes à Claude-Albert Colliard, Droit et libertés à la fin du xxe siècle, 1984, pp. 361-381; Guttry, A., Some Recent Cases of Unilateral Countermeasures and the Problem of their Lawfulness in International Law, 7 IYIL 1986-1987, pp. 169-189.

[14] Kuyper, P., Sanctions against Rhodesia, The EEC and the Implementation of General International Legal Rules, 12 CMLR 1975, pp. 231-244; Schröder, M., Wirtschaftssanktionen der Europäischen Gemeinschaften gegenüber Drittstaaten, dagestellt am Beispiel des Iranembargos, 23 GYIL 1980, pp. 111-125; Petersmann, E., Internationale Wirtschaftssanktionen als Problem des Völkerrecht und des Europarechts, 80 ZVR 1981, pp. 1-28; Kuyper, P., Community Sanctions against Argentina: Lawfulness under Community and Interna-

tional Law, in O'Keeffe, D., and Schermers, H. (Eds.), Essays in European Law and Integration, Kluwer, Deventer, 1982, pp. 141-166; Dewost, J.-L., La Communauté, les dix, et les «sanctions» économiques: De la crise Iranienne à la crise des Malouines, 28 AFDI 1982, pp. 215-232; Meng, W., Die Kompetenz der EWG zur Verhängung von Wirtschaftssanktionen gegen Drittländer, 42 ZAORV 1982, pp. 780-803; Kißler, K.-P., Die Zulässigkeit von Wirtschaftssanktionen der Europäischen Gemeinschaft gegenüber Drittstaaten, Verlag Peter Lang, Frankfurt am Main, 1984, especially 92-99 and 179-185; Verhoeven, J., Sanctions internationales et Communautes Europeennes, A propos de l'affaire des îles Falkland (Malvinas), 19 CDE 1984, pp. 259-290.

[15] It may be noted that the Charter itself does not contain any reference to the word "sanctions". The 1945 Charter of the United Nations, 39 AJIL 1945, Supplement, pp. 190-215.

[16] There is only one other Charter provision, article 94, paragraph 2, concerning measures to give effect to judgments of the Court, that authorizes the Security Council to decide upon sanctions.

[17] Commentary Article 30, Part One, 121. Ago, Eighth Report, 44.

[18] Commentary Article 30, Part One, 121.

[19] Commentary Article 30, Part One, 121.

[20] Arangio-Ruiz, G., Third Report on State Responsibility, 19 July 1991, A/CN.4/440, 46 pp., 13-15.

[21] The 1969 Vienna Convention on the Law of Treaties, 63 AJIL 1969, pp. 875-903.

[22] Simma, B., Reflections on Article 60 of the Vienna Convention on the Law of Treaties and Its Background in General International Law, 20 OZOR 1970, pp. 5-83, 8, 15, 59-60. Inconclusive Mazzeschi, R., Termination and Suspension of Treaties for Breach in the ILC Works on State Responsibility, in Spinedi, M., and Simma, B. (Eds.), United Nations Codification of State Responsibility, Oceana Publications, Inc., New York, 1987, pp. 57-94, 83.

[23] See Arangio-Ruiz, Third Report, 4-6; and also Third Report on State Responsibility, 19 July 1991, A/CN.4/440/Add.1, 25 pp., 8-16; Fourth Report on State Responsibility, 1 June 1992, A/CN.4/444/Add.1, 37 pp., 5-16; Fifth Report on State Responsibility, 24 June 1993, A/CN.4/453/Add.3, 36 pp., 7-9. Note draft article 14 (a), Part Two, in Fourth Report, 34; and Drafting Committee's article 14 (a), 5 EJIL 1994, 118-119.

[24] Arangio-Ruiz, Fourth Report, 2-5.

[25] Note Arangio-Ruiz' division of responsibility consequences into substantive and instrumental consequences. Arangio-Ruiz, Preliminary Report, 5 and 9; and Third Report, 1.

[26] Case concerning the Factory at Chorzów (Claim for Indemnity) (The Merits), Publications PCIJ, 1928, Series A, No. 17, p. 4, 47.

[27] Arangio-Ruiz, Fourth Report, 2. Footnote omitted. He went on to consider issues of punishment and punitive intent, on which see next subsection.

[28] Arangio-Ruiz, Fourth Report, 3. Stein (Ted), Observations on "Crimes of States", in Weiler, J., Cassese, A., and Spinedi, M. (Eds.), International Crimes of State: A Critical Analysis of the ILC's Draft Article 19 on State Responsibility, Walter de Gruyter, Berlin, 1989, pp. 194-200, 195, asserted: "(...) countermeasures that are purely punitive in function are excluded even in response to a crime of State."

[29] C.f. Malanczuk, P., Countermeasures and Self-Defence as Circumstances Precluding Wrongfulness in the International Law Commission's Draft Articles on State Responsibility, 43 ZAORV 1983, pp. 705-812, 721.

[30] Text Article 11, Part Two, in Report of the International Law Commission on the work of its forty-sixth session, 2 May – 22 July 1994, General Assembly, Official Records, Forty-ninth Session, Supplement No. 10 (A/49/10), p. 365, footnote 362. Based on a text proposed by the Drafting Committee, 5 EJIL 1994, 118-119. Arangio-Ruiz' very similar proposal ran: "An injured State whose demands under articles 6 to 10 have not met with adequate response from the State which has committed the internationally wrongful act is entitled, subject to the conditions and restrictions set forth in the following articles, not to comply with one or more of its obligations towards the said State." Arangio-Ruiz, Fourth Report, 40.

[31] Arangio-Ruiz, Fourth Report, 3-4.

[32] Commentary Article 30, Part One, 116. Ago, Eighth Report, 39.

[33] Indeed, as has been noted in chapter three, subsection 3.6.3, a rule providing for the imposition of damages reflecting the gravity of the infringement of rights has been proposed by the Commission. But such a rule has not been laid down in positive international law, and should be rejected as a matter of progressive development, because it would amount to unjust enrichment for the injured State.

[34] Arangio-Ruiz, Fourth Report, 3-4, and footnote 7.

[35] Arangio-Ruiz, Fourth Report, 5. Underlining in the original. Also quite rightly he rejects the elaboration *de lege ferenda*, of such a rule in the draft articles.

[36] Austin, J., Lectures on Jurisprudence or the Philosophy of Positive Law, volume 1, (Reprint of Fifth Edition, Revised and Edited by Campbell, R., John Murray, Albemarle Street, London, 1885, Originally Printed 1832), Verlag Detlev Auvermann KG, Glashütten im Taumus, 1972, 87-88, and also 96-100.

[37] Austin, Lectures on Jurisprudence, 452-457.

[38] Arbitrage entre le Portugal et l'Allemagne, Sentence arbitrale du 30 juin 1930 (de Meuron, Fazy, Guex), Affaire Cysne, in United Nations, RIAA, volume II, Sijthoff, Leyden, 1949, pp. 1037-1077, 1077.

[39] C.f. Boutros-Ghali, B., Supplement to An Agenda for Peace, Position Paper of the Secretary-General on the Occasion of the Fiftieth Anniversary of the United Nations, 3 January 1995, S/1995/1, paragraph 66, who states as to the legal basis of article 41 measures: "(...) the purpose of sanctions is to modify the behaviour of a party that is threatening international peace and security and not to punish or otherwise exact retribution." See also paragraph 68. And Combacau, J., Le pouvoir de sanction de l'O.N.U., Étude théorique de la coercition non militaire, Editions A. Pedone, Paris, 1974, 18; Zoller, E., Peacetime Unilateral Remedies: An Analysis of Countermeasures, Transnational Publishers, Inc., Dobbs Ferry, New York, 1984, 105-108.

[40] Commentary Article 1, Part One, 178. Ago, R., Second report on State responsibility, YBILC 1970, Volume II, pp. 177-197, 182-183. Note also Commentary Article 30, Part One, 116: "The countermeasures with which this article is concerned are measures the object of which is, by definition, to inflict punishment or to secure performance (...)". A little bit later on it goes on to say: "A measure such as the application of economic reprisals, for example, involves no use of force, but its object is nonetheless to punish the perpetrator of an internationally wrongful act, (...)." Ago, Eighth Report, 39.

[41] *E.g.* Kelsen, H., Principles of International Law, Rinehart & Company Inc., New York, 1952 (Third Printing 1959), 4: "The use of physical force ensues if the application of the sanction meets with resistance." It may be noted that Kelsen similarly confuses the idea of punishment with physical compulsion, as he states (*ibid.*, 5): "Punishment is forcible deprivation of life – capital punishment; or forcible deprivation of freedom – imprisonment; or forcible deprivation of property – fine." Further on, however, he notes (*ibid.*, 117): "Even if an international delict – as, for instance, resort to an illegal war – is sometimes called a 'crime,' the collective responsibility of the state for such delict is not a criminal responsibility, because reprisals and war have not the specific character of punishment." Footnote omitted.

[42] Kelsen, Principles, 4-5, observes with regard to individuals: "In order to induce individuals to a certain conduct, an authority may threaten them with an evil to be forcibly inflicted upon them in case they act contrarily. The threatened evil consists of depriving men of certain possessions, such as life, freedom, property, or other values. (...) The threatened evil we call a sanction. (...) Such sanctions have the character of acts of coercion; for they are to be carried out against the will of those subject to the order, by the employment of physical force, if necessary. The use of physical force ensues if the application of the sanction meets with resistance, which is only exceptionally the case where the authority applying the sanction has sufficient power. (...) Only if the employment of physical force is admissible we speak of a sanction as of a coercive act or enforcement action."

[43] Arangio-Ruiz, Preliminary Report, 5.

[44] Kelsen, H., Unrecht und Unrechtsfolge im Völkerrecht, Verlag von Julius Springer, Wien, 1932 (Reprint from 12 ZOR 1932); and Kelsen, Principles, 18-64.

[45] Kelsen, Principles, 3-5.

[46] Kelsen, Unrecht, 88-128; Principles, 23-33.

[47] Kelsen, Principles, 115-116.

[48] Barcelona Traction, Light and Power Company, Limited, Judgment, ICJ Reports 1970, p. 3, 32.

[49] Secretary-General Boutros-Ghali observed in relation to sanctions by the Security Council: "They raise the ethical question of whether suffering inflicted on vulnerable groups in the target country is a legitimate means of exerting pressure on political leaders whose behaviour is unlikely to be affected by the plight of their subjects." Position Paper, paragraph 70.

[50] Take for instance the suspension of development aid to Surinam by the Netherlands after the killing of a number of journalists in 1981. See Lindemann, H.-H., Die Auswirkungen der Menschenrechtsverletzungen in Surinam zwischen den Niederlanden und Surinam, 44 ZAORV 1984, pp. 64-93; and Vierdag, E., Spanningen tussen recht en praktijk in het verdragenrecht, in Mededelingen NVIR 1989, pp. 3-87, 74-87.

[51] See basic resolutions 661 on Iraq; 757 on Serbia and Montenegro; and 841 on Haiti.

[52] Generally Ago, Eighth Report, 27-30; and Commentary Circumstances Precluding Wrongfulness, YBILC 1979, Volume II, Part Two, pp. 106-109.

[53] Respectively Ago, Eighth Report, 30-39, 39-47, 47-66 for consent, countermeasures, *force majeure* and fortuitous events; and Ago, R., Addendum to the eighth report on State responsibility, YBILC 1980, Volume II, Part One, pp. 1-70, 14-51, 51-70 for state of necessity and self-defence.

[54] Ago, Eighth Report, 27.

[55] Ago, Eighth Report, 30.

[56] With regard to countermeasures the Commission has used the phrases to the effect that "the obligation is rendered inoperative" and "the obligation is set aside", and it concluded "hence the obligation is not breached". Commentary Article 30, Part One, 116.

[57] Text and Commentary Article 35, Part One, YBILC 1980, Volume II, Part Two, pp. 61-62.

[58] Those who argue in favour of the imposition of punitive damages would not object to the liquidation of funds, but as noted in chapter three, subsection 3.6.3, punitive damages are not admitted under international law. Furthermore, even punitive damages would be part of the law on reparation and would have to be agreed upon between the injured and author States.

[59] Riphagen, Fifth Report, 3. Riphagen's commentary to articles 8 and 9 does not elaborate on this choice of words. Riphagen, Sixth Report, 10-11. Nor was the incompatibility of his choice of words with Ago's terminology commented upon in the discussions following his fifth and sixth reports.

[60] Arangio-Ruiz, Fourth Report, 40; Drafting Committee, 5 EJIL 1994, 118-119.

[61] The commentary testifies to the idea that the circumstances later to be described in Chapter V, Part One, preclude the wrongfulness rather than the responsibility of the injured State. Commentary Article 1, Part One, 176.

[62] Commentary Circumstances Precluding Wrongfulness, 107. Also Ago, Eighth Report, 28-29.

[63] Military and Paramilitary Activities in and against Nicaragua (Nicaragua *v.* United States of America, Merits, Judgment, ICJ Reports 1986, p. 14, 147-148.

[64] Dissenting Opinion Schwebel, Nicaragua Case, Merits, 378-381. The justifying ground of self-defence could only be deduced from his text, it was not invoked explicitly. See also Dissenting Opinion Oda, *ibid.*, 214, where he explained that his decision to vote against operative paragraph 8 (and he was the only one to vote against) was due to the fact that a decision by the Court on a breach of obligations *erga omnes* was out of place in the judgment.

[65] This example mentioned by Ago illustrates the point: "But what happens if, in the legitimate application by State A of a sanction against State B, the action of A has the effect of infringing the rights of State C? (...) There is no doubt that the existence of the earlier wrongful act by State B may preclude the wrongfulness of A's reaction towards B, it cannot, however, in any way preclude the wrongfulness of the injury caused to C in connection with this reaction." Ago, Eighth Report, 45. He went on to discuss the Cysne Award. *Ibid.*, 45-47.

[66] The Cysne Award, 1057. Emphasis in the original.

[67] Commentary Article 30, Part One, 116. Ago, Eighth Report, 39.

[68] Arangio-Ruiz, Third Report, 8.

[69] Commentary Article 30, Part One, 119. Ago, Eighth Report, 43-44.

[70] Arangio-Ruiz, Third Report, 10. The intrinsically lawful character of acts of retortion nevertheless does not stand in the way of considering possible restrictions. *Ibid.*, 9-10.

[71] Commentary Article 30, Part One, 115. On the next page the Commission observed: "(...) the 'measures' considered here always involve action which under different conditions (...) would represent a breach of an international obligation and the infringement of another's subjective right."

[72] Commentary Circumstances Precluding Wrongfulness, 109. Emphasis added. Also Commentary Article 30, Part One, 116 and 120. Observe that Vereshchetin agreed with the special rapporteur that: "(...) countermeasures could only be justified in very few cases." YBILC 1992, Volume I, 73; and Güney, *ibid.*, 132-133.

[73] Kelsen, Principles, 5.

[74] Kelsen, Principles, 6-7.

[75] Kelsen, Principles, 7.

[76] Commentary Article 30, Part One, 116.

[77] On preconditions see draft articles 11 and 12, Part Two, proposed by Arangio-Ruiz, Fourth Report, 40; and his introduction of his fourth report in YBILC 1992, Volume I, 126-128.

[78] Kelsen, Principles, 25 as regards reprisals; 34 on war; and most explicit, 13, by reference to the force monopoly under national law. One may note, however, that he refers to the "usual" definition (without indicating approval or disapproval) of reprisals as being exceptionally permitted. *Ibid.*, 23.

[79] Note Arbitrage entre le Portugal et l'Allemagne, Sentence arbitral du 31 juillet 1928 (de Meuron, Fazy, Geux), Responsabilité de l'incident de Naulilaa, in United Nations, RIAA, volume II, pp. 1013-1033, 1027: "La première condition – *sine qua non* – du droit d'exercer des répresailles est un *motif* fourni par un acte préalable, contraire au droit des gens." Emphasis in the original. The Cysne Award, 1056-1057, repeated that stance. In agreement also Elagab, O., The Legality of Non-Forcible Counter-Measures in International Law, Clarendon Press, Oxford, 1988, 47-51 and 52-55.

[80] Arangio-Ruiz, Fourth Report, 40; Drafting Committee, 5 EJIL 1994, 118-119; discussion reported in YBILC 1992, Volume I, 69-91, 126-181, and 185-190; and Commission Report 1994, 365, footnote 362.

[81] Commission Report 1994, 365, footnote 362; originally Drafting Committee, 5 EJIL 1994, 118-119. Delbrück has argued that in cases where a State reacts to the breach of an obligation *erga omnes* and the reaction would constitute a breach of obligation towards a third State, that should not lead to the conclusion that the countermeasure is unlawful *vis-à-vis* that third State. That conclusion is based on the fact that the third State

is interested in, or even obliged to support, the enforcement measure. Delbrück, J., International Economic Sanctions and Third States, 30 ADV 1992, pp. 86-100, 95-96. See also Reed, K., Reviving the Doctrine of Non-Forcible Countermeasures: Resolving the Effect of Third Party Injuries, 29 VJIL 1988, pp. 175-209.

82 The Air Services Agreement Award appeared to support that position. Case concerning the Air Services Agreement of 27 March 1946, United States *v.* France, Arbitral Tribunal (Riphagen, Ehrlich, Reuter), 9 December 1978, 54 ILR 1979, pp. 303-349, 336. Discussed by Arangio-Ruiz, Third Report, 18-19. See also his Fourth Report, 2; and also Elagab, The Legality, 47-51. The question whether resort to countermeasures is possible with regard to minor breaches should be answered in the affirmative. C.f. Elagab, *ibid.*, 51-52. The question whether there is any room under international law for resort to anticipatory countermeasures should be answered in the negative. C.f. Elagab, *ibid.*, 52-55.

83 Commentary Circumstances Precluding Wrongfulness, 107.

84 C.f. Graefrath, B., Ausschluß der Völkerrechtswidrigkeit – Selbstverteidigung – Sanktion, in Durchsetzungsprobleme des Völkerrechts, Wissenschaftliche Schriftenreihe der Humboldt-Universität, Berlin, 1983, pp. 13-26, 25; and Cassese, A., La Communaute internationale et le genocide, in Le droit au service de la paix, de la justice et du développement, Mélanges Michel Virally, Éditions A. Pedone, Paris, 1991, pp. 183-194, 186-187, in relation to the crime of genocide. Some base the right to adopt countermeasures in case of armed attacks on the idea that who can do more, can do less. Kuyper, P., Community Sanctions, 162; and Frowein, J., Die Verpflichtungen *erga omnes* im Völkerrecht und ihre Durchsetzung, in Völkerrecht als Rechtsordnung, Internationale Gerichtsbarkeit, Menschenrechte, Festschrift für Hermann Mosler, Springer-Verlag, Berlin, 1983, pp. 241-262, 254 and 258.

85 Arangio-Ruiz, G., Seventh Report on State Responsibility, 24 May 1995, A/CN.4/469/Add.1, 4 pp., 2. Malanczuk, Countermeasures and Self-Defence, 747 (more broadly 742-747), claims that measures can only lawfully be adopted on the basis of an authorization of an international institution. Cassese, A., International Law in a Divided World, Clarendon Press, Oxford, 1986, 244, asserts that measures, to be legitimate, must rest upon an authoritative pronouncement by a representative body. In a similar sense Quigley, J., The International Law Commission's Crime-Delict Distinction: A Toothless Tiger?, 66 RDISDP 1988, pp. 117-161, 150; and Dupuy, P.-M., Implications of the Institutionalization of International Crimes of States, in Weiler *et al*, International Crimes, pp. 170-185, 182-183.

86 Arangio-Ruiz, Seventh Report, Addendum 1, 3.

87 Arangio-Ruiz, Seventh Report on State Responsibility, 9 May 1995, A/CN.4/469, 49 pp., 17.

88 Arangio-Ruiz, Seventh Report, 20-21; article 17, paragraph 1, in Seventh Report, Addendum 1, 2.

89 Commented upon in Hoogh, A. de, Comments, in Post, H. (Ed.), International Economic Law and Armed Conflict, Martinus Nijhoff Publishers, Dordrecht, 1994, pp. 43-46. See generally the interesting studies of Gross, L., States as Organs of International Law and the Problem of Autointerpretation, in Lipsky, A. (Ed.), Law and Politics in the World Community, Essays on Hans Kelsen's Pure Theory and Related Problems in International Law, University of California Press, Berkely, 1953, pp. 59-89 and 336-351 (notes); and Cheng, B., Flight from justiciable to auto-interpretative international law: From the Jay Treaty to the Schultz letter, in Liber Amicorum Elie van Bogaert, Kluwer rechtswetenschappen, Antwerpen, 1985, pp. 1-18.

90 C.f. Leben, Les sanctions privatives, 41-44, who argues that countermeasures cannot be considered "sanctions", though subjectively they might constitute reactions against wrongful acts.

91 Kelsen for instance observes that: "It is, however, possible that in a concrete case the obligation to make reparation, stipulated *in abstracto* by general international law, cannot come into existence. For an obligation to make reparation exists only if an international delict has been committed, and there is, under general international law, no objective authority, especially no court, competent to ascertain the existence of a delict. This function is left by general international law to the states concerned. Consequently a state may consider itself to be under an obligation to make reparation only if it admits that is has committed a delict; that is to say, if there is an agreement of the states concerned in this respect, and such agreement might not be reached. Even if it has been reached, it does not suffice to establish the concrete obligation to make reparation. The state responsible for a delict is not obliged to comply with any unilateral demand for reparation made by the injured State." Kelsen, Principles, 21.

92 Oddly enough Kelsen seems to hold inconsequential positions on reparation and sanctions. He observes (quoted in previous note) that a State may consider itself not to be under any obligation to repair the damage unless it admits that it has committed a delict. At the same time he stipulates the existence of a delict as condition for the application of a sanction. On the one hand therefore a State has to admit to having committed a delict for purposes of reparation, while on the other hand an injured State may apply a sanction to a State irrespective of its having admitted committing a delict. Kelsen, Principles, 20-23.

[93] Kelsen, Principles, 22, notes with regard to the necessity of unilateral enforcement by States: "For this legal community, constituted by general international law, being completely decentralized, has no special organs for the creation and application of the law."

[94] Arangio-Ruiz, Fourth Report, 2.

[95] Arangio-Ruiz, Fourth Report, 2; and Hoogh, Comments, 45.

[96] As Arangio-Ruiz, Fourth Report, 2, observes, a good faith belief of another State's wrongful conduct may be taken into consideration in determining the degree of responsibility incurred by a State's wrongful resort to (counter)measures.

[97] Arangio-Ruiz, Seventh Report, 26.

[98] A contrary conclusion might be reached on the basis of an interpretation of article 42. This provision foresees action by the military forces of members which might be seen as breaches of obligation under article 2, paragraphs 3 and 4, of the Charter. However, any such action is not action by members, but action by the Security Council. And the prohibitions under article 2, paragraphs 3 and 4, apply to members, not to the United Nations itself.

[99] Dissenting Opinion Weeramantry, Questions of Interpretation and Application of the 1971 Montreal Convention arising from the Aerial Incident at Lockerbie (Libyan Arab Jamahiriya *v.* United Kingdom), Provisional Measures, Order, ICJ Reports 1992, p. 3, 67.

[100] Lockerbie Case, Provisional Measures, 15. The Court's order seems to give precedence to the obligations (established under resolution 748) over the rights of Libya: "(...) the rights claimed by Libya under the Montreal Convention cannot now be regarded as appropriate for protection by the indication of provisional measures." And it added (*ibid.*): "(...) an indication of the measures requested by Libya would be likely to impair the rights which appear prima facie to be enjoyed by the United Kingdom by virtue of Security Council resolution 748 (1992);" These United Kingdom rights amount to the negation of its obligations to respect Libya's exercise of rights under the Montreal Convention.

[101] Note the remarks of Gowlland-Debbas, V., Security Council Enforcement Action and Issues of State Responsibility, 43 ICLQ 1994, pp. 55-98, 78, in this respect.

[102] Note that Kelsen, Principles, 46, with respect to article 41 of the Charter, observes: "The enforcement measures not involving the use of armed force have the technical character of reprisals."

[103] Commentary Article 30, Part One, 119, footnote 599.

[104] Gowlland-Debbas, Security Council Enforcement, 61-63; Sinclair, I., State Responsibility and the Concept of Crimes of States, in Weiler *et al*, International Crimes, pp. 223-225, 224.

[105] On discretion see Gaja, G., Reflexions sur le role du Conseil de Securite dans le nouvel ordre mondial, A propos des rapports entre maintien de la paix et crimes internationaux des Etats, 97 RGDIP 1993, pp. 297-320, 306.

[106] Again the view of Gowlland-Debbas, Security Council Enforcement, 72 and 74.

[107] In agreement Starace, V., La responsabilité résultant de la violation des obligations à l'égard de la communauté internationale, 153 RDC ADI 1976-V, pp. 263-317, 294-296. Contrary Kelsen, H., The Law of the United Nations, A Critical Analysis of Its Fundamental Problems, Stevens & Sons Limited, London, 1951, 724-730. But see also 732-737. At 725 he observes: "The Charter, however, does not prescribe that the enforcement actions provided for in Chapter VII shall be taken exclusively against a Member which has violated its obligations;" See also Gaja, Reflexions, 300-301.

[108] C.f. Frowein, J., Article 39, in Simma, B. (Ed.), The Charter of the United Nations, A Commentary, Oxford University Press, Oxford, 1994, pp. 605-616, 609-610. Generally Goodrich, L., and Hambro, E., Charter of the United Nations, Commentary and Documents, Second and Revised Edition, Stevens & Sons Limited, London, 1949, 262-272; Cohen Jonathan, G. Article 39, in Cot, J.-P., and Pellet, A. (Eds.), La Charte des Nations Unies, Commentaire article par article, 2e édition, revue et augmentée, Economica, Paris, 1991, pp. 644-666, 658-662; Kelsen, The Law of the United Nations, 930-931.

[109] Generally Cohen Jonathan, Article 39, 655-658; Kelsen, The Law of the United Nations, 724-730, and 930-931.

[110] Note especially Gaja, Reflexions, 301, who claims: "Il ne semble pas que la notion de menace à la paix puisse être dissociée de l'existence du risque d'un conflit armé international. Il est vrai que les causes de ce risque peuvent être appréciées de manières différentes; on ne peut donc pas exclure que la violation d'une obligation d'une certaine importance entraîne une menace contre la paix. Encore faut-il que le risque d'un conflit soit véritablement pris en considération par le Conseil et qu'il ne soit pas un prétexte invoqué pour lui permettre d'exercer des pouvoirs qui ne lui auraient pas été attribués." He goes on to examine the specific resolutions of the Security Council on Rhodesia (217, 221, 232, 253, 277), South Africa (418), Iraq (688), Somalia (794, 733), Libya (731, 748). *Ibid.*, 302-307.

[111] *E.g.* Kelsen, The Law of the United Nations, 729, observes that the Charter: "(...) does not even prescribe that the enforcement measures shall be directed only against a Member guilty of a threat to, or breach of, the peace." In a similar sense McDougal, M., and Reisman, W., Rhodesia and the United Nations: The Lawfulness of International Concern, 62 AJIL 1968, pp. 1-19, 8.

[112] Kelsen, The Law of the United Nations, 730, claims that the Security Council: "(...) might consider it to be just to direct enforcement action against a Member which legally, that is, from the point of view of international law, is not wrong, since it has not violated any obligation expressly imposed upon it by the text of the Charter." In the footnote attached to these lines he observes: "According to the wording of Article 39, the Security Council is not bound to determine the aggressor. But if the enforcement measure to be taken under this Article shall have the character of a sanction it must not be directed against a state which is not guilty of a violation of its obligations. If the violation consists in an act of aggression, the enforcement action as a true sanction must be directed against the aggressor. If Article 39 is interpreted to provide for sanctions, the Security Council is bound to determine who is the aggressor."

[113] Resolution 748 is problematical to the extent that it relates to Libya's involvement in acts of terrorism as a threat to the peace and because the remedy sought therefore constitutes a denial of Libya's right to choose for the prosecution of its nationals.

[114] Note Leben, Les sanctions privatives, 270, on organizations as *judex in causa sua*; and Hoogh, Comments, 43-46.

[115] Note that Kelsen, The Law of the United Nations, 372-450, discusses the Security Council's quasi-judicial settlement of disputes.

[116] Contrary Gowlland-Debbas, Security Council Enforcement, 73-74: "Second, whilst collective responses are to be preferred to the more arbitrary, anarchic and possibly more destabilising unilateral ones, the problem is that whilst the qualification of an act as a prior condition to the application of unilateral countermeasures by a State may eventually (though not necessarily) be opened to challenge by the judge or arbitrator, those taken by the Council in connection with its primary responsibility in peace maintenance are authoritative and binding and when linked to determinations under Article 39 not subject, *as such*, to judicial review." Emphasis in the original; footnote omitted.

[117] That is not to say of course that there may not be any such problems. In the context of Security Council action under Chapter VII see Gaja, Reflexions, 300-301.

[118] Arangio-Ruiz, Fifth Report, Addendum 3, 14. Similar observations have been made within the Commission. See Commission Report 1994, 350.

[119] Arangio-Ruiz, Fifth Report, Addendum 3, 17.

[120] Leaving aside here Covenant provisions (articles 12, 13 and 15) stipulating that war could only be waged by one State against another if the latter refused to implement an award or recommendations in a unanimous Council report. The 1919 Covenant of the League of Nations, 13 AJIL 1919, Supplement, pp. 128-140.

[121] And one may note his stance to the effect that: "The only existing permanent body possessing, in principle, the competence and technical means to determine the existence, attribution and consequences of an internationally wrongful act – including possibly a crime of State – is the International Court of Justice." Arangio-Ruiz, Fifth Report, Addendum 3, 15.

[122] Arangio-Ruiz acknowledges this: "In such hypotheses, where a timely reaction is indispensable, one can accept to sacrifice, in a measure, objective assessment of any guilt and liability to the compelling necessity of safeguarding the peace, reducing bloodshed and destruction and maintaining a minimum degree of order. One is very close here to that function which is typical of self-defence (...) and one can accept, for lack of a better solution, that the political body's vis be employed without the guarantees of a judicial process, which is inevitably problematic and mainly too slow." Arangio-Ruiz, Fifth Report, Addendum 3, 17.

[123] Arangio-Ruiz, Fifth Report, Addendum 3, 16.

[124] Arangio-Ruiz, Fifth Report, Addendum 3, 17-18.

[125] Arangio-Ruiz, Fourth Report, 25. Underlining in the original. Generally *ibid.*, 20-39; Arangio-Ruiz, G., Sixth Report on State Responsibility, 19 April 1994, A/CN.4/461, 28 pp., 3-28 (especially 21), and Sixth Report on State Responsibility, 14 June 1994, A/CN.4/461/Add.2, 5 pp., 2-5.

[126] His originally proposed article 12, paragraph 1 (a), Part Two, ran: "Subject to the provisions set forth in paragraphs 2 and 3, no measure of this kind shall be taken by an injured State prior to: (a) the exhaustion of all the amicable settlement procedures available under general international law, the United Nations Charter or any other dispute settlement instrument to which it is a party;" Text to be found in Arangio-Ruiz, Fourth Report, 40.

[127] Note that it is stated in the Naulilaa Award, 1026, that: "La *représaille* est un acte de propre justice (Selbsthilfehandlung) de l'État lésé, (...)." Emphasis in the original.

[128] Arangio-Ruiz, Sixth Report, 8.

[129] Arangio-Ruiz, Sixth Report, 8.

[130] Note the very pertinent remark by Simma, B., Counter-Measures and Dispute Settlement: A Plea for a Different Balance, 5 EJIL 1994, pp. 102-105, 102-103, to the effect that: "We have to keep in mind that recourse to counter-measures not involving the threat or use of force is in itself a *peaceful* means of settling a dispute arising from an internationally wrongful act." Emphasis in the original.

[131] Arangio-Ruiz, Sixth Report, 9. Underlining in the original.

[132] The Naulilaa Award, 1026, states that an act of reprisal is an: "(...) acte répondant – *après sommation restée infructueuse* – à un acte contraire au droit des gens de l'État offenseur." Emphasis in the original. See also especially Arangio-Ruiz, Fourth Report, 19. To say that there must be some attempt to obtain reparation before adopting countermeasures is not the same as saying, as Hakenberg does, that they can only be adopted as a last resort. Hakenberg, M., Die Iran-Sanktionen der USA während der Teheraner Geiselaffäre aus völkerrechtlicher Sicht, Verlag Peter Lang, Frankfurt am Main, 1988, 206-207 and 245-247.

[133] Arangio-Ruiz, Sixth Report, 25-26. He originally voiced such criticism in relation to the draft proposed by the Drafting Committee. Note also Fourth Report, 6-19, on the requirement of prior demands of reparation.

[134] Text in 5 EJIL 1994, 118-119.

[135] Arangio-Ruiz, Sixth Report, 3-28; Sixth Report, Addendum 2, 2-5.

[136] Arangio-Ruiz, G., Sixth Report on State Responsibility, 21 July 1994, A/CN.4/461/Add.3, 2 pp., 2. His proposed paragraph 2 to the same article provides that the conditions of paragraph 1 do not apply to: "(...) urgent, temporary measures as are required to protect the rights of the injured State or limit the damage caused by the internationally wrongful act;", and also not if the author State does not accept the offer for dispute settlement, does not co-operate in good faith in the implementation thereof, fails to honour a request or order emanating from the procedure, or does not comply with a decision rendered by the procedure. Paragraph 3 (discussed below) stipulates that the injured State must communicate its intention to resort to countermeasures to the author State.

[137] Tomuschat, C., Are Counter-Measures Subject to Prior Recourse to Dispute Settlement Procedures?, 5 EJIL 1994, pp. 77-88, 87, observes: "It is submitted that it would be better to require the (alleged) wrongdoer to take the initiative in instituting dispute settlement procedures. It is the State author of the initial act that has stirred up the conflict. The burden should therefore be incumbent on its government to take steps to avert the negative effect of a counter-measure." And Simma, Counter-Measures, 104, stated: "As a matter of principle, to require the (alleged) wrong-doer to take the initiative in instituting dispute settlement procedures, is more equitable and just than to put the burden upon the injured State." Note also Dominicé, C., Die internationalen Verbrechen und deren rechtliches Regime, in Fischer, P., Koeck, H., and Verdross, A. (Eds.), Völkerrecht und Rechtsphilosophie, Internationale Festschrift für Stephan Verosta zum 70. Geburstag, Duncker & Humblot, Berlin, 1980, pp. 227-248, 247-248, who observes that countermeasures could be taken if an author State of a crime would refuse to accept dispute settlement.

[138] Air Services Agreement Award, 338-341.

[139] Arangio-Ruiz, Sixth Report, Addendum 3, 2. Earlier Arangio-Ruiz, Fourth Report, 18-19, had observed as to Riphagen's proposals regarding notifications: "A less cumbersome solution might be to impose upon the allegedly injured State the duty to submit its protest or demands to the alleged law-breaking State together with the indication of the essential facts and any suitable warning of possible countermeasures."

[140] Or by preparing for resort to countermeasures without actually implementing them. Consider the measures prepared by the United States with regard to its dispute with France regarding changes of gauge in third countries. Air Services Agreement Award, 325-326, and also 339-340.

[141] Arangio-Ruiz indicated with regard to this issue: "A State which has committed or is committing a wrongful act of the degree of gravity of the crimes singled out in article 19, presumably involving a measure of wilful intent, should not be entitled to a warning that might reduce the effectiveness of countermeasures." Arangio-Ruiz, Seventh Report, 17.

[142] In agreement Arangio-Ruiz, Fourth Report, 19.

[143] Note however the pause of goodwill in resolution 678, and the delays regarding the time of imposition of sanctions expressed in resolutions 748, 820, 841, 864, 873, 883, and 917.

[144] In that sense Gowlland-Debbas, Security Council Enforcement, 62: "Moreover, the Security Council is not hampered by any of the conditions which, debatedly, are said to govern unilateral countermeasures. There is no requirement for prior exhaustion of peaceful settlement mechanisms of Chapter VI, or for a prior demand for reparation. There is no need for a graduated or proportionate response." Two footnotes omitted.

[145] *E.g.* Dissenting Opinion El-Kosheri, Lockerbie Case, Provisional Measures, 105-106.

[146] See the statements in A/46/827. See also A/46/425 and A/46/828.

[147] Resolution 731 also mentions the attack against the "Union de transports aérens" flight and the request made by France in connection therewith. See A/46/825.

[148] For history see Lockerbie Case, Provisional Measures, 4-8.

[149] The 1945 Statute of the International Court of Justice, 39 AJIL 1945, Supplement, pp. 215-229.

[150] Note the conflicting opinions expressed within the Commission. Commission Report 1994, 343.

[151] Arangio-Ruiz, Seventh Report, 16-17; and Seventh Report, Addendum 1, 2-3.

[152] Arangio-Ruiz, Sixth Report, 9.

[153] Arangio-Ruiz, Seventh Report, Addendum 1, 3. C.f. Arangio-Ruiz, Fifth Report, Addendum 3, 20. In that context he made the argument that crimes related to a state of necessity or *détresse* situation.

[154] Arangio-Ruiz, Fifth Report, Addendum 3, 19-20; and Seventh Report, 16-17.

[155] Arangio-Ruiz, Fifth Report, Addendum 3, 19-20; and Seventh Report, 16-17. Discussing notification demands in case of delicts (Fourth Report, 6-19) he pointed out, at 10, that: "(...) the fact that a protest or intimation to cease seems to be lacking, may well be justified by the urgency of a remedy and the persistence of the injurious conduct."

[156] Arangio-Ruiz, Seventh Report, respectively 40 and 17; and article 19 in Seventh Report, Addendum 1, 4.

[157] Arangio-Ruiz, Fifth Report, Addendum 3, 20.

[158] Note the remarks by Graefrath, B., Mohr, M., and Oeser, E., Rechtsfolgen bei völkerrechtlicher Verantwortlichkeit, 31 SR 1982, pp. 1073-1086, 1083-1084.

[159] Arangio-Ruiz, Fourth Report, 2-4. Also Third Report, 24-26; and Fifth Report on State Responsibility, 8 June 1993, A/CN.4/453/Add.2, 35 pp., 24.

[160] Commentary Article 30, Part One, 119. Apparently supported by Malanczuk, Countermeasures and Self-Defence, 747-753; and Skubiszewski, K., The Application of Non-Military Measures by the General Assembly of the United Nations, 1 PYIL 1966/67, pp. 110-135, 117, as he observes: "In cases where the breach of the law results from compliance with the Assembly's request, the measure involved is exceptionally permissible and does not constitute an international tort." At 134 he observes: "The collective and non-military action recommended by the General Assembly are not enforcement action of the United Nations. Enforcement measures remain, (...), within the sole competence of the Security Council. The application of coercion is neither the prerogative nor the function of the General Assembly." Footnote omitted.

[161] Action: articles 5, 37 (paragraph 2), 42, 48, 53 (paragraph 1), 56, 106 and 107. Measures: articles 39, 50, and 53 (paragraph 1).

[162] C.f. Kelsen, The Law of the United Nations, 204-205 (see generally 198-211). At pages 269-270, on self-help, he uses the phrase "enforcement action" as synonym to "use of force". At page 98 he mentions the existence of obligations with respect to enforcement action only in relation to articles 43, 44, 45 and 48. In his chapter on sanctions, on the other hand, enforcement action is defined in relation to articles 41, 42 and 45 (at pages 724-725).

[163] Certain expenses of the United Nations (Article 17, paragraph 2, of the Charter), Advisory Opinion, ICJ Reports 1962, p. 151, 165.

[164] Kelsen, The Law of the United Nations, 195-196. Relevant footnote omitted.

[165] The Court observed in the Lockerbie Case, Provisional Measures, 15, that, on first sight, article 25 applied to resolution 748, and that: "(...) an indication of the measures requested by Libya would be likely to impair the rights which appear prima facie to be enjoyed by the United Kingdom by virtue of Security Council resolution 748 (1992);"

[166] It may be noted that the Commission has refrained from considering the instigation to commit wrongful acts as implication in the commission of wrongful acts. Text and Commentary Article 27, Part One, YBILC 1978, Volume II, Part Two, pp. 99-105, 99-101.

[167] Eisemann, P., Article 41, in Cot and Pellet, La Charte, pp. 691-704, 704.

[168] Expenses Opinion, 163. Emphasis added. Quoted by Eisemann, Article 41, 704. The English equivalent for "prescrire" was "require".

[169] See also Kelsen, The Law of the United Nations, 95-98 and 444-450. He states (445-446): "However, under Article 39, the Security Council may consider non-compliance with its recommendation a threat to the peace and resort to enforcement action against the recalcitrant state. If such enforcement action is interpreted to be a sanction, a recommendation of the Security Council may constitute the obligation to comply with the recommendation, that is to say, the so-called recommendation may have the same character as a 'decision' of the Security Council, binding upon Members under Article 25." Two footnotes omitted. To this one may counter that it is not intrinsically a member's non-compliance with the recommendation that constitutes the threat to the peace. Rather it is the targeted State's conduct itself which contributes to the existence of a threat to the peace.

[170] *E.g.* Kelsen, The Law of the United Nations, 439-440 and 728. Inconclusive Eisemann, Article 41, 696-697.

[171] Goodrich and Hambro, Charter of the United Nations, 277.

[172] C.f. Frowein, J., Article 40, in Simma, The Charter, pp. 617-621, 618, regarding provisional measures. Apparently contrary Simon, D., Article 40, in Cot and Pellet, La Charte, pp. 667-689, 670-676.

[173] Note Quigley, The International Law Commission's Distinction, 134-137 (especially 136).

[174] Arangio-Ruiz, G., Fourth Report on State Responsibility, 1 June 1992, A/CN.4/444/Add.2, 37 pp., 36. Footnote omitted.

[175] Nicaragua Case, Merits, 127. The Court considered the trade embargo, imposed by the United States on Nicaragua as of 1 May 1985, to amount to a violation by the United States of the obligation not to defeat the object and purpose of the 1956 FCN Treaty and a breach of obligation under article XIX. It rejected the American claim that the measures could be taken on the basis of article XXI, that is, as measures for the protection of essential security interests. Nicaragua Case, Merits, 135-142. The Court did not examine specifically whether the embargo might be justified under the heading of resort to non-armed countermeasures. The conclusions of the Court can only be based on either one of two arguments: first, that there had not been any internationally wrongful act committed by Nicaragua; secondly, that the United States did not possess injured State status. In view of the text accompanying this note the arguments by the Court seem to tend towards the latter view.

[176] Nicaragua Case, Merits, 104-105.

[177] Tomuschat, YBILC 1992, Volume I, 167. Bowett, *ibid.*, 82, seemed to take the opposite position: "(...) an injured State could not be denied the right to take countermeasures simply because a State which was more directly or more seriously affected did not do likewise." His formulation appears more apt to describe the situation in which all States are affected by a breach of obligations and some more than others. Note also Arangio-Ruiz, Fourth Report, Addendum 2, 35, footnote 303; and Dominicé, Die internationalen Verbrechen, 245. Mohr, M., The ILC's Distinction between "International Crimes" and "International Delicts" and its Implications, in Spinedi and Simma, United Nations Codification, pp. 115-141, 131, acknowledges the right of "third" States to adopt countermeasures, but notes that this is dependent on the consent of the victim State or people. Contrary Annacker, C., The Legal Régime of *Erga Omnes* Obligations in International Law, 46 AJPIL 1994, pp. 131-166, 161.

[178] Arangio-Ruiz, Third Report, Addendum 1, 2-7; Fourth Report, Addendum 2, 20-37.

[179] Arangio-Ruiz, Fourth Report, Addendum 2, 24-26.

[180] The situation of the American hostages in Iran presents some odd features. The issues at stake had to do, primarily, with Iran's breaches of obligation under rules of diplomatic law. As such only the United States could be considered an injured State. Nevertheless EEC member States took action and adopted certain measures towards Iran. Since Iran's conduct did not constitute uses of force amounting to an armed attack, such States would not enjoy injured State status under article 5, paragraph 3. The only correct manner of approaching those measures then is to view them as reactions to breaches of human rights obligations by Iran. In that sense Hoogh, A. de, Book Review: Sachariew, K., Die Rechtstellung der betroffenen Staaten bei Verletzungen multilateraler Verträge, Fragen der Aktivlegitimation und der völkerrechtlich zugelassenen Rechtsfolgen, 38 NILR 1991, pp. 104-109, 106. Note also Arangio-Ruiz, Fourth Report, Addendum 2, 32, footnote 295; Gaja, G., Obligations *Erga Omnes*, International Crimes and *Jus Cogens*: A Tentative Analysis of Three Related Concepts, in Weiler *et al*, International Crimes, pp. 151-160, 153-154; Graefrath, B., International Crimes – A Specific Regime of International Responsibility of States and its Legal Consequences, in *ibid.*, pp. 161-169, 168, and footnote 2.

[181] Arangio-Ruiz, Fourth Report, Addendum 2, 26-27, footnote 280.

[182] Arangio-Ruiz, Fourth Report, Addendum 2, 26-27, footnote 280.

[183] Arangio-Ruiz, Fourth Report, Addendum 2, 26-27, footnote 280.

[184] Note Arangio-Ruiz' interpretation of the Court's observations in the Nicaragua Case. He quite correctly stated that the Court's aim was to condemn measures involving the use of force prohibited by international law (self-defence excluded). More particularly he claimed that the acts of which Nicaragua was accused involved breaches of the obligation of non-intervention (and minor uses of force). These, so he claims, only involve a bilateral structure and not an *erga omnes* one. For that reason, he notes, third States simply do not have a right to respond to such acts. Now if intervention and minor uses of force take place within a bilateral context, why then does he consider that serious uses of force, in the sense of aggression, do not take place within a bilateral context? Naturally, the more serious the acts, the more serious the consequences that may flow from them, including more serious effects on other States. Yet it is submitted that this still does not explain the transformation from bilateral to *erga omnes* structures.

[185] YBILC 1992, Volume I, 144. Note also Bowett's remarks, *ibid.*, 153-154.

[186] For the 1947 General Agreement on Tarifs and Trade see 55 UNTS, pp. 194-285.

[187] Boisson de Chazournes, L., Les contre-mesures dans les relations internationales économiques, Editions A. Pedone, Paris, 1992, 136-139; Kuyper, P., Het GATT en het Volkenrecht, De gevolgen van toenemende juridificering, Mededelingen NVIR 1993, pp. 3-60, 39-41 and 59. He asserts that the GATT, in the absence of

organs charged to uphold the general interest, could envisage an *actio popularis*, but that panels have instead opted for reducing the impact of the damage condition. Note however the formulation of article XXIII, which states that a contracting party may make representations to another contracting party also should it consider that the attainment of the objectives of the GATT are being impeded. These may be found in the preamble and are very broad: raising standards of living, ensuring full employment and a large and steadily growing volume of real income and effective demand, developing full use of the resources of the world and expanding the production and exchange of goods.

188 Nicaragua Case, Merits, 127.

189 Bowett, YBILC 1992, Volume I, 153-154. He asserts, correctly in the mind of the present writer (though not in the context of further or more severe measures going beyond those of the Security Council), that the Security Council cannot demand a State not to take lawful countermeasures. The remarks by Arangio-Ruiz appear to lead to the opposite conclusion. *Ibid.*, 163.

190 Riphagen, YBILC 1982, Volume I, 202.

191 Simma, B., Self-Contained Regimes, 16 NYIL 1985, pp. 111-136, 117.

192 Simma, Self-Contained Regimes, 117.

193 Note Bowett's claim, YBILC 1992, Volume I, 82, with regard to self-contained régimes: "In short, it would be necessary to determine whether the particular treaty involved a renunciation on the part of the parties to that treaty of the right to take countermeasures under general international law, assuming that the measures provided for under the treaty were inadequate."

194 The 1961 Vienna Convention on Diplomatic Relations, 55 AJIL 1961, pp. 1064-1077.

195 United States Diplomatic and Consular Staff in Tehran, Judgment, ICJ Reports 1980, p. 3, 38-41.

196 Diplomatic Staff Case, Judgment, 40.

197 Commission Report 1994, 366, footnote 362. Also Arangio-Ruiz, Third Report, Addendum 1, 21-23; Fourth Report, Addendum 1, 27-29 and 34.

198 Diplomatic Staff Case, Judgment, 40.

199 The 1961 Optional Protocol Concerning the Compulsory Settlement of Disputes, 55 AJIL 1961, pp. 1078-1080.

200 The Court recognized as much since it decided that Iran was under an obligation to provide reparation to the United States as a result of its violations of "international conventions in force between the two countries". Diplomatic Staff Case, Judgment, 44-45, operative paragraphs 1 and 5. The late judge Lachs voted against the latter paragraph because he felt it to be redundant, and that a reservation for further procedure would have sufficed. Separate Opinion Lachs, *ibid.*, 47.

201 C.f. Simma, Self-Contained Regimes, 120-121; Dominicé, C., Représailles et droit diplomatique, in Recht als Prozess und Gefüge, Festschrift für Hans Huber zum 80. Geburtstag, Verlag Stämpfli & Cie AG, Bern, 1981, pp. 541-552, 549-552; and Barnhoorn, L., Diplomatic Law and Unilateral Remedies, 25 NYIL 1994, pp. 39-81, 61. Apparently contrary Dissenting Opinion Morozov, Diplomatic Staff Case, Judgment, 53: "But taking into account the extraordinary circumstances which occurred during the period of judicial deliberation on the case, when the Applicant itself committed many actions which caused enormous damage to the Islamic Republic of Iran, the Applicant has forfeited the legal right as well as the moral right to expect the Court to uphold any claim for reparation." The deciding issue is whether the actions of the United States were justifiable or not. In his mind they were not (*ibid.*, 52-57). Similarly Dissenting Opinion Tarazi, *ibid.*, 58 and 65.

202 C.f. Graefrath, B., Das Verantwortlichkeitsverhältnis im Völkerrecht und die Definition des "Verletzten Staates", in Graefrath, B. (Ed.), Probleme des Völkerrecht, Akademie-Verlag, Berlin, 1987, pp. 107-138, 126-128; Frowein, Die Verpflichtungen *erga omnes*, 255-256; and Frowein, J., Das Staatengemeinschaftsinteresse – Probleme bei Formulierung und Durchsetzung, in Hailbronner, K., Ress, G., and Stein, Torsten (Eds.), Staat und Völkerrechtsordnung, Festschrift für Karl Doehring, Springer-Verlag, Berlin, 1989, pp. 219-228, 227. For the contrary position see Henkin, L., Human Rights and "Domestic Jurisdiction", in Buergenthal, T. (Ed.), Human Rights, International Law and the Helsinki Accord, Alanheld, Osmun & Co. Publishers, Montclair (New Jersey), 1977, pp. 21-40, 25 and 29-33; Tanzi, A., Is Damage a Distinct Condition for the Existence of an Internationally Wrongful Act?, in Spinedi and Simma, United Nations Codification, pp. 1-33, 28-29. He does consider however that in view of the obligation to settle disputes peacefully, recourse to the mechanism of specific treaties would satisfy the requirements of that obligation after which resort to countermeasures could take place.

203 Nicaragua Case, Merits, 134.

204 The 1969 American Convention on Human Rights, 65 AJIL 1971, pp. 679-701.

205 Nicaragua Case, Merits, 134.

206 Nicaragua Case, Merits, 134.

[207] Nicaragua Case, Merits, 92-97. The multilateral treaties considered by the Court to come under the reservation were the Charters of the United Nations and of the Organization of American States, as well as the GATT and the Geneva Conventions.

[208] The *ad hoc* Conciliation Commission that may be established, with the prior consent of the States parties in dispute, under article 42, may go one step further and submit a report containing findings of all relevant facts and its views on the possibilities for reaching an amicable solution. After that States parties are expected to notify, within three months, whether or not they accept the report.

[209] C.f. Simma, Self-Contained Regimes, 132-135. At page 133 he observes, however, that: "(...) it is quite obvious that specific mechanisms of supervision and control, as well as complaint procedures available to States and individuals, enjoy priority over any attempts at enforcing human rights obligations on the inter-State level."

[210] Simma correctly holds that countermeasures not involving the threat or use of force, in themselves, are peaceful means of settling a dispute. Simma, Counter-Measures, 102-103.

[211] Commission Report 1994, 366, footnote 362.

[212] C.f. Bowett, YBILC 1992, Volume I, 153.

[213] Bowett, YBILC 1992, Volume I, 154. Note also his claim that the Security Council would not have the power to demand an injured State to refrain from lawful countermeasures in case the author State proved recalcitrant.

[214] In the affirmative Mavroidis, P., Das GATT als "self-contained" Regime, 37 RIW 1991, pp. 497-501; and Arangio-Ruiz, Fourth Report, Addendum 2, 12-13. In the negative Boisson de Chazournes, Les contre-mesures, 183-186. Non-committed Kuyper, Het GATT en het Volkenrecht, 52; and Kuyper, P., The Law of GATT as a Special Field of International Law, Ignorance, Further Refinement or Self-Contained System of International Law?, 25 NYIL 1994, pp. 227-257, 251-252.

[215] C.f. Nicaragua Case, Merits, 136.

[216] The Court discussed essential security interests in the Nicaragua Case, Merits, 115-117, 136, and 140-142.

[217] The situation prevailing in Central America appears to be typical in this respect. Mavroidis discusses two panel reports related to disputes between Nicaragua and the United States. The second decided not to review the legality of United States' measures under article XXI. It stated that it could not do so since its mandate prohibited such course of action. Mavroidis, Das GATT, 499-501.

[218] Reported by Mavroidis, Das GATT, 499.

[219] Mavroidis, Das GATT, 501. At the same page he observes that State practice under the GATT does not support the conclusion that the GATT constitutes a self-contained régime.

[220] The 1993 agreement on the Multilateral Trade Organization and the understanding on rules and procedures governing the settlement of disputes have not in any way changed this picture. Texts in ILM 1994, pp. 15-23 and 114-131.

[221] Contrary Boisson de Chazournes, Les contre-mesures, 183-184.

[222] Commission Report 1994, 366, footnote 362.

[223] Commission Report 1994, 366, footnote 362.

[224] Arangio-Ruiz, Third Report, Addendum 1, 16-21.

[225] Naulilaa Award, 1026.

[226] Quoted by Arangio-Ruiz, Third Report, Addendum 1, 17.

[227] Within the Commission Tomuschat addressed the argument that an injured State could not resort to countermeasures affecting an author State's nationals, because technically such measures could not be justified towards the other States parties. Nevertheless he claimed that a State whose nationals were denied human rights in another State party could adopt countermeasures affecting the human rights of the author State's nationals. He asserted that a State, injured by another State's restrictions on the freedom of movement of the injured State's nationals under article 12 of the Covenant, could respond in kind. That claim was not however based on arguments regarding countermeasures derived from the Covenant, but on the consideration that a special relationship would exist between the two States. Tomuschat, YBILC 1992, Volume I, 86 and especially 167. It may be pointed out that the right to freedom of movement would not appear to be, under the Covenant, a basic or fundamental right: it is not included in the non-derogable list of article 4, paragraph 2. Gaja, Obligations *Erga Omnes*, 156, also points to this technical argument and draws the opposite conclusion, that is, countermeasures are generally prohibited.

[228] Arangio-Ruiz, YBILC 1992, Volume I, 70 and 188; Jacovides, *ibid.*, 73; Tomuschat, *ibid.*, 86 and 167; a little bit less clear Razafindralambo, *ibid.*, 177; and Vargas Carreño, *ibid.*, 180.

[229] Bennouna, YBILC 1992, Volume I, 81; Villagran Kramer, *ibid.*, 87; and Rao, *ibid.*, 163.

[230] Article 46 of the 1949 Geneva Convention I for the Amelioration of the Condition of the Wounded and Sick in Armed Forces in the Field, in Roberts, A., and Guelff, R. (Eds.), Documents on the Laws of War, Clarendon Press, Oxford, 1982, pp. 171-192; article 33 of the 1949 Geneva Convention IV Relative to the

Protection of Civilian Persons in Time of War, *ibid.*, pp. 272-326. See also articles 20, 51, paragraph 6, 52, paragraph 1, 53 (C), 54, paragraph 4, 55, paragraph 2, and 56, paragraph 4 of the 1977 Protocol Additional to the Geneva Conventions of 12 August 1949, and relating to the protection of victims of international armed conflicts (Protocol I), 16 ILM 1977, pp. 1391-1433.

231 The preparatory works of the Covenant do not seem to shed any light on the issue. See Bossuyt, M., Guide to the "*Travaux Préparatoires*" of the International Covenant on Civil and Political Rights, Martinus Nijhoff Publishers, Dordrecht, 1987, 85-96, and 635-715.

232 The Case of the S.S. Lotus, Publications PCIJ, 1927, Series A, No. 10, p. 4, 18.

233 Arangio-Ruiz, Third Report, Addendum 1, 17. Relevant footnote omitted. Note also Alland, D., La légitime défense et les contre-mesures dans la codification du droit international de la responsabilité, 110 JDI 1983, pp. 728-762, 754.

234 Arangio-Ruiz, Third Report, Addendum 1, 20-21.

235 Arangio-Ruiz, Fourth Report, Addendum 1, 26-27.

236 Arangio-Ruiz, Fourth Report, Addendum 1, 22-25 and 34. Zemanek claims that the Universal Declaration of Human Rights is considered to form part of *jus cogens* and that such norms cannot be suspended by way of reprisal. Zemanek, K., La responsabilité des États pour faits internationalement illicites, ainsi que pour faits internationalement licites, in Weil, P. (Ed.), Responsabilité internationale, Éditions A. Pedone, Paris, 1987, pp. 3-88, 85.

237 Arangio-Ruiz, Fourth Report, Addendum 1, 25.

238 Barcelona Traction Case, Judgment, 32.

239 Arangio-Ruiz, Third Report, Addendum 1, 20-21. Crawford stated, YBILC 1992, Volume I, 154, that countermeasures generally had to be restricted to reversible acts. Al-Khasawneh, observed, *ibid.*, 159, that the right of property should be protected (excluding nationalization and freezing of assets), and that countermeasures affecting individuals should be kept to a minimum. Mikulka noted, *ibid.*, 172, that countermeasures had to be temporary in nature and end as soon as the author State accepted its obligations. Arangio-Ruiz, *ibid.*, 186, also supported the position that countermeasures ought to be reversible in character.

240 Arangio-Ruiz, Seventh Report, 21-22.

241 Air Services Agreement Award, 338-340.

242 Air Services Agreement Award, 340-341.

243 South West Africa Cases (Ethiopia *v.* South Africa; Liberia *v.* South Africa), Preliminary Objections, Judgment, ICJ Reports 1962, p. 319; South West Africa, Second Phase, Judgment, ICJ Reports 1966, p. 6.

244 South West Africa Cases, Preliminary Objections, 326-327. Note also the scant majorities in both cases. South West Africa Cases, Preliminary Objections, 347; and South West Africa Cases, Second Phase, 51.

245 Military and Paramilitary Activities in and against Nicaragua (Nicaragua *v.* United States of America), Jurisdiction and Admissibility, Judgment, ICJ Reports 1984, p. 392. For text withdrawal from proceedings, 24 ILM 1985, pp. 246-263. Later on the United States went on to terminate its declaration under article 36, paragraph 2, of the Statute with effect as of six months. Text in 24 ILM 1985, p. 1742 (see also 1743-1745).

246 Arangio-Ruiz, Third Report, 32-36; Fourth Report, Addendum 1, 2-4; and Seventh Report, 17-20. Delbrück, J., Proportionality, in Bernhardt, R. (Ed.), EPIL, Instalment 7, Elsevier Science Publishers B.V., Amsterdam, 1984, pp. 396-400.

247 Arangio-Ruiz, Fourth Report, Addendum 1, 2, noted that: "The function of the principle is to avoid the possible inequitable result of the use of countermeasures, (...)." Repeated, *ibid.*, 3.

248 Riphagen, W., Second report on the content, forms and degrees of international responsibility (part 2 of the draft articles), YBILC 1981, Volume II, Part One, pp. 79-101, 100. In agreement Stein (Ted), Observations, 195-196.

249 Text Article 13, Part Two, in Commission Report 1994, 365, footnote 362; originally Drafting Committee, 5 EJIL 1994, 118-119.

250 Arangio-Ruiz, Third Report, 35-36; and Fourth Report, Addendum 1, 3-4. In his latest report he doubts the advisability of mentioning the effects on the injured State in addition to the gravity of the wrongful act, because this would neglect certain other elements such as fault, the importance of the rules, and the effects on the object of protection (*e.g.* on individuals, peoples or the environment). Arangio-Ruiz, Seventh Report, 17-20.

251 The arbitrators in the Naulilaa Award, 1028, claimed: "Même si l'on admettait que le droit des gens n'exige pas que la répresaille se mesure approximativement à l'offense, on devrait certainement considérer, comme excessives et partant illicites, des représailles hors de toute proportion avec l'acte qui les a motivées." The arbitrators in the Air Services Agreement Award, 338, noted the existing general agreement that: "(...) all counter-measures must, in the first instance, have some degree of equivalence with the alleged breach;" It added that the measures adopted by the United States did not appear "clearly disproportionate" compared to those of France.

[252] C.f. Air Services Agreement Award, 338.

[253] The Court pointed to the United States' belief of grave and manifest violations on the part of Iran, to the extent and seriousness of the conflict between Iran's conduct and its obligations, and to the particular gravity due to the involvement of the Iranian government itself. Diplomatic Staff Case, Judgment, 28 and 42.

[254] The Court stated in the Diplomatic Staff Case, Judgment, 42: "At the same time the Court finds itself obliged to stress the cumulative effect of Iran's breaches of its obligations when taken together."

[255] In agreement Arangio-Ruiz, Seventh Report, 18-19.

[256] Generally Lindemann, Die Auswirkungen, 64-93; and Vierdag, Spanningen, 74-87.

[257] Arangio-Ruiz, Fourth Report, Addendum 1, 4.

[258] Air Services Agreement Award, 338.

[259] C.f. Arangio-Ruiz, Seventh Report, 17-20. Note the Court's statements as to the fundamental character of the inviolability of diplomats' immunities, the imperative character of Iran's obligations, and the extreme importance of the principles it had to apply. Diplomatic Staff Case, Judgment, 40-43. At this last page the Court went so far as to consider it its duty to call the attention of the entire international community to the irreparable harm that could be caused by the events before the Court.

[260] Commission Report 1994, 366, footnote 362. Arangio-Ruiz proposed to deal with economical coercion as forming part of the prohibition of the use of force under article 2, paragraph 4, of the Charter. Third Report, Addendum 1, 14-16; Fourth Report, Addendum 1, 17-22. That position was not reflected in the formulated text of his proposed draft article 14 (b). *Ibid.*, 34.

[261] C.f. Nicaragua Case, Merits, 138.

[262] Arangio-Ruiz, Fifth Report, Addendum 3, 20-23. Note also Commission Report 1994, 344.

[263] Arangio-Ruiz, Seventh Report, 20-21.

CHAPTER 5

THE RIGHT OF (AN) INJURED STATE(S) AND THE UNITED NATIONS TO RESORT TO ARMED FORCE IN RESPONSE TO INTERNATIONAL CRIMES

5.1. Introduction

A first clarification regarding the scope of the present chapter relates to the meaning of the word "force" as employed in article 2, paragraph 4, of the Charter.[1] The neutral formulation of that provision could open the way to an interpretation that threats or uses of force other than military in character are covered by the prohibition. Thus the threat or use of economic coercion would constitute a breach of obligation under that article. Such kind of coercion may certainly threaten the territorial integrity or political independence of a State,[2] but a contextual reading of the Charter militates against such an interpretation.

The preamble for instance notes the aim to "save succeeding generations from the scourge of war". Paragraph 3 of article 2 stipulates that: "All members shall settle their international disputes by peaceful means in such a manner that international peace and security, and justice, are not endangered." Article 24 of the Charter bestows the task of maintaining international peace and security primarily on the Security Council. The main powers of the Security Council in that field are laid down in Chapter VII under which it can opt to "decide what measures not involving the use of armed force are to be employed" (article 41), or to have resort to "action by sea, air or land forces" (article 42). Article 43 in turn stipulates that members "undertake to make available to the Security Council, on its call and in accordance with a special agreement or agreements, armed forces, assistance and facilities, (...)." Finally article 44 mentions that the Security Council may have "decided to use force".[3]

The interpretation of "force" in article 2, paragraph 4, as meaning armed force is to some extent confirmed by the preparatory works of the Charter. In this regard authors generally refer to the rejection of a Brazilian amendment intended to have the prohibition cover economic force.[4]

The circumstances preceding and surrounding the conclusion of the Charter likewise point to this interpretation. Almost the whole of the first half of the 20th century has been devoted to restricting the prevailing freedom of States to resort to military force. The 1907 Hague Convention (II) respecting the Limitation of the Use of Force for the Recovery of Contract Debts (Porter-Drago Convention) was the first treaty ever to impose a restriction regarding the legitimate causes to use armed force. Its parties were bound not to use force for the recovery of contractual debts.[5] The Covenant on the League of Nations proceeded, in articles 12, 13 and 15, to put procedural limits on resort to war.[6] War by one State against another could only be resorted to, at the earliest, three months after the failure of that other State to honour the outcome of Council of the League of Nations or arbitral procedures. Article 1 of the Kellogg-Briand Pact finally provided that:[7]

> "The High Contracting Parties solemnly declare in the name of their respective peoples that they condemn recourse to war for the solution of international controversies, and renounce it as an instrument of national policy in their relations with one another."

For such reasons this chapter will only discuss the actual use of armed force in response to the commission of an international crime.

An important aspect of article 2, paragraph 4, of the Charter is that it not only prohibits the actual use of armed force, but also threats to use armed force. One might argue that there does not exist any necessity for such an explicit rule. By way of logical implication the threat to engage in certain particular conduct could be considered illegal if actually adopting the conduct in question is prohibited. Others might say, on the basis of an *a contrario* argument, that if a rule only prohibits the use of force, the threat to use force remained lawful. That claim would be bolstered by reference to the Lotus Case, in which the Permanent Court noted that restrictions to the independence of States could not be presumed.[8] Opponents might be tempted to argue that the object and purpose of a rule prohibiting the use of force would be defeated if threats were considered lawful. The weaker States would then be liable to being coerced into accepting certain demands by the stronger States. The draftsmen of the Charter clearly were foresighted to include a prohibition of threats to use force.

Question is of course what may constitute a threat to use force.[9] On this count the clearest example will naturally constitute the outright verbal assurance or promise, with or without an ultimatum, that force will be used. But such blunt behaviour will undoubtedly not be the rule but the exception. The disguised threat will be more typical, necessitating reading between the lines of diplomatic intercourse. Besides verbal threats the outright military kind are frequently made. A State might for instance direct its troops or crafts to certain areas, or it might hold large scale manoeuvres in the vicinity of the targeted State.

Though article 2, paragraph 4, prohibits the threat to use force this does not necessarily mean that any display of military force will constitute an illegal threat. Preparation for self-defence, for instance, is perfectly legitimate. The decisions of the Court in the Corfu Channel Case and the Nicaragua Case show that not just any display of force amounts to a breach of obligation under article 2, paragraph 4. The incidents related to the first case concerned the United Kingdom sending ships at action stations through the Corfu Channel, an international strait, in order to affirm its right of innocent passage. Such action was considered not to amount to a violation of Albanian sovereignty.[10] In the second case the Court was not satisfied, considering the circumstances, that the military manoeuvres held by the United States near the borders of Nicaragua constituted a prohibited threat of force.[11]

In the context of international crimes it is not to be expected that an author State will be impressed by mere verbal rhetoric. In the nature of things it is engaging, wilfully and with premeditation, in acts of such seriousness that it will not likely be deterred from continuing to commit the crime. Even a display of military power might not suffice to put an end to the crime. The end result will most likely be that armed force will be necessary if the commission of the crime is to be stopped. The author State, in turn, may be tempted to resist by all the means at its disposal. For this reason the present chapter will concern only the actual use of armed force against a State committing an international crime.

Subject to the foregoing the following issues will be addressed in this chapter. Section 5.2 will examine the scope of the prohibition of the use of armed force in international law. In section 5.3 certain arguments regarding the function and nature of resort to armed force will be discussed. The preconditions for resort to armed force will form the subject of section 5.4. In derogation from previous chapters sections 5.5 and 5.6 will examine the use of force in response to particular international crimes, or at least separate the crime of aggression from the other crimes. The necessity for this is dictated by the explicit regulation of the use of armed force in the Charter of the United Nations. Section 5.7 finally will discuss certain possible restrictions regarding resort to armed force.

5.2. The scope of the prohibition of the use of armed force in international law

5.2.1. THE SCOPE OF ARTICLE 2, PARAGRAPH 4, OF THE CHARTER

It is generally recognized that the Charter of the United Nations prohibits members to threaten or use force against any State, and reliance is placed, for the most part, on the text of article 2, paragraph 4, which runs:

> "All Members shall refrain in their international relations from the threat or use of force against the territorial integrity or political independence of any state, or in any manner inconsistent with the Purposes of the United Nations."

There is no need to examine all problems of interpretation arising from this text. At this point the only object is to ascertain the scope of the prohibition of the use of force as applicable between States.[12] The major differences of opinion relate to whether "against the territorial integrity or political independence" reduces the scope of the prohibition of the use of force, and what interpretation should be given to "or in any manner inconsistent with the Purposes of the United Nations".

The interpretation of "force against the territorial integrity or political independence of any state"

As a preliminary the issue arises whether, as has indeed been claimed,[13] this text conveys some ambiguity, or leaves the meaning obscure. For if that were the case this would certainly justify recourse to the preparatory works of the Charter (article 32, Vienna Convention on the Law of Treaties).[14] It is submitted that such is not the case, and that the ordinary meaning to be attached to the first part of article 2, paragraph 4, is that only force against the territorial integrity or political independence of States is prohibited. That is not the same as saying that force which is not against the territorial integrity or political independence of States would be permissible. Rather this means that any such use of force is not covered by this specific part of the prohibition of article 2, paragraph 4, and that it consequently would not on that count entail a breach of obligation under that provision.

That conclusion cannot be set aside, moreover, by making references to conflicting texts found in the preparatory works.[15] That smaller States wanted more specific safeguards, and that the phrase was not therefore intended to have any qualifying effect,[16] is irrelevant from the viewpoint of treaty interpretation. It is the intention of the States parties as manifested in the text which must take precedence.[17] What remains to be examined, then, is the meaning that must be attached to "territorial integrity" and "political independence".

As to the former it has been asserted that this is equivalent to territorial inviolability.[18] That stance is inspired, once more, by the desire to argue the comprehensive nature of the ban on the use of force under article 2, paragraph 4, of the Charter. If the two terms were identical in meaning any cross-border incursion by military or paramilitary elements would amount to a breach of obligation under article 2, paragraph 4. In support of such argument one could refer to the Declaration on Principles of International Law (General Assembly resolution 2625 (XXV)), which proclaimed that:[19]

> "Every State has the duty to refrain from the threat or use of force to violate the existing international boundaries of another State (...)."

Though this appears to lend credibility to the argument, it is submitted that the Declaration in fact goes beyond an authoritative interpretation of article 2, paragraph 4, of the Charter.[20] It may be noted for instance that all the principles elaborated upon start off by stipulating that "States" shall do, or not do, something. The text is clearly intended to reflect rules of customary international law.

A State's threat or use of force to violate international boundaries will not, generally, lead to a loss of territory or disrupt the territorial "unity" of another State. Only if it could have such an effect, irrespective of the size of the territory endangered, is there a breach of obligation in this respect under article 2, paragraph 4, of the Charter. The decisive criterion, however, does not lie with the intention of the State threatening or using force, but with the actual or even potential effects of such threats or uses of force. Yet even if a State's use of force could not be said to entail, potentially, a loss of territory, still such use of force would not on that count become lawful under international law.[21] The prohibition of the use of force rests on more broad foundations than that.

The prohibition to use force against the "political independence" of a State is linked to the prohibition of intervention in international law.[22] That this is so may be deduced especially from the observations of the Court in the Nicaragua Case:[23]

> "(...) the principle forbids all States or groups of States to intervene directly or indirectly in internal or external affairs of other States. A prohibited intervention must accordingly be one bearing on matters in which each State is permitted, by the principle of State sovereignty, to decide freely. One of these is the choice of a political, economic, social and cultural system, and the formulation of foreign policy. Intervention is wrongful when it uses methods of coercion in regard to such choices, which must remain free ones. The element of coercion, which defines, and indeed forms the essence of, prohibited intervention, is particularly obvious in the case of an intervention which uses force, either in the

direct form of military action, or in the indirect form of support for subversive or terrorist armed activities within another State."

By reference to this text it seems appropriate to define the adjective "political" in the sense that the independence of a State, against which States may not use force, concerns the freedom to order one's internal affairs (the political, economic, social, and cultural system) and external affairs (formulation of foreign policy).[24] Once certain choices can no longer be made in freedom due to the existence of an international obligation, the subject-matter on which that choice turns has left the realm of domestic jurisdiction. In such a case, to paraphrase the Permanent Court in the Lotus Case, a restriction has been placed on the independence of a State.[25] The use of armed force will not necessarily in every case be directed against the political independence of a State. Force used to pressure a State into compliance with its international obligations will therefore not of necessity constitute a breach of obligation under article 2, paragraph 4. But again this does not entail the conclusion that the use of force in pursuit of another State's compliance with its obligations becomes lawful by definition. It remains to be considered to what extent uses of armed force are illegal due to inconsistency with the purposes of the United Nations.

The interpretation of "force (...) in any other manner inconsistent with the Purposes of the United Nations"

A first remark concerns the stance that some uses of force are lawful because they further the realization of the purposes of the United Nations. Such an argument obviously misconstrues the text of article 2, paragraph 4. The text of this article clearly deals only with *illegal* uses of force. The argument turns the ordinary meaning of the words around. It is not possible to claim that a use of force is lawful under article 2, paragraph 4, because it enhances the realization of a purpose of the United Nations. The phrase "inconsistent with the Purposes of the United Nations" can only be taken to mean a broadening of the scope of the prohibition.[26]

A second observation relates to the already noted circumstance that the members are under the obligation to abstain from the use of force *in their international relations.* In this context "their" can only refer back to members of the United Nations. Since membership in the United Nations is only open to entities that are States (articles 3 and 4), the obvious deduction ought to be that article 2, paragraph 4, only covers inter-State threats or uses of force.

Taking a look at the purposes of the United Nations laid down in article 1, paragraphs 2 and 3, it seems hardly likely that any use of force inconsistent with those purposes will, or even can, take place in the members' international relations. Denying a people the exercise of its right to self-determination appears to be possible only within one and the same State. It is possible, yet somewhat difficult, to imagine a State going into the territory of another State in order to frustrate, militarily, the exercise of a right of self-determination of a people living there.[27] Similarly it is hard to envisage a State engaging in cross-border military incursions with the purpose of breaching human rights obligations in another State. A denial of self-determination, or human rights violations, could of course take place as a side-effect of a cross-border use of force. With regard to the prohibition of force inconsistent with the purpose of article 1, paragraph 1, it must be said that that seems to coincide almost completely with the obligation under article 2, paragraph 3, that members must settle their disputes peacefully (discussed in the next subsection). Only the purpose of the United Nations to take effective *collective* measures for the prevention and removal of threats to the peace appears to have some added value in this respect. It might be interpreted to rule out any unilateral recourse to armed force.

However, account must be taken of the interpretation rule that a provision, or even part of it, should not be construed in such a way as to deprive it of all meaning. The more literal interpretation must therefore be abandoned in favour of one more in accordance with the spirit of the text. As a result one should consider the threat or use of armed force in denial of the right of self-determination of peoples or human rights to fall under the scope of the prohibition of article 2, paragraph 4.[28] To what measure it is possible to use force to uphold the right to self-determination and human rights will be discussed in section 5.6.

5.2.2. THE SCOPE OF ARTICLE 2, PARAGRAPH 3, OF THE CHARTER

Article 2, paragraph 3, of the Charter requires that:

> "All Members shall settle their international disputes by peaceful means in such a manner that international peace and security, and justice, are not endangered."

The most striking feature of studies on the subject of peaceful settlement of disputes, in accordance with article 2, paragraph 3, of the Charter, is that they tend to focus on the *peaceful* means to settle disputes.[29] Hardly ever does one find a discussion of *non-peaceful* means to settle disputes, that is, in which circumstances one could say that there is a breach of obligation in this respect. This lack of attention by scholars is noteworthy also considering that the principle (obligation) involved is often claimed to be the complement of the prohibition of the use of force.[30] An explanation for this might be the argument that the two rules substantially cover the same ground and that therefore the negative aspect of the rule of peaceful settlement of disputes might be regarded as being redundant in relation to the prohibition of force.[31] However, that view is based on the partly erroneous belief (as shown in the previous subsection) that article 2, paragraph 4, of the Charter prohibits any kind of threat or use of cross-border armed force.

As to the content of this specific obligation placed on members of the United Nations, that may be divided into two categories. As a positive duty members are required to make attempts to settle their international disputes peacefully if, and to the extent that, an unsettled dispute would be likely to endanger the maintenance of international peace and security. That conclusion flows from the combined effect of articles 2, paragraph 3, and 33 of the Charter.[32] The negative duty of the provision of article 2, paragraph 3, is that members must refrain from all acts which are not peaceful in character. Basically then members are enjoined to refrain from any kind of armed action.[33] The prohibition of armed reprisals, so often founded on article 2, paragraph 4,[34] could more confidently be based on article 2, paragraph 3, of the Charter.[35] Paragraph 13 (I) of the Manila Declaration, adopted by the General Assembly, quite accurately states:[36]

"Neither the existence of a dispute nor the failure of a procedure of peaceful settlement of disputes shall permit the use of force or threat of force by any of the States parties to the dispute."

A final issue in this subsection lies with the text of article 2, paragraph 3, which is confined to the settlement of "international disputes". Would it be possible to argue that a particular dispute is not international in character or that there is no dispute, and that therefore the obligation to settle through peaceful means is not relevant?

Regarding the first issue it may be said that what is international and what is not depends on the development and state of international law.[37] Any matter which is not regulated by international law will fall, essentially, within the domestic jurisdiction of States.[38] When a State uses force to settle a particular matter falling essentially within its domestic jurisdiction, any dispute resulting therefrom with another State will not be international in character if the first State was not required to act otherwise. If the second State makes claims on such matters and applies coercion to the first State, it will be in breach of its obligation under the prohibition of intervention. Nowadays the issue is less crucial since many matters previously falling within the domestic jurisdiction of States have been regulated through the conventional and customary rules on human rights.

As to the second question it may be said that any cross-border use of armed force in the absence of a pre-existing dispute must be considered, *prima facie*, a breach of obligation under article 2, paragraph 3. The fact that a State has not pronounced itself as to its position on the facts or the law cannot be taken to mean that therefore another State can use force against it. Indeed the non-existence of a dispute between two States may be due exactly because the State resorting to force did not at any time take any precise position on the situation.[39] Adhering to such a stance would imply that surprise uses of force would not be contrary to the obligation to settle disputes by peaceful means. It is submitted that such an interpretation would defeat the object and purpose of article 2, paragraph 3, or even the whole Charter, and cannot be admitted.

5.2.3. THE PROHIBITION OF THE USE OF ARMED FORCE, CUSTOMARY INTERNATIONAL LAW, AND *JUS COGENS*

The use of armed force and customary international law

In the Nicaragua Case, due to the operation of the multilateral treaty reservation, the Court had to judge the conduct of the United States almost exclusively in terms of customary international law.[40] The Court did indeed find that the prohibition of the threat or use of force against the territorial integrity or political independence of any State had been enshrined in customary international law.[41] Its examination on these matters focused on the rule prohibiting armed force against the territorial integrity or political independence of States. It did not distinguish between uses of force generally breaching article 2, paragraph 3, and those specifically against the territorial integrity or political independence of States violating article 2, paragraph 4.[42] However, the Court extensively discussed the prohibition of intervention, and as already noted, in subsection 5.2.1, that concerns the "political independence" of States.[43]

The absence of any particular argument devoted to breaches of obligation under the rule stipulating the settlement of disputes by peaceful means may be explained also by reference to the constellation of facts underlying the case. The United States' attacks and acts of intervention involving the use of force were part of a scheme to put pressure on Nicaragua to change its policies on militarization, human rights, and democracy.[44] Nicaragua did not claim that the United States acted contrary to article 2, paragraph 3, but only against article 2, paragraph 4, and it did not distinguish between any such uses of force under customary international law.[45] For obvious reasons the Court did not therefore address the alleged uses of force from the viewpoint of the forcible settlement of disputes.

Although the Court therefore did not address the question whether there had been any breach of the obligation to settle disputes peacefully, it observed that it had to recall another principle involved:[46]

> "(...) respect for which is essential in the world of today: the principle that the parties to any dispute, particularly any dispute the continuance of which is likely to endanger the maintenance of international peace and security, should seek a solution by peaceful means. Enshrined in Article 33 of the United Nations Charter, (...), this principle has also the status of customary law."

It is submitted that the rule of customary international law not merely imposes the positive duty to settle disputes peacefully, but also the negative duty to refrain from forcible action intended to settle a dispute. A further argument may be advanced in that the obligation applies equally where there is a dispute and where there is none. It even applies in the absence of mounting tension between States. In sum, a breach of the obligation to settle disputes peacefully, or to act peacefully, occurs whenever a State uses armed force wilfully as against another State.

The use of armed force and jus cogens

The Commission, in its commentary to draft article 50 on the law of treaties (now 53), claimed:[47]

> "(...) the law of the Charter concerning the prohibition of the use of force in itself constitutes a conspicuous example of a rule in international law having the character of *jus cogens*."

This statement was quoted by the Court, in the Nicaragua Case, so as to validate the customary law nature of the principle laid down in article 2, paragraph 4, of the Charter.[48] In chapter three it has extensively been argued that the rule prohibiting the threat or use of force against the territorial integrity or political independence of States constitutes a peremptory norm of general international law. As a result the reparation obligations resulting from a committed internationally wrongful act, whether a delict or a crime, could not involve any loss of territory or downgrading of the political independence of any State. The latter would have to be understood in the sense that, notwithstanding certain limits flowing from the rules on guarantees against repetition, (the population of) a State would be free to determine its own future.

Yet the quoted part seems inevitably to lead to the conclusion that the rule prohibiting the use of force, generally, constitutes a peremptory norm. That would mean that any treaty, for example the Charter, contemplating the (lawful) use of force, *e.g.* articles 42 and 51, would be void for conflict with a rule of *jus cogens*. As already noted such a conclusion would be manifestly absurd. A further text of the Commission also does not testify to any such intention. Article 33, Part One, of the ILC-draft on State responsibility, stipulates that a state of necessity cannot be invoked as a ground precluding wrongfulness if the obligation arises out of a peremptory norm. Yet the commentary to that article makes clear that there may be:[49] "(...) doubt on the question whether all international obligations concerning respect for territorial sovereignty of States have really become obligations of *jus cogens*, (...)."

In relation more specifically to the rule prescribing the peaceful settlement of disputes the obvious claim, enunciated by Charpentier, must be that:[50]

> "On ne saurait toutefois aller au-delà, et lui reconnaître, à la différence de ce qui est généralement admis pour l'article 2, paragraphe 4, la valeur impérative d'un principe de *jus cogens*;"

In certain cases the Charter clearly allows the Security Council (article 42) or (a) (group of) State(s) (article 51) to have resort to the use of force in order to impose a return to a previously existing status quo. In such cases it is possible to argue that such use of force may be justified under the rules of State responsibility notwithstanding the rule stipulating the peaceful settlement of disputes. Whether there exist any other possible justifications, besides the two mentioned, will be seen later on. Preliminary to that issue is the question whether the Charter based derogations or exceptions would be, legally speaking, the only ones admissible under either the Charter or customary international law.

5.2.4. EXCLUSIVENESS OF CHARTER BASED DEROGATIONS AND EXCEPTIONS TO THE PROHIBITION OF THE USE OF ARMED FORCE?

The Charter leaves room for the justifiable use of armed force by either the Security Council or members acting individually or collectively. Article 42 is noteworthy in this respect because it is the only provision that refers in a more explicit manner to the possibility of armed action. Other provisions suffer, to some extent, from obscurity. Article 51 limits itself to affirming the inherent right of individual or collective "self-defence"; article 53, paragraph 1, notes that regional arrangements or agencies shall not resort to "enforcement action" without authorization of the Security Council; article 94, paragraph 2, confers on the Security Council the power to decide on "measures" to give effect to a judgment of the Court;[51] in article 106 it is said that the Four Powers and France shall consult with one another and, as required, with other members of the United Nations, pending the coming into force of the agreements of article 43, with a view to such "joint action" as may be necessary for the purpose of the maintenance of international peace and security; and article 107 finally states that nothing in the Charter shall invalidate or preclude "action" in relation to enemy States (defined in article 53, paragraph 2) taken or authorized by governments, having responsibility for such action, as a result of the second world war. Can it be said that the Charter limitatively provides for derogations or exceptions to the prohibition of the use of military force? Or is it possible to infer other such derogations or exceptions under either the Charter or customary international law?

In relation to these questions an interpretation of the Charter would not seem to open up to any use of armed force other than that in application of the provisions mentioned. Two issues tend to qualify an absolute stance in this respect.

First there is the occurrence of peace-keeping operations. Military forces established under such operations are stationed on the territory of a State only with its consent.[52] The legitimacy of establishing such forces has been questioned mainly insofar as they were created by the General Assembly and not by the Security Council. Any doubts in relation thereto were, however, authoritatively dispelled by the Court. Troops acting under a peace-keeping operation are allowed to use force only to the extent that such force operates within the bounds of the consent given.[53] It should be noted though that force can always be resorted to in the exercise of a right of self-defence. Regarding the subject under review, whether the Charter allows for the use of force other than based on specific provisions, the example of peace-keeping operations does not provide an answer. Although there has been a trend to have such operations based upon specific Charter provisions or the Charter generally, it is submitted that their existence can in addition be based on the customary rule allowing States to consent to the stationing of armed forces on their territories.

Secondly attention may be drawn to the practice of the Security Council by which it grants an authorization to use all necessary means in order to reach certain goals. Such authorization was first granted by way of resolution 678 to the "Member States co-operating with the Government of Kuwait", and has been granted on a number of occasions since. The phrase "to use all necessary means" had been intended, and therefore interpreted, to include resort to armed force. Any specific Charter basis for such authorizations to States cannot be found. The question of their legal basis will be explored more thoroughly in subsection 5.4.3.

Does, or even can, customary international law contain rules derogating from the prohibition of the use of force?

A preliminary question is whether the rights of States under customary international law pertaining to the use of force have survived the conventional limitations imposed upon members by virtue of the Charter. The guiding principle, to quote the Court in the Expenses Opinion, is that:[54] "Save as they have entrusted the Organization with the attainment of these common ends, the Member States retain their freedom of action." Fundamentally there does not exist, therefore, any objection to recognizing the possibility of the continued validity of a rule of customary international law providing for a right to use military force. However, as Bowett quite correctly observes:[55]

> "We must presuppose that rights formerly belonging to member states continue except in so far as obligations inconsistent with those existing rights are assumed under the Charter."

It follows that any use of armed force against the territorial integrity or political independence of a State, or in any manner inconsistent with the purposes of the United Nations, or contrary to the peaceful settlement of disputes, cannot be justified by reference to any customary law right predating the introduction of the basic Charter obligations under article 2, paragraphs 3 and 4.[56]

While this argument does away with the stance that there would be room for the continued exercise of customary law rights predating the Charter, the question whether any such right could come into existence considering the broad Charter prohibition of the use of force remains to be answered. The answer may be in the affirmative. In the Nicaragua Case the Court discussed not only whether a right of self-defence existed in customary international law, but also whether there existed a right to intervene, without or with the use of force, in support of the opposition within a State.[57] Similarly it considered whether force could be used, collectively, against a State which itself used force falling below the threshold of an armed attack.[58] It denied the existence, in law, of either of those justifications, but noted in respect of a potential right to intervene:[59] "For such a general right to come into existence would involve a fundamental modification of the customary law principle of non-intervention." The Court followed through on this by saying that:[60] "Reliance by a State on a novel right or an unprecedented exception to the principle might, if shared in principle by other States, tend towards a modification of customary international law." Clearly then the conclusion must be drawn that customary international law might develop a rule justifying the use of force in situations other than those justifying the use of force by States under Charter provisions. If the existence of such a rule could be established it would constitute a defence against charges of breaches of obligation under the Charter in relation to States against which force is used, against other States, and in relation to the United Nations.

5.3. The function and nature of resort to armed force

With regard to this section most of the considerations related to countermeasures contained in chapter four, section 4.2, will apply, *mutatis mutandis*, to the function and nature of resort to armed force.

The goal to be attained through recourse to armed force will be, as with resort to countermeasures, to obtain reparation. Any idea of punishment or punitive intent, other than in the "minds" of the State resorting to armed action or the State targeted by it, lies with the nature of the specific forms of reparation. The author State's psychologically (mis)perceived perception of ideas of punishment or punitive intent on the part of the injured State, as a consequence of the application against it of armed force, rests on the setting aside of an obligation by the injured State. The coercive element thus inherent in an injured State's recourse to armed force does not constitute an end in itself, but a means to obtain reparation. To the extent that recourse to armed force might be resorted to in particular circumstances, those circumstances would justify, in international law, the suspension of the injured State's obligation not to resort to force against the author State.

Though the observations on the function and nature of countermeasures apply for the most part to resort to armed force, some additional remarks are necessary on the relation between reparation and armed force and on the issue whether armed force would involve exceptional measures.

The object to be attained by an injured State's resort to countermeasures or armed force will generally be to obtain reparation. However, in case of resort to countermeasures this objective can be accomplished only with the co-operation of the author State.

That conclusion would be different only if one accepted the notion, rejected earlier, that countermeasures could involve irreversible acts such as nationalization or the confiscation of assets and property.

Resort to armed force by an injured State against an author State for the purpose of enforcing the latter State's international responsibility will not necessitate the co-operation of the author State. In such circumstances the goal of the injured State by having resort to armed force will normally be to impose upon the author State respect for its reparation obligations. The imposition, by way of armed force, of respect for reparation obligations may be effected either in the absence or in the face of armed opposition by the author State. For that reason resort to armed force by an injured State against an author State takes away the choice the latter might have had in the matter: which would have been either to accede to reparation demands or to refuse them. The use of armed force to impose respect for reparation obligations by an injured State therefore constitutes forcible implementation of the international responsibility of an author State, and, as such, amounts to the forced settlement of reparation disputes between the injured and author States.

The object of an injured State by using force against an author State of an international crime will be, in first instance,[61] to effect the cessation of the conduct constituting the crime and also, in case of continuing occupation due to aggression, to impose restitution of territory. Whether or not the performance of other reparation obligations (compensation, satisfaction, and guarantees against repetition) may be enforced through the use of armed force will be discussed separately in sections 5.5 and 5.6.[62]

In regard to self-defence it has been claimed by Ago that state of necessity and self-defence are:[63] "(...) expressions that connote a situation or *de facto* conditions, not a subjective right." He continued on the next page:[64]

> "It would be quite wrong to think that self-defence can also be defined as a kind of sanction, even if it were described as a sanction applicable to a specific kind of wrong. 'Self-defence' and 'sanction' are reactions relevant to different moments and, above all, are distinct in logic. Besides, action in a situation of self-defence, is as its name indicates, action taken by a State in order to defend its territorial integrity or its independence against violent attacks; it is action whereby 'defensive' use of force is opposed to an 'offensive' use of comparable force, with the object – and this is the core of the matter – of preventing another's wrongful action from proceeding, succeeding and achieving its purpose. Action taken in the form of a sanction on the other hand involves the application *ex post facto* to the State committing the international wrong of one of the possible consequences that international law attaches to the commission of an act of this nature."

A first remark here would be that is difficult to see why it would be wrong to think of self-defence in terms of rights. Assuredly action taken by a State in response to an armed attack is defensive in character. Yet a State need not necessarily act in self-defence if it is attacked, that is, it may refrain from exercising its right. States are under the obligation not to use armed force against other States, which includes an obligation not to initiate an armed attack. Against a breach of obligation in the form of an armed attack is then set the right to take cross-border action in self-defence.

In the second place it is not clear what distinguishes (aside from a possible temporal difference) self-defence from sanctions. Self-defence action by definition involves a reaction against a continuing breach of obligation by the attacking State. In that sense the use of force is intended to effect a cessation of wrongful conduct. To the extent that a State is attempting to regain occupied territory, notwithstanding that hostilities had come to an end (if only temporarily), such a use of force is generally regarded as self-defence. Yet at that point in time the action is no longer, strictly speaking, defensive in character. Consequently, it would not be inappropriate to consider such action as a sanction.

As to the nature of use of armed force the question arises whether this kind of enforcement constitutes a generally applicable means to ensure an author State's compliance with its reparation obligations, or whether it would only exceptionally be justified to resort to armed force for such purposes.

The reparation obligations established in consequence of the commission of an international delict cannot ordinarily be enforced through use of armed force.[65] Article 14 (a), Part Two, provisionally adopted by the Commission, provides:[66] "An injured State shall not resort by way of countermeasure, to: (a) the threat or use of force as prohibited by the Charter of the United Nations." Since the use of force for the settlement of disputes, including disputes related to reparation obligations, is prohibited under article 2, paragraph 3, of the Charter, the Commission's proposal confirms the prohibition of armed reprisals.

In relation to international crimes Arangio-Ruiz put forward the question, first of all:[67] "(...) whether armed measures are not admissible also in order to bring about the cessation of crimes other than aggression."; and secondly:[68]

> "(...) whether this would constitute the 'typical' sanction of a crime (...), or whether it would correspond to a different ratio. We have in mind, for example, the ratio underlying the 'state of necessity' or 'distress' – circumstances which do indeed rule out illegitimacy but, unlike self-defence, are not characterized by the fact of authorizing a direct reaction against the perpetrator of a particularly serious international breach."

It is clearly possible to, and it is submitted that one should, envisage the use of armed force as the "typical" response to an international crime. In that sense there would be nothing exceptional about making the general statement that the commission, and perpetuation, of an international crime ought to be prevented or suppressed through the use of armed force. Within the Commission there is, however, a trend which would extend the prohibition of countermeasures involving the use of force applicable to delicts to international crimes.[69] Arangio-Ruiz has proposed, apparently on that basis, that the prohibition of countermeasures involving the threat or use of armed force applicable in case of delicts should apply also in case of crimes.[70] In the event that such a trend, and his proposal, would be laid down in a text adopted by the Commission, it would follow that the only permissible unilateral or concerted reaction involving the use of force would be self-defence against an armed attack. In a factual sense then justifiable uses of force by way of self-defence would certainly be exceptional. However, the right of self-defence as an exceptional right flows not from the fact that there exists a general prohibition of the use of armed force as such. Rather it is the competence of the Security Council to act against uses of force generally, and by the use of force if necessary, that accounts for the exceptional and temporary character of the right of self-defence.[71]

It is not possible to claim, as to military action by the Security Council under article 42 of the Charter, that armed force would only exceptionally be permitted for the restoration of international peace and security.[72] For the Security Council is entitled to initiate such action not only if it considers that the measures under article 41 have proved to be inadequate, but also if it considers, from the start, that they would be inadequate.[73] Furthermore, such action may be taken not only to maintain or restore international peace and security in consequence of a breach of the peace or act of aggression, but also in circumstances where there is a (mere) threat to the peace. A very wide measure of discretion is thus granted to the Security Council.[74] To the extent then that it determines the existence of a threat to the peace substantially unrelated to the use of force, it certainly possesses the competence to resort to military action under article 42 in response to international crimes other than that of aggression.

5.4. Preconditions for resort to armed force

5.4.1. THE COMMISSION OF AN INTERNATIONALLY WRONGFUL ACT, REPARATION DEMANDS, DISPUTE SETTLEMENT AND ARMED FORCE

The arguments forwarded in relation to resort to countermeasures in regard to the basic precondition of an internationally wrongful act apply also in relation to resort to armed force and need not detain us for long. Clearly the existence of an internationally wrongful act is fulfilled in case of committed international crimes. As pointed out in relation to countermeasures the basic content of the rules under which international crimes can take place is not disputed. As to the existence of the wrongful acts constituting crimes, the criterion of "serious" breaches of obligation under such rules makes any assessment as to their existence an easy task.

The international crime of aggression warrants some additional remarks in view of the fact that article 51 of the Charter stipulates that nothing will impair the right of self-defence against an armed attack until the Security Council has taken measures necessary to maintain international peace and security. The implication resulting from the text of this provision must be that if there is no armed attack there does not exist any right of self-defence, and if there is an armed attack a right of self-defence exists.[75] It follows also that from the moment of attack a right of self-defence may be exercised until the Security Council has taken measures.[76] In case the Security Council does not take any measures the exercise of the right of self-defence may be continued for as long as the objects of self-defence have not been accomplished (see *infra* subsection 5.5.1).[77] The conclusion must be that for as long as the Security Council has not taken measures any individual, or group of, State(s) may judge whether an armed attack has taken place.[78] Since an armed attack by one State against another will of necessity be inconsistent with the obligations under article 2, paragraphs 3 or 4, this amounts to a competence, for purposes of self-defence, to determine the existence of an internationally wrongful act. A right of self-defence will exist only in the presence of an internationally wrongful act constituting an armed attack (on which more in subsection 5.5.1). Whether the assessment of a State claiming the existence of an armed attack is correct, and consequently whether its use of force constitutes self-defence, again depends on the interpretation of the legal rules and the verification of the facts by the Security Council and all States concerned alike.[79]

It has been argued by Dallal:[80]

> "However, because the Security Council is a political body and not a court of justice, its actions are of necessity political and not judicial. While the U.N. Security Council's decision to condemn Iraq's invasion of Kuwait may have been unavoidable politically, such condemnation was probably premature and perhaps unjustified legally. It would have been justified legally only if it were coupled with an advisory opinion by the International Court of Justice (ICJ) that Iraq's invasion of Kuwait was in fact an act of aggression."

These propositions are legally insupportable. Article 39 of the Charter clearly confers the power on the Security Council to determine that an act of aggression has taken place. One cannot find any provision in the Charter restricting that competence. Article 36, paragraph 3, which states that "legal disputes should as a rule be referred by the parties to the International Court of Justice", cannot be seen to curtail the Security Council's powers. That provision belongs to Chapter VI on the peaceful settlement of disputes. The determination of an act of aggression by the Security Council under article 39 presupposes that a dispute between certain parties has resulted in such tense relations that the use of its recommendatory powers under Chapter VI would not suffice to deal with the situation. If that is the case the Security Council may judge it opportune to resort to measures under articles 41 or 42 against one, several, or all, of the parties to the dispute. Furthermore, article 36, paragraph 3, concerns the peaceful settlement of disputes between the parties only, not the settlement of a dispute between the Security Council and one of the parties as to whether an act of aggression has taken place. The provision of article 96, paragraph 1, moreover, clearly establishes only the right of the Security Council to request advisory opinions. There is no indication whatsoever that an obligation to do so, whether general or specific, would exist.
As to the political nature of the Security Council's actions, that is no different than the nature of State actions. A State is no more than a political (and legal) entity. However, decisions on State actions are made not by the legal but by the political organs of a State. On the international plane a State under attack clearly can defend itself notwithstanding the fact that the existence of such an armed attack has not been verified by the Court. Such an armed attack may eventually be judged by the Court to be nonexistent.[81] Yet in first instance the political organ of a State provisionally determines the existence of an armed attack. Could the Security Council do less? Certainly not.

As to the question whether any obligation to demand reparation or to have recourse to dispute settlement can be imposed on an injured State before it resorts to armed force, the answer must again, as with resort to countermeasures, be in the negative.

The intentional, wilful, and clearly premeditated character of international crimes destroys any hope of voluntary compliance by the author State with its reparation obligations or that any peaceful settlement of disputes could be effected.[82] It is for those reasons that one ought to view resort to armed force as the "typical" reaction to international crimes. Such response to international crimes, that is, use of armed force, is the only totally and completely efficacious means to effect cessation of, and restitution in regard to, wrongful conduct.[83] That is not to say that no settlement at all ought to be effected. Eventually one would at least expect the conclusion of a treaty of some kind related to the troops occupying territory (if there are any) of the author State, a cease-fire, and possibly on withdrawal of troops.

In regard to the Iraq-Kuwait crisis it has been alleged that the failure by the Security Council to have recourse to the peaceful means of dispute settlement under article 33 amounted to a violation of the Charter.[84] A contextual interpretation of the Charter must lead to the conclusion that once the Council determines a threat to the peace, breach of the peace, or act of aggression under Chapter VII of the Charter, procedures under Chapter VI need no longer be applied by it.[85] While such a conclusion could arguably be assailed where the Council determines a "mere" threat to the peace, it certainly cannot be opposed in case of breaches of the peace or acts of aggression.[86] The fact that the Security Council, in resolution 660, operative paragraph 3, called upon Iraq and Kuwait to "begin immediately intensive negotiations for the resolution of their differences" is similarly beside the point. First, because it is placed after operative paragraph 2 which "demands that Iraq withdraw immediately and unconditionally all its forces to the positions in which they were located on 1 August 1990". The call for negotiations is thus clearly subordinated to the withdrawal of Iraqi forces. Secondly, because the call for negotiations does not concern the disputes on withdrawal or sovereignty over Kuwait,[87] but the frontier disputes and differences over oil and debts between the two States on which negotiations had broken down just before the Iraqi invasion.

The situation is certainly different if a party to a dispute has already initiated recourse to dispute settlement. The United States, for instance, brought its dispute with Iran regarding the American hostages in Tehran before the Court. After the indication of provisional measures by the Court,[88] but before its judgment on the merits, the United States attempted to free the hostages by way of armed force.[89] The Court in this respect felt:[90] "(...) bound to observe that an operation undertaken in those circumstances, from whatever motive, is of a kind calculated to undermine respect for the judicial process in international relations;" In addition to the provisional measures indicated (mainly the release of hostages; facilities to leave Iran; and no action which might aggravate tension) the circumstances referred to concerned the request by the United States to the Court to obtain an early judgment. However, the Court noted that its findings on the conduct of the Iranian government six months earlier were not affected by United States' actions.[91] The conclusion appears justified that the fact that armed force is being used during arbitral or judicial proceedings does not prejudge the legality of such armed force. An obligation to abstain from such force consequently cannot be presumed.

5.4.2. ARMED ACTION BY THE SECURITY COUNCIL UNDER ARTICLE 42 OF THE CHARTER

Article 42 of the Charter provides:

> "Should the Security Council consider that the measures provided for in Article 41 would be inadequate or have proved to be inadequate, it may take such action by air, sea, or land forces as may be necessary to maintain or restore international peace and security. Such action may include demonstrations, blockade, and other operations by air, sea, or land forces of Members of the United Nations."

A number of issues arises with regard to this provision: the relationship to article 39, the relationship to article 41, and the relationship to article 43.

The relationship to article 39 of the Charter

The first question is whether the Security Council could take action under article 42 without first having determined, under article 39, the existence of a threat to the peace, breach of the peace, or act of aggression. In regard to the analogous question on measures under article 41 the answer was in the negative, and so it must also be in regard to action under article 42.[92]

The contrary position, adopted by Fischer,[93] does not convince. He claims that under article 39 the Security Council only determines threats to the peace, breaches of the peace, or acts of aggression. Article 42 on the other hand speaks about the maintenance or restoration of "international" peace and security. Accordingly, so he claims, the differing formulations militate in favour of the separability of the texts.[94] That stance neglects that article 39 provides that the Security Council "shall decide what measures shall be taken in accordance with Articles 41 and 42, to maintain or restore *international* peace and security." Essentially this means that the Security Council's competence regarding threats to the peace should be exercised in order to maintain or restore "international" peace.[95] Whatever meaning ought to be attached generally to "threats to the peace", clearly any threat to "international" peace will generate a threat to the peace.

Another argument mentioned by Fischer to support his position, that article 94, paragraph 2, allows for action under article 42 in the absence of a threat to the peace,[96] is even less convincing. Action by the Security Council under article 42 must be "necessary to maintain or restore international peace and security". The measures decided on under article 94, paragraph 2, on the other hand must be "to give effect to the judgment". The objectives to be reached through the exercise of the competencies under the two provisions are obviously not cognate. Measures under article 94, paragraph 2, may be similar to the measures under Chapter VII, but recourse to them is not subordinated to the procedures of Chapter VII.

A more difficult question is whether the Security Council could resort to armed force with regard to each and any of the situations envisaged under article 39. The construction and formulation of the provisions under Chapter VII do not support a restrictive view on the matter. Breaches of the peace and acts of aggression can surely be addressed through action under article 42. It is less easy to conceive of armed action with regard to just any kind of threat to the peace.

One may consider, as an example, the case of Libya. By way of resolution 748 the Security Council determined that Libya's continued failure to demonstrate by concrete actions its renunciation of terrorism constituted a threat to the peace. It then decided (paragraphs 1 and 2) that Libya had to comply with requests by France, the United States and the United Kingdom (basically the handing over of suspects);[97] that it had to commit itself to cease all forms of terrorist action and assistance to terrorist groups; and that it must demonstrate its renunciation of terrorism through concrete actions. In the event that Libya did not comply with these paragraphs by 15 April 1992, all States were to take certain measures against Libya (operative paragraphs 3 to 6). Although Libya has not complied, until now, with the requests of France, the United Kingdom and the United States, it is hard to imagine the Security Council taking action under article 42 of the Charter (or authorizing armed force by those States) for the purpose of going into Libya and taking hold of the suspects. It might not be too farfetched to claim that the measures imposed on Libya by way of resolution 748 have proved to be inadequate to maintain international peace and security. Yet not many would argue that armed force could now be used against Libya. It may be submitted that the basis for denying the possibility of using force against Libya would lie with the perceived disproportionality of using force in relation to Libya's conduct, which has been determined to constitute no more than a threat to the peace.

The relationship to article 41 of the Charter

Another issue is whether the Security Council ought to proceed to take action under article 42 only after having attempted to enforce its decisions through measures under article 41. The text of article 42 does not support such an interpretation: the Security Council may take action if it considers that measures under article 41 would be inadequate.[98] Consequently a large measure of discretion has been endowed on the Security Council. In this respect one may note that the Court, in the Nicaragua Case, distinguished between treaty provisions related to "necessary measures" and "measures considered necessary", and it observed:[99]

> "(...) whether a measure is necessary to protect the essential security interests of a party is not (...) purely a question for the subjective judgment of the party; the text does not refer to what the party 'considers necessary' for that purpose."

Apparently a provision stipulating that a State party may consider measures to be necessary allows for a subjective appraisal, and it is unlikely that the Court would easily substitute that by its own. The Security Council, then, has been given the competence to evaluate, subjectively, whether or not the measures of article 41 would be adequate. A decision to the effect that they would not be adequate evidently could not easily be censured.

It has been observed, however, by Eisemann:[100]

> "Mais on peut également soutenir avec quelque légitimité que, hormis des situations exceptionelles dans lesquelles la force doit répondre à la force, c'est recours à des mesures non militaires qui *politiquement* s'impose en premier lieu."

Political expediency as to which kind of measures ought to be resorted to always imposes itself, though such considerations necessarily do not qualify as legal restrictions. For reasons similar to those expressed in the previous paragraph the question whether or not action under article 42 may be taken, either with or without previously imposed measures under article 41, ought to depend on considerations of proportionality.

Another hypothesis covered by article 42 lies with previously attempted enforcement by the Security Council of its decisions through the imposition of measures against a State under article 41. In such a case, article 42 states, the Security Council may take action should it consider that such measures "have proved to be inadequate". Here too, one would say, the Security Council enjoys a wide measure of discretion.

In relation to the Iraq-Kuwait crisis it has been suggested, by Weston, that the decision to forego reliance on the non-military measures of article 41 in favour of military confrontation was premature.[101] Admittedly the sanctions of resolution 661 had only been in place a bare three and a half months when resolution 678 was adopted. At the same time it has been conceded, seemingly also by Weston, that the sanctions probably would not have produced any decisive results for at least another year.[102] It might be pointed out that the armed attack by Iraq against Kuwait, even though consummated, could have led, immediately, to the use of military force against Iraq in the exercise of a right of collective self-defence. Seen in this light the Security Council unquestionably could have adopted a decision to resort to armed action at once. That it decided that armed force could be used some four months later cannot then, in the light of the circumstances, be called in question.

The relationship to article 43 of the Charter

It was said just now that the Security Council could have resorted to armed action at once in relation to Iraq's attack on Kuwait. That surely constitutes an accurate assessment of the facts of the case and of the Security Council's competence under article 42. There is, however, one problem: the Security Council generally cannot take action under article 42 due to the absence of the special agreements contemplated by article 43 of the Charter.[103] To put it simply: it does not hold or control any air, sea or land forces with which to take action.

The view has been put forward, by Franck and Patel, that there has been armed action by the Security Council under article 42 in relation to the situations in Korea and Kuwait.[104] That view appears incorrect. On the legal level the interpretation of article 42, and its context (especially articles 46 and 47), clearly shows that it must be the Security Council which initiates and controls action under article 42.[105] The military operations against North Korea and Iraq assuredly were not under Security Council control. True, the forces in Korea were authorized by the Security Council to use the United Nations flag, members providing military forces and assistance were recommended to place these under the unified command of the United States, and the United States was requested to designate the commander of the forces.[106] In spite of these indications the action against North Korea cannot be seen to have been transformed into Security Council action under article 42.[107] For similar reasons the action taken in regard to Iraq cannot be considered Security Council action under article 42 of the Charter.[108]

Although the Security Council cannot currently take action under article 42 (given the absence of the agreements envisaged in article 43), there is nothing to prevent it to utilize such forces put at its disposal, by members, in an *ad hoc* fashion.[109] That has not happened so far. Another option presents itself. This concerns the possible transformation of a peace-keeping force into forces by which the Security Council takes action under article 42. Certainly, the Court held in the Expenses Opinion that peace-keeping forces did not imply enforcement action under Chapter VII.[110] There are, nevertheless, some Security Council resolutions which testify, to a limited degree, to this possibility. The mandates of some peace-keeping operations have thus been expanded to cover the use of force in circumstances going beyond, strictly speaking, self-defence.[111]

5.4.3. RECOMMENDATIONS AND AUTHORIZATIONS TO USE ARMED FORCE

Though the Security Council presently cannot act under article 42, that does not necessarily mean that no action at all can be taken by members. The competence of the General Assembly to recommend armed action and the competence of the Security Council to authorize, or recommend, members to use all necessary means, need to be discussed.

In chapter four it was claimed (subsection 4.3.3) that the General Assembly could recommend the adoption of countermeasures for as long as there would not be any cause for action by the Security Council under Chapter VII of the Charter. The question is whether the Assembly should be held competent, generally, to recommend to members the use of armed force. The Assembly itself appeared to think so, as it resolved in resolution 377 that:[112]

> "(...) if the Security Council, because of lack of unanimity of the permanent members, fails to exercise its primary responsibility for the maintenance of international peace and security in any case where there appears to be a threat to the peace, breach of the peace, or act of aggression, the General Assembly shall consider the matter immediately with a view to making appropriate recommendations to Members for collective measures, including in the case of a breach of the peace or act of aggression the use of armed force when necessary, to maintain or restore international peace and security."

Under this resolution the General Assembly claims the competence to recommend to members the use of armed force in case of breaches of the peace and acts of aggression. Apparently it does not claim any competence to recommend the use of armed force in respect of threats to the peace or situations which would not even qualify as such. The Court, in the Expenses Opinion, noted that the sentence "Any such question on which action is necessary shall be referred to the Security Council either before or after discussion." contained in article 11, paragraph 2, refers to coercive or enforcement action under Chapter VII of the Charter.[113] Such action is, indisputably, within the province of the Security Council.[114] However, when read in conjunction to article 12, paragraph 1, the conclusion will remain that as long as the Council is not exercising its functions the Assembly can recommend members to use armed force in regard to

breaches of the peace or acts of aggression. For if there truly was a situation amounting to a breach of the peace or act of aggression one would expect the Council to exercise its functions under Chapter VII. It may be noted that the Security Council itself has called for the emergency sessions of the Assembly under Uniting for Peace resolution 377 in order for the latter to make the appropriate recommendations.[115]
The Assembly can also express its support for the exercise of any specific right to use armed force, for instance as an exercise of the right of self-defence. Should the Assembly however recommend the use of armed force, action taken in pursuit of such recommendation can be justified only if there is some other legal basis either under the Charter or customary international law.[116]

In resolution 678 the Security Council demanded Iraq's compliance with its resolution 660 and all subsequent relevant resolutions, and:[117]

> "Authorizes Member States co-operating with the Government of Kuwait, unless Iraq on or before 15 January 1991 fully implements, as set forth in paragraph 1 above, the foregoing resolutions, to use all necessary means to uphold and implement resolution 660 (1990) and all subsequent relevant resolutions and to restore international peace and security in the area;"

The discussion in the Security Council meeting surrounding the adoption of resolution 678 makes clear that the phrase "all necessary means" included the use of armed force.[118] The initiation of the action by Coalition forces against Iraq on January 16th, 1991, was fully covered by the terms of resolution 678.[119] Whether all the separate military actions can be legally justified under this heading rather depends on the requirements of necessity and proportionality, as well as compliance with rules of international humanitarian law.
The term "authorizes" raises more difficult issues, since it does not as such feature in the Charter. It has been claimed that the Security Council, not being able to take action itself, also is not competent to authorize members to use armed force. This has aroused disquiet as to the legal basis of resolution 678,[120] and more so because the Security Council has since granted a number of authorizations.[121]

Any discussion of Security Council powers ought to proceed on the basis of the Court's dictum, in the Expenses Opinion, that the argument that measures for the maintenance of international peace and security had to be financed through the agreements of article 43:[122]

> "(...) would seem to exclude the possibility that the Security Council might act under some other Article of the Charter. The Court cannot accept so limited a view of the powers of the Security Council under the Charter. It cannot be said that the Charter has left the Security Council impotent in the face of an emergency situation when agreements under Article 43 have not been concluded. Articles of Chapter VII of the Charter speak of 'situations' as well as disputes, and it must lie within the power of the Security Council to police a situation even though it does not resort to enforcement action against a State."

The Court suggests that the Security Council could act under some other article of the Charter. With due caution, considering the context of peace-keeping operations, the Court envisages action by the Security Council on some basis other than article 42 (and article 43). The problem is that such a Charter basis cannot even be found for peace-keeping operations, let alone for armed action by members. At first glance such a basis might be thought to exist in article 48, paragraph 1, of the Charter:

> "The action required to carry out the decisions of the Security Council for the maintenance of international peace and security shall be taken by all the Members of the United Nations or by some of them, as the Security Council may determine."

This provision seems to endow the Security Council with the competence to determine that action shall be taken by all the members or by some of them. This article must, however, be read in its context. There appears to be general recognition that the Security Council cannot require a member to contribute armed forces in the absence of the agreements of article 43.[123] If that interpretation is accepted, as it should, then any argument based on the text of article 48 would circumvent the meaning and scope of article 43. For that would place members under an obligation to take action directly, by way of their military forces, even though they would not be under an obligation to do so in the absence of an agreement based on article 43. The power of the Security Council under article 48 to determine which members shall take action applies only in relation to the armed forces, assistance, and facilities made available by members to the Security Council *on its call*. Since there are no such forces made available to the Security Council, article 48, paragraph 1, functions only in regard to the measures of article 41.[124] Moreover, not one of the resolutions authorizing the use of force *requires* a member to take action.[125] As it is the Security Council cannot be said to have *determined* that any member shall take action.

Naturally article 51 of the Charter was discussed in regard to the legal basis of the authorization of resolution 678. Whatever the arguments on that count (next section), they cannot have any relevance in situations other than armed conflict. For authorizations such as those related to Somalia, Rwanda and Haiti, the Charter does not offer any provision that could stand at the (legal) basis of military operations. However, it may be submitted that the requisite basis ought to be found in the Council's power to delegate its powers, under its authority, to its members. The provision of article 53, paragraph 1, specifically testifies to that possibility:[126]

> "The Security Council shall, where appropriate, utilize such regional arrangements or agencies for enforcement action under its authority. But no enforcement action shall be taken under regional arrangements or by regional agencies without the authorization of the Security Council, (...)."

It may be deduced from this that regional arrangements or agencies may take "enforcement action" upon authorization of the Security Council. The phrase "enforcement action" is generally interpreted to mean Security Council measures under articles 39, 41 and 42.[127] It must be stressed that article 53, paragraph 1, allows the Security Council to authorize regional arrangements or agencies to resort to armed force. Analogously to this provision the Security Council ought to be considered competent also to authorize individual members, or members acting collectively, to resort to armed force. Should one insist on a specific legal basis it is submitted that by now a customary rule has developed within the United Nations validating the Council's competence to grant authorizations to members.[128]

An important observation on authorizations is due, and that concerns the scope and meaning of the word. Regional arrangements and agencies do not require any authorization to resort to armed force if their action constitutes the exercise of a right of collective self-defence. States, acting in self-defence under article 51 of the Charter, also do not need any authorization to react by way of armed force to an armed attack. The interpretation of a resolution in which an "authorization" (or the word "authorizes") to use all necessary means features must be in accordance with the ordinary meaning of the word, that is, that those "authorized" would not otherwise be entitled to resort to armed force. The authorization granted by the Security Council must then be seen as a basis for precluding the wrongfulness of the conduct of a member using force contrary to its obligations under article 2 of the Charter. In the absence of such a basis the use of armed force would constitute an internationally wrongful act. A prime example of such a basis constitutes resolution 678, because Kuwait's and the Coalition's rights of self-defence had been suspended due to the imposition of sanctions in resolution 661.

Penultimately to be discussed in this section are Security Council resolutions which "call" upon members to use such measures commensurate to the specific circumstances. This poses a problem to the extent that the Security Council appears to call for the use of force in circumstances which would not, under the Charter or rules of customary international law, justify unilateral action. The Security Council has done this so far particularly in order to provide for the maritime enforcement of measures imposed by it under article 41 of the Charter.[129]
The Security Council possesses the general competence to recommend the use of armed force by members.[130] Article 39 provides that the Security Council shall make recommendations, or decide upon the measures of articles 41 and 42, to maintain or restore international peace and security. Contrary to what has been suggested the recommendations of article 39 are not confined to the action contained in Chapter VI of the Charter.[131] That chapter only deals with disputes the continuance of which is likely to endanger the maintenance of international peace and security. The recommendations of article 39 on the other hand concern situations in which the maintenance of international peace and security is not merely endangered, but has in effect proven to be unsuccessful. Such situations call for either measures or recommendations to restore international peace and security.
Furthermore, the use of the words "call upon" rather than "to authorize", or even "to recommend", suggests that the Council wants certain specified action to take place. While the latter phrases clearly leave the States addressed free to take or not take action, the former expresses the will of the Security Council that such action actually takes place. Similarly it might be remarked that the words "call upon" feature in article 41 and are commonly interpreted as indicating the mandatory character of measures decided upon.[132] However, since members are not under any obligation to provide military contingents in the absence of article 43 agreements, they also cannot be under an obligation to take the action "called upon".[133] It would seem then that resolutions which call upon States to take certain action ought to be seen to embody implicit authorizations.[134]

Finally it may be noted that there is a certain lacuna regarding the circumstances precluding wrongfulness enumerated in Chapter V, Part One, of the ILC-draft.

And this is not remedied by the Commission's observation that the list of such circumstances is not absolutely exhaustive.[135] In the commentary to article 30 the Commission has indicated that measures adopted pursuant to a decision of the Security Council under article 41 of the Charter fall within the category of countermeasures.[136] In consequence the wrongfulness of such measures will be precluded. However, if a State resorts to force upon authorization of the Security Council, or in application of a Security Council decision under article 42, no comparable circumstance precluding wrongfulness is provided for in Chapter V, Part One, of the ILC-draft.[137] Only unilateral resort to armed force is covered, in article 34, under the heading of self-defence. One would think therefore that either countermeasures would be defined anew, excluding measures adopted pursuant to a decision of the competent organs of an international organization, or that another circumstance precluding wrongfulness would be added covering resort to armed force pursuant to a Security Council authorization or decision.[138]

5.5. Resort to armed force in response to the international crime of aggression

In the previous section it has been noted that the existence of the basic precondition for the use of armed force could easily be verified in case of international crimes. Earlier (chapter one, subsection 1.9.2, and chapter two, subsection 2.6.1) it had been noted that the international crime of aggression ought to be seen in terms of an armed attack by one State against another. That conclusion is bolstered by the requirement that there must be a *serious* breach of an international obligation essential for the maintenance of international peace and security. The dividing line between serious and non-serious breaches is not an easy one to draw. Similarly it is hard to find any kind of hard and fast rule as to what constitutes an armed attack. Since the latter is apparently the only type of use of force to give rise to a right to take armed action, individually or collectively, in self-defence (article 51 Charter; article 34, Part One, ILC-draft), it will be discussed first. In this connection will be discussed some conditions, under customary international law and the Charter, for a lawful exercise of the right of self-defence. Observations regarding immediacy, necessity and proportionality, requests for assistance and "until the Security Council has taken measures" will be postponed until section 5.7. Lastly some of the issues surrounding past authorizations in this field by the Security Council will be dealt with.

5.5.1. THE EXERCISE OF THE RIGHT OF INDIVIDUAL OR COLLECTIVE SELF-DEFENCE

The interpretation of armed attack ("agression armée")

A preliminary observation is in order regarding the divergence in the English and French texts of article 51. While the English version mentions self-defence against an "armed attack", the French text stipulates the right of defence against "une agression armée". This discrepancy has in the past been interpreted to justify the use of force in circumstances other than an all out armed attack. Proponents of a broad right of self-defence have been able to point to the Definition of Aggression which defines that term in such a manner as to include, for example, any kind of attack on the military forces of a State.[139] Whatever may be thought of this, it is possible to assert that the right of self-defence laid down in article 51 generally must be interpreted restrictively due to its exceptional character. Support for this may be found in the Nicaragua Case. Thus the Court noted that:[140]

> "(...) it will be necessary to distinguish between the most grave forms of the use of force (*those constituting an armed attack*) from other less grave forms."

As a follow-up the Court observed that some of the rules contained in the Declaration on Principles of International Law referred to aggression, while others concerned only less grave forms of the use of force.[141] Obviously then only the most grave forms of the use of armed force are considered an armed attack and give rise to a right of self-defence. This latter proposition must be qualified however.

As to the kind of uses of force which constitute armed attacks the Court observed:[142]

> "(...) an armed attack must be understood as including not merely action by regular armed forces across an international border, but also 'the sending by or on behalf of a State of armed bands, groups, irregulars or mercenaries, which carry out acts of armed force against another State of such gravity as to amount to' *(inter alia)* an actual armed attack conducted by regular forces, 'or its substantial involvement therein'."

And it continued:[143]

> "The Court sees no reason to deny that, in customary law, the prohibition of armed attacks may apply also to the sending by a State of armed bands to the territory of another State, if such an operation, because of its scale and effects, would have been classified as an armed attack rather than as a mere frontier incident had it been carried out by regular armed forces. But the Court does not believe that the concept of 'armed attack' includes not only acts by armed bands where such acts occur on a significant scale but also assistance to rebels in the form of the provision of weapons or logistical or other support. Such assistance may be regarded as a threat or use of force, or amount to intervention in the internal or external affairs of other States."

The Court thus establishes a dichotomy between uses of force or acts of intervention which constitute armed attacks and those which do not. The former comprises action by regular forces across international borders and the sending of armed bands which carry out acts of armed force of such particular gravity as to amount to an armed attack (or a State's substantial involvement therein). The latter consists of uses of force or acts of intervention amounting to assistance to rebels in the form of the provision of weapons and/or logistical or other support. The one kind does give rise to a right of self-defence, while the other kind would not.[144]

However, matters are complicated due to the Court's claim that:[145]

> "While an armed attack would give rise to an entitlement to collective self-defence, a use of force of a lesser degree cannot, as the Court has already observed (paragraph 211 above), produce any entitlement to take collective counter-measures involving the use of force. The acts of which Nicaragua is accused, even assuming them to have been established and imputable to that

> State, could only have justified proportionate counter-measures on the part of the State which had been the victim of these acts, namely El Salvador, Honduras or Costa Rica. They could not justify counter-measures taken by a third State, and particularly could not justify intervention involving the use of force."

A few conclusions can be drawn from this statement. First, that an armed attack gives rise to a right of collective self-defence. Secondly, that a use of force of a lesser degree than an armed attack does not give rise to a right to take collective counter-measures involving the use of force. Thirdly, that such uses of force of a lesser degree do in fact give rise to a right of States to take, for themselves, proportionate countermeasures. What is meant by "proportionate countermeasures" is not defined by the Court.[146] The term "countermeasure" is generally reserved for measures not involving the use of force, but the conclusion seems inescapable that the Court acknowledges the right of a directly injured State to use force in regard to uses of force and/or acts of intervention which do not constitute an armed attack. If that is truly the case it is difficult to see how such an entitlement could be characterized other than as a right of individual self-defence. It cannot be denied that a right of individual self-defence exists also with regard to frontier incidents and isolated attacks on the military forces of a State. One would think that such defence could be carried out also, under certain circumstances, on the territory of the State whose forces first attacked.[147] To name such acts of defence proportionate countermeasures would be a misnomer. Countermeasures in response to an internationally wrongful act generally need not be resorted to immediately. Reactions to frontier incidents on the other hand, involving a cross-border use of force, must take place at once. Should the fighting have stopped and no foreign troops remain on the territory, an injured State can no longer invoke a right to use force across the international border. Ultimately the Court appears to make a distinction between uses of force of a lesser degree that give rise to a right of individual self-defence, and uses of force constituting an armed attack which give rise, over and above the right of individual self-defence, to a right of collective self-defence.[148] The right laid down in article 51 of the Charter would then by definition only concern the latter category of uses of force, since it provides for a right of collective self-defence.

That a right of individual self-defence would exist in response to uses of force falling short of an armed attack does not come as a surprise. The Court, however, in the consideration quoted at the beginning of the previous paragraph, spoke of the alleged acts imputable to Nicaragua conceivably justifying proportionate countermeasures on the part of the victims of such acts, notably El Salvador, Honduras or Costa Rica. To the extent that such countermeasures could involve a cross-border use of force on the part of Honduras and Costa Rica, this could be viewed as the exercise of a right of individual self-defence.[149]

The same cannot as easily be said in relation to the alleged Nicaraguan acts regarding El Salvador. In the abstract the Court had stated that the concept of an armed attack does not include "assistance to rebels in the form of the provision of weapons or logistical or other support".[150] In this particular case the Court only discussed the alleged, though subsequently proven as between July 1979 and early 1981, provision of arms by Nicaragua to the opposition in El Salvador.[151] As to the kind of breaches of obligation such support (provision of arms, logistical or other) would amount to, the Court, again in the abstract, noted that they could be considered uses of force or intervention in the internal or external affairs.[152] The Court nowhere elaborates which kind of support would amount to a use of force, and which kind ought to be considered intervention. However, it may be deduced that the arming and training of irregular forces or armed bands, if the purpose is incursion into the territory of another State, would constitute a threat or use of force.[153] The Court claimed that support in the order of financing, intelligence, logistics, and even humanitarian assistance if rendered on a discriminatory basis, constitutes intervention in the internal or external affairs.[154]

It may be wondered whether the arming and training of irregulars or armed bands should be considered a use of force. It may reasonably be argued that this may amount to a threat to use force. One may hesitate to conclude that such acts would give rise, by themselves, to a right of individual self-defence. That would open the door, for instance, to allow a State to engage in air strikes against training camps in another State. The situation changes, one would think, where the irregulars or armed bands are caught crossing the border. In such cases a right of individual self-defence, involving a cross-border use of force, may be exercised, subject however to requirements of necessity and proportionality.

Taking the issue back one would have to say that the Court's construction of the customary rules regarding the use of armed force appears to accord with the Commission's view that injured State status in respect of uses of force accrues to all States only in relation to the crime of aggression. And the Commission has advocated this example only in relation to a *serious* breach of an essential obligation for the maintenance of international peace and security. The serious breach mentioned in article 19, paragraph 3 (a), Part One, of the ILC-draft, must involve a transgression of the prohibition of aggression. It stands to reason then that the need for a serious breach is tantamount to posing the requirement of an armed attack. If such a serious breach occurs all States are endowed with injured State status entitling them to resort to countermeasures and, since there is an armed attack, to take military action in collective self-defence. Should a use of force fall below the threshold of an armed attack, only the State affected by the use of force in question will be entitled to react thereto by means of countermeasures and armed force as an exercise of the right of individual self-defence.[155]

The object of self-defence

It has been argued, notably by judge Schwebel,[156] that the overthrow of an aggressor government may be a necessary and proportionate act of self-defence. This raises the question of the object of self-defence. The text of article 51 of the Charter may usefully serve as a starting-point for remarks on this score. Nothing in the Charter, so it stipulates, shall impair "the inherent right of individual or collective self-defence if an armed attack occurs against a Member of the United Nations". The right of self-defence, as noted earlier, exists only in relation to an armed attack. Furthermore, the use of force resorted to as an exercise of the right of self-defence must be directed against the armed attack. The justification for any use of armed force under the Charter or customary rules lies with the necessity of defence against attack. Nothing more, nothing less. Any use of force must have as a goal to obtain reparation. Yet the goal to be reached by resorting to force as an exercise of the right of self-defence is limited by the ordinary meaning of the word "defence". In essence then resort to the use of force as an exercise of the right of self-defence must be geared towards the cessation of wrongful conduct, that is, it must counter the armed attack. Should the attack have stopped, there is no longer any necessity to defend oneself, and consequently the right of self-defence will have been extinguished.

However, it is tempting and to some extent unavoidable to link the right to self-defence to the substantial right of territorial integrity possessed by the injured State. To the extent that the injured State's territory, or any part thereof, remains occupied by the State that initiated the armed attack, the right to self-defence is left unimpaired.

Certainly it would be an absurd and unreasonable interpretation of the law to state that a State's right to self-defence would have lapsed on the basis that hostilities had ended and the injured State no longer possessed the means to fight on. Practically the consequence of such a situation would be an impossibility for the injured State to continue any defence. Legally on the other hand the injured State's right of individual defence is matched by the complementary right of collective defence. If the injured State finds (an)other State(s) willing and capable to continue its defence measures, those may be undertaken as an exercise of the right of collective self-defence. This was of course the position of Kuwait after Iraq's invasion and occupation of its territory.[157] Its defence was immediately taken over by the United States and others.

The right of individual or collective self-defence against armed attacks constitutes a power to take such military measures to impose upon the author State a withdrawal of its occupation forces. It thus amounts to the right of the directly injured State and others to forcibly effect restitution in kind and impose upon the author State respect for this specific reparation obligation. This argument is buttressed by the consideration that the circumstances under which a right of self-defence can be exercised only constitute circumstances precluding wrongfulness in relation to measures which would otherwise be considered wrongful. Since every State has a force monopoly regarding its own territory, any force resorted to against invading or occupying forces on the injured State's territory would not need any separate justification under international law. Only force resorted to on the territory of the author State is in need of the justification of self-defence.[158]

It is frequently argued, though not without limitations, that the right to self-defence may be exercised by the injured State also to ward off future attacks by the author State. That claim is surely correct insofar as the cross-border use of force by the injured State would be directed towards fending off impending attacks by the author State in cases in which it could not be said that hostilities had ended.[159]

What should be understood by "future" attacks?[160] Would the goal of prevention of future attacks include, for instance, forced execution of the reparation obligations to provide guarantees against repetition? If that were the case an almost unrestricted right to use force would exist for a State acting in self-defence against an armed attack. As noted in chapter three the author State of an international crime is under an obligation to change its government. In such a light the State under attack would be entitled to continue measures for as long as the government of the author State had not stepped down and made way for another that was both more peace-loving and bore no blame for the attack in the first place. Similarly the right to continue self-defence measures for the purpose of imposing respect for the obligations to provide guarantees against repetition would involve the right of the injured State to impose measures of disarmament.

Although there exists a legitimate concern of the injured State to obtain assurances or guarantees against repetition, indeed it has the right to obtain those, it may be suggested that the use of force by a State in the exercise of a right of self-defence is not the appropriate means to execute the author State's obligations in this respect.[161] It must be kept in mind that the right of self-defence constitutes an exception of a temporary nature to the otherwise existing near exclusive competence of the Security Council to resort to armed force. And exceptions must be interpreted restrictively. Indeed if one were to claim the right to continue self-defence measures against future attacks generally, the limitless temporal sense of such an assertion could imply a right to use force even though the author State of the attack was in no position to contemplate further attacks.

On the same level any right of the injured State to occupy, in whole or in part, the territory of an author State of the international crime of aggression, as a measure of self-defence, must be rejected. Naturally this does not mean that a defending State could not temporarily take hold of the territory of the attacking State as may be strictly necessary for purposes of self-defence. Similarly, but *a fortiori*, annexation of territory would, and could, not be justified as a measure of self-defence.[162]

In conclusion it can be said that the objects of measures of self-defence must be defence against ongoing attacks, impending attacks in case hostilities have not ended, or the restoration of territorial status quo *ante*. This amounts, under the law of State responsibility, to the right to effect cessation and restitution in kind. Although the injured State may demand from the author State of an armed attack the performance of other reparation obligations, it does not possess the right to use force in order to effect or obtain such performance.

Conditions under the Charter and customary international law

The Court examined, in the Nicaragua Case, which conditions had to be fulfilled for the right of (collective) self-defence to be lawfully exercised. The basic condition for a lawful exercise of the right to self-defence, an armed attack, has been discussed above (subsection 5.5.1). The conditions of immediacy, necessity and proportionality will be addressed in subsection 5.7.2. The request for assistance, in case of collective self-defence, and the phrase "until the Security Council has taken measures" will be argued on in subsection 5.7.1. This leaves the discussion of the requirements of a report and the declaration of an armed attack for present consideration.

The right of self-defence exists, and can be exercised, only in the presence of an armed attack. The Court added to this that:[163]

> "It is also clear that it is the State which is the victim of an armed attack which must form and declare the view that it has been so attacked. There is no rule in customary international law permitting a State to exercise the right of collective self-defence on the basis of its own assessment of the situation. Where collective self-defence is invoked, it is to be expected that the State for whose benefit this right is used will have declared itself to be the victim of an armed attack."

A few remarks are in order. In subsection 5.4.1 it has been argued that article 51 confers the power on an individual, or group of, State(s) to judge whether an armed attack exists. These observations of the Court provide a limit in the sense that the State under attack must form and declare the view that it is under attack. In the absence of such a declaration other States cannot exercise any right of collective self-defence. That proposition would appear to be unassailable. However, should this condition be fulfilled even if the attacked State had been overrun in such a short time that it had had no opportunity to declare the existence of an armed attack? Ideally the Security Council would determine the existence of a breach of the peace or act of aggression, and would proceed to take measures for the restoration of international peace and security. However, the Council might be blocked by virtue of a permanent member's veto against such action. If that were to be the case the right to self-defence would not be impaired, since the Council would still not have taken measures in the sense of article 51. It is submitted that in such circumstances other States might assess the situation independently from the attacked State and exercise their rights of collective self-defence. In the world today, considering the manifold communication channels, such a situation is luckily not likely to occur.

Following up on the preceding observations it may be noted that the Court held that, under customary international law, the lawfulness of the use of force in self-defence does not depend on measures of self-defence being reported to the Security Council.[164] It may be submitted that this is the case even insofar as the Charter is concerned. Thus the use of force in self-defence will not become unlawful merely because it has not been reported to the Council. The purpose of the requirement in article 51 is to enable the Council to assess for itself the existence of an alleged attack, and whether it should adopt measures under articles 39, 41 or 42. If there is an armed attack failure to report measures of self-defence may well constitute a breach of obligation under the Charter, but this will not render the use of force in self-defence unlawful. The decisive criterion of the lawfulness of the use of force in self-defence must lie with the existence of an armed attack. Additionally it may be noted that the Court treated the absence of a report to the Security Council as one of the factors indicating whether the State claiming to have acted in self-defence was itself convinced that it was acting in self-defence.[165]

5.5.2. SECURITY COUNCIL ACTION UNDER CHAPTERS VII AND VIII OF THE CHARTER

In the scheme of the Charter the Security Council is the organ which has been conferred the power to take military action in respect of threats to the peace, breaches of the peace or acts of aggression. In addition it possesses the power to authorize individual States, or regional arrangements or agencies, to use of force. Individual States and regional arrangements or agencies have the right to use cross-border force only, autonomously, in cases of self-defence against armed attacks. The Security Council on the other hand can resort to, or authorize, force where there is only a threat to the peace, that is, in the absence of armed incidents or hostilities. As such it has been given the power to use force not only in case of a serious breach of an obligation essential for the maintenance of international peace and security, but also in regard to minor breaches, the threat of such breaches, or breaches of other obligations that might lead to such breaches. In relation to issues of State responsibility this means that the Security Council's competence is not restricted to the international crime of aggression, but extends to all kinds of breaches of obligation to the extent that those affect the maintenance of international peace and security.

As reactions against illegal uses of force the Security Council can be said, first, to have taken military action itself; secondly, to have endorsed the use of force in self-defence; or thirdly, to have authorized the use of force.

An example of the first category is that in which the Security Council has authorized peace-keeping forces to use force in circumstances going beyond self-defence in the strict sense. In resolution 161, paragraph 1, the Security Council urges the United Nations to take all appropriate measures, including the use of force (if necessary, in the last resort) to prevent the occurrence of civil war in Congo. Resolution 169, paragraph 4, could arguably viewed as such, because it authorizes the Secretary-General to use requisite force for the apprehension, detention and deportation of foreign military and paramilitary personnel in Congo. More recently UNPROFOR has been authorized to use force acting in self-defence against bombardments of, or incursions into, safe areas; against deliberate obstruction regarding its freedom of action in and around those areas; against the deliberate obstruction of protected humanitarian convoys; and to ensure its security and freedom of movement.[166]

The only clear example of the second category is resolution 83 by which the Security Council recommended members to furnish such assistance to South Korea as necessary to repel the armed attack by North Korea and to restore international peace and security in the area.

In a broad sense all the resolutions on the Iraq-Kuwait crisis and on the former Yugoslavia authorizing States or regional arrangements or agencies to use force fall in the third category.[167] However, those concerning the former Yugoslavia need not detain us, since most of them are geared towards establishing humanitarian relief and cannot be regarded as responses to illegal uses of force. Resolutions providing for a limited use of force to ensure the effective application of embargo measures adopted under article 41 also need not be taken into account. The only true examples of authorizations to use force in response to an illegal use of force lie with resolutions 678, 686 and 687.

It is noteworthy that the Iraqi invasion of Kuwait provides an example of the commission of the supreme international crime: aggression. It should not have come as a surprise then that resolution 678 did not confine itself to authorizing the use of armed force for purposes otherwise associated with self-defence, but that the object for which force could be used was to uphold and implement earlier Security Council resolutions (especially 660) and to restore international peace and security in the area. In effect the members co-operating with Kuwait could impose upon Iraq all those measures which could be considered necessary for the restoration of international peace and security in the area, provided of course that such measures would relate, and amount, to the implementation of Iraq's responsibility. As argued in chapter three, on reparation for international crimes, the author State's secondary obligations regarding guarantees against repetition could include the reconstitution of government and of armed, paramilitary or police forces, disarmament, and the conviction and punishment of those responsible for the commission of the crime. As rightly noted by some the terms of resolution 678 would have justified a "march on Baghdad" to overthrow Saddam Hussein's régime,[168] as well as the imposition of a régime of military occupation so as to ensure the effective implementation of Iraq's responsibility in the field of guarantees against repetition.

In the event neither the Coalition forces, nor the Security Council, did go as far as that. Resolution 686, in the preamble, noted Iraq's agreement to comply fully with all previous Council resolutions, the suspension of all offensive combat operations by the Coalition forces, and the intention of the States of the Coalition to bring their military presence in Iraq to an end as soon as possible consistent with the objectives of resolution 678. In paragraphs 2 and 3 of the former resolution the Council set out a number of demands with which Iraq had to comply. These were that it had to: rescind its actions to annex Kuwait; accept its responsibility; release Kuwaiti and foreign nationals and any remains; return Kuwaiti property; cease hostile and provocative acts; designate military commanders in order to arrange for military aspects of a cessation of hostilities; provide access to and release prisoners of war and remains; provide information on mines, booby traps, explosives, and chemical and biological weapons in territory occupied by Coalition forces. Paragraph 4 importantly recognized that as long as Iraq had not complied with paragraphs 2 and 3 the authorization to use all necessary means remained valid.

Resolution 687 contained a number of additions with regard to the demands made of Iraq under resolution 686. These concerned mostly measures of disarmament. In paragraph 33 the Security Council decided that once Iraq officially notified its acceptance of the provisions of resolution 687 a formal cease-fire would be effective between Iraq and the Coalition forces. It is to be noted that resolution 687 does not contain any paragraph similar to paragraph 4 of resolution 686. Paragraph 1 comes closest in that it affirms "all thirteen resolutions above, except as expressly changed below to achieve the goals of this resolution". It might conceivably be argued that the authorization to use force has survived the adoption of resolution 687.[169] It is submitted that such is only partly the case, that is, only until Iraq communicated its acceptance of the terms of the resolution. It is not unlikely that the effective implementation of Iraq's responsibility, especially on compensation, might take decades.[170] It would be unreasonable to claim that the Coalition forces might for instance ten years later invade Iraq to pressure it into fulfilling its compensation obligations. Furthermore, it may be argued that since the establishment of the formal cease-fire between Iraq and the Coalition forces the Charter provisions on the peaceful settlement of disputes have regained their efficacy. So the original disputes between Iraq and Kuwait and those arising directly from the crisis, or their settlement by way of Security Council resolution 687, must be solved through peaceful means. Individual States can therefore only use force against Iraq if it launches another armed attack, or if the Security Council decides anew that an authorization to use force is necessary.

5.6. Resort to armed force in response to the international crimes of denial of self-determination of peoples and widespread breaches of basic human rights obligations

5.6.1. THE SCOPE AND CONTENT OF THE RIGHT OF SELF-DETERMINATION OF PEOPLES AND THE NECESSITY OF A CONNECTION TO SOME OF THE OTHER CRIMES OF ARTICLE 19

Article 19, paragraph 3 (b), Part One, of the ILC-draft confirms that there is an international crime when there exists "a serious breach of an international obligation of essential importance for safeguarding the right of self-determination of peoples, such as that prohibiting the establishment or maintenance by force of colonial domination". This formulation raises a number of difficult questions. The first relates to the scope of the right of self-determination of peoples: what is a people? The second concerns the specification made: "the establishment or maintenance by force of colonial domination". Does this mean that there would not be an international crime where the domination could not be said to be colonial in character? Thirdly, what is a people entitled to by virtue of the right of self-determination, that is, what would constitute a breach of obligation? In the fourth place, what should be considered a "serious breach" and what reach should be given to the words "by force"? The fifth question would be: by what means can a people itself attempt to effect the realization of its right? And finally, in the context of the use of force, by what means could States further the cause of a people unjustly denied the exercise of its right to self-determination. This latter issue will be addressed in the following subsection. Not all of these questions can be treated in depth. Some pertinent remarks will be made though.

As to the definition of "people" no attempt is made in the commentary, or elsewhere, to identify characteristics in order to arrive at the conclusion that a certain group of individuals would constitute a people. In the literature a number of elements are mentioned:[171] a common historical tradition; racial or ethnic identity; cultural homogeneity; linguistic unity; religious or ideological affinity; territorial connection; and common economic life. For a group of individuals to constitute a people some or all of those elements would have to be present.

As a follow-up one has to observe that the right to self-determination is said to apply to *all* peoples. The example mentioned of colonial domination has illustrative value only. The commentary makes clear that neither the categories of crimes listed, nor the specific examples mentioned in relation to any particular category, are meant to be exhaustive.[172]

The third question concerns the content of the right of self-determination of peoples. What obligation would a State be under if a people lived on its territory? Article 1, paragraph 1, of the International Covenant on Civil and Political Rights, states on self-determination that:[173] "By virtue of that right they freely determine their political status and freely pursue their economic, social and cultural development." But what does it mean that peoples "freely determine their political status"? Does this include the right to choose for independence and the creation of a new State? In other words does a people have the right to secede?

The language of article 1 of the Covenant is reminiscent of resolution 1514 regarding self-determination for colonial countries and peoples.[174] There the goal was independence. However, by reason of its title already the Declaration only applied to colonial situations. Steps were to be taken (paragraph 5) in Trust Territories, Non-Self-Governing Territories, and other territories which had not yet attained independence, to transfer all powers to the peoples and enable them to enjoy complete independence and freedom. The operative word here is "territories". Only peoples living in a specific territory, under colonial domination, had to be enabled to freely determine their political status. In effect the Declaration, in paragraph 6, significantly stated that:

> "Any attempt aimed at the partial or total disruption of the national unity and the territorial integrity of a country is incompatible with the purposes and principles of the Charter of the United Nations."

Within the context of the Charter it may be a reasonable inference that a State which becomes a member of the United Nations does so as a territorial unit, and the fact that a people lives on a specific part of the territory may not lead to loss of such territory. It would seem rather inappropriate to allow a people to attempt to do what States themselves could not attempt to do. Some other resolutions adopted by the General Assembly seem to lead to the same conclusion.[175]

However, the picture is rather less clear, and in fact becomes muddy, if one reads the relevant sections of resolution 2625 on Principles of International Law.[176] Under the heading of "The principle of equal rights and self-determination of peoples" one may find the following:

> "The establishment of a sovereign and independent State, the free association or integration with an independent State or the emergence into any other political status freely determined by a people constitute modes of implementing the right of self-determination by that people."

By virtue of this provision a people is apparently entitled to make a free choice for the establishment of a new State. It must be noted that this implies, necessarily, that the creation of such a new State would take place on that part of the territory on which the people lives. That observation is bolstered by one of the subsequent paragraphs:

> "Nothing in the foregoing paragraphs shall be construed as authorizing or encouraging any action which would dismember or impair, totally or in part, the territorial integrity or political unity of sovereign and independent States conducting themselves in compliance with the principle of equal rights and self-determination of peoples as described above and thus possessed of a government representing the whole people belonging to the territory without distinction as to race, creed, or colour."

The obvious deduction must be, on the basis of a very strong *a contrario* argument, that if a State does not act in accordance with the principle of self-determination its territorial integrity may be put in jeopardy.[177] The criterion for deciding whether such could justifiably be the case constitutes the absence of a "government representing the whole people belonging to the territory without distinction as to race, creed, or colour." It cannot but be noted that there appears to be a discrepancy between the two paragraphs quoted above. The first envisages the exercise by a people of its right to self-determination by means of a choice for, among others, the establishment of a sovereign and independent State. Under the second such a result could only come about if the whole people, including especially the people that may claim the right to self-determination, is not adequately represented in the government.

There are strong objections to this approach, and these bring us to the next questions. The criterion of a "government representing the whole people" insufficiently takes into account that there may be, and are, differing degrees of seriousness characterizing denials of self-determination. Under article 19, Part One, of the ILC-draft, only a serious breach of an obligation essential for safeguarding the right of self-determination will constitute an international crime. Can it really be said that the lack of a representative government would entail a serious breach of that obligation? In the past there have been many, and in the present there still are, governments which could not really be said to represent the people, let alone the "whole" people. It is therefore suggested that the absence of representation in the political organs of a State alone should not be considered a serious breach of the obligation. Indeed, the essence of a denial of self-determination consists by definition in the denial of political rights for the people concerned. It is possible to go even further than that. The fact that such a lack of representation is due to discriminatory practices still would not entail the conclusion that a serious breach of the obligation to promote self-determination had taken place. Again, a denial of self-determination by definition involves discriminatory practices, on the political plane, in regard to the specific people.

In this context the words "by force" featuring in regard to the establishment or maintenance of colonial domination deserve attention. As noted before (chapter two, subsection 2.6.1) the use of those words create the impression that the domination has to take place by way of armed force. The commentary to article 19, however, has indicated that:[178]

> "The expression 'by force' should be understood as meaning against the will of the subject population, even if that will is not manifested, or has not yet been manifested, by armed opposition."

It may be assumed that this explanation applies equally to the category of denials of self-determination of peoples generally. This comment then makes it impossible to determine the difference between "ordinary" breaches and "serious" breaches of the obligation to promote a people's right to self-determination. To refer to the need of (colonial) domination similarly does not help. It may be assumed that domination takes place against the will of those dominated. If that were not so it would not be possible to speak of domination. In that sense the word "domination" has the same meaning as the meaning attributed by the Commission to the words "by force". It is submitted that in order to be able to distinguish between ordinary and serious breaches, and to do justice to the idea of international "crimes", the words "by force" should be understood to involve the application of armed, military, or physical force in regard to (individuals of) the people concerned.[179]

These observations are reinforced by reference to considerations regarding the next question: by what means can a people attempt to realize its right to self-determination? To put it differently: under which circumstances could one assert a people's right to armed resistance against authorities? The above quoted part of the commentary to article 19, Part One, notes that by force means against the will of the people "even if that will is not manifested, or has not yet been manifested, by armed opposition." Again: there is no indication that the words "by force" would not apply to denials of self-determination generally. So it seems, in the light of the commentary, that a people could have recourse to armed opposition whenever there is a denial of self-determination. In this context reference may be made once more to resolutions of the Security Council recognizing the legitimacy of struggles by peoples or liberation movements,[180] and the urges to members to render moral and material support regarding such struggles.[181] Pertinent to this issue is again General Assembly resolution 2625, in which it is noted that:

> "Every State has the duty to refrain from any forcible action which deprives peoples (...) of their right to self-determination and freedom and independence. In their actions against, and resistance to, such forcible action in pursuit of the exercise of their right to self-determination, such peoples are entitled to seek and receive support in accordance with the purposes and principles of the Charter."

It is not too farfetched to claim that this provision only confirmed a people's right to resist against "forcible action".[182] Clearly then there is no right to resist against non-forcible action. The central issue is what should be considered "forcible action". Following in this respect the previous paragraph, this ought to be seen as resort to armed, military, or physical force only, affecting, by its very nature, individuals belonging to the people that is denied self-determination. That is not, however, where it ends.

If a right to armed resistance does not exist generally for peoples suffering a denial of self-determination, this implies that in a general sense the laws applicable within the territory must be obeyed.[183] This does not mean that a people denied self-determination would have to stand idly by. But in the choice of means to effect the realization of self-determination they are limited to peaceful alternatives, such as campaigns of civil disobedience and the organization of demonstrations. This limitation would naturally not take away the right to defend oneself, in the individual case, against unlawful violent acts committed by authorities.

Furthermore, a connection should be made specifically to breaches of basic human rights obligations. If armed opposition is legitimate only in response to the use of armed, military or physical force against individuals of a people, this implies that the acts of organs of the author State amount to breaches of basic human rights obligations. It is submitted that only breaches of obligation such as violations of the right to life, and of the right to physical and psychological integrity, ought to give rise to a right of resistance.[184] Mere denial of political rights, such as the right to vote, to be elected, to express one's opinions, and to peaceful assembly, does not entail a right to armed opposition if such a denial is not coupled to resort to armed, military or physical force.[185] It cannot but be noted that none of these rights are non-derogable under article 4 of the International Covenant on Civil and Political Rights. Admittedly derogable rights are subject to suspension only in cases of emergency which threaten the life of the nation. But the fact already that a distinction is made shows that some rights are considered more important than others.

In addition, and in relation to the observation that a crime must involve elements of intent and premeditation, one would have to say that such breaches of basic human rights obligations in respect of individuals of a people ought to take place pursuant to government policies. Consequently they must be widespread and systematic and testify to government involvement in them or an unwillingness or inability to do anything about them. If such is the case a right of armed opposition cannot be denied to a people targeted by an oppressive government or State. Where the breaches of basic human rights obligations in respect of a people are decidedly widespread and systematic and allow for the conclusion that a genocide is either attempted or in effect committed, the right to self-determination includes the right to opt for the creation of a new State. Naturally such could only be the case if the geographical and demographical circumstances are such that a specific part of the territory is inhabited, in large majority, by the people concerned. The example of the Kurds in Northern Iraq imposes itself.

5.6.2. WIDESPREAD BREACHES OF BASIC HUMAN RIGHTS OBLIGATIONS AND HUMANITARIAN INTERVENTION

The question whether a State can intervene to put a stop to human rights violations has been discussed over and over again. Though most people would agree that something ought to be done about such situations, States themselves appear to have been reluctant to intervene for such purposes. And if they did intervene they have tended to rely, exclusively or mainly, not on a right of humanitarian intervention, but on other justifications (mainly self-defence). First some arguments will be devoted to issues under the Charter of the United Nations and customary international law. In the second place a few observations will be made on proposed conditions.

Under article 2, paragraph 4, of the Charter members are prohibited, in their international relations, to use force against the territorial integrity or political independence of States, or inconsistent with the purposes of the United Nations. That provision is complemented by article 2, paragraph 3, which stipulates that members shall settle their disputes peacefully in such a manner that international peace and security, and justice, are not endangered. The Charter, read in its entirety, clearly does not provide States with a unilateral right of humanitarian intervention. The only (unilateral) rights to use force come under the headings of self-defence, joint action by the permanent members for the purpose of maintaining international peace and security (on behalf of the United Nations), or action against former enemy States. No other right is provided for under the Charter.[186] There is no need here to present extensive argument on stances claiming that force used under the heading of humanitarian intervention would not be a prohibited use of force under article 2, paragraphs 3 or 4, of the Charter.[187] Suffice it to say that humanitarian intervention in fact amounts, at the very least, to the forced settlement of disputes contrary to article 2, paragraph 3, of the Charter. It is not redundant to note that any use of armed force across international frontiers, for whatever purposes,[188] endangers international peace and security (if not necessarily justice). Since the Charter does not recognize any right of humanitarian intervention the existence of any such right could only be based on a rule of customary international law. As noted above (subsection 5.2.4) the rules of customary international law existing prior to 1945 have not survived the coming into force of the Charter.[189] Whether it is possible to say that such a rule has come into existence since will be discussed next.

In subsection 5.2.4 it has been observed that the Court did not deny that, in principle, a rule of customary international law might develop allowing a State to intervene by the use of armed force within the territory of another State. But it noted that for such a rule to develop would constitute a fundamental modification of the customary law principle of non-intervention.[190] In applying the law to the facts of the case it further held:[191]

> "In any event, while the United States might form its own appraisal of the situation as to respect for human rights in Nicaragua, the use of force could not be the appropriate method to monitor or ensure such respect."

It is not quite clear why the use of force could not be an appropriate method to ensure respect for human rights obligations. Indeed, should armed force be resorted to, and operations carried out in compliance with rules of humanitarian law, it could constitute the most effective means to bring about an end to human rights violations. Perhaps the Court made this statement exclusively in the light of the facts of the case. In that context it claimed that the humanitarian objective of protection of human rights could not be considered compatible with:[192] "(...) the mining of ports, the destruction of oil installations, or again with the training, arming and equipping of the *contras*."
Be that as it may, it is difficult to see much in recent State practice that would allow for the conclusion that a rule of customary international law exists, or is in the process of being created,[193] justifying unilateral humanitarian intervention. The most recent intervention by the United States, the United Kingdom, France and the Netherlands in Northern Iraq for the protection of the Kurds, in the aftermath of the Gulf war, must be disregarded in view of the special circumstances surrounding that particular intervention.[194] In addition to the insufficiency of State practice, *opinio juris* that such a practice could be based on an (allegedly) existing rule justifying humanitarian intervention appears to be lacking.[195] Last but not least the already earlier mentioned trend within the Commission may be recalled to the effect that the unilateral use of force would be restricted, even in case of crimes, to individual or collective self-defence.[196]

However, the Commission, in its commentary to article 33, Part One, has hinted at the possibility, though not in so many words, that a state of necessity might be invoked in order to justify the cross-border use of force in cases where there was a:[197]

> "(...) grave and imminent danger to the State, to some of its nationals or simply to human beings – a danger of which the territory of the foreign State is either the theatre or the place of origin, and which the foreign State has a duty to avert by its own actions, but which its unwillingness or inability to act allows to continue."

This has led some to assert that a State's use of force might be justified, under the heading of state of necessity, in order to protect its nationals in a foreign State,[198] or to protect the author State's nationals.[199]
A preliminary remark would be that the Commission itself observes that after World War II (up to 1980) only one example of State practice existed, the 1960 Congo crisis, regarding which a State (Belgium) had claimed to be acting "in a situation of absolute

necessity".[200] Although the state of necessity, as a circumstance precluding wrongfulness, constitutes an open-ended category, it may be suggested that some more evidence of a "general practice" might be required to show that these kinds of cross-border incursions would come under the heading of a state of necessity.
Furthermore, in article 33, paragraph 1 (a), the Commission stipulates that a state of necessity cannot be invoked unless "the act was the only means of safeguarding an essential interest of the State against a grave and imminent peril;" In its commentary the Commission specifies that the essential interest at stake does not have to relate to the "existence" of the State.[201] It also considered that it did not have to spell out, in the abstract, categories of essential interests.[202] It is not hard to imagine that violent attacks on a State's nationals in the territory of another State could constitute an essential interest.[203] It is much more difficult to conceive that an essential interest of the State would relate to attacks by another State on its own nationals and on its own territory.[204] That all States are in possession of a legal interest regarding such breaches of basic human rights obligations cannot be taken to mean that therefore an essential interest of a State is at risk. By definition a State is not affected by such breaches of obligation, and any interest it has in the matter flows from the nature of the rules concerned. Of course certain obligations are essential for the protection of the fundamental interests of the international community. But this does not signify that therefore States themselves are in possession of an essential interest which would warrant a use of force on their part to ward off any grave and imminent peril to such interest. Certainly the current trend within the Commission testifies against any such possibility.

In conclusion it may be said that there does not exist, under customary international law, any justification, whether in the form of humanitarian intervention or state of necessity, that would validate a cross-border use of force for the protection of the basic human rights of the nationals of the author State. It may be opportune, nevertheless, to devote some argument to the conditions allegedly applicable to intervention for the protection of the basic human rights of the author State's nationals.

Humanitarian intervention by a State allegedly would be justified if a number of conditions were met: a relative disinterest on the part of the intervening State; the existence of an emergency situation in which especially the right to life is (about to be) violated on a massive scale; exhaustion of peaceful means, that is, intervention only as a last resort; the impact of the intervention upon the target State would have to be confined to a minimum; and proportionality.[205] Only some of these conditions will be discussed.

A first remark concerns the alleged requirement of exhaustion of other means, including for instance recourse to the mechanisms of human rights treaties and the Charter.[206] It may be submitted that this by far constitutes the most unrealistic condition suggested by the proponents of a right of humanitarian intervention. If a situation develops in which there is a risk that the rights to life of individuals will be violated on a widespread scale, recourse to other means will most likely not lead to averting the risk. The situation in Rwanda in 1994 is typical in this respect. France, with the authorization of the Security Council, intervened at the end of a massacre lasting already two and a half months at a point in time that most of the country had been taken over by the RPF. By that time, it has been estimated, over 500,000 people had been killed. If a situation of this magnitude develops, the obvious reaction would be to engage in a full-scale military intervention within a matter of days. Recourse to other procedures cannot be awaited. Although it might be possible to attempt to obtain a Security Council resolution authorizing the operation, the example of Rwanda again does not inspire much hope in this respect. After the outbreak of massacres on April 6th, 1994, the Security Council did not take any decisive action until June 22nd,[207] when it adopted resolution 929 in which it authorized France to go ahead with its proposed intervention. By then, it cannot but be noted, it was too late.

A second observation relates to the conditions of disinterest on the part of the intervening State,[208] and the minimum impact on the target State. The goal of the intervention, so it is said, among others by Duke, is to protect human lives, and it is not to go beyond that purpose:[209]

> "Humanitarian intervention is however a response to the immediate needs of people and not an answer to the longer-term stability of a regime or country. The political solutions to human rights abuses are beyond the scope of humanitarian intervention and fall into the realm of peacekeeping, peacemaking and peace enforcement. This is an important distinction, since, the moment humanitarian intervention is perceived to be part of a political solution, claims of neutrality and impartiality may be forfeited."

Here we have the underlying cause of much misunderstanding: the idea that those applying and enforcing the law must remain neutral and impartial. It has to be understood that the law itself remains neutral only for as long as it is not transgressed. As soon as there is a (threat of) violation of the law, it provides the law enforcers with an authorization to do something about it: the threat or use of force against the author of the violation. There can be no doubt that it might be wise to remain neutral. In national societies police forces generally may command overwhelming force that can be applied as against individuals. In the international community, in contrast, there is no equivalence of such overwhelming force that can, in a general sense, be applied to States. It is suggested, nevertheless, that those engaged in humanitarian intervention could not be expected to stand idly by while those responsible walk away from them, or even worse, prepare themselves to start off where they left. To impose conditions of neutrality and impartiality, minimum impact upon State structures, intervention for the shortest time possible, and with as few troops as possible, implies that those responsible remain in power, that they continue to control the military command structures, in short, that no guarantees whatsoever exist that the crime(s) will not be repeated.[210]

It has been argued, in chapter three, that the main difference between international delicts and international crimes, insofar as reparation is concerned, should lie with the requisite guarantees against repetition. For the reasons stated those should include, in case of crimes, disarmament, implementation of individual responsibility, a change of government, and possibly also certain changes in the State's legal structures. Obviously, none of these will be forthcoming merely because they are demanded. The threat of force alone will most likely not be sufficient. Only the actual use of force against, and subsequent occupation of, the author State will do. The tasks of peace-keeping, peacemaking and peace enforcement must be taken up by the intervening State(s), and taken over by the international community.

5.6.3. SECURITY COUNCIL ACTION UNDER CHAPTERS VII AND VIII OF THE CHARTER

In the recent past the Security Council has authorized the use of all necessary means in response to some crises which did not involve any cross-border use of force: Somalia, Rwanda, and Haiti.[211] Preliminary is the observation that the threats to international peace are not altogether obvious in those instances.

In resolution 794 regarding Somalia the Security Council determined a threat to international peace and security on the basis of the magnitude of the tragedy (exacerbated by obstacles created to the distribution of humanitarian assistance). That alone, one would think, would not have threatened international peace and security. The Council also recognized the unique character of the situation which required an immediate and exceptional response. The humanitarian tragedy was due, at least in part, to the fact that a civil war was raging and that there was a threat that Somalia might disintegrate. That prospect by itself could already be said to constitute a threat to international peace and security.

The situation in Rwanda would also not seem to qualify, at first sight, as a threat to international peace and security. However, an indication against any hasty conclusion in this respect would be that renewed fighting broke out, after the outbreak of massacres on a massive scale, between the Rwandese Patriotic Front and government forces. Another circumstance is that the situation caused extreme tension in Burundi, where the population is also divided in Hutus and Tutsis, with the latter in control of the army. Furthermore, at the time of adoption of resolution 929 a massive flow of refugees, of Hutu origin, existed towards the bordering countries causing unrest and chaos. The French intervention to some extent calmed emotions and high strung nerves.

The Security Council based its determination of a threat to international peace and security in resolution 940 mainly on the breaches of the Governors Island Agreement and the Pact of New York,[212] the systematic violations of civil liberties in Haiti, and the plight of Haitian refugees. One would guess that the latter circumstance tended to cause international tension, as most of the refugees tried to reach the United States. It may not be farfetched to speculate that eventually the United States would have been tempted to intervene in Haiti, in disregard of its obligations under the Charter and customary international law, to put a stop to the refugee flow.[213] This of course might constitute the basis for a Security Council determination that there exists a threat to international peace and security. To some extent this is a twisted argument, since the measures would be taken against the refugee creating State, even though the actual threat of armed intervention originated in another State. Nevertheless Security Council competence has to be recognized in such circumstances.

One final observation needs to be made regarding the Security Council's punctilious tendency towards neutrality and impartiality. In the heat of the crisis, with the Rwandese Patriotic Front fighting government forces and massacres being carried out by the Interhamwe, the Security Council demanded, by way of resolution 912 (paragraph 6), an immediate cessation of hostilities between these two parties and, admittedly, an end to the mindless violence and carnage. That demand is to be found also in later resolutions.[214] Yet, as noted above, a people or the civilian population which is the target of widespread breaches of basic human rights obligations possesses a right of armed resistance. Similarly the armed opposition force, the Rwandese Patriotic Front, consisting mainly of Tutsis, could not be denied the right to attempt to end the genocidal acts being committed against its people. The Security Council's demand for a cessation of hostilities, in addition to its demand for an end to the carnage, was therefore inappropriate. It may be suggested that instead it should have supported the Front's armed struggle and called upon States to provide material support to that effect.

5.7. Restrictions regarding resort to armed force

5.7.1. RESTRICTIONS REGARDING RESORT TO ARMED FORCE, MULTIPLICITY OF INJURED STATES, AND THE ORGANIZATIONAL INTEREST IN ARMED FORCE

Restrictions based on the absence of specially affected States

In chapter four, subsection 4.4.1, it was noted that breaches of obligation constituting a denial of self-determination and violations of human rights need not affect any State specifically. For that reason the faculty of resort to countermeasures ought to be recognized to all States. However, as recorded in section 5.6, there does not exist any right of unilateral humanitarian intervention under international law, nor can the circumstance precluding wrongfulness "state of necessity" be invoked to justify the use of force in this respect. Clearly that is not because States would not be in possession of a legal interest regarding the breaches of obligations committed by the author State. Rather this is due to the Charter's harsh prohibitions regarding the use of force, and the fact that those have not been moderated by rules of customary international law providing for the possibility of unilateral humanitarian intervention. Should a right of humanitarian intervention be established under customary international law it will accrue to all States individually, though doubtless the collective exercise of such a right will be preferred. In the meanwhile we are witnessing State practice inconsistent with the basic Charter prohibitions, and an *opinio juris* consistent with those prohibitions. While this writer would personally support, or even advocate, an intervention in particular instances, the legal justification for such an intervention will be found, still, to be lacking.

Restrictions based on the presence of a directly injured State

The international crime of aggression is the only one that always involves a directly injured State, which will by definition be the State that is the victim of an armed attack. The question arises whether States other than the directly injured State can exercise a right of collective self-defence in the absence of a request to that effect. The Court concluded in the Nicaragua Case, assuming the presence of an armed attack and a report by the victim State to the Security Council of its measures of self-defence, that:[215]

> "(...) the requirement of a request by the State which is the victim of the alleged attack is additional to the requirement that such a State should have declared itself to have been attacked."

That statement by the Court was a logical follow-up to the Court's earlier observation that a State wanting to use force in collective self-defence could not do so on the basis of its own assessment.[216] If it could exercise a right to collective self-defence without any specific request to that effect by the State that is the victim of the attack, this would be tantamount to allowing it to assess the situation autonomously. The Court's remarks bear out that the right to collective self-defence constitutes an accessory right. It can only be exercised in a situations of armed attack by one State against another State and then on the latter's request only.

In the specific context of State responsibility for the commission of the international crime of aggression, some observations by judge Jennings on collective self-defence are pertinent:[217]

> "It seems to be based almost upon an idea of vicarious defence by champions: that a third State may lawfully come to the aid of an authenticated victim of armed attack provided that the requirements of a declaration of attack and a request for assistance are complied with. But whatever self-defence means, it does not mean vicarious defence; for that way the notion is indeed open to abuse. The assisting State is not an authorized champion, permitted under certain conditions to go to the aid of a favoured State. The assisting State surely must, by going to the victim State's assistance, be also, and in *addition* to other requirements, in some measure defending itself. There should even in 'collective self-defence' be some real element of 'self' involved with the notion of defence. This is presumably also the philosophy which underlies mutual security arrangements, such as the system of the Organization of American States, for which indeed Article 51 was specifically designed. By such a system of collective security, the security of each member State is meant to be involved with the security of the others;"

As a matter of Charter interpretation this proposition appears untenable. It may be acknowledged, and it is widely reported, that the reference to collective self-defence was inserted in the Charter to safeguard the mutual security arrangements in the Americas. At the same time it has to be noted that the provision on collective self-defence was not placed in Chapter VIII, on regional arrangements, but in Chapter VII. Yet inclusion in Chapter VIII would have sufficed to validate the collective "self"-defence provisions of the Charter of the Organization of American States. Moreover, the Charter of the United Nations itself constitutes a global collective security arrangement. Clearly the whole idea behind it is that each and every State has an interest in the security of any other State. True, for that reason States parties have conferred the primary responsibility for the maintenance and restoration of international peace and security on the Security Council. The latter has been given the power to act on their behalf and to bind them legally to take action irrespective of whether they consider their security to be in

jeopardy.[218] However, the inclusion of the provision on collective self-defence in Chapter VII rather than Chapter VIII testifies to the possibility of vicarious defence.
If one were to insist on a pre-existing link between the defending State and (an)other(s) coming to its rescue, the result would be that any State which had not in the past joined a mutual security arrangement would not be entitled to receive assistance in self-defence.[219] Such an outcome would be even less acceptable if the Security Council could not act under Chapter VII due to the exercise of a veto. The whole scheme of the Charter would fall to the ground, and a vanquished State would be obliterated because of the absence of a right to accept assistance in defence.
Furthermore, the adoption of article 5, paragraph 3, Part Two of the ILC-draft, points in the same direction.[220] It provides that, in addition, if the internationally wrongful act constitutes an international crime, all States are injured States. That surely points to an interest of such States to respond to the crime by all lawful means open to them. Whether collective self-defence in the absence of a direct and personal interest would constitute a lawful means is another matter. Yet within the Commission it is often claimed that States can only resort to armed force as an exercise of the right of individual or collective self-defence. It does not therefore seem that other injured States would be prevented from taking part in defence actions merely because they had not beforehand agreed to mutual assistance.[221]

Restrictions based on the exercise of Security Council powers
Article 51 of the Charter states that the right of individual or collective self-defence against an armed attack will not be impaired *until the Security Council has taken measures necessary to maintain international peace and security.* The ordinary meaning of this phrase must be that the right of self-defence will be impaired once the Security Council has taken measures necessary to maintain international peace and security. The right of self-defence will be impaired, so article 51 states, but this does not necessarily mean that the adoption by the Security Council of necessary measures will terminate the right to self-defence. It may be supposed however that the adoption of necessary measures will, as a minimum, lead to a suspension of the right to use force in self-defence.[222] What remains to be seen then is what should be considered necessary measures taken by the Security Council.

A preliminary remark concerns Greig's opinion that "necessary" measures must mean "effective" measures.[223] A relation is perhaps seen to exist with the purpose of article 1, paragraph 1, that the United Nations ought to "take effective collective measures for the prevention and removal of threats to the peace, and for the suppression of acts of aggression or other breaches of the peace". Equating necessary measures to effective measures would open the door to an interpretation that the right of self-defence would not be impaired for as long as the objectives set by the Security Council,[224] or the objectives held by the State acting in self-defence, would not have been accomplished. It may be assumed that the objectives set by the Security Council will substantially match those held by the defending State: in particular the cessation of hostilities, the restoration of the territorial status quo *ante*, and the absence of any threat of further attacks. Should one consider that the measures taken by the Security Council must be effective, this amounts to saying that the State defending itself can prolong its use of force in self-defence for as long as its objectives have not been accomplished. However, as soon as the objectives of self-defence have been accomplished the right to self-defence lapses.[225] Requiring Security Council measures to be effective in order for the right to self-defence to be impaired, amounts, realistically speaking, to posing no restriction at all.[226] Only if the Security Council would set less far-reaching objectives would the right to self-defence be impaired before it could be terminated due to the accomplishment of objectives. It would seem, in consequence, that one ought to reject any interpretation to the effect that Security Council measures must be effective in order to impair the right to self-defence.

Rather more important is the question what kind of Security Council measures would impair the right of self-defence. A first remark would be that the mere adoption of a resolution by the Security Council does not qualify as a measure. Secondly, it may be pointed out that a decision of the Security Council requiring the attacking State to effect a withdrawal of its forces also could not be considered as such.[227] Thirdly, in the light of the observations in the previous subsection, one would have to say that even if a demand for withdrawal by the Security Council was coupled to a demand for cessation of hostilities (the latter addressed to both States), this would still not impair the right of a State to use force in self-defence in order to restore the territorial status quo *ante*. Such a demand for cessation of hostilities may constitute a decision of the Security Council which, in the words of article 25, members have agreed to accept and carry out. Flouting a demand for cessation of hostilities by the Security Council will constitute a breach of obligation under the Charter. Yet it is submitted that such a demand does not *ipso jure* entail an obligation to end resort to the use of force in self-defence. Such an obligation could be said to exist only where there is no longer any attack, the absence of any territorial gains by the attacking State, and no threat of imminent future attacks.

Furthermore, any interpretation of the word "measures" in article 51 must take account of the fact that other Charter provisions mention this word on a number of occasions in a very specific manner. First there is of course article 39 which authorizes the Security Council to decide on the measures of articles 41 or 42. Secondly article 2, paragraph 7, makes a cross-reference to Chapter VII and its "enforcement measures". Thirdly article 50 mentions "preventive or enforcement measures". And fourthly there is article 94, paragraph 2, which authorizes the Council to decide on measures to give effect to a judgment of the Court. Additionally it may be noted that the latter part of the second sentence of article 51 provides that measures of self-defence taken by members "shall not in any way affect the authority and responsibility of the Security Council under the present Charter to take at any time such action as it deems necessary to maintain or restore international peace and security." The action referred to must be read in conjunction with similar terms featuring in other provisions.[228] All this points to an interpretation that Security Council measures capable of impairing the right of self-defence must be either measures adopted under article 41 or action resorted to under article 42.[229]

With regard to the Iraq-Kuwait crisis it has been claimed that resolution 678, which authorized the States co-operating with Kuwait to use all necessary means to implement earlier resolutions and to restore international peace and security in the area, was not necessary to justify the use of force against Iraq. The Security Council had not taken the necessary measures, and the right to self-defence, so they say, could therefore still be exercised.[230] It has already been pointed out that the criterion of effectiveness cannot serve as a guide for deciding whether the Council has taken the necessary measures in the sense of article 51. It is hard to see how the measures adopted by the Council in resolution 661 would not be necessary measures. They formed the basis of an almost complete isolation of Iraq. If such measures did not constitute necessary measures, which would? One would have to say then that the measures adopted by way of resolution 661 led to the suspension of Kuwait's right of individual or collective self-defence.[231]

That position is not affected by the fact that resolution 661 affirms, in the preamble, the right of individual or collective self-defence in response to the armed attack by Iraq against Kuwait.[232] Provisions in preambles cannot give rise to either obligations or rights. If Kuwait could not exercise its right of self-defence on the basis of Charter provisions, it certainly also could not do so on the basis of a preamble provision of a Security Council resolution. It is possible to argue that the intent of the Security Council is relevant in deciding whether there have indeed been "necessary measures".[233] However, the terminology of article 51 does not contain any indication that the Security Council must express its opinion on whether the measures taken by it are necessary measures in the sense used in article 51. If the word "measures" is interpreted consistently as measures under articles 41 or 42, the suspension of action in self-defence ensues automatically unless the Security Council decides that such action can still be taken. The Security Council taketh, the Security Council giveth. Such a decision, however, cannot be considered present on the basis of a mere preambular paragraph, but would have to be contained in one of the operative paragraphs.

Subsequent practice supports this interpretation. Resolution 665, paragraph 1, called upon States co-operating with Kuwait to use such measures commensurate to the circumstances to halt inward and outward shipping for purposes of implementation of resolution 661. Apparently a separate resolution was required to justify such force. While this would not as such be decisive, resolution 678 "authorizes" the States co-operating with Kuwait to use all necessary means to implement earlier resolutions and to restore international peace and security in the area. As noted above the word "authorizes" implies that those authorized would not be authorized to take action in the absence of such an authorization. In addition resolution 678 authorizes States to resort to force for purposes other than self-defence. The object of self-defence is to defend against continuing or impending future attacks or to restore the territorial status quo *ante*. A use of force for purposes of implementation of Security Council resolutions already would not qualify as self-defence.[234] The use of all necessary means for the restoration of international peace and security in the area, quite arguably encompassing such measures as the overthrow of the Iraqi government, disarmament, and the prosecution of persons accused of crimes, could certainly not be justified under the heading of self-defence.

In conclusion it may be said that the phrase "until the Security Council has taken measures necessary for the maintenance of international peace and security" refers to the measures of articles 41 and 42. If measures thereunder have been taken by the

Council the exercise of the right to self-defence will be suspended unless the Security Council decides otherwise.

In relation to the other crimes, denial of self-determination and widespread breaches of basic human rights obligations, the question arises whether action by the Security Council will preclude unilateral action. The answer will have to be in the affirmative. It has been argued that States do not possess any right of unilateral intervention in respect of those crimes. Whether or not the Security Council has in fact resorted to enforcement action makes no difference then. Should the Security Council have authorized the use of all necessary means to achieve a certain purpose, that means that force cannot be used for other purposes. Of course the Security Council provided Kuwait and member States co-operating with it with an almost blanket authorization to use all necessary means: not only for the implementation of the twelve antecedent resolutions of the Council, but also to restore international peace and security in the area. All the other Council authorizations to use force, for States, peace-keeping forces, or the Secretary-General, were less sweeping.[235]

The relevance of such Security Council action lies in the circumstance that while the authorized party can resort to force, all those not so authorized cannot join in. Thus, to use once again the example of resolution 678, only those member States co-operating with Kuwait could use force against Iraq. Others, which had not offered any assistance, consequently were barred from taking forcible action against Iraq. In the same line of thought it is to be noted that some authorizations are granted to member States,[236] while others are conferred generally on States.[237] Obviously non-member States can partake in armed action only if the authorization relates to "States".

5.7.2. GENERAL RESTRICTIONS REGARDING RESORT TO ARMED FORCE

Necessity and immediacy

The condition of necessity assumes the utmost importance in relation to the question whether there is any need to envisage the use of force for the suppression of continuing international crimes.[238] In chapter four it was claimed that the right to resort to countermeasures could be exercised immediately in case of international crimes. The basis for that observation lay with the intentional and premeditated nature of the acts committed by the author State, and the resultant inability to obtain compliance with those reparation obligations most wanted. It may not be exaggerated to claim that even the most comprehensive set of trade, communication, travel and diplomatic measures will not be sufficient to achieve the primary objective sought to be attained: cessation of wrongful conduct. It may be admitted such a claim cannot be absolute. In the long run economic and other measures might result in discontinuance of crimes being committed. Yet to pose a requirement to sit out a period of time in order for economic and other sanctions or countermeasures to kick in would be to neglect that in the meanwhile irreparable harm will be done. That such is the case may be illustrated especially by reference to the crime of widespread breaches of basic human rights obligations (especially genocide). But the argument may apply also regarding the crimes of aggression and denial of self-determination if those are coupled to breaches of obligation under the basic rules of humanitarian and/or human rights law intended for the protection of the population (in occupied territories).

It has been seen however, in the previous section, that international law does not allow for the unilateral use of force to enforce reparation obligations based on the international crimes of denial of self-determination and widespread breaches of basic human rights obligations. It certainly is one of the most undesirable features of international law that even though the necessity of the use of force cannot be denied with regard to the suppression of those crimes, the state of the law does not allow such use of force. The crime of aggression, not by definition the most heinous one, on the other hand can be countered by way of individual and collective self-defence, and lesser uses of force by way of individual self-defence.

With regard to the right of self-defence the argument has been made that its exercise is conditioned by the requirement of immediacy.[239] In a sense such a condition amounts to no more than saying that whenever an armed attack or use of force has stopped there no longer exists any necessity to use force in response.[240] That stance cannot remain unqualified. First of all it implies that the only lawful purpose of self-defence is to repel the attack. As has been seen above the objects of self-defence include the restoration of the territorial status quo *ante* and the fending off of impending attacks.[241] Whether the use of force is necessary depends on the circumstances,[242] and especially on whether any foreign troops remain on the victim State's territory, whether actual fighting is going on, and whether there are indications that the author State intends to renew its aggressive policies.

In the end the necessity of the use of force also depends on whether the injured State is capable of acting in self-defence but refrains from doing so. Eventually a claim to be acting in self-defence loses its credibility if no action has been undertaken for a considerable period of time. The example of the Falklands shows that it may take quite some time to organize action in self-defence.[243] But clearly no condition of absolute immediacy could have been imposed regarding the British actions to regain the Falklands.[244]

To the extent that an injured State is no longer capable of resisting the attack and (part of) its territory remains occupied, other States may come to the rescue. The logistical side of collective self-defence operations may require time, yet the right to collective self-defence does not lapse merely because it is not exercised immediately. In this respect one would have to say that especially preparation for the exercise of the right of collective self-defence, if announced within a reasonable period of time after the attack and occupation, prevents termination of the right. Suspension of the right of individual and collective self-defence may come about as a result of the Security Council adopting measures under articles 41 and 42 of the Charter.

In chapter four, subsection 4.3.2, it was noted that the Security Council is not bound to pursue the Charter provisions on the peaceful settlement of disputes once it determines the existence of a threat to the peace, breach of the peace, or act of aggression. Similarly it was noted above in subsection 5.4.2 that the Security Council is not legally bound to pursue the non-military measures of article 41 before taking or authorizing armed action. The Security Council's discretion as to whether specific action is necessary to achieve a certain goal cannot easily be challenged. One would think that a decision of the Council could not be assailed on the basis of necessity considerations, since any appraisal of necessity hinges on an evaluation not only of the present but also the future state of affairs. Hypothetically speaking a decision of the Security Council to authorize the use of force against an aggressor State might conflict with considerations of necessity if that State was, at the time, actively withdrawing its forces from occupied territory, taking positions well off the frontier, and providing assurances of non-repetition.[245] However, since the Security Council may involve itself with the whole gambit of reparation forms, including such guarantees against repetition as changes of government, the conclusion that the use of force would not be necessary might still not be reached. If the Security Council authorizes certain States or organizations to use force to enforce its decisions, any such force resorted to must be necessary to attain the goals set by the Security Council. Security Council practice in this respect shows that those goals may be very general, and consequently a broad competence to use force has been delegated at times.

Proportionality

So far the Commission has envisaged the lawful use of force only as a measure of self-defence taken in conformity with the Charter of the United Nations (article 34, Part One, of the ILC-draft). In relation to the use of force in self-defence the Court has acknowledged, in the Nicaragua Case, that the condition of proportionality applies.[246] In chapter four, subsection 4.4.3, it was argued that the application of the condition of proportionality must involve a comparison between the internationally wrongful act committed and the response thereto. It was further stressed that the proportionality of countermeasures was not to be judged in relation to the aim sought to be attained. For if that were the case the response would remain proportional to the wrongful act for as long as the aim (reparation) was not in fact obtained. However, it may be noted that then special rapporteur Ago claimed in relation to self-defence:[247]

> "The requirement of *proportionality* of the action taken in self-defence, as we have said, concerns the relationship between that action and its purpose, namely (...) that of halting and repelling the attack or even, in so far as preventive self-defence is recognized, of preventing it from occurring. It would be mistaken, however, to think that there must be proportionality between the conduct constituting the armed attack and the opposing conduct. The action needed to halt and repulse the attack may well have to assume dimensions disproportionate to those of the attack suffered."

It is submitted that the criterion to determine the (dis)proportional character of acts of self-defence should not lie with the goal of the measures. First of all it may be noted that Ago seems to be saying that self-defence may acquire disproportionate dimensions in relation to the original attack. One may wonder, if that is so, how one could still argue that proportionality functions as a restriction to the use of force in self-defence. Furthermore, as self-defence by definition involves the right to engage in cross-border use of force, that would appear to account for his opinion that there might be disproportionate dimensions. However, if an attack is still continuing any use of force to halt and/or repel the attack, including the use of force at different sites than where the actual hostilities are taking place, would not appear to be disproportionate.[248]

In the end it seems preferable to remain within the framework of a comparison between the internationally wrongful act (an armed attack) and the reaction thereto (acts of self-defence) taking into account the elements discussed in chapter four, subsection 4.4.3. Those were the degree of gravity of the wrongful act, the degree of fault on the part of the author State, and the importance of the rules at stake. The first element involves the scale of the acts, effects, damage or injury done. As to the second element it was pointed out that this concerned questions of negligence, wilful intent, or premeditation. The third element involves the importance of rules as evidenced by widespread ratification of multilateral treaties, elevation to the rank of peremptory norms, and recognition of particular conduct as an international crime. The question of occupation of territory is especially relevant in relation to self-defence. As long as territory of the injured State remains occupied force can be used against the author State to regain such territory. Similarly the use of force to forestall impending attacks in circumstances where hostilities have not come to an end ought not to be viewed as disproportionate.

In regard to Security Council action the obvious conclusion must be that any armed action it authorizes ought to be seen in relation to the goals set by it. Thus the proportionality of action adopted pursuant to an authorization depends very much on an evaluation whether such action could be considered apt to achieve the goals laid down in the resolution. As a matter of fact the condition of proportionality would appear to operate more strongly before any authorization is granted. That is, it takes on importance at the moment in time at which the Security Council has to decide whether or not the use of armed force would be the appropriate means to remedy a certain situation. This does not amount to an evaluation as to whether or not certain action is necessary. As pointed out in the previous subsection, whether or not specific action is necessary depends on whether other, less far-reaching, means could still be resorted to. The situation of Libya may serve as an example once more. On the assumption that the Council would have expanded the measures of article 41 so as to amount to a complete embargo against Libya, it might be argued that after a period of time there would be sufficient grounds to conclude on their inadequacy. Other, armed, action might be considered necessary then. However, though the gravity of alleged Libyan involvement in acts of terrorism cannot be denied, it is hard to see how its continued refusal to hand over the individuals suspected of having caused the crash at Lockerbie could justify armed action against it.[249] If one were to reject the proposition that armed action could be taken as against Libya, whether unilaterally or authorized by the Security Council, that would not be because such action would not be necessary, but because the use of force would be disproportionate in view of the circumstances. Naturally the conduct allegedly imputed to Libya could not be said to constitute an international crime.

In relation to international crimes the use of force authorized by the Security Council could certainly not be considered disproportional to the acts concerned.

Resort to armed force, peremptory norms, and human rights

Enough has been said already regarding the peremptory norm on the use of force against the territorial integrity and political independence of States. It may be repeated here that only the attempted genocide on a specific people could lead to a disruption of the territorial integrity of a State, and that no State could be put into a position of subordination towards other States for reasons unrelated to the performance of international obligations (whether those originate from primary or secondary rules of international law).

The peremptory norm of self-determination of peoples obviously places a restriction on the use of force to the effect that it may not be used to prevent a people from deciding on its own future. As such it constitutes, partly, the counterpart of the peremptory norm prohibiting the use of force against the political independence of States.

In regard to issues of self-determination the previous section made clear that a people living within the territory of an existing State cannot claim the right to secede from that State and form its own State. Also it could not claim any general right of armed opposition against the government of that State. Only when the denial of self-determination constitutes serious breaches of obligation by a State, involving widespread and systematic breaches of basic human rights obligations regarding individuals of the people, is there any right of armed opposition. Should a State resort to force, either as a lawful exercise of the right to self-defence, or as an unlawful humanitarian intervention, it must refrain from using force to suppress a people's legitimate aspirations to self-determination.

With regard to the peremptory norm stipulating respect for basic human rights obligations similar observations apply. A State resorting to force must refrain from violating basic human rights. It is here that a link exists with international humanitarian law. Any cross-border use of force brings into operation the conventional and customary rules and principles regarding hostilities between States. It is to be noted moreover that those rules and principles function as special rules which take precedence over the general rules of human rights law (*lex specialis derogat legi generalis*).

The basic tenet of humanitarian law, enunciated for the first time in article 22 of the Regulations Respecting the Laws and Customs of War on Land, is that:[250] "The right of belligerents to adopt means of injuring the enemy is not unlimited." One of the most important among the rules formulated in pursuit of that principle is the fundamental distinction between combatants and non-combatants.[251] In general terms it is possible to say that the use of force should as least as possible affect the civilian population.[252] In furtherance of specifically that cause a treaty has been drafted, namely the 1949 Geneva Convention IV.[253]

With regard to combatants the situation is generally different. The rule protecting the right to life under human rights law essentially does not operate in relation to persons taking part in hostilities. Thus it is lawful for individuals that are part of the armed forces (in a broad sense) of a party to the conflict to (attempt to) kill persons forming part of the armed forces of the other party (and vice versa). Restrictions have been placed on this right both from a general and specific point of view. Generally speaking persons can no longer be killed if they no longer take part in hostilities. Such is especially the case if they are no longer in any position to do any harm, or if they have surrendered.[254] Specific restrictions have been established with regard to the means and methods of killing individuals of the armed forces of the opposite party. These concern mostly restrictions regarding prohibited weapons.

5.8. Summary

The scope of the rule prohibiting the threat or use of force in international law, whether under the Charter or customary international law, is quite comprehensive. States are under the obligations to refrain from the threat or use of force against the territorial integrity or political independence of other States, in any manner inconsistent with the purposes of the United Nations, or contrary to the peaceful settlement of disputes. However, in contrast with the rule prohibiting the use of force against the territorial integrity or political independence of States, the rule prohibiting the use of force to settle disputes does not constitute a peremptory norm. The Charter provisions allowing the use of force, basically articles 42 and 51, replaced the rules of customary international law in that respect. It is possible, though, that other derogations from the prohibition on the use of force would have come, or will come, into existence under customary international law.

The considerations in subsection 4.2.1, chapter four, apply *mutatis mutandis* to the function of resort to armed force. However, in contrast to the function of countermeasures, the function of resort to armed force constitutes the forced settlement of reparation disputes between the injured State and the author State. On the other hand resort to countermeasures constitutes a general option in response to internationally wrongful acts. Resort to armed force, in self-defence, constitutes an exceptional option for States. In contrast armed force may be resorted to, generally, by the Security Council.

The basic precondition for the lawful resort to armed force lies, as with lawful resort to countermeasures, with the prior commission of a wrongful act. As an armed attack will necessarily constitute a breach of obligation, as a minimum, under article 2, paragraph 3, of the Charter, the resort to force in self-defence is based, if only provisionally, on a determination by the injured State of a wrongful act on the part of the author State. The Security Council possesses the competence to determine the existence of a threat to the peace, breach of the peace, or act of aggression, and as such does not need to have recourse to the Court in order to establish the existence of an internationally wrongful act. Due to the intentional, wilful and premeditated character of breaches of obligation constituting crimes there is no need, for either injured States or the Security Council, to demand reparation or resort to dispute settlement procedures prior to the use of armed force against the author State. As such resort to armed force should be considered typical in case of crimes. Resort to armed force during arbitral or judicial proceedings is not prohibited just because of the existence of such proceedings.

As a matter of Charter interpretation resort to armed force by the Security Council must be preceded by a determination under article 39 of the Charter. In deciding on the measures necessary to restore international peace and security the Council is not bound to resort to article 41 before taking action under article 42. Nor is it bound to refrain from taking action under article 42 until the measures adopted under article 41 would have proved to be inadequate. In view of the lack of the agreements envisaged in article 43, however, the Security Council cannot generally resort to action under article 42. The interpretation of article 12, paragraph 1, of the Charter, shows that the General Assembly possesses the competence to recommend the use of armed force if the Security Council is not exercising its functions under the Charter. As the Assembly cannot decide on action, the lawfulness of armed force resorted to pursuant to a recommendation depends on the presence of a legal basis under the Charter or customary international law. The same argument applies to Security Council recommendations. The practice of the Security Council shows that it can, analogous to the provision of article 53, paragraph 1, on regional arrangements, authorize individual members of the United Nations to resort to armed force. However, no obligation can be inferred to actually resort to force in pursuit of such an authorization.

In view of the Court's statements in the Nicaragua Case a right to resort to collective self-defence can be asserted only against an armed attack. Where a use of armed force, whether carried out by the regular armed forces or by armed bands, is not of sufficient gravity, only a right of individual self-defence can be exercised. In the light of article 19, paragraph 3 (a), Part One, and article 5, paragraph 3, Part Two, of the ILC-draft on State responsibility, only an armed attack should be considered a crime of aggression giving rise to injured State status for all States. The object of self-defence must be to impose performance of the author State's obligations regarding cessation and restitution in kind. To the extent that hostilities are continuing, force may be resorted to to fend off impending attacks. A right of collective self-defence can be exercised only if the victim State declared itself under attack (provided it had not been overrun). Such a State must also report to the Security Council, though failure to report will not invalidate any action taken in self-defence.

In contrast the Security Council's competence under article 39 extends to all kinds of uses of force, whether of minor importance or not, and to breaches of obligation which could lead to such uses of force. The Security Council can authorize the use of force to maintain or restore international peace and security. In contrast to the object to be pursued by force in self-defence, resort to force under the authority of the Security Council may involve the forced implementation of all the author State's reparation obligations.

A denial of self-determination implies the denial of the political rights of the individuals of a people on a discriminatory basis. For that reason a serious breach of obligation for safeguarding the right to self-determination exists only if a State is violating, on a widespread scale and in a systematic fashion, the basic human rights of individuals of a specific people. If such is the case the people concerned has a right of armed assistance against the authorities of the author State. Should the conduct of authorities of the author State allow for the conclusion that genocide is attempted or has been committed, the targeted people may, subject to geographical and demographical factors, exercise its right to self-determination and opt for the establishment of a new State.

At present there does not exist any rule of international law that would justify a cross-border use of force, whether in the form of humanitarian intervention or state of necessity, to end the commission of human rights violations in another State. A right of humanitarian intervention in response to widespread breaches of basic human rights obligations ought to exist under international law. However, in such a case one should not require the exhaustion of other means, nor that it should be undertaken for the shortest possible of times and with a minimum impact on the State organization. In the long run all the reparation obligations of the author State of a crime, especially those on guarantees against repetition, must be implemented.

The Security Council has determined a threat to the peace regarding the crises in Somalia, Rwanda and Haiti. Though the threats to "international" peace cannot be said to have been overly obvious regarding those situations, the competence of the Security Council must be recognized regarding these kinds of emergencies.

No restriction on the basis of the absence of specially affected States would apply to the right to resort to force, if such a right were to come into existence, in response to the crimes of denial of self-determination and widespread breaches of basic human rights obligations. Regarding the crime of aggression the presence of a directly injured State leads to the restriction that other States' resort to force must have been requested. Furthermore, and also in relation to the crime of aggression, it may be said that the right of self-defence can be exercised only for as long as the Security Council has refrained from taking measures under articles 41 or 42 of the Charter.

The requirements of immediacy and necessity must be evaluated in the light of the objects of self-defence, especially whether the use of force is still continuing, whether territory of the directly injured State remains occupied, and whether a renewal of aggressive policies on the part of the author State is imminent. Since the Security Council may involve itself with the whole gambit of reparation obligations, the argument that an authorization to use force is not necessary cannot easily be made.

The proportionality of the use of force must take into account the elements discussed in chapter four, namely the gravity of the wrongful act, the degree of fault on the part of the author State, and the importance of the rules at stake. The evaluation of proportionality of action by the Security Council is relevant especially before any action is implemented. Thus it would be hard to envisage, for instance, that the Security Council would authorize the use of force against Libya notwithstanding the obvious inadequacy of measures under article 41 of the Charter.

The use of force may not lead to situations contrary to those desired under peremptory norms. Resort to the use of force must not, generally, lead to the disruption of the territorial integrity of the author State, to domination over it unrelated to the performance of obligations, to the suppression of legitimate aspirations of a people to self-determination, or to violations of the basic rules of humanitarian or human rights law.

Disputes or questions regarding the matters discussed in this chapter or those of the other chapters may call for adjudication by the Court. That brings us to the next chapter.

NOTES

[1] The 1945 Charter of the United Nations, 39 AJIL 1945, Supplement, pp. 190-215. In contrast to Bowett, D., Self-Defence in International Law, Manchester University Press, Manchester, 1958, 148, it is not especially self-evident to the present writer that the plain, common-sense meaning of threat or use of force will not apply

to: "(...) economic or political pressure but only to physical, armed force." Footnote omitted. Generally also Brownlie, I., International Law and the Use of Force by States, Clarendon Press, Oxford, 1963, 361-362; Calogeropoulos-Stratis, S., Le recours à la force dans la société internationale, Editions L.E.P., Lausanne, and Librairie Generale de Droit et de Jurisprudence, Paris, 1986, 62-66; Cassese, A., Article 51, in Cot, J.-P., and Pellet, A. (Eds.), La Charte des Nations Unies, Commentaire article par article, 2e édition, revue et augmentée, Economica, Paris, 1991, pp. 771-792, 789-790; and Randelzhofer, A., Article 2(4), in Simma, B. (Ed.), The Charter of the United Nations, A Commentary, Oxford University Press, Oxford, 1994, pp. 106-128, 112-115.

[2] Bowett, Self-Defence, 148-149. Ranging economic coercion under force are Paust, J., and Blaustein, A., The Arab Oil Weapon – A Threat to International Peace, 68 AJIL 1974, pp. 410-439, 415-419 and 439.

[3] Article 46 states, on the other hand, that: "Plans for the application of armed force shall be made by the Security Council with the assistance of the Military Staff Committee."

[4] Bowett, Self-Defence, 148, footnote 3; Calogeropoulos-Stratis, 63-64; Virally, M., Article 2, Paragraphe 4, in Cot and Pellet, La Charte, pp. 115-128, 122-123.

[5] Text of basic article 1 in Calogeropoulos-Stratis, Le recours, 42. This limitation would be removed if a State refused to accept an offer for arbitration, did not co-operate in good faith in establishing the compromis, or did not implement the arbitration award.

[6] The 1919 Covenant of the League of Nations, 13 AJIL 1919, Supplement, pp. 128-140.

[7] The 1928 General Pact for the Renunciation of War, 22 AJIL 1928, Supplement, pp. 171-173; and Note sent by the United States to a number of governments. *Ibid.*, pp. 174-176. Article 2 ran: "The High Contracting Parties agree that the settlement or solution of all disputes or conflicts of whatever nature or of whatever origin they may be, which may arise among them, shall never be sought except by pacific means."

[8] The Case of the S.S. Lotus, Publications PCIJ, 1927, Series A, No. 10, p. 4, 18: "International law governs relations between independent States. The rules of law binding upon States therefore emanate from their own free will as expressed in conventions or by usages generally accepted as expressing principles of law and established in order to regulate the relations between these co-existing independent communities or with a view to the achievement of common aims. Restrictions upon the independence of States cannot therefore be presumed."

[9] Generally Sadurska, R., Threats of Force, 82 AJIL 1988, pp. 239-268.

[10] Corfu Channel case, Judgment, ICJ Reports 1949, p. 4, 30-31.

[11] Military and Paramilitary Activities in and against Nicaragua (Nicaragua *v.* United States of America), Merits, Judgment, ICJ Reports 1986, p. 14, 118.

[12] This excludes an in depth discussion of the phrase "in their international relations". One may note however that the word "their" relates to members of the United Nations. As membership of the Organization is open only to peace-loving States (article 4, paragraph 1), the obvious deduction should be that the prohibition of article 2, paragraph 4, only covers inter-State threats or uses of force. See Bowett, Self-Defence, 149-150. That conclusion entails some ambiguity regarding the interpretation "or in any manner inconsistent with the Purposes of the United Nations". See next subsections.

[13] Brownlie, International Law, 267, claimed in this respect: "If it is asserted that the phrase may have a qualifying effect then writers making this assertion face the difficulty that it involves an admission that there is an ambiguity, and in such a case recourse may be had to the *travaux préparatoires*, which reveal a meaning contrary to that asserted." Two footnotes omitted.

[14] The 1969 Vienna Convention on the Law of Treaties, 63 AJIL 1969, pp. 875-903.

[15] According to article 32 of the Vienna Convention the preparatory works may also be consulted to confirm the meaning resulting from the application of article 31. It is not clear what should happen if the meaning flowing from the preparatory works contradicts the ordinary meaning of the terms employed in the treaty. Judge Schwebel has addressed this issue. See Dissenting Opinion Schwebel, Maritime Delimitation and Territorial Questions between Qatar and Bahrain, Jurisdiction and Admissibility, Judgment, ICJ Reports 1995, p. 6, 31-32 and 39. Though he appears to grant precedence to the demonstrated lack of common intentions of the parties in the preparatory works, it may be submitted that in the particular case at hand, the interpretation(s) of the Doha Minutes, the disputed phrase did not carry with it any specific ordinary meaning. Recourse to the preparatory works should have been based on the fact that the interpretation(s) under article 31 left the meaning ambiguous and obscure. The purpose of such recourse would have had to be to determine the meaning rather than to confirm it. Note Dissenting Opinion Shahabuddeen, *ibid.*, 58 (more broadly 55-59) to this effect.

[16] Bowett, Self-Defence, 150-152; Brownlie, International Law, 265-268.

[17] C.f. Bowett, Self-Defence, 152; Virally, Article 2, Paragraphe 4, 117 and 125. Apparently contrary Brownlie, International Law, 265-268; Verwey, W., Humanitarian Intervention under International Law, 32 NILR 1985, pp. 357-418, 379-380, 389, and 406.

[18] Ronzitti, N., Rescuing Nationals Abroad through Military Coercion and Intervention on Grounds of Humanity, Martinus Nijhoff Publishers, Dordrecht, 1985, 8-9; Implicitly Schachter, O., The Lawful Use of Force by a State against Terrorists in Another Country, 19 IYHR 1989, pp. 209-231, 213-214. and Schachter, O., Just War and Human Rights, 1 PUSL YIL 1989, pp. 1-19, 5-6; Randelzhofer, Article 2(4), 117-118. Verwey, Humanitarian Intervention, 406, expresses the view that arguments supporting an extensive interpretation of the prohibition of article 2, paragraph 4, are more convincing.

[19] Declaration on Principles of International Law concerning Friendly Relations and Co-operation among States in accordance with the Charter of the United Nations, First Principle (States shall refrain in their international relations from the threat or use of force against the territorial integrity or political independence of any State, or in any other manner inconsistent with the Purposes of the United Nations). Note also that the Definition of Aggression, General Assembly resolution 3314 (XXIX), states: "Aggression is the use of armed force by a State against the sovereignty, territorial integrity or political independence of another State, (...)."

[20] C.f. Nicaragua Case, Merits, 100: "The effect of consent to the text of such resolutions cannot be understood merely that of a 'reiteration or elucidation' of the treaty commitment undertaken in the Charter. On the contrary, it may be understood as an acceptance of the validity of the rule or set of rules declared by the resolution by themselves."

[21] Goodrich, L., and Hambro, E., Charter of the United Nations, Commentary and Documents, Second and Revised Edition, Stevens & Sons Limited, London, 1949, 104-105.

[22] Especially Declaration on the Inadmissibility of Intervention in the Domestic Affairs of States and the Protection of their Independence and Sovereignty, General Assembly resolution 2131 (XX); and Bowett, Self-Defence, 42-50.

[23] Nicaragua Case, Merits, 108.

[24] Observations Kellogg, Case of the Free Zones of Upper Savoy and the District of Gex (Second Phase), Publications PCIJ, 1930, Series A, No. 24, p. 4, 41; Goodrich and Hambro, Charter, 105, observe: "Clearly the 'political independence' of a state is in fact violated if a state is coerced through the threat or use of force by a more powerful state into taking action which it would not otherwise take."

[25] Lotus Case, Judgment, 18.

[26] Brownlie, International Law, 268; Verwey, Humanitarian Intervention, 381.

[27] Though one might consider the situation, in relation to the Kurds, prevailing in Turkey and Iraq to come close to such an hypothesis. Turkish action, however, appears not to involve the Iraqi Kurds, but only the Turkish Kurd armed opposition.

[28] C.f. Verwey, Humanitarian Intervention, 381-383.

[29] *E.g.* Merrills, J., The Principle of Peaceful Settlement of Disputes, in Lowe, V., and Warbrick, C. (Eds.), The United Nations and the Principles of International Law, Essays in memory of Michael Akehurst, Routledge, London, 1994, pp. 49-65; and Tomuschat, C., Article 2(3), in Simma, The Charter, pp. 97-106. The latter mentions that measures inconsistent with the ban of article 2, paragraph 4, are not peaceful.

[30] Nicaragua Case, Merits, 145; Brownlie, International Law, 113; Charpentier, J., Article 2, Paragraphe 3, in Cot and Pellet, La Charte, pp. 103-113, 103-105; and Virally, Article 2, Paragraphe 4, 116. See also Gray, C., The Principle of Non-Use of Force, in Lowe and Warbrick, The United Nations, pp. 33-48.

[31] Arangio-Ruiz, G., Fourth Report on State Responsibility, 12 May 1992, A/CN.4/444, 40 pp., 25. Note also the arguments recorded in Verwey, Humanitarian Intervention, 378-379 and 383.

[32] Note also especially Manila Declaration on the Peaceful Settlement of International Disputes, A/RES/37/10.

[33] Charpentier, Article 2, Paragraphe 3, 106, observes: "(...) il est relativement indifférent à la Charte que les Etats trouvent une solution à leur différends: ce qui lui importe, c'est que ces différends ne s'enveniment pas au point de les conduire à les régler par la force."

[34] Note its place in the Declaration on Principles of International Law concerning Friendly Relations and Co-operation among States in Accordance with the Charter of the United Nations, General Assembly resolution 2625 (XXV); also Verwey, Humanitarian Intervention, 378-379 and 383.

[35] Goodrich and Hambro, Charter, 102, note: "Interpreted in the light of paragraph 4, this principle would seem to prohibit any method of settlement involving the use of force short of war. The use of armed reprisals, for example, is not to be regarded as a peaceful means, though technically it may not be war." See generally Bowett, D., Reprisals involving Recourse to Armed Force, 66 AJIL 1972, pp. 1-36.

[36] Manila Declaration on the Peaceful Settlement of International Disputes, A/RES/37/10.

[37] Nationalities Decrees in Tunis and Morocco, Publications PCIJ, Series B, No. 4, 23-26.

[38] Charpentier, Article 2, Paragraphe 3, 109.

[39] On situations and disputes see Kelsen, H., The Law of the United Nations, A Critical Analysis of Its Fundamental Problems, Stevens & Sons Limited, London, 1951, 359-362. Charpentier, Article 2, Paragraphe 3, 108, observes: "La notion de différend implique donc un objet suffisamment circonscrit. Mais elle implique aussi des parties, entre lesquelles a surgi une divergence de points de vue;"

[40] Nicaragua Case, Merits, 92-97.

[41] Nicaragua Case, Merits, 97-102.

[42] Operative paragraph 4 bears witness to this absence of differentiation, as it stated that the United States had "acted, against the Republic of Nicaragua, in breach of its obligation under customary international law not to use force against another State;" Nicaragua Case, Merits, 146-147. In the same vein the Court quoted indiscriminately from General Assembly resolution 2625 (XXV). *Ibid.*, 101-102.

[43] Nicaragua Case, Merits, 106-111, 123-127, and 130-135.

[44] Nicaragua Case, Merits, 123-124 and 130-135. The Court observed, moreover, that the goal of the *Contras* was the violent overthrow of the Nicaraguan government.

[45] Nicaragua Case, Merits, 18-20.

[46] Nicaragua Case, Merits, 145.

[47] Commentary Article 50, Law of Treaties, YBILC 1966, Volume II, pp. 247-249, 247. Generally Dinstein, Y., War, Aggression and Self-Defence, Grotius Publications Limited, Cambridge, 1988, 98-103.

[48] Nicaragua Case, Merits, 100. The Court referred to the apparently concurring views of the parties to the case in this respect. *Ibid.*, 100-101. C.f. Thirlway, H., The Law and Procedure of the International Court of Justice, 1960-1989 (Part Two), 61 BYBIL 1990, pp. 1-133, 108-110.

[49] Text and Commentary Article 33, Part One, YBILC 1980, Volume II, Part One, pp. 34-52, 44. The Commission contemplated that there might be situations in which conduct infringing the territorial sovereignty of a State would not be necessarily considered acts of aggression. It referred to (*ibid.* and 43): "(...) incursions into foreign territory to forestall harmful operations by an armed group which was preparing to attack the territory of the State, or in pursuit of an armed band or gang of criminals who had crossed the frontier and perhaps had their base in that foreign territory, or to protect the lives of nationals or other persons attacked or detained by hostile forces or groups not under the authority and control of the state, or to eliminate or neutralize a source of troubles which threatened to occur or to spread across the frontier." *Ibid.*, 43-44. In support Verwey, Humanitarian Intervention, 416-417; and Schachter, The Lawful Use of Force, 227-228.

[50] Charpentier, Article 2, Paragraphe 3, 105, and also 112. In his opinion this is because a proposal (related to the Declaration on Friendly Relations), to the effect that the principle on the peaceful settlement of disputes constituted the expression of a universal conviction of the international community, was rejected. Such denial of *jus cogens* status was due, in his opinion, because (*ibid.*, 105): "(...) les Etats ont sans aucun doute voulu sauvegarder le large pouvoir discrétionnaire que leur laisse, comme nous le verrons, le texte de l'article 2, paragraphe 3, sur le choix de moyens et sur l'appréciation des résultats."

[51] Fischer, G., Article 42, in Cot and Pellet, La Charte, pp. 705-716, 709.

[52] C.f. Certain expenses of the United Nations (Article 17, paragraph 2, of the Charter), Advisory Opinion, ICJ Reports 1962, p. 151, 164, in which the Court noted that article 11, paragraph 2: "(...) in its first sentence empowers the General Assembly, by means of recommendations to States or to the Security Council, or to both, to organize peace-keeping operations, *at the request, or with the consent, of the States concerned.*" Emphasis added.

[53] Definition of Aggression, General Assembly resolution 3314 (XXIX), article 3 (e); Text and Commentary Article 29, Part One, YBILC 1979, Volume II, Part Two, pp. 109-115, 113.

[54] Expenses Opinion, 168.

[55] Bowett, Self-Defence, 184-185. He added (185): "It is, therefore, fallacious to assume that members have only those rights which the Charter accords to them; on the contrary they have those rights which general international law accords to them except in so far as they have surrendered them under the Charter." It may be noted that he otherwise takes a broad view on the circumstances which justify the exercise of the right of self-defence. *Ibid.*, 269-275. Similar broad views are to be found in Bowett, D., The Use of Force for the Protection of Nationals Abroad, in Cassese, A. (Ed.), The Current Legal Regulation of the Use of Force, Martinus Nijhoff Publishers, Dordrecht, 1986, pp. 39-55. An analogous argument is made by Cassese, Article 51, 778, in regard to anticipatory self-defence: "(...) l'article 51 a de toute façon effacé tout le droit préexistant, sans laisser aucun espace à la legitime défense contemplée par le droit coutumier si ce n'est dans les limites où elle est explicitement autorisée par la Charte de l'ONU." Similarly Brownlie, International Law, 272-275.

[56] C.f. Malanczuk, P., Humanitarian Intervention and the Legitimacy of the Use of Force, Het Spinhuis, Amsterdam, 1993, 27.

[57] Nicaragua Case, Merits, 108-111, 126-127, 130-135.

[58] Nicaragua Case, Merits, 106, 110-111, 126-128.

[59] Nicaragua Case, Merits, 108. In the same line of reasoning article 53 of the Vienna Convention, while positing an almost absolute prohibition to derogate from peremptory norms, envisages the possibility that such norms can be modified by others having the same character.

[60] Nicaragua Case, Merits, 109. The Court found that States had not, in actual fact, justified their conduct by reference to a right to intervene. *Ibid.*

[61] Arangio-Ruiz' first observation, after discussing self-defence, concerned the question whether armed force could be used to obtain cessation of other crimes than aggression. Arangio-Ruiz, G., Fifth Report on State Responsibility, 24 June 1993, A/CN.4/453/Add.3, 36 pp., 8.

[62] Arangio-Ruiz raised the issue in Fifth Report, Addendum 3, 9 and footnote 117.

[63] Ago, R., Addendum to the eighth report on State responsibility, YBILC 1980, Volume II, Part One, 1-70, 53. Relevant footnote omitted.

[64] Ago, Eighth Report, Addendum, 54. After the text quoted here Ago continues once more to argue the essentially punitive or repressive object of sanctions. The Commission substantively took over Ago's remarks, but did not state that it would be wrong to view self-defence as a kind of sanction. Text and Commentary Article 34, Part One, YBILC 1980, Volume II, Part Two, pp. 52-61, 53-54.

[65] "Ordinarily" because a right to use force in individual self-defence against uses of force staying below the threshold of an armed attack exists under customary international law (see subsection 5.5.1).

[66] Report of the International Law Commission on the work of its forty-sixth session, 2 May – 22 July 1994, General Assembly, Official Records, Forty-ninth Session, Supplement No. 10 (A/49/10), 366, footnote 362.

[67] Arangio-Ruiz, Fifth Report, Addendum 3, 8.

[68] Arangio-Ruiz, Fifth Report, Addendum 3, 9. Underlining in the original. Note these remarks by Rasy: "S'il y a une chose incompatible avec le droit, c'est l'absence de force. Car le faible, si faible au point de ne pouvoir se prévaloir de son propre droit, sera pour toujours l'éternel frustré." Rasy, D., Le droit et la force dans le monde contemporain, in Recueil d'études en hommage a Charles Eisenmann, Éditions Cujas, Paris, 1975, pp. 419-421, 421. And note the critical remarks by Scelle, G., Quelques réflexions sur l'abolition de la compétence du guerre, 58 RGDIP 1954, pp. 5-22, 12; and Fitzmaurice, G., The Foundations of the Authority of International Law and the Problem of Enforcement, 19 MLR 1956, pp. 1-13, 4-6.

[69] Commission Report 1994, 344-345, and 362.

[70] Arangio-Ruiz, G., Seventh Report on State Responsibility, 9 May 1995, A/CN.4/469, 49 pp., 20-21; and proposed article 17, paragraph 1, Part Two, in Seventh Report on State Responsibility, 24 May 1995, A/CN.4/469/Add.1, 4 pp., 2. One may note that he has indicated that injured States could adopt urgent, interim measures aimed at (Seventh Report, 17): "(...) securing immediate access to the victims for purposes of rescue and/or aid or preventing the continuation of a genocide, measures concerning humanitarian convoys, anti-pollution action, passage facilities, etc." As noted earlier, in chapter four, subsection 4.3.1, it is not clear how injured States would secure immediate access to victims or prevent the continuation of genocide, etc., in view of the proposed prohibition of measures involving the threat or use of armed force.

[71] The Commission noted: "Another element (...) is that the use of force, even for strictly defensive purposes, is likewise admitted not as a general rule, but only as an exception to a rule under which a central authority has a monopoly on the use of force so as to guarantee respect by all for the integrity of others. Only in specific situations where, by its very nature, the use of force by the agencies of the central authority cannot be resorted to promptly and efficiently enough to protect a subject against an attack by another does the use of means of defence involving force by the subject in question remain legitimate." Commentary Article 34, Part One, 52. C.f. Brownlie, International Law, 273; Bowett, Self-Defence, 195 (generally 195-197). Contrary Graefrath, B., Ausschluß der Völkerrechtswidrigkeit – Selbstverteidigung – Sanktion, in Durchsetzungsprobleme des Völkerrechts, Wissenschaftliche Schriftenreihe der Humboldt-Universität, Berlin, 1983, pp. 13-26, 21, who notes that the right to resort to self-defence and other sanctions are rights of the victim against the law-breaker for the enforcement of international law, and for that reason should not simply be seen as exceptions to the rule.

[72] Contrary Frowein, J., Article 42, in Simma, The Charter, pp. 628-636, 631, who claims that the principle of proportionality applies, since article 42 concerns such action "as may be necessary".

[73] C.f. Goodrich and Hambro, Charter, 279.

[74] C.f. Fischer, Article 42, 707-710.

[75] C.f. Brownlie, International Law, 265, 269-270, and 278-279; Cassese, Article 51, 774-775. Contrary Bowett, Self-Defence, 187-193.

[76] Generally Bowett, Self-Defence, 195-197; Franck, T., and Patel, F., UN Police Action in Lieu of War: "The Old Order Changeth", 85 AJIL 1991, pp. 63-74, 63.

[77] Cassese, Article 51, 774-775; Rostow, E., Until What?, Enforcement Action or Self-Defense?, 85 AJIL 1991, pp. 506-516, 510-514; Greig, D., Self-Defence and the Security Council: What Does Article 51 Require?, 40 ICLQ 1991, pp. 366-402, 392-393.

[78] C.f. Greig, Self-Defence, 392 and 401.

[79] C.f. Ago, Eighth Report, Addendum, 70.

[80] Dallal, S., International Law and the United Nations' Role in the Gulf Crisis, 18 SJILC 1992, pp. 111-140, 125. Also *ibid.*, 126. He claims the necessity of an advisory opinion on the basis that otherwise Iraq's claim on Kuwaiti territory remains unadjudicated. If that claim were valid, so he seems to say, Iraq's use of force against Kuwait would not constitute an act of aggression. In that connection he claims that Iraq's recognition of Kuwait in 1963 was made by an unrepresentative government, was not ratified by a representative body, and not supported by a popular plebiscite. *Ibid.*, 127. To that one could counter that the present Iraqi government would also not appear to be a very representative government.

[81] Nicaragua Case, Merits, 118-123.

[82] Schachter, The Lawful Use of Force, 221-222, correctly states in regard to the possible insufficiency of peaceful means: "However, in some cases this does not make sense. Not only does an ongoing attack require armed defence at the time but the relations between the parties may be so implacably hostile as to render futile any attempt at peaceful settlement." Footnote omitted. He continues (222) however: "These difficulties do not dispose of the basic idea that force should not be used if other means can be effective. It should not be assumed, a priori, that measures of a non-military nature will fail to deter State support of terrorism (...)." Footnote omitted.

[83] Giraud, E., Le droit international public et la politique, 110 RDC ADI 1963-III, pp. 419-809, 664, observes: "Quelle est la valeur de la guerre comme sanction du droit international? C'est sans doute une sanction beaucoup plus efficace que les mesures de rétorsion et de représailles, (...)." Also *ibid.*, 678.

[84] Dallal, International Law, 122-123 and footnotes 66 and 68; in a similar sense, Weston, B., Security Council Resolution 678 and Persian Gulf Decision Making: Precarious Legitimacy, 85 AJIL 1991, pp. 516-535, 528-532, especially 530.

[85] Note also Military and Paramilitary Activities in and against Nicaragua (Nicaragua *v.* United States of America), Jurisdiction and Admissibility, Judgment, ICJ Reports 1984, p. 392, 434.

[86] Resolution 660. It may be asserted, *a fortiori*, that the Council would have been fully justified to determine the Iraqi invasion of Kuwait an act of aggression.

[87] Contrary Dallal, International Law, 123-124 and especially footnote 71, in which he claims: "These differences stem from Iraq's claim that Kuwait is part of Iraqi territory. (...) They also stem from Iraq's claim that Kuwait was waging "economic war against Iraq'." It is highly unlikely that such are the differences which the Security Council had in mind. Would it have determined a breach of the peace if Kuwait should indeed be considered part of Iraq? The more plausible interpretation of paragraph 3 is that it relates to the differences on which negotiations were broken off in the days immediately preceding the Iraqi invasion. See Rousseau, C., Chronique, 94 RGDIP 1990, 1091-1093.

[88] United States Diplomatic and Consular Staff in Tehran, Provisional Measures, Order, ICJ Reports 1979, p. 7, 20-21.

[89] United States Diplomatic and Consular Staff in Tehran, Judgment, ICJ Reports 1980, p. 3, 17-18.

[90] Diplomatic Staff Case, Judgment, 43.

[91] Diplomatic Staff Case, Judgment, 43-44. The Court observed that the legality of the United States' actions, or any question of responsibility flowing from it, was not before it. *Ibid.*, 43.

[92] C.f. Frowein, J., Article 39, in Simma, The Charter, pp. 605-616, 612-613; and Frowein, Article 42, 631.

[93] Fischer, Article 42, 708-710.

[94] Fischer, Article 42, 709.

[95] C.f. Kelsen, The Law of the United Nations, 731.

[96] Fischer, Article 42, 709.

[97] See A/46/825 (France); and A/46/827 (United Kingdom and United States).

[98] C.f. Lapidoth, R., Some Reflections on the Law and Practice Concerning the Imposition of Sanctions by the Security Council, 30 ADV 1992, pp. 114-127, 117.

[99] Nicaragua Case, Merits, 141. Also 116.

[100] Eisemann, P., Article 41, in Cot and Pellet, La Charte, pp. 691-704, 696. Emphasis in the original. Fischer, Article 42, 708, notes that the stance that article 41 measures must be resorted to first is not legally defensible.

[101] Weston, Security Council Resolution 678, 528-532. Kaikobad claims that the Council should have clarified that the sanctions were, or had proved to be, inadequate. Kaikobad, K., Self-Defence, Enforcement Action and the Gulf Wars, 1980-88 and 1990-91, 63 BYBIL 1992, pp. 299-366, 353.

[102] Weston, Security Council Resolution 678, 528-529. He observes (529) that critics noted that the United States had been extremely patient in regard to sanctions against South Africa, and that: "(...), over time, the international crimes committed by Pretoria matched – indeed exceeded – those committed by Baghdad." That com-

parison is completely lame. The crimes committed by South Africa by far do not match the crimes of Iraq, especially not when considered over time.

[103] C.f. Boutros-Ghali, B., An Agenda for Peace, Preventive Diplomacy, Peacemaking and Peace-Keeping, 17 June 1992, A/47/277, reprinted in 31 ILM 1992, pp. 956-975, paragraphs 42 and 43. Generally on article 43 Goodrich and Hambro, Charter, 281-287; Kelsen, The Law of the United Nations, 756-768; Furet, M.-F., Article 43, in Cot and Pellet, La Charte, pp. 717-723.

[104] Franck and Patel, UN Police Action in Lieu of War, 66 and 70.

[105] C.f. Fischer, Article 42, 707 and 714-716. Contrary Schachter, O., United Nations Law in the Gulf Conflict, 85 AJIL 1991, pp. 452-473, 462, who claims that resolution 678 constitutes an example of "action" involving the use of military forces under article 42, and that such "action" need not be under the control of the Security Council. Also *ibid.*, 469-460. In this sense also Malanczuk, Humanitarian Intervention, 15.

[106] Resolution 84, paragraphs 3 to 5.

[107] Apparently in agreement Kelsen, The Law of the United Nations, 936-940; Furet, Article 43, 721; Klein, E., Sanctions by International Organizations and Economic Communities, 30 ADV 1992, pp. 101-113, 105; and Frowein, Article 39, 614.

[108] C.f. Warbrick, C., The Invasion of Kuwait by Iraq, 40 ICLQ 1991, pp. 482-492, 486-487; Rostow, Until What?, 508-509; Weston, Security Council Resolution 678, 519; implicitly Dallal, International Law, 137-138.

[109] Goodrich and Hambro, Charter, 281; Kelsen, The Law of the United Nations, 756; Franck and Patel, UN Police Action in Lieu of War, 66; Schachter, United Nations Law, 463-464. Contrary, though implicitly, Weston, Security Council Resolution 678, 519, who speaks of article 42 as a dead letter and of its dependent relationship to article 43.

[110] Expenses Opinion, 166 and 177. The Court also quoted the following (170-171) from a Secretary-General plan: "While the General Assembly is enabled to *establish* the Force with the consent of those parties which contribute units to the Force, it could not request the Force to be *stationed* or *operate* on the territory of a given country without the consent of the Government of that country. This does not exclude the possibility that the Security Council could use such a Force within the wider margins provided under Chapter VII of the United Nations Charter." Emphasis in the original.

[111] Security Council resolutions 836, paragraph 9, and 871, paragraph 9 (UNPROFOR); 918, paragraph 4, and 925, paragraph 5 (UNAMIR). Also resolutions 459, 467, 488, 498, and 501 (UNIFIL).

[112] General Assembly resolution 377 (V), Uniting for Peace, paragraph 1. For general comment see Kelsen, The Law of the United Nations, 953-990; Giraud, Le droit international public et la politique, 678-681.

[113] Expenses Opinion, 164-165.

[114] Expenses Opinion, 165.

[115] Security Council resolutions 119, 120, 129, 157, 303, 462, 500, 571, 572, 573, 577, 580, and 612.

[116] C.f. Frowein, J., Legal Consequences for International Law Enforcement in Case of Security Council Inaction, in Delbrück, J. (Ed.), The Future of International Law Enforcement, New Scenarios – New Law?, Duncker & Humblot, Berlin, 1993, pp. 111-124, 118-119; Klein, Sanctions by International Organizations, 106; and Lapidoth, Some Reflections, 125. Kelsen, H., Collective Security and Collective Self-Defense under the Charter of the United Nations, 42 AJIL 1948, pp. 783-796, 796, noted: "The only organ competent to determine, in a way binding upon the members, the existence of an armed attack within the meaning of Article 51, is the Security Council, and not the General Assembly."

[117] It may be noted that earlier on, in resolution 221, paragraph 5, the Security Council had called upon the government of the United Kingdom to: "(...) prevent, by the use of force if necessary, the arrival at Beira of vessels reasonably believed to be carrying oil destined for Southern Rhodesia, and empowers the United Kingdom to arrest and detain the tanker known as the *Joanna V* upon her departure from Beira in the event her oil cargo is discharged there." In resolution 665, paragraph 1, the Security Council called upon: "(...) those Member States co-operating with the Government of Kuwait which are deploying maritime forces to the area to use such measures commensurate to the specific circumstance as may be necessary under the authority of the Security Council to halt all inward and outward maritime shipping, in order to inspect and verify their cargoes and destinations and to ensure strict implementation of the provisions related to such shipping laid down in resolution 661 (1990);"

[118] S/PV.2963 (English version), 6 and 103 (USA); 19-20 (Kuwait); 41 (Colombia); 62-63 (China); 71 (Canada); 74 and 76 (Malaysia); 81-82 (UK). Iraq disputed the validity of the authorization on the ground that it was not covered by any one of the three exceptions (articles 51, 42 or 106) in the Charter. *Ibid.*, 19-20 to 21. Yemen voted against the resolution because it was so broad and vague and was not limited to the enforcement of the 10 earlier resolutions. It noted also that it was not related to any specific article under Chapter VII, that the Security Council would not control the forces, and that this amounted to a classic exam-

ple of "authority without accountability". *Ibid.*, 32-33. Cuba claimed that the text of the resolution violated the Charter by authorizing some States to use military force in total disregard of the procedures under the Charter. *Ibid.*, 58. Discussed by Lavalle, R., The Law of the United Nations and the Use of Force, under the Relevant Security Council Resolutions of 1990 and 1991, to Resolve the Persian Gulf Crisis, 23 NYIL 1992, pp. 3-65, 31-33.

119 Weston, Security Council Resolution 678, 525-528, admits that military action by the Coalition forces can be said to have been "technically" legal, but apparently he wishes to take some of that back in denying the legitimacy of such action.

120 *E.g.* Weston, Security Council Resolution 678, 518-519.

121 Resolutions 816, 836, 871, 908, 958, and 981 (former Yugoslavia); 794 (Somalia); 929 (Rwanda); and 940 (Haiti).

122 Expenses Opinion, 167.

123 Glennon, M., The Constitution and Chapter VII of the United Nations Charter, 85 AJIL 1991, pp. 74-88, 77 and 88; Schachter, United Nations Law, 464-465; implicitly Warbrick, The Invasion of Kuwait, 487.

124 C.f. Schachter, United Nations Law, 463.

125 C.f. Glennon, The Constitution and Chapter VII, 75, 77-78, 81-82 and 88; Warbrick, The Invasion of Kuwait, 487; Schachter, United Nations Law, 463 and 464-465.

126 As does also, by now, the practice of the Security Council: earlier mentioned resolutions 816, 836, 871, 908, 958, and 981 (former Yugoslavia); 794 (Somalia); 929 (Rwanda); and 940 (Haiti).

127 Implicitly Goodrich and Hambro, Charter, 316; Kodjo, E., Article 53, in Cot and Pellet, La Charte, pp. 816-831, 819 and 824.

128 C.f. Freudenschuß, H., Between Unilateralism and Collective Security: Authorizations of the Use of Force by the UN Security Council, 5 EJIL 1994, pp. 492-531, 526. The Court recalled the practice of the Security Council to the effect that abstentions by permanent members do not prevent the adoption of resolutions, and noted as to this procedure that it: "(...) has been generally accepted by Members of the United Nations and evidences a general practice of that Organization." Legal Consequences for States of the Continued Presence of South Africa in Namibia (South West Africa) notwithstanding Security Council Resolution 276 (1970), Advisory Opinion, ICJ Reports 1971, p. 16, 22. See also articles 5 and 31, paragraph 3 (b) and (c), Vienna Convention on the Law of Treaties, and article 38, paragraph 1 (b), of the Statute of the Court. The 1945 Statute of the International Court of Justice, 39 AJIL 1945, Supplement, pp. 215-229.

129 Resolutions 221 (Rhodesia); 665 (Iraq-Kuwait); 787 (former Yugoslavia); 875 and 917 (Haiti). Resolution 770, paragraph 2, is similar in wording, but calls upon States to take all measures necessary to facilitate delivery of humanitarian assistance to Sarajevo and other parts of Bosnia.

130 Contrary Weston, Security Council Resolution 678, 521, who states that the recommendations of article 39 relate to the pacific settlement of disputes under Chapter VI. Generally Cohen Jonathan, G., Article 39, in Cot and Pellet, La Charte, pp. 644-666, 662-663; and Fischer, Article 42, 709-710. In resolution 83 the Security Council recommended members to furnish such assistance to the Republic of Korea as necessary to repel the armed attack. The wording suggests that such assistance would amount to collective self-defence. Resolution 84 authorizes forces under a unified command to fly the United Nations flag.

131 Weston, Security Council Resolution 678, 521.

132 Goodrich and Hambro, Charter, 277; Eisemann, Article 41, 695-696.

133 C.f. Glennon, The Constitution, 82, in regard to resolution 665.

134 C.f. Lavalle, The Law of the United Nations, 21.

135 Commentary Article 34, Part One, 61.

136 Text and Commentary Article 30, Part One, YBILC 1979, Volume II, Part Two, pp. 115-122, 121.

137 The Commission, noting the differences between self-defence and countermeasures, claimed: "Armed reprisals cannot now be considered legitimate. (...) The prevailing view nowadays is that only the sanctions referred to in Chapter VII of the Charter of the United Nations can entail a lawful use of force." Commentary Article 34, Part One, 54.

138 Proposed by Schwebel, YBILC 1980, Volume I, 192: "Hence, it might be necessary to include in the draft an article which, in substance, provided that, where a State used force in a manner that would breach an international obligation were it not for the fact that the State was responding to a requirement or authorization of the United Nations or a regional organization acting pursuant to the Charter of the United Nations, that State did not incur international responsibility." Note also Commentary Article 34, Part One, 54.

139 Definition of Aggression, General Assembly resolution 3314 (XXIX), Annex.

140 Nicaragua Case, Merits, 101. Emphasis added.

141 Nicaragua Case, Merits, 101.

[142] Nicaragua Case, Merits, 103. Generally on armed attack Gill, T., The Law of Armed Attack in the Context of the Nicaragua Case, 1 HYIL 1988, pp. 30-58; Schachter, The Lawful Use of Force, 215-219; Sohn, L., The International Court of Justice and the Scope of the Right of Self-Defense and the Duty of Non-Intervention, in Dinstein, Y. (Ed.), Essays in Honour of Shabtai Rosenne, International Law at a Time of Perplexity, Martinus Nijhoff Publishers, Dordrecht, 1989, pp. 869-878, 871-875; Guillaume, G., Terrorisme et droit international, 215 RDC ADI 1989-III, pp. 287-416, 405-406; and Randelzhofer, A., Article 51, in Simma, The Charter, pp. 661-678, 668-675.

[143] Nicaragua Case, Merits, 103.

[144] Vigorously criticized by Dissenting Opinion Schwebel, Nicaragua Case, Merits, 331-352; also by Dissenting Opinion Jennings, Nicaragua Case, Merits, 542-544. Note Gill, The Law of Armed Attack, 38-44 and 50-52.

[145] Nicaragua Case, Merits, 127. The Court earlier stated, in paragraph 211, that (*ibid.*, 110): "Thus the lawfulness of the use of force by a State in response to a wrongful act of which it is has not itself been the victim is not admitted when this wrongful act is not an armed attack. In the view of the Court, under international law in force today – whether customary international law today or that of the United Nations system – States do not have a right of 'collective' armed response to acts which do not constitute an 'armed attack'."

[146] Noted by Dissenting Opinion Schwebel, Nicaragua Case, Merits, 349-350.

[147] C.f. Gill, T., The Forcible Protection, Affirmation and Exercise of Rights by States under Contemporary International Law, 23 NYIL 1992, pp. 105-173, 111-113; And note Gill, T., The Second Gulf Crisis and the Relation between Collective Security and Collective Self-Defense, 10 Grotiana 1989, pp. 47-76, 63 (especially footnote 31), and 66 (especially footnote 38).

[148] Especially Gill, The Second Gulf Crisis, 66, footnote 38. Apparently contrary Randelzhofer, Article 51, 667.

[149] In the Nicaragua Case there was only question of Nicaraguan incursions into the territory of Honduras and Costa Rica. The Court did not investigate any allegation of Nicaraguan support for opposition forces in those countries. Nicaragua Case, Merits, 86-87, and 119-121.

[150] Nicaragua Case, Merits, 103-104.

[151] Nicaragua Case, Merits, especially 82-86, and 119.

[152] Nicaragua Case, Merits, 103-104. Generally Lowe, V., The Principle of Non-Intervention: Use of Force, in Lowe and Warbrick, The United Nations, pp. 66-84; Lauterpacht, H., The Development of International Law by the Court, Stevens & Sons Limited, London, 1958, 316-318; and Henkin, L., Use of Force: Law and U.S. Policy, in Right *v.* Might: International Law and the Use of Force, Council on Foreign Relations Press, New York, 1991, pp. 37-69, 47.

[153] Nicaragua Case, Merits, 118-119.

[154] Nicaragua Case, Merits, 119, 124-125, and 146, paragraph 3. Some acts of intervention have not been considered as they were claimed by the Court also to amount to a threat or use of force.

[155] Apparently in agreement Guillaume, Terrorisme et droit international, 401. Contrary Sohn, The International Court of Justice, 877-878.

[156] Dissenting Opinion Schwebel, Nicaragua Case, Merits, 299-300.

[157] In that sense earlier Hoogh, A. de, Book Review: Sachariew, K., Die Rechtstellung der betroffenen Staaten bei Verletzungen multilateraler Verträge, Fragen der Aktivlegitimation und der völkerrechtlich zugelassenen Rechtsfolgen, 38 NILR 1991, pp. 104-109, 107-108.

[158] C.f. Gill, The Forcible Protection, Affirmation and Exercise of Rights, 120.

[159] C.f. Kaikobad who states that the objective of self-defence may be the "fending off and protection from further attacks which constitute an integral part of the continuum of hostilities". He also mentions two other objectives of self-defence: fending off current attacks; and restoration of the territorial status quo. Kaikobad, K., "*Ius Ad Bellum*": Legal Implications of the Iran-Iraq War, in Dekker, I., and Post, H. (Eds.), The Gulf War of 1980-1988, The Iran-Iraq War in International Legal Perspective, Martinus Nijhoff Publishers, Dordrecht, 1992, pp. 51-70, 63.

[160] Rostow argued in connection to the goals of resolution 678: "But the Security Council resolutions also contemplate 'measures to restore international peace and security in the area.' This phrase is not a rhetorical flourish. It has always been an essential ingredient of the law of self-defense. (...) It means that the lawful goal of the war, viewed as a war of self-defense, was not simply to force Iraq out of Kuwait, so that it could wait, fully armed, until the United States and other coalition forces went home and it perfected its nuclear, chemical and biological warfare capabilities. The customary international law of self-defense, and therefore the law of Article 51 of the Charter, means that the coalition fighting Iraq could seek not simply to liberate Kuwait, but to make it impossible for Iraq to continue the extraordinary career of conquest it has pursued since 1979." Rostow, Until What?, 514.

[161] Contrary Klein, E., Völkerrechtliche Aspekte des Golfkonflikts 1990/91, 29 ADV 1991, pp. 421-435, 431-432, who claims that a march on Baghdad would have constituted a lawful measure of self-defence.

[162] On these latter issues see Cassese, A., International Law in a Divided World, Clarendon Press, Oxford, 1986, 230; and Cassese, Article 51, 774-775.

[163] Nicaragua Case, Merits, 104.

[164] Nicaragua Case, Merits, 105. On the reporting requirement see Greig, Self-Defence, 384-388.

[165] Nicaragua Case, Merits, 105. Later on in the judgment the Court examined other evidence related to the (alleged) armed attack and (unreported) acts of self-defence, and found that neither had been claimed or indeed taken place. *Ibid.*, 119-122.

[166] Respectively resolutions 836 (Bosnia) and 871 (Croatia). Similarly it has been recognized that UNAMIR may need to take action in self-defence against persons or groups that threaten protected sites or populations, United Nations or other humanitarian personnel, or the means of delivery and distribution of humanitarian relief. Resolutions 918 and 925.

[167] In an even broader sense one might say that similar resolutions on Somalia, Rwanda and Haiti also fall within this category, since they too concern responses to illegal uses of force. As those all find their cause within one State they are excluded here.

[168] Raic, D., The Gulf Crisis and the United Nations, 4 LJIL 1991, pp. 119-134, 132. Contrary Lavalle, The Law of the United Nations, 48.

[169] That appears to be Graefrath and Mohr's interpretation of resolutions 686 and 687, though they claim that to provide for a right to use force to enforce compliance with Iraq's obligations has no basis in the Charter. Graefrath, B., and Mohr, M., Legal Consequences of an Act of Aggression: The Case of the Iraqi Invasion and Occupation of Kuwait, 43 AJPIL 1992, pp. 109-138, 121-123.

[170] C.f. Graefrath and Mohr, Legal Consequences, 121. Note that the Iran-USA Claims Tribunal has been handling compensation claims since the early eighties on the basis of apparently less grave disputes between the United States and Iran.

[171] Thornberry, P., The Principle of Self-Determination, in Lowe and Warbrick, The United Nations, pp. 175-203, 187.

[172] Text and Commentary Article 19, Part One, YBILC 1976, Volume II, Part Two, pp. 95-122, 120. Note especially Palmisano, G., Les causes d'aggravation de la responsabilite des etats et la distinction entre «crimes» et «delits» internationaux, 98 RGDIP 1994, pp. 629-673, 647-652, in this respect.

[173] The 1966 International Covenant on Civil and Political Rights, 61 AJIL 1967, pp. 870-887. Paragraph 3 of the same provision stipulates that: "The States Parties to the present Covenant, including those having responsibility for the administration of Non-Self-Governing and Trust Territories, shall promote the realization of the right of self-determination, and shall respect that right, in conformity with the provisions of the Charter of the United Nations."

[174] Declaration on the granting of independence to colonial countries and peoples, General Assembly resolution 1514 (XV).

[175] Resolution 2131 concerns the prohibition of intervention in the internal or external affairs of States. The prohibition encompasses the lending of all kinds of support for terrorist or armed activities, as well as interference in civil strife. Declaration on the Inadmissibility of Intervention in the Domestic Affairs of States and the Protection of Their Sovereignty and Independence, General Assembly resolution 2131 (XX), paragraphs 1 and 2. Note also paragraph 6 on self-determination. Note further the remark of Pomerance, M., Self-Determination in Law and Practice, Martinus Nijhoff Publishers, The Hague, 1982, 73 (more broadly 63-76), that: "(...) self-determination claims will frequently conflict with other, no less sacred, rights and principles, such as sovereign equality, non-intervention, the non-use of force, and the maintenance of territorial integrity and political independence;"

[176] Declaration on Principles of International Law concerning Friendly Relations and Co-operation among States in accordance with the Charter of the United Nations, General Assembly resolution 2625 (XXV).

[177] C.f. Thornberry, The Principle of Self-Determination, 181-183.

[178] Commentary Article 19, Part One, 121.

[179] Such a meaning would seem to accord also with the terms of article 2, paragraph 4, of the Charter, which prohibits the threat or use of force inconsistent with the purposes of the United Nations, *e.g.* inconsistent with the principle of equal rights and self-determination of peoples. Admittedly article 2, paragraph 4, applies equally to the threat of force. Yet the question whether the mere threat to use force in denial of self-determination constitutes a serious breach of obligation depends on the answer to the question, to be discussed next, by what means a people may try to effect the exercise of its right.

[180] Resolutions (reaffirmations omitted): 312 (Portuguese colonies); 232 (Rhodesia); 269 (Namibia); 282 (South Africa).

[181] Resolution 253 (reaffirmed in resolutions 277 and 411). With regard to the people of Namibia see resolution 269 (reaffirmed in resolution 566).

[182] Schachter, Just War and Human Rights, 8, claims: "The resolution recognizes, clearly enough, that people may use force to resist governments which deprive them of self-determination. This can be read as recognizing the *right to revolt*; a right that does not involve the use of force in 'international relations' and, therefore, is not within the terms of Article 2(4)." Emphasis in the original.

[183] C.f. Doehring, K., Self-Determination, in Simma, The Charter, pp. 56-72, 66: "(...) not every kind of discrimination can legitimize a secession. As already pointed out, all citizens are in principle obliged to maintain loyalty towards their State, and they must accept certain limitations of their freedom." Some provisions regarding the protection of the population in occupied territories contained in the 1949 Geneva Convention IV Relative to the Protection of Civilians Persons in Time of War, notably articles 64 to 68, envisage the continued application of legal regulations within occupied territories, as well as the competence of the Occupying Power to prosecute individuals for violent acts against the occupying forces. Text in Roberts, A., and Guelff, R. (Eds.), Documents on the Laws of War, Clarendon Press, Oxford, 1982, pp. 272-326. Note also article 48 of the 1907 Regulations Respecting the Laws and Customs of War on Land, in *ibid.*, pp. 48-57.

[184] Note Doehring, Self-Determination, 66: "(...) a right to secession could, however, nevertheless be recognized if the minority discriminated against is exposed to actions by the sovereign state power which consist in an evident and brutal violation of fundamental human rights, *e.g.* through killing or unlimited imprisonment without legal protection, through destroying family relations, through expropriation without any regard for the necessities of life, through special prohibitions against following religious professions or using one's own language, and, lastly, through executing all these prohibitions with brutal methods and measures." See also 70.

[185] C.f. Starace, V., La responsabilité résultant de la violation des obligations à l'égard de la communauté internationale, 153 RDC ADI 1976-V, pp. 263-317, 299. Apparently contrary Cassese, A., Remarks on the Present Legal Regulation of Crimes of States, in Etudes en l'honneur de Roberto Ago, Le droit international à l'heure de sa codification, volume III, Giuffrè, Milano, 1987, pp. 49-64, 51-54, who claims (53): "«Forcible action» (...) means the establishment of a repressive régime which does not allow the oppressed people to choose its lot by free means. That expression does not necessarily entail that the State should continuously use military violence against the oppressed people: the existence of institutionalized violence (such as that obtaining in South Africa) is sufficient to establish the right of the people to resort to force." Note also articles 19, 21 and 25 of the International Covenant on Civil and Political Rights.

[186] C.f. Adviescommissie Mensenrechten en Buitenlands Beleid (AMBB), and Commissie van Advies voor Volkenrechtelijke Vraagstukken (CAVV), Het gebruik van geweld voor humanitaire doeleinden, Dwangmaatregelen voor humanitaire doeleinden en humanitaire interventie, Advies nummer 15, Den Haag, 1992, 5.

[187] Note for instance the discussion between Reisman and Schachter on the issue of pro-democratic invasions and ongoing self-determination. Reisman, M., Coercion and Self-Determination: Construing Charter Article 2(4), 78 AJIL 1984, pp. 642-645; and Schachter, O., The Legality of Pro-Democratic Invasion, 78 AJIL 1984, pp. 645-650.

[188] Article 2 of the Definition of Aggression, General Assembly resolution 3314 (XXIX), states that: "The first use of force by a State in contravention of the Charter shall constitute *prima facie* evidence of an act of aggression (...)." As the Charter does not provide for any first use of force other than that by the Security Council, the permanent members, or action against enemy States, humanitarian intervention would qualify as an act of aggression. The Definition goes on to say, in article 5, paragraph 1, that: "No consideration of whatever nature, whether political, economic, military or otherwise, may serve as a justification for aggression."

[189] Cautiously in the latter sense, AMBB and CAVV, Het gebruik van geweld, 7. The advice disputes that a rule of customary international law was ever developed, especially in the pre-Charter period, that could constitute the legal basis for humanitarian intervention.

[190] Nicaragua Case, Merits, 106-110.

[191] Nicaragua Case, Merits, 134.

[192] Nicaragua Case, Merits, 134-135.

[193] C.f. Genugten, W. van, Mensenrechten tussen staatssoevereiniteit en internationale jurisdictie, 21 NTRR 1992, pp. 204-223, 213-214. The AMBB and CAVV have argued that presently international law does not know of any clear legal basis for the threat or use of force, outside Chapter VII of the Charter, to combat widespread violations of fundamental human rights. At the same time they note that the obligation to protect and promote fundamental human rights provides a basis for the development of a legal justification in this respect. Therefore, so they claim, a State may be justified, in extremely exceptional circumstances to resort to humanitarian intervention in another State, provided the following conditions are met: that fundamental human rights are being violated on a large scale; that the intervening State has attempted in vain to activate all appropriate effective procedures to come to responses against the State which is violating human rights (including attempts to activate existing instruments, the United Nations, or a regional organization with authorization of the United Nations); and that the intervention does not amount to a larger threat to international peace and secu-

rity than the violations of human rights which the intervention attempts to end. AMBB and CAVV, Het gebruik van geweld, 8.

[194] Note Malanczuk, Humanitarian Intervention, 27.

[195] C.f. Randelzhofer, Article 2(4), 123-124. Apparently contrary Henkin, Use of Force, 41-42; Beres, L., Genocide, State and Self, 18 DJILP 1989, pp. 37-57, 46.

[196] Commission Report 1994, 344 (see also 347 and 361-362). In favour of the continued prohibition of armed measures Dominicé, C., Die internationalen Verbrechen und deren rechtliches Regime, in Fischer, P., Koeck, H., and Verdross, A. (Eds.), Völkerrecht und Rechtsphilosophie, Internationale Festschrift für Stephan Verosta zum 70. Geburstag, Duncker & Humblot, Berlin, 1980, pp. 227-248, 244. The stance that peoples struggling for self-determination can invoke the right to individual and collective self-defence must be discarded. The argument fails basically because under the Charter the right accrues to member States only, and such a right of peoples does not seem to have been established under customary international law. For discussion see Verwey, Humanitarian Intervention, 395-398 and 407-409.

[197] Commentary Article 33, Part One, 44 (generally 43-45).

[198] *E.g.* Raby, J., The State of Necessity and the Use of Force to Protect Nationals, 26 CYIL 1988, pp. 253-272, 265-271.

[199] Verwey, Humanitarian Intervention, 413-418.

[200] Commentary Article 33, Part One, 45.

[201] Commentary Article 33, Part One, 49.

[202] Commentary Article 33, Part One, 49.

[203] In this sense Bowett, The Use of Force, 40-41, though he regards attacks against a State's nationals as an attack on the State regarding which a right of self-defence could be exercised; and Raby, The State of Necessity, 266.

[204] Contrary Verwey, Humanitarian Intervention, 414-416.

[205] Verwey, Humanitarian Intervention, 418. Duke, S., The State and Human Rights: Sovereignty *Versus* Humanitarian Intervention, 12 IR 1994, pp. 25-48, 44-47, adheres to these conditions, but adds that humanitarian intervention should be for the shortest possible period, that it should generally take place under Chapter VII procedures, and that it should involve, when possible, the consent of the target State. Similar criteria may be found with Lillich, R., Forcible Self-Help by States to Protect Human Rights, 53 IowaLR 1967-1968, pp. 325-351, 347-351.

[206] AMBB and CAVV, Het gebruik van geweld, 8, 11 and 13-14. Duke, The State and Human Rights, 45, mentions that armed humanitarian intervention should be considered only after the measures of article 41 of the Charter have been exhausted.

[207] In resolution 912 the Security Council adjusted UNAMIR's mandate to the effect that it could act as an intermediary between the fighting parties in order to bring about a cease-fire, to assist in the resumption of humanitarian relief operations, and to monitor events. It also authorized an increase in the force level. In resolution 918 it expanded UNAMIR's mandate again and authorized an increase of the force level up to 5,500. It recognized that UNAMIR could act in self-defence against persons or groups that threatened sites, the population, United Nations and other humanitarian personnel, and the delivery and distribution of humanitarian relief. Finally, it decided on an embargo of arms and related material in respect of Rwanda. Resolution 925 did not add anything substantial to the foregoing resolutions.

[208] This condition is claimed to exist especially because intervening States tend to have ulterior motives for intervening. See Verwey, Humanitarian Intervention, 399-404.

[209] Duke, The State and Human Rights, 45-46. He deduces from the above quoted part (*ibid.*, 46): "Thus, it follows that humanitarian forces should be as small as possible but sufficient to complete their tasks." In the same line of thought he claims (*ibid.*) that intervention must be for the shortest possible time and should not become long-term.

[210] In their advice to the Dutch government, in 1992, the AMBB and CAVV indicated that a quick intervention and a fast withdrawal entails the risk that the action only produces short-term effects and that an even more dangerous situation might ensue. To prevent this from happening the intervention could also relate to the construction of administrative structures and the organization of elections. AMBB and CAVV, Het gebruik van geweld, 11-12. Also Tomuschat, in Delbrück, The Future, 83-84.

[211] Respectively resolutions 794, 929 and 940. Note also resolution 688, paragraph 1, in which the Security Council condemned the "repression of the Iraqi civilian population in many parts of Iraq, including most recently in Kurdish populated areas, the consequences of which threaten international peace and security in the region;" It has been claimed by the States intervening in Northern Iraq for the protection of the Kurds that their action was not inconsistent with resolution 688. See generally Charpentier, C., La résolution 688 (1991) du Conseil de Securité: quel devoir d'ingérence?, 23 EI 1992, pp. 279-317, 315, who denies that the resolu-

tion recognizes a right to intervene for humanitarian purposes. In the same sense Scheffer, D., Use of Force After the Cold War: Panama, Iraq and the New World Order, in Right *v.* Might, pp. 109-172, 144-147. It is to be noted similarly that the "consequences" of the Iraqi repression threatened international peace and security in the region, not the repression itself.

[212] The 1993 Governors Island Agreement, reprinted in Report of the Secretary-General, A/47/975, 2-3; and the 1993 New York Pact, reprinted in A/47/1000, Annex. See also the 1992 Protocol between President Jean-Bertrand Aristide and the Parliamentary Negotiating Commission to find a Definitive Solution to the Haitian Crisis, reprinted in A/46/891, Annex I; and the 1992 Protocol between President Jean-Bertrand Aristide and Prime Minister-Designate, Rene Theodore, under the Auspices of the Organization of American States (OAS), reprinted in *ibid.*, Annex II.

[213] Note Frowein's pertinent remark that: "Serious violations of international law which could provoke armed counter-measures may generally be seen as a threat to the peace even when the admissibility of the counter-measures may be doubtful." Frowein, Article 39, 612.

[214] Resolutions 918, paragraph 1; and 925, paragraph 6. In resolution 929 the Security Council dropped the demand for an immediate cessation of hostilities (see paragraph 9).

[215] Nicaragua Case, Merits, 105 (see also 104). In the event the Court found (*ibid.*, 120-121) that no such requests had been made by Honduras or Costa Rica, and that there was no evidence of requests by El Salvador earlier than the one contained in its Declaration of Intervention.

[216] Nicaragua Case, Merits, 104.

[217] Dissenting Opinion Jennings, Nicaragua Case, Merits, 545 (also 546). Emphasis in the original; relevant footnote omitted. See also the statements of a similar kind reported in Commission Report 1994, 346.

[218] Commentary Article 30, Part One, 119, which claims that the competent organs of the United Nations are: "(...) empowered in certain circumstances not simply to authorize, but even to direct a Member State other than the one directly injured by a particular international offence, or a group of States, or at times all Member States, to apply certain sanctions, including measures involving the use of armed force, against a State which has committed an offence of a specified content and gravity."

[219] C.f. Ago, Eighth Report, Addendum, 68.

[220] Though the Commission pointed out: "This temporary exception applies to a Member State which is the victim of an armed attack, as well as other Members which consider themselves threatened by the acts of the aggressor or are merely associated by collective security agreements, (...)." Commentary Article 19, Part One, 105. The Commentary Article 34, Part One, does not shed any further light on this.

[221] C.f. Kelsen, The Law of the United Nations, 792 and 795-798; Brownlie, International Law, 329-331; Cassese, Article 51, 787; Schachter, United Nations Law, 457. Contrary Bowett, Self-Defence, 200-247 (especially 200-207 and 215-218); Weston, Security Council Resolution 678, 520.

[222] C.f. Bowett, Self-Defence, 195.

[223] Argument found with Kaikobad, "*Ius Ad Bellum*", 68-70; implicitly Weller, M., The Use of Force and Collective Security, in Dekker and Post, The Gulf War, pp. 71-90, 87-90; note also Siekmann, R., Comments, in *ibid.*, pp. 91-94, 93; and Greig, Self-Defence, 389.

[224] Note Warbrick, The Invasion of Kuwait, 487-488.

[225] C.f. Greig, Self-Defence, 393-394, and more generally 393-399; and Cassese, Article 51, 774-775.

[226] Rostow, Until What?, 511, on the contrary claims: "To me, what Article 51 and resolution 661 seem to say is just the opposite – that the customary law of self-defense is not impaired in any way by the Charter but remains intact until the Council has *successfully* dealt with the controversy before it." Emphasis in the original.

[227] C.f. Schachter, United Nations Law, 458. Bowett, Self-Defence, 196, claims: "Yet the decision of the Council without more cannot, one would suppose, terminate action in self-defence, for the phrase 'measures necessary' implies positive action. Whether such positive action by the Council, or by member states pursuant to its decisions or recommendations, does in fact constitute the necessary measures must be decided on the facts of the individual situation. It may well be that in some circumstances an order to the attacking state which is obeyed so as to end the attack will be sufficient; in other circumstances nothing less than the use of armed force will suffice." Relevant footnote omitted. It may be suggested that the basis for concluding on the termination of the right of self-defence where the attacking State obeys an order of the Council lies with the accomplishment of the objectives of self-defence rather than with the taking of necessary measures by the Security Council.

[228] Notably article 2, paragraph 5 (preventive or enforcement action); article 5 (preventive or enforcement action); article 11, paragraph 2 (action); article 24 (action); article 42 (action); article 48, paragraph 1 (action); and finally article 54, paragraph 1 (enforcement action). Note also articles 53 and 107 which respectively mention "measures against any enemy state" and "action, in relation to any state which during the Second World War has been an enemy"; and article 106 which mentions "joint action on behalf of the Organization".

[229] Both Bowett and Kelsen, refer to articles 39, 41 and 42. Bowett, Self-Defence, 197; Kelsen, The Law of the United Nations, 801. The latter goes on to say however (*ibid.*, 801-802; Bowett appears to take the same stance, *ibid.*, 196): "These measures need not necessarily be enforcement measures. They may be 'recommendations' made under Article 39." This latter stance must be rejected. Article 51 refers to "measures", and article 39 distinguishes between the Security Council making recommendations, *or* deciding on measures under articles 41 or 42. Note also Stein, in Delbrück, The Future, 161-162.

[230] Schachter, United Nations Law, 457-463; Warbrick, The Invasion of Kuwait, 486-488. In a similar sense, categorically, Frowein, in Delbrück, The Future, 183.

[231] C.f. Dallal, International Law, 136-137.

[232] Contrary Schachter, United Nations Law, 457-461. In an earlier published book review the present writer adhered to Schachter's stance. See Hoogh, Book review: Sachariew, 108.

[233] Schachter, United Nations Law, 458.

[234] Resolutions 664, paragraph 1; 667, paragraphs 2 to 4; and 674, paragraphs 1 and 5, basically demand of Iraq the release, freedom of action and departure of third-State nationals, Kuwaitis and diplomatic and consular agents, as well as to refrain from action that would jeopardize their safety and well-being.

[235] Resolutions 665 (Iraq); 770, 787, 816, 836, 871, 908, 958, and 981 (former Yugoslavia); 794 and arguably 814 (Somalia) (note Freudenschuß, Between Unilateralism, 515-516, in this respect); 837 (Somalia); 875 and 940 (Haiti); 929 (Rwanda). Resolution 221 is somewhat odd in this respect as it called upon the United Kingdom to prevent, by the use of force if necessary, vessels from carrying oil to Rhodesia. Odd because the Council had not, to that date, imposed a mandatory oil embargo, under article 41 of the Charter, regarding Rhodesia.

[236] Resolutions 665, 678, 794, 816, 836, 875, 929, 940, 958, and 981.

[237] Resolutions 770 and 787.

[238] As to necessity reference may be made here to the Caroline incident regarding which secretary of state Webster wrote: "It will be for (...) Her Majesty's Government to show a necessity of self-defence, instant, overwhelming, leaving no choice of means, and no moment for deliberation. It will be for it to show, also, that the local authorities of Canada, even supposing the necessity of the moment authorized them to enter the territories of The United States at all, did nothing unreasonable or excessive; since the act, justified by the necessity of self-defence, must be limited by that necessity, and kept clearly within it. It must be shown that admonition or remonstrance to the person on board the *Caroline* was impracticable, or would have been unavailing; it must be shown that day-light could not be waited for; that there could be no attempt at discrimination between the innocent and the guilty; that it would not have been enough to seise and detain the vessel; but that there was a necessity, present and inevitable, for attacking her in the darkness of the night, while moored to the shore, and while unarmed men were asleep on board, killing some and wounding others, and drawing her into the current, above the cataract, setting her on fire, and, careless to know whether there might not be in her the innocent with the guilty, or the living with the dead, committing her to a fate which fills the imagination with horror. A necessity for all this, the Government of The United States cannot believe to have existed." Text in Harris, D., Cases and Materials on International Law, Sweet & Maxwell, London, 1983, 656. Also Ago, Eighth Report, Addendum, 69.

[239] Ago, Eighth Report, Addendum, 70.

[240] The Court noted, at the end of the paragraph largely devoted to questions of necessity and proportionality, that: "(...) the Court must also observe that the reaction of the United States in the context of what it regarded as self-defence was continued long after the period in which any presumed armed attack by Nicaragua could reasonably be contemplated." Nicaragua Case, Merits, 122-123.

[241] It is to be noted again that the use of force by the injured State on its own territory does not need any separate justification under international law. It can resort to force on its own territory on the basis of its territorial sovereignty. Gill has argued this point convincingly. Gill, The Forcible Protection, Affirmation and Exercise of Rights, 127-131.

[242] In the Nicaragua Case the Court observed in regard to United States' action: "First, these measures were only taken, and began to produce their effects, several months after the major offensive of the armed opposition against the Government of El Salvador had been completely repulsed (...), and the actions of the opposition considerably reduced in consequence. Thus it was possible to eliminate the main danger to the Salvadorian Government without the United States embarking on activities in and against Nicaragua. Accordingly, it cannot be said that these activities were undertaken in the light of necessity." Nicaragua Case, Merits, 122.

[243] C.f. Rostow, Until What?, 513-514, with regard to the Iraq-Kuwait conflict.

[244] C.f. Malanczuk, P., Countermeasures and Self-Defence as Circumstances Precluding Wrongfulness in the International Law Commission's Draft Articles on State Responsibility, 43 ZAORV 1983, pp. 705-812, 767-768.

[245] The situation prevailing in Kuwait on 16 January 1991 could not have justified the revocation of the authorization to use all necessary means on the basis that armed action was no longer necessary.

[246] Nicaragua Case, Merits, 103 and 122. The Court did not go into any detail. It noted the concurrence of views of the parties regarding the applicability of the condition (103), and stated (122): "Whether or not the assistance to the *contras* might meet the criterion of proportionality, the Court cannot regard the United States activities (...), i.e. those relating to the mining of the Nicaraguan ports, oil installations, etc., as satisfying that criterion. Whatever uncertainty may exist as to the exact scale of the aid received by the Salvadorian armed opposition from Nicaragua, it is clear that these latter United States activities in question could not have been proportionate to that aid." The Court further referred to the possibility of the acts of Nicaragua justifying proportionate countermeasures on the part of El Salvador, Honduras and Costa Rica, without indicating what would constitute such proportionate countermeasures. *Ibid.*, 127. Note also Dissenting Opinion Schwebel, *ibid.*, 299-300, on the overthrow of an aggressor government as a (dis)proportionate act of self-defence.

[247] Ago, Eighth Report, Addendum, 69 (see also 70). Emphasis in the original. Ago's observations on the requirements of immediacy, necessity and proportionality were not inserted into the commentary on article 34, and consequently there is no indication to what extent the Commission would have endorsed those. See Commentary Article 34, Part One, 60. Discussed by Malanczuk, Countermeasures and Self-Defence, 796-798.

[248] Ago noted (Eighth Report, Addendum, 70) that: "Moreover, the limits inherent in the requirement of proportionality are clearly meaningless where the armed attack and the likewise armed resistance to it lead to a state of war between the countries." He probably meant to refer to a state of hostilities between two States, since the existence of a state of war could not as such give rise to the right to act in self-defence. Also it seems inappropriate to say that proportionality would no longer function as a limit in such circumstances.

[249] One may note that provisional measures were requested by Libya also because it considered that the United Kingdom (and the United States) had "refused to rule out the use of armed force against Libya." Questions of Interpretation and Application of the 1971 Montreal Convention arising from the Aerial Incident at Lockerbie (Libyan Arab Jamahiriya *v.* United Kingdom), Provisional Measures, Order, ICJ Reports 1992, p. 3, 7.

[250] The word "enemy" in article 22 of the Regulations does not appear to be limited to military and paramilitary personnel, since it is prohibited in the following article, among others, to treacherously wound or kill individuals of the hostile nation or army, and to abolish, suspend, or declare inadmissible in a court of law, the rights and actions of nationals of the hostile party.

[251] This distinction goes back to article 3 of the Regulations, which stated: "The armed forces of the belligerent parties may consist of combatants and non-combatants. In the case of capture by the enemy, both have a right to be treated as prisoners of war." Apparently the category of non-combatants was not identical to the category of civilians. It is noteworthy that articles 1 and 2 defined the word "belligerents", which included armies, and, under certain conditions, militia and volunteer corps, and inhabitants of unoccupied territory which spontaneously take up arms at the approach of the enemy. Article 48 of the 1977 Protocol Additional to the Geneva Conventions of 12 August 1949, and relating to the protection of victims of international armed conflicts (Protocol I), 16 ILM 1977, pp. 1391-1433, states: "In order to ensure respect for and protection of the civilian population and civilian objects, the Parties to the conflict shall at all times distinguish between the civilian population and combatants and between civilian objects and military objectives and accordingly shall direct their operations only against military objectives."

[252] Note for instance article 13, paragraph 1, first sentence, of the 1977 Protocol Additional to the Geneva Conventions of 12 August 1949, and relating to the protection of victims of non-international armed conflicts (Protocol II), 16 ILM 1977, pp. 1442-1449: "The civilian population and individual civilians shall enjoy general protection against the dangers arising from military operations."

[253] Complemented by articles 48 to 79 Protocol I, and 13 to 18 Protocol II. To the extent that situations would arise not covered by these provisions the so-called Martens clause, contained in the preamble of the 1907 Hague Convention IV Respecting the Laws and Customs of War on Land, in Roberts and Guelff, Documents, pp. 44-47, stipulates: "Until a more complete code of the laws of war has been issued, the High Contracting Parties deem it expedient to declare that, in cases not included in the Regulations adopted by them, the inhabitants and the belligerents remain under the protection and the rule of the principles of the law of nations, as they result from the usages established among civilized peoples, from the laws of humanity, and the dictates of the public conscience." Reiterated in article 1, paragraph 2, Protocol I; and the preamble of Protocol II.

[254] Article 23 (c), Regulations Respecting the Laws and Customs of War on Land. Article 23 (d) forbids to issue a declaration that no quarter shall be given.

CHAPTER 6

THE RIGHT OF (AN) INJURED STATE(S) AND THE UNITED NATIONS TO HAVE RECOURSE TO THE INTERNATIONAL COURT OF JUSTICE IN RELATION TO INTERNATIONAL CRIMES

6.1. Introduction

In the preceding chapters the substantive law regarding the international responsibility of States was discussed. The first two chapters were devoted to exploring the legal interests of States and the United Nations. The third chapter then examined what could be demanded, as reparation, of the author State of an international crime. Chapters four and five finally investigated issues of enforcement by way of countermeasures and the use of force. Any dispute or question on these subjects, real or imagined, could be put before the Court for settlement or advice.

As a matter of fact Arangio-Ruiz has proposed, in his seventh report, to subject the exercise of rights to demand reparation and rights to resort to countermeasures to a prior determination by the Court that a crime has been or is being committed (articles 16 and 17, read together with 19, paragraph 5, Part Two).[1] His choice for the Court is dictated mainly by the fact that the General Assembly and the Security Council are political organs, which: tend to act neither necessarily or systematically regarding situations that call for the exercise of their competence; are not bound to use uniform criteria; and need not motivate their choices.[2] Furthermore, the determination to be made would not result from the Court's exercise of its advisory jurisdiction, but would have to be the outcome of the Court's exercise of its contentious jurisdiction.[3] States parties to a future convention on State responsibility would not, however, be entitled to seize the Court simply on their own initiative. The construction of proposed article 19, Part Two, entails that any unilateral application to the Court would have to be based upon a prior decision of the Assembly or the Council, adopted by qualified majority, that the allegation of the existence of a crime is sufficiently substantiated to justify the grave concern of the international community.[4] Arangio-Ruiz has further proposed, in view of the gravity of crimes, to establish the Court's compulsory jurisdiction in relation to any disputes over the implementation of the legal consequences of a crime.[5]

The purpose of this chapter will not be to discuss all of the substantive law in the light of the Court's jurisprudence and the substantive legal rules highlighted by it. Nor will this chapter discuss, argue on, or dispute, Arangio-Ruiz' choice for the Court rather than the Security Council as the appropriate organ to determine the existence of an international crime. Rather the goal will be to focus on a number of substantive issues, correlated mostly to procedural obstacles, that may prevent the Court from settling a dispute or giving advice regarding international crimes.

It may be noted here that the Court's proceedings may be subdivided according to whether they relate to an exercise of its contentious or advisory jurisdiction. Thus the Court performs two functions. According to article 38, paragraph 1, of the Statute it is "to decide in accordance with international law such disputes as are submitted to it";[6] and according to article 65, paragraph 1, of the Statute it may give "an advisory opinion on any legal question". It flows from the provisions of the Statute that the former function can currently only be activated by States (article 34, paragraph 1, of the Statute);[7] whereas the latter function can be activated by "whatever body may be authorized by or in accordance with the Charter of the United Nations" (article 65, paragraph 1, of the Statute).[8] According to article 96 of the Charter such bodies are the General Assembly and the Security Council (paragraph 1), or other organs of the United Nations and specialized agencies when so authorized by the Assembly (paragraph 2).[9] At appropriate places issues related to advisory proceedings will be discussed.

The obstacles regarding contentious proceedings before the Court relate mainly to the jurisdiction of the Court and the admissibility of the claim of the applicant State. In this respect article 79, paragraph 1, of the Rules of Court (established pursuant to article 30, paragraph 1, of the Statute) provides for the possibility of a State filing preliminary objections.[10] If that occurs the proceedings on the merits will be suspended (paragraph 3), and the Court, in deciding upon any objection, nowadays has three options (paragraph 7). First, to uphold the objection, in which case the proceedings will be terminated; secondly, to reject the objection, in which case proceedings on the merits will be resumed; and thirdly, to declare that the objection does not possess, in the circumstances of the case, an exclusively preliminary character, in which case proceedings on the merits will also be resumed. The Court's decision on preliminary objections is to be laid down in the form of a judgment (paragraph 7).[11]

In contrast the Rules do not envisage the filing of preliminary objections in respect of advisory proceedings. Of course article 68 of the Statute (reproduced in article 102, paragraph 2, of the Rules) provides:

> "In the exercise of its advisory functions the Court shall further be guided by the provisions of the present Statute which apply in contentious cases to the extent to which it recognizes them to be applicable."

But this has not so far led to separate phases and decisions on objections to jurisdiction and admissibility regarding requests for advisory opinions.[12] However, the Court has on occasion in its opinions countered certain arguments directed against its competence and the admissibility of the request.[13]

Another topic relevant to the exercise of jurisdiction by the Court concerns its relation to the Security Council. This may relate to problems of concurrent jurisdiction and justiciability, as well as the possibility of a clash between their respective decisions. The issue is all the more important as they are the only two organs of the United Nations regarding which, in general, member States have agreed to be legally bound by the decisions they may take (articles 25 and 94, paragraph 1, of the Charter; and articles 59 and 60 of the Statute).

More substantively speaking the question is whether the Security Council can legitimately take decisions requiring a member State to act in a certain way notwithstanding a member State's right, under international law, to act in another. If the Security

Council ought not to be considered competent to do this, the question would then be whether the Court could challenge the validity of that decision.

From the viewpoint of a State's responsibility for international crimes there is still another interesting matter. That concerns the indication of provisional measures in contentious proceedings. Provisional measures would not appear to play any role in advisory proceedings.[14] Article 68 of the Statute might be invoked in that regard, but the advisory character of the Court's opinion and the absence of real parties militates against the analogous indication of provisional measures. Certainly the Court has so far not developed any practice related to the indication of provisional measures other than in contentious proceedings.[15]

One particular issue will not be discussed in this chapter, and that concerns the question of legal interest as a condition for the admissibility of the claim, or the possibility to claim, of an injured State. Though of course the question of legal interest forms a central part of this thesis, no additional useful purpose would be served in going over all the aspects of that question again in the context of proceedings before the Court: the extensive discussion in chapters one and two should suffice in this regard.

This chapter will therefore deal with the following sections. Section 6.2 will be devoted to the jurisdiction of the Court, and the possibility that its exercise will be hampered given the absence of affected States. This is followed in section 6.3 by a discussion of the admissibility of claims, particularly in relation to disputes, negotiations and justiciability. Section 6.4 will explore the relation between the Court and the Security Council, especially the question of review. Finally aspects related to the indication of provisional measures and enforcement will be examined in section 6.5.

6.2. The jurisdiction of the Court

6.2.1. GENERAL OBSERVATIONS

It is undisputed that the Court only possesses the requisite jurisdiction to decide the merits of a case if the parties to that case have, in some manner, consented to such jurisdiction.[16] Already the Permanent Court had stated in one of its first cases:[17]

> "For this reason the Court, bearing in mind that its jurisdiction is limited, that it is invariably based on the consent of the respondent and only exists in so far as this consent has been given, cannot content itself with the provisional conclusion that the dispute falls or not within the terms of the Mandate."

The Court cannot, of course, exercise its jurisdiction unless a party (or both parties) to a dispute bring(s) the case before the Court.[18] This aspect concerns the so-called seisin of the Court,[19] and is born out by article 40, paragraph 1, of the Statute:

> "Cases are brought before the Court, as the case may be, either by the notification of the special agreement or by a written application addressed to the Registrar. In either case the subject of the dispute and the parties shall be indicated."

It is important to note that the requisite consent concerns the jurisdiction of the Court and not the exercise of such jurisdiction. Thus no further show of consent is required once the Court determines that it has jurisdiction.[20] That the Court is empowered to determine the scope of its jurisdiction flows from article 36, paragraph 6, of the Statute, which records that:[21]

> "In the event of a dispute as to whether the Court has jurisdiction, the matter shall be settled by the decision of the Court."

The use of the word "decision" could lead one to conclude that article 36, paragraph 6, must be read in conjunction to article 59 which stipulates the binding force of the decision of the Court. That conclusion is confirmed by reference to article 79, paragraph 7, of the Rules, which states that the Court shall rule on objections through a decision in the form of a judgment.

Article 36, paragraphs 1 and 2, of the Statute, establishes three different ways by which States may consent to the jurisdiction of the Court. The first two ways both generally concern the treaty form and have been referred to, in article 36, paragraph 1, of the Statute, as follows:[22]

> "The jurisdiction of the Court comprises all cases which the parties refer to it and all matters specially provided for in the Charter of the United Nations or in treaties and conventions in force."

Cases which the parties refer to the Court are generally held to find their basis in a special agreement (compromis). The object of a special agreement is to found the jurisdiction of the Court regarding a predetermined dispute or controversy between the parties to the special agreement. With respect to matters specially provided for in treaties or conventions in force it may be said that these concern provisions which subject a certain generalized category of disputes, with or without conditions, to the jurisdiction of the Court. If such is the case the seisin of the Court takes place by way of application. The categories included within the jurisdiction of the Court usually comprise disputes regarding the interpretation or application of the treaty, or disputes regarding breaches of obligations under the treaty.[23]

The third way of constituting the jurisdiction of the Court concerns the making of a declaration by States parties to the Statute under article 36, paragraph 2, to the effect that they:[24]

> "(...) recognize as compulsory *ipso facto* and without special agreement, in relation to any other state accepting the same obligation, the jurisdiction of the Court in all legal disputes concerning:
> (a) the interpretation of a treaty;
> (b) any question of international law;
> (c) the existence of any fact which, if established, would constitute a breach of an international obligation;
> (d) the nature or extent of the reparation to be made for the breach of an international obligation."

Cases brought before the Court under article 36, paragraph 2, of the Statute are made by way of application, and may involve any legal dispute between States that have made declarations under that paragraph.

A fourth way of establishing the jurisdiction of the Court concerns the so-called *forum prorogatum*. In such a case a State brings a case before the Court by way of application, without specifying any basis of jurisdiction, or a basis which even on a *prima facie* view simply does not confer any jurisdiction on the Court. Should the respondent State appear before the Court and fail to argue, in a timely fashion, the Court's lack of jurisdiction, such jurisdiction will have been established notwithstanding the absence of any pre-existing basis to that effect.[25]

Regarding these means of establishing the Court's jurisdiction it may be said that the first, the special agreement, and the latter, *forum prorogatum*, are unlikely to provide jurisdictional bases in case of international crimes. As to the first it is not to be expected that an author State of an international crime will consent, by way of special agreement, to adjudication.[26] The situation might be different of course if a change of government had occurred within the author State. As to the latter, *forum prorogatum*, it is not to be expected that any State accused of having committed an international crime will appear before the Court without at the same time arguing its lack of jurisdiction.[27] Indeed, it is far more likely that an author State of an international crime will fail to show up. If that is the case the Court will have no other choice but to take note of the absence of any (arguable) basis of jurisdiction and remove the case from the General List.

The second means of providing the Court with jurisdiction, provisions in treaties, may more fruitfully be resorted to by injured States. Since the requisite consent (to the treaty and hence to the Court's jurisdiction) will have been given, in advance, to the settlement of prospective disputes regarding the subject-matter of the treaty, the possibility of an author State of a crime being called before the Court is far from negligible. In this respect there is one basic condition, namely that the dispute and the injured State's claims, fall within the jurisdiction *ratione materiae* created through the jurisdictional clause.[28] As an application of this condition may be mentioned the Court's refusal, twice in a row, to indicate some of the provisional measures requested by Bosnia and Herzegovina, because and to the extent that they were substantially unrelated to the subject-matter, and hence the jurisdiction conferred by article IX, of the Genocide Convention.[29]

The subject-matter of the international crimes enumerated in article 19, Part One, of the ILC-draft, is to some extent covered by existing jurisdictional clauses in treaties.

The rules stipulating obligations for the maintenance of international peace and security are not, on the universal level, covered by any jurisdictional clause. However, regionally the Pact of Bogotá, in article XXXI, vests the Court with jurisdiction regarding disputes of a juridical nature concerning the categories mentioned in article 36, paragraph 2, of the Statute.[30] The Pact is peculiar in this respect, since it does not restrict the Court's jurisdiction *ratione materiae* to the subject-matter of the treaty.

The International Covenants on Civil and Political Rights and on Economic, Social and Cultural Rights,[31] confirming the right to self-determination in their articles 1, similarly do not provide for jurisdiction of the Court. On the regional level human rights treaties establish political rights which, when violated, may amount to a denial of self-determination. However, while the intent to commit a denial of self-determination may be present, the jurisdiction extant in such treaties will be grafted upon the substantive human rights safeguarded under the treaty. Such jurisdiction is moreover not conferred on the International Court of Justice, but on the institutions created by the treaty.

The foregoing considerations apply similarly to the crime of widespread breaches of basic human rights obligations. Breaches of certain particular human rights obligations are covered by treaties intended for the suppression of such breaches. In the context of the international crime of widespread breaches of basic human rights obligations, those relate to slavery, genocide and *apartheid*. All three treaties contain jurisdictional clauses.[32] So far there has only been one case in which the Court's jurisdiction has been invoked: the pending case of Bosnia and Herzegovina against Yugoslavia (Serbia and Montenegro).

In the context of this study it would go too far to examine all the jurisdictional obstacles related to that case. It may be noted however that Maison claims, on the basis of the Court's orders on provisional measures, that the Court holds that genocide cannot be committed by States, and that consequently it does not possess jurisdiction under article IX of the Genocide Convention.[33] His assertion is based on the Court's rejection of the Bosnian request for the indication of a measure safeguarding Bosnia's right to self-defence:[34]

> "Puisque l'Etat ne peut être l'auteur du génocide, la Bosnie n'est pas autorisée à l'utiliser, pour sanctionner ce crime, son droit de légitime défense, car celui-ci s'entend comme une mesure dirigée contre un Etat."

The reason why a State cannot be the author of a genocide lies, according to Maison,[35] in the fact that the Genocide Convention imposes but two obligations on States parties: to prevent genocide and to punish those who commit genocide; and so States are not supposed to commit direct acts of genocide.[36] This view appears unduly restrictive and cannot be said to underlie the Court's orders. If persons within a State commit genocide, that State will certainly have breached its obligation to prevent acts of genocide. But article 4 of the Genocide Convention stipulates:

> "Persons committing genocide or any of the other acts enumerated in Article 3 shall be punished, whether they are constitutionally responsible rulers, public officials or private individuals."

This provision clearly foresees the possibility that the organs of a State may engage in acts of genocide. That article 4 is directed towards the punishment of persons individually cannot contradict the obvious conclusion that the Convention envisages the possibility that a State may commit genocide. The jurisdiction of the Court regarding disputes related to the responsibility of a State for genocide is not therefore restricted to situations in which a State fails to prevent the commission of genocide by "private individuals" or isolated "public officials", but relates also to situations in which "constitutionally responsible rulers" directly engage in the acts punishable under the Convention. The Court's refusal to indicate measures safeguarding Bosnia's right of self-defence (and the concomitant refusal to declare that the arms embargo of resolution 713 does not apply to Bosnia and Herzegovina) is based on the lack of jurisdiction under the Genocide Convention, since the Convention does not name the means by which States are to prevent genocide.[37]

The jurisdiction of the Court founded on declarations made pursuant to article 36, paragraph 2, of the Statute, allows most broadly the seisin of the Court by way of unilateral application. Contrary to the previously discussed means of conferring jurisdiction on the Court, the jurisdiction *ratione materiae* conferred on the Court by way of declarations under article 36, paragraph 2, appears virtually unlimited. Restrictions may nevertheless be imposed by a State by entering reservations to its declaration, and those may in turn be invoked by any respondent State. However, jurisdiction over disputes regarding responsibility for an alleged international crime can, in principle, be based on declarations under article 36, paragraph 2.

It may be noted in this respect that authors claiming the impossibility of an *actio popularis* in international law generally argue such impossibility by reference to the absence of universal compulsory jurisdiction.[38] However, as observed in chapter one, if one can establish a customary law obligation imposing respect for any particular human right, any State similarly bound by the same obligation would be in possession of a legal interest pursuant to the breach of such an obligation. Since the obligation exists under customary international law the only way of acting, on the judicial plane,[39] upon such a legal interest would have to be based either on jurisdiction under a compromis, by virtue of *forum prorogatum*, or under the declarations based on article 36, paragraph 2, of the Statute.[40] The crimes of aggression and denial of self-determination do indeed pose problems due to the absence of universal compulsory jurisdiction, but the problems on that count, to be discussed next, occur only if some States are not before the Court.

6.2.2. PROBLEMS CONCERNING STATES ABSENT FROM PROCEEDINGS BEFORE THE COURT

States absent from contentious proceedings before the Court

It is quite likely that the author State of an international crime, dragged before the Court against its (contemporary) will, will fail to show up at all. If that happens the Court will have three options. In the absence of any plausible jurisdictional basis it will, after a reasonable period of time, remove the case from the General List.[41] However, should a *prima facie* arguable case exist in favour of jurisdiction, it will proceed to set dates for memorials by the applicant State and the respondent State. Clearly a respondent State that persists in its attitude not to appear will not be in a position to avail itself of the possibility of filing preliminary objections. Consequently proceedings on the merits will not be suspended, and oral hearings will take place after which the Court will withdraw to consider its judgment (article 54). In the light of the non-appearance of a respondent State, or its failure to defend its case, the applicant State may call upon the Court to decide in favour of its claim (article 53, paragraph 1). In such circumstances the Court is bound to apply article 53, paragraph 2, which stipulates that it must satisfy itself that "it has jurisdiction in accordance with Articles 36 and 37". At this point the Court has two options. Either to find that it has jurisdiction, or that it has not.

Another far more serious problem occurs when a State, though not a party to a certain case before the Court, may be affected by the Court's exercise of jurisdiction. The most famous example of this problem up till recently has been presented by the Monetary Gold Case.[42] There the Court was asked to decide whether the United Kingdom or Italy could appropriate gold, in possession of the United Kingdom, for compensation purposes. The United Kingdom claimed the gold as compensation on the basis of the

Court's judgment in the Corfu Channel Case; Italy claimed the gold as compensation for wrongful acts by Albania; and Albania had owned the gold. Both Italy and Albania were granted the right to apply to the Court, and Italy exercised that right. In doing so it raised the question, the one and only preliminary objection ever to be filed by an applicant State, whether the Court could decide the priority of the Italian claim over the British claim in the absence of Albania from the proceedings. In order to determine the issue it seemed to the Court that it would have to assess the validity of the Italian claim against Albania, and so it observed:[43]

> "To adjudicate upon the international responsibility of Albania without her consent would run counter to a well-established principle of international law embodied in the Court's Statute, namely, that the Court can only exercise jurisdiction over a State with its consent."

The Court added to this in relation to the phrasing of article 62 of the Statute and Albania's non-intervention:[44] "In the present case, Albania's legal interests would not only be affected by a decision, but would form the very subject-matter of the decision."

The argument has been made a number of times since that the Court could not decide a case, or not fully so, in the absence of certain States from the proceedings.[45] There can be no question that the Court has been unwilling, in general,[46] to let any such circumstance hamper the exercise of its jurisdiction. From the perspective of international crimes two cases are of particular interest: the Nicaragua Case and the East Timor Case.

In the Nicaragua Case the Court had to decide whether the United States could justify its conduct towards Nicaragua on the basis of a right of collective self-defence. To do this the Court had to determine whether acts allegedly committed by Nicaragua could be said to constitute an armed attack against either El Salvador, Honduras or Costa Rica. The Court found against this contention of the United States. In doing so it in fact determined that El Salvador, Honduras and Costa Rica had not been, in the relevant time span, the victims of an armed attack, and consequently could not have exercised any right of collective self-defence.[47] The United States' argument, that El Salvador, Honduras and Costa Rica were indispensable parties, and that the Court could not settle the dispute in their absence, had been previously rejected in the judgment on jurisdiction and admissibility. In rejecting that plea the Court pointed to article 59 of the Statute and noted that the implicated States could institute separate proceedings or intervene under articles 62 or 63 of the Statute. Also, so the Court claims, none of those States was in the same position as Albania, that is to say, their legal interests could not be considered to form the very subject-matter of the case before the Court.[48]

Another relevant case concerns that between Portugal and Australia. In 1989 Australia concluded a treaty with Indonesia regarding the exploration and exploitation of the Timor Gap.[49] This area constitutes part of the continental shelf of the territory of East Timor, which had been administered by Portugal unto 1975. In that year the Portuguese abandoned the territory, troubled as they were by civil disorder, after which Indonesia invaded.[50] Portugal claims that Australia, by negotiating, concluding, and initiating performance of the Timor Gap treaty, is in breach of its obligation to respect the right of self-determination of the people of East Timor; its obligation to respect

Portugal's rights as administering authority; and its obligation to conform to Security Council resolutions 384 and 389 in accordance with article 25 of the Charter.[51]
Jurisdiction for this case was based upon Portugal's and Australia's declarations under article 36, paragraph 2, of the Statute. It seemed obvious that if the Court would investigate the Portuguese charges, it would first have to determine the legality of Indonesia's invasion into, and occupation of, East Timor. For if that invasion had been lawful, or if the occupation had had the effect of providing Indonesia with a title to the territory valid under international law, such would constitute a comprehensive defence against the breaches of obligation alleged by Portugal.[52] It is for those reasons that the Court observed that:[53]

> "(...) Australia's behaviour cannot be assessed without first entering into the question why it is that Indonesia could not lawfully have concluded the 1989 treaty, while Portugal allegedly could have done so; the very subject-matter of the Court's decision would necessarily be a determination whether, having regard to the circumstances in which Indonesia entered and remained in East Timor, it could or could not have acquired the power to enter into treaties on behalf of East Timor relating to the resources of its continental shelf. The Court could not make such a determination in the absence of the consent of Indonesia."

And since Indonesia, in contrast with Australia, had never consented to the Court's jurisdiction, the Court quite rightly found that it could not exercise the jurisdiction conferred upon it by the declarations of the parties under article 36, paragraph 2, of the Statute.[54]

The Nicaragua Case showed that a State which claims to exercise a right of collective self-defence, but which is not itself attacked, may be brought before the Court as a respondent. Apparently a State arguably injured in the sense of article 5, paragraph 3, Part Two, of the ILC-draft, may be forced to account for its conduct notwithstanding that the directly injured State is not sued at the same time. Question is whether the situation may be reversed, that is, whether a State injured in that way may sue the author State of an armed attack notwithstanding the absence of the directly injured State from the proceedings. It would not have been too difficult to imagine the United States bringing a case against Nicaragua, as an applicant, in respect of the latter's intervention in El Salvador.[55] Assuming for the sake of argument that El Salvador had not in the past accepted the Court's jurisdiction in relation to Nicaragua, and that the latter's action did amount to an armed attack, one might wonder whether the Court could have granted any claims brought before it by the United States. That would mean accepting that Nicaragua could be forced to account for its action towards a third State (not before the Court), in relation to which it had not consented to the settlement of disputes, and in relation to which it could not make any counter-claims.[56] It may not be too farfetched to consider such to be an encroachment on the consensual and reciprocal character of the Court's jurisdiction.

States implicated in advisory proceedings before the Court

Similar problems as those discussed in the previous paragraphs may arise in the context of advisory proceedings. Of course the jurisdiction of the Court to render an advisory opinion is triggered as soon as a request is made. Though, as in contentious proceedings, the Court can only exercise such jurisdiction once the request is communicated to it. In relation to the Court's advisory jurisdiction it has been claimed that judicial proceedings on legal questions pending between States could not take place without the consent of the relevant or affected States.[57] According to the Court this objection confuses the principles applicable to contentious proceedings and those applicable to advisory procedure:[58]

> "The consent of States, parties to a dispute, is the basis of the Court's jurisdiction in contentious cases. The situation is different in regard to advisory proceedings even where the Request for an Opinion relates to a legal question actually pending between States. The Court's reply is only of an advisory character: as such, it has no binding force. It follows that no State, whether a Member of the United Nations or not, can prevent the giving of an Advisory Opinion which the United Nations considers to be desirable in order to obtain enlightenment as to the course of action it should take. The Court's Opinion is given not to States, but to the organ which is entitled to request it."

By this token the Court appeared, to some extent, to back away from the opinion delivered by the Permanent Court regarding Eastern Carelia. In that opinion the latter had stated:[59]

> "The question put to the Court is not one of abstract law, but concerns directly the main point of the controversy between Finland and Russia, (...). Answering the question would be substantially equivalent to deciding the dispute between the parties."

The Permanent Court's reason for denying that it could answer the question was only marginally based on the circumstance that this required the actual or real consent of the parties to the dispute. Rather it depended on the circumstance that Russia was not a member of the League of Nations, and because, therefore, article 17 of the Covenant applied.[60] That provision stipulated that in case of a dispute between a member of the League and a State which is not a member, the latter would be invited to accept the obligations of membership (under articles 12 to 16) of the League for purposes of such a dispute. While the members of the League are bound by the obligations regarding the pacific settlement of disputes, non-members are not, and since Russia had declared its opposition to intervention by the League it could not be said to have consented to such settlement.[61]

In the event it was the lack of competence of the League, not of the Court, which led the Permanent Court to decline to answer the question in the Eastern Carelia Opinion.

The Court has argued, on the other hand, that States by becoming members of the United Nations have agreed to the Court giving opinions on questions affecting their legal disputes with other members.[62] The operative condition as to the propriety of the Court's exercise of its advisory jurisdiction is that the question submitted lies within the competence of the organ requesting it.[63]

The Court has indicated only one specific circumstance in which the rendering of an advisory opinion would be incompatible with its judicial character, namely when:[64]

> "(...) the circumstances disclose that to give a reply would have the effect of circumventing the principle that a State is not obliged to allow its disputes to be submitted to judicial settlement without its consent."

It has been claimed, by Akhavan, that in view of the inadequacy of international judicial remedies the advisory jurisdiction of the Court could be fruitfully used for purposes of enforcement under the Genocide Convention.[65] In view of the object to induce compliance with the Genocide Convention, so he said, the question:[66]

> "(...) must not be at a level of abstraction where it would be ineffective for the practical purposes of condemning states in international delinquency. Nor should it be so factually specific that it would be tantamount to a clear contentious dispute and a manifest abuse of the advisory opinion jurisdiction."

He continues to state that the question could be framed in terms of applicability rather than in terms of consequences deriving from such applicability.[67] Yet one would think that this would constitute the exact point made by the Court, namely that the power to demand advisory opinions should not be used to circumvent the requirement of consent to judicial settlement. Admittedly, it is hardly possible, in view of the Court's advisory practice, to deny that a thin line exists between answering a question, and settling a dispute between States. However, the Court has conceded that the same principles which apply to rendering advice in the presence of a dispute between States, apply also in regard to disputes between the United Nations and a (member) State.[68] The Court would therefore appear to rule out giving a reply to any question that would involve a determination of a State's responsibility.

6.3. Admissibility of claims

A preliminary question is when it is appropriate to speak of an objection against the jurisdiction of the Court and when of an objection against the admissibility of the claim of the applicant.[69] The distinguishing factor between the two lies with the phrasing of the jurisdictional basis. Should the jurisdictional basis make a reference to a condition to be fulfilled before the Court is seized, then any objection related to that condition is directed towards denying the existence of jurisdiction. Should such a condition be absent from the jurisdictional basis, the same condition may be claimed to exist under a rule of treaty or customary international law. Objections to the effect that a condition posed by a rule of treaty or customary international law is not fulfilled are directed against the admissibility of the claim. Traditionally, for instance, there have been conditions attached to the exercise of the right of diplomatic protection: the exhaustion of local remedies and the nationality of the claim.[70] Other conditions posed either in jurisdictional bases or under treaty or customary international law relate to the existence of a dispute or to negotiations leading up to it. These will be discussed subsequently. As a follow-up the legal or political character of disputes or questions will be discussed as an introduction to the final issue of justiciability.

6.3.1. DISPUTES AND NEGOTIATIONS

The first and foremost condition applicable to the exercise of the right to claim lies with the necessity of there being a dispute between the applicant and respondent States.[71] Many jurisdictional clauses in treaties provide for the jurisdiction of the Court concerning disputes regarding the interpretation or application of the treaty, or regarding alleged breaches of obligation under the treaty. However, even without any reference to disputes in such clauses, one would think that a claim could not be entertained by the Court if there did not exist any dispute between the applicant and respondent States at the time of seisin. Article 36, paragraph 2, of the Statute for instance envisages declarations accepting the compulsory jurisdiction of the Court regarding (legal) disputes only. Article 36, paragraph 1, on the other hand merely mentions that the jurisdiction of the Court comprises cases referred to it by the parties, or matters provided for in treaties in force. Notwithstanding the absence of any reference to disputes there, article 38, paragraph 1, of the Statute states, in a somewhat haphazard manner, that the Court's function is to decide (in accordance with international law) such disputes as are submitted to it. And article 40, paragraph 1 (chapter on procedure) provides that both in case of notification of the special agreement and of written application the subject of the dispute shall be indicated.[72] Question is of course what is to be considered a dispute for purposes of adjudication.

In this regard the often quoted dictum of the Permanent Court in the Mavrommatis Case is still relevant:[73]

> "A dispute is a disagreement on a point of law or fact, a conflict of legal views or of interests between two persons."

It is somewhat difficult to conceive of two States coming before the Court and asking it to decide on a disagreement on a point of fact or on a conflict of interests without at the same time arguing legal issues.[74] That might perhaps be imagined regarding a conflict of interests should the parties authorize the Court to decide *ex aequo et bono* (article 38, paragraph 2, of the Statute).[75] As this has never happened, the Court so far has always been obliged to decide disputes in accordance with international law.[76] Yet how is one to decide that a dispute does indeed exist? That question was answered by the Court in 1962, when it held:[77]

> "In other words it is not sufficient for one party to a contentious case to assert that a dispute exists with the other party. A mere assertion is not sufficient to prove the existence any more than a mere denial of the existence of a dispute proves its non-existence. Nor is it adequate to show that the interests of the two parties to such a case are in conflict. It must be shown that the claim of one party is positively opposed by the other."

The idea that a dispute involves a claim by a State that is positively opposed by another State raises the questions what kind of opposition is required, and in which way it is to be ascertained. This poses the issue, relevant in relation to international crimes, whether negotiations ought to be conducted before bringing a case to the Court.

The opposition required to show the existence of a dispute must concern a claim by one State which is contested by another State. Since the dispute must exist at the time the Court is seized, this seems to imply that an exchange of views must have occurred previously. Some writers contend, notably Cassese, that the purpose aimed at by subordinating proceedings before the Court to the existence of a dispute, is that:[78]

> "(...) the prestige and interests of States should not be harmed by a summons to appear before an international tribunal and the consequential opening of a long and costly trial when the State concerned could easily have acceded to the demands of the complainant State before being made answerable in court."

The consequence is, so he claims, that there must be a clash between a demand to adopt a certain juridical attitude and another State's refusal to comply with the demand.[79] The refusal can be explicit or implicit (through conclusive facts or omissive behaviour), and must expose an unwillingness to accede to the demand.[80]
In the Mavrommatis Case the Permanent Court postulated that diplomatic negotiations were necessary in order to define the subject-matter of a dispute.[81] Although this appeared to be an absolute condition, both the Permanent Court and the Court have tended to be little formalistic on this score. In the Mavrommatis Case the Permanent Court went on to say that the criterion might be that a deadlock had been reached in the negotiations.[82] The present Court similarly did not require extensive negotiations between the parties, and likewise adopted the criterion of a deadlock.[83] Whether the negotiations concern diplomatic exchanges defining the dispute, or negotiations intended to bring about a settlement of the dispute, the materialization of a deadlock regarding the perspective positions is decisive: it makes the dispute one that is not any longer capable of being settled through negotiations.

Disputes regarding the commission of an international crime will concern legal and factual controversies as to the international responsibility of the author State, inclusive its reparation obligations, or alternatively controversies related to enforcement, through countermeasures or the use of force, by injured States. In chapters four and five it was argued that, in case of crimes, neither injured States, nor the Security Council, would be under any obligation to resort to dispute settlement before resorting to countermeasures or the use of armed force. The most that could be required was that they indicate the specific demands made of the author State of an international crime at the time of their resort to countermeasures or force. This stance implies, negotiation being one of the means of dispute settlement, that substantively speaking one should not require an injured State to attempt to negotiate with the author State of an international crime. In the same vein an injured State's claim should not be found inadmissible by the Court on the ground that there had not been any negotiations, or that they had not been sufficiently exhausted. Where the condition of negotiations is imposed by the terms of a jurisdictional clause of a particular treaty, one ought to proceed from the view that a mere offer, by the author State, to have resort to dispute settlement or to conduct direct negotiations is insufficient to cut through a deadlock. The refusal by a State to negotiate could also render inoperative the condition to negotiate contained in a jurisdictional basis.[84] Similarly the mere verbal assurance, unaccompanied by concrete action, that the demands of the injured State will be complied with, does not constitute evidence that there is room for negotiations. These arguments all tend to the conclusion that a provision conferring jurisdiction on the Court in a future convention on State responsibility ought to dispense with any condition to resort to dispute settlement generally, and negotiations in particular, in case of international crimes.[85]

6.3.2. POLITICAL *VERSUS* LEGAL DISPUTES AND ISSUES OF JUSTICIABILITY

Quite often the distinction between legal and political disputes is equated to the respective categories of justiciable and non-justiciable disputes.[86] Some preliminary remarks are directed therefore to the question of determining the legal or political character of disputes, before entering into issues of justiciability.

Political versus *legal disputes*
The phrase "legal disputes" appears in article 36, paragraph 3, of the Charter, and article 36, paragraph 2, of the Statute. Yet no indication is to be found as to what would make a dispute legal in character,[87] or what would make it political in character.[88] Now the Court, in the Armed Actions Case, claimed:[89]

> "(...) the Court is aware that political aspects may be present in any legal dispute brought before it. The Court, as a judicial organ, is however only concerned to establish, first, that the dispute before it is a legal dispute, in the sense of a dispute capable of being settled by the application of principles and rules of international law, (...)."

It is similarly possible, with regard to determining the legal character of a dispute, to find numerous references to the idea of a dispute being apt to be settled by application of legal rules. Thus the phrase on the Court "whose function it is to decide disputes in accordance with international law", contained in article 38 of the Statute, does no more than to exclude political controversies, and indicates that the Court can only take note of, and settle, disputes which are legal in character.

The Court has dealt with objections, in both its contentious and advisory jurisprudence, to the effect that a dispute or question was political in character, or that the legal aspects could not be divorced from their political context.[90] The Court, in its Admission Opinion and Expenses Opinion, observed that a request for the interpretation of a treaty provision involved an essentially judicial task.[91] And in the former opinion it stated that it was not concerned with the motives underlying the request, nor with the considerations advanced before the Security Council in relation to concrete cases.[92] In the latter opinion it took note of an argument that it ought to decline to answer because the question was intertwined with political questions, but held that, in the nature of things, most interpretations of the Charter had political significance.[93]
The issue arose once more in the Diplomatic Staff Case. There the Court rejected an objection by Iran to the effect that the Court could not take cognizance of the American claims, because this would involve an examination of the issue:[94] "(...) divorced from its proper context, namely the whole political dossier of the relations between Iran and the United States over the last 25 years." In its letter to the Court, Iran, remaining absent from the proceedings, had not made any attempt to explain or define the connection between the separate dispute and the overall problem, but according to the Court:[95]

> "This was the more necessary because legal disputes between sovereign States by their very nature are likely to occur in political contexts, and often form only one element in a wider and long-standing political dispute between the States concerned. Yet never has the view been put forward that, because a legal

dispute submitted to the Court is only one aspect of a political dispute, the Court should decline to resolve for the parties the legal questions at issue between them."

Justiciability of disputes

Another question concerns the meaning to be attached to the "(non-) justiciability" of disputes.[96] The more usual formulation is that a dispute may, or may not, be suitable for judicial decision.[97] The problem with that, of course, is that it does not specify why the dispute would, or would not, be suitable for adjudication. Since, as noted in the previous paragraphs, a dispute which cannot be settled by way of the application of rules of international law is by definition a political dispute, it is also by definition a dispute which is not suitable for adjudication. Yet the dispute's unsuitability for judicial decision lies with the impossibility of the Court to decide in accordance with international law, not because the dispute would be non-justiciable if legal rules could be found applicable to it.[98]

Another criterion sometimes put forward concerns the unwillingness of one of the parties to have the dispute settled by the Court. Such arguments have not, however, gained any weight over the years. It is widely accepted, in relation to issues of jurisdiction, that consent once given cannot be revoked at the moment one State invokes its own and another State's consent to have a particular dispute settled by the Court.[99] Indeed, the Statute envisages this type of situation by providing, in article 53, paragraph 1, that in cases of non-appearance of the respondent State, or failure to defend its position, the applicant State may call upon the Court to decide in favour of its claim. Paragraph 2 of the same article enjoins the Court to satisfy itself that it has jurisdiction, and that the claim of the applicant State is well founded in fact and law. The Court's case law furthermore testifies to the fact that the Court has tended to adjudicate disputes notwithstanding a respondent's failure to show up.[100] Clearly unwillingness to appear or to defend, or generally to have the dispute adjudicated, cannot transform the dispute into a non-justiciable one.[101]

If the idea of justiciability is to have any place in the jurisprudence of the Court, it must mean that a dispute, though legal in character, ought not to be settled by the Court due to circumstances substantially extraneous to the substantive law.[102]
One such circumstance, particularly interesting from the viewpoint of international crimes, was argued by the United States:[103]

> "The resort of force during ongoing armed conflict lacks the attributes necessary for the application of the judicial process, namely that a pattern of legally relevant facts discernible by the means available to the adjudicating tribunal, establishable in conformity with applicable norms of evidence and proof, and not subject to further material evolution during the course of, or subsequent to, the judicial proceedings."

The Court had no problem in refuting the primary argument that it would be unable to establish the facts, as well as the subsidiary argument that the judgment might not be capable of implementation.[104] Another argument was not really countered by the Court, namely that allegations of ongoing use of unlawful armed force were never intended by the draftsmen of the Charter to be covered by article 36, paragraph 2, of the Statute.[105]

In the light of the text of article 36, paragraph 2, such an argument appears somewhat odd, since its terms, establishing the jurisdiction of the Court regarding legal disputes,[106] cover any question of international law, and any fact which may constitute the breach of an international obligation. The fact however that a dispute can be settled by reference to rules of international law would not be decisive in order to conclude on the non-justiciability of the dispute. As pointed out even legal disputes may be non-justiciable. However, the Court did not have to search for long to come up with precedents regarding the adjudication of disputes involving the use of force.[107]

The connected argument that those precedents were all retrospective in character, and did not relate to a fluid situation, did not persuade the Court to refrain from deciding the issues. As judge Schwebel aptly observed, in the merits phase of the Nicaragua Case, the provision on the Court's power to indicate provisional measures would not make sense if ongoing cases were excluded.[108] In this connection one may note that Nicaragua disputed that the Court's judicial function was "inherently retrospective".[109] In view of the accepted forms of reparation (*supra* chapter three) there appears no reason to deny the Court's power to settle disputes involving claims for cessation of wrongful conduct and restitution. These may involve putting a stop to (a) continuing wrongful act(s) or ending an illegal situation, and in that sense the Court's judgment would invariably be prospective.

There is one aspect regarding the issue of (non-) justiciability that deserves closer scrutiny. It concerns judge Schwebel's stance that the Court cannot, and could not, judge the necessity of United States' action in self-defence partly in view of the insufficiency of the evidence, and partly because of the difficulty of establishing the true motives and reasonableness of the policy of a party.[110] The Court, in a very limited way, judged United States' action to be in conflict with the condition of necessity, mainly because it was initiated several months after a major offensive by the armed opposition in El Salvador had been repulsed.[111] If it is recognized that the Court can assess whether a right of self-defence can be exercised in the circumstances of the case,[112] fluid and ongoing as they may be, it would seem contradictory to claim that it could not assess, at the same time, whether other conditions for the lawful exercise of that right are fulfilled.[113]

Two final issues, relevant from the viewpoint of international crimes, warrant discussion. First, can the Court uphold claims demanding, as guarantees against repetition, a change of government or the implementation of individual responsibility for crimes under international law? Secondly, can the Court issue a declaration affirming the right to take countermeasures or to use force by one party against another if the countermeasures or the use of force have not yet occurred?

A serious problem of justiciability may exist regarding claims for guarantees against repetition, especially those relating to a change of government and the implementation of individual responsibility. It is not to be expected, generally, that an author State will implement such specific and far-reaching guarantees of its own free will.[114] But that is not really the issue. The implementation of a change of government and the individual responsibility of public officials may involve not merely the dismissal of the government, but also a complete re-organization of the police, paramilitary and armed forces. It is also recognized that ultimate responsibility for the political reconstitution of a particular State lies with the people of that State. In the end then it is not merely a question of disposing of those who bear the ultimate responsibility for the commission of an international crime, but of a complete turnabout including the organization of elections to enhance the legitimacy of the new government. It may be submitted that disputes regarding such complex issues, encompassing the making of choices regarding the future political and constitutional structures of a State, could not be settled by the Court.

As to the second question, it is possible to claim that the Court cannot authorize resort to countermeasures or the use of force. It is generally accepted that the Court should not take into account, at any stage of its deliberations, the distinct possibility that a party would act in disregard of its obligation to comply with the judgment of the Court (article 94 Charter).[115] Should a party nevertheless fail to honour its obligation, enforcement of the author State's responsibility may come about on the basis of a Security Council decision under article 94, paragraph 2, of the Charter, or by virtue of the injured State's exercise of its right to resort to countermeasures or to use force (should the latter be lawful under international law). It is to be assumed that the Court would have established the author State's responsibility and its obligation to provide reparation to the injured State. If the Court would issue a declaration that a State possesses, or would possess, the right to resort to countermeasures or to use force, this would amount to positing a party's future disregard of the judgment of the Court. At the same time this would implicate the Court in the injured State's decision to exercise its rights. Furthermore, as the parties will be free, subject to considerations of *jus cogens*, to opt for a settlement of their dispute on some other basis than the Court's judgment, such a declaration by the Court would prejudice the position of the author State in any negotiations following the judgment.

6.4. Relations between the Court and the Security Council

6.4.1. THE CONCURRENT EXERCISE OF JURISDICTION BY THE COURT AND THE SECURITY COUNCIL

The non-justiciability of a dispute has been claimed to exist on the basis of the exercise by the Security Council of its powers regarding the maintenance of international peace and security.[116] Article 24, paragraph 1, of the Charter confers on the Security Council primary responsibility for the maintenance of international peace and security. It has been argued that if and when the Security Council is exercising its functions in that field, the Court should refrain from exercising contentious jurisdiction. With respect to these issues the Court had already stated in the Expenses Opinion that the Security Council's primary responsibility could not be considered to constitute an exclusive responsibility.[117] Hence the General Assembly could take such action as did not come within the province of the Security Council.[118]

In so far as the Council's relation to the Court is concerned the starting-point of the discussion must lie with article 12, paragraph 1, of the Charter:

"While the Security Council is exercising in respect of any dispute or situation the functions assigned to it in the present Charter, the General Assembly shall not make any recommendation with regard to that dispute or situation unless the Security Council so requests."

As the Court has noted a few times already,[119] there is no equivalent rule to be found anywhere in the Charter or the Statute limiting the freedom of the Court to exercise the functions assigned to it. It is to be observed that this limitation on the Assembly's competence comes into operation already as soon as the Security Council is seized of a situation or dispute under Chapter VI (article 12, paragraph 2, read together with article 24, paragraph 2), and not merely if it exercises its powers under Chapter VII (in which case article 11, paragraph 2, final sentence, may apply). For obvious reasons no such limit could be imposed on the Court, since under Chapter VI it has a role to play regarding the peaceful settlement of disputes (articles 33 and 36, paragraph 3).[120] Additionally it may be noted that the Security Council cannot adopt binding decisions under Chapter VI of the Charter, and that the concurrent exercise of jurisdiction by the two organs will probably, but not necessarily, develop in parallel directions.[121]

Should the Court's position be any different if the Council is exercising its powers under Chapter VII of the Charter? The United States argued that Nicaragua's complaint about the use of force against its territorial integrity and national independence amounted to a charge of aggression and armed conflict which could only be dealt with by the Security Council under Chapter VII, and not by the Court as part of the pacific settlement of disputes under Chapter VI. The Court retorted:[122]

"But, if so, it has to be noted that, while the matter has been discussed in the Security Council, no notification has been given to it in accordance with Chapter VII of the Charter, so that the issue could be tabled for full discussion before a decision were taken for the necessary enforcement measures to be authorized. It is clear that the complaint by Nicaragua is not about an ongoing armed conflict between it and the United States, but one requiring, and indeed demanding, the peaceful settlement of disputes between the two States."

It is not clear what kind of notification in accordance with Chapter VII is meant. Yet what is clear is that the Court's construction of the dispute between the two parties is somewhat artificial. Can it really be doubted that the mutual allegations of intervention and use of force concern situations appropriate for Security Council action under Chapter VII? The mere fact that the matter has not been tabled for discussion under Chapter VII, or that the Security Council has not adopted any resolution under that chapter, cannot mean that consequently there is no Chapter VII type of situation. Even the fact that a draft resolution determining a threat to the peace, breach of the peace, or act of aggression, fails to acquire the requisite votes does not mean that consequently there is no threat to the peace, breach of the peace, or act of aggression. It simply means that the Security Council has been prevented from exercising its powers on political grounds,[123] and that it has not adopted any legally binding decision(s). The Court's argument did not address the issue whether it could adjudicate disputes that fall within the Security Council's province of Chapter VII. Substantially the answer of the Court is that the Security Council had not exercised its responsibility under Chapter VII in regard to the dispute between Nicaragua and the United States. And, again, this constitutes a reliance on the lack of any provision analogous to article 12, paragraph 1, of the Charter.

Apparently the Court will not refrain from adjudicating a dispute on the sole ground that the Council is simultaneously exercising its responsibility under Chapter VI, nor when there is a Chapter VII type of situation regarding which the Council has failed to exercise its responsibility. It remains to be seen whether the Court will exercise its contentious jurisdiction if the Council has made use of its powers under Chapter VII.[124] It may be noted that the Court has made use of its power to indicate provisional measures in relation to the disputes between Bosnia and Herzegovina and Yugoslavia (Serbia and Montenegro), and regarding which the Security Council has been, and is, exercising its powers under Chapter VII.[125]

6.4.2. JUDICIAL REVIEW OF SECURITY COUNCIL RESOLUTIONS

The issue to be discussed in this subsection, review of decisions of the Security Council, is of the utmost importance in relation to international crimes. As argued in the previous section questions regarding the prospective exercise of rights of enforcement are non-justiciable. Not because they would not entail the interpretation or application of legal rules, but because the Court would, by affirming the existence of enforcement rights prior to their exercise, be implicated as to the political decision to exercise such rights. It has been claimed by some that the Court could not settle certain disputes between States on the basis that such would encroach upon the powers of the Security Council under Chapter VII of the Charter. Of course, as noted in the previous subsection, there does not exist any danger of encroachment in cases in which the decisions of the two organs run in the same direction.

On the other hand, the Court's eventual decision could, hypothetically at least, be at variance with an existing Council decision. The question then arises whether the Court could review the earlier decision of the Council as to its conformity with the Charter or international law in general. The Court can be confronted with the issue of review through the exercise of both its contentious and advisory jurisdiction. However, since the Court's exercise of its advisory jurisdiction does not lead to any binding result for organs of the United Nations or member States, one could not consider such exercise a review of a decision properly speaking. The Court's jurisprudence in the field of advisory opinions has, however, proved relevant to the issue, and will be discussed first.

Review in advisory proceedings before the Court

In its very first opinion, on the admission of States to the United Nations, the Court noted that:[126]

> "The political character of an organ cannot release it from the observance of the treaty provisions established by the Charter when they constitute limitations on its powers or criteria for its judgment."

It would certainly not be too farfetched to claim that the phrase "threat to the peace, breach of the peace, or act of aggression", featuring in article 39 of the Charter, presents criteria for the Council's judgment. Indeed, the term "peace-loving" which formed the subject of this opinion of the Court could not be said to allow for any less wide appreciation of relevant circumstances than the phrase "threat to the peace". As argued before, especially in chapter two, the Council's determination of a threat to the peace under article 39, though undoubtedly constituting the exercise of a discretionary power and as such subject at the most to marginal scrutiny, involves not merely a factual, military, and political evaluation, but allows for the application of legally relevant criteria.

Subsequently, in its Expenses Opinion, the Court observed:[127]

> "But when the Organization takes action which warrants the assertion that it was appropriate for the fulfilment of one of the stated purposes of the United Nations, the presumption is that such action is not *ultra vires* the Organization."

It is in the nature of a presumption that it can be rebutted, just as much as a doctrine of *ultra vires* acts constitutes a legal doctrine. If there is a presumption that certain action is not *ultra vires*, then the rebuttal of that presumption must take place by reference to legal limitations on the powers conferred. Admittedly, the Court went on to point out that proposals to vest the ultimate authority to interpret the Charter in the Court were rejected, and that it was restricted to rendering an "advisory" opinion.[128] At the same time one cannot but take note that it further observed that:[129] "(...) each organ must, in the first place at least, determine its own jurisdiction." According to Watson the Court did assert a power of review in the Expenses Opinion, mainly because it stated that it could consider whether the expenses were "decided on in conformity with the provisions of the Charter".[130]

In the Namibia Opinion the Court, finally, pronounced itself more clearly on an argument against review (unless specifically so requested):[131]

> "Undoubtedly, the Court does not possess powers of judicial review or appeal in respect of the decisions taken by the United Nations organs concerned."

Although the question submitted to the Court was what legal consequences ensued, for States, of the continued presence of South Africa in Namibia notwithstanding Security Council resolution 276,[132] the Court went on, in detail, to examine the legal justification for the General Assembly's action in terminating the mandate.[133] While thus affirming the non-existence of any power of review, it at the same time took a broad approach regarding the issues to be argued and in actual fact undertook action that amounted to judicial review of Generally Assembly resolution 2145 (XXI).[134]

Review in contentious proceedings before the Court

Gowlland-Debbas has argued that the Court could not review decisions of the Security Council under article 39 of the Charter. Her position in this respect follows from her claim that determinations under that article involve a factual and political judgment, and not a legal one.[135] This latter claim was discussed and rejected in chapter two. The Charter and the Statute do not really provide any guidance as to questions of review, and the preparatory works of the Charter may be interpreted to go either way.[136]
Although the question of review has not been the subject of any explicit statement by the Court, some of the Court's positions in contentious cases are relevant. The Court has had the opportunity to discuss its relation to the Security Council in four cases.

In the Diplomatic Staff Case the Court observed that:[137]

> "(...) it does not seem to have occurred to any member of the Council that there was or could be anything irregular in the simultaneous exercise of their respective functions by the Court and the Security Council. Nor is there in this any cause for surprise. Whereas Article 12 of the Charter expressly forbids the General Assembly to make any recommendation with regard to a dispute or situation while the Security Council is exercising its functions in respect of that dispute or situation, no such restriction is placed upon the functioning of the Court by any provision of either the Charter or the Statute of the Court. The reasons are clear. It is for the Court, the principal judicial organ of the United Nations, to resolve any legal questions that may be in issue between parties to a dispute;"

This quotation indicates that the Court will not be hampered by the fact that the Security Council is exercising its functions under the Charter in respect of (partially) the same dispute. But that is of course not the same as saying that the Court has the power to review a determination of the Security Council under article 39.

In the jurisdiction and admissibility phase of the Nicaragua Case the Court was faced with the claim advanced by the United States that the Court would be in need to determine that United States' activities complained of by Nicaragua constituted a threat to the peace, breach of the peace, or act of aggression. Nicaragua had earlier presented corresponding claims, as advanced to the Court, in a draft resolution to the Security Council which failed to acquire the requisite majority, and the United States, as part of a larger issue, argued that:[138]

> "(...) the Nicaraguan Application requires the Court to determine that the activities complained of constitute a threat to the peace, a breach of the peace, or an act of aggression, (...). Since Nicaragua's Application in effect asks the Court for a judgment in all material respects identical to the decision which the Security Council did not take, it amounts to an appeal to the Court from an adverse consideration in the Security Council."

The Court responded to this specific point by saying:[139]

> "Nor can the Court accept that the present proceedings are objectionable as being in effect an appeal to the Court from an adverse decision of the Security Council. The Court is not asked to say that the Security Council was wrong in its decision, nor that there was anything inconsistent with law in the way in which the members of the Council employed their right to vote. The Court is asked to pass judgment on certain legal aspects of a situation which has also been considered by the Security Council, a procedure which is entirely consonant with its position as the principal judicial organ of the United Nations."

Again this does not amount to an unambiguous assertion that the Court possesses the power to review a decision of the Security Council under article 39. Here the Court merely proceeds to examine the legality of certain acts which beforehand had been presented to the Security Council with the claim that they constituted a breach of the peace, or an act of aggression. It may be said here, somewhat in the form of an obiter dictum, that the Court was certainly right to ignore the fact that the Security Council had not taken any decision under article 39. As is known the draft resolution was not adopted due to the United States voting against.[140] Apart from the obvious fact that no determination under article 39 took place, no other consequences attach to the so-called power of veto. The exercise of the right to vote in the Security Council concerns a political act and a vetoed resolution cannot prejudice, in any way, the legal position with respect to a certain situation.[141]

The third case in which acts of the Security Council have been implicated concerns the Lockerbie Case.[142] The United Kingdom and the United States demanded from Libya the surrender of two individuals, of Libyan nationality,[143] and secured the support of the Security Council for its demands. Libya brought a case against the two States before the Court under the jurisdictional clause of the Montreal Convention, and asked the Court to issue provisional measures ordering the United Kingdom and the United States to refrain from putting any pressure on it, individually or through means of their positions in the Security Council, to surrender the individuals concerned. Before the Court had completed its deliberation on the Libyan requests, the Security Council took a resolution under Chapter VII of the Charter ordering Libya to surrender the individuals. The Court had to face a new situation, and reacted as follows:[144]

> "39. Whereas both Libya and the United Kingdom, as Members of the United Nations, are obliged to accept and carry out the decisions of the Security Council in accordance with Article 25 of the Charter; whereas the Court, which is at the stage of proceedings on provisional measures, considers that prima facie this obligation extends to the decision contained in resolution 748 (1992); and whereas, in accordance with Article 103 of the Charter, the obligations of the Parties in that respect prevail over their obligations under any other international agreement, including the Montreal Convention;
>
> 40. Whereas the Court, while thus not at this stage called upon to determine definitively the legal effect of resolution 748 (1992), considers that, whatever the situation previous to the adoption of that resolution, the rights claimed by Libya under the Montreal Convention cannot now be regarded as appropriate for protection by the indication of provisional measures;
>
> 41. Whereas, furthermore, an indication of the measures requested by Libya would be likely to impair the rights which appear prima facie to be enjoyed by the United Kingdom by virtue of Security Council resolution 748 (1992);"

While it is clear that the Court here refrains from reviewing the validity of Security Council resolution 748, that in itself is not sufficient evidence to conclude that the Court denies itself the power to review the resolution. Indeed, there are a number of indications that the Court could possibly, probably in its deliberations on the merits of the case (if it reaches that stage), proceed to such review. Thus, first of all, the Court makes a reference to the fact that, at the stage of provisional measures, the obligation of article 25 *prima facie* extends to the decision contained in resolution 748. It seems to imply that, at a later phase of proceedings, it could examine whether resolution 748 really lays down any decision, or whether it should be considered to merely lay down a recommendation. Furthermore, and more importantly, it appears to leave open the possibility of reviewing the validity of resolution 748 when it remarks that it is not called upon at the stage of provisional measures to "determine definitively the legal effect of resolution 748".[145] It may be submitted that part of the problem regarding this particular order lies with the incidental nature of provisional measures. Could one expect the Court to proceed with a review of resolution 748, considering that it had not at such a stage determined its jurisdiction and is enjoined to refrain from prejudging the merits? Certainly not.[146]

Finally the Genocide Convention Case presents some relevant indications as to the question of review. Bosnia and Herzegovina had requested the Court, *inter alia*, to indicate provisional measures to the effect that it could receive the supply of arms and assistance.[147] In its first order the Court observed that such requests dealt with matters outside the jurisdiction of the Genocide Convention and could not be entertained.[148] In its second order the Court added that the intention of the applicant was not the indication of measures to be taken by the respondent, but a declaration of rights possessed by Bosnia and Herzegovina so as to clarify the legal situation to the entire international community; accordingly, so the Court noted, the request had to be regarded as outside the scope of article 41 of the Statute.[149] Yugoslavia (Serbia and Montenegro) in turn claimed that since the Security Council had been acting under Chapter VII of the Charter, and had taken decisions on the basis of article 25, the indication of provisional measures by the Court, of the type requested, would be premature.[150] The Court understood that objection to be directed to those measures requested "which go beyond matters within the scope of the Genocide Convention", and it considered, for that reason alone, that it could not indicate those measures.[151] However, it went on to quote the passage from the Nicaragua Case which noted the absence of any provision analogous to article 12, paragraph 1, of the Charter.[152] The inference to be drawn from the orders is that the Court's refusal to indicate measures affecting resolution 713 does not hinge on its inability or incompetence to assess its validity, but rather reflects the limited scope of jurisdiction under the Genocide Convention.

It may be said, in conclusion, that the question of review of Security Council determinations under article 39 of the Charter is still open. There are ample grounds for finding that determining the existence of a threat to the peace involves the application of legal criteria. A future decision by the Court in the Lockerbie Case could put the matter beyond doubt.[153]

6.5. Indication of provisional measures under article 41 of the Statute

Article 41, paragraph 1, of the Statute establishes that:

> "The Court shall have the power to indicate, if it considers that circumstances so require, any provisional measures which ought to be taken to preserve the respective rights of either party."

A few aspects of this power of the Court stand out in the context of the present discussion on international crimes. These concern the preservation of rights, irreparable prejudice to rights, and arguments on equality, neutrality and impartiality. Other aspects relate to the possible timeliness of any indication of provisional measures, and issues of (non-) compliance and enforcement of provisional measures.

6.5.1. THE PRESERVATION OF RIGHTS, IRREPARABLE PREJUDICE, AND EQUALITY, NEUTRALITY AND IMPARTIALITY

Article 41, paragraph 1, of the Statute contemplates the indication of such provisional measures which "ought to be taken to preserve the respective rights of either party." The Court, in its practice on article 41, has specified that this:[154]

> "(...) presupposes that irreparable prejudice should not be caused to rights which are the subject of dispute in judicial proceedings;"

From the perspective of international responsibility, and in particular the rules on reparation, there is but one possibility of irreparable prejudice to rights.[155] Any internationally wrongful act gives rise to the obligation of the author State to provide reparation to the injured State. As argued in chapter three, section 3.4, the obligation to provide restitution should be accorded preference if either the injured or the author State so prefers. In the nature of things compensation is always possible,[156] even if the determination of the amount of compensation may prove difficult. Restitution on the other hand may prove absolutely impossible in cases of destruction of property and the killing of people. In this respect the Court's observation made in its judgment on the merits of the Nicaragua Case is noteworthy. It referred to its provisional measure to refrain from action that might prejudice the rights of the other party related to the carrying out of its prospective decision, and it then stated:[157]

> "When the Court finds that the situation requires that measures of this kind should be taken, it is incumbent on each party to take the Court's indications seriously into account, and not to direct its conduct solely by reference to what it believes to be its rights. *Particularly is this so in a situation of armed conflict where no reparation can efface the results of conduct which the Court may rule to have been contrary to international law.*"

Conduct found to have been contrary to international law may still be compensated. Yet it may prove to be impossible to efface the results of such conduct. It may not be possible, to use the words of the Permanent Court, to:[158] "(...) wipe out all the consequences of the illegal act and re-establish the situation which would, (...), have existed if that act had not been committed." It is typically this impossibility which lies at the basis of any indication of provisional measures by the Court. Obviously irreparable prejudice will almost inevitably be caused when an international crime is committed. By referring to the impossibility of reparation in cases of armed conflict the Court already implied as much as to uses of force in general. In its second order on provisional measures in the Genocide Convention Case the Court repeated this formula.[159] Obviously the same considerations apply regarding the international crimes of denial of self-determination and widespread breaches of basic human rights obligations.

As a follow-up to this there is the consideration that the Court, by indicating provisional measures, might cause irreparable prejudice to the "rights" of the target State. That might be the case, for instance, if the Court would order measures that amount to restitution. Should the target State comply with the order, and subsequently it were to be found either that the Court lacked jurisdiction or that the respondent party had acted lawfully, then it might no longer be possible (at least politically) to return to the situation before restitution. The Diplomatic Staff Case is illustrative in this respect. Should

Iran have released the hostages and allowed their leaving the country, it is clear that no matter how the eventual judgment of the Court would turn out, they would not have returned to Iran. Surely this constituted the basis for the Iranian argument that the Court's indication of the measures requested by the United States would amount to passing judgment on the substance of the case in breach of the norms governing its jurisdiction.[160] The Court retorted that provisional measures must relate to the substance of the case, since they are designed to preserve the rights of either party (pending final decision).[161] Logically the conclusion is that the indication of provisional measures may prejudge the outcome of the jurisdictional or the merits phase.

In the past allegations have been made that indicated measures came close to constituting a prejudgment on the merits.[162] A big part of the criticism voiced in this respect was based on the perceived one-sidedness, or unbalanced character, of the Court's order.[163] That measures have been directed at one party raises questions regarding the equality of the parties, neutrality, and the impartiality of the Court. However, doubts in this regard are misguided.

Merrills has claimed, regarding the issue of equality of treatment, that:[164]

> "Interim measures, however, exist to protect the rights of *both* parties. In deciding what action is called for by the circumstances it is therefore essential for the Court to ensure that any impression of bias is avoided."

In a similar vein Iran argued that provisional measures could not be unilateral,[165] meaning of course that they could not be directed against one party only. The Court countered this position by noting that provisional measures are designed to preserve the rights of *either* party, and that the concept of provisional measures (as recognized by article 73 of the Rules of Court) implies a request by one of the parties for measures to preserve its rights against conduct calculated to prejudice those rights.[166]

The equality of parties before the Court relates basically to affording the parties equal opportunities to exercise procedural rights and to present and argue their case. Thus the issue of bias could arise only if the other party (usually the respondent) also requested the indication of provisional measures. But even if it could be said that a substantive obligation applies to both parties, this does not mean that provisional measures must be directed at both of them. For it is in the light of the facts of the case that the Court must appreciate the likelihood of action threatening irreparable prejudice. It is in this light that one has to see the Court's rejection of the request by Yugoslavia (Serbia and Montenegro) to indicate more specific measures, other than the general measure directed at both parties in the first order,[167] to be directed at Bosnia and Herzegovina alone.[168]

The real reason for caution lies with the fact that the Court at the stage of provisional measures has not yet determined its jurisdiction,[169] or heard sufficient argument on the law or the facts. It is for that reason that it cannot make definite findings on either the law or the facts, and that the rights of parties to contest such issues remains unaffected.[170] Provisional measures must, as noted, be grafted upon the substantive law to be applied and the facts of the case.[171] It would be a mistake to confuse the impartiality inherent in judicial proceedings with the apparent neutrality ascribed to the law. Essentially law is designed to be applied and complied with. Once a situation evolves that could be described as unlawful and involves breaches of obligation, the law's neutrality is dropped in favour of a very partisan attitude towards establishing the illegality, preventing repetition, and enforcement. Provisional measures clearly must favour the safeguarding of substantive rights and compliance with obligations for the period up to decisions on the jurisdiction or the merits.[172]

6.5.2. TIMELINESS, (NON-) COMPLIANCE AND THE ENFORCEMENT OF PROVISIONAL MEASURES

The Rules of Court provide that requests for the indication of provisional measures have priority over all other cases (article 74, paragraph 1), and that the Court shall proceed to a decision on the request as a measure of urgency (article 74, paragraph 2). The jurisprudence of the Court witnesses that the object of provisional measures, to preserve the respective rights of either party, presupposes that irreparable prejudice should not be caused to rights which are the subject of dispute in judicial proceedings.[173] It is clear that the threat of such irreparable prejudice accounts for the urgency with which the Court proceeds to consider and indicate provisional measures.[174] One may wonder nevertheless whether the Court is sufficiently equipped, from the legal point of view, to prevent the occurrence of such harm.

First of all it may be noted that even the priority accorded to the consideration of requests for indication of provisional measures does not, in general,[175] lead to the indication of provisional measures within two weeks of the date of the request. It may be surmised that within such a time span a substantial risk of irreparable harm could well have turned into actual fact. That argument is even stronger in respect of international crimes, since the acts complained of are being committed in a premeditated and intentional fashion. It may be noted, on the other hand, that irreparable harm may of course also take place after the indication of provisional measures, that is, if a State does not comply with the measures indicated. It may be speculated that whenever a State intentionally adopts a certain conduct, irrespective of whether the conduct would be characterized as lawful, a delict, or a crime, that the more likely scenario is a defiant attitude towards indicated provisional measures.[176] This brings us to issues of enforcement.

Secondly, and this does not so much concern the Court as the structure of the international legal order, there are only limited possibilities to enforce provisional measures in case of non-compliance. The Security Council's power under article 94, paragraph 2, of the Charter may be invoked only in case of non-compliance with a judgment of the Court.[177] Whether or not the Court's orders indicating provisional measures would be covered by article 94, paragraph 1, of the Charter, and whether or not one considers them binding on the parties, the choice of form, order instead of judgment, militates against the applicability of paragraph 2. The only form of organized collective enforcement left would lie with the Security Council determining conduct constituting non-compliance with provisional measures a threat to the peace under article 39 of the Charter.[178] Article 41, paragraph 2, of the Statute runs:

> "Pending the final decision, notice of the measures suggested shall forthwith be given to the parties and to the Security Council."

This paragraph probably was inserted to provide the Security Council with adequate information, so that it may take appropriate action, if the circumstances so require, to maintain or restore international peace and security.

Would an applicant or respondent State be entitled to resort to enforcement measures in case of non-compliance by the other State? It may be suggested that such is not the case. However, Sztucki has argued the contrary:[179]

> "Even if the indication of interim measures does not impose a formal obligation, and thus creates only a kind of *lex imperfecta* as between the parties, it still constitutes a formal recognition of the right to interim protection of the disputed rights. Consequently, order creditors should be in a position lawfully to assert that right by all the means otherwise admissible in international law."

The latter sentence reveals the crux of the matter: means admissible in international law. From the theoretical perspective any measure involving a breach of obligation is in need of justification, and in the absence of such justification will constitute an internationally wrongful act.

If one considers an order indicating provisional measures to impose an obligation to comply with it, the possibility of enforcement in case of breach would be open to the injured (creditor) State.[180] Yet one is hard pressed to find arguments in favour of the binding force of orders other than numerous allusions to the need for effectiveness.[181] An order indicating provisional measures does not constitute a decision of the Court either under article 94, paragraph 1, of the Charter, or under article 59 of the Statute. Even though the Rules of Court state that the Court decides on the indication of provisional measures, it is noteworthy that it does not enunciate them in a judgment. By doing exactly that it would place the matter beyond doubt. But generally speaking the only judgments by the Court, other than those on the merits, concern decisions on objections and on requests for intervention under article 62. The Statute envisages decisions on disputes regarding jurisdiction (article 36, paragraph 6), and on certain other matters (articles 16, paragraph 2; 17, paragraph 2; 24, paragraph 3; 31, paragraph 5; 46; 48; 62, paragraph 2; and 64). Article 41, paragraph 1, proclaims the power of the Court to indicate provisional measures, but it does not stipulate that the Court decides on provisional measures. Furthermore, most decisions of the Court are put down in the form of orders. Article 79, paragraph 7, of the Rules of Court singularly stands out in that it provides that decisions on objections will be given in the form of a judgment. Nevertheless decisions under article 62, paragraph 2, of the Statute have been laid down in judgments;[182] in contrast decisions on provisional measures have not.

Since the indication of provisional measures by the Court cannot be said to carry with it the force of legal obligation for the target States,[183] this means that conduct inconsistent with such measures cannot provide any justification for the State injured by such conduct to act in breach of its international obligations. Simply put: there are no admissible means to enforce provisional measures.

Thirdly, the possibility of unilateral enforcement by the injured State, or applicant State, of its substantive rights runs counter to the tendency of the Court to indicate that the parties ought not to take any action, and ensure that no action is taken, which might aggravate the dispute, or render it more difficult of solution.[184] It would seem obvious that all kinds of economic, and other, measures resorted to by an injured State against an author State may indeed aggravate the dispute and render it more difficult of solution. During the hostages crisis, and after the indication of provisional measures, the United States resorted to economic and other kinds of measures against Iran.[185] But the closest the Court came in relation to those was a remark to the effect that:[186]

> "They were measures taken in response to what the United States believed to be grave and manifest violations of international law by Iran, (...)."

No other specific observations were made by the Court on this issue.[187] It may not be too farfetched to claim that the Court apparently did not consider resort to such measures to be inadmissible.[188]

The situation is somewhat more complicated as regards military action. The Court, in the Diplomatic Staff Case, took note of the United States' requests for a delay and later for an early judgment, and then, in relation to the American military incursion into Iran, felt bound to observe:[189]

> "(...) that an operation undertaken in those circumstances, from whatever motive, is of a kind calculated to undermine respect for the judicial process in international relations; and to recall that (...) the Court had indicated that no action was to be taken by either party which might aggravate the tension between the two countries."

Immediately after, in the following paragraph, it noted that the legality of the operation under the Charter or general international law, or any issue of responsibility, was not before the Court.[190] Apparently the Court did not seem inclined to judge the American actions in the light of their discernible inconsistency with the indicated provisional measures. As noted in relation to countermeasures and the use of force, prior recourse to dispute settlement procedures should not be considered a condition for lawful resort in case of international crimes. Their lawfulness similarly should not be considered impaired on the basis of any inconsistency with provisional measures indicated by the Court. The lawfulness of the use of force should in fact be decided solely in relation to the substantive rules under the Charter or customary international law.[191]

6.6. Summary

One of the main obstacles that may induce the Court to refrain from settling a dispute lies in the absence of jurisdiction, generally, regarding the author State of an international crime. It is very unlikely that an author State of an international crime will agree, by special agreement, or through application of *forum prorogatum*, to adjudication by the Court. To the extent that the specific international crimes of article 19, paragraph 3, Part One, of the ILC-draft on State responsibility, are covered by existing jurisdictional clauses, recourse to the Court could be envisaged. So far only one case, that between Bosnia and Herzegovina against Yugoslavia (Serbia and Montenegro), has been brought before the Court. The rejection by the Court of certain provisional measures requested by Bosnia and Herzegovina, twice in a row, was based on the fact that the measures requested were substantially unrelated to the subject-matter, and hence jurisdiction *ratione materiae*, of the Genocide Convention.

The jurisdiction conferred on the basis of declarations under article 36, paragraph 2, of the Statute, allows for the settlement of disputes regarding international crimes. That no universal compulsory jurisdiction exists under international law cannot hinder any State in possession of a legal interest from requesting the Court to settle any dispute related to human rights generally, or international crimes in particular, if a basis of a jurisdiction exists.

Serious problems may arise when the Court is confronted with a request to settle a dispute, and acceding to that request would implicate the rights or obligations of a State that is not a party to the proceedings. The Court recognized in the Monetary Gold Case that it could not exercise jurisdiction over disputes in the absence of consent on the part of a third State if the legal interests of that third State would form the very subject-matter of the proceedings. The precedent has been slow to be repeated, though it found partial application in the Continental Shelf Case between Libya and Tunisia. From the viewpoint of international crimes especially the Nicaragua Case and the East Timor Case are interesting. In the former case the United States invoked a plea of collective self-defence, and claimed that the Court could not adjudicate in the absence of, particularly, El Salvador. The Court refused to admit the existence of a rule of indispensable parties and asserted that the limits of its jurisdiction, as defined in the Monetary Gold Case, had not been reached. In the East Timor Case, which involved basically the right to self-determination of the people of East Timor, the Court explicitly reverted to its precedent in the Monetary Gold Case, and ruled that it could not settle the legal dispute(s) between Portugal and Australia in view of Indonesia's absence from the proceedings.

In the Eastern Carelia Opinion the Permanent Court decided to refrain from rendering advice to the League in view of the lack of consent by Russia required under article 17 of the Covenant of the League of Nations. As no similar condition has been inserted into the Charter, the Court has not refrained from rendering advice to the United Nations as long as the request came within the competence of the requesting organ. The Court has recognized, however, that it would be incompatible with its judicial character to give a reply to a question if the circumstances disclose that the request constitutes an attempt to circumvent the principle that a State is not obliged to have its disputes submitted to judicial settlement without its consent. This would seem to rule out any exercise of its advisory jurisdiction to the extent that giving a reply would involve establishing the responsibility of a State.

The primary condition regarding the existence and exercise of jurisdiction or the admissibility of a claim is constituted by the requirement of a dispute, which must be shown to exist by reference to a claim by one party that is positively opposed by the other party. Generally the subject-matter of a dispute must have been defined through negotiations between the States concerned. In chapters four and five it was argued that injured States should not be held bound to resort to dispute settlement in case of international crimes before having recourse to countermeasures or the use of force. Similarly claims by an injured State before the Court should not be found inadmissible simply because there had not been any direct negotiations or because they, arguably, had not been sufficiently exhausted.

In relation to issues of justiciability the character of a dispute, whether legal or political, is determined according to the perception that it can be solved by application of legal rules and principles. Consequently the distinction between justiciable and non-justiciable disputes is not equivalent to that between legal and political disputes. By definition the latter kind of dispute is non-justiciable because it cannot be settled in accordance with international law. The jurisprudence of the Court also testifies to the fact that the unwillingness of a State to appear, to defend its case, or to have the dispute adjudicated, cannot transform the dispute into a non-justiciable one. If the idea of non-justiciability of disputes is to have a place within the jurisprudence of the Court, it must mean that the Court ought not to settle a dispute due to circumstances substantially unrelated to the substantive law to be applied.

In the Nicaragua Case the Court rejected a number of arguments based on the alleged non-justiciability of the dispute. It found that the ongoing nature of an armed conflict did not hinder it in such a way as to prevent it to verify the existence of a pattern of legally discernible facts. It also found, in accordance with established jurisprudence, that disputes involving the use of armed force were capable of adjudication. The argument that earlier precedents concerned inherently retrospective situations and did not concern a fluid situation of armed conflict similarly did not persuade the Court to refrain from settling the dispute. Having regard furthermore to the reparation forms of cessation and restitution in kind, decisions of the Court on that score would necessarily be prospective in character.

In relation to international crimes it may be argued that the guarantees against repetition concerning a change of government and implementation of the responsibility of individuals are non-justiciable. Linked as those are to other issues such as the re-organization of police, paramilitary and armed forces, the organization of elections, and constitutional changes, adjudication by the Court would involve taking a stand on complex choices regarding the future organization of the State. Such choices are not necessarily and inevitably decided by way of application of legal rules and principles.

Another question of non-justiciability may be identified in that the Court should not be considered competent to rule that one of the parties would be justified, prospectively, in resorting to countermeasures or the use of force. The Court cannot assume that a party would act in disregard of its obligation to comply with the judgment of the Court. Such would also prejudice the position of the author State in future negotiations with the injured State.

A particular claim of non-justiciability has been claimed to exist to the effect that the Court should refrain from exercising its contentious jurisdiction if the Security Council is exercising its primary responsibility regarding the maintenance of international peace and security. The Court has refuted that argument basically by relying on the absence of a provision analogous to that of article 12, paragraph 1, of the Charter. That position of the Court cannot be challenged to the extent that the Security Council would exercise its primary responsibility under Chapter VI of the Charter. The Court has indicated provisional measures regarding the dispute between Bosnia and Herzegovina and Yugoslavia (Serbia and Montenegro), regarding which the Security

Council has exercised powers under Chapter VII. As this did not constitute an exercise of conferred jurisdiction under article 36 of the Statute, the issue has not been decided yet in regard to the Council's exercise of responsibility under Chapter VII.

It cannot be said, on the basis of either the Court's advisory or contentious jurisprudence, that the Court has assumed any power of review regarding Security Council determinations under article 39 of the Charter. Such jurisprudence does contain indications that it might assume a power of review under the appropriate circumstances.

The indication of provisional measures by the Court presupposes that irreparable prejudice should not be caused to the rights in dispute. From the legal point of view only the destruction of property or the killing of persons amounts to irreparable prejudice, since this brings about the absolute impossibility to effect restitution in kind. As much was recognized by the Court in relation to the use of armed force generally, and may therefore be claimed to extend to the commission of international crimes generally. The indication of provisional measures itself may cause irreparable prejudice to the "rights" of the target State, since measures ordered, such as for instance the release of persons, may amount to restitution. If the targeted party complies with such measures, the release of such persons will most likely not be reversed, notwithstanding the possibility of a lack of jurisdiction or a judgment on the merits in favour of the targeted party. This shows that the indication of provisional measures is grafted upon the substance of the case, and may prejudice the decisions on jurisdiction and the merits. In the same vein the Court has rightly not let itself be hindered by allegations that the measures indicated were one-sided. Considerations of neutrality and impartiality must be taken into account only having regard to the fact that the Court has not yet, at the stage of provisional measures, determined its jurisdiction or ruled upon the admissibility of the claim.

Although requests for the indication of provisional measures are handled as a matter of urgency, orders are rarely forthcoming within two weeks. In such a time span irreparable prejudice may already have been caused. Such may result also due to non-compliance with provisional measures, which is most likely to occur in cases of intentional conduct by a party. Since the Court indicates provisional measures in the form of an order, article 94, paragraph 2, of the Charter does not apply. Consequently Security Council enforcement regarding conduct inconsistent with provisional measures could only be effected through application of article 39 of the Charter. The enforcement by one party of the measures targeted at the other party cannot be admitted. The Statute and the practice of the Court do not testify to the existence of any legal obligation on the part of the targeted party. Consequently the basic precondition for resort to countermeasures or armed force, the existence of an internationally wrongful act, will be lacking. However, since provisional measures should not be considered binding on the parties, enforcement of the author State's obligations by an injured State can only take place on the basis of those substantive rules establishing a right to resort to countermeasures, or to use armed force, in order to obtain reparation.

NOTES

[1] Arangio-Ruiz G., Seventh Report on State Responsibility, 24 May 1995, A/CN.4/469/Add.1, 4 pp., 2-4.

[2] Arangio-Ruiz, G., Seventh Report on State Responsibility, 9 May 1995, A/CN.4/469, 49 pp., 36. He adds to these that the discretionary and possibly arbitrary character of their choices is aggravated by the absence of legal motivation, which prevents verification of the legitimacy of, or comparison between, such choices. *Ibid.*

[3] Arangio-Ruiz, Seventh Report, 38-40. As arguments in favour of contentious proceedings he mentions the consultative nature of advisory opinions; the importance of questions of fact; the differing purpose of advisory proceedings, namely to give guidance to the addressee; and the fact that advisory proceedings do not involve full-fledged proceedings between litigant States. *Ibid.*, 39-40.

[4] Arangio-Ruiz, Seventh Report, Addendum 1, 4. Arguments in Seventh Report, 43-44.

[5] Proposed Article 7, Part Three, in Arangio-Ruiz, G., Seventh Report on State Responsibility, 29 May 1995, A/CN.4/469/Add.2, 3 pp., 3.

[6] The 1945 Statute of the International Court of Justice, 39 AJIL 1945, Supplement, pp. 215-229.

[7] Article 35, paragraph 1, of the Statute states: "The Court shall be open to the states parties to the present Statute." Paragraph 2 runs: "The conditions under which the Court shall be open to other states shall, subject to the special provisions contained in treaties in force, be laid down by the Security Council, (...)." The Court has reflected upon issues of capacity (or as it itself stated its jurisdiction *ratione personae*), in the case brought before it by Bosnia and Herzegovina against Yugoslavia (Serbia and Montenegro). Application of the Convention on the Prevention and Punishment of the Crime of Genocide, Provisional Measures, Order of 8 April 1993, ICJ Reports 1993, p. 3, 11-14. See also Visscher, C. de, Aspects récents du droit procédural de la Cour internationale de Justice, Éditions A. Pedone, Paris, 1966, 75; Mabrouk, M., Les exceptions de procédure devant les juridictions internationales, Librairie Générale de Droit et de Jurisprudence, Paris, 1966, 78-79; Bos, M., Les conditions du procès en droit international public, E.J. Brill, Leiden, 1957, 23-26; Jenks, W., The Prospects of International Adjudication, Stevens & Sons Limited, London, 1964, 185-186.

[8] Especially Jenks, The Prospects, 185-189, and 208-224, has argued on the desirability of allowing international organizations to become parties to cases before the Court. Also Lauterpacht, E., Aspects of the Administration of International Justice, Grotius Publications Limited, Cambridge, 1991, 59-66.

[9] The 1945 Charter of the United Nations, 39 AJIL 1945, Supplement, pp. 190-215.

[10] The 1978 Rules of Court, 17 ILM 1978, pp. 1286-1304. It is noteworthy that the Statute itself does not envisage the filing of objections. See generally on preliminary objections Visscher, Aspects récents, 99-113; Grisel, E., Les exceptions d'incompétence et d'irrecevabilité dans la procédure de la Cour internationale de Justice, Éditions Herbert Lang & Cie SA, Berne, 1968; Malloy, M., Objections to Adjudication in Contentious Cases before the International Court of Justice, 5 BJIL 1979, pp. 262-347; Rosenne, S., Procedure in the International Court, A Commentary on the 1978 Rules of the International Court of Justice, Martinus Nijhoff Publishers, The Hague, 1983, 158-170; and Annacker, C., Die Durchsetzung von *erga omnes* Verpflichtungen vor dem Internationalen Gerichtshof, Verlag Dr. Kovac, Hamburg, 1994, 95-96.

[11] Article 36, paragraph 6, of the Statute provides that: "In the event of a dispute as to whether the Court has jurisdiction, the matter shall be settled by the decision of the Court." Article 59 in turn states that: "The decision of the Court has no binding force except between the parties and in respect of that particular case." Finally article 60, first sentence, claims: "The judgment is final and without appeal." Article 79, paragraph 7, of the Rules, by mentioning a decision in the form of a judgment, seems to emphasize not only the binding force of the decision for the parties, but also the finality of the judgment on preliminary objections in general. The words "in the form of a judgment" first appeared in article 67, paragraph 7, of the 1972 Rules of Court (see ICJ Yearbook 1971-1972, no. 26, 8). The 1966 judgment on South West Africa has been criticized because it appeared to reverse or overrule the 1962 judgment on the subject of the applicants' legal interest. See South West Africa Cases (Ethiopia *v.* South Africa; Liberia *v.* South Africa), Preliminary Objections, Judgment, ICJ Reports 1962, p. 319, 342-344; and South West Africa, Second Phase, Judgment, ICJ Reports 1966, p. 6, 18-19, 36-38, 42-43, and 51. For criticism see Dissenting Opinion Koretsky, *ibid.*, 239-242; and Dissenting Opinion Jessup, *ibid.*, 331-338.

[12] The Court rejected a suggestion to the effect that it might devote a separate phase to questions of competence and admissibility. Western Sahara, Advisory Opinion, ICJ Reports 1975, p. 12, 17.

[13] Admission of a State to the United Nations (Charter, Art. 4), Advisory Opinion, ICJ Reports 1948, p. 57, 61-62; Interpretation of Peace Treaties, Advisory Opinion, ICJ Reports 1950, p. 65, 70-72; Reservations to the Convention on Genocide, Advisory Opinion, ICJ Reports 1951, p. 15, 19-20; Certain expenses of the United Nations (Article 17, paragraph 2, of the Charter), Advisory Opinion, ICJ Reports 1962, p. 151, 155-156; Legal Consequences for States of the Continued Presence of South Africa in Namibia (South West Africa) notwithstanding Security Council Resolution 276 (1970), Advisory Opinion, ICJ Reports 1971, p. 16, 21-27;

Western Sahara Opinion, 18-29; Applicability of Article VI, Section 22, of the Convention on the Privileges and Immunities of the United Nations, Advisory Opinion, ICJ Reports 1989, p. 177, 188-191.

[14] Extensively discussed by Sztucki, J., Interim Measures in the Hague Court, An Attempt at a Scrutiny, Kluwer Law and Taxation Publishers, Deventer, 1983, 136-143.

[15] See Obligation to Arbitrate under Section 21 of the United Nations Headquarters Agreement of 26 June 1947, Advisory Opinion, ICJ Reports 1988, p. 12. See Merrills, J., Interim Measures of Protection in the Recent Jurisprudence of the International Court of Justice, 44 ICLQ 1995, pp. 90-146, 145, footnote 157.

[16] Anglo-Iranian Oil Co. case (jurisdiction), Judgment, ICJ Reports 1952, p. 93, 102-103; Case of the monetary gold removed from Rome in 1943 (Preliminary Question), Judgment, ICJ Reports 1954, p. 19, 32-33; Frontier Dispute, Judgment, ICJ Reports 1986, p. 554, 579; Certain Phosphate Lands in Nauru (Nauru *v.* Australia), Preliminary Objections, Judgment, ICJ Reports 1992, p. 240, 260; Case concerning East Timor, Judgment, 30 June 1995, paragraphs 26, 28-29, and 33-35. Also Salvioli G., Problèmes de procédure dans la jurisprudence internationale, 91 RDC ADI 1957-I, pp. 553-617, 587-588; Seidl-Hohenveldern, I., *Actio Popularis* im Völkerrecht?, in Il processo internazionale, Studi in onore di Gaetano Morelli, Comunicazioni e Studi, volume 14, Giuffrè, Milano, 1975, pp. 803-813, 806-809; Silagi, M., Die Popularklage als Fremdkörper im Völkerrecht, 4 SAYIL 1978, pp. 10-28, 14-15, notes that jurisdiction under international law is consensual, whereas jurisdiction under national law is imposed; Malloy, Objections to Adjudication, 341-343; Annacker, Die Durchsetzung, 89-90.

[17] The Mavrommatis Concessions, Publications PCIJ, 1924, Series A, No. 2, p. 6, 16. Also Rights of Minorities (Minority Schools), Publications PCIJ, 1928, Series A, No. 15, p. 4, 22 and 22-26 (*forum prorogatum*); Case concerning the Factory at Chorzów (Claim for Indemnity) (The Merits), Publications PCIJ, 1928, Series A, No. 17, p. 4, 37.

[18] The judgment of the Court on the disputes between Qatar and Bahrain revolved around the question whether the Court could be seized by either of the parties or both of the parties. Maritime Delimitation and Territorial Questions between Qatar and Bahrain, Jurisdiction and Admissibility, Judgment, ICJ Reports 1995, p. 6, 14-24.

[19] See Maritime Delimitation Case, Jurisdiction and Admissibility, 23-24. On seisin see further Fitzmaurice, G., The Law and Procedure of the International Court of Justice, volume 2, Grotius Publications Limited, Cambridge, 1986, 440-447.

[20] To decide issues of jurisdiction the Court may need to go into the facts of the case and legal arguments applicable to the dispute. This it can do as long as it does not thereby pronounce on the merits of the case. C.f. Fitzmaurice, The Law and Procedure, volume 2, 449-450; and Salvioli, Problèmes de procédure, 596-601 and 602-603.

[21] See Nottebohm case, Preliminary Objection, Judgment, ICJ Reports 1953, p. 111, 118-120, on this.

[22] It is to be noted that the reference to the Charter serves no useful purpose, as the Charter does not provide for matters that fall under the jurisdiction of the Court.

[23] See generally Charney, J., Compromissory Clauses and the Jurisdiction of the International Court of Justice, 81 AJIL 1987, pp. 855-887.

[24] Paragraph 3 of article 36 adds to this that such declarations may be made: "(...) unconditionally or on condition of reciprocity on the part of several or certain states, or for a certain time." It may be noted that States have attached reservations to such declarations imposing restrictions other than those mentioned in paragraph 3. The Court has not disavowed such a practice by claiming the incompatibility of such reservations with paragraph 3.

[25] First discussed in Minorities Case, 22-26. Huber dissented on this point. See Dissenting Opinion Huber, *ibid.*, 50-54. See also Salvioli, Problèmes de procédure, 588.

[26] C.f. Hoogh, A. de, The Relationship between *Jus Cogens*, Obligations *Erga Omnes* and International Crimes: Peremptory Norms in Perspective, 42 AJPIL 1991, pp. 183-214, 196-197, regarding obligations *erga omnes.*

[27] Note that recently the Court refused to accept the Bosnian plea, in relation to its second request for provisional measures, that Yugoslavia (Serbia and Montenegro), by requesting provisional measures going beyond the scope of jurisdiction laid down in article IX of the Genocide Convention, had agreed on wider jurisdiction in accordance with the doctrine of *forum prorogatum.* Application of the Convention on the Prevention and Punishment of the Crime of Genocide, Provisional Measures, Order of 13 September 1993, ICJ Reports 1993, p. 325, 341-342; and also Separate Opinion Shahabuddeen, *ibid.*, 353-355; Separate Opinion Lauterpacht, *ibid.*, 416-421, apparently disagreeing with the Court.

[28] Dupuy, P.-M., Action publique et crime international de l'état: A propos de l'article 19 du projet de la Commission du Droit International sur la responsabilite des états, 25 AFDI 1979, pp. 539-554, 551-552.

[29] The measures requested related to issues of self-defence, the arms embargo of Security Council resolution 713, the sovereignty, territorial integrity and political independence of Bosnia, and self-determination of the

Bosnian people. Genocide Convention Case, Provisional Measures, 8 April 1993, 8 (Bosnian requests), and 19-20 (the Court's observations); and more fully argued by the Court in Genocide Convention Case, Provisional Measures, 13 September 1993, 332-333, 343-344 (Bosnian requests), 344-346 (the Court's observations). The basic consideration underlying the Court's refusal is worded as follows: "(...) the Court, having established the existence of a basis on which its jurisdiction might be founded, ought not to indicate measures for the protection of any disputed rights other than those which ultimately form the basis of a judgment in the exercise of that jurisdiction; whereas the Court will confine its examination of the measures requested, and of the grounds asserted for the request for such measures, to those which fall within the scope of the Genocide Convention;" Genocide Convention Case, Provisional Measures, 8 April 1993, 19. Commented upon by Maison, R., Les ordonnances de la CIJ dans l'affaire relative à l'application de la Convention sur la prévention et la répression du crime de génocide, 5 EJIL 1994, pp. 381-400.

[30] The Court assumed jurisdiction under this provision in the Border and Transborder Armed Actions (Nicaragua *v.* Honduras), Jurisdiction and Admissibility, Judgment, p. 69, 82-90 and 107.

[31] The 1966 International Covenant on Civil and Political Rights, 61 AJIL 1967, pp. 870-887; and the 1966 International Covenant on Economic, Social and Cultural Rights, 61 AJIL 1967, pp. 861-870.

[32] Article 9 of the 1948 Convention on the Prevention and Punishment of the Crime of Genocide, adopted by way of General Assembly resolution 260 (III), reprinted in 45 AJIL 1951, Supplement, pp. 7-10; article 10 of the 1957 Convention supplémentaire relative à l'abolition de l'esclavage, de traite des esclaves et des institutions et pratiques analogues à l'esclavage, 61 RGDIP 1957, pp. 137-142; article 12 of the 1973 International Convention on the Suppression and Punishment of the Crime of *Apartheid*, adopted by way of General Assembly resolution 3068 (XXVIII), reprinted in 13 ILM 1974, pp. 50-57. The latter does not allow unilateral application to the Court.

[33] Maison, Les ordonnances, 394-400.

[34] Maison, Les ordonnances, 398.

[35] Maison, Les ordonnances, 395 and 396.

[36] Maison, Les ordonnances, 396.

[37] Though article 8 states that any contracting party may call upon the competent organs of the United Nations to take appropriate action to prevent and suppress acts of genocide.

[38] Seidl-Hohenveldern, *Actio Popularis*, 806 and 809; Dupuy, P.-M., Observations sur le "crime international de l'etat", 84 RGDIP 1980, pp. 449-486, 481-484. Less clear Silagi, Die Popularklage, 14-21.

[39] The possibility of acting upon a legal interest is not restricted to judicial action, as may be seen from this observation by the Court: "Competence to bring an international claim is, for those possessing it, the capacity to resort to the customary methods recognized by international law for the establishment, the presentation and the settlement of claims. Among these methods may be mentioned protest, request for an inquiry, negotiation, and request for submission to an arbitral tribunal or the Court in so far as this may be authorized by the Statute. This capacity certainly belongs to the State; a State can bring a claim against another State. (...) It is dealt with by means of negotiations, and cannot, in the present state of the law as to international jurisdiction, be submitted to a tribunal, except with the consent of the States concerned." Reparation for injuries suffered in the service of the United Nations, Advisory Opinion, ICJ Reports 1949, p. 174, 177-178. Note Silagi, Die Popularklage, 20: "Im Völkerrecht entfällt hingegen die Frage nach einer 'Prozessführungsbefugnis' wegen der prinzipiellen Unklagbarkeit von Ansprüchen." Similar remarks may be found with Annacker, Die Durchsetzung, 103.

[40] Mann, F., The Doctrine of *Jus Cogens* in International Law, in Festschrift für Ulrich Scheuner, Duncker & Humblot, Berlin, 1973, pp. 399-418, 406, more pertinently observes regarding obligations *erga omnes*: "But it would probably also mean that every State has a cause of action and can exercise judicial remedies. If this is the Court's intention the Foreign Offices of the world will be well advised to review their acceptances of the optional clause."

[41] The Court noted that it had in the past exercised its power to remove cases from the General List in circumstances in which an applicant State itself recognized the absence of any existing title of jurisdiction. Military and Paramilitary Activities in and against Nicaragua (Nicaragua *v.* United States of America), Provisional Measures, Order, ICJ Reports 1984, p. 169, 178.

[42] Monetary Gold Case, Preliminary Question, 32-33. See Salvioli, Problèmes de procédure, 606-608 and 613-614; Visscher, Aspects récents, 40-41 and 111-113; and Malloy, Objections, 426-427.

[43] Monetary Gold Case, Preliminary Question, 32.

[44] Monetary Gold Case, Preliminary Question, 32.

[45] The issue of (third) States absent from proceedings has risen generally and in the context of intervention. See Separate Opinion Nagendra Singh, Trial of Pakistani Prisoners of War, Interim Protection, Order, ICJ Reports 1973, p. 328, 332; Continental Shelf (Libyan Arab Jamahiriya Malta), Application to Intervene, Judgment,

ICJ Reports 1984, p. 3, 24-27; Nicaragua Case, Jurisdiction and Admissibility, 430-431; Frontier Dispute, Judgment, 576-580; Land, Island and Maritime Frontier Dispute (El Salvador Honduras), Application to Intervene, Judgment, ICJ Reports 1990, p. 92, 114-116; Phosphate Lands Case, Preliminary Objections, 258-262.

[46] The Court partially applied the Monetary Gold doctrine by restricting the scope of its judgment between Libya and Malta in the light of Italian claims brought to its notice as a result of the (rejected) Italian request for permission to intervene in the case. Continental Shelf (Libyan Arab Jamahiriya Malta), Judgment, ICJ Reports 1985, p. 13, 26; and it refused to adjudicate Portuguese claims against Australia. East Timor Case, paragraphs 28-29 and 33-35.

[47] Military and Paramilitary Activities in and against Nicaragua (Nicaragua *v.* United States of America), Merits, Judgment, ICJ Reports 1986, p. 14, 119-122.

[48] Nicaragua Case, Jurisdiction and Admissibility, 430-431. One may note that the United States formulated its argument as a ground of inadmissibility. Commented upon by Damrosch, L., Multilateral Disputes, in Damrosch, L. (Ed.), The International Court of Justice at a Crossroads, Transnational Publishers, Inc., Dobbs Ferry, New York, 1987, pp. 376-400, 389-393.

[49] The 1989 Treaty between Australia and the Republic of Indonesia on the Zone of Cooperation in an Area between the Indonesian Province of East Timor and Northern Australia, 29 ILM 1990, pp. 475-537.

[50] See East Timor Case, paragraphs 11-18; Clark, R., Some International Law Aspects of the East Timor Affair, 5 LJIL 1992, pp. 265-271; and Stern, B., L'affaire du Timor oriental, 119 JDI 1992, pp. 740-745.

[51] East Timor Case, paragraph 19.

[52] Note the Australian claims to that effect registered in East Timor Case, paragraphs 27 and 30.

[53] East Timor Case, paragraph 28. See further paragraphs 29 and 33-35. A decision to this effect was anticipated by Greig, D., Third Party Rights and Intervention before the International Court, 32 VJIL 1992, pp. 285-376, 346-347 and 375 (note also his argument at 352, and footnote 238); and Hoogh, A. de, Intervention under Article 62 of the Statute and the Quest for Incidental Jurisdiction without the Consent of the Principal Parties, 6 LJIL 1993, pp. 17-46, 44.

[54] East Timor Case, paragraph 38. Judge Oda considered that the dismissal of the Portuguese claims had to be based on that State's lack of standing, since Portugal could no longer be considered the administrative power. Separate Opinion Oda, East Timor Case, paragraphs 1, 3, and 18-20. In contrast to this latter stance see Dissenting Opinion Skubiszewski, *ibid.*, paragraphs 100-104. Judge Vereshchetin claims that the Court should have based its refusal, at least partly, on the fact that there was no credible evidence of the support of the people of East Timor for the case brought by Portugal, and that the mere denomination of a State as administering power does not automatically confer the right to take action on behalf of the people concerned. Separate Opinion Vereshchetin, *ibid.*, 1-4.

[55] Or even to have exercised its faculty to bring counter-claims against Nicaragua in the already existing, and now closed, proceedings. See article 80 Rules of Court.

[56] Note in this respect the critical remarks by Mann, The Doctrine, 406.

[57] Peace Treaties Opinion, 71; Namibia Opinion, 23-24; Western Sahara Opinion, 22-28; Privileges and Immunities Opinion, 188-191. To some extent the argument has its basis in article 102, paragraph 2, second sentence, of the Rules of Court, which specifies that the Court shall consider: "(...) whether the request of the advisory opinion relates to a legal question actually pending between two or more States."

[58] Peace Treaties Opinion, 71 (also 72).

[59] Status of Eastern Carelia, Publications PCIJ, 1923, Series B, No. 5, p. 7, 28-29.

[60] Eastern Carelia Opinion, 27. For article 17 see the 1919 Covenant of the League of Nations, 13 AJIL 1919, Supplement, pp. 128-140.

[61] Eastern Carelia Opinion, 27-28.

[62] Namibia Opinion, 23-24; Western Sahara Opinion, 23-24. Note Seidl-Hohenveldern, *Actio Popularis*, 807. See also Visscher, Aspects récents, 41-43 and 195-202.

[63] In the Western Sahara Opinion, 24, the Court claimed regarding Spain's opposition: "It has not objected, and could not validly object, to the General Assembly's exercise of its powers to deal with the decolonization of a non-self-governing territory and to seek an opinion on questions relevant to the exercise of those powers."

[64] Western Sahara Opinion, 25. More broadly 25-27.

[65] Akhavan, P., Enforcement of the Genocide Convention Through the Advisory Opinion Jurisdiction of the International Court of Justice, 12 HRLJ 1991, pp. 285-299.

[66] Akhavan, Enforcement of the Genocide Convention, 293.

[67] Akhavan, Enforcement of the Genocide Convention, 296. Relying in this respect on the Court's Privileges and Immunities Opinion, 191.

[68] Privileges and Immunities Opinion, 189 read together with 191.

69 Generally Iwanejko, M., The Jurisdiction of the International Court of Justice: The Plea to the Admissibility, 1 PYIL 1966 67, pp. 164-182; Fitzmaurice, The Law and Procedure, volume 2, 438-440; Visscher, Aspects récents, 95-113; Annacker, Die Durchsetzung, 96-101. On these distinctions in relation to the merits see Fitzmaurice, *ibid.*, 448-451; and Mabrouk, Les exceptions de procédure, 278-291.

70 However, that is not to say that there could not be any claim, or that there had not been any internationally wrongful act. Contrary the Commission who claims, in article 22, Part One: "When the conduct of a State has created a situation not in conformity with the result required of it by an international obligation concerning the treatment to be accorded to aliens, whether natural or juridical persons, but the obligation allows that this or an equivalent result may nevertheless be achieved by subsequent conduct of the State, there is a breach of the obligation only if the aliens concerned have exhausted the effective local remedies available to them without obtaining the treatment called for by the obligation or, where that is not possible, an equivalent treatment." Text and Commentary Article 22, Part One, YBILC 1977, volume II, Part Two, pp. 30-50. It may be deduced from the position adopted here that the rule on the exhaustion of local remedies does not belong to the rules of Part One, but to the rules of Part Two of the ILC-draft.

71 The Court stated in Nuclear Tests (Australia *v.* France), Judgment, ICJ Reports 1974, p. 253, 270-271: "Thus the existence of a dispute is the primary condition for the Court to exercise its judicial function;" See Bos, Les conditions, 26-27; Aslaoui, O., Les conclusions et leurs modifications en procédure judiciaire internationale, Librairie Droz, Genève, 1963, 38-41; Mabrouk, Les exceptions de procédure, 134-135; Scandamis, N., Le jugement déclaratoire entre états, La séperabilité du contentieux international, Éditions A. Pedone, Paris, 1975, 181-186 and 249-252; Donner, R., International Adjudication: Using the International Court of Justice, with special reference to Finland, Suomalainen Tiedeakatemia, Helsinki, 1988, 90-91; Annacker, C., The Legal Régime of *Erga Omnes* Obligations in International Law, 46 AJPIL 1994, pp. 131-166, 162-163; Annacker, Die Durchsetzung, 100-101.

72 C.f. Visscher, Aspects récents, 30-31.

73 Mavrommatis Case, 11. For a critical comment see Cassese, A., The Concept of «Legal Dispute» in the Jurisprudence of the International Court, in Il processo internazionale, pp. 173-200, 179-182.

74 Though the Permanent Court contemplated as much. Case concerning the Payment of Various Serbian Loans issued in France, Publications PCIJ, 1929, Series A, No. 20, p. 5, 19 (and also 20). Abi-Saab, G., Les exceptions preliminaires dans la procédure de la Cour internationale, Étude des notions fondamentales de procédure et des moyens de leur mise en oeuvre, Éditions A. Pedone, Paris, 1967, 122, notes: "En droit international, le désaccord sur les faits est moins commun qu'en droit interne. En général, les différends portent sur des points de droit, c'est-à-dire soit sur l'interprétation d'une règle par rapport à une situation de fait non contestée, soit sur la qualification juridique d'une telle situation, ce qui, logiquement, revient au même." Cassese, The Concept, 179-180, claims: "(...) it is wrong to extend the concept of dispute to include the conflict of interests as a *separate issue* in respect of the conflict of legal views. Were this so, every instance of opposing interests should give rise to a legal dispute." Emphasis in the original.

75 See Dissenting Opinion Novacovitch, Serbian Loans Case, 80, on this issue.

76 The Permanent Court has claimed that it could decide disputes on some other basis than international law. It referred to the wide wording of article 36, paragraph 1, and to the possibility of it possessing jurisdiction to determine a fact under article 36 (c), of its Statute. Serbian Loans Case, 19-20. Pessôa and Novacovitch disagreed. Dissenting Opinion Pessôa, *ibid.*, 62-64; and Dissenting Opinion Novacovitch, *ibid.*, 79. Of course the phrase contained in article 38, paragraph 1, of the Statute "whose function is to decide in accordance with international law such disputes as are submitted to it" did not feature in the Statute of the Permanent Court. See Gordon, E., "Legal Disputes" Under Article 36(2) of the Statute, in Damrosch, The International Court, pp. 183-222, 192-195. On the other hand it may be noted that the Permanent Court disclaimed any power to prescribe a settlement on the basis of considerations of expediency only in the absence of any clear and explicit provision to that effect. Case of the Free Zones of Upper Savoy and the District of Gex (Second Phase), Publications PCIJ, 1930, Series A, No. 24, p. 4, 10 (also 11); also Observations Kellogg, *ibid.*, 32-42; and Case of the Free Zones of Upper Savoy and the District of Gex, Publications PCIJ, 1932, Series A B, No. 46, p. 96, 153 and 162.

77 South West Africa Cases, Preliminary Objections, 328. Earlier on, in 1950, the Court had observed: "Whether there exists an international dispute is a matter for objective determination. The mere denial of the existence of a dispute does not prove its non-existence. (...) There has thus arisen a situation in which the two sides hold clearly opposite views concerning the question of the performance or non-performance of certain treaty obligations." Peace Treaties Opinion, 74.

78 Cassese, The Concept, 176-177. The Permanent Court considered in relation to disputes: "In so far as concerns the word 'dispute', the Court observes that according to the tenor of Article 60 of the Statute, the manifestation of the existence of the dispute in a specific manner, as for instance by diplomatic negotiations, is

not required. It would no doubt be desirable that a State should not proceed to take as serious a step as summoning another State before the Court without having previously, within reasonable limits, endeavoured to make it quite clear that a difference of views is in question which has not been capable of being overcome otherwise. But in view of the wording of the article the Court considers that it cannot require that the dispute should have manifested itself in a formal way; according to the Court's view, it should be sufficient if the two Governments have in fact shown themselves as holding opposite views in regard to the meaning and scope of a judgment of the Court." Interpretation of Judgments Nos. 7 and 8 (The Chorzów Factory), Publications PCIJ, 1927, Series A, No. 13, p. 4, 10-11. Also Joint Dissenting Opinion Spender Fitzmaurice, South West Africa Cases, Preliminary Objections, 563.

[79] The Court observed in the East Timor Case: "Portugal has, rightly or wrongly, formulated complaints of fact and law against Australia which the latter has denied. By virtue of this denial, there is a legal dispute." East Timor Case, paragraph 22.

[80] Cassese, The Concept, 173-178 (especially 176-178), and 186. Similarly Visscher, Aspects récents, 31-33.

[81] Mavrommatis Case, 15: "The Court realises to the full the importance of the rule laying down that only disputes which cannot be settled by negotiation should be brought before it. It recognises, in fact, that before a dispute can be made the subject of an action at law, its subject matter should have been clearly defined by means of diplomatic negotiations." Cassese criticizes these observations on the basis that the object of the rule on diplomatic negotiations is to arrive at an out of court settlement, and not to define the subject-matter of the dispute. Cassese, The Concept, 181-182 and 184. See also Visscher, Aspects récents, 81-87; Abi-Saab, Les exceptions preliminaires, 120-130; and Ghozali, N.-E., La négociation diplomatique dans la jurisprudence internationale, Essai d'analyse, 25 RBDI 1992, pp. 323-350.

[82] Mavrommatis Case, 13. See also Donner, International Adjudication, 92. In a later case, in relation to the question whether a difference of opinion existed, the Permanent Court noted that one exists as soon as a government contends that an attitude adopted conflicts with its own views. It further held that even if one were to require the existence of a definite dispute, such a condition could be fulfilled: "(...) by means of the unilateral action on the part of the applicant Party." And it added: "The Court cannot allow itself to be hampered by a mere defect of form, the removal of which depends solely on the Party concerned." Case concerning certain German Interests, Publications PCIJ, 1926, Series A, No. 6, p. 4, 14. See also South West Africa Cases, Preliminary Objections, 345.

[83] South West Africa Cases, Preliminary Objections, 345-346; United States Diplomatic and Consular Staff in Tehran, Judgment, ICJ Reports, p. 3, 27. For comments on the latter case see Folz, H.-E., Bemerkungen zur völkerrechtlichen Beurteilung der Vorgänge um die amerikanischen Geiseln im Iran, in Münch, I. von (Ed.), Staatsrecht – Völkerrecht – Europarecht, Festschrift für Hans-Jürgen Schlochauer zum 75. Geburtstag am 28 März 1981, Walter de Gruyter, Berlin, 1981, pp. 271-288; Röling, B., Aspects of the Case concerning United States Diplomatic and Consular Staff in Tehran, 11 NYIL 1980, pp. 125-153; Stein (Ted), Contempt, Crisis, and the Court: the World Court and the Hostage Rescue Attempt, 76 AJIL 1982, pp. 499-533. In the Nicaragua Case the Court held that although Nicaragua had not in previously held negotiations referred to the 1956 treaty, it was not debarred from invoking its compromissory clause. Nicaragua Case, Jurisdiction and Admissibility, 428-429. The arguments on negotiations in these cases all relate to jurisdictional clauses. On negotiations required by a provision other than the jurisdictional clause itself see Armed Actions Case, Jurisdiction and Admissibility, 92-99.

[84] Note Declaration Oda, Questions of Interpretation and Application of the 1971 Montreal Convention arising from the Aerial Incident at Lockerbie (Libyan Arab Jamahiriya *v.* United Kingdom), Provisional Measures, Order, ICJ Reports 1992, p. 3, 18; Dissenting Opinion Bedjaoui, *ibid.*, 35-37; inconclusive Dissenting Opinion Weeramantry, *ibid.*, 51-52; Dissenting Opinion Ajibola, *ibid.*, 82-84; and Dissenting Opinion El-Kosheri, *ibid.*, 108-109.

[85] Salvioli acknowledged that the Permanent Court did not impose any condition to negotiate, but considered nevertheless that it applied unless a treaty excluded the need for negotiations. Salvioli, Problèmes de procédure, 565-566.

[86] Note Acevedo, D., Disputes Under Consideration by the U.N. Security Council or Regional Bodies, in Damrosch, The International Court, pp. 242-263, 244-248.

[87] Discussed by Scandamis, Le jugement déclaratoire, 181-186; and Gordon, Legal Disputes, 183-222.

[88] In the Haya de la Torre Case, Judgment, ICJ Reports 1951, p. 71, 79, the Court observed that the parties wanted it to: "(...) make a choice amongst the various courses by which the asylum may be terminated. But these courses are conditioned by the facts and by possibilities which, to a very large extent, the Parties are alone in a position to appreciate. A choice among them could not be based on legal considerations, but only on considerations of practicability or of political expediency; it is not part of the Court's judicial function to make such a choice." Note also Kellogg: "What is a political question? It is a question which is exclusively within

the competence of a sovereign State. (...) In passing upon a political question there is no rule or principle of law, no norm of equity, justice, or even good conscience, which the Court can apply;" Observations Kellogg, Free Zones Case, Second Phase, 41 (more generally 32-42).

[89] Armed Actions Case, Jurisdiction and Admissibility, 91. It added (*ibid.*, 106): "Nor should it be thought that the Court is unaware that the Application raises juridical questions which are only elements of a larger political situation. Those wider issues are however outside the competence of the Court, which is obliged to confine itself to these juridical questions."

[90] Admission Opinion, 61; Diplomatic Staff Case, Judgment, 19-20; Armed Actions Case, Jurisdiction and Admissibility, 91-92.

[91] Admission Opinion, 61; Expenses Opinion, 155.

[92] Admission Opinion, 61. In the Nicaragua Case the Court noted that if Nicaraguan support to the armed opposition in El Salvador constituted an armed attack, and if the other conditions for the exercise of a right of collective self-defence were met, the United States could invoke that justification notwithstanding the existence of an additional, perhaps even more decisive, motive derived from the political orientation of the Nicaraguan government. Nicaragua Case, Merits, 70-71.

[93] Expenses Opinion, 155.

[94] Diplomatic Staff Case, Judgment, 19. Immediately after Iran pointed to crimes committed by the United States in Iran (the 1953 *coup d'état*), its direct intervention in its internal affairs, and violations of other norms. The Court later on in its judgment rejected these considerations as possible justification of Iran's conduct. *Ibid.*, 37-41.

[95] Diplomatic Staff Case, Judgment, 20.

[96] McWhinney, E., Judicial Settlement of Disputes, Jurisdiction, Justiciability and Judicial Law-Making on the Contemporary International Court, Martinus Nijhoff Publishers, Dordrecht, 1991, 44, has put the issue as follows: "If it be accepted, then, that there is no objective, *a priori* basis for separating 'legal' from 'political' disputes, and the 'legal' disputes today are, if not also inherently 'political' then at least mixed, 'political'-and-'legal', then the criteria for separating the justiciable from the non-justiciable, and the exercise of Court jurisdiction from its non-exercise, become essentially pragmatic in character. Such criteria would involve judicial policy conclusions as to whether, and when, and in what degree, judicial interventionism on a particular tension-issue of contemporary international relations will help or hinder actual community problem-solving." More generally 37-46. In a later chapter he then goes on to identify basically three indices for guiding the Court as to justiciability: timing, fact-finding, and separation of powers. *Ibid.*, 134-147.

[97] *E.g.* Gordon, Legal Disputes, 189-190. See also Anand, R., International Courts and Contemporary Conflicts, Asia Publishing House, London, 1974, 228-241; and Mosler, H., Political and Justiciable Legal Disputes: Revival of an Old Controversy?, in Cheng, B., and Brown, E. (Eds.), Contemporary Problems: Essays in Honour of Georg Schwarzenberger on his eightieth birthday, Stevens & Sons Limited, London, 1988, pp. 216-229.

[98] Gordon, Legal Disputes, 191, observes: "Accordingly, if a claim based on international law cannot be judged objectively on the basis of the sources enumerated in Article 38(1), it must fail. In this event, however, it fails on its merits, not because it is unsuited for judgment."

[99] In the Case concerning right of passage over Indian territory (Preliminary Objections), Judgment, ICJ Reports 1957, p. 125, 142, the Court observed: "It is a rule of law generally accepted, as well as one acted upon in the past by the Court, that, once the Court has been validly seised of a dispute, unilateral action by the respondent State in terminating its Declaration, in whole or in part, cannot divest the Court of jurisdiction."

[100] Corfu Channel case, Judgment, ICJ Reports 1949, p. 244, 248; Fisheries Jurisdiction (United Kingdom *v.* Iceland), Merits, Judgment, ICJ Reports 1974, p. 3, 8-10; Nuclear Tests Case, Judgment, 257; Aegean Continental Shelf, Judgment, ICJ Reports 1978, p. 3, 20; Diplomatic Staff Case, Judgment, 9-10. In the Nicaragua Case, Merits, 23-24, the Court observed: "Furthermore the Court is bound to emphasize that the non-participation of a party in the proceedings at any stage of the case cannot, in any circumstances, affect the validity of its judgment. Nor does such validity depend upon the acceptance of that judgment by one party. The fact that a party purports to 'reserve its rights' in respect of a future decision of the Court, after the Court has determined that it has jurisdiction, is clearly of no effect on the validity of that decision. Under article 36, paragraph 6, of its Statute, the Court has jurisdiction to determine any dispute as to its own jurisdiction, and its judgment on that matter, as on the merits, is final and binding on the parties under Articles 59 and 60 of the Statute (...)."

[101] In agreement Schachter, O., Disputes involving the Use of Force, in Damrosch, The International Court, pp. 223-241, 238-239.

[102] An example may be found in the Northern Cameroons Case, in which the Court refused to adjudicate on the basis that: "The function of the Court is to state the law, but it may pronounce judgment only in connection with concrete cases where there exist at the time of the adjudication an actual controversy involving a conflict of legal interests between the parties. The Court's judgment must have some practical consequence in the sense that it can affect existing legal rights or obligations of the parties, thus removing uncertainty from their legal relations." Case concerning the Northern Cameroons (Cameroon *v.* United Kingdom), Preliminary Objections, Judgment, ICJ Reports 1963, p. 15, 33-34. More generally see 31-38. Another example might be seen to exist in the Nuclear Tests Case. There the Court declined to adjudicate Australian and New Zealand claims on the basis of its assessment that by virtue of French unilateral statements those claims no longer had any object. Nuclear Tests Case, Judgment, 262-263 and 267-272. See also Annacker, Die Durchsetzung, 100-103.

[103] Nicaragua Case, Jurisdiction and Admissibility, 436.

[104] Nicaragua Case, Jurisdiction and Admissibility, 437-438.

[105] To the extent that the argument was based on the alleged exclusive competence of the Security Council the Court of course did address it. See *infra* next section.

[106] Judge Oda claimed that the dispute did not constitute a "legal" dispute under article 36, paragraph 2, of the Statute. Dissenting Opinion Oda, Nicaragua Case, Merits, 233-236 (generally 219-246). At page 245 judge Oda concluded: "The present case is characterized by the fact that the dispute at issue, not being a *legal* dispute within the demonstrable meaning of article 36, paragraph 2, of the Statute, is one which the Respondent had never imagined as falling under the jurisdiction which it had voluntarily accepted." Emphasis in the original.

[107] The Court, discussing its relation to the Security Council, referred to the Corfu Channel Case and the Aerial Incident Cases. Nicaragua Case, Jurisdiction and Admissibility, 435. See generally Schachter, Disputes involving the Use of Force, 223-241.

[108] Dissenting Opinion Schwebel, Nicaragua Case, Merits, 294.

[109] Nicaragua Case, Jurisdiction and Admissibility, 437.

[110] Dissenting Opinion Schwebel, Nicaragua Case, Merits, 293-296. His position presupposes that a right of self-defence could be exercised in the circumstances of the case. The Court majority took the opposite position. Nicaragua Case, Merits, 122-123 and 146.

[111] Nicaragua Case, Merits, 122. The Court added (123) that United States action continued long after the period in which any presumed armed attack could be contemplated.

[112] Acevedo, Disputes under Consideration, 260, claims: "(...) it is difficult to imagine how the existence of such a fundamental right could be subject to adjudication by the I.C.J., particularly if one considers that the U.N. Charter itself prescribes that 'nothing in the present Charter shall impair the inherent right of individual or collective self-defense;' but the Court is, however, competent to adjudicate a dispute resulting from allegations, made by one of the parties, of improper or unlawful *exercise* of the right of self-defense." Emphasis in the original. The Court rejected the United States' justification of collective self-defence. Nicaragua Case, Merits, 123 and 146. And it stated (*ibid.*, 122) that the condition *sine qua non* (an armed attack) for the exercise of a right of collective self-defence was lacking. Nicaragua observed that there is no generalized right of self-defence; but only a right if an armed attack occurs. Nicaragua Case, Jurisdiction and Admissibility, 433. See also generally Rostow, E., Disputes involving the Inherent Right of Self-Defense, in Damrosch, The International Court, pp. 264-287.

[113] C.f. Schachter, Disputes involving the Use of Force, 229-231.

[114] Note for instance that Iraq's compliance with its disarmament obligations under resolution 687 is being enforced by the continuance of the general embargo instituted by resolution 661.

[115] *E.g.* Nicaragua Case, Jurisdiction and Admissibility, 437-438.

[116] Generally Klein, E., Paralleles Tätigwerden von Sicherheitsrat und Internationalem Gerichtshof bei Friedensbedrohenden Streitigkeiten, Zu Fragen der Zuständigkeit und Organtreue, in Bernhardt, R. (Ed.), Völkerrecht als Rechtsordnung – Internationale Gerichtsbarkeit – Menschenrechte, Festschrift für Hermann Mosler, Springer-Verlag, Berlin, 1983, pp. 468-491.

[117] Expenses Opinion, 163; repeated in the Nicaragua Case, Jurisdiction and Admissibility, 434.

[118] Expenses Opinion, 163-165.

[119] Diplomatic Staff Case, Judgment 21-22; Nicaragua Case, Jurisdiction and Admissibility, 434-435.

[120] Diplomatic Staff Case, Judgment, 21-22. Contrary the United Kingdom on Libya's request for provisional measures. Reported by Beveridge, F., The Lockerbie Affair, 41 ICLQ 1992, pp. 907-920, 918.

[121] Though it may be noted that resolution 731, adopted under Chapter VI, could have led to some conflict of opinion between the Court and the Security Council. In the light of the non-binding character of recommendations under that Chapter it is unlikely that the Court would have given that resolution precedence over rights

enjoyed by Libya. Comment by Beveridge, The Lockerbie Affair, 909-912 and 917-918; and Gowlland-Debbas, V., The Relationship between the International Court of Justice and the Security Council in the light of the *Lockerbie* Case, 88 AJIL 1994, pp. 643-677, 647 and footnote 26.

[122] Nicaragua Case, Jurisdiction and Admissibility, 434.

[123] Judge Schwebel observed: "Moreover, while the Security Council is invested by the Charter with the authority to determine the existence of an act of aggression, it does not act as a court in making such a determination. It may arrive at a determination of aggression – or, as more often is the case, fail to arrive at a determination of aggression – for political rather than legal reasons. However compelling the facts which could give rise to a determination of aggression, the Security Council acts within its rights when it decides that to make such a determination will set back the cause of peace rather than advance it. In short, the Security Council is a political organ which acts for political reasons. It may take legal considerations into account but, unlike a court, it is not bound to apply them." Dissenting Opinion Schwebel, Nicaragua Case, Merits, 290. Similar observations were made in Joint Dissenting Opinion Basdevant Winiarski McNair Read, Admission Opinion, 85.

[124] Gowlland-Debbas, The Relationship, 656, claims that the Court has stated in the jurisdiction and admissibility phase of the Nicaragua Case, that: "(...) even after a determination under Article 39, there is no necessary inconsistency between Security Council action and adjudication by the Court." However, it must be pointed out that that phrase reflects the Court's summary of the Nicaraguan point of view and not the view of the Court itself. See Nicaragua Case, Jurisdiction and Admissibility, 432.

[125] Genocide Convention Case, Provisional Measures, 8 April 1993, 18-19.

[126] Admission Opinion, 64.

[127] Expenses Opinion, 168.

[128] Expenses Opinion, 168.

[129] Expenses Opinion, 168.

[130] Watson, G., Constitutionalism, Judicial Review, and the World Court, 34 HILJ 1993, pp. 1-45, 15 (generally 14-17). The reference is to Expenses Opinion, 157.

[131] Namibia Opinion, 45.

[132] Text of the question in Namibia Opinion, 17.

[133] Namibia Opinion, 45-50.

[134] C.f. Watson, Constitutionalism, 17-22.

[135] Gowlland-Debbas, V., Collective Responses to Illegal Acts in International Law, United Nations Action in the Question of Southern Rhodesia, Martinus Nijhoff Publishers, Dordrecht, 1990, 451-452. Also Gowlland-Debbas, Security Council Enforcement, 72, 74, and 97-98.

[136] Watson, Constitutionalism, 4-14.

[137] Diplomatic Staff Case, Judgment, 21-22.

[138] Nicaragua Case, Jurisdiction and Admissibility, 432-433.

[139] Nicaragua Case, Jurisdiction and Admissibility, 436.

[140] See Patil, A., The UN Veto in World Affairs 1946-1990, A Complete Record and Case Histories of the Security Council's Veto, Unifo Publishers, Sarasota, Florida, 1992, 348-354.

[141] See also Reisman, W., The Legal Effect of Vetoed Resolutions, 74 AJIL 1980, pp. 904-907. Note also Graefrath, B., Oeser, E., and Steiniger, P., Internationale Verbrechen – Internationale Delikte, 22 DA 1977, pp. 90-101, 96, who observe that the existence of aggression is not dependent on a prior determination to that effect by the Security Council.

[142] Comments by McGinley, G., The I.C.J.'s Decision in the Lockerbie Cases, 22 GJICL 1992, pp. 577-601; Kooijmans, P., Zwijgt het recht als de Veiligheidsraad spreekt?, Uitspraak van het Internationaal Gerechtshof in de Lockerbie-zaak van 14 april 1992, 67 NJB 1992, pp. 847-851; Beveridge, The Lockerbie Affair, 907-920; and Gowlland-Debbas, The Relationship, 643-677. See also Osieke, E., The Legal Validity of *Ultra Vires* Decisions of International Organizations, 77 AJIL 1983, pp. 239-256; Lauterpacht, Aspects of the Administration, 37-54 and 112-114; Franck, T., The "Powers of Appreciation": Who is the Ultimate Guardian of UN Legality?, 86 AJIL 1992, pp. 519-523; Bloed, A., "Toetsing" van besluiten Veiligheidsraad, 67 NJB 1992, pp. 661-663; Watson, Constitutionalism, 1-45; Bedjaoui, M., Du contrôle de légalité des actes du Conseil de Securité, in Nouveaux itinéraires en droit, Hommage à François Rigaux, Bruylant, Bruxelles, 1993, pp. 69-110.

[143] See A 46 827.

[144] Lockerbie Case, Provisional Measures, 15.

[145] That phrase could be intended to convey merely the same meaning as the one spoken of earlier, namely that the Court, at the stage of provisional measures, considered that *prima facie* the obligation of article 25 extends to resolution 748. The separate and dissenting opinions indicate that at least some judges have in mind the possibility of review of resolution 748. See Declaration Oda, Lockerbie Case, Provisional Measures, 17;

Separate Opinion Lachs, *ibid.*, 27; Separate Opinion Shahabuddeen, *ibid.*, 28, 29 and 32; Dissenting Opinion Bedjaoui, *ibid.*, 35 and 41-46; Dissenting Opinion Weeramantry, *ibid.*, 50 and 55-67; Dissenting Opinion Ajibola, *ibid.*, 91-92; Dissenting Opinion El-Kosheri, *ibid.*, 101-107.

146 C.f. Dissenting Opinion Bedjaoui, Lockerbie Case, Provisional Measures, 41 and 46.

147 Genocide Convention Case, Provisional Measures, 8 April 1993, 8; and *ibid.*, Provisional Measures, 13 September 1993, 332-333.

148 Genocide Convention Case, Provisional Measures, 8 April 1993, 18-20.

149 Genocide Convention Case, Provisional Measures, 13 September 1993, 345.

150 Genocide Convention Case, Provisional Measures, 8 April 1993, 18-19.

151 Genocide Convention Case, Provisional Measures, 8 April 1993, 19.

152 Genocide Convention Case, Provisional Measures, 8 April 1993, 19.

153 Note the opinions indicating that the question of review may come up in the remainder of the proceedings of the case. Declaration Oda, Lockerbie Case, Provisional Measures, 17; Separate Opinion Lachs, *ibid.*, 26-27; Separate Opinion Shahabuddeen, *ibid.*, 28-29; Dissenting Opinion Bedjaoui, *ibid.*, 41-47; Dissenting Opinion Weeramantry, *ibid.*, 50; Dissenting Opinion Ajibola, *ibid.*, 91-92. See also Hoogh, A. de, Comments, in Post, H. (Ed.), International Economic Law and Armed Conflict, Martinus Nijhoff Publishers, Dordrecht, 1994, pp. 43-46, 45-46.

154 United States Diplomatic and Consular Staff in Tehran, Provisional Measures, Order, ICJ Reports 1979, p. 7, 19; repeated, in somewhat changed form, in the Passage through the Great Belt, Provisional Measures, Order, ICJ Reports 1991, p. 12, 17; Genocide Convention Case, Provisional Measures, 8 April 1993, 19; Genocide Convention Case, Provisional Measures, 13 September 1993, 342. It is often indicated that provisional measures are to protect rights "pending final decision". Arbitral Award of 31 July 1989, Provisional Measures, Order, ICJ Reports 1990, p. 64, 69-70; Great Belt Case, Provisional Measures, 17-20; Genocide Convention Case, Provisional Measures, 8 April 1993, 19. The Permanent Court has observed that the provision on provisional measures applies in principle to the effect that: "(...) the parties to a case must abstain from any measure capable of exercising a prejudicial effect in regard to the execution of the decision to be given (...)." The Electricity Company of Sofia and Bulgaria, Publications PCIJ, Series A B, No. 79, p. 194, 199.

155 Generally see Sztucki, Interim Measures, 106-112. The Permanent Court has observed that provisional measures were to preserve rights in so far as: "(...) the damage threatening these rights would be irreparable in fact or in law;" Legal Status of the South-Eastern Territory of Greenland, Publications PCIJ, 1932, Series A B, No. 48, p. 268, 284.

156 Sztucki, Interim Measures, 109, quite correctly notes: "Indeed, there are no violations of rights which could not be made good *in law* by a reparation. This is true not only of financial or other economic injury but also of all other injuries not measurable in pecuniary terms." It is odd to note that some writers discussing the issue of irreparable prejudice state that this involves the impossibility of compensating the requesting party. Haver, P., The Status of Interim Measures of the International Court of Justice after the Iranian-Hostage Crisis, 11 CWILJ 1981, pp. 515-542, 517 and 534-535; and Merrills, Interim Measures, 108-109 (generally 107-110). In this they can rely on the observations of the Permanent Court to the effect that the infraction of rights: "(...) could not be made good simply by the payment of an indemnity or by compensation or restitution in some other material form." Sino-Belgian Treaty Case, Series A, No. 8, p. 6, 7.

157 Nicaragua Case, Merits, 144. Emphasis added.

158 Chorzów Factory Case, Merits, 47.

159 Genocide Convention Case, Provisional Measures, 13 September 1993, 349.

160 Diplomatic Staff Case, Provisional Measures, 11.

161 Diplomatic Staff Case, Provisional Measures, 16. This shows that the power to indicate provisional measures constitutes an example of incidental jurisdiction. On incidental jurisdiction generally Briggs, H., La compétence incidente de la Cour internationale de Justice en tant que compétence obligatoire, 64 RGDIP 1960, pp. 217-229.

162 Declaration Tarassov, Genocide Convention Case, Provisional Measures, 8 April 1993, 26-27; Dissenting Opinion Tarassov, *ibid.*, Provisional Measures, 13 September 1993, 449-452. Dissenting Opinion Kreca, *ibid.*, 462-463. See further Separate Opinion Shahabuddeen, *ibid.*, 355-356; Separate Opinion Lauterpacht, *ibid.*, 409-412. The Permanent Court had once refused to indicate provisional measures because they were: "(...) designed to obtain an interim judgment in favour of a part of the claim (...)." Case concerning the Factory at Chorzów (Indemnities), Publications PCIJ, Series A, No. 12, p. 9, 10.

163 Declaration Tarassov, Genocide Convention Case, Provisional Measures, 8 April 1993, 26-27; Dissenting Opinion Tarassov, *ibid.*, Provisional Measures, 13 September 1993, 449-452.

[164] Merrills, Interim Measures, 119. He further noted, however, that it would be absurd to suggest that the Court ought to make orders affecting both sides equally, and also that the presence of counter allegations is not a good enough reason to direct measures to both parties. *Ibid.*, 118-119.

[165] Diplomatic Staff Case, Provisional Measures, 11.

[166] Diplomatic Staff Case, Provisional Measures, 16-17.

[167] Genocide Convention Case, Provisional Measures, 8 April 1993, 24.

[168] Genocide Convention Case, Provisional Measures, 13 September 1993, 346-347.

[169] On jurisdiction in relation to provisional measures see Aegean Sea Continental Shelf, Interim Protection, Order, ICJ Reports 1976, p. 3, 13; Nicaragua Case, Provisional Measures, 178-179; Arbitral Award Case, Provisional Measures, 68-69; The Great Belt Case, Provisional Measures, 15; Genocide Convention Case, Provisional Measures, 8 April 1993, 11-18.

[170] Nicaragua Case, Provisional Measures, 182; Lockerbie Case, Provisional Measures, 14; Genocide Convention Case, Provisional Measures, 8 April 1993, 22; Genocide Convention Case, Provisional Measures, 13 September 1993, 347. In the two latter orders the Court added issues of imputability.

[171] They are further circumscribed by the respective claims of the parties. The Permanent Court refused to indicate measures since those: "(...) would result in a general suspension of the agrarian reform in so far as concerns Polish nationals of German race, and cannot therefore be regarded as solely designed to protect the subject of the dispute and the actual object of the principal claim (...)." Case concerning the Polish Agrarian Reform and the German Minorities (Interim Measures of Protection), Publications PCIJ, Series A B, No. 58, p. 175, 178. The Court refused to indicate a provisional measure requested by Greece because it did not form the subject of any claim set out in the application; and it refused the provisional measures requested by Guinea-Bissau because they did not relate to that State's claims. Respectively Aegean Sea Case, Interim Protection, 11; and Arbitral Award Case, Provisional Measures, 69-70. See also Haver, The Status, 517-518.

[172] Provisional measures are intended to protect rights "pending final decision". See Arbitral Award Case, Provisional Measures, 69; The Great Belt Case, Provisional Measures, 17; Genocide Convention Case, Provisional Measures, 8 April 1993, 19; and *ibid.*, Provisional Measures, 13 September 1993, 342.

[173] Diplomatic Staff Case, Provisional Measures, 19; The Great Belt Case, Provisional Measures, 16; Genocide Convention Case, Provisional Measures, 8 April 1993, 19.

[174] On urgency see the Great Belt Case, Provisional Measures, 17-18; and Merrils, Interim Measures, 110-113.

[175] The order of the Court in the Frontier Dispute Case followed within 8 days of the request. See Merrills, Interim Measures, 142, footnote 153.

[176] Exception made in this regard to the dispute between Burkina Faso and Mali. See Frontier Dispute, Provisional Measures, Order, ICJ Reports 1986, p. 3, 8-12.

[177] On this see Separate Opinion Ajibola, Genocide Convention Case, Provisional Measures, 13 September 1993, 400-403.

[178] C.f. Sztucki, Interim Measures, 294-298. Oxman, B., Jurisdiction and the Power to Indicate Provisional Measures, in Damrosch, The International Court, pp. 323-354, 331-332, observes that the failure to comply with provisional measures coupled to other circumstances could be considered to constitute a threat to the peace.

[179] Sztucki, Interim Measures, 299.

[180] On enforcement see Haver, The Status, 526-541; and Sztucki, Interim Measures, 294-302.

[181] On binding nature see Haver, The Status, 518-526; and Sztucki, Interim Measures, 280-294.

[182] Continental Shelf (Tunisia Libyan Arab Jamahiriya), Application to Intervene, Judgment, ICJ Reports 1981, p. 3; Continental Shelf (Libyan Arab Jamahiriya Malta), Application to Intervene, Judgment, ICJ Reports 1984, p. 3; Land, Island and Maritime Frontier Dispute (El Salvador Honduras), Application to Intervene, Judgment, ICJ Report 1990, p. 92. The two cases of intervention under article 63 of the Statute were decided without any separate order or judgment being made by the Court. The S.S. Wimbledon, Publications PCIJ, 1923, Series A, No. 1, p. 6, 9-14; Haya de la Torre Case, Judgment, 73-77. The Court decided, by way of order, that El Salvador's Declaration of Intervention under article 63 was inadmissible. Military and Paramilitary Activities in and against Nicaragua (Nicaragua *v.* United States of America), Declaration of Intervention, Order, ICJ Reports 1984, p. 215, 216.

[183] C.f. Rosenne, Procedure, Commentary, 149, footnote 1. Contrary Separate Opinion Weeramantry, Genocide Convention Case, Provisional Measures, 13 September 1993, 374-389; Separate Opinion Ajibola, *ibid.*, 397-400.

[184] Diplomatic Staff Case, Provisional Measures, 21; with a less standard formulation Nicaragua Case, Provisional Measures, 187; Genocide Convention Case, Provisional Measures, 8 April 1993, 24; Genocide Convention Case, Provisional Measures, 13 September 1993, 350. Some have thought to deny the legality of unilateral measures for the enforcement of substantive obligations in view of the existence of judicial

proceedings alone, or because of provisional measures rendered in pursuit thereof. *E.g.* Hakenberg, M., Die Iran-Sanktionen der USA während der Teheraner Geiselaffäre aus völkerrechtlicher Sicht, Verlag Peter Lang, Frankfurt am Main, 1988, 255-257. At this latter page, and at 259, he observes that Iran's non-compliance with the indicated provisional measures revived the right to self-help.

[185] Noted by the Court in the Diplomatic Staff Case, Judgment, 17.

[186] Diplomatic Staff Case, Judgment, 28. The Court made this observation in relation to the question whether the United States, notwithstanding its measures, could still invoke the Treaty of Amity, Economic Relations, and Consular Relations. *Ibid.*, 27-28.

[187] Judges Lachs, Morozov (implicitly), and Tarazi claimed that an applicant State could not lawfully exercise any right to resort to countermeasures or to use force pending proceedings before the Court. Separate Opinion Lachs, Diplomatic Staff Case, Judgment, 48; Dissenting Opinion Morozov, *ibid.*, 53 and 55; Dissenting Opinion Tarazi, *ibid.*, 63-64.

[188] C.f. Sztucki, Interim Measures, 299-302.

[189] Diplomatic Staff Case, Judgment, 43.

[190] Diplomatic Staff Case, Judgment, 43.

[191] Sztucki appears to doubt the legality of the use of force on the territory of the other party on the basis of provisional measures indicated by the Court. Sztucki, Interim Measures, 301-302. On this latter page he states: "The Court's position also seems to indicate that the limits of tolerable self-help in connection with the indication of provisional measures do not differ from what is regarded as admissible in this field in international law in general."

FINAL OBSERVATIONS

In the Introduction to this thesis it has been noted that the Commission envisaged the elaboration of more severe consequences applicable to those internationally wrongful acts defined as international crimes in article 19, paragraph 2, Part One, of the ILC-draft on State responsibility.[1] It has further been indicated that the purpose of the research underlying this thesis has been to examine whether it is possible to envisage a régime of responsibility applicable to international crimes that would be substantially aggravated compared to the régime of responsibility applicable to international delicts. To that end it was proposed to attempt to identify the aggravated consequences of the régime of responsibility applicable to crimes. In consequence the first two chapters investigated questions of legal interest, and rights to invoke the responsibility of an author State, on the part of States and the international community personified in the United Nations. The third chapter went on to discuss whether an extended scope of obligations under the specific forms of reparation could be envisaged in case of crimes. Chapters four and five approached the issue of aggravated consequences from the viewpoint of enforcement by way of countermeasures or the use of armed force directed against the author State of a crime. In chapter six the obstacles which could prevent the Court from settling a dispute, or giving advice, regarding international crimes were looked into. The more salient conclusions on the aggravated consequences under a possible régime applicable to international crimes will now be put into a somewhat more broad perspective.

The investigation of the first chapter has shown that all States are in possession of a legal interest, and that they are entitled to invoke the responsibility of an author State, regarding international crimes. That conclusion is reflected in article 5, paragraph 3, Part Two, of the ILC-draft, which defines all States as injured in case of international crimes.[2] However, the injured State status consequent upon the commission of a crime only constitutes an aggravated consequence in regard to the crime of aggression. Obligations underlying the other crimes, regarding self-determination and basic human rights, are of such a nature that their breach, whether of minor or serious character, entails the right to invoke the responsibility on the part of all States bound by the rule. As the rules on the right of self-determination and basic human rights exist also under universal customary international law, all States possess the right to invoke the responsibility of an author State for breaches of obligation not amounting to international crimes. Article 5, paragraph 2 (e) (iii), Part Two, supports that conclusion.

For these reasons the dictum of the Court in the Barcelona Traction Case on obligations *erga omnes* does not really add anything to solving questions of legal interest.[3] That obligations *erga omnes* (or, as it was also put, to the international community as a whole) are the concern of all States and that they all have a legal interest regarding genocide and the protection of basic rights of the human person (including freedom from slavery and racial discrimination) flows from the nature of the rules for the protection of human rights generally. As no State will be affected if another State violates the human rights of its nationals, all States bound by the particular rule in question must logically be deemed to possess the right to invoke the responsibility of the State breaching its human rights obligations. Only the legal interest of all States pursuant to the commission of the crime of aggression can then be considered to relate to a true obligation *erga omnes*.

The United Nations similarly are in possession of a legal interest pursuant to the commission of an international crime. However, the practice of the Security Council does not support the conclusion that a situation in which a crime is committed will necessarily be considered, as a minimum, a threat to the peace under article 39 of the Charter.[4] For that reason claims by some that reactions to international crimes should exclusively take place through action of the Security Council under Chapter VII could not, and should not, form the basis for the régime applicable to crimes. In this respect Arangio-Ruiz has proposed to allow every State to bring allegations of the commission of a crime before the Court if the General Assembly or the Security Council had previously resolved that the allegations were substantial enough to warrant the grave concern of the international community.[5] The Court's judicial determination of the existence of a crime would constitute a prerequisite for States to demand reparation or to resort to countermeasures.[6]

His arguments to opt in favour of a determination by the Court rather than the Assembly or the Council fail to convince.[7] As he observes, the Assembly is by far the more representative organ of the United Nations, but the absence of any decision-making power on its part makes it difficult to envisage a more substantial role for the Assembly within the organized international community. Arangio-Ruiz has further pointed to the Security Council's less democratic, and hence less representative, character. But the main reason brought forward by Arangio-Ruiz against letting the Council determine the existence of a crime is its political character. Yet the Council has been allotted the function of guardian of international peace and security, and in that capacity has been given the power to determine any threat to the peace, breach of the peace, or act of aggression. Far-reaching consequences, on the factual as well as the legal plane, may entail for States consequent upon such a determination by the Council: the imposition of measures against a targeted State, and the possibility of armed action against such a State. But all this has not prevented States from conferring those powers on the Security Council notwithstanding its political character.

Turning now to substantive issues of reparation, the conclusion must be that the extended scope of guarantees against repetition forms an aggravated consequence of the régime of crimes. Two main categories may be identified. Guarantees related to the police, paramilitary and armed forces, which may include, *inter alia*, disarmament, destruction of weapons, and the re-organization of such forces. And guarantees related to the State organization, which may include, among others, the prosecution and punishment of responsible individuals, governmental and constitutional change, free elections, and respect for human rights. In the extreme case of an attempt at genocide, an affected people may, subject to geographical and demographical circumstances, exercise its right to self-determination.

Considering the far-reaching character of such guarantees it would seem obvious that they cannot simply be demanded, imposed, or implemented, whether by way of countermeasures or the use of armed force, by States individually. Though this has been the practice related to the peace treaties after World Wars I and II, the more recent example of Security Council resolution 687, sometimes called the modern equivalent of a peace treaty, constitutes an improvement. However, while not denying in any way the necessity of a large part of the measures imposed by means of that resolution, it cannot but be noted that there is no possibility whatsoever of dispute settlement on points regarding which Iraq might have legitimate grievances. Certainly one of these concerned the demarcation of its border with Kuwait, which turned out not just to be a case of demarcation but also, at least partly, one of delimitation.[8]

Even more serious concerns may be voiced regarding the way in which the implementation and enforcement of Iraq's disarmament obligations have been taken on. For four years now Iraq and its population have been subjected to a comprehensive trade embargo on the ground that Iraq has not in any satisfactory manner fulfilled its disarmament obligations. It is an open secret however that the continued rule of Saddam Hussein in Iraq constitutes the main reason for the United Kingdom and the United States to oppose, within the Security Council, the lifting of the sanctions.[9] While the plight of the Iraqi population is to a large extent due to Iraq's obstinate refusal to accept the offer to export oil for purposes of humanitarian relief, all this could have been prevented if the Coalition forces had marched on to Baghdad and taken it upon themselves to implement Iraq's obligations in the field of guarantees against repetition. Admittedly, the implementation of guarantees regarding the Iraqi State organization probably would have posed serious problems. The reasons for not taking on that task must have been the fear of chaos due to potential claims of self-determination by the Kurdish people, the likelihood of Shiite rule analogous to that in Iran, and the resultant necessity for the prolonged occupation of Iraq as a whole. Yet even so one might have expected a reconsideration of the available options when the Kurds and the Shiites rose against the government in Baghdad.

In this relation it may be noted that the Security Council later on established the Tribunals on the former Yugoslavia and Rwanda,[10] but that no tribunal was created to prosecute, convict and punish those individuals responsible for the commission of Iraq's crime of aggression or Somalia's crime of widespread breaches of basic human rights obligations. With regard to Iraq one explanation may be that since there was not going to be any occupation of Iraq, there would also not be any real possibility of ever laying hands on the guilty persons. Yet that does not seem to have stopped the Security Council in relation to the former Yugoslavia: it remains to be seen whether Karadzic or Mladic will ever appear before the Tribunal notwithstanding their indictments of 25 July 1995. Another explanation may be that if a tribunal would have been set up to prosecute Iraqi crimes, there might have been a call to also prosecute those responsible for war crimes on the side of the Coalition forces. From a public relations point of view no victorious army wants to be subjected to slurs on the record of its success story.

On a more general note it may be observed that the major obstacle regarding the prosecution of individuals lies with the impossibility of getting hold of them. Even a transition from a military government to a civilian one, or from a dictature to a democracy, will not necessarily change that picture. As experience has shown, especially in Latin America, but also in relation to Cambodia and South Africa, the prosecution of former political and military leaders after a negotiated deal remains problematical. This latter aspect also explains the difficulties encountered, with respect to the former Yugoslavia as well as Somalia, during negotiations or attempts at reconciliation, since the same people who could be accused of having committed serious crimes are the ones whose co-operation may be essential or necessary to bring the negotiations or attempts at reconciliation to a successful close.

It has also been argued by the present writer that all States can exercise their rights to resort to countermeasures against the author State of a crime. This constitutes a special or supplementary consequence regarding the crime of aggression, though a request by the directly injured State, if possible, must precede such exercises. In view of the nature and gravity of international crimes neither injured States, nor the Security Council, are under any obligation to refrain from adopting countermeasures on the basis of a mere verbal admission of responsibility, or offer of dispute settlement, on the part of the author State. The latter's adequate performance of reparation obligations may terminate the right to adopt countermeasures. In view of the potentially long time span necessary to implement the appropriate guarantees, the right to resort to countermeasures may revive in cases of serious set-backs. The adoption of countermeasures by injured States or the Security Council may not, however, infringe the basic human rights of the nationals of the author State.

The existence of any faculty of unilateral resort to countermeasures has been disputed especially by non-Western States. They aptly perceived that only Western States could muster the necessary, sufficiently large scale, and hence relatively more effective, economic power to make a difference in regard to issues of enforcement. In view of the large degree of cohesion within the Western block, they similarly descried that exercises of rights to resort to countermeasures would most likely be directed against non-Western States. Such proved to be the case especially in relation to the Falklands, hostages, Afghan and Polish crises, in response to which Western States adopted measures against Argentina, Iran and the Soviet Union respectively. While denying the legality as well as the legitimacy of recourse to unilateral, or concerted, economic countermeasures by Western States, non-Western States insisted on such measures against the territory of Rhodesia and South Africa. The Security Council over time adopted comprehensive sanctions against the former,[11] but in face of Western opposition came no further than a broad arms embargo regarding the latter.[12] Due to the coming into power of Gorbachov and the resultant end of the Cold War, the Iraq-Kuwait and Yugoslav crises have led to the imposition of comprehensive sanctions by the Security Council.[13]

However, as noted some time ago by Secretary-General Boutros-Ghali, sanctions constitute a blunt instrument.[14] Within a targeted State they will affect the least influential groups the first and the most. And, as observed also by the Secretary-General, the behaviour of the political leaders of a State is not likely to be affected by the plight of their people.[15] The more pertinent examples in this respect are provided by Iraq, and, independently from any countermeasures issue, by Somalia. It follows from this that the instrument of countermeasures is most unlikely to be very effective in obtaining cessation and restitution in case of crimes, let alone the far-reaching guarantees against repetition necessary to prevent repetition of the crime. Though the arms destruction programme regarding Iraq, set out in resolution 687, seems almost to have been completed, the accomplishment of the more covert goal of disposing Saddam Hussein as political leader of Iraq may still take some more time.

The right of collective self-defence, which may be exercised against armed attacks, bears witness to, and constitutes, the supplementary consequence in respect of the crime of aggression. Under contemporary international law the other international crimes, denial of self-determination and widespread breaches of basic human rights obligations, cannot be countered by the use of armed force in the exercise of any right of humanitarian intervention or by invoking a state of necessity. The Security Council possesses the power under article 39 of the Charter to determine a threat to the peace, breach of the peace, or act of aggression, and to decide on the measures of article 41, or take action under article 42, to maintain or restore international peace and security. In view of the lack of the agreements anticipated in article 43 it has not been able to take direct action under article 42. Yet it has overcome that obstacle by authorizing States to resort to the use of armed force against particular States. Thus armed action could lawfully be taken by States against Iraq, and in Somalia, Rwanda, and Haiti. These decisions by the Security Council to authorize the use of armed force furthermore show that the use of armed force may be appropriate also in circumstances other than armed conflict between States.

Be that as it may, practice has shown that States are not altogether eager to take part in armed enforcement action, or for that matter in peace-keeping operations.[16] There can be little doubt that the experience in Somalia has contributed significantly to the unwillingness of States to engage in what they consider to be risky business. Perhaps this may provide the explanation for the tardy and in essence ineffective response to the commission of genocide in Rwanda. The Somalian and Rwandan crises show however, at least in the mind of the present writer, that the use of armed force should not be considered only in the last resort, but rather, and in fact predominantly, as the typical response to the international crime of widespread breaches of basic human rights obligations.

Within the Commission there appears to be a body of opinion that wishes to reaffirm, express and establish the prohibition of countermeasures involving the threat or use of armed force also in regard to responses against international crimes. Arangio-Ruiz has proposed to allow the adoption of urgent, interim measures to protect the right of the injured State or to limit the damage caused by the crime. Such measures could be aimed at securing immediate access to victims or preventing the continuation of genocide. Yet at the same time he has not challenged the applicability in case of crimes of the prohibition of armed countermeasures, and it is therefore difficult to see how urgent, interim measures could involve the use of armed force. While prohibiting armed action in response to crimes would conform to the present state of international law, it may be submitted that present-day realities allow for the progressive development of the law in this respect. Any future convention on State responsibility would be less than ideal if it failed to provide for resort to armed force in order to ensure the effective suppression of conduct constituting crimes.

Of course, as indicated above, the far-reaching character of the guarantees necessary to prevent repetition should lead one to conclude that they should not be imposed by States unilaterally. If a unilateral right to resort to armed force were to be envisaged in response to the crime of widespread breaches of basic human rights obligations, it would have to be restricted to the goal of effecting cessation of the crime, restitution, and disarmament. As the implementation of the other guarantees against repetition, especially guarantees regarding the State organization, may in themselves already necessitate a prolonged presence in the targeted State, the forces of any (group of) State(s) should be relieved by a United Nations force as soon as a secure and stable environment would have been created. It must be stressed that such a United Nations force could be a peace-keeping force based on the consent of the State or parties involved, or a peace-enforcing unit based on the Council's exercise of powers under Chapter VII. The guarantees against repetition envisaged in case of crimes, whether related to the police, paramilitary or armed forces or to the State organization, may be demanded in law, and may be enforced or implemented by way of countermeasures or the use of armed force.

Special rapporteur Arangio-Ruiz has proven to be particularly progressive on issues of adjudication. As already noted he has proposed to have the Court determine the existence (and attribution) of a crime on the request of any State, subject to a prior decision of the General Assembly or the Security Council that the allegations warrant the grave concern of the international community. In view of the gravity of international crimes he has further proposed to confer jurisdiction on the Court to settle any dispute on the implementation of the legal consequences of crimes.

Although the present writer has nothing but praise for the envisaged broad role to be played by the Court in relation to crimes, it may be submitted that the Court would not be right organ of the United Nations to concern itself with the subject of guarantees against repetition. First of all any dispute on such issues would be likely to come before the Court only if there is still some sort of effective government capable of representing the targeted State. Yet the guarantees that may be demanded relate to the prosecution of responsible individuals, a change of government and the organization of free elections. It would be odd if the agents of the State before the Court would be the same whose prosecution is demanded. If there is no effective government, as in Somalia for instance, any dispute would not come before the Court until after the re-establishment of such a government. Yet that, as has also been noted earlier, might take quite some time.

More importantly, the implementation of the specific guarantees against repetition would seem to require the making of choices which are not inherently decided by application of legal rules or principles. What kind of coercion, countermeasures or the use of armed force, will be necessary to prevent repetition of the crime; if there is to be any resort to armed force, will it be necessary to occupy the territory and how many troops would that take; which kind of weapons are to be destroyed; which political groups or parties would have to be outlawed; which individuals would have to be prosecuted; what kind of political or constitutional structures would best prevent repetition; what long-term arrangements would have to be put in place to monitor possible set-backs? All these questions, and more besides, would have to be decided on the basis of expediency and the circumstances prevailing within the territory. It may be submitted that, if there is to be any role for the Court in this respect, it must be fully retrospective. A way out of these difficulties would be the existence of any agreement between the parties within the State, or between the government or the parties within a State and the United Nations, formulating the necessary goals, measures and guarantees. The interpretation and application of such an agreement would be a suitable subject for adjudication by the Court.

In the light of the foregoing there can be no doubt that a substantially aggravated régime of responsibility applicable to international crimes may fruitfully be elaborated. The essential features of such a régime would relate to the reparation obligations of the author State and the possibility of resort to armed force by injured States or the United Nations. The goal of resort to armed force would be to impose cessation of criminal conduct, restitution, and the implementation of far-reaching guarantees against repetition.

It is submitted furthermore that the assumptions which formed the basis of the research have been proved correct.

The first assumption was that the consequences applicable in case of delicts attach also to crimes. In this respect the prohibition of the threat or use of armed force does present some problems. However, from a purely theoretical point of view the use of armed force could be envisaged also against the author State of a delict. Under Chapter VII the Security Council is not, moreover, restricted to reacting against conduct constituting crimes.

The assumption that there are only two régimes of responsibility would appear to be sound. Though it may be difficult to draw a precise line between where a delict stops and a crime starts, it may be submitted that the application of the criteria to determine the existence of a crime, the essential importance of the obligation, the seriousness of the breach, and premeditation on the part of the author State, could lead to substantially similar results.

Finally the assumption that the régime of responsibility applicable to international crimes would apply in a uniform manner to all the crimes mentioned in article 19, paragraph 3, Part One, should be upheld. Though from a *de lege lata* view the use of armed force cannot be resorted to in respect of the crime of widespread breaches of basic human rights obligations, that possibility should be envisaged as a matter of progressive development.

As noted earlier Arangio-Ruiz has proposed to let the Court determine the existence of a crime at the request of any State, provided that the General Assembly or the Security Council decided previously that the allegations warrant the grave concern of the international community.

A problematical aspect of the proposed construction is that the experience in the last fifty years related to cases before the Court on breaches of human rights obligations has not been exactly favourable. Even if the Assembly or the Council would have resolved that the allegations warrant the grave concern of the community, that is not to say that consequently any State will bring the matter before the Court. And even if any particular State would claim the existence of a crime, and the Court determined its existence, this would not necessarily mean that other States, that is, all the injured States, would exercise their rights to invoke the author State's responsibility.

On the basis of their rights to invoke the responsibility of the author State, the crime having been determined by the Court, other States could demand reparation and resort to countermeasures. However, under Arangio-Ruiz' proposals they would not be under any obligation to do so. In view of such freedom the author State might first of all be confronted by a variety of differing reparation demands and all kinds of divergent countermeasures. The proposed supplementary obligations for injured States (non-recognition; abstention regarding assistance; assist each other in these fields; not hinder the exercise of reparation and countermeasures rights; implement the prosecute or extradite principle; take part in lawful measures decided or recommended by an international organization; and facilitate the adoption of lawful measures to cope with emergency situations), will most likely not be sufficient to assure the effective suppression of the crime.

Lastly, but not the least, the proposals as they stand suspend injured States' rights to demand reparation and to resort to countermeasures till after the closure of, to use the words of Arangio-Ruiz, full-fledged contentious proceedings before the Court. If the proposal to have the Court determine the existence of a crime were to be accepted, it might be worthwhile to have the Court decide by way of summary procedure (article 29 of the Statute). As that procedure is ordinarily open only at the request of the parties, the future convention would have to provide in advance and expressly that the States parties to the convention accept summary procedure to determine the existence of a crime. As the ordinary kind of contentious proceedings generally takes a long period of time, the only reaction immediately open to injured States would be to resort to urgent, interim countermeasures to protect the rights of an injured State or to limit the damage caused by the crime. Though such measures may aim at securing access to victims or at preventing the continuation of genocide, the proposal would not appear to justify recourse to armed force to achieve such goals.

In conclusion, serious misgivings may be expressed regarding the proposal to subject demands for reparation and resort to countermeasures to a prior decision of the Court to the effect that an international crime has been, or is being, committed. Indeed, already the formulation alone, that a crime *has been* committed, raises the issue whether the proposed construction could adequately lead to the suppression of the crime. Though Arangio-Ruiz has proposed an article 20, Part Two, stipulating that the provisions of Part Two of the ILC-draft are without prejudice to measures decided upon by the Security Council in the exercise of its functions under the Charter and the inherent right of self-defence as provided in article 51 of the Charter, this will most likely not bring about the effective suppression of crimes. The Council is the only standing organ of the United Nations empowered to initiate enforcement action within a matter of hours, days or weeks. For that reason the more appropriate course of action, considering the essential goal of suppressing conduct which simply cannot be tolerated, would appear to be to enlarge the competence of the Council by conferring it the power to determine the existence of an international crime, and the power to decide on any coercive measures, including the use of armed force, necessary to ensure the suppression of an international crime.

There is one issue left for discussion and that concerns the question, posed in the Introduction to this thesis, whether the "New World Order" would be grafted upon the old legal structures, or whether new legal structures would have to be created, necessitating, possibly, amendments to the Charter or the Statute. The Commission observed in relation to this issue:[17]

> "The Commission is in no way called upon to interpret or to supplement the Charter by the rules which it formulates, and still less to derogate from the Charter."

And Arangio-Ruiz has opted, by proposing the determination of a crime by the Court based upon a prior decision of the Assembly or the Council that the grave concern of the international community is warranted, to stay within the existing contemporary legal structures.

To begin with the Statute, the jurisdiction of the Court will necessarily be based upon existing bases of jurisdiction,[18] or upon the jurisdiction conferred through a future convention on State responsibility. Considering the far-reaching consequences attached to crimes it is not to be expected that it will be widely ratified. Nevertheless it might be worthwhile to propose amending article 34 of the Statute so as to allow international organizations to appear before the Court in contentious proceedings. Jurisdiction conferred by the future convention on State responsibility could then also cover disputes between the United Nations and any targeted author State.

The position is far more difficult as the Charter is concerned. It has shown itself to be abundantly clear, to laymen and specialists alike, that international law is in need of something more than enforcement based on national policies and interests. Thus the aftermath of the (armed) conflict regarding the Iraq-Kuwait crisis calls for reflections regarding the role of the United Nations in the future enforcement of international law. For it has been aptly perceived that the argument made by president Bush concerning the creation of a New World Order hinged upon the good will, good faith and detente between the permanent members of the Security Council.[19] Though the decision-making under Chapter VII of the Charter with regard to the Iraq-Kuwait crisis, and the armed conflict resulting therefrom, did not provoke too many dissents, it has been doubted whether such quasi-unanimity could be expected to continue even in the near future. Yet even if the Security Council will not again be paralyzed by any inappropriate use of the veto power, that does not necessarily mean that it will function effectively. Sensibilities between the permanent members, and (member) States in general, may delay action by the Council to such an extent that the delay becomes unacceptable. The situation in Rwanda has been a case in point. Doing away with the veto power would solve some problems, but this will not likely take place if regard is had to articles 108 and 109, paragraph 2, of the Charter. Even so, proposals for the enlargement of the Security Council, including the number of (semi-) permanent seats, should not lead to an increase of the number of States holding the veto power.

Another problem lies with the fact that the responsibility of the Security Council concerns the maintenance or restoration of "international" peace and security. The examination of the practice of the Security Council shows that it will not necessarily consider an international crime to constitute a threat to the peace. For that reason it would seem to be desirable that the competence of the Security Council would be established beyond any doubt also in relation to the crimes of denial of self-determination and widespread breaches of basic human rights obligations. In view of the recent practice of the Security Council a proposed amendment of article 39 of the Charter to that effect would not in advance be chanceless.
Far more important, at least at this moment, is the non-existence of any military forces at the disposal of the Security Council. In his Agenda for Peace Secretary-General Boutros-Ghali recommended that negotiations begin to conclude the agreements envisaged in article 43 of the Charter.[20] In his supplement to the Agenda he pointed to the desirability, in the long run, for a capacity of the United Nations to deploy, direct, command, and control forces to engage in enforcement action against those responsible for threats to the peace, breaches of the peace, or acts of aggression, but he noted that:[21]

> "(...) it would be folly to attempt to do so at the present time when the Organization is resource-starved and hard pressed to handle the less demanding peacemaking and peace-keeping responsibilities entrusted to it."

It seems obvious then that any enforcement action taken in response to international crimes will have to rely upon the good will of States, and particularly those accounted of major military power. One may doubt however whether the United States, the major military power in the world today, will be willing and capable of facing crises in every backward corner of the world.[22] Apart from the fact that only States with military power are able to carry out armed action in an effective manner, it would in effect be harsh to let only those States bear the burden of grief inevitably resulting from any military conflict. Clearly it would be desirable henceforth to institute the system of the Charter of the United Nations as it had been envisaged from the start. Yet it seems doubtful whether implementation of the scheme envisaged in the Charter will be held feasible any time in the near future.

The effective suppression of conduct constituting international crimes necessitates recourse to armed force to impose cessation, restitution, and guarantees against repetition. Obviously this will not be feasible if there is a lack of financial and material resources. The effective functioning of the United Nations is impeded not merely because there is too much red tape involved, but because important and well-off member States fail to pay their assessed contributions.[23] More importantly member States must have the will and determination to contribute to the maintenance of international peace and security, as well as to the suppression of international crimes. In the absence of centralized forces that may be put into action independently from the will of the contributing States, the goal of effective suppression of future international crimes will probably not be accomplished. An effective international order based on respect for international law will come into effect only if States are willing to contribute militarily to the elimination of such crises whose continued existence cannot be borne. Secretary-General Boutros-Ghali observed in his Agenda for Peace:[24]

> "In these past months a conviction has grown, among nations large and small, that an opportunity has been regained to achieve the great objectives of the Charter – a United Nations capable of maintaining international peace and security, of securing justice and human rights and of promoting, in the words of the Charter, 'social progress and better standards of life in larger freedom'. This opportunity must not be squandered."

In his supplement to the Agenda for Peace he further reiterated the need for hard decisions, and he stated:[25]

> "As understanding grows of the challenges to peace and security, hard decisions, if postponed, will appear in retrospect as having been relatively easy when measured against the magnitude of tomorrow's troubles."

With another four years to go before the close of the United Nations Decade on International Law, and the completion of the Commission's draft on State responsibility coming up, member States of the United Nations will have to make up their minds on the matter of a "New World Order". The years to come will be critical.

NOTES

1 Text and Commentary Article 19, Part One, YBILC 1976, Volume II, Part Two, pp. 95-122.

2 Text and Commentary Article 5, Part Two, YBILC 1985, Volume II, Part Two, pp. 25-27.

3 Barcelona Traction, Light and Power Company, Limited, Judgment, ICJ Reports 1970, p. 3, 32.

4 The 1945 Charter of the United Nations, 39 AJIL 1945, Supplement, pp. 195-215.

5 Proposed Article 19, Part Two, in Arangio-Ruiz, G., Seventh Report on State Responsibility, 24 May 1995, A/CN.4/469/Add.1, 4 pp., 4.

6 Arangio-Ruiz, Seventh Report, Addendum 1, 2-3.

7 See Arangio-Ruiz, G., Seventh Report on State Responsibility, 9 May 1995, A/CN.4/469, 49 pp., 25-49.

8 C.f. Mendelson, M., and Hulton, S., The Iraq-Kuwait Boundary, 64 BYBIL 1993, pp. 135-195, 192-195.

9 See Sur, S., La résolution 687 (3 avril 1991) du Conseil de Securité dans l'affaire du Golfe: Problèmes de rétablissement et de garantie de la paix, 37 AFDI 1991, pp. 25-97, 70-71.

10 Resolutions 827 and 955.

11 Resolutions 232, 253, 277, 388, and 409.

12 Resolution 418.

13 Basic resolution 661, (Iraq); and basic resolution 757 (Yugoslavia, Serbia and Montenegro).

14 Boutros-Ghali, B., Supplement to an Agenda for Peace, Position Paper of the Secretary-General on the Occasion of the Fiftieth Anniversary of the United Nations, 3 January 1995, S/1995/1, paragraph 70.

15 Boutros-Ghali, Position Paper, paragraph 70.

16 The Secretary-General observed in his paper: "(...) when in May 1994 the Security Council decided to expand the United Nations Assistance Mission for Rwanda (UNAMIR), not one of the 19 Governments that at that time had undertaken to have troops on stand-by agreed to contribute." Boutros-Ghali, Position Paper, paragraph 43.

17 Commentary Article 19, Part One, 118.

18 Secretary-General Boutros-Ghali recommended that member States should accept, without any reservation, the general jurisdiction of the Court under article 36 of the Statute before the end of the United Nations' Decade on International Law in the year 2000. Boutros-Ghali, B., An Agenda for Peace, Preventive Diplomacy, Peacemaking and Peace-Keeping, 17 June 1992, A/47/277, reprinted in 31 ILM 1992, pp. 956-975, paragraph 39.

[19] Secretary-General Boutros-Ghali stated: "Never again must the Security Council lose the collegiality that is essential for its proper functioning, an attribute that it has gained after such trial. A genuine sense of consensus deriving from shared interests must govern its work, not the threat of veto or the power of any group of nations." Boutros-Ghali, An Agenda for Peace, paragraph 78.

[20] Boutros-Ghali, An Agenda for Peace, paragraph 43. He further noted that the forces anticipated in article 43 of the Charter were not likely to be established for some time yet, and recommended the creation of so-called peace-enforcement units, more heavily armed and extensively trained volunteers, to assist in the tasks of peace-keeping troops. See *ibid.*, paragraph 44.

[21] Boutros-Ghali, Position Paper, paragraph 77. He also argued in favour of the creation of a rapid reaction force intended for peace-keeping purposes. *Ibid.*, paragraph 44.

[22] Note the restrictive policy formulated with regard to peace-keeping operations by the United States government. See The Clinton Administration's Policy on Reforming Multilateral Peace Operations, 33 ILM 1994, pp. 798-813. Note also the official statements by Warner, E., Coalition Defense and Reinforcing Forces, *ibid.*, pp. 815-820; and Harper, C., Legal Authority for UN Peace Operations, *ibid.*, pp. 822-829.

[23] Generally Boutros-Ghali, An Agenda for Peace, paragraphs 69-74; and Position Paper, paragraphs 97-101.

[24] Boutros-Ghali, An Agenda for Peace, paragraph 3.

[25] Boutros-Ghali, Position Paper, paragraph 104.

APPENDIX

DRAFT ARTICLES ON STATE RESPONSIBILITY

Draft articles (provisionally) adopted by the Commission
(Texts in YBILC 1980, Volume II, Part Two, pp. 30-34; Report of the International Law Commission on the work of its forty-fifth session, 3 May - 23 July 1993, General Assembly, Official Records, Forty-eighth Session, Supplement No. 10, (A/48/10), pp. 128-132; and Report of the International Law Commission on the work of its forty-sixth session, 2 May - 22 July 1994, General Assembly, Official Records, Forty-ninth Session, Supplement No. 10, (A/49/10), pp. 365-366, footnote 362)

Part 1. *The origin of international responsibility*

Chapter I

GENERAL PRINCIPLES

Article 1, Part One, Responsibility of a State for its internationally wrongful acts
Every internationally wrongful act of a State entails the international responsibility of that State.

Article 2, Part One, Possibility that every State may be held to have committed an internationally wrongful act
Every State is subject to the possibility of being held to have committed an internationally wrongful act entailing its international responsibility.

Article 3, Part One, Elements of an internationally wrongful act of a State
There is an internationally wrongful act of a State when:
(a) conduct consisting of an action or omission is attributable to the State under international law; and
(b) that conduct constitutes a breach of an international obligation of the State.

Article 4, Part One, Characterization of an act of a State as internationally wrongful
An act of a State may only be characterized as internationally wrongful by international law. Such characterization cannot be affected by the characterization of the same act as lawful by internal law.

Chapter II

THE "ACT OF THE STATE" UNDER INTERNATIONAL LAW

Article 5, Part One, Attribution of the State of the conduct of its organs
For the purposes of the present articles, conduct of any State organ having that status under the internal law of that State shall be considered as an act of the State concerned under international law, provided that organ was acting in that capacity in the case in question.

Article 6, Part One, Irrelevance of the position of the organ in the organization of the State
The conduct of an organ of the State shall be considered as an act of that State under international law, whether that organ belongs to the constituent, legislative, executive, judicial or other power, whether its functions are of an international or an internal character, and whether it holds a superior or a subordinate position in the organization of the State.

Article 7, Part One, Attribution to the State of the conduct of other entities empowered to exercise elements of the government authority
1. The conduct of an organ of a territorial governmental entity within a State shall also be considered as an act of that State under international law, provided that organ was acting in that capacity in the case in question.
2. The conduct of an organ of an entity which is not part of the formal structure of the State or of a territorial governmental entity, but which is empowered by the internal law of that State to exercise elements of the governmental authority, shall also be considered as an act of the State under international law, provided that organ was acting in that capacity in the case in question.

Article 8, Part One, Attribution to the State of the conduct of persons acting in fact on behalf of the State
The conduct of a person or group of persons shall also be considered as an act of the State under international law if:
(a) it is established that such persons or group of persons was in fact acting on behalf of that State; or
(b) such person or group of persons was in fact exercising elements of the governmental authority in the absence of the official authorities and in circumstances which justified the exercise of those elements of authority.

Article 9, Part One, Attribution to the State of the conduct of organs placed at its disposal by another State or by an international organization
The conduct of an organ which has been placed at the disposal of a State by another State or by an international organization shall be considered as an act of the former State under international law, if that organ was acting in the exercise of elements of the governmental authority of the State at whose disposal it has been placed.

Article 10, Part One, Attribution to the State of the conduct of organs acting outside their competence or contrary to instructions concerning their activity
The conduct of an organ of a State, of a territorial governmental entity or of an entity empowered to exercise elements of the governmental authority, such organ having acted in that capacity, shall be considered as an act of the State under international law even if, in the particular case, the organ exceeded its competence according to internal law or contravened instructions concerning its activity.

Article 11, Part One, Conduct of persons not acting on behalf of the State
1. The conduct of a person or group of persons not acting on behalf of the State shall not be considered as an act of the State under international law.
2. Paragraph 1 is without prejudice to the attribution to the State of any other conduct which is related to that of the persons or group of persons referred to in that paragraph and which is to be considered as an act of the State by virtue of articles 5 to 10.

Article 12, Part One, Conduct of organs of another State
1. The conduct of an organ of a State acting in that capacity which takes place in the territory of another State or in any other territory under its jurisdiction shall not be considered as an act of the latter State under international law.
2. Paragraph 1 is without prejudice to the attribution to a State of any other conduct which is related to that referred to in that paragraph and which is to be considered as an act of that State by virtue of articles 5 to 10.

Article 13, Part One, Conduct of organs of an international organization
The conduct of an organ of an international organization acting in that capacity shall not be considered as an act of a State under international law by reason only of the fact that such conduct has taken place in the territory of that State or in any other territory under its jurisdiction.

Article 14, Part One, Conduct of organs of an insurrectional movement
1. The conduct of an organ of an insurrectional movement which is established in the territory of a State or in any other territory under its administration shall not be considered as an act of that State under international law.
2. Paragraph 1 is without prejudice to the attribution to a State of any other conduct which is related to that of the organ of the insurrectional movement and which is to be considered as an act of that State by virtue of articles 5 to 10.
3. Similarly, paragraph 1 is without prejudice to the attribution of the conduct of the organ of the insurrectional movement to that movement in any case in which such attribution may be made under international law.

Article 15, Part One, Attribution to the State of the act of an insurrectional movement which becomes the new government of a State or which results in the formation of a new State
1. The act of an insurrectional movement which becomes the new government of a State shall be considered as an act of that State. However, such attribution shall be without prejudice to the attribution to that State of conduct which would have been previously considered as an act of the State by virtue of articles 5 to 10.
2. The act of an insurrectional movement whose action results in the formation of a new State in part of the territory of a pre-existing State or in a territory under its administration shall be considered as an act of the new State.

Chapter III

BREACH OF AN INTERNATIONAL OBLIGATION

Article 16, Part One, Existence of a breach of an international obligation
There is a breach of an international obligation by a State when an act of that State is not in conformity with what is required of it by that obligation.

Article 17, Part One, Irrelevance of the origin of the international obligation breached
1. An act of a State which constitutes a breach of an international obligation is an internationally wrongful act regardless of the origin, whether customary, conventional or other, of that obligation.
2. The origin of the international obligation breached by a State does not affect the international responsibility arising from the internationally wrongful act of that State.

Article 18, Part One, Requirement that the international obligation be in force for the State
1. An act of the State which is not in conformity with what is required of it by an international obligation constitutes a breach of that obligation only if the act was performed at the time when the obligation was in force for that State.
2. However, an act of the State which, at the time when it was performed, was not in conformity with what was required or it by an international obligation in force for that State, ceases to be considered an internationally wrongful act if, subsequently, such an act has become compulsory by virtue of a peremptory norm of general international law.
3. If an act of the State which is not in conformity with what is required of it by an international obligation has a continuing character, there is a breach of that obligation only in respect of the period during which the act continues while the obligation is in force for that State.
4. If an act of the State which is not in conformity with what is required of it by an international obligation is composed of a series of actions or omissions in respect of separate cases, there is a breach of that obligation if such an act may be considered to be constituted by the actions or omissions occurring within the period during which the obligation is in force for that State.

5. If an of the State which is not in conformity with what is required of it by an international obligation is a complex act constituted by actions or omissions by the same or different organs of the State in respect of the same case, there is a breach of that obligation if the complex act not in conformity with it begins with an action or omission occurring within the period during which the obligation is in force for that State, even if that act is completed after that period.

Article 19, Part One, International crimes and international delicts
1. An act of a State which constitutes a breach of an international obligation is an internationally wrongful act, regardless of the subject-matter of the obligation breached
2. An internationally wrongful act which results from the breach by a State of an international obligation so essential for the protection of fundamental interests of the international community that its breach is recognized as a crime by that community as a whole constitutes an international crime.
3. Subject to paragraph 2, and on the basis of the rules of international law in force, an international crime may result, *inter alia*, from:
(a) a serious breach of an international obligation of essential importance for the maintenance of international peace and security, such as that prohibiting aggression;
(b) a serious breach of an international obligation of essential importance for safeguarding the right of self-determination of peoples, such as that prohibiting the establishment or maintenance by force of colonial domination;
(c) a serious breach on a widespread scale of an international obligation of essential importance for safeguarding the human being, such as those prohibiting slavery, genocide and *apartheid*;
(d) a serious breach of an international obligation of essential importance for the safeguarding and preservation of the human environment, such as those prohibiting massive pollution of the atmosphere or the seas.
4. Any internationally wrongful act which is not an international crime in accordance with paragraph 2 constitutes an international delict.

Article 20, Part One, Breach of an international obligation requiring the adoption of a particular course of conduct
There is a breach by a State of an international obligation requiring it to adopt a particular course of conduct when the conduct of that State is not in conformity with that required of it by that obligation.

Article 21, Part One, Breach of an international obligation requiring the achievement of a specified result
1. There is a breach by a State of an international obligation requiring it to achieve, by means of its own choice, a specified result if, by the conduct adopted, the State does not achieve the result required of it by that obligation.
2. When the conduct of the State has created a situation not in conformity with the result required of it by an international obligation, but the obligation allows that this or an equivalent result may nevertheless be achieved by subsequent conduct of the State,

there is a breach of the obligation only if the State also fails by its subsequent conduct to achieve the result required of it by that obligation.

Article 22, Part One, Exhaustion of local remedies
When the conduct of a State has created a situation not in conformity with the result required of it by an international obligation concerning the treatment to be accorded to aliens, whether natural or juridical persons, but the obligation allows that this or an equivalent result may nevertheless be achieved by subsequent conduct of the State, there is a breach of the obligation only if the aliens concerned have exhausted the effective local remedies available to them without obtaining the treatment called for by the obligation or, where that is not possible, an equivalent treatment.

Article 23, Part One, Breach of an international obligation to prevent a given event
When the result required of a State by an international obligation is the prevention, by means of its own choice, of the occurrence of a given event, there is a breach of that obligation only if, by the conduct adopted, the State does not achieve that result.

Article 24, Part One, Moment and duration of the breach of an international obligation by an act of the State not extending in time
The breach of an international obligation by an act of the State not extending in time occurs at the moment when that act is performed. The time of commission of the breach does not extend beyond that moment, even if the effects of the act of the State continue subsequently.

Article 25, Part One, Moment and duration of the breach of an international obligation by an act of the State extending in time
1. The breach of an international obligation by an act of the State having a continuing character occurs at the moment when that act begins. Nevertheless, the time of commission of the breach extends over the entire period during which the act continues and remains not in conformity with the international obligation.
2. The breach of an international obligation by an act of the State, composed of a series of actions or omissions in respect of separate cases, occurs at the moment when that action or omission of the series is accomplished which establishes the existence of the composite act. Nevertheless, the time of commission of the breach extends over the entire period from the first of the actions or omissions constituting the composite act not in conformity with the international obligation and so long as such actions or omissions are repeated.
3. The breach of an international obligation by a complex act of the State, consisting of a succession of actions or omissions by the same or different organs of the State in respect of the same case, occurs at the moment when the last constituent element of that complex act is accomplished. Nevertheless, the time of commission of the breach extends over the entire period between the action or omission which initiated the breach and that which completed it.

Article 26, Part One, Moment and duration of the breach of an international obligation to prevent a given event
The breach of an international obligation requiring a State to prevent a given event occurs when the event begins. Nevertheless, the time of commission of the breach extends over the entire period during which the event continues.

Chapter IV

IMPLICATION OF A STATE IN THE INTERNATIONALLY WRONGFUL ACT OF ANOTHER STATE

Article 27, Part One, Aid or assistance by a State to another State for the commission of an internationally wrongful act
Aid or assistance by a State to another State, if it is established that it is rendered for the commission of an internationally wrongful act carried out by the latter, itself constitutes an internationally wrongful act, even if, taken alone, such aid or assistance would not constitute the breach of an international obligation.

Article 28, Part One, Responsibility of a State for an internationally wrongful act of another State
1. An internationally wrongful act of a State committed by a State in a field of activity in which that State is subject to the power of direction or control of another State entails the international responsibility of that other State.
2. An internationally wrongful act committed by a State as the result of coercion exerted by another State to secure the commission of that act entails the international responsibility of that other State.
3. Paragraphs 1 and 2 are without prejudice to the international responsibility, under the other articles of the present draft, of the State which has committed the internationally wrongful act.

Chapter V

CIRCUMSTANCES PRECLUDING WRONGFULNESS

Article 29, Part One, Consent
1. The consent validly given by a State to the commission by another State of a specified act not in conformity with an obligation of the latter State towards the former State precludes the wrongfulness of the act in relation to that State to the extent that the act remains within the limits of that consent.
2. Paragraph 1 does not apply if the obligation arises out of a peremptory norm of general international law. For the purposes of the present draft articles, a peremptory norm of general international law is a norm accepted and recognized by the international community of States as a whole as a norm from which no derogation is permitted and which can be modified only by a subsequent norm of general international law having the same character.

Article 30, Part One , Countermeasures in respect of an internationally wrongful act
The wrongfulness of an act of a State not in conformity with an obligation of that State towards another State is precluded if the act constitutes a measure legitimate under international law against that other State, in consequence of an internationally wrongful act of that other State.

Article 31, Part One, *Force majeure* and fortuitous event
1. The wrongfulness of an act of a State not in conformity with an international obligation of that State is precluded if the act was due to an irresistible force or to an unforeseen external event beyond its control which made it materially impossible for the State to act in conformity with that obligation or to know that its conduct was not in conformity with that obligation.
2. Paragraph 1 shall not apply if the State in question has contributed to the occurrence of the situation of material impossibility.

Article 32, Part One, Distress
1. The wrongfulness of an act of a State not in conformity with an international obligation of that State is precluded if the author of the conduct which constitutes the act of that State had no other means, in a situation in extreme distress, of saving his life or that of persons entrusted to his care.
2. Paragraph 1 shall not apply if the State in question has contributed to the occurrence of the situation of extreme distress or if the conduct in question was likely to create a comparable or greater peril.

Article 33, Part One, State of necessity
1. A state of necessity may not be invoked by a State as a ground for precluding the wrongfulness of an act of that State not in conformity with an international obligation of the State unless:
(a) the act was the only means of safeguarding an essential interest of the State against a grave and imminent peril; and
(b) the act did not seriously impair an essential interest of the State towards which the obligation existed.
2. In any case, a state of necessity may not be invoked by a State as a ground for precluding wrongfulness:
(a) if the international obligation with which the act of the State is not in conformity arises out of a peremptory norm of general international law; or
(b) if the international obligation with which the act of the State is not in conformity is laid down by a treaty which, explicitly or implicitly, excludes the possibility of invoking the state of necessity with respect to that obligation; or
(c) if the State in question has contributed to the occurrence of the state of necessity.

Article 34, Part One, Self-defence
The wrongfulness of an act of a State not in conformity with an international obligation of that State is precluded if the act constitutes a lawful measure of self-defence taken in conformity with the Charter of the United Nations.

Article 35, Part One, Reservation as to compensation for damage
Preclusion of the wrongfulness of an act of a State by virtue of the provisions of articles 29, 31, 32 or 33 does not prejudge any question that may arise in regard to compensation for damage caused by that act.

Part 2. ***The content, forms and degrees of international responsibility***

Article 1, Part Two
1. The international responsibility of a State which, pursuant to the provisions of Part One, arises from an internationally wrongful act committed by that State, entails legal consequences as set out in the present part.
2. The legal consequences referred to in paragraph 1 are without prejudice to the continued duty of the State which has committed the internationally wrongful act to perform the obligation it has breached.

Article 2, Part Two
Without prejudice to the provisions of articles 4 and [12], the provisions of this Part govern the legal consequences of any internationally wrongful act of a State, except where and to the extent that those legal consequences have been determined by other rules of international law relating specifically to the internationally wrongful act in question.

Article 3, Part Two
Without prejudice to the provisions of articles 4 and [12], the rules of customary international law shall continue to govern the legal consequences of an internationally wrongful act of a State not set out in the provisions of the present Part.

Article 4, Part Two
The legal consequences of an internationally wrongful act of a State set out in the provisions of the present Part are subject, as appropriate, to the provisions and procedure of the Charter of the United Nations relating to the maintenance of international peace and security.

Article 5, Part Two
1. For the purposes of the present articles, "injured State" means any State a right of which is infringed by the act of another State, if that act constitutes, in accordance with Part One of the present articles an internationally wrongful act of that State.
2. In particular, "injured State" means:
(a) if the right infringed by the act of a State arises from a bilateral treaty, the other State party to the treaty;
(b) if the right infringed by the act of a State arises from a judgment or other binding dispute-settlement decision of an international court or tribunal, the other State or States parties to the dispute and entitled to benefit of that right;

(c) if the right infringed by the act of a State arises from a binding decision of an international organ other than an international court or tribunal, the State or States which, in accordance with the constituent instrument of the international organization concerned, are entitled to the benefit of that right;
(d) if the right infringed by the act of a State arises from a treaty provision for a third State, that third State;
(e) if the right infringed by the act of a State arises from a multilateral treaty or from a rule of customary international law, any other State party to the multilateral treaty or bound by the relevant rule of customary international law, if it is established that:
(i) the right has been created or is established in its favour;
(ii) the infringement of the right by the act of a State necessarily affects the enjoyment of the rights or performance of the obligations of the other State parties to the multilateral treaty or bound by the rule of customary international law; or
(iii) the right has been created or is established for the protection of human rights and fundamental freedoms;
(f) if the right infringed by the act of a State arises from a multilateral treaty, any other State party to the multilateral treaty, if it is established that the right has been expressly stipulated in that treaty for the protection of the collective interests of the State parties thereto.
3. In addition, "injured State" means, if the internationally wrongful act constitutes an international crime [and in the context of the rights and obligations of States under articles 14 and 15], all other States.

Article 6, Part Two, Cessation of wrongful conduct
A State whose conduct constituting an internationally wrongful act having a continuing character is under the obligation to cease that conduct, without prejudice to the responsibility it has already incurred.

Article 6 *bis*, Part Two, Reparation
1. The injured State is entitled to obtain from the State which has committed an internationally wrongful act full reparation in the form of restitution in kind, compensation, satisfaction and assurances and guarantees on non-repetition, as provided in articles 7, 8, 10 and 10 bis, either singly or in combination.
2. In the determination of reparation, account shall be taken of the negligence or the wilful act or omission of:
(a) the injured State; or
(b) a national of that State on whose behalf the claim is brought;
which contributed to the damage.
3. The State which has committed the internationally wrongful act may not invoke the provisions of its internal law as justification for the failure to provide full reparation.

Article 7, Part Two, Restitution in kind
The injured State is entitled to obtain from the State which has committed an internationally wrongful act restitution in kind, that is, the re-establishment of the situation that existed before the wrongful act was committed, provided and to the extent that restitution in kind:
(a) is not materially impossible;
(b) would not involve a breach of an obligation arising from a peremptory norm of general international law;
(c) would not involve a burden out of all proportion to the benefit which the injured State would gain from obtaining restitution in kind instead of compensation; or
(d) would not seriously jeopardize the political independence or economic stability of the State which has committed the internationally wrongful act, whereas the injured State would not be similarly affected if it did not obtain restitution in kind.

Article 8, Part Two, Compensation
1. The injured State is entitled to obtain from the State which has committed an internationally wrongful act compensation for the damage caused by that act, if and to the extent that the damage is not made good by restitution in kind.
2. For the purposes of the present article, compensation covers any economically assessable damage sustained by the injured State, and may include interest and, where appropriate, loss of profits.

Article 10, Part Two, Satisfaction
1. The injured State is entitled to obtain from the State which has committed an internationally wrongful act satisfaction for the damage, in particular moral damage, caused by that act, if and to the extent necessary to provide full reparation.
2. Satisfaction may take the form of one or more of the following:
(a) an apology;
(b) nominal damages;
(c) in cases of gross infringement of the rights of the injured State, damages reflecting the gravity of the infringement;
(d) in cases where the internationally wrongful act arose from the serious misconduct of officials or from criminal conduct of officials or private parties, disciplinary action against, or punishment of, those responsible.
3. The right of the injured State to obtain satisfaction does not justify demands which would impair the dignity of the State which has committed the internationally wrongful act.

Article 10 *bis*, Part Two, Assurances and guarantees of non-repetition
The injured State is entitled, where appropriate, to obtain from the State which has committed an internationally wrongful act assurances or guarantees of non-repetition of the wrongful act.

Article 11, Part Two, Countermeasures by an injured State
1. As long as the State which has committed an internationally wrongful act has not complied with its obligations under Articles 6 to 10 bis, the injured State is entitled to take countermeasures, that is, subject to the conditions and restrictions set forth in articles 12, 13 and 14, not to comply with one or more of its obligations towards the State which has committed the internationally wrongful act, as necessary in the light of the response to its demands by the State which has committed the internationally wrongful act in order to induce it to comply with its obligations under articles 6 to 10 bis.
2. Where a countermeasure against a State which has committed an internationally wrongful act involves a breach of an obligation towards a third State, such a breach cannot be justified as against the third State by reason of paragraph 1.

Article 13, Part Two, Proportionality
Any countermeasure taken by an injured State shall not be out of proportion to the degree of gravity of the internationally wrongful act and the effects thereof on the injured State.

Article 14, Part Two, Prohibited countermeasures
An injured State shall not resort, by way of countermeasure, to:
(a) the threat or use of force as prohibited by the Charter of the United Nations;
(b) extreme economic or political coercion designed to endanger the territorial integrity or political independence of the State which has committed an internationally wrongful act;
(c) any conduct which infringes the inviolability of diplomatic or consular agents, premises, archives and documents;
(d) any conduct which derogates from basic human rights; or
(e) any other conduct in contravention of a peremptory norm of general international law.

Draft article proposed by the Drafting Committee
(Text in 5 EJIL 1994, pp. 118-119)

Article 12, Part Two, Conditions relating to resort to counter-measures
1. An injured State may not take counter-measures unless:
(a) it has recourse to a [binding/third party] dispute settlement procedure which both the injured State and the State which has committed the internationally wrongful act are bound to use under any relevant treaty to which they are parties; or
(b) in the absence of such a treaty, it offers a [binding/third party] dispute settlement procedure to the State which has committed the internationally wrongful act.
2. The right of the injured State to take counter-measures is suspended when and to the extent that an agreed [binding] dispute settlement procedure is being implemented in

good faith by the State which has committed the internationally wrongful act, provided that the internationally wrongful act has ceased.
3. A failure by the State which has committed the internationally wrongful act to honour a request or order emanating from the dispute settlement procedure shall terminate the right of suspension of the right of the injured State to take countermeasures.

Draft articles proposed by special rapporteur Arangio-Ruiz
(Texts in Arangio-Ruiz, G., Seventh Report of State Responsibility, A/CN.4/469/ Add.1, 4 pp., 2-4; and Arangio-Ruiz, G., Seventh Report of State Responsibility, A/CN.4/469/Add.2, 3 pp., 3)

Article 15, Part Two
Without prejudice [In addition] to the legal consequences entailed by an international delict under articles 6 to 14 of the present Part, an international crime as defined in article 19 of Part One entails the special or supplementary consequences set forth in articles 16 to 19 below.

Article 16, Part Two
1. Where an internationally wrongful act of a State is an international crime, every State is entitled, subject to the condition set forth in paragraph 5 of article 19 below, to demand that the State which is committing or has committed the crime should cease its wrongful conduct and provide full reparation in conformity with articles 6 to 10 bis, as modified by paragraphs 2 and 3 below.
2. The right of every injured State to obtain restitution in kind as provided in article 7 shall not be subject to the limitations set forth in subparagraphs (c) and (d) of paragraph 1 of the said article, except where restitution in kind would jeopardize the existence of the wrongdoing State as an independent member of the international community, its territorial integrity or the vital needs of its people.
3. Subject to the preservation of its existence as an independent member of the international community and to the safeguarding of its territorial integrity and the vital needs of its people, a State which has committed an international crime is not entitled to benefit from any limitations of its obligation to provide satisfaction and guarantees of non-repetition as envisaged in articles 10 and 10 bis, relating to the respect of its dignity, or from any rules or principles of international law relating to the protection of its sovereignty and liberty.

Article 17, Part Two
1. Where the internationally wrongful act of a State is an international crime, every State whose demands under article 16 have not met with an adequate response from the State which has committed or is committing the crime is entitled, subject to the condition set forth in paragraph 5 of article 19 below, to resort to countermeasures

under the conditions and restrictions set forth in articles 11, 13 and 14 as modified by paragraphs 2 and 3 of the present article.
2. The condition set forth in paragraph 5 of article 19 below does not apply to such urgent, interim measures as are required to protect the rights of an injured State or to limit the damage caused by the international crime.
3. The requirement of proportionality set forth in article 13 shall apply to counter-measures taken by any State so that such measures shall not be out of proportion to the gravity of the international crime.

Article 18, Part Two
1. Where an internationally wrongful act is an international crime, all States shall, subject to the condition set forth in paragraph 5 of article 19 below:
(a) refrain from recognizing as legal or valid, under international or national law, the situation created by the international crime;
(b) abstain from any act or omission which may assist the wrongdoing State in maintaining the said situation;
(c) assist each other in carrying out their obligations under subparagraphs (a) and (b) and, in so far as possible, coordinate their respective reactions through available international bodies or ad hoc arrangements;
(d) refrain from hindering in any way, by act or omission, the exercise of the rights or powers provided for in articles 16 and 17;
(e) fully implement the aut dedere aut judicare principle, with respect to any individuals accused of crimes against the peace and security of mankind the commission of which has brought about the international crime of the State or contributed thereto;
(f) take part, jointly or individually, in any lawful measures decided or recommended by any international organization of which they are members against the State which has committed or is committing the international crime;
(g) facilitate, by all possible means, the adoption or implementation of any lawful measures intended to remedy any emergency situations caused by the international crime.
2. Subject to the conditions set forth in paragraph 5 of article 19 below, the State which has committed or is committing an international crime shall not oppose fact-finding operations or observer missions in its territory for the verification of compliance with its obligations of cessation or reparation.

Article 19, Part Two
1. Any State Member of the United Nations Party to the present Convention claiming that an international crime has been or is being committed by one or more States shall bring the matter to the attention of the General Assembly or the Security Council of the United Nations in accordance with Chapter VI of the United Nations Charter.
2. If the General Assembly or the Security Council resolves by a qualified majority of the Members present and voting that the allegation is sufficiently substantiated as to justify the grave concern of the international community, any Member State of the United Nations Party to the present Convention, including the State against which the

claim is made, may bring the matter to the International Court of Justice by unilateral application for the Court to decide by a judgment whether the alleged international crime has been or is being committed by the accused State.
3. The qualified majority referred to in the preceding paragraph shall be, in the General Assembly, a two-thirds majority of the members present and voting, and in the Security Council, nine members present and voting including permanent members, provided that any members directly concerned shall abstain from voting.
4. In any case where the International Court of Justice is exercising its competence in a dispute between two or more Member States of the United Nations Parties to the present Convention, on the basis of a title of jurisdiction other than paragraph 2 of the present article, with regard to the existence of an international crime of State, any other Member State of the United Nations which is a party to the present Convention shall be entitled to join, by unilateral application, the proceedings of the Court for the purpose of paragraph 5 of the present article.
5. A decision of the International Court of Justice that an international crime has been or is being committed shall fulfil the condition for the implementation, by any Member State of the United Nations Party to the present Convention, of the special or supplementary legal consequences of international crimes of States as contemplated in articles 16, 17 and 18 of the present Part.

Article 20, Part Two
The provisions of the articles of the present Part are without prejudice to:
(i) any measures decided upon by the Security Council of the United Nations in the exercise of its functions under the provisions of the Charter;
(ii) the inherent right of self-defence as provided in Article 51 of the Charter.

Article 7, Part Three
1. Any dispute which may arise between any States with respect to the legal consequences of a crime under articles 6 to 19 of Part Two shall be settled by arbitration on either party's proposal.
2. Failing referral of the dispute to an arbitral tribunal within four months from either party's proposal, the dispute shall be referred unilaterally, by either party, to the International Court of Justice.
3. The competence of the Court shall extend to any issues of fact or law under the present articles other than the question of existence and attribution previously decided under article 19 of Part Two.

REFERENCES

Abi-Saab, G., Les exceptions preliminaires dans la procédure de la Cour internationale, Étude des notions fondamentales de procédure et des moyens de leur mise en oeuvre, Éditions A. Pedone, Paris, 1967.

Abi-Saab, G., The Concept of "International Crimes" and its Place in Contemporary International Law, in Weiler, J., Cassese, A., and Spinedi, M. (Eds.), International Crimes of States, A Critical Analysis of the ILC's Draft Article 19 on State Responsibility, Walter de Gruyter, Berlin, 1989, pp. 141-150.

Acevedo, D., Disputes Under Consideration by the U.N. Security Council or Regional Bodies, in Damrosch, L. (Ed.), The International Court of Justice at a Crossroads, Transnational Publishers, Inc., Dobbs Ferry, New York, 1987, pp. 242-263.

Adviescommissie Mensenrechten en Buitenlands Beleid, and Commissie van Advies inzake Volkenrechtelijke Vraagstukken, Het gebruik van geweld voor humanitaire doeleinden, Dwangmaatregelen voor humanitaire doeleinden en humanitaire interventie, Den Haag, 1992.

Ago, R., Second report on State responsibility, YBILC 1970, Volume II, pp. 177-197.

Ago, R., Third report on State responsibility, YBILC 1971, Volume II, Part One, pp. 199-274.

Ago, R., Fifth report on State responsibility, YBILC 1976, Volume II, Part One, pp. 3-54.

Ago, R., Sixth report on State responsibility, YBILC 1977, Volume II, Part One, pp. 3-43.

Ago, R., Seventh report on State responsibility, YBILC 1978, Volume II, Part One, pp. 31-60.

Ago, R., Eighth report on State responsibility, YBILC 1979, Volume II, Part One, pp. 3-66.

Ago, R., Addendum to the eighth report on State responsibility, YBILC 1980, Volume II, Part One, pp. 1-70.

Ago, R., The International Community and International Organizations, in Dupuy, R.-J. (Ed.), Handbook on International Organizations, Martinus Nijhoff Publishers, Dordrecht, 1988, pp. 3-12.

Ago, R., Remarks on Some Classes of Crimes by States, in Weiler, J., Cassese, A., and Spinedi, M. (Eds.), International Crimes of States, A Critical Analysis of the ILC's Draft Article 19 on State Responsibility, Walter de Gruyter, Berlin, 1989, p. 215.

Ago, R., Obligations *Erga Omnes* and the International Community, in Weiler, J., Cassese, A., and Spinedi, M. (Eds.), International Crimes of States, A Critical Analysis of the ILC's Draft Article 19 on State Responsibility, Walter de Gruyter, Berlin, 1989, pp. 237-239.

Ago, R., The Concept of "International Community as a Whole": A Guarantee to the Notion of State Crimes, in Weiler, J., Cassese, A., and Spinedi, M. (Eds.), International Crimes of States, A Critical Analysis of the ILC's Draft Article 19 on State Responsibility, Walter de Gruyter, Berlin, 1989, pp. 252-253.

Akehurst, M., Reprisals by Third States, 44 BYBIL 1970, pp. 1-18.

Akhavan, P., Enforcement of the Genocide Convention Through the Advisory Opinion Jurisdiction of the International Court of Justice, 12 HRLJ 1991, pp. 285-299.

Alland, D., La légitime défense et les contre-mesures dans la codification du droit international de la responsabilité, 110 JDI 1983, pp. 728-762.

Anand, R., International Courts and Contemporary Conflicts, Asia Publishing House, London, 1974.

Annacker, C., The Legal Régime of *Erga Omnes* Obligations in International Law, 46 AJPIL 1994, pp. 131-166.

Annacker, C., Die Durchsetzung von *erga omnes* Verpflichtungen vor dem Internationalen Gerichtshof, Verlag Dr. Kovac, Hamburg, 1994.

Anzilotti, D., La responsabilité internationale des états a raison des dommages soufferts par des étrangers, 13 RGDIP 1906, pp. 5-29.

Arangio-Ruiz, G., Preliminary Report on State Responsibility, 18 May 1988, A/CN.4/416, 34 pp.; and 27 May 1988, A/CN.4/416/Add.1, 53 pp.

Arangio-Ruiz, G., Second Report on State Responsibility, 9 June 1989, A/CN.4/425, 125 pp.; and 22 June 1989, A/CN.4/425/Add.1, 25 pp.

Arangio-Ruiz, G., State Fault and the Forms and Degrees of International Responsibility: Questions of Attribution and Relevance, in Le droit au service de la paix, de la justice et du développement, Mélanges Michel Virally, Éditions A. Pedone, Paris, 1991, pp. 25-41.

Arangio-Ruiz, G., Third Report on State Responsibility, 19 July 1991, A/CN.4/440, 46 pp.; and 19 July 1991, A/CN.4/440/Add.1, 25 pp.

Arangio-Ruiz, G., Fourth Report on State Responsibility, 12 May 1992, A/CN.4/444, 40 pp.; 25 May 1992, A/CN.4/444/Add.1, 37 pp.; and 1 June 1992, A/CN.4/444/Add.2, 37 pp.

Arangio-Ruiz, G., Fifth Report on State Responsibility, 12 May 1993, A/CN.4/453, 63 pp.; 8 June 1993, A/CN.4/453/Add.2, 35 pp.; and 24 June 1993, A/CN.4/453/Add.3, 36 pp.

Arangio-Ruiz, G., Sixth Report on State Responsibility, 19 April 1994, A/CN.4/461, 28 pp.; 26 April 1994, A/CN.4/461/Add.1, 7 pp.; 14 June 1994, A/CN.4/461/Add.2, 5 pp.; and 21 July 1994, A/CN.4/461/Add.3, 2 pp.

Arangio-Ruiz, G., Seventh Report on State Responsibility, 9 May 1995, A/CN.4/469, 49 pp.; 24 May 1995, A/CN.4/469/Add.1, 4 pp.; 29 May 1995, A/CN.4/469/Add.2, 3 pp.

Arató, S., Die völkerrechtliche Haftung, Nyomatott Taizs József könyvnyoamdában, Pécs, 1937.

Aslaoui, O., Les conclusions et leurs modifications en procédure judiciaire internationale, Librairie Droz, Genève, 1963.

Aulagnon, L., Aperçus sur la force dans la regle de droit, in Mélanges en l'honneur de Paul Roubier, volume 1, Théorie générale du droit et droit transitoire, Librairies Dalloz & Sirey, Paris, 1961, pp. 29-37.

Austin, J., Lectures on Jurisprudence or the Philosophy of Positive Law, volume 1 (Reprint of Fifth Edition, Revised and Edited by Campbell, R., John Murray, London, 1885, originally printed in 1832), Verlag Detlev Auvermann KG, Glashütten im Taumus, 1972.

Barile, G., The Protection of Human Rights in Article 60, Paragraph 5 of the Vienna Convention of the Law of Treaties, in Etudes en l'honneur de Roberto Ago, Le droit international à l'heure de sa codification, volume II, Giuffrè, Milano, 1987, pp. 3-14.

Barnhoorn, L., Diplomatic Law and Unilateral Remedies, 25 NYIL 1994, pp. 39-81.

Bastid, S., L'affaire du Sud-Ouest africain devant la Cour internationale de justice, 94 JDI 1967, pp. 571-583.

Bedjaoui, M., Droit au developpement et *jus cogens*, 54/55/56 YAAA 1984/85/86, pp. 275-299.

Bedjaoui, M., Du contrôle de légalité des actes du Conseil de Securité, in Nouveaux itinéraires en droit, Hommage à François Rigaux, Bruylant, Bruxelles, 1993, pp. 69-110.

Beres, L., Genocide, State and Self, 18 DJILP 1989, pp. 37-57.

Beveridge, F., The Lockerbie Affair, 41 ICLQ 1992, pp. 907-920.

Bilge, A., La Responsabilité Internationale des Etats et son Application en Matière d'Actes Legislatifs, Imprimerie Tsitouris Frères, Istanbul, 1950.

Bindschedler, R., Das Problem der Beteiligung der Schweiz an Sanktionen der Vereinten Nationen, besonders im Falle Rhodesiens, 28 ZAORV 1968, pp. 1-15.

Bindschedler, R., Völkerrechtliche Verantwortlichkeit als Verbrechen, in Dutoit, B., and Grisel, E. (Eds.), Mélanges Georges Perrin, Diffusion Payot, Lausanne, 1984, pp. 51-61.

Birkás, G., Das Staatsinteresse als Grundlage des Völkerrechts, Carl Heymanns Verlag, Berlin, 1933.

Bleckmann, A., Probleme der Anwendung multilateraler Verträge, Gegenseitigkeit und Anwendbarkeit der Vertragspartner, Duncker & Humblot, Berlin, 1974.

Bleckmann, A., Zur Verbindlichkeit des allgemeinen Völkerrechts für internationale Organisationen, 37 ZAORV 1977, pp. 107-121.

Bleckmann, A., The Subjective Right in Public International Law, 28 GYIL 1985, pp. 144-162.

Bloed, A., "Toetsing" van besluiten Veiligheidsraad, 67 NJB 1992, pp. 661-663.

Boisson de Chazournes, L., Les contre-mesures dans les relations internationales économiques, Editions A. Pedone, Paris, 1992.

Bollecker Stern, B., Le préjudice dans la théorie de la responsabilité internationale, Éditions A. Pedone, Paris, 1973.

Booysen, H., Convention on the Crime of *Apartheid*, 2 SAYIL 1976, pp. 56-96.

Bos, M., Les conditions du procès en droit international public, E.J. Brill, Leiden, 1957.

Bossuyt, M., Guide to the "*Travaux Préparatoires*" of the International Covenant on Civil and Political Rights, Martinus Nijhoff Publishers, Dordrecht, 1987.

Bowett, D., Self-Defence in International Law, Manchester University Press, Manchester, 1958.

Bowett, D., Economic Coercion and Reprisals by States, 13 VJIL 1972, pp. 1-12.

Bowett, D., Reprisals Involving Recourse to Armed Force, 66 AJIL 1972, pp. 1-36.

Bowett, D., The Use of Force for the Protection of Nationals Abroad, in Cassese, A. (Ed.), The Current Legal Regulation of the Use of Force, Martinus Nijhoff Publishers, Dordrecht, 1986, pp. 39-55.

Boyle, A., State Responsibility for Breach of Obligations to Protect the Global Environment, in Butler, W. (Ed.), Control and Compliance with International Law, Martinus Nijhoff Publishers, Dordrecht, 1991, pp. 69-81.

Briggs, H., La compétence incidente de la Cour internationale de Justice en tant que compétence obligatoire, 64 RGDIP 1960, pp. 217-229.

Briggs, H., Barcelona Traction: The *Jus Standi* of Belgium, 65 AJIL 1971, pp. 327-345.

Brown Weiss, E., In Fairness to Future Generations, International Law, Common Patrimony and Intergenerational Equity, The United Nations University Press, Tokyo, 1989.

Brownlie, I., International Law and the Use of Force by States, Clarendon Press, Oxford, 1963.

Brownlie, I., State Responsibility, System of the Law of Nations, Part I, Clarendon Press, Oxford, 1983.

Brownlie, I., Principles of Public International Law, Fourth Edition, Clarendon Press, Oxford, 1990.

Brownlie, I. (Ed.), Basic Documents on Human Rights, Third Edition, Clarendon Press, Oxford, 1992.

Brunnée, J., "Common Interest" – Echoes from an Empty Shell?: Some Thoughts on Common Interest and International Environmental Law, 49 ZAORV 1989, pp. 791-808.

Butkiewicz, E., The Premisses of International Responsibility of Inter-Governmental Organizations, 11 PYIL 1981-1982, pp. 117-140.

Buxbaum, H., Das völkerrechtliche Delikt, Druck der Universitäts-Buchdruckerei von E. Th. Jacob, Erlangen, 1915.

Calogeropoulos-Stratis, S., Le recours à la force dans la société internationale, Editions L.E.P., Lausanne, and Librairie Generale de Droit et de Jurisprudence, Paris, 1986.

Cassese, A., The Concept of «Legal Dispute» in the Jurisprudence of the International Court, in Il processo internazionale, Studi in onore di Gaetano Morelli, Comunicazioni e Studi, volume 14, Giuffrè, Milano, 1975, pp. 173-200.

Cassese, A., International Law in a Divided World, Clarendon Press, Oxford, 1986.

Cassese, A., Remarks on the Present Legal Regulation of Crimes of States, in Etudes en l'honneur de Roberto Ago, Le droit international à l'heure de sa codification, volume III, Giuffrè, Milano, 1987, pp. 49-64.

Cassese, A., La communaute internationale et le genocide, in Le droit au service de la paix, de la justice et du développement, Mélanges Michel Virally, Éditions A. Pedone, Paris, 1991, pp. 183-194.

Cassese, A., Article 51, in Cot, J.-P., and Pellet, A. (Eds.), La Charte des Nations Unies, Commentaire article par article, 2e édition, revue et augmentée, Economica, Paris, 1991, pp. 771-792.

Cepelka, C., Les conséquences juridiques du délit en droit international contemporain, Universita Karlova, Praha, 1965.

Chandrasekhara Rao, P., South West Africa Cases: Inconsistent Judgments from the International Court of Justice, 6 IJIL 1966, pp. 383-394.

Charlesworth, H., and Chinkin, C., The Gender of *Jus Cogens*, 15 HRQ 1993, pp. 63-76.

Charney, J., Compromissory Clauses and the Jurisdiction of the International Court of Justice, 81 AJIL 1987, pp. 855-887.

Charney, J., Third State Remedies in International Law, 10 MJIL 1989, pp. 57-101.

Charpentier, C., La résolution 688 (1991) du Conseil de Sécurité: quel devoir d'ingerence?, 23 EI 1992, pp. 279-317.

Charpentier, J., Affaire de la Barcelona Traction, Arrêt de 5 février 1970, 16 AFDI 1970, pp. 307-328.

Charpentier, J., Article 2, Paragraphe 3, in Cot, J.-P., and Pellet, A. (Eds.), La Charte des Nations Unies, Commentaire article par article, 2e édition, revue et augmentée, Economica, Paris, 1991, pp. 103-113.

Cheng, B., General Principles of Law as applied by International Courts and Tribunals, Stevens & Sons Limited, London, 1953.

Cheng, B., The 1966 South-West Africa Judgment of the World Court, 5 ACSIL 1968, pp. 4-31.

Cheng, B., Flight from justiciable to auto-interpretative international law: From the Jay Treaty to the Schultz letter, in Liber Amicorum Elie van Bogaert, Kluwer rechtswetenschappen, Antwerpen, 1985, pp. 1-18.

Christenson, G., The World Court and *Jus Cogens*, 81 AJIL 1987, pp. 93-101.

Clark, R., Some International Law Aspects of the East Timor Affair, 5 LJIL 1992, pp. 265-271.

Cohen Jonathan, G. Article 39, in Cot, J.-P., and Pellet, A. (Eds.), La Charte des Nations Unies, Commentaire article par article, 2e édition, revue et augmentée, Economica, Paris, 1991, pp. 644-666.

Colliard, C., and Manin, A. (Eds.), Droit International et Histoire Diplomatique, Documents choisi, volume II, Europe, Éditions Montchrestien, Paris, 1976.

Combacau, J., Le pouvoir de sanction de l'O.N.U., Étude théorique de la coercition non militaire, Editions A. Pedone, Paris, 1974.

Condorelli, L., To Continuity between certain Principles of Humanitarian Law and the Concept of Crimes of States, in Weiler, J., Cassese, A., and Spinedi, M. (Eds.), International Crimes of States, A Critical Analysis of the ILC's Draft Article 19 on State Responsibility, Walter de Gruyter, Berlin, 1989, pp. 233-237.

Condorelli, L., Measures Available to Third States Reacting to Crimes of State, in Weiler, J., Cassese, A., and Spinedi, M. (Eds.), International Crimes of States, A Critical Analysis of the ILC's Draft Article 19 on State Responsibility, Walter de Gruyter, Berlin, 1989, pp. 264-266.

Cot, J.-P., and Pellet, A. (Eds.), La Charte des Nations Unies, Commentaire article par article, 2e édition, revue et augmentée, Economica, Paris, 1991.

Cottereau, G., De la responsabilité de l'Iraq selon la résolution 687 du Conseil de Sécurité, 37 AFDI 1991, pp. 99-117.

Crawford, J., Democracy and International Law, 64 BYBIL 1993, pp. 113-133.

D'Amato, A., It's a Bird, It's a Plane, It's *Jus Cogens*!, 6 CJIL 1990, pp. 1-6.

Dallal, S., International Law and the United Nations' Role in the Gulf Crisis, 18 SJILC 1992, pp. 111-140.

Damrosch, L., Multilateral Disputes, in Damrosch, L. (Ed.), The International Court of Justice at a Crossroads, Transnational Publishers, Inc., Dobbs Ferry, New York, 1987, pp. 376-400.

Damrosch, L. (Ed.), The International Court of Justice at a Crossroads, Transnational Publishers, Inc., Dobbs Ferry, New York, 1987.

Dehaussy, J., Le problème de la classification des traités et le projet de convention établi par la Commission du Droit International des Nations Unies, in Recueil d'études de droit international en hommage à Paul Guggenheim, Imprimerie de la Tribune de Genève, Genève, 1968, pp. 305-326.

Dekker, I., Criminal Responsibility and the Gulf War of 1980-1988: The Crime of Aggression, in Dekker, I., and Post, H. (Eds.), The Gulf War of 1980-1988, The Iran-Iraq War in International Legal Perspective, Martinus Nijhoff Publishers, Dordrecht, 1992, pp. 249-268.

Dekker, I., and Post, H. (Eds.), The Gulf War of 1980-1988, The Iran-Iraq War in International Legal Perspective, Martinus Nijhoff Publishers, Dordrecht, 1992.

Delbez, L., Les principes généraux du contentieux international, Librairie Générale de Droit et de Jurisprudence, Paris, 1962.

Delbrück, J., Proportionality, in Bernhardt, R. (Ed.), EPIL, Instalment 10, Elsevier Science Publishers B.V., Amsterdam, 1987, pp. 396-400.

Delbrück, J., International Economic Sanctions and Third States, 30 ADV 1992, pp. 86-100.

Deman, C., La cessation de l'acte illicite, 23 RBDI 1990, pp. 476-495.

Detter De Lupis, I., The Concept of International Law, Norstedts Förlag, Stockholm, 1987.

Dewost, J.-L., La Communauté, les dix, et les «sanctions» économiques: De la crise Iranienne à la crise des Malouines, 28 AFDI 1982, pp. 215-232.

Dinstein, Y., War, Aggression and Self-Defence, Grotius Publications Limited, Cambridge, 1988.

Doehring, K., Die Selbstdurchsetzung völkerrechtliche Verpflichtungen, Einige Einzelprobleme der Repressalie, 47 ZAORV 1987, pp. 44-55.

Doehring, K., Self-Determination, in Simma, B. (Ed.), The Charter of the United Nations, A Commentary, Oxford University Press, Oxford, 1994, pp. 56-72.

Dominicé, C., Die internationale Verbrechen und deren rechtliches Regime, in Fischer, P., Koeck, H., and Verdross, A. (Eds.), Völkerrecht und Rechtsphilosophie, Internationale Festschrift für Stephan Verosta zum 70. Geburstag, Duncker & Humblot, Berlin, 1980, pp. 227-248.

Dominicé, C., Représailles et droit diplomatique, in Recht als Prozess und Gefüge, Festschrift für Hans Huber zum 80. Geburtstag, Verlag Stämpfli & Cie AG, Bern, 1981, pp. 541-552.

Dominicé, C., La satisfaction en droit des gens, in Dutoit, B., and Grisel, E. (Eds.), Mélanges Georges Perrin, Diffusion Payot, Lausanne, 1984, pp. 91-121.

Donner, R., International Adjudication: Using the International Court of Justice, with special reference to Finland, Suomalainen Tiedeakatemia, Helsinki, 1988.

Drost, P., The Crime of State, volume 1, Humanicide, A.W. Sijthoff, Leyden, 1959.

Duckwitz, E., Rechtsfolgen bei Verletzung völkerrechtlicher Verträge, Duncker & Humblot, Berlin, 1975.

Duke, S., The State and Human Rights: Sovereignty *Versus* Humanitarian Intervention, 12 IR 1994, pp. 25-48.

Duléry, F., L'affaire du Lac Lanoux, 62 RGDIP 1958, pp. 469-516.

Dupuy, P.-M., L'affaire des essais nucléaires français et le contentieux de la responsabilité internationale publique, 20 GYIL 1977, pp. 375-405.

Dupuy, P.-M., Action publique et crime international de l'état: A propos de l'article 19 du projet de la Commission du Droit International sur la responsabilite des états, 25 AFDI 1979, pp. 539-554.

Dupuy, P.-M., Observations sur le "crime international de l'état", 84 RGDIP 1980, pp. 449-486.

Dupuy, P.-M., Observations sur la pratique récente des "sanctions" de l'illicite, 87 RGDIP 1983, pp. 505-548.

Dupuy, P.-M., Implications of the Institutionalization of International Crimes of States, in Weiler, J., Cassese, A., and Spinedi, M. (Eds.), International Crimes of States, A Critical Analysis of the ILC's Draft Article 19 on State Responsibility, Walter de Gruyter, Berlin, 1989, pp. 170-185.

Dupuy, P.-M., The International Law of State Responsibility: Revolution or Evolution?, 11 MJIL 1990, pp. 105-128.

Dupuy, P.-M., Apres la guerre du Golfe..., 95 RGDIP 1991, pp. 621-638.

Dupuy, P.-M., Responsabilite et legalite, Société Française pour le Droit International, Colloque Du Mans, La responsabilité dans le système international, Editions A. Pedone, Paris, 1991, pp. 263-297.

Eagleton, C., International Organization and the Law of Responsibility, 76 RDC ADI 1950-I, pp. 319-425.

Eisemann, P., Article 41, in Cot, J.-P., and Pellet, A. (Eds.), La Charte des Nations Unies, Commentaire article par article, 2e édition, revue et augmentée, Economica, Paris, 1991, pp. 691-704.

Elagab, O., The Legality of Non-Forcible Counter-Measures in International Law, Clarendon Press, Oxford, 1988.

Falk, R., The South West Africa Cases: An Appraisal, 21 IO 1967, pp. 1-23.

Falsafi, H., L'affaire des Essais nucléaires devant la Cour Internationale de Justice, Imprimerie H. Messeiller S.A., Neuchatel (Suisse), 1978.

Fischer, G., Article 42, in Cot, J.-P., and Pellet, A. (Eds.), La Charte des Nations Unies, Commentaire article par article, 2e édition, revue et augmentée, Economica, Paris, 1991, pp. 705-716.

Fitzmaurice, G., The Foundations of the Authority of International Law and the Problem of Enforcement, 19 MLR 1956, pp. 1-13.

Fitzmaurice, G., Third Report on the Law of Treaties, YBILC 1958, Volume II, pp. 20-46.

Fitzmaurice, G., Fourth Report on the Law of Treaties, YBILC 1959, Volume II, pp. 37-81.

Fitzmaurice, G., Fifth Report on the Law of Treaties, YBILC 1960, Volume II, pp. 69-107.

Fitzmaurice, G., The Law and Procedure of the International Court of Justice, volume 2, Grotius Publications Limited, Cambridge, 1986.

Folz, H.-E., Bemerkungen zur völkerrechtlichen Beurteilung der Vorgänge um die amerikanischen Geiseln im Iran, in Münch, I. von (Ed.), Staatsrecht–Völkerrecht–Europarecht, Festschrift für Hans-Jürgen Schlochauer zum 75. Geburtstag am 28 März 1981, Walter de Gruyter, Berlin, 1981, pp. 271-288.

Francescakis, Ph., Lueurs sur le droit international des sociétés: L'arrêt «Barcelona» de la Cour internationale de justice, 59 RCDIP 1970, pp. 609-664.

Francioni, F., and Scovazzi, T. (Eds.), International Responsibility for Environmental Harm, Graham & Trotman, London, 1991.

Franck, T., The Emerging Right to Democratic Governance, 86 AJIL 1992, pp. 46-91.

Franck, T., The "Powers of Appreciation": Who Is the Ultimate Guardian of UN Legality?, 86 AJIL 1992, pp. 519-523.

Franck, T., and Patel, F., UN Police Action in Lieu of War: "The Old Order Changeth", 85 AJIL 1991, pp. 63-74.

Freudenschuß, H., Between Unilateralism and Collective Security: Authorizations of the Use of Force by the UN Security Council, 5 EJIL 1994, pp. 492-531.

Fritzemeyer, W., Die Intervention vor dem Internationalen Gerichtshof, Eine international-verfahrensrechtliche Untersuchung auf rechtsvergleichender Grundlage, Nomos Verlagsgesellschaft, Baden-Baden, 1984.

Frowein, J., Die Verpflichtungen *erga omnes* im Völkerrecht und ihre Durchsetzung, in Bernhardt, R. (Ed.), Völkerrecht als Rechtsordnung – Internationale Gerichtsbarkeit – Menschenrechte, Festschrift für Hermann Mosler, Springer-Verlag, Berlin, 1983, pp. 241-262.

Frowein, J., *Jus Cogens*, in Bernhardt, R. (Ed.), EPIL, Instalment 7, Elsevier Science Publishers B.V., Amsterdam, 1984, pp. 327-330.

Frowein, J., Das Staatengemeinschaftsinteresse – Probleme bei Formulierung und Durchsetzung, in Hailbronner, K., Ress, G., and Stein, Torsten (Eds.), Staat und Völkerrechtsordnung, Festschrift für Karl Doehring, Springer-Verlag, Berlin, 1989, pp. 219-228.

Frowein, J., Legal Consequences for International Law Enforcement in Case of Security Council Inaction, in Delbrück, J. (Ed.), The Future of International Law Enforcement, New Scenarios – New Law?, Duncker & Humblot, Berlin, 1993, pp. 111-124.

Frowein, J., Article 39, in Simma, B. (Ed.), The Charter of the United Nations, A Commentary, Oxford University Press, Oxford, 1994, pp. 605-616.

Frowein, J., Article 40, in Simma, B. (Ed.), The Charter of the United Nations, A Commentary, Oxford University Press, Oxford, 1994, pp. 617-621.

Frowein, J., Article 42, in Simma, B. (Ed.), The Charter of the United Nations, A Commentary, Oxford University Press, Oxford, 1994, pp. 628-636.

Furet, M.-F., Article 43, in Cot, J.-P., and Pellet, A. (Eds.), La Charte des Nations Unies, Commentaire article par article, 2e édition, revue et augmentée, Economica, Paris, 1991, pp. 717-723.

G.P.R., Torture and Other Violations of Human Rights as International Crimes, 17 RICJ 1976, pp. 41-50.

Gaja, G., *Jus Cogens* Beyond the Vienna Convention, 172 RDC ADI 1981-III, pp. 271-316.

Gaja, G., Obligations *Erga Omnes*, International Crimes and *Jus Cogens*: A Tentative Analysis of Three Related Concepts, in Weiler, J., Cassese, A., and Spinedi, M. (Eds.), International Crimes of States, A Critical Analysis of the ILC's Draft Article 19 on State Responsibility, Walter de Gruyter, Berlin, 1989, pp. 151-160.

Gaja, G., Reflexions sur le role du Conseil de Securite dans le nouvel ordre mondial, A propos des rapports entre maintien de la paix et crimes internationaux des Etats, 97 RGDIP 1993, pp. 297-320.

Gangl, W., The *Jus Cogens* Dimensions of Nuclear Technology, 13 CJIL 1980, pp. 63-87.

García-Amador, F., Sohn, L., and Baxter, R., Recent Codification of the Law of State Responsibility for Injury to Aliens, Oceana Publications, Inc., Dobbs Ferry, New York, 1974.

Geffcken, H., Das Gesamtinteresse als Grundlage des Staats- und Völkerrechts, Prolegomena eines Systems, A. Deichert'sche Verlagsbuchhandlung Nachf. (Georg Böhme), Leipzig, 1908.

Genugten, W. van, Mensenrechten tussen staatssoevereiniteit en internationale jurisdictie, 21 NTRR 1992, pp. 204-223.

Gervais, A., L'affaire du Lac Lanoux, Étude critique de la sentence du Tribunal arbitral, 6 AFDI 1960, pp. 372-434.

Gervais, A., Quelques reflexions a propos de la distinction des «droits» et des «interets», in Mélanges en l'honneur de Paul Roubier, volume 1, Théorie générale du droit et droit transitoire, Librairies Dalloz & Sirey, Paris, 1961, pp. 241-252.

Ghozali, N.-E., La négociation diplomatique dans la jurisprudence internationale, Essai d'analyse, 25 RBDI 1992, pp. 323-350.

Gilbert, G., The Criminal Responsibility of States, 39 ICLQ 1990, pp. 345-369.

Gill, T., The Law of Armed Attack in the Context of the Nicaragua Case, 1 HYIL 1988, pp. 30-58.

Gill, T., The Second Gulf Crisis and the Relation between Collective Security and Collective Self-Defense, 10 Grotiana 1989, pp. 47-76.

Gill, T., The Forcible Protection, Affirmation and Exercise of Rights by States under Contemporary International Law, 23 NYIL 1992, pp. 105-173.

Giraud, E., Le droit international public et la politique, 110 RDC ADI 1963-III, pp. 419-809.

Glennon, M., The Constitution and Chapter VII of the United Nations Charter, 85 AJIL 1991, pp. 74-88.

Gómez Robledo, A., Le *jus cogens* international: sa genèse, sa nature, ses fonctions, 172 RDC ADI 1981-III, pp. 9-217.

Goodrich, L., and Hambro, E., Charter of the United Nations, Commentary and Documents, Second and Revised Edition, Stevens & Sons Limited, London, 1949.

Gordon, E., "Legal Disputes" Under Article 36(2) of the Statute, in Damrosch, L. (Ed.), The International Court at a Crossroads, Transnational Publishers, Inc., Dobbs Ferry, New York, 1987, pp. 183-222.

Gormley, W., The Legal Obligation of the International Community to Guarantee a Pure and Decent Environment: The Expansion of Human Rights Norms, 3 GIELR 1990, pp. 85-116.

Gounelle, M., Quelques remarques sur la notion de «crime international» et sur l'évolution de la responsabilité internationale de l'état, in Le droit international: unité et diversité, Mélanges offerts à Paul Reuter, Pedone, Paris, 1981, pp. 315-326.

Gowlland-Debbas, V., Collective Responses to Illegal Acts in International Law, United Nations Action in the Question of Southern Rhodesia, Martinus Nijhoff Publishers, Dordrecht, 1990.

Gowlland-Debbas, V., Security Council Enforcement Action and Issues of State Responsibility, 43 ICLQ 1994, pp. 55-98.

Gowlland-Debbas, V., The Relationship between the International Court of Justice and the Security Council in the Light of the *Lockerbie* Case, 88 AJIL 1994, pp. 643-677.

Graefrath, B., Zur Geschichte der Reparationen, VEB Deutscher Zentralverlag, Berlin, 1954.

Graefrath, B., Verantwortlichkeit und Wiedergutmachung bei Apartheidverbrechen, 35 NJ 1981, pp. 115-117.

Graefrath, B., Ausschluß der Völkerrechtswidrigkeit – Selbstverteidigung – Sanktion, in Durchsetzungsprobleme des Völkerrechts, Wissenschaftliche Schriftenreihe der Humboldt-Universität, Berlin, 1983, pp. 13-26.

Graefrath, B., Responsibility and Damages Caused: Relationship between Responsibility and Damages, 185 RDC ADI 1984-II, pp. 9-150.

Graefrath, B., Völkerrechtliche Verantwortlichkeit für internationale Verbrechen, in Graefrath, B. (Ed.), Probleme des Völkerrechts, Akademie-Verlag, Berlin, 1985, pp. 89-110.

Graefrath, B., Das Verantwortlichkeitsverhältnis im Völkerrecht und die Definition des "verletzten Staates", in Graefrath, B. (Ed.), Probleme des Völkerrechts, Akademie-Verlag, Berlin, 1987, pp. 107-138.

Graefrath, B., International Crimes – A Specific Regime of International Responsibility of States and its Legal Consequences, in Weiler, J., Cassese, A., and Spinedi, M. (Eds.), International Crimes of States, A Critical Analysis of the ILC's Draft Article 19 on State Responsibility, Walter de Gruyter, Berlin, 1989, pp. 161-169.

Graefrath, B., and Mohr, M., Völkerrechtliche und strafrechtliche Verantwortlichkeit für internationale Verbrechen, 35 SR 1986, pp. 29-40.

Graefrath, B., and Mohr, M., Legal Consequences of an Act of Aggression: The Case of the Iraqi Invasion and Occupation of Kuwait, 43 AJPIL 1992, pp. 109-138.

Graefrath, B., Mohr, M., and Oeser, E., Rechtsfolgen bei völkerrechtlicher Verantwortlichkeit, 31 SR 1982, pp. 1073-1086.

Graefrath, B., Oeser, E., and Steiniger, P., Internationale Verbrechen – Internationale Delikte, 22 DA 1977, pp. 90-101.

Graefrath, B., Oeser, E., and Steiniger, P., Völkerrechtliche Verantwortlichkeit der Staaten, Staatsverlag der DDR, Berlin, 1977.

Gray, C., The Principle of Non-Use of Force, in Lowe, V., and Warbrick, C. (Eds.), The United Nations and the Principles of International Law, Essays in memory of Michael Akehurst, Routledge, London, 1994, pp. 33-48.

Green, L., New Trends in International Criminal Law, 11 IYHR 1981, pp. 9-40.

Greig, D., Self-Defence and the Security Council: What Does Article 51 Require?, 40 ICLQ 1991, pp. 366-402.

Greig, D., Third Party Rights and Intervention Before the International Court, 32 VJIL1992, pp. 285-376.

Grisel, E., Les exceptions d'incompétence et d'irrecevabilité dans la procédure de la Cour internationale de Justice, Éditions Herbert Lang & Cie SA, Berne, 1968.

Grisel, E., L'arrêt de la Cour internationale de justice dans l'affaire de la Barcelona Traction, (seconde phase): problèmes de procédure et de fond, 27 SJIR 1971, pp. 31-48.

Gros Espiel, H., Self-Determination and *Jus Cogens*, in Cassesse, A. (Ed.), UN Law/Fundamental Rights, Two Topics in International Law, Sijthoff and Noordhoff, Alphen aan den Rijn, 1979, pp. 167-173.

Gross, E., The South West Africa Case: What Happened?, 45 FA 1966-1967, pp. 36-48.

Gross, L., States as Organs of International Law and the Problem of Autointerpretation, in Lipsky, A. (Ed.), Law and Politics in the World Community, Essays on Hans Kelsen's Pure Theory and Related Problems in International Law, University of California Press, Berkely, 1953, pp. 59-89 and 336-351 (notes).

Guillaume, G., Terrorisme et droit international, 215 RDC ADI 1989-III, pp. 287-416.

Guttry, A. de, Some Recent Cases of Unilateral Countermeasures and the Problem of their Lawfulness in International Law, 7 IYIL 1986-1987, pp. 169-189.

Haasdijk, S., The Lack of Uniformity in the Terminology of the International Law of Remedies, 5 LJIL 1992, pp. 245-263.

Hafner, G., Bermerkungen zur Funktion und Bestimmung der Betroffenheit im Völkerrecht anhand des Binnenstaates, 31 GYIL 1989, pp. 187-229.

Hakenberg, M., Die Iran-Sanktionen der USA während der Teheraner Geiselaffäre aus völkerrechtlicher Sicht, Verlag Peter Lang, Frankfurt am Main, 1988.

Halderman, J., Some Legal Aspects of Sanctions in the Rhodesian Case, 17 ICLQ 1968, pp. 672-705.

Hannikainen, L., Peremptory Norms (*Jus Cogens*) in International Law, Historical Development, Criteria, Present Status, Finnish Lawyers' Publishing Company, Helsinki, 1988.

Harris, D., Cases and Materials on International Law, Sweet & Maxwell, London, 1983.

Hart, H., The Concept of Law, Second Edition, Clarendon Press, Oxford, 1994.

Haver, P., The Status of Interim Measures of the International Court of Justice after the Iranian-Hostage Crisis, 11 CWILJ 1981, pp. 515-542.

Henkin, L., Human Rights and "Domestic Jurisdiction", in Buergenthal, T. (Ed.), Human Rights, International Law and the Helsinki Accord, Alanheld, Osmun & Co. Publishers, Montclair (New Jersey), 1977, pp. 21-40.

Henkin, L., Use of Force: Law and U.S. Policy, in Right *v.* Might: International Law and the Use of Force, Council on Foreign Relations Press, New York, 1991, pp. 37-69.

Higgins, R., Conflict of Interests, International Law in a Divided World, A Background Book, The Bodley Head, London, 1965.

Higgins, R., The Place of International Law in the Settlement of Disputes by the Security Council, 64 AJIL 1970, pp. 1-18.

Higgins, R., Aspects of the Case Concerning the Barcelona Traction, Light and Power Company, Ltd., 11 VJIL 1970, pp. 327-343.

Hofmann, R., Zur Unterscheidung Verbrechen und Delikt im Bereich der Staatenverantwortlichkeit, 45 ZAORV 1985, pp. 195-231.

Hoof, G. van, Rethinking the Sources of International Law, Kluwer, Deventer, 1983.

Hoogh, A. de, Book Review: Sachariew, K., Die Rechtstellung der betroffenen Staaten bei Verletzungen multilateraler Verträge, Fragen der Aktivlegitimation und der völkerrechtlich zugelassenen Rechtsfolgen, 38 NILR 1991, pp. 104-109.

Hoogh, A. de, The Relationship between *Jus Cogens*, Obligations *Erga Omnes* and International Crimes: Peremptory Norms in Perspective, 42 AJPIL 1991, pp. 183-214.

Hoogh, A. de, Intervention under Article 62 of the Statute and the Quest for Incidental Jurisdiction without the Consent of the Principal Parties, 6 LJIL 1993, pp. 17-46.

Hoogh, A. de, Comments, in Post, H. (Ed.), International Economic Law and Armed Conflict, Martinus Nijhoff Publishers, Dordrecht, 1994, pp. 43-46.

Hutchinson, D., Solidarity and Breaches of Multilateral Treaties, 59 BYBIL 1988, pp. 151-215.

Iwanejko, M., The Jurisdiction of the International Court of Justice: The Plea to the Admissibility, 1 PYIL 1966/67, pp. 164-182.

Janis, M., The Nature of *Jus Cogens*, 3 ConnJIL 1988, pp. 359-363 and 370.

Jenks, C., The General Welfare as a Legal Interest, in Wilner, G. (Ed.), *Jus et Societas*, Essays in Tribute to Wolfgang Friedmann, Martinus Nijhoff Publishers, The Hague, 1979, pp. 151-158.

Jenks, W., The Prospects of International Adjudication, Stevens & Sons Limited, London, 1964.

Jennings, R., The Acquisition of Territory in International Law, Manchester University Press, Manchester, 1963.

Jiménez de Aréchaga, E., and Tanzi, A., International State Responsibility, in Bedjaoui, M. (Ed.), International Law: Achievement and Prospects, Martinus Nijhoff Publishers, Dordrecht, and UNESCO, Paris, 1991, pp. 347-380.

Kadelbach, S., Zwingendes Völkerrecht, Duncker & Humblot, Berlin, 1992.

Kaikobad, K., "*Ius Ad Bellum*": Legal Implications of the Iran-Iraq War, in Dekker, I., and Post, H. (Eds.), The Gulf War of 1980-1988, The Iran-Iraq War in International Legal Perspective, Martinus Nijhoff Publishers, Dordrecht, 1992, pp. 51-70.

Kaikobad, K., Self-Defence, Enforcement Action and the Gulf Wars, 1980-88 and 1990-91, 63 BYBIL 1992, pp. 299-366.

Kamminga, M., Inter-State Accountability for Violations of Human Rights, 1990.

Kawasaki, K., Crimes of State in International Law, 15 SLR 1993, pp. 27-45.

Kelsen, H., Unrecht und Unrechtsfolge im Völkerrecht, Verlag von Julius Springer, Wien, 1932 (Reprint from 12 ZOR 1932).

Kelsen, H., Collective Security and Collective Self-Defense under the Charter of the United Nations, 42 AJIL 1948, pp. 783-796.

Kelsen, H., The Law of the United Nations, A Critical Analysis of Its Fundamental Problems, Stevens & Sons Limited, London, 1951.

Kelsen, H., Principles of International Law, Rinehart & Company Inc., New York, 1952 (Third Printing 1959).

Kißler, K.-P., Die Zulässigkeit von Wirtschaftssanktionen der Europäischen Gemeinschaft gegenüber Drittstaaten, Verlag Peter Lang, Frankfurt am Main, 1984.

Klein, E., Beihilfe zum Völkerrechtsdelikt, in Münch, I. von (Ed.), Staatsrecht – Völkerrecht – Europarecht, Festschrift für Hans-Jürgen Schlochauer zum 75. Geburtstag am 28 März 1981, Walter de Gruyter, Berlin, 1981, pp. 425-438.

Klein, E., Paralleles Tätigwereden von Sicherheitsrat und Internationalem Gerichtshof bei Friedensbedrohenden Streitigkeiten, Zu Fragen der Zuständigkeit und Organtreue, in Bernhardt, R. (Ed.), Völkerrecht als Rechtsordnung – Internationale Gerichtsbarkeit – Menschenrechte, Festschrift für Hermann Mosler, Springer-Verlag, Berlin, 1983, pp. 468-491.

Klein, E., Völkerrechtliche Aspekte des Golfkonflikts 1990/91, 29 ADV 1991, pp. 421-435.

Klein, E., Sanctions by International Organizations and Economic Communities, 30 ADV 1992, pp. 101-113.

Ko Swan Sik, De Verplichting in het Volkenrecht, T.M.C. Asser Instituut, 's-Gravenhage, 1991.

Kodjo, E., Article 53, in Cot, J.-P., and Pellet, A. (Eds.), La Charte des Nations Unies, Commentaire article par article, 2e édition, revue et augmentée, Economica, Paris, 1991, pp. 816-831.

Kooijmans, P., Actie, harde actie: Enkele opmerkingen over de volkenrechtelijke toelaatbaarheid van eenzijdige sanctiemaatregelen, 37 IS 1983, pp. 771-777.

Kooijmans, P., Zwijgt het recht als de Veiligheidsraad spreekt?, Uitspraak van het Internationaal Gerechtshof in de Lockerbie-zaak van 14 april 1992, 67 NJB 1992, pp. 847-851.

Kraus, H., Interesse und zwischenstaatliche Ordnung., 49 NZIR 1934, pp. 22-65.

Kunz, J., Sanctions in International Law, 54 AJIL 1960, pp. 324-347.

Kuyper, P., Sanctions against Rhodesia, The EEC and the Implementation of General International Legal Rules, 12 CMLR 1975, pp. 231-244.

Kuyper, P., Community Sanctions against Argentina: Lawfulness under Community and International Law, in O'Keeffe, D., and Schermers, H. (Eds.), Essays in European Law and Integration, Kluwer, Deventer, 1982, pp. 141-166.

Kuyper, P., Het GATT en het Volkenrecht, De gevolgen van toenemende juridificering, Mededelingen NVIR 1993, pp. 3-60.

Kuyper, P., The Law of GATT as a Special Field of International Law, Ignorance, Further Refinement or Self-Contained System of International Law?, 25 NYIL 1994, pp. 227-257.

Lachs, M., Slavery: The Past and the Present, in Delissen, A., and Tanja, G. (Eds.), Humanitarian Law of Armed Conflict, Essays in Honour of Fritz Kalshoven, Martinus Nijhoff Publishers, Dordrecht, 1991, pp. 613-625.

Laïs, R., Die Rechtsfolgen völkerrechtliche Delikte, Verlag von Georg Stilke, Berlin, 1932.

Lapidoth, R., Some Reflections on the Law and Practice Concerning the Imposition of Sanctions by the Security Council, 30 ADV 1992, pp. 114-127.

Lauterpacht, E., Aspects of the Administration of International Justice, Grotius Publications Limited, Cambridge, 1991.

Lauterpacht, H., First Report on the Law of Treaties, YBILC 1953, Volume II, pp. 90-162.

Lauterpacht, H., The Development of International Law by the International Court, Stevens & Sons Limited, London, 1958.

Lavalle, R., The Law of the United Nations and the Use of Force, under the Relevant Security Council Resolutions of 1990 and 1991, to Resolve the Persian Gulf Crisis, 23 NYIL 1992, pp. 3-65.

Leben, C., Les sanctions privatives de droits ou de qualité dans les organisations internationales specialisées, Recherches sur les sanctions internationales et l'évolution du droit des gens, Établissements Émile Bruylant, Bruxelles, 1979.

Leben, C., Les contre-mesures inter-étatiques et les réactions à l'illicite dans la société internationale, 28 AFDI 1982, pp. 9-77.

Lefeber, R., The Exercise of Jurisdiction in the Antarctic Region and the Changing Structure of International Law, The International Community and Common Interests, 21 NYIL 1990, pp. 81-137.

Lillich, R., Forcible Self-Help by States to Protect Human Rights, 53 IowaLR 1967-1968, pp. 325-351.

Lindemann, H.-H., Die Auswirkungen der Menschenrechtsverletzungen in Surinam auf die Vertragsbeziehungen zwischen den Niederlanden und Surinam, 44 ZAORV 1984, pp. 64-93.

Lowe, V., The Principle of Non-Intervention: Use of Force, in Lowe, V., and Warbrick, C. (Eds.), The United Nations and the Principles of International Law, Essays in memory of Michael Akehurst, Routledge, London, 1994, pp. 66-84.

Lukashuk, I., International Organizations and the Functioning of International Law, 24 IJIL 1984, pp. 68-76.

Mabrouk, M., Les exceptions de procédure devant les juridictions internationales, Librairie Générale de Droit et de Jurisprudence, Paris, 1966.

Macdonald, R., Fundamental Norms in Contemporary International Law, 25 CYIL 1987, pp. 115-149.

Maison, R., Les ordonnances de la CIJ dans l'affaire relative à l'application de la Convention sur la prévention et la répression du crime de génocide, 5 EJIL 1994, pp. 381-400.

Malanczuk, P., Countermeasures and Self-Defence as Circumstances Precluding Wrongfulness in the International Law Commission's Draft Articles on State Responsibility, 43 ZAORV 1983, pp. 705-812.

Malanczuk, P., Zur Repressalie im Entwurf der International Law Commission zur Staatenverantwortlichkeit, 45 ZAORV 1985, pp. 293-323.

Malanczuk, P., Humanitarian Intervention and the Legitimacy of the Use of Force, Het Spinhuis, Amsterdam, 1993.

Malekian, F., International Criminal Responsibility of States, Borgstroms Trycker AB, Stockholm, 1985.

Malloy, M., Objections to Adjudication in Contentious Cases before the International Court of Justice, 5 BJIL 1979, pp. 262-347.

Mann, F., The Doctrine of *Jus Cogens* in International Law, in Festschrift für Ulrich Scheuner, Duncker & Humblot, Berlin, 1973, pp. 399-418.

Mann, F., The Consequences of an International Wrong in International and National Law, 48 BYBIL 1976-1977, pp. 1-65.

Marauhn, T., The Implementation of Disarmament and Arms Control Obligations Imposed upon Iraq by the Security Council, 52 ZAORV 1992, pp. 781-803.

Marek, K., Criminalizing State Responsibility, 14 RBDI 1978-1979, pp. 460-485.

Mavroidis, P., Das GATT als "self-contained" Regime, 37 RIW 1991, pp. 497-501.

Mavroidis, P., Government Procurement Agreement, The Trondheim case: the Remedies Issue, 48 ASZIW 1993, pp. 77-93.

Mazov, V., Responsibility for Aggression in International Law, 6 IA (Moscow) 1972, pp. 43-48.

Mazzeschi, R., Termination and Suspension of Treaties for Breach in the ILC Works on State Responsibility, in Spinedi, M., and Simma, B. (Eds.), United Nations Codification of State Responsibility, Oceana Publications, Inc., New York, 1987, pp. 57-94.

Mbaye, K., L'intérêt pour agir devant la Cour internationale de Justice, 209 RDC ADI 1988-II, pp. 223-345.

McCaffrey, S., *Lex Lata* or the Continuum of State Responsibility, in Weiler, J., Cassese, A., and Spinedi, M. (Eds.), International Crimes of States, A Critical Analysis of the ILC's Draft Article 19 on State Responsibility, Walter de Gruyter, Berlin, 1989, pp. 242-244.

McDougal, M., and Reisman, W., Rhodesia and the United Nations: The Lawfulness of International Concern, 62 AJIL 1968, pp. 1-19.

McGinley, G., The I.C.J.'s Decision in the Lockerbie Cases, 22 GJICL 1992, pp. 577-601.

McNair, A., The Law of Treaties, Oxford University Press, Oxford, 1961.

McWhinney, E., Judicial Settlement of International Disputes, Jurisdiction, Justiciability and Judicial Law-Making on the Contemporary International Court, Martinus Nijhoff Publishers, Dordrecht, 1991.

Medina Quiroga, C., The Battle of Human Rights, Gross, Systematic Violations and the Inter-American System, Martinus Nijhoff Publishers, Dordrecht, 1988.

Mendelson, M., and Hulton, S., The Iraq-Kuwait Boundary, 64 BYBIL 1993, pp. 135-195.

Meng, W., Die Kompetenz der EWG zur Verhängung von Wirtschaftssanktionen gegen Drittländer, 42 ZAORV 1982, pp. 780-803.

Meng, W., Internationale Organisationen im völkerrechtlichen Deliktsrecht, 45 ZAORV 1985, pp. 324-357.

Meron, T., On a Hierarchy of International Human Rights, 80 AJIL 1986, pp. 1-23.

Meron, T., Human Rights and Humanitarian Norms as Customary Law, Clarendon Press, Oxford, 1989.

Meron, T., Common Rights of Mankind in Gentili, Grotius and Suárez, 85 AJIL 1991, pp. 110-116.

Merrills, J., The Principle of Peaceful Settlement of Disputes, in Lowe, V., and Warbrick, C. (Eds.), The United Nations and the Principles of International Law, Essays in memory of Michael Akehurst, Routledge, London, 1994, pp. 49-65.

Merrills, J., Interim Measures of Protection in the Recent Jurisprudence of the International Court of Justice, 44 ICLQ 1995, pp. 90-146.

Mestre, A., Quelques remarques sur l'affaire du lac Lanoux, in Mélanges offerts à Jacques Maury, volume I, Droit international privé et public, Librairie Dalloz & Sirey, Paris, 1960, pp. 261-271.

Minagawa, T., *Jus Cogens* in Public International Law, 6 HJLP 1968, pp. 16-28.

Minagawa, T., Essentiality and Reality of International *Jus Cogens*, 12 HJLP 1984, pp. 1-15.

Mohr, M., The ILC's Distinction between "International Crimes" and "International Delicts" and its Implications, in Spinedi, M., Simma, B. (Eds.), United Nations Codification of International Responsibility, Oceana Publications, Inc., New York, 1987, pp. 115-141.

Morgenstern, F., Legal Problems of International Organizations, Grotius Publications Limited, Cambridge, 1986.

Morgenthau, H., Theorie des sanctions internationales, 62 RDILC 1935, pp. 474-503 and 809-836.

Mosler, H., Political and Justiciable Legal Disputes: Revival of an Old Controversy?, in Cheng, B., and Brown, E. (Eds.), Contemporary Problems: Essays in Honour of Georg Schwarzenberger on his eightiest birthday, Stevens & Sons Limited, London, 1988, pp. 216-229.

Mosler, H., Article 94, in Simma, B. (Ed.), The Charter of the United Nations, A Commentary, Oxford University Press, Oxford, 1994, pp. 1003-1007.

Nagy, K., Forms of Legal Relationship in International Responsibility, in Haraszti, G. (Ed.), Questions of International Law, Volume 2, Sijthoff and Noordhoff International Publishers, Alphen a/d Rijn, 1981, pp. 129-145.

Nagy, K., The Problem of Reparation in International Law, in Bokor-Szego, H. (Ed.), Questions of International Law, volume 3, Martinus Nijhoff Publishers, Dordrecht, 1986, pp. 173-190.

Napel, H.-M. ten, The Concept of International Crimes of States: Walking the Thin Line between Progressive Development and Disintegration of the International Legal Order, 1 LJIL 1988, pp. 149-169.

Onuf, N., Reprisals, Rituals, Rules, Rationales, Center of International Studies, Princeton University, 1974.

Osieke, E., The Legal Validity of *Ultra Vires* Decisions of International Organizations, 77 AJIL 1983, pp. 239-256.

Osieke, E., Sanctions in International Law: The Contributions of International Organizations, 31 NILR 1984, pp. 183-198.

Oxman, B., Jurisdiction and the Power to Indicate Provisional Measures, in Damrosch, L. (Ed.), The International Court of Justice at a Crossroads, Transnational Publishers, Inc., Dobbs Ferry, New York, 1987, pp. 323-354.

Palmisano, G., Les causes d'aggravation de la responsabilite des etats et la distinction entre «crimes» et «delits» internationaux, 98 RGDIP 1994, pp. 629-673.

Patil, A., The UN Veto in World Affairs 1946-1990, A Complete Record and Case Histories of the Security Council's Veto, Unifo Publishers, Sarasota, Florida, 1992.

Paust, J., and Blaustein, A., The Arab Oil Weapon – A Threat to International Peace, 68 AJIL 1974, pp. 410-439.

Peaslee, A., The Sanction of International Law, 10 AJIL 1916, pp. 328-336.

Perez Gonzalez, M., Les organisations internationales et le droit de la responsabilité, 92 RGDIP 1988, pp. 63-102.

Personnaz, J., La Réparation du Préjudice en Droit International Public, Librairie du Recueil Sirey, Paris, 1939.

Petersmann, E., Internationale Wirtschaftssanktionen als Problem des Völkerrechts und des Europarechts, 80 ZVR 1981, pp. 1-28.

Pillepich, A., Article 94, in Cot, J.-P., and Pellet, A. (Eds.), La Charte des Nations Unies, Commentaire article par article, 2e édition, revue et augmentée, Economica, Paris, 1991, pp. 1275-1285.

Pomerance, M., Self-Determination in Law and Practice, Martinus Nijhoff Publishers, The Hague, 1982.

Przetacznik, F., La responsabilité internationale de l'état a raison des préjudices de caractère moral et politique causés a un autre état, 78 RGDIP 1974, pp. 917-974.

Quigley, J., Complicity in International Law: A New Direction in the Law of State Responsibility, 57 BYBIL 1986, pp. 77-131.

Quigley, J., The International Law Commission's Crime-Delict Distinction: A Toothless Tiger?, 66 RDISDP 1988, pp. 117-161.

Raby, J., The State of Necessity and the Use of Force to Protect Nationals, 26 CYIL 1988, pp. 253-272.

Raic, D., The Gulf Crisis and the United Nations, 4 LJIL 1991, pp. 119-134.

Randelzhofer, A., Article 2(4), in Simma, B. (Ed.), The Charter of the United Nations, A Commentary, Oxford University Press, Oxford, 1994, pp. 106-128.

Randelzhofer, A., Article 51, in Simma, B. (Ed.), The Charter of the United Nations, A Commentary, Oxford University Press, Oxford, 1994, pp. 661-678.

Rasy, D., Le droit et la force dans le monde contemporain, in Recueil d'études en hommage a Charles Eisenmann, Éditions Cujas, Paris, 1975, pp. 419-421.

Reed, K., Reviving the Doctrine of Non-Forcible Countermeasures: Resolving the Effect of Third Party Injuries, 29 VJIL 1988, pp. 175-209.

Reisman, W., Revision of the South West Africa Cases, An Analysis of the Grounds of Nullity in the Decision of July 18th, 1966 and Methods of Revision, 7 VJIL 1966, pp. 3-90.

Reisman, W., The Legal Effect of Vetoed Resolutions, 74 AJIL 1980, pp. 904-907.

Reisman, W., Coercion and Self-Determination: Construing Charter Article 2(4), 78 AJIL 1984, pp. 642-645.

Reuter, P., Le dommage comme condition de la responsabilité internationale, in Homenaja al profesor Miaja de la Muela, volume II, 1979, pp. 837-846.

Reuter, P., Trois observations sur la codification de la responsabilite internationale des etats pour fait illicite, in Le droit au service de la paix, de la justice et du développement, Mélanges Michel Virally, Éditions A. Pedone, Paris, 1991, pp. 389-398.

Riedel, E., Satisfaction, in Bernhardt, R. (Ed.), EPIL, Instalment 10, Elsevier Science Publishers B.V., Amsterdam, 1987, pp. 383-384.

Rigaux, F., Le crime d'etat, Reflexions sur l'article 19 du projet d'articles sur la responsabilite des etats, in Etudes en l'honneur de Roberto Ago, Le droit international à l'heure de sa codification, volume III, Giuffrè, Milano, 1987, pp. 301-325.

Riphagen, W., Over concentratie en delegatie bij internationale instellingen, in *Varia Juris Gentium*, Questions of International Law, Liber Amicorum presented to Jean Pierre Adrien François, A.W. Sijthoff, Leyden, 1959, pp. 229-253.

Riphagen, W., The Legal Consequences of Illegal Acts under Public International Law (Advisory Opinion I.C.J. of June 21, 1971), 20 NTIR 1973, pp. 27-36.

Riphagen, W., Second report on the content, forms and degrees of international responsibility (part 2 of the draft articles), YBILC 1981, Volume II, Part One, pp. 79-101.

Riphagen, W., Third report on the content, forms and degrees of international responsibility (part 2 of the draft articles), YBILC 1982, Volume II, Part One, pp. 22-50.

Riphagen, W., Fourth report on the content, forms and degrees of international responsibility (part 2 of the draft articles), YBILC 1983, Volume II, Part One, pp. 3-24.

Riphagen, W., Fifth report on the content, forms and degrees of international responsibility (part 2 of the draft articles), YBILC 1984, Volume II, Part One, pp. 1-4.

Riphagen, W., Sixth report on the content, forms and degrees of international responsibility (part 2 of the draft articles); and "Implementation" (*mise en oeuvre*) of international responsibility and the settlement of disputes (part 3 of the draft articles), YBILC 1985, Volume II, Part One, pp. 3-19.

Riphagen, W., Seventh Report on State Responsibility, 4 March 1986, A/CN.4/397, 29 pp.

Roberts, A., and Guelff, R. (Ed.), Documents on the Laws of War, Clarendon Press, Oxford, 1982.

Röling, B., Aspects of the Case concerning United States Diplomatic and Consular Staff in Tehran, 11 NYIL 1980, pp. 125-153.

Ronzitti, N., Rescuing Nationals Abroad through Military Coercion and Intervention on Grounds of Humanity, Martinus Nijhoff Publishers, Dordrecht, 1985.

Ronzitti, N., Use of Force, *Jus Cogens* and State Consent, in Cassese, A. (Ed.), The Current Legal Regulation of the Use of Force, Martinus Nijhoff Publishers, Dordrecht, 1986, pp. 147-166.

Root, E., The Outlook for International Law, 10 AJIL 1916, pp. 1-11.

Rosenne, S., Bilateralism and Community Interest in the Codified Law of Treaties, in Friedmann, W., Henkin, L., and Lissitzyn, O. (Eds.), Transnational Law in a Changing Society, Essays in Honor of Philip C. Jessup, Colombia University Press, New York, 1972, pp. 202-227.

Rosenne, S., Procedure in the International Court, A Commentary on the 1978 Rules of the International Court of Justice, Martinus Nijhoff Publishers, The Hague, 1983.

Rosenne, S., Developments in the Law of Treaties 1945-1986, Cambridge University Press, Cambridge, 1989.

Rostow, E., Disputes involving the Inherent Right of Self-Defense, in Damrosch, L. (Ed.), The International Court of Justice at a Crossroads, Transnational Publishers, Inc., Dobbs Ferry, New York, 1987, pp. 264-287.

Rostow, E., Until What?, Enforcement Action or Collective Self-Defense?, 85 AJIL 1991, pp. 506-516.

Rousseau, C., L'application des sanctions contre l'Italie et le droit international, 63 RDILC 1936, pp. 5-64.

Ruzié, D., Organisations internationales et sanctions internationales, Librairie Armand Colin, Paris, 1971.

Sachariew, K., State Responsibility for Multilateral Treaty Violations: Identifying the "Injured State" and its Legal Status, 35 NILR 1988, pp. 273-289.

Sachariew, K., Norm und Rechtsverhältnis im Völkerrecht, 37 SR 1988, pp. 495-501.

Sadurska, R., Threats of Force, 82 AJIL 1988, pp. 239-268.

Sahovic, M., Le concept du crime international de l'etat et le developpement du droit international, in Etudes en l'honneur de Roberto Ago, Le droit international à l'heure de sa codification, Giuffrè, Milano, volume III, 1987, pp. 363-369.

Salmon, J., L'intention en matiere de responsabilite internationale, in Le droit au service de la paix, de la justice et du développement, Mélanges Michel Virally, Éditions A. Pedone, Paris, 1991, pp. 413-422.

Salvioli, G., Problèmes de procédure dans la jurisprudence internationale, 91 RDC ADI 1957-I, pp. 553-617.

Saulle, M., *Jus Cogens* and Human Rights, in Etudes en l'honneur de Roberto Ago, Le droit international à l'heure de sa codification, volume II, Giuffrè, Milano, 1987, pp. 385-396.

Scandamis, N., Le jugement déclaratoire entre états, La séperabilité du contentieux international, Éditions A. Pedone, Paris, 1975.

Scelle, G., Quelques réflexions sur l'abolition de la compétence du guerre, 58 RGDIP 1954, pp. 5-22.

Schachter, O., The Quasi-Judicial Role of the Security Council and the General Assembly, 58 AJIL 1964, pp. 960-965.

Schachter, O., The Legality of Pro-Democratic Invasion, 78 AJIL 1984, pp. 645-650.

Schachter, O., Disputes involving the Use of Force, in Damrosch, L. (Ed.), The International Court of Justice at a Crossroads, Transnational Publishers, Inc., Dobbs Ferry, New York, 1987, pp. 223-241.

Schachter, O., Just War and Human Rights, 1 PUSL YIL 1989, pp. 1-19.

Schachter, O., The Lawful Use of Force by a State against Terrorists in Another Country, 19 IYHR 1989, pp. 209-231.

Schachter, O., United Nations Law in the Gulf Conflict, 85 AJIL 1991, pp. 452-473.

Scheffer, D., Use of Force After the Cold War: Panama, Iraq and the New World Order, in Right *v.* Might: International Law and the Use of Force, Council on Foreign Relations Press, New York, 1991, pp. 109-172.

Schermers, H., Inleiding tot het Internationale Institutionele Recht, Kluwer, Deventer, 1983.

Schermers, H., The Obligation to Intervene in the Domestic Affairs of States, in Delissen, A., and Tanja, G. (Eds.), Humanitarian Law of Armed Conflict, Essays in Honour of Fritz Kalshoven, Martinus Nijhoff Publishers, Dordrecht, 1991, pp. 583-593.

Schröder, M., Wirtschaftssanktionen der Europäischen Gemeinschaften gegenüber Drittstaaten, dargestellt am Beispiel des Iranembargos, 23 GYIL 1980, pp. 111-125.

Schütz, H.-J., Article 5, in Simma, B. (Ed.), The Charter of the United Nations, A Commentary, Oxford University Press, Oxford, 1994, pp. 175-185.

Schwelb, E., Termination or Suspension of the Operation of a Treaty as a Consequence of its Breach, 7 IJIL 1967, pp. 309-334.

Schwelb, E., Some Aspects of International *Jus Cogens* as Formulated by the International Law Commission, 61 AJIL 1967, pp. 946-975.

Schwelb, E., The *Actio Popularis* and International Law, 2 IYHR 1972, pp. 46-56.

Seidl-Hohenveldern, I., Der Barcelona-Traction-Fall, 22 OZOR 1971, pp. 255-309.

Seidl-Hohenveldern, I., *Actio Popularis* im Völkerrecht?, in Il processo internazionale, Studi in onore di Gaetano Morelli, Comunicazioni e Studi, volume 14, Giuffrè, Milano, 1975, pp. 803-813.

Seidl-Hohenveldern, I., Das Recht der Internationalen Organisationen einschließlich der Supranationalen Gemeinschaften, Dritte, vermehrte Auflage, Carl Heymanns Verlag KG, Köln, 1979.

Siekmann, R., Comments, in Dekker, I., and Post, H. (Eds.), The Gulf War of 1980-1988, The Iran-Iraq War in International Legal Perspective, Martinus Nijhoff Publishers, Dordrecht, 1992, pp. 91-94.

Silagi, M., Die Popularklage als Fremdkörper im Völkerrecht, 4 SAYIL 1978, pp. 10-28.

Simma, B., Reflections on Article 60 of the Vienna Convention on the Law of Treaties and Its Background in General International Law, 20 OZOR 1970, pp. 5-83.

Simma, B., Das Reziprozitätselement im Zustandekommen völkerrechtliche Verträge, Duncker & Humblot, Berlin, 1972.

Simma, B., Zur bilateralen Durchsetzung vertraglich verankerter Menschenrechte: Aktivlegitimation und zulässige Mittel nach allgemeinem Völkerrecht, in Schreuer, C. (Ed.), Autorität und internationale Ordnung, Duncker & Humblot, Berlin, 1979, pp. 129-154.

Simma, B., Fragen der zwischenstaatlichen Durchsetzung vertraglich vereinbarter Menschenrechte, in Staatsrecht – Völkerrecht – Europarecht, Festschrift für Hans-Jürgen Schlochauer, Walter de Gruyter, Berlin, 1981, pp. 635-648.

Simma, B., Self-Contained Regimes, 16 NYIL 1985, pp. 111-136.

Simma, B., Bilateralism and Community Interest in the Law of State Responsibility, in Dinstein, Y. (Ed.), Essays in Honour of Shabtai Rosenne, International Law at a Time of Perplexity, Martinus Nijhoff Publishers, Dordrecht, 1989, pp. 821-844.

Simma, B., Does the UN Charter Provide and Adequate Legal Basis for Individual or Collective Responses to Violations of Obligations *Erga Omnes*?, in Delbrück, J. (Ed.), The Future of International Law Enforcement, New Scenarios – New Law?, Duncker & Humblot, Berlin, 1993, pp. 125-146.

Simma, B., Counter-Measures and Dispute Settlement: A Plea for a Different Balance, 5 EJIL 1994, pp. 102-105.

Simon, D., Article 40, in Cot, J.-P., and Pellet, A. (Eds.), La Charte des Nations Unies, Commentaire article par article, 2e édition, revue et augmentée, Economica, Paris, 1991, pp. 667-689.

Sinclair, I., The Vienna Convention on the Law of Treaties, Second Edition, Manchester University Press, Manchester, 1984.

Sinclair, I., State Responsibility and the Concept of Crimes of States, in Weiler, J., Cassese, A., and Spinedi, M. (Eds.), International Crimes of States, A Critical Analysis of the ILC's Draft Article 19 on State Responsibility, Walter de Gruyter, Berlin, 1989, pp. 223-225.

Skubiszewski, K., The Application of Non-Military Measures by the General Assembly of the United Nations, 1 PYIL 1966/67, pp. 110-135.

Smith, B., State Responsibility and the Marine Environment, The Rules of Decision, Clarendon Press, Oxford, 1988.

Sohn, L., The International Court of Justice and the Scope of the Right of Self-Defence and the Duty of Non-Intervention, in Dinstein, Y. (Ed.), Essays in Honour of Shabtai Rosenne, International Law at a Time of Perplexity, Martinus Nijhoff Publishers, Dordrecht, 1989, pp. 869-878.

Sperduti, G., Les obligations solidaires en droit international, in Makarczyk, J. (Ed.), Essays in International Law in Honour of Judge Manfred Lachs, Martinus Nijhoff Publishers, The Hague, 1984, pp. 271-275.

Spinedi, M., International Crimes of State, The Legislative History, in Weiler, J., Cassese, A., and Spinedi, M. (Eds.), International Crimes of States, A Critical Analysis of the ILC's Draft Article 19 on State Responsibility, Walter de Gruyter, Berlin, 1989, pp. 7-138.

Spinedi, M., Convergences and Divergencies on the Legal Consequences of International Crimes of States: With whom Should Lie the Right of Response?, in Weiler, J., Cassese, A., and Spinedi, M. (Eds.), International Crimes of States, A Critical Analysis of the ILC's Draft Article 19 on State Responsibility, Walter de Gruyter, Berlin, 1989, pp. 244-249.

Spinedi, M., and Simma, B. (Eds.), United Nations Codification of State Responsibility, Oceana Publications, Inc., New York, 1987.

Starace, V., La responsabilité résultant de la violation des obligations à l'égard de la communauté internationale, 153 RDC ADI 1976-V, pp. 263-317.

Stein, Ted, Contempt, Crisis and the Court: The World Court and the Hostage Rescue Attempt, 76 AJIL 1982, pp. 499-533.

Stein, Ted, Observations on "Crimes of States", in Weiler, J., Cassese, A., and Spinedi, M. (Eds.), International Crimes of States, A Critical Analysis of the ILC's Draft Article 19 on State Responsibility, Walter de Gruyter, Berlin, 1989, pp. 194-200.

Stern, B., L'affaire du Timor oriental, 119 JDI 1992, pp. 740-745.

Stone, J., *De Victoribus Victis*: The International Law Commission and Imposed Treaties of Peace, 8 VJIL 1968, pp. 356-373.

Strydom, H., *Ius Cogens*: Peremptory Norm or Totalitarian Instrument?, 14 SAYIL 1988-1989, pp. 42-58.

Sucharitkul, S., Terrorism as an International Crime: Questions of Responsibility and Complicity, 19 IYHR 1989, pp. 247-258.

Sur, S., La résolution 687 (3 avril 1991) du Conseil de Sécurité dans l'affaire du Golfe: Problèmes de rétablissement et de garantie de la paix, 37 AFDI 1991, pp. 25-97.

Sztucki, J., *Jus Cogens* and the Vienna Convention on the Law of Treaties, A Critical Appraisal, Springer-Verlag, Wien, 1974.

Sztucki, J., Interim Measures in the Hague Court, An Attempt at a Scrutiny, Kluwer Law and Taxation Publishers, Deventer, 1983.

Tanzi, A., Is Damage a Distinct Condition for the Existence of an Internationally Wrongful Act?, in Spinedi, M., Simma, B. (Eds.), United Nations Codification of International Responsibility, Oceana Publications, Inc., New York, 1987, pp. 1-33.

Thirlway, H., The Law and Procedure of the International Court of Justice 1960-1989 (Part One), 60 BYBIL 1989, pp. 1-157.

Thirlway, H., The Law and Procedure of the International Court of Justice 1960-1989 (Part Two), 61 BYBIL 1990, pp. 1-133.

Thomsen, S., Restitution, in Bernhardt, R. (Ed.), EPIL, Instalment 10, Elsevier Science Publishers B.V., Amsterdam, 1987, pp. 375-378.

Thornberry, P., The Principle Self-Determination, in Lowe, V., and Warbrick, C. (Eds.), The United Nations and the Principles of International Law, Essays in memory of Michael Akehurst, Routledge, London, 1994, pp. 175-203.

Tomuschat, C., Repressalie und Retorsion, Zu einigen Aspekten ihrer innerstaatlichen Durchführung, 33 ZAORV 1973, pp. 179-222.

Tomuschat, C., Are Counter-Meaures Subject to Prior Recourse to Dispute Settlement Procedures?, 5 EJIL 1994, pp. 77-88.

Tomuschat, C., Article 2(3), in Simma, B. (Ed.), The Charter of the United Nations, A Commentary, Oxford University Press, Oxford, 1994, pp. 97-106.

Tunkin, G., International Law, A Textbook, Progress Publishers, Moscow, 1986.

Tunkin, G., The Legal Bases of International Organization Action, in Dupuy, R.-J. (Ed.), A Handbook on International Organizations, Martinus Nijhoff Publishers, Dordrecht, 1988, pp. 261-276.

Turpel, M., and Sands, P., Peremptory International Law and Sovereignty: Some Questions, 3 ConnJIL 1988, pp. 364-369 and 371.

Union Académique Internationale, Dictionnaire de la terminologie du droit international, Sirey, Paris, 1959.

United Nations, The Work of the International Law Commission, Fourth Edition, New York, 1988.

Valki, L., Does International Law Contain Sanctions?, in Annales Universitatis Scientiarum Budapestinensis de Rolando Eötvös nominatae, Separatum, Sectio Iuridica, Tomus XXI, 1979, pp. 255-275.

Venezia, J.-C., La notion des représailles en droit international public, 64 RGDIP 1960, pp. 465-498.

Verhoeven, J., Sanctions internationales et Communautes Europeennes, A propos de l'affaire des îles Falkland (Malvinas), 19 CDE 1984, pp. 259-290.

Verma, D., The Nuclear Tests Cases: an Inquiry into the Judicial Response of the International Court of Justice, 8 SAYIL 1982, pp. 20-57.

Verwey, W., Humanitarian Intervention under International Law, 32 NILR 1985, pp. 357-418.

Verzijl, J., The South West Africa Cases (Second Phase), IR 1966, pp. 87-97.

Vierdag, E., Spanningen tussen recht en praktijk in het verdragenrecht, in Mededelingen NVIR 1989, pp. 3-87.

Virally, M., Sur la classification des traites, A propos du projet d'articles de la Commission du Droit International, in Comunicazioni e Studi, Volume 13, 1969, pp. 17-35.

Virally (M.), Article 2, Paragraphe 4, in Cot, J.-P., and Pellet, A. (Eds.), La Charte des Nations Unies, Commentaire article par article, 2e édition, revue et augmentée, Economica, Paris, 1991, pp. 115-128.

Visscher, C. de, Aspects récents du droit procédural de la Cour internationale de Justice, Éditions A. Pedone, Paris, 1966.

Waldock, H., Second Report on the Law of Treaties, YBILC 1962, Volume II, pp. 27-80.

Waldock, H., Third Report on the Law of Treaties, YBILC 1964, Volume II, pp. 5-65.

Waldock, H., Fifth Report on the Law of Treaties, YBILC 1966, Volume II, pp. 1-50.

Warbrick, C., The Invasion of Kuwait by Iraq, 40 ICLQ 1991, pp. 482-492.

Watson, G., Constitutionalism, Judicial Review, and the World Court, 34 HILJ 1993, pp. 1-45.

Weckel, P., Le chapitre VII de la Charte et son application par le Conseil de Sécurité, 37 AFDI 1991, pp. 165-202.

Weil, P., Towards Relative Normativity in International Law?, 77 AJIL 1983, pp. 413-442.

Weiler, J., Cassese, A., and Spinedi, M. (Eds.), International Crimes of States, A Critical Analysis of the ILC's Draft Article 19 on State Responsibility, Walter de Gruyter, Berlin, 1989.

Wellens, K., *Apartheid*, An International Crime, in Heyde, L., Leijten, J., Mertens, Th., and Vermeulen, B. (Eds.), Begrensde Vrijheid, Opstellen over mensenrechten aangeboden aan Prof. Dr. D.F. Scheltens bij zijn afscheid als hoogleraar aan de Katholieke Universiteit Nijmegen, Tjeenk Willink, Zwolle, 1989, pp. 288-311.

Wellens, K., Diversity in Secondary Rules and the Unity of International Law: Some Reflections on Current Trends, 25 NYIL 1994, pp. 3-37.

Weller, M., The Use of Force and Collective Security, in Dekker, I., and Post, H. (Eds.), The Gulf War of 1980-1988, The Iran-Iraq War in International Legal Perspective, Martinus Nijhoff Publishers, Dordrecht, 1992, pp. 71-90.

Weston, B., Security Council Resolution 678 and Persian Gulf Decision Making: Precarious Legitimacy, 85 AJIL 1991, pp. 516-535.

Whiteman, M., *Jus Cogens* in International Law, With a Projected List, 7 GJICL 1977, pp. 609-626.

Willisch, J., State Responsibility for Technological Damage in International Law, Duncker & Humblot, Berlin, 1987.

Wolfrum, R., Purposes and Principles of International Environmental Law, 33 GYIL 1990, pp. 308-330.

Yokota, K., War as an International Crime, in Constantopoulos, D., Eustathiades, C., and Fragistas, C. (Eds.), Grundprobleme des internationalen Rechts, Festschrift für Jean Spiropoulos, Schimmelbusch & Co., Bonn, 1957, pp. 453-460.

Zacklin, R., Responsabilite des organisations internationales, in SFDI, Colloque Du Mans, La responsabilité dans le système international, Editions A. Pedone, Paris, 1991, pp. 91-100.

Zemanek, K., Das Problem der Beteiligung des immerwährend neutralen Österreich an Sanktionen der Vereinten Nationen, besonders im Falle Rhodesiens, 28 ZAORV 1968, pp. 16-32.

Zemanek, K., Die völkerrechtliche Verantwortlichkeit und die Sanktionen des Völkerrecht, in Neuhold, H. (Ed.), Österreichisches Handbuch des Völkerrecht, volume 1, Wien, 1983, pp. 368-388.

Zemanek, K., La responsabilité des États pour faits internationalement illicites, ainsi que pour faits internationalement licites, in Weil, P. (Ed.), Responsabilité internationale, Éditions A. Pedone, Paris, 1987, pp. 3-88.

Zoller, E., Quelques réflexions sur les contre-mesures en droit international public, in Études offertes à Claude-Albert Colliard, Droit et libertés à la fin du XXe siècle, 1984, pp. 361-381.

Zoller, E., Peacetime Unilateral Remedies: An Analysis of Countermeasures, Transnational Publishers, Inc., Dobbs Ferry, New York, 1984.

Zoller, E., Enforcing International Law through U.S. Legislation, Transnational Publishers, Inc., Dobbs Ferry, New York, 1985.

INDEX

A

B

C

H

I

Q

R

S